SECOND EDITION

# Direct Marketing

HERBERT KATZENSTEIN
St. John's University

WILLIAM S. SACHS
Eastern New Mexico University

MACMILLAN PUBLISHING COMPANY
New York
MAXWELL MACMILLAN CANADA
Toronto
MAXWELL MACMILLAN INTERNATIONAL
New York Oxford Singapore Sydney

*This book is dedicated to our wives, Claire and Joyce, for their constant support and encouragement.*

Editor: Fred Easter
Production Supervision: Publication Services, Inc.
Cover Design and Illustration: Publication Services, Inc.

This book was set in Palatino by Publication Services, Inc., and was printed and bound by Book Press. The cover was printed by Lehigh Press.



Printed in the United States of America


Macmillan Publishing Company
866 Third Avenue, New York, New York 10022

Macmillan Publishing Company is part of the
Maxwell Communication Group of companies.

Maxwell Macmillan Canada, Inc.
1200 Eglinton Avenue East
Suite 200
Don Mills, Ontario M3C 3N1

Library of Congress Cataloging-in-Publication Data

Katzenstein, Herbert.
Direct marketing / Herbert Katzenstein, William S. Sachs. –2nd ed.
p. cm.
Includes index.
ISBN 0-02-362425-6
1. Direct marketing. I. Sachs, William S., 1919– . II. Title.
HF5415.126.K38 1992 91-25146
658.8′4–dc20 CIP

Printing: 1 2 3 4 5 6 7 Year: 2 3 4 5 6 7 8

# PREFACE

*Direct Marketing* was written for a basic course on the subject at the college level. Its immediate requirements are appropriateness to a business school curriculum and relevancy to a professional orientation, both of which are geared toward understanding the art as currently practiced in the outside world.

The past decade has witnessed strong and consistent growth of direct marketing. This expansion was fueled mainly by large companies adopting direct marketing techniques. These activities were not added as separate and unrelated inputs to company operations. Rather, they were incorporated as part of companies' selling and distributive efforts. In accordance with this trend, the book accepts the underlying philosophy that regards direct marketing as a subfunction of total marketing.

Within this framework of total marketing, the subject of direct marketing is handled from a managerial point of view. But our emphasis transcends the strictly how-to-do-it approach that is often associated with management. We have attempted to focus on the whys and wherefores of decisions. We have given preference, where possible, to the analytical aspects of decision making. Our rationale for doing so is the belief that an understanding of basic principles comes from analysis of relevant variables in the decision process. To discuss what is done without a discussion of why portrays managerial decisions as thoughtless or unreasoned acts.

The book is divided into five parts. The first, entitled "Framework for Direct Marketing," includes Chapters 1, 2, and 3. It discusses the scope of direct marketing, which sets the parameters for the activity, and the organization of direct marketing, which describes the institutional arrangements under which activities are carried out. The third chapter covers the social and legal environment.

The second section deals with the planning process. Though strategic planning is included, it is the author's view that direct marketing is primarily tactical in nature. This section thus emphasizes such aspects as the strategy concept and segmentation approaches.

The third section, spanning Chapters 6 to 9 inclusive, describes the implementation of marketing programs. These encompass database marketing, financial aspects of direct marketing programs, the role of marketing research, fulfillment, and customer service.

The fourth section discusses uses of media. These include direct mail to consumers, list management, catalogs, telemarketing, consumer publications, and direct response in electronic media.

The last section focuses on direct marketing in different markets. Included here are business-to-business marketing and international direct marketing.

---

## THE SECOND EDITION

The second edition has been extensively updated from the first. In this edition we have set out to include new material and features requested by professors and students, changes in business technology, and new opportunities. The major objectives of our text are to enable readers to learn the basics in direct marketing, to familiarize them with the many opportunities in the field, and to provide an advantage to them when they look for an entrance-level position.

The following new features have been added:

- New chapters: The Social and Legal Environment
  Database Marketing
  List Management
  International Direct Marketing
- New appendixes: Some General Patterns of Direct Response Advertising
  PRIZM
  Circulation Analysis
  Legal Aspects of International Direct Marketing
  Careers in Direct Marketing
- All-new projects: Enrollment problems at a university
  Cleopatra Hotel and Casino
  King Henry Teas
  Jose Quality Auto Parts
  Bueno Supermarkets
  Doug Merriam, entrepreneur
  Kenneth Burkhardt, entrepreneur
  Goldmark Gasket Company
- All-new cases: Arts & Entertainment Network, Part A: Choices for Developing A&E
  Arts & Entertainment Network, Part B: Implementation of A&E Strategy
  Ford New Holland, Inc.: Full-Line Insert
  Kayeville College Rescinds Its Decision to Admit Men
  Golf View Village

**ACKNOWLEDGMENTS**

The responsibility for *Direct Marketing* is ours alone. But we owe a deep debt of gratitude to many people both in and out of the academic environment. Richard S. Hodgson, Richard L. Montessi, Pierre A. Passavant, Paul Sampson, and Laurie Spar opened the field of direct marketing to us through their interesting and exciting DMA workshops.

The book also bears the imprint of many friends and colleagues who made important contributions. These include ideas they supplied from the business world, reviews of our initial chapters, and materials on direct marketing. Our sincere thanks go to Irving Chernow, president of Van Heusen Markets Company; Nickolas Davatzes, president and CEO, Arts & Entertainment Network; Peter S. Goodrich, professor at Providence College; Henry R. Hoke, president, Hoke Communications, Inc.; Alex MacRae, director of marketing and sales development, National Geographic Society; John S. Manna, J.D., professor at St. John's University; Jerome W. Pickholz, chairman and CEO, Ogilvy & Mather Direct; James W. Prendergast, president, W. Prendergast Associates; Lewis B. Tucker, professor at Clark University; George S. Wiedemann, president, Grey Direct.

Of enduring benefit have been the comments of reviewers, especially those of Herbert Brown, Wright State University; Robert Dwyer, University of Cincinnati; John D. Jenks, the University of Wisconsin; Norman Leebron, Drexel University; and William Brunsen, Eastern New Mexico University. We want to acknowledge the fine editorial work of Joyce M. Sachs, who edited the initial manuscript, and Jennifer McNab of Macmillan Publishing Company; and Karen Hawk of Publication Services, who prepared the final manuscript for publication. We are grateful to Claire Katzenstein, who chipped in with editorial help, proofread the material, and managed releases.

We are greatly indebted to Elizabeth McCall, who helped enormously with logistical and clerical chores in getting the manuscript ready for publication. We thank Dorothy Burns and Anna Agnetti for inputting our text and laboring over our revisions.

H. K.

W. S. S.

# CONTENTS

PART I

# FRAMEWORK FOR DIRECT MARKETING

## PROFILES

CHAPTER 1

# The Scope of Direct Marketing

## PROFILE

**HENRY REED HOKE, JR.**

**The Voice of the Industry.** Henry R. Hoke, Jr., known in the direct marketing industry as "Pete," is president of Hoke Communications, Inc., and publisher of the industry's leading trade journal. He is holder of the Miles Kimball Award, the highest honor accorded by the direct mail industry for outstanding contributions.

Pete literally grew up in direct marketing. His father published *The Reporter of Direct Mail Advertising,* a trade journal. After serving in the U.S. Navy during World War II, young Pete completed his education at the Wharton School of the University of Pennsylvania. With the polish acquired from an Ivy League college, he joined his father in the family business.

Pete assumed command of the journal in 1955. He expanded the editorial content to all aspects of direct marketing. In 1968 the magazine's name became *Direct Marketing* to reflect its broadened scope and to popularize new concepts. The next year witnessed the launching of a bimonthly magazine, *Fund Raising Management,* and of an audiovisual division. In 1977 Hoke Communications started yet another publication, *FRM Weekly.*

Hoke's long and productive career has been punctuated with many awards and honors. But the most eloquent testimony to his editorial excellence is his publication record—the thousands of printed pages that report on, describe, and analyze events in a dynamic industry. If any man can lay claim to being the voice of direct marketing, it is surely Henry Reed Hoke, Jr. ■

# What Is Direct Marketing?

It is only within the past 10 or 15 years that direct marketing has come of age. It has grown faster than almost every other marketing activity for nearly two decades. Most companies that make up the Fortune 500 use some form of it, as do the largest firms in the service sector of our economy. It is extensively practiced by retailers, banks, and other local businesses.

What is direct marketing? It is many things. The full answer to this question is the theme of this book, which, it is hoped, will yield valuable insights as to how business can profitably use direct marketing in its operations.

Although direct marketing has come to prominence in recent times, the activity is old and has been described in many ways. The most common definitions include direct mail, mail order, and direct response advertising. All three of these concepts are related to each other.

*Direct mail* is a promotional medium whereby postal services provide the means of communicating with would-be buyers. These commercial messages come in different shapes and sizes—letters, postcards, catalogs, leaflets, coupons. Hardly a mailbox in America has escaped the vigorous assaults of these promotions. Advertisers in 1989 spent just short of $22 billion for direct mail, putting it behind only newspapers and television in terms of expenditures in measured media.[1]

*Mail order* is a device for advertising goods and services through any medium: television, magazines, or newspapers. But orders are fulfilled by mail. Today, mail order has been expanded to telephone. The modern customer finds it easier to phone in an order than to write it out on a standard form, stuff it into an often ill-fitting envelope, and remember to drop it into a mailbox on the way to work. Whether the response is written or oral, the mail order technique is basically a method of product distribution and accounts for a little less than 10 percent of all retail sales.[2]

*Direct response advertising* sends out sales messages by any medium, like mail order, but does not confine fulfillment to the narrow post office boundaries. In that respect, direct response advertising embraces the broadest range of activities.

Direct marketing includes all three of these somewhat overlapping concepts, and more. To put it into one succinct statement, *direct marketing* is paid-for communication in media, expressly eliciting a direct,

1. Robert J. Coen, "Estimated Annual U.S. Advertising Expenditures 1980–1989," prepared for *Advertising Age*. (Unpublished.) (Also see Table 1-1.)
2. Dorothy Rogers and Mercia M.T. Grassi, *Retailing: New Perspective* (Hinsdale, IL: Dryden Press, 1988), pp. 194–195.

measurable response, such as an order, an inquiry, or a visit to a store or showroom. *Direct Marketing* magazine defines it as follows:

> Direct Marketing is an interactive system of marketing that uses one or more advertising media to effect a measurable response and/or transaction at any location.

# Characteristics of Direct Marketing

A definition is like a reference file. It differentiates a thing from all other things in one clear statement and makes it easier to look up particular subjects. But it tells little about content, the inner workings of what has been defined. For a better understanding of direct marketing, we must cross the boundary of definition and go from outward to inward, from lookup labels to functioning details, from superficial titles to practical elements used in the day-to-day conduct of business.

Direct Marketing is an obvious tool of promotion. Like most promotions, it tries to make things happen by affecting customer behavior. Yet direct marketing also contains qualities that set it apart from other forms of promotion. What are they? Three in particular come to the fore: advertising-action unity, specificity, and feedback.

## Unity of Advertising and Action

Insofar as direct marketing communicates through paid media, it differs little from advertising. Messages in both direct marketing and advertising are sponsored by an interested source, usually a firm selling a good or service, that identifies itself as such. Then how does one distinguish direct marketing and general advertising?

The biggest difference lies in communication objectives. Direct marketing unites advertising with action; it solicits an immediate response. The typical national advertisment does not do that. Rather, it is part of a campaign, a series of ads, aimed at creating some desired image, favorable attitude, or buying predisposition.

Actually, general and direct-response advertising have the same ultimate goal—making sales. But the former sees the road to sales as indirect, a devious passageway winding through the confusing and little-understood labyrinths of consumer minds. It presumes that the right mental image must exist prior to purchase; attitudes precede purchases. In accordance with this philosophy, advertising is often produced as an arousal device. The link between arousal and action, however, remains obscure. After about a century of consistent effort, general advertisers have yet to prove a strong connection between their messages and the sales they are supposed to generate.

Direct marketing makes no claim that carefully built-up attitudes are prerequisites to sales. They help, yes. Direct marketers do not deny that. But they do not concern themselves much with gentle appeals to consumer psyches and shun everything else. They forgo oblique innuendoes and ask directly for orders. Every direct marketing message focuses on performance. It pleads with customers to do something, to act. Now!

Indeed, direct marketing has much in common with retailing, whose advertising often exudes a keen sense of urgency. Headlines scream at their audiences to buy now.

> Oriental Rug Sale. Fantastic Supervalues!
> No limitations, not machine-made, no look-alikes . . .
> Limited quantities!!!
> Largest Sale Ever, Plus . . . No Interest & No Payments 'til July!
>
> Our Deals Make the Difference!!!
> Every car will be sold at prices in this ad . . . on a first–come, first–choice basis.
>
> 90 Days No Payment!
> The biggest sale of the year! Sale ends March 25!
>
> Price Slasher Sale! But hurry, this sale gets cut off Wednesday at 9 P.M.!

The marriage of advertising and selling goes a long way toward explaining why direct marketing holds great attraction for retailers. Of the 300 leading mail order houses listed in the Scroge Directory, almost one-fourth run retail operations. The sales volume of these establishments is proportionately greater than their numbers, for they include such giants as Sears, J.C. Penney, Neiman-Marcus, Marshall Fields, Bloomingdale's and Saks Fifth Avenue. All these stores conduct extensive mail order businesses. J.C. Penney reports more than 300 million catalogs distributed each year. Sears does not release figures on the number of annual mailings. But it issues more than 50 full-color catalogs per year, in addition to brochures and newspaper inserts across the country. Catalog supplements alone total more than 300 million copies annually, and in 1985 the firm's catalog sales amounted close to $7 billion.[3]

By combining advertising and selling, direct marketing eliminates the need for personal selling or, for that matter, shopping at sellers' premises. In many merchandise lines direct marketing thus acts as a substitute for retailing. The two rivals—direct marketing and retailing—vie for sales in ready-to-wear apparel, sporting goods, books, records, tapes, and crafts.

At the same time, direct marketing complements retailing in many ways. A symbiotic relationship exists in which both distribution systems

3. *Scroge Directory.*

draw support and sustenance from each other. Dependence flows in two directions, from retailing to direct marketing and vice versa.

In the first instance, retailers can extend their trading zones without incurring large capital expenditures. J.C. Penney, for example, sent catalogs into Texas and fulfilled orders from out-of-state distribution centers before any stores were opened in the Lone Star State.[4] Brooks Brothers, long known for quality men's clothing, tapped new markets by an aggressive program of specialty catalogs in the 1980s.[5] Offerings such as "Brookgate," geared to young male executives, attracted customers living beyond easy traveling distance to Brooks Brothers stores. The groups of new catalogs filled huge gaps between the firm's major trading zones and increased the number of customers on a national scale.[6]

Another way in which in-store operations breed mail order is when retailers seek better returns from shelf space. Large department stores carry as many as 50,000 items or more but find space limited. All possible variations in a line, or even just the profitable ones, cannot be displayed in the store. Generally speaking, replacing low-turnover products with better-selling ones produces more revenue per linear foot of space. If that is the name of the game, a retailer has two choices: drop the slow mover or sell the vacated merchandise by direct marketing. The latter alternative gives retailers the option of maintaining full product lines without sacrificing economical use of space. It also yields incremental revenue by adding products that would ordinarily not be offered.

The other scenario is retailing that follows direct marketing. Spiegel, one of the largest mail order companies in the United States, opened more than a half-dozen outlet stores for overstocks. Here the retail store is used as a device to move excess merchandise resulting from direct marketing. Likewise, Lillian Vernon in 1985 opened a test store in New Rochelle, New York, to see if its 3,000-plus items sold by catalog can form a base for a retail business.[7]

Sharper Image provides another example of retail following direct marketing. The firm originally sold consumer electronics, apparel, and health-related products. In the early 1980s, it decided to use its mail order facilities as a springboard into retailing. The first store opened in San Francisco in 1983, and within five years some 15 outlets came into existence.[8]

---

4. Don Abramson, "What Retailers Must Learn About Fulfillment," *DM News* (June 1, 1984), p. 28.
5. *Scroge Directory*, pp. 73–74.
6. Al Schmidt, "Key to Some Retail Problems: Direct Marketing Concept," *Direct Marketing* (October 1982), p. 106.
7. See *Scroge Directory*.
8. *Ibid*.

No matter which comes first, direct marketing and retailing are often inseparable. As so aptly phrased in a Royal Silk management report, stores generate new customers for catalog mailings and, in turn, catalogs serve as in-home advertisments for the stores.[9]

The marriage of retailing and direct marketing does not always have a fairy-tale ending. The Royal Silk cohabitants did not live happily ever after; in December of 1988 the company filed for bankruptcy under Chapter 11. Having leveraged itself to ride the swelling waves of growth, the corporation foundered when unforseen events hit.[10] Royal Silk sold off its 17 retail stores and, at this writing, is busy trimming off the corporate fat that it added imprudently in the go-go days of the 1980s.

Royal Silk's failure does not discredit the mutual benefits of direct marketing and retailing that management described in an hour of optimism. The majority of such ventures perform satisfactorily. All business holds risk, but that is no reason to avoid business undertakings.

## Specificity

A second characteristic unique to direct marketing is the use of media to transmit messages to specific, preselected individuals. For lack of a better word, we call this feature *specificity*.

Some idea of the scope of direct marketing can be gotten by examining advertising expenditures. These are given in Table 1-1, which shows advertising expenditures in measured media.

Except for direct mail, which forms the backbone of direct marketing, and the Yellow Pages, all media in Table 1-1 reflect general advertising. Some print and broadcast advertising solicits direct response, but such ads make up an insignificant proportion of the total.

Such means of general advertising, both national and local, are "open systems." Messages cannot be directed precisely to particular individuals. Rating surveys give broadcasters estimates of audience, but they cannot tell exactly who watches and who does not. People are treated as a mass and are given probabilities, which apply to no particular individuals. The audience for magazines is a little more precise, especially those that distribute a goodly portion of their copies by subscription. Yet all subscribers do not read every issue, and for many magazines the major part of their readership is composed of nonsubscribers. At least that is the conclusion of the syndicated audience studies, such as Simmons and MRI. Unless delivered directly to homes, newspapers similarly cannot direct advertising to particular homes or individuals, and under no circumstances can they control readership.

9. Quoted in *ibid.*, p. 468.

10. Arnold Fishman, "Mail Order, Top 250+," *Direct Marketing* (July 1989), pp. 42–43.

**TABLE 1.1. Estimated U.S. Advertising Expenditures (1989) (in millions of dollars).**

| Medium | Expenditures |
|---|---|
| Newspapers | 32.368 |
| Television | 26,891 |
| Direct mail | 21,945 |
| Yellow Pages | 8,330 |
| Radio | 8,323 |
| Magazines* | 6,928 |
| Business publications | 2,763 |
| Outdoor | 1,111 |
| Miscellaneous** | 15,271 |
| Total | 123,930 |

*The total for magazines includes both consumer and farm publications. The latter accounted for $212 million.

**"Miscellaneous" includes such media as transportation, weekly newspapers, and free shopper advertising and advertising material distributed at the point of purchase.

SOURCE: Prepared for *Advertising Age* by Robert J. Coen, McCann-Erickson, Inc. Reprinted with permission.

Outdoor advertisers also reckon circulation in terms of broad, overall averages. They make counts of road traffic but cannot say exactly who drives past a billboard, let alone who sees it and takes note. Advertisements in these media take on the characteristics of their carriers. Marshall McLuhan many years ago epitomized this tendency: "The medium is the message."[11]

Media that convey general advertising reach out in unrestricted fashion to find audiences, and the coupling is a chance encounter. Advertisements thus are generalized messages, addressed "to whom it may concern."

In contrast, direct mail and telephone calls, the two pillars that support the direct marketing edifice, go to specific homes. A mailout must have an exact address to be delivered, even if sent to an unnamed "occupant." A phone call is made to a specific number and is answered only by a person in that home—or sometimes by an answering machine. But that automaton is nevertheless an extension of a person. These media, direct mail and telephone, account for some 85 percent of total direct marketing expenditures.

These specifically directed media have obvious advantages over their generalized cousins. Messages are not transmitted haphazardly. They are finely focused. They communicate one on one. But control extends only to transmission, not reception. People may throw mailings into a trash can without reading them. They may hang up on telephone solicitors, not wanting to be disturbed at home. Marketers thus control

11. Marshall McLuhan, *Understanding Media: The Extensions of Man* (New York: McGraw-Hill, 1965) p. 7.

only one part of a communication system. The firm produces and sends out commercial messages, but cannot control how these messages are received or acted on.

However, although marketers cannot mandate customer response, they can influence it. This is done in two main ways. The first way is to segment the marketplace so as to appeal to those sectors of the general population that are most likely to buy. Putting this notion into practice calls for market analysis, product design, and media selection. The idea is to offer the most appropriate products to the "right" audiences.[12]

Specificity gives direct marketing the ability to fulfill individual tastes and demands, to tailor products to particular customers.[13] The one-on-one approach is perhaps best exemplified by GM's Saturn model. Customers can choose from many alternative features, and cars are manufactured to order by programmable robots. The "have it your way" concept has come full circle from simple hamburgers to complex products such as automobiles.

The second way of influencing response is by presenting the offer in an attractive and interesting manner. This job entails creativity and skill of copywriters, layout specialists, art directors, and production people and goes under the name of copy development.

## Feedback

Direct marketing gives its practitioners the ability to measure response objectively. An order for goods or a request for information is a hard, indisputable fact. By keying advertisements, these actions can be traced directly to a particular communication source. When carrying direct response advertising, even such generalized media as print and broadcast identify buyers by name and address and specify the source of such response.

Tracking individual transactions is often referred to as *feedback*. This term came from cybernetics, the science of control, and applies strictly to mechanical systems. Whether ideas of the physical sciences can be carried over to marketing is debatable. For one thing, marketing lacks the high degree of regulation that is inherent in a mechanical system. Unlike engineers, marketers cannot control every part of the communication system with which they are involved. Governance of output is especially weak, although that is the most vital part of a marketing system. The vast majority of consumers who receive a telephone call or a mailing piece do not respond in a positive way. After all, isn't all marketing geared toward accomplishing some predetermined result?

---

12. For more details on segmentation, see Chapter 5.
13. For a fuller development of this thesis, see Stan Rapp and Tom Collins, *Maximarketing* (New York: McGraw-Hill, 1987).

Yet direct marketing, more than any other branch of selling or advertising, can rightly claim the advantages of feedback. Direct marketers don't have to fall back on John Wanemaker's oft-quoted remark to evaluate their efforts: "I know that half my advertising works, but I don't know which half." They know what worked, what didn't, and how much response came from each ad.

Direct marketing measures advertising results specifically and objectively. There are no inferences drawn from sets of disputable assumptions. Advertising thus becomes more accountable. A firm can judge the value of its advertising by comparing expenditures with returns.

Feedback is enhanced by the ever-decreasing costs of data processing. Computerized databases have enormously expanded capacities to record and store information. Companies can track individual transactions as never before, and many experts think that this development forms the essence of direct marketing.[14]

## Products and Markets

Many practitioners insist that almost any product can be sold by direct marketing. The goods and services sold by this method, however, are not random. Some items rely heavily on direct marketing, and others not at all. When would a business lean toward direct marketing, and when would it move away from it? The answer depends on the nature of the products and the markets the firm enters.

On the whole, specialties and general merchandise make up a substantial portion of the goods category. Insurance and credit cards hold prominent positions in the services area. Exact figures are hard to come by, but a number of consumer surveys provide estimates. Table 1-2 presents a select list of items ordered by mail or phone, as reported by Simmons Market Research Bureau. These figures are based on a national probability sample of some 38,000 interviews conducted over a two-year period.

The percentages are small, but when they are projected to the entire adult population, the numbers become imposing. For example, the 4.2 percent who bought audio cassette tapes translates into more than 7 million customers 18 years of age or older. According to Simmons Market Research Bureau, roughly 45 percent of adults bought something by mail or phone during a 12-month span.[15]

The products listed in Table 1-2, excluding insurance, were the most commonly mentioned in the Simmons survey. Insurance is bought less frequently than magazines, books, or records, but prices of insurance

14. Herbert E. Brown and Roger W. Brucker, "Just What Is a Direct Marketing Offer?" *Direct Marketing* (November 1988), pp. 68–75.
15. *DMA Statistical Fact Book* (New York: DMA, 1989), p. 7.

**TABLE 1.2. Products Ordered by Mail or Phone in Last 12 Months.**

| Product | Percent of Adults Ordering |
|---|---|
| Magazines | 13.3 |
| Clothing | 11.6 |
| Books from book clubs | 5.3 |
| Other books | 4.1 |
| Travel information | 4.2 |
| Audio cassette tapes | 4.2 |
| Records | 3.6 |
| Credit cards | 3.5 |
| Toys | 3.4 |
| Plants, trees, seeds | 3.3 |
| Insurance | 1.9 |

SOURCE: Simmons Market Research Bureau, as reported in *DMA Statistical Fact Book* (New York: DMA, 1989) pp.4–5.

policies are much higher. Consequently, insurance vaults to the top of direct marketing sales in terms of dollar volume. This conclusion is buttressed by examining the companies—12 in all—whose mail order sales in 1988 amounted to $1 billion or more (see Table 1-3). Of the 12 leading mail order operators, five offer insurance. General merchandise, publishing materials, apparel, and entertainment rank among the top sellers.

**TABLE 1.3. Leading U.S. Companies in Mail Order Sales, 1988 and 1989 (in $ millions).**

| Company | Products Offered | Sales | |
|---|---|---|---|
| | | *1988* | *1989* |
| United Automobile Association Services | Insurance | 2,180 | 2,738 |
| Time, Inc. | Books, magazines, cable TV | 1,997 | 2,636 |
| Sears, Roebuck & Co. | Insurance, auto club, general merchandise | 1,597 | 3,280 |
| Tele-Communications | Cable TV | 1,468 | |
| GEICO | Insurance | 1,430 | |
| Reader's Digest | Books, magazines, collectibles, general merchandise | 1,420 | 1,584 |
| Spiegel | General merchandise, apparel | 1,384 | |
| Fingerhut | Audio-video, food, insurance, general merchandise | 1,146 | |
| AT&T | Service, consumer electronics | 1,132 | |
| American Cable & Communication | Cable TV | 1,021 | |
| J.C. Penney | General merchandise, insurance | 1,021 | 3,170 |
| American Auto Association | Auto clubs | 1,000 | |

SOURCE: Arnold Fishman, "Mail Order, Top 250+," *Direct Marketing* (July 1989) p. 20; (October 1990), p. 48.

What do these leading products have in common? What generalizations apply to items that lend themselves to direct marketing?

PRODUCTS WITH GAPS IN DISTRIBUTION. The most popular items sold by direct marketing lack wide, extensive coverage in distribution. Products available everywhere are more conveniently purchased at local stores—drug outlets, supermarkets, variety stores. Packaged goods are a prime example. Why wait for such merchandise to arrive by mail or private carrier when it can be obtained with so little effort, and cheaper?

PRODUCTS WHOSE CUSTOMERS ARE WIDELY DISPERSED. Low customer density makes retailing uneconomical, especially for low-priced goods and services. Consumers order in small quantities, and store traffic is a major contributor to profitability. When demand is low, nonstore selling becomes a viable alternative.

The same holds for industrial goods. Firms cannot support personal selling when customers are scattered and unit prices are low—unless order size is large. In the absence of quantity orders, direct marketing offers an attractive way of overcoming spatial gaps in demand.

FAMILIAR PRODUCTS WITH STANDARD SPECIFICATIONS. By the very nature of direct marketing, customers buy sight unseen. A picture in print or on television is not the same as the actual product, and people have a natural reluctance to order things when they are not sure exactly what they are getting.

Buyers want dependability and freedom from risk. "I usually buy from companies I have heard of before." That refrain was sounded most often in a recent Gallup purchase survey of more than 1,550 consumers.[16] A good reputation is a valuable corporate asset, not only in direct marketing but in all fields of business. But reputation does not come about overnight; it matures over a lengthy period of time.

To reduce risks of sight-unseen buying, unconditional guarantees have become an almost permanent feature of direct marketing. Ads frequently assure buyers of satisfaction (see Figure 1-1) or money back. This has been a long-standing policy of Sears, Penney, and many other resellers.

Another way of lessening buyer risk is to offer products for examination, on a trial basis (see Figure 1-2). Many books and records, the contents of which are not precisely known, are sold in this manner. Such items can be returned within a specific period free of charge if a buyer isn't satisfied.

16. "Familiarity Breeds Orders Survey," *Target Marketing* (August 1987), p. 11.

## *We make shopping easier!*

**We promise complete satisfaction on absolutely everything**...including personalized products. If you're unhappy with anything you order, don't keep it...return it for a replacement, refund or credit!

**Shop by phone anytime!** Our operators are here 7 days a week, 24 hours a day to take credit card orders when it's convenient for you! Call 914-633-6300, and please have your charge card and catalog handy. Sorry, we don't accept collect calls.

**Let us send your gifts!** Just tell us the recipient's name and address, and the items you want sent. Add $2.00 for each address you're mailing to, we'll do the rest!

**Our Customer Service Representatives** will be happy to answer any questions you have. Call 804-430-1500, Monday through Friday, 9 a.m. to 5 p.m., E.T. If you're inquiring about an order you've received, be sure to have the packing slip ready—we'll ask for the 9-digit order number at the top of the form.

**At Lillian Vernon, personalization is FREE!** You can "customize" any item we offer personalized—be it with initials, monograms, a name or saying—at no extra charge! Just provide us with the information on the order form (list initials in usual order). Please note: monograms have the last-name intials centered (we'll be sure it's properly done). We offer ALL personalized items plain, too.

**To return an item,** just fill in the reverse side of the packing slip, and send it along with your return. If you no longer have the packing slip, don't worry— write all the pertinent information on a piece of paper. Send all returns to: Lillian Vernon Distribution Center, Virginia Beach, VA 23479-0001.

**Our refund policy is simple!** If you paid for your order with a personal check, money order or Lillian Vernon gift certificate, we'll issue you a refund check. If your order was paid for using any major credit card, we'll credit your account.

**We sometimes share our mailing lists** with other reputable companies. If you'd prefer not to receive these mailings, send us a note with your name and address exactly as it appears on the back cover of your catalog. Tell us whether you want your name removed only from outside mailings, or from all mailings, including ours. Send to: Lillian Vernon Mail Preference, Virginia Beach, VA 23479-0004.

**FIGURE 1-1 Lillian Vernon Ad Promising Complete Satisfaction**
*Source:* Reprinted with permission of Lillian Vernon.

# It's time to re-order

☐ Please send ______ Qty. 1991 Re-Markable Calendars.
☐ Please send ______ Qty. Marker Sets.
☐ Please send ______ Qty. Easy Wipe-Offs.
☐ Charge my ☐ Visa ☐ American Express ☐ MasterCard
Card # ______
Expiration Date ______
Signature ______
☐ Bill me later.
Purchase order number ______ (necessary to fill order)

**DC90**

**1991 Re-Markable Calendar**

*Only $12.95 for the first Re-Markable (plus $3.00 S&H).*
*Only $9.95 for each additional Re-Markable (plus $1.50 S&H).*
*FREE fine tip black marker included with each Re-Markable.*
*Marker Set (set of 8) only $4.95 (plus $.95 S&H).*

**Telephone: (201) 784-0900  Fax: (201) 767-7463**

Name MS. CLAIR KATZENTSIN
Company PAR ASSOCIATES INC.
Address 500 BARNETT PLACE
City HO-HO-KUS State NJ Zip 07423

Please correct if necessary  0049274  CODE RC90  CODE DC90

**Remarkable Products**
245 Pegasus Avenue, Northvale, New Jersey 07647
**Forwarding Postage Guaranteed**
**Address Correction Requested**

Presorted First Class Mail U.S. Postage Paid Remarkable Products

Use the convenient order form above to receive your 1991 Re-Markable Calendars in plenty of time to plan your schedule without interruption. Take advantage of our two Guarantees:

## 30-day No-Risk trial offer

If you are not satisfied, simply return the Re-Markables and there will be no charge – No Questions Asked!

## 48 Hour Shipping Guarantee

All orders are shipped within 48 hours (Via UPS whenever possible)

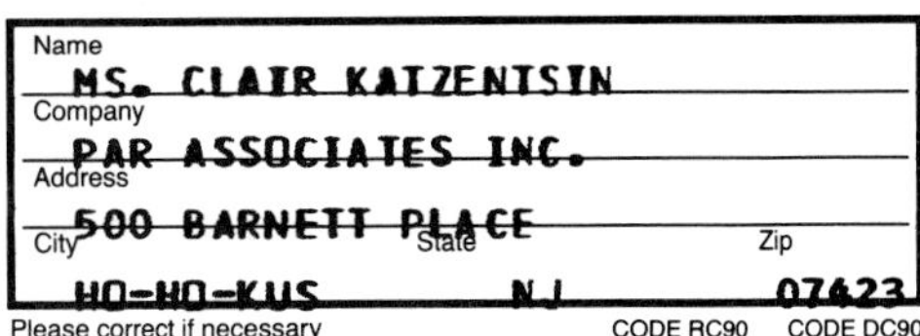
Name MS. CLAIR KATZENTSIN
Company PAR ASSOCIATES INC.
Address 500 BARNETT PLACE
City HO-HO-KUS State NJ Zip 07423
Please correct if necessary  CODE RC90  CODE DC90
D24*3/8

**FIGURE 1-2 An Example of a No-Risk Trial Offer**
*Source:* Reprinted with permission of Remarkable Products.

Nevertheless, steps to assure consumers that their expectations will be met encounter various obstacles. Many consumers regard nonstore buying as a hassle.[17] Most companies issuing unconditional guarantees stand behind their products but do not pay for returned merchandise.[18]

Product familiarity is closely related to questions of standardization. If a size 10 shoe varies from one manufacturer to another, there is no telling whether the footwear will fit. Similarly, purchasing agents are not prone to order goods for their companies if product specifications are not standardized.

Company familiarity is not the only quality that breeds orders. Product awareness is also a prominent factor. Items must have common meanings among consumers with respect to product features and specifications.

DELIVERY TIME. Delivery time looms important in business-to-business transactions, especially with the growing trend toward just-in-time inventories. The most popular items sold to industry through direct marketing are standardized, off-the-shelf supplies. When they are produced for future demand, they can be shipped in minimum time.

Likewise, consumer markets may make stringent demands on delivery time. Almost 50 percent of consumers surveyed by the Gallop Organization agreed with the statement: "I find it difficult to order products through the mail because of the time it takes to get them."[19] The telephone has shortened the time from order placement to receipt of goods, and the toll-free 800 numbers encourage consumers to call from a distance. Yet time of delivery has remained a major concern. Consumer complaints about delays in shipments have occasioned a host of federal and state regulations.[20]

## Tasks of Direct Marketing

Like other businesses, direct marketing is a performance system. It is called on to perform certain tasks, which are quite diverse. From a marketing perspective, we can group tasks into two broad categories: those that are product-related and those that are not. Each of these categories, in turn, can be subdivided into two parts.

Product-related ads can do the entire selling job or play a supportive role. Advertisements that do not feature products can have commercial transactions as their goals, or they can be devised with no commercial transaction in mind. These tasks are illustrated in Figure 1-3.

---

17. Quoted in *DMA Statistical Fact Book, op. cit.*, p. 27.
18. *Ibid.*, p. 73.
19. *Ibid.*, p. 63.
20. For more details, see Chapter 3.

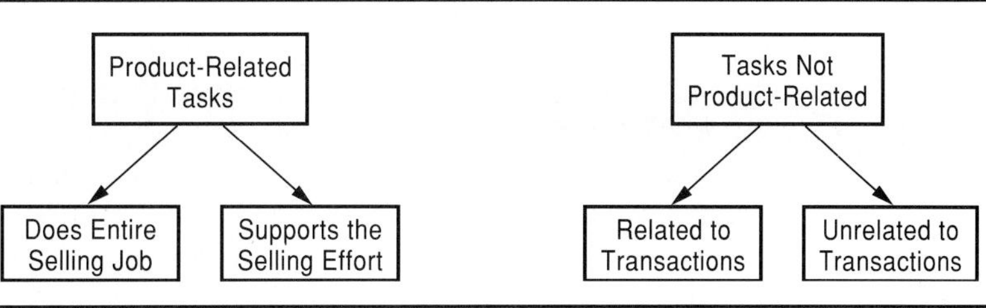


**FIGURE 1-3 The Tasks of Direct Marketing**

## Product-Related Tasks

Most direct marketing efforts are geared toward sales in the short run. No matter what the long-term strategy may be, the operational focus is on the present.

Results can come in one of two ways. First, a direct response ad can do the entire selling job. For example, direct mail pieces have merchandise order forms. Telephone solicitors frequently try to close sales. Printed ads with coupons and TV commercials with 800 numbers urge people to buy goods and services directly.

On the other hand, a number of direct marketing techniques are designed as supportive devices. That is, they work with other elements of the marketing mix in a somewhat subordinate role. Business-to-business marketing, for example, often confines direct marketing to lead generation, leaving closing to sales personnel. Service industries such as airlines employ direct marketing in much the same way. Advertisments for special tours and flights direct interested prospects to get in touch with their nearest travel agent or airline representative. Auto manufacturers and real estate operators may run sweepstakes, contests, and incentive offers to increase traffic at sellers' premises. Here, direct marketing functions like lead-generation programs, relying on personal selling to bring about the transaction.

## Nonproduct Tasks

Some direct marketing solicitations, probably about 10 percent, feature neither goods nor services. Then what sort of response do they seek?

One kind promotes an organization. Such advertising aims at inducing requests for company brochures, annual reports, and information about corporate projects and related company concerns.

These activities have two prime objectives. One involves transactions of some sort, but the route is indirect. For example, utilities may offer free literature on energy conservation. Whether such promotions eventually result in less electric or gas usage, additional insulation, or installation of storm windows, they effect transactions.

Another objective of transaction-related activity is to enhance the value of a corporation, usually the value of its stock. This job must be done circumspectly, for it is illegal to tout company stock by advertising or promotion.

Regardless of whether objectives encompass products or financial assets, products are not featured. Rather, the focus rests on the corporation. Results ensue indirectly; they are not measurable. In that respect, the approach is not much different from that of general advertising. The response is an intermediate one and not traceable to eventual action.

A second sort of solicitation involves no commercial transaction whatsoever. These direct marketing messages concern themselves with social or political issues, such as fund raising for charities (see Figure 1-4), political and social causes, and candidates running for office. Although direct marketing techniques are commonly used in these endeavors, there are serious questions as to whether they can really be called marketing. These actions, which have the same outward form as product advertising, do not give rise to exchange in a marketplace.

## The Flow of Influence

Tasks are duties that people set for themselves or for others. They arise from a set of objectives, which can be laid out formally, as in a marketing plan, or simply kept in an individual's head. It matters little whether these objects are formal or private. In either case, they depend heavily on products and markets. These relationships suggest a flow of influence illustrated by a familiar planning model, portrayed in Figure 1-5.[21]

The general planning model shown in Figure 1-5 depicts objectives as dependent on analyses of a firm's products and markets. This view accords with a management science philosphy of decision making, in which procedures follow a rational, problem-solving approach.

Every "problem" in the context of decision theory must specify a goal or objective, something management wants to attain. In keeping with rationalism, goal setting takes place after in-depth analysis of the marketing context. For example, a goal to generate a certain number of leads for an industrial product assumes that personal selling is the best instrument for closing sales. This is based on an intimate knowledge of an industry, of both its products and its markets. An objective to renew a certain proportion of magazine subscriptions has some realistic basis—either past experience, new knowledge about renewal trends, a market test, or any combination of these information sources.

---

21. This section is based on Peter S. Goodrich and William S. Sachs. "Patterns of Direct Response Advertising," *Discussion Paper 89-1*, Providence College.

# Here's your chance to achieve a small moral victory.

**What would you do if you saw a lost, frightened child?**

You'd probably stop, pick him up, brush away his tears, and help him find his way. Without even thinking about it. And there's a reason.

**You know what's right.**

And right now, you can do just that. You can act on instinct...by reaching out to *one* desperately poor child, thousands of miles away.

As a Childreach Sponsor, you can help a child who may not have enough to eat. A decent place to sleep. Medical care. The chance to go to school. Or hope.

**It's your choice.**

You can even choose the child you'd like to sponsor. A boy or girl. In a country where *you'd* like to help. You'll be helping that child within his own family. And more, helping that family to work with other families to make a better life for their children.

In return, you'll receive pictures of the child. Personal reports from our on-site overseas staff. And letters written in the child's or family's own words. You'll see for yourself what a difference your personal caring is making.

In fact, for just $22 a month, you'll make it possible for a child to have better nutrition, health programs, schooling — and hope. That's only 72 cents a day. Imagine. Your spare change could change a child's life.

**Please don't wait.**

If you saw a helpless child on the street, you wouldn't wait. You'd help that instant. Please don't wait now, either. Achieve a small moral victory!

**Become a Childreach Sponsor with PLAN International USA.**

**Call 1-800-225-1234 Now.**
**In RI call 738-5600**

**Yes, I want to reach out and make a difference.**

**Enroll me as a Childreach Sponsor to...**
☐ **The child who needs my help most.**
☐ Girl ☐ Boy ☐ Either
☐ SOUTH AMERICA
☐ CENTRAL AMERICA/CARIBBEAN
☐ ASIA
☐ AFRICA

☐ Please send my New Sponsor Kit with my sponsored child's photo and case history.
☐ My check for $22 for the first month's sponsorship is enclosed.
☐ Bill me.

☐ I'm interested, but not yet sure if I want to be a sponsor. Please send me information about the child I would be sponsoring.

☐ I can't sponsor right now, but I want to help. Enclosed is a contribution to the Children's Emergency Fund for $______.

☐ Mr. ☐ Mrs. ☐ Miss ☐ Ms.

ADDRESS

CITY

STATE ZIP

Mail to: Childreach Sponsorship
C/O PLAN International USA
157 Plan Way, Warwick, RI 02886
**Or Call TOLL-FREE 1-800-225-1234**

Childreach Sponsorship is a program of PLAN International USA, formerly Foster Parents Plan—one of the oldest and most respected sponsorship organizations in the world, with over 53 years as a leader in linking caring sponsors with needy children and their families overseas. Non-profit. Non-political. Non-sectarian. Tax deductible. A copy of our financial report is available upon request from N.Y. Dept. of State, Office of Charities Registration Albany, N.Y., or PLAN International USA.

**FIGURE 1-4 Example of a Nontransactional Message**
*Source:* Reprinted with permission of PLAN International USA.

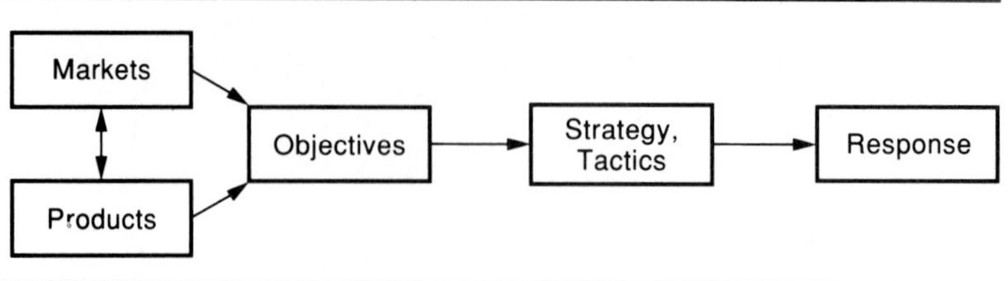


**FIGURE 1-5 A Flow-of-Influence Model**

Strategies and tactics are ways of accomplishing objectives. Strategies are long-term plans. Tactics are means of implementing a strategy. Consider the following:

> *Objective:* To increase sales of our product by X amount
>
> *Strategy:* To generate more leads so as to give our sales force more opportunities to make sales
>
> *Tactics:* A saturation campaign in the business press, offering free brochures and literature through reader service cards
>
> Installation of an 800 number to handle requests for information
>
> A follow-up program whereby outgoing phone calls are used to qualify these leads
>
> Integration of this program with personal selling, so that qualified prospects can be contacted by our sales personnel in *Y* days at the latest.

The type of response is largely a consequence of the tactics employed. A mailing of cents-off coupons results only in redemptions at the store. An offer of a prospectus by a mutual fund yields only requests for the financial literature. What ensues depends on the actions that are called for.

The level of response is another matter. Several factors have a bearing on results: what is offered, to whom the offer is made, and how it is presented.

An offer is what a seller proposes in an exchange. The more attractive its terms, the higher the level of response. A free catalog will bring a greater response than one for which consumers must pay.

Determining who gets the offer involves media selection—the choice between mailing lists, magazines, and TV shows, for example. The better an offer is matched with markets, the higher the response. An ad read by interested prospects will get a more favorable reception than one seen by the general public.

A bigger response, however, is not necessarily a more profitable response. The free catalog offer, for instance, may produce more requests for the publication, but it may lead to fewer orders than a catalog for which consumers pay. The marketer must consider the trade-off between a larger market potential with lower purchase probabilities and a more selective market with more likely buyers.

Finally, the way an offer is presented influences the level of response. In advertising parlance, this refers to *copy quality*, a unique combination of verbal and visual elements that make up a message.

Response is not uniform. It varies markedly across products and markets. A coupon for 50 cents off will bring in more redemptions than a $1,000 rebate on an automobile. In part, this is because the market potentials of the two products are very unequal. Second, 50 cents may represent a higher proportion of the respective product's price than the $1,000 rebate. Each product market has its own range of effective response, and planning for direct marketing requires an understanding of the limitations.

The flow-of-influence model implies that response is a mix of various activities, including both planning and implementation. The job of coordinating these widely diverse activities falls to marketing management.

# Direct Marketing Is Dynamic

So far, direct marketing has been portrayed in accordance with its mainstream features. Yet direct marketing is not a body of unchanging practices. Although its growth slowed toward the end of 1989, direct response is still expanding at a faster rate than other major phases of marketing. After adjustment for inflation, direct marketing advanced more than 5 percent per annum during the entire decade of the 1980s. That rate of increase is about double the real growth of the total economy.

Growth usually breeds change. For one thing, the more an idea is used, the more it is altered. Although mail and telephone are still mainstays of the industry, direct marketing is slowly changing its face.

Among the emerging agents of change is technology. The computer has introduced completely new ways of doing business. It has allowed databases to be used in new and profitable ways, such as identifying prospective customers through a wider range of demographic and purchasing criteria. The following are just a few concrete examples of how the computer has impacted the industry.

- Supermarkets have begun "frequent shopping" programs. With the use of cards that are electronically scanned with purchases at checkout counters, retailers can get a more accurate picture of individual or household buying habits.[22]

---

22. Lena H. Sun, "Checking Out the Customers," *Washington Post* (July 9, 1989), pp. H1, H4; Gerald McMahon, "Grocers Need Shopper Data Base to Build Strong Relationships," *Marketing News* (March 19, 1990), p. 26.

- More firms are adopting computer-aided telemarketing systems. These handle towering amounts of information, including customer profiles, past contracts and purchases, daily call reports, progress reports on leads, and statistical summaries of activities, campaigns, and results.[23]
- More than 300 billion coupons, or some 3,600 per home, are distributed each year. Advances in computer technology have made this gigantic volume easily manageable.
- Although the industry is littered with past failures, home electronic information services keep appearing. The most notable is that of Trintex, a joint venture of Sears and IBM, whose developmental costs are estimated at better than $250 million. The service, called Prodigy, made its market entry in the latter part of 1988. It offers computer owners access to news from USA Today and The Associated Press, stock quotations from Dow Jones, and merchandise orders conducted electronically.

Other changes have come from technological developments and innovations in business practice. Cable TV systems sport "alphanumeric" channels. These are basically text services that keep consumers informed on special events and promotions. More relevant to direct marketing are shopping programs that allow viewers to order by dialing an 800 number.

Some marketers have begun to exploit videocassettes as a selling tool. Real estate developers send out videos to brokers, who can show different properties to clients. Some have marketed these videos directly to individuals, who can inspect homes of various styles and prices in the comfort of their living rooms. Cadillac in 1987 demonstrated its new ultra-luxury model, Allente, in videotapes mailed to upscale homes. Several large retailers have developed videocassette catalogs to expand marketing alternatives.[24] Video stores are even renting tapes with coupons and direct response offers inside video boxes.

Many of these changes were occasioned by large national advertisers embracing direct marketing in major ways. Indeed, these large companies have acted as a powerful force in propelling the rapid growth of direct response.

When large companies adopt direct marketing, they seldom substitute it completely for other selling techniques. Rather, they add direct marketing to their already-bulging bag of tools, incorporating it into

23. See Sam L. Gallucci, "Automated Telemarketing Has Benefits Manual Systems Lack," (August 15, 1988), p. 9. For a more detailed analysis and a discussion of problems on implementation, see Api Ruzdic, "Potential Barriers to the Implementation of Computer-Aided Direct Marketing Systems," *Review of Business* (Fall 1989), pp. 13–20.

24. Scott Hume, "Sears Tests Video Catalog," *Advertising Age* (November 9, 1987), p. 46.

their marketing mix. For example, the Allente videotape promotion ran side by side with a heavy schedule of television spots and printed advertisements that extolled the graceful lines created by the famous Italian designer Sergio Pininfarina. In a similar vein, Visa, Master Card, and American Express spent millions on television advertising at the same time American consumers were being deluged by various mail offers of credit cards.

When direct marketing is part of an integrated advertising program, its results are difficult, if not impossible, to measure. What proportion of Allente's sales resulted from videotapes as opposed to the TV ads? How many cardholders were brought in by direct mail when ad campaigns were saturating other media, such as television and top-selling magazines? Like the mythical Gordian knot, the combination of direct marketing with other types of promotion cannot be disentangled to measure results by source of expenditure. Feedback acquires murky boundaries.

This trend of multiple resource usage is apparent in Table 1-4, which shows the percentage of money expended on the major medium used by the top 10 direct response agencies. Most of their clients are large companies.

Fifteen years ago, direct mail usage would have approached 100 percent in virtually every case. Direct mail still reigns as the top direct response medium, but its eminence is weakening. Table 1-4 indicates that two agencies give top billing to television and print. Two other organizations show less than 50 percent of total volume accounted for by direct mail. The industry statistics may contain ambiguities because firms use different accounting and reporting methods, but the overall trend is clear. In the years ahead, the share of direct mail can be expected to shrink as direct marketing becomes more diverse.

**TABLE 1.4. Expenditures of Top 10 Direct Response Agencies (1988).**

| Agency | Chief Medium, as a Percent of Total Volume |
|---|---|
| Ogilvy & Mather Direct Response | Direct mail, 65.6 |
| Wunderman Worldwide | Direct mail, 45.8 |
| Rapp Collins Marcoa | Direct mail, 31.1 |
| Foote, Cone, Belding | Direct mail, 80.2 |
| Direct Marketing Group | Direct mail, 68.0 |
| Grey Direct International | Print, 29.1 |
| Kobs & Draft Advertising | Television, 13.4 |
| Barry Blau & Partners | Direct mail, 100.0 |
| Chapman Stone | Direct mail, 85.5 |
| Devon Direct Marketing & Advertising | Direct mail, 96.8 |

SOURCE: Based on *Advertising Age* (May 15, 1989), p. 8–2.

# Summary

Direct marketing is paid-for communication in media that expressly elicits a direct, measurable response, such as an order, an inquiry, or a visit to a store or showroom. It has three outstanding characteristics that set it apart from other types of promotional activities:

1. Advertising and action are combined as a single function.
2. Promotional messages are primarily directed to specific, preselected targets.
3. Operations contain built-in procedures for feedback.

Approximately 85 percent of media expenditures go to direct mail and telephone. According to Arnold Fishman, it is estimated that $62.076 billion was spent on direct response advertising in 1989. Some 83 percent of this total occurred in the consumer sector of the economy; the remaining 17 percent took place in the industrial sector. Although direct marketing has a long history, its major growth came during the 1980s. It is still growing, but at a much slower pace. As reported by Simmons Market Research Bureau, roughly 45 percent of adults bought something by mail or phone during 1988.

Of the 12 leading mail order firms, 5 offer insurance. Books, magazines, general merchandise, and entertainment make up the balance of the sales. All of these products share the following characteristics:

1. They have gaps in distribution.
2. Their customers are widely dispersed.
3. They are familiar products with standard specifications.

Direct marketing is a tool utilized by many organizations with differing perspectives and diverse goals. It is therefore called upon to perform a variety of tasks. The objective of the promotion is always to produce some kind of response. Direct marketing is still growing at a faster rate than other major phases of marketing. The factors responsible for its expansion are technology, increased credit card usage, changing lifestyles, and growth.

**REVIEW QUESTIONS**

1. How and when did direct marketing start? Explain.
2. Describe the various charateristics of direct marketing. Provide current examples of each.
3. Describe how each of the following media applies direct marketing techniques: newspapers, television, consumer magazines, and business publications.

4. Describe the differences between general advertising and direct response advertising. Provide two examples of each.
5. Direct marketing has sometimes been called a "control" system because its messages are pinpointed to specific individuals and because of feedback. Comment.
6. Why is an unconditional guarantee such an important axiom of direct marketing?
7. Why does a good with wide gaps in distribution lend itself to direct marketing?
8. The greatest importance of computers lies in their use by companies rather than by consumers. Comment.
9. How do firms use direct marketing to promote themselves? Explain.
10. Marketers are spouting the benefits of videocassettes as a selling tool. Comment.

# APPENDIX A

# Some General Patterns of Direct Response Advertising

Peter S. Goodrich and William S. Sachs

## INTRODUCTION

The database is the hallmark of direct marketing. It is so closely entwined with practice that it is often thought of as direct marketing itself. Individual companies analyze databases to hammer out their programs, control their operations, and evaluate performance.[1] If firms can derive such benefits from customer databases, why can't they obtain similar value from industry databases? Is it possible to obtain useful insights from databases that relate to behavior of an entire industry?

We think so. For that purpose we have selected the Echo Award entries, a competitive contest sponsored by the Direct Marketing Association (DMA). These entries make up the largest body of information about direct marketing practices. Well over 1,200 entries come in each year, providing a wide range of experience. Since these data are continuous, gathered from year to year, they allow comparison of succeeding periods. Shifts in strategies and tactics are readily observable.

This analysis is based on 1,286 entries submitted in 1987. A random sample of 304 cases representing the entry universe revealed that 92

---

This appendix is based on Peter S. Goordich and William S. Sachs, "Patterns of Direct Response Advertising," Discussion Paper 89-1, Providence College.

1. Mary Lou Roberts and Paul D. Berger, *Direct Marketing Management* (Englewood Cliffs, NJ: Prentice-Hall, 1989).

percent of all submisssions contained product offers. A product here is defined as a good or a service that commands money in exchange. The 8 percent that did not feature a product were primarily fund-raising offers for various causes and charities.

An insignificant proportion of entrants—4 percent—advertised products in foreign countries. These were mainly English firms with business connections in the United States or American companies selling abroad.

Of all offers, some 62 percent were directed toward consumer markets. The remainder went to the business sector. Since the Echo Awards allow multiple entries, a certain amount of duplication exists. It is estimated that roughly 16 percent of Echo competitors submitted more than one entry.

A key issue relates to representatives. To what extent is the Echo database representative of the entire direct marketing industry? Of all business units offering products, 9 percent were among the top 100 leading national advertisers. Each of these organizations spent better than $83 million a year on advertising. Another 5 percent were firms ranked from 101 to 200 in advertising volume. The lowest budget in this group was $33.1 million.[2] In terms of entries rather than business units, about 19 percent were among the 100 largest advertisers. This calculation still understates the share of the top spenders by not giving full weight to volume. However, this underestimate is not too far below the 25 percent share of the $109.7 billion recorded by the leading 100 companies.[3]

Although large advertisers are major players in direct marketing, packaged goods manufacturers are underrepresented in the Echo database. Services and high-ticket items receive better-than-average emphasis. This does not mean, however, that packaged goods firms refrain from heavy usage of direct marketing.[4] Their focus is on promotion, through such means as redeemable coupons, where direct marketing is a subordinate element in the marketing mix. This sort of advertising does not win awards for exemplifying outstanding copy, so such advertisements are not entered in the Echo competition. The same is true of telephone solicitations. Business-to-business advertising seems overrepresented. Despite these deviations from overall experience, the Echo entries have many things in common with other direct response messages and yield valuable insights.

---

2. "Leading National Advertisers," *Advertising Age* (November 21, 1988), pp. S1-S34.
3. Robert J. Coen, "Ad Spending Outlook Brightens," *Advertising Age* (May 15, 1989), p. 24; Craig R. Endicott, "Philip Morris Unseats P&G as Top Advertising Spender," *Advertising Age* (September 28, 1988), pp. 1–2, 158.
4. See Dan Bencivenga, "Packaged Goods Manufacturers Think Direct" *Target Marketing* (October 1988), pp. 59–60.

## CODING

The first step in analysis is to bring the raw data into some form of order. This arrangement is called *coding*. The 1,286 records were first encoded into dBase III, a management program for handling large amounts of data. Statistical information was then generated by SYSTAT, a computer program that is compatible with personal computers.

All Echo data were categorized into 12 sets of variables. All categories, it was decided, had to be based on objective criteria. These were either stated explicitly on the entry forms or were readily inferred from observation. Subjective criteria can be useful, but when used as a first attempt, they did not seem appropriate for analysis. This decision narrowed the scope of analysis, but it increased accuracy and gave greater uniformity to the meaning of data. Table A-1 summarizes the classification scheme.

Direct marketers pretty much control all variables except two: markets and response. They can influence demand but cannot control it. They can influence the type of response but cannot set its level. The other factors depend entirely on the decision of sellers. They choose products and match them to markets. They set goals for themselves and then devise ways for meeting those objectives—formulating offers, creating advertisements, selecting media, and so on.

The variables analyzed in Table A-1 relate mainly to what is called an offer. There is no universal agreement as to the meaning of this term, but practically everyone includes products and transactional terms as

**TABLE A.1. Summary of Variable Codes.**

| Variable | Categories Tabulated |
|---|---|
| 1. Market type | Consumer, business |
| 2. Customer target | Present customer, new buyer |
| 3. Product class (LNA)* | 35 classes, grouped by product type: apparel, business and consumer services, financial, office equipment and computers, media and publishing, travel, and other, nonproducts |
| 4. Product summary | Goods, services, nonproducts |
| 5. Primary objectives | Order generation, inquiries, traffic building |
| 6. Conditional incentive | Used incentive, did not use |
| 7. Unconditional incentive | Used incentive, did not use |
| 8. Continuity of offer | One time, continuous |
| 9. Number of contacts | One, more than one |
| 10. Specific media used | Newspapers, magazines, direct mail, TV, radio, telephone |
| 11. Number of media used | One, multiple |
| 12. Response type | Direct sales, inquiries, other |

*Products were classified in accordance with categories as defined by Leading National Advertisers, Inc. (LNA).

parts of an offer.[5] We have used this minimal definition. We regard the presentation as advertising copy—window dressing, so to speak—and not part of the offer itself.[6]

## ANALYSIS

The primary purpose of any analysis is to understand causal relationships—how things work, and how things relate to other things in producing an outcome.

These relationships can be shown in many ways. One way is to proceed from simple to complex displays. Therefore, we begin with "marginals," shown as percentages. Table A-2 indicates the components of each variable and their frequencies.

As seen in the table, financial and other services make up the largest categories of Echo offers. Services, both to businesses and consumers, represent more than half the products offered. This is in line with our service economy, in which the value of services exceeds that of goods. More than three-fourths of all advertisements are directed to new customers, despite the fact that response is higher for present customers. This reflects customer attrition as well as single, stand-alone offers. Incentives apparently are an important part of direct marketing selling, especially conditional ones. They are given only if the prospect does something—goes to a dealer's showroom and takes a test drive, visits a recreational community and agrees to tour the property, and so forth.

Table A-2 represents one-way tabulations. Each variable is examined separately, as though independent of all other variables. This is a useful beginning, but it is not enough to illuminate relationships.

Caldwell and Sachs examined the data by using cross-tabulations.[7] This mechanism treats two or more variables simultaneously to study relationships. It addresses the problem as one of "conditional probabilities"—the likelihood of an event, given some other event, which is called the independent variable. The Caldwell-Sachs analysis designated "markets" as the independent or causal factor. The cross-tabulations thus show how all other factors are affected by the type of market, consumer or business.

Cross-tabulations yield more meaningful inferences than the one-way analysis. They reveal whether a relationship exists, in a statistical

5. See, for example, Herbert Katzenstein and William S. Sachs, *Direct Marketing* (Columbus, OH: Merrill, 1986); Edward L. Nash, *Direct Marketing: Strategy-Planning-Execution* (New York: McGraw-Hill, 1985); and Bob Stone, *Successful Direct Marketing Methods* (Chicago: Crain Books, 1986).
6. See Herbert E. Brown and Roger W. Brucker, "Just What Is a Direct Marketing Offer?" *Direct Marketing* (November 1988), pp. 68–75.
7. Peter Caldwell and William S. Sachs, "Echo Award Entries, 1987," *Journal of Direct Marketing* (Summer 1988), pp. 35–41.

**TABLE A.2. Frequency Distribution for Each Variable.**

| | | | | | |
|---|---|---|---|---|---|
| 1. | Markets | | 7. | Unconditional incentive | |
| | Consumer | 63.1 | | Yes | 10.0 |
| | Business | 36.9 | | No | 90.0 |
| 2. | Customer Type | | 8. | Continuity | |
| | New customer | 77.2 | | Single offer | 75.3 |
| | Old customer | 22.8 | | Continuous | 24.7 |
| 3. | Product classification | | 9. | Number of contacts | |
| | Financial | 21.0 | | One | 64.6 |
| | Services | 15.6 | | Two or more | 35.4 |
| | Publishing media | 9.7 | 10. | Media used | |
| | Office equipment | 6.7 | | Mail only | 76.5 |
| | Travel | 4.8 | | Magazines only | 6.7 |
| | Apparel | 3.9 | | TV only | 3.3 |
| | Other | 29.6 | | Other single | 3.3 |
| | Nonproducts | 8.7 | | Multiple | 10.2 |
| 4. | Product summary | | 11. | Number of media | |
| | Services | 52.0 | | Single | 89.8 |
| | Goods | 39.3 | | Multiple | 10.2 |
| | Nonproducts | 8.7 | 12. | Response | |
| 5. | Primary objective | | | Direct sales | 54.6 |
| | Orders | 53.8 | | Requests | 34.8 |
| | Inquiries | 35.1 | | Indirect sales | 10.6 |
| | Traffic | 11.1 | | | |
| 6. | Conditional incentive | | | | |
| | Yes | 38.2 | | | |
| | No | 61.8 | | | |

sense. But not all associations are relevant in an operational sense. A relationship may be "statistically significant," meaning that it cannot happen by pure chance. But it may be completely insignificant in terms of profit contribution, market share, returns on investment, or a dozen other criteria in judging a business operation. Cross-tabs do not reveal the strength of relationships that exist between attributes. To what degree are they associated with each other? How strongly?

Measurements of association imply some form of correlation analysis. The Echo database, however, is nonmetric. It has no numerical or rank-order values. A financial product is neither greater nor less than an item of apparel. The phi statistic, a nonmetric measure, was therefore used to assess the strength of various relationships.

A total of 12 variables yields 66 correlations. Degree of association was measured by the Cramer *V* coefficient, a modified version of the phi statistic. The Cramer *V* measure ranges from 0 (complete independence, or no association) to 1 (complete dependence). The advantage of this approach is that *V* coefficients have the same upper and lower limits regardless of the number of cells in cross-tabulations.[8]

8. Hubert E. Blalock, Jr., *Social Statistics* (New York: McGraw-Hill, 1972).

**TABLE A.3. Correlation Matrix of 12 Variables.**

| Variables | 1 | 2 | 3 | 4 | 5 | 6 | 7 | 8 | 9 | 10 | 11 | 12 |
|---|---|---|---|---|---|---|---|---|---|---|---|---|
| 1. Markets | – | | | | | | | | | | | |
| 2. Customers | .11 | – | | | | | | | | | | |
| 3. Products | .45 | .17 | – | | | | | | | | | |
| 4. Summary | .15 | .10 | .83 | – | | | | | | | | |
| 5. Objectives | .37 | .21 | .31 | .20 | – | | | | | | | |
| 6. Incentive, conditional | .08 | .02 | .21 | .12 | .14 | – | | | | | | |
| 7. Incentive, unconditional | .10 | .09 | .11 | .06 | .10 | .02 | – | | | | | |
| 8. Continuity | .08 | .06 | .39 | .24 | .13 | .04 | .03 | – | | | | |
| 9. Contacts | .33 | .21 | .33 | .24 | .87 | .12 | .07 | .08 | – | | | |
| 10. Media | .22 | .27 | .16 | .17 | .17 | .19 | .09 | .20 | .20 | – | | |
| 11. Number of media | .00 | .14 | .07 | .12 | .10 | .07 | .00 | .10 | .12 | .98 | – | |
| 12. Response | .37 | .21 | .26 | .20 | .93 | .13 | .09 | .12 | .84 | .17 | .10 | – |

The formula for Cramer $V$ is

$$V = \frac{\phi^2}{\min[(r-1),(c-1)]}, \text{ where}$$

$$\phi = (\chi^2/N)^{1/2}$$

$$r = \text{Number of rows}$$

$$c = \text{Number of columns}$$

The values of $V$ are displayed as a matrix in Table A-3.

Table A-3 indicates that markets are, at best, only moderately related to products offered, objectives, the number of contacts, and type of response. This suggests that the division of consumer versus business markets may be adequate for some sort of macro-analysis, but should be more specific when used by an individual company.

The nature of products has some link to continuity programs. That is, some products lend themselves better than others to this form of offer. Again, more specification would give more meaning, such as examining individual product categories. This, in turn, would necessitate accumulation of more data in order to obtain statistical reliability.

Objectives, which are somewhat related to markets, have extremely high correlations with the number of contacts and response type. It is readily seen that once marketers agree on what they want to accomplish, they create the means of achieving those goals. For example, an objective to solicit inquiries automatically leads to two or more contacts with prospective buyers, or a multiple-step approach to marketing. It also leads to a response that involves requests for information, literature, or a catalog. In this situation, there is little likelihood of a direct order. Objectives are strong determinants of the type of response. The Echo database, however, gives no evidence about the level of response.

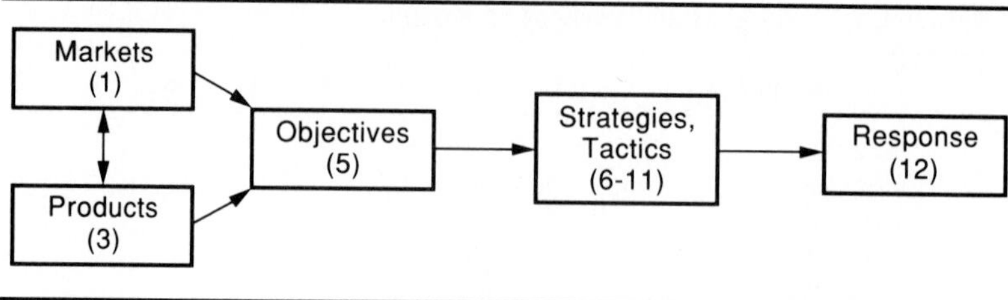


**FIGURE A-1 A General Planning Model**

## THE FLOW OF INFLUENCE

The observed correlations in Table A-3 provide strong support for applying the familiar general planning model. In its simplest form, this model can be visualized as shown in Figure A-1. According to this model, markets and products are regarded as independent variables in the short run. They make up the first four variables of the matrix in Table A-3 and are looked on as "states of being." Although products can be altered, they are "givens" in the short run. Resellers have more flexibility than producers, but even they, in most instances, choose from product sets that exist at a certain point in time. Objectives are influenced by product-market availabilities and, in turn, affect operational procedures.

The two sources of influence flows—products and markets—go together, like two sides of a coin. The flow can move in any direction. It can begin with products, the vendors of which go looking for markets. Usually, however, markets are primary, and products are matched to them. The effect of both variables on objectives, expressed as an unadjusted multiple $R$, is equal to .38. The partitioned variation for this two-factor model is shown in Table A-4. This table was obtained by the use of dummy variables, an acceptable statistical procedure when intervally ordered data are not available.[9]

**TABLE A.4. Primary Objectives = Constant + Product Class + Market.**

| Source of Variation | Sum of Squares | Degrees of Freedom | Mean Square | F-Ratio | Probability |
|---|---|---|---|---|---|
| Product class | 58.79 | 7 | 8.40 | 20.82 | .000 |
| Market | 12.64 | 1 | 12.84 | 31.34 | .000 |

9. *Ibid.*; Norman H. Nie *et al.*, *Statistical Package for the Social Sciences* (New York: McGraw-Hill, 1975).

## CONCLUSIONS

This analysis suggests that broad, industry-wide databases are capable of revealing general practices. Both environmental and operational factors, however, produce weak to moderate relationships with actual results. The analysis thus explains rather than predicts. This has been the experience of other broad industrial databases. The PIMS project at the Wharton School, the largest body of information concerning business practices, has indicated similar findings.[10]

Such results can be expected because large databases of this type contain many heterogeneous elements. Objectives are stated as generalities so that diverse parts can be united by common bonds. In addition, there is usually more than one way to reach an objective, even when choices are highly specific. In using such a database, an individual firm should narrow its scope to reflect more relevant experience.

A second shortcoming, largely one of analysis, is omission of copy elements. Models contain sizable unexplained variances when relevent factors are left out, and copy is probably one such element. The analysis has heroically ignored copy treatment because subjective methods are necessary in classifying advertisements. Some copy elements lend themselves to easy classification, such as size of advertising units, color treatment, themes, or selling propositions in a message. These are the "whats" of an ad. But the same theme can be presented in many ways, and the "hows" are much more difficult to pigeonhole into the neat compartments of a classification chart. If creative outputs are unique arrangements of thoughts, words, and graphics, by definition they are novel. How, then, does one classify them, especially in view of their large numbers? In this sense, the analysis is incomplete and should be regarded as a preliminary attempt to understand a bewildering array of experience.

Finally, the database itself can yield much more valuable information if responses are stated in a uniform manner. To safeguard confidentiality, entrants are allowed to record performance in various ways, such as "our response was 50 percent higher than our control." But what is the control? This laxity prohibits common metric measures. Estimates of response level thus become impossible. And this is what marketers want more than anything else—some way to gauge the returns that can be expected in a given situation. Not until some system of metric measures is included, even if adroitly disguised to safeguard confidentiality, can we begin to approach the subject of performance level.

Although the Echo database has a present value and can be used by individual firms with adjustments, it can be much more than it is.

10. Robert D. Buzzell and Bradley T. Gale, *The PIMS Principles* (New York: Free Press, 1987).

CHAPTER 2

# Organization for Direct Marketing

## PROFILE

C. JAMES SCHAEFER

**Proprietor to Corporate Management.** C. James Schaefer is former president of the DR Group, Inc. and executive vice president of Needham, Harper Worldwide. He typifies a small group of individual proprietors who have taken the old, direct response agency, actually a letter shop, into the modern world of advertising.

Schaefer attended Dartmouth and later its Amos Tuck School of Business Administration. Shortly after graduating in 1948, he served as sales promotion manager at Beechnut Company until 1952.

His first real contact with direct marketing was when he took a job as an account executive at Dickie Raymond, a direct mail agency that, for a while in the 1960s, was part of Metromedia. Schaefer rose to senior vice president of the parent's Metromail Division. In this position, he melded the simplistic letter shop operations with direct mail techniques geared to the broader world of marketing. In 1969 Schaefer was responsible for taking the direct response company out of the parent corporation. He, along with several other owner-operators, struck out on their own under the name of The DR Group.

Under Schaefer's leadership, the small mail order agency built up a reputation in the broader field of direct marketing. It first became well known for its business-to-business marketing. Among its blue-chip clients were such firms as Pitney Bowes, Pan American World Airways Cargo, Western Union, and the First National Bank of Boston. Gradually, the agency branched out into the consumer field, with Ramada Inn becoming the biggest account. At the same time, annual billings grew steadily, reaching more than $25 million in 1983. This put The DR Group among the top 10 direct marketing agencies.

By the late 1970s, a number of large general advertising agencies began looking to get into the direct marketing area. In early 1984 The DR Group became a member company of Needham, Harper Worldwide. As head of his old subsidiary and now an officer of the parent company, Schaefer symbolizes the marriage of general advertising organizations with a direct marketing company. It remains only a matter of time until both companies begin servicing the same clients, adopt each others' procedures and practices, and become integrated into a more effective form of total marketing. ■

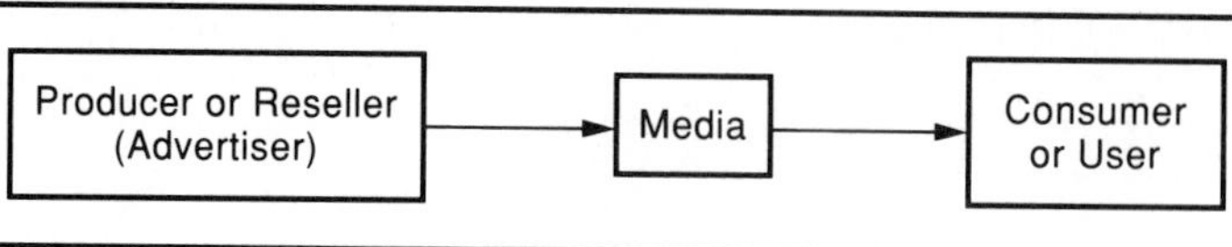


**FIGURE 2-1** **The Direct Marketing Channel**

## Direct Marketing as a Distribution Channel

The previous chapter described direct marketing as a function of total marketing. A function implies an action or activity. The activities of direct marketing are brought about by organized efforts. A prime objective of these efforts is to create a transaction, an exchange of a good or a service for money. As such, the organized efforts of direct marketing can be viewed as forming a channel of distribution.

Yet the direct marketing channel is somewhat different from traditional distribution forms. As the term *direct marketing* implies, there are no intermediaries separating sellers from buyers. The distribution channel is short and direct, involving no organization other than the seller. This relationship is depicted in Figure 2-1. As shown in the chart, the source or initiator of the transaction can be a producer or reseller. Their respective roles are not perfectly structured or mutually exclusive. Resellers are often producers, such as retailers who offer private labels. Such firms either produce these items themselves or obtain them through contract manufacturing and offer them in catalogs and brochures. Sometimes producers act as resellers. For example, credit card companies offer goods made by other firms in bills and brochures they mail out to their customers. Financial houses stuff offers of other firms into their bills and receive commissions on sales. This ambiguity between producers and resellers often makes direct marketing appear as a channel segment, a part of a larger distribution system.

Designations of consumer and user in Figure 2-1 refer to buyers in different markets. Consumer markets are composed of end users and make up the last stage of the distribution process. Once merchandise gets into consumers' hands, it is consumed privately by individuals. The term *users* refers to buyers in organizational markets, who use the good or service as an input in further production.

## Channel Organizations

Direct marketing sells products by paid communication in media, and the messages transmitted must be identified as advertisements by their sponsors. These practices conform to the standard definition of advertising.[1] In many ways, the structure of the direct marketing industry resembles that of the advertising industry.

In a delightful little book written more than three decades ago, Martin Mayer quotes an executive describing a meeting of the Advertising Research Foundation:

> The media people come first, usually about 10 minutes early. Then about the time the meeting is supposed to start, the agency people show up and start kicking the media people around. The advertisers come about 15 minutes late and for the rest of the meeting they kick the agency people around. Then everybody goes out for a drink.[2]

This tongue-in-cheek vignette is an analogy of the real world, where advertisers order, agencies suggest, and media request. It still represents the basic structure of the industry and, superficially, the commercial relationships of clients, agents, and suppliers. The advertisers are the producers of the goods and services they pay to have promoted. The advertising agencies work under contract as agents of the advertisers, on whose behalf they prepare and place ads and commercials. Media are the carriers of these printed and broadcast messages.

While Mayer's organizational core is still recognizable today, the face of the direct marketing industry has changed. In Mayer's day, direct marketing was virtually synonymous with mail order. Today, marketing practices are much more varied. New media have sprung up to challenge once-traditional forms, especially in electronic fields—cable TV, kiosks, videos. The telephone, ignored as a marketing tool before 1960, is as pervasive a means of doing business as negotiating rental agreements or billing for deliveries of goods sold.

Perhaps the greatest change in direct marketing over the last quarter-century has been the proliferation of facilitating agencies, of which media is only a part. A facilitating agency does not participate directly in a transaction. It supplies either goods or services associated with transactions. The leading types of such companies are listed in Table 2-1.

As the direct marketing industry expands, the numbers and types of facilitating agencies continue to grow. These firms are actually narrow specialists whose particular skills depend upon the size of the market. The larger the industry, the more it is able to support specialization and division of labor.

A major change in the industry's structure came with the development of modern direct marketing agencies. Before 1970 these firms were small undertakings, mainly proprietorships or partnerships, concerned with single functions. They concentrated on mail order, writing copy,

---

1. See American Marketing Association, "Report of the Definitions Committee," *Journal of Marketing* (October 1948), p. 202.
2. Martin Mayer, *Madison Avenue, U.S.A.* (New York: Pocket Books, 1959), p. 15.

**TABLE 2.1. Main Facilitating Agencies in Direct Marketing.**

- Media companies
- Direct marketing agencies
- Telemarketing service bureaus
- Fulfillment services
- Transportation agencies
- Public warehouses
- List compilers and brokers
- TV and video production houses
- Printing plants
- Freelance writers, artists, designers

or functioning as letter shops. Since then the leaders have grown in size and operate as subsidiaries or divisions of large advertising agencies.

These changes came primarily from budgeting trends of national advertisers. As late as 1970 almost two thirds of their promotional outlays went into general advertising. By the beginning of the 1980s budgets had done a complete flip-flop—more than 60 percent went toward sales promotion and less than 40 percent toward general advertising. The era of building brand loyalty by advertising was over. Rebates, cents-off coupons, sweepstakes, and premiums were the new engines that drove sales.[3]

As national advertisers waded deeper into promotional waters, they parceled out new assignments to their advertising agencies. In the beginning these jobs were handled like any others, going through regular account management. Eventually they drifted to specialized departments. These were thinly staffed and soon proved inadequate to service their clients properly.

The result was a wave of mergers and acquisitions. Advertising agencies picked up the smaller direct marketing firms by dangling hefty premiums in front of their owners. These owner-managers stepped gingerly into new roles of senior executives in larger, and often public, corporations. Noncompetitive clauses in merger agreements usually tied down the shifts in jobs. For example, WCRS, a British company that owned the agencies Della, Femina, Travisano & Partners, and HBM/Creamer, acquired Cohn & Wells, a San Francisco direct marketing agency that was billing about $20 million. The two partners who sold their agency signed a five-year contract to continue with the company at an initial salary of $3.2 million plus further payments, depending on performance.[4]

Most large advertising agencies with direct marketing sections separate these components from general advertising. They commonly struc-

3. B. G. Yovovich, "Stepping into a New Era," *Advertising Age* (August 22, 1983), p. M-30.

4. Jennifer Pendleton, "WCRS Broadens DM Base," *Advertising Age* (December 21, 1987), p. 16.

ture the direct marketing branches as independent subsidiaries. The parent thus becomes a holding company, in many instances operating other units. There are two reasons for the separation of direct marketing from advertising. First, the two kinds of marketing are disparate. Although a national advertiser may treat them as an integral part of a marketing plan, the goals of each division are different. General advertising focuses its efforts on image creation and aims for rewards in the long run. Direct marketing wants returns now, directly traceable to its current actions.

Second, the divorce of direct marketing from general advertising is meant to minimize account conflicts. That agencies shall not handle competitive accounts is an almost universally accepted rule. An agent, acting in the interests of a principal, cannot serve two rival masters at the same time. Since advertisers' assignments do not always pair direct marketing and advertising, agencies have difficulties keeping both types of activity under the same roof. Advertising may be farmed out to one agency and direct marketing to another. In this way, agencies have more opportunities to handle accounts of competitors. However, this strategy frequently does not work. Regardless of organization charts on paper, clients may not see subsidiaries as independent firms when their top executives report to the same parent and sit on the same board of directors. Table 2-2 lists the top 10 direct response agencies, along with their billings for 1990.

An exception to the separation of advertising and direct marketing within a company is the giant Leo Burnett agency, with billings of more than $2.5 billion in advertising. In 1986 Burnett was the first major ad agency to develop direct marketing internally as part of its advertising functions. Its direct marketing structure differs from the rest of the industry in several ways. Direct response is not organized as a separate profit center. It is neither a subsidiary nor a division. The same staff handles both direct marketing and general advertising. Direct marketing

**TABLE 2.2. Billings of Top Direct Response Agencies in 1990.**

| Agency | Billings ($ millions) |
|---|---|
| Ogilvy & Mather Direct Response | 855.2 |
| Wunderman Worldwide | 567.0 |
| Rapp Collins Marcoa | 398.2 |
| Foote, Cone, Belding | 319.3 |
| Kobs & Draft Advertising | 300.2 |
| Grey Direct International | 206.7 |
| McCann Direct | 191.0 |
| The Direct Marketing Group, Inc. | 146.2 |
| Bronner Slosberg Humphrey, Inc. | 127.2 |
| Lintas: Marketing Communications | 123.0 |

SOURCE: *DM News* (June 11, 1990), p. 10.

people are distributed throughout agency accounts. As put by a Burnett spokesperson, "If new employees are taught . . . that direct marketing is one of many skills you have to have, you'll end up with marketers who have no idea there's any other way to consider the relationship between direct marketing and general advertising."[5]

The Leo Burnett approach departs from the mainstream practice in other ways besides organizational structure. It not only does things differently, but it does different things. It assumes that direct marketing is a subfunction of advertising, not a distribution channel. Problems are likely to be seen from an advertising perspective and are likely to have advertising solutions.

## Use of Direct Marketing Agencies

Not all companies use direct marketing agencies. The decision to use or not to use an agency hinges on several factors: the tasks to be done, how capable the firm is of doing those tasks, and relative costs.

Few firms would give work to an outside agency if they had the capacity to do as good a job themselves. Companies that traditionally sell to customers directly, such as retail organizations, have less need to employ an outside agency. The core of their business is product policy or merchandising. Activities are product-driven. Promotions use local media, particularly newspapers, which allow no commissions to ad agencies. Many production functions, such as ad layout and typesetting, are included in advertising rates. A one day ad life does not warrant sophisticated graphics and expensive copy treatment. Consequently, most retailers have their own internal advertising and promotion departments. These groups usually create catalogs and mailings at periodic intervals.

The same departments also operate in electronic media. Local broadcasters, like newspapers, make production facilities available to retailers. Their personnel shoot and edit commercials in accordance with advertiser specifications. Retailers may hire outside creative specialists for specific jobs, especially when commercials need more professionalism and better quality than those produced by local talent. One option is the sandwich commercial. The outside agency does the opening and closing parts, and the retailer's promotion department fills in the middle with individual items and merchandise tidbits. The retailer might employ an outside service bureau, not a direct marketing company, to receive telephone orders that come in from the broadcasts.[6]

The exact manner of carrying out promotional activity depends on the size of the retail company and its line of business. Generally, the

---

5. Julie L. Erickson, "Burnett Pulls Clients into Direct Response," *Advertising Age* (October 17, 1988), p. 10.
6. See Chapter 13.

smaller the organization, the "flatter" the organizational structure. That is, there are few—perhaps one or two—organizational levels. In this sort of retail setup, direct marketing functions are apt to be found in the merchandise department and joined with newspaper advertising and sales promotion.

As retail organizations get larger, their organizational structures become "taller." They acquire more management and organizational levels. Promotion breaks off from merchandising, and jobs take on specialized functions. The promotion department might have different groups handling catalogs, mailing pieces, TV, and print media. Or a direct marketing section might be completely separated from general advertising. Because the variety of jobs is greater, larger organizations are more likely to employ direct marketing agencies for special functions. These may include such specialized tasks as particular promotions, broadcast production services, media placements, and package designs.[7]

Many publishers, who depend heavily on direct mail, also have internal direct marketing facilities. Magazines that distribute copies by subscription normally handle their own renewal notices. The vast majority of publishers refuse to report subscription renewals, but estimates for individual magazines run from roughly one-half to four-fifths of all subscriptions sold. A number of publishers employ outside direct marketing agencies when they solicit new customers in mass media and their messages require a certain touch of artistic skill and craftsmanship. In that event, they buy services a la carte. The relationship is one of buyer and supplier rather than of principal and client.

A third broad group of businesses with less need of direct marketing agencies is industrial marketers. They work with small promotional budgets, compared with sellers of consumer products, and their marketing expenditures go mainly toward personal selling. Impersonal communication, such as advertising in the trade press, is a nickel-and-dime business. Media charges are comparatively small. Ad agencies cannot afford to assign highly paid personnel to these accounts, and even then often ask for above-standard fees. Since commercial messages, both of general and direct marketing kinds, do not require refined artistic quality, many industrial firms maintain in-house facilities for making ads and mailing brochures.

Such companies augment their limited skills by buying outside services piecemeal. For example, industrial firms hire telemarketing firms to screen leads for the sales force. To prepare for a trade show, they might hire specialists to prepare material requiring skills that they lack. Direct marketing agencies also perform such services as creating a mailing package, designing a sales promotion, and building an exhibit for

---

7. D. M. Lewison and M. W. DeLozier, *Retailing*, 3rd ed. (Columbus, OH: Merrill, 1989), pp. 242–277.

a trade show. In most instances, they are willing to take these assignments on a project-by-project basis.

The main thrust of agency growth has come from large general advertisers who added direct marketing to their operations. They have practically no internal capability, especially in the area of creative skills. They are the largest users of advertising agencies. As they expanded into direct marketing, they went outside their companies for talent. Many of them first gave such assignments to their ad agencies, who in turn were encouraged to acquire direct marketing firms.

Regardless of how the blend of general advertising and direct marketing came about, the two forms of activity have become integrated, as they must. Clients don't care about agency organization charts. They just care about doing a complete marketing job. General advertising, direct marketing, and sales promotion might all show up in their marketing plans. What matters is that those plans be carried out.

A number of options are available for implementing a marketing plan. It might be assigned to one organization, such as an advertising agency, or the job might be awarded to several promotional agencies. In the event that assignments are given to firms not affiliated with each other, the client company must manage the diverse efforts. When tasks are handled by different divisions or subsidiaries of the same company, work is more highly integrated. In most cases, the advertising agency will act as the main contractor and coordinate all tasks. The direct marketing subsidiary will assume a role of supplier. The important point, however, is that the marketing mix used should work in a coherent manner. In this situation, direct marketing becomes integrated into the overall operation. It no longer stands by itself.

## Client Organization

An organizational structure is an arrangement for getting things done. Clients rely on two structural forms: functional departments and management teams. Most organizations combine the two forms in various ways.

The functional department is the older, traditional form of handing out job responsibilities. Direct marketing is usually included in the advertising or sales promotion department. The use of functional departments prevails when the firm has:

- Narrow product lines
- Diversified lines that are closely related
- Unrelated lines that benefit from similar promotional methods

In this type of organization, responsibility for any job, whether in-house or out-of-house, resides with a department. A mailing, a contest, a coupon, or any other promotion is run from a designated section of the

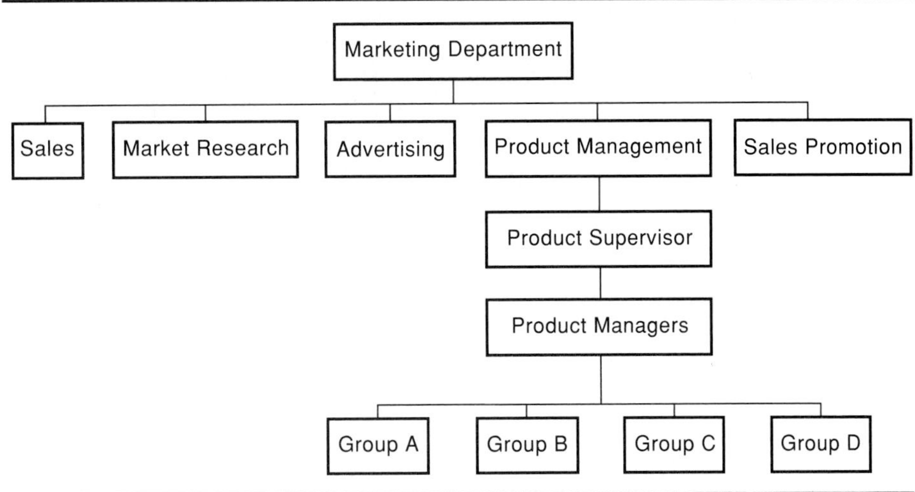


**FIGURE 2-2 Product Management System in a Consumer Goods Company**

company. This arrangement first took hold in single-line businesses and is still often associated with small firms.[8]

Large firms are much more likely to have product management systems. Promotional activities are handled by a team charged with managing one or more products. This team may call on internal departments to perform certain tasks, or it may work with outside agencies. The product manager assumes the responsibility of all marketing functions. A common form of a product management system in a consumer goods division is depicted in Figure 2-2.

When working with outside agencies, the product manager guides and integrates the various efforts. With respect to direct advertising, that executive establishes the goals of all projects or campaigns. As the delegated representative of the client organization, the product manager must also approve all plans and work undertaken by the agency. This includes creative outputs, production and media contracts, out-of-pocket payments to third parties, and any other obligation undertaken by an agency on behalf of a principal. Clients also set budgets for direct advertising assignments, and product managers track expenditures to make sure that spending remains related to returns. Finally, client organizations monitor and evaluate agency efforts continuously.

# Direct Marketing Agencies

A direct marketing agency, like its general advertising cousin, brings together a group of specialists concerned primarily with communication

8. Alfred E. Chandler, *Strategy and Structure* (Cambridge, MA: MIT Press, 1962).

functions. These include copywriters, artists, audiovisual specialists, television producers, photocomposition and print production experts, graphic designers, and others. The typical direct marketing agency is divided into three major parts: creative, media, and account management. Figure 2-3 shows an organization chart of the American direct marketing branch of Ogilvy & Mather Direct.

The creative function is the heart of the direct marketing agency. It is the only unique service an agency has to offer. All other tasks can be done by the advertiser. Many companies with large promotional budgets have their own media departments, maintain their own databases, and plan their own marketing and sales promotion efforts. But they lack creative talent, especially artistic skills of high quality.

Agencies can afford to pay top dollar for top talent by spreading costs among many different accounts. Innovative ideas can be imitated, but they cannot be anticipated except by their creators. The Ogilvy & Mather organization chart clearly shows creative groups not beholden to account executives, but to a creative director who reports directly to the president. All other functional groups, such as media, traffic, and technical, are under the general supervision of account groups.

Media functions are concerned with the placement of commercial messages. The placement of ads in media involves a multistage process. It begins with media planning—devising a schedule to attain a

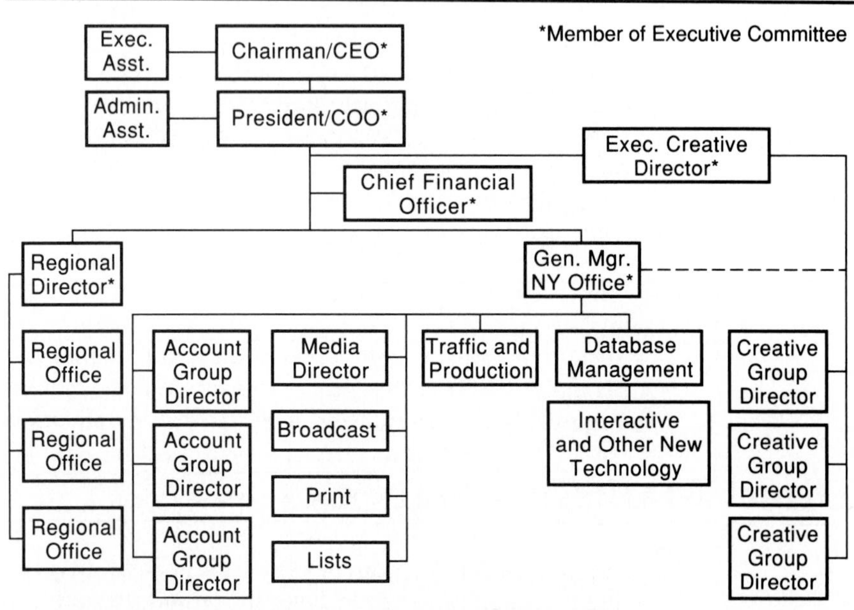


**FIGURE 2-3 Organization Chart: US Direct-Marketing Agency**
*Source:* Reprinted with permission of Ogilvy & Mather Direct.

predetermined goal. The selection process entails the matching of media with markets, as well as negotiating for space and time in general media. For direct mail, agencies may also be involved in negotiating list rentals for clients.

Traffic departments service media planners and are often part of media departments proper. Traffic personnel follow the progress of every job in an agency, making sure the right material gets to the right place at the right time. No matter where traffic is placed in the organization, it represents a routine, logistical function.

The account group is the coordinating mechanism. The account executive usually has a marketing background and familiarity, if not expertise, with the client's line of business. The makeup of an account group depends on the size of a budget. Big-budget accounts are headed by more experienced executives, assisted by adequate staffs. Low-budget accounts may use as few as one person sharing a secretary from a typing pool. Labor hours are related to budgets, since wages and salaries make up the major part of agency expenditures.

The account executive is the counterpart of the product manager. He or she is the liaison to the client organization, receiving all requests and complaints on the account. That individual presents all agency proposals for approval—strategies, creative efforts, media schedules, contracts, and bills. More than anyone else, this person becomes identified with the success or failure of direct marketing activities.

Agencies that go beyond the twin functions of creating messages and placing them in media are referred to as *full-service*. The additional services usually cover marketing research, campaign planning, database management, interactive systems, merchandising, sales promotion, and even narrow specialties such as product testing and creating exhibits and trade shows. To offer such a wide span of services, an agency must do a sufficient volume of business to support these lavish overhead functions. Only the very large direct marketing agencies, or those affiliated with sizable organizations, can truly offer full service.

## Specialized Services

The direct marketing landscape is spotted by firms selling ancillary services, such as list brokerage houses, telemarketing firms, and film production companies. These services complement the work of direct marketing agencies. They tend to locate near areas where advertising agencies cluster, such as Madison Avenue in New York, Michigan Avenue in Chicago, and Wilshire Boulevard in Los Angeles. Patterns of cohesion provide such narrow specialists with markets large enough to support their activities. At the same time, direct marketing agencies can purchase specialties at a reasonable cost. They would certainly pay more if they had to buy such customized services at a distance.

**TABLE 2.3. Sales Promotion Agencies by Service (1988).**

| | Service Sales (000) | | Service Sales (000) |
|---|---|---|---|
| *Strategic planning* | | *Creative services* | |
| Impact | $10,935 | Einson Freeman | $7,200 |
| CCG/TCA | 7,391 | OLM Associates (FKB) | 4,928 |
| Marketing Corporation of America | 4,675 | Guild Group | 4,800 |
| D.L. Blair Corp. | 4,598 | Merchandising Workshop | 2,465 |
| Sage Worldwide | 4,359 | Saugatuck Group | 1,372 |
| *Point of purchase* | | *Direct marketing* | |
| Sage Worldwide | 7,477 | D.L. Blair | 4,356 |
| Columbia Advertising Corporation | 4,557 | Flair Communications | 1,902 |
| Comart-KLP | 4,521 | CCG/TCA | 1,643 |
| CCG/KLP | 4,106 | Promotion Group | 1,543 |
| Flair Communications | 3,170 | Columbia Advertising Corporation | 1,519 |
| *Production* | | *Sweepstakes, games, and contests* | |
| American Consulting | 10,935 | D.L. Blair | 6,292 |
| Merchandising Workshop | 5,738 | Flair Communications | 2,536 |
| Einson Freeman | 2,880 | Smiley Promotion | 2,186 |
| R.P. Klein Associates | 2,625 | Don Jagoda Associates | 1,838 |
| R.H. Meyer & Associates | 1,926 | American Marketing Association | 1,072 |

SOURCE: *Advertising Age* (May 1, 1989), p. S-20.

But other specialty shops compete with direct marketing agencies, especially those that list themselves as full-service. Among them are sales promotion agencies that specialize in such activities as strategic planning and consulting, point-of-purchase activities, production, creative services, direct marketing, sweepstakes, games, and contests. The large, full-service agencies have been acquiring promotion and public relations agencies to round out their service mix. Nevertheless, these "boutique" shops have multiplied and although small, pose a formidable competitive threat to the all-purpose giants in the industry. They give national-brand producers more choices in selecting firms that supply business services. They also give small direct marketing agencies ready access to needed specialty skills. Table 2-3 shows the five leading firms in various specialties of sales promotion. The table shows in order of importance the top services of sales promotion agencies: strategic planning, point-of-purchase, production, creative, direct marketing, and sweepstakes and contests. Other areas with total 1988 revenues of $10 million or more are graphics, incentives, audiovisual, and event marketing.[9]

9. *Advertising Age* (May 1, 1989), p. S-19.

The increase of specialization has been accompanied by "scrambled services." As is evident in Table 2-3, promotion agencies take on various specialties, even when services are dissimilar, such as consulting on strategic planning and running sweepstakes. Full-service agencies are quite willing to contract on specific jobs so that they compete with limited function shops. This trend has blurred traditional product lines in marketing services and has widened the range of alternatives of doing business for all firms in the industry.

# Agency Compensation

Because direct marketing agencies are tied to those doing general advertising, both organizationally and functionally, compensation methods for the two activities are similar. Methods of paying agencies doing general advertising were actually carried over into direct marketing.

There are basically two methods: billings-based and cost-based. The first is a commission system. The second is popularly known as the fee system. Both methods have numerous variations. Choice of the method used is the result of negotiation between client and agency. Agencies are flexible, and will work under almost any system that yields what they consider a "fair return." Demand on part of clients is determined by the kind of work needed and the type of relationship a company is seeking.

## Commission System

The commission system is the oldest method of agency compensation, dating back to the nineteenth century. This method has become known as the "standard 15 percent commission system." The agency bills the client 15 percent of the gross value of time or space. Supplies and services paid for out of pocket are marked up 17.65 percent.

To illustrate how this procedure works, suppose an agency contracts to run print ads in a magazine for a total cost of $100,000. Out-of-pocket expenditures for such components as art, typesetting, and film negatives amount to $10,000. The resulting agency billings and payments are shown in Table 2-4.

Cash discounts, usually given by media at 2/10/net 30 (2 percent discount if paid in 10 days, net due in 30 days), are turned over to the client. Agencies typically get the money from clients before bills are due. They do not have the funds to pay in advance out of their operating capital. The standard procedure is for agencies to bill clients all estimated charges for a month and adjust the totals later in accordance with actual expenses incurred. When a commission system is used, current practice does not adhere to the standard 15 percent. Most advertisers pay smaller commissions, either reduced to a fixed percentage or to a sliding scale that lowers rates after spending reaches certain levels.

**TABLE 2.4. Agency Billings and Payments Under a Standard Commission System.**

| | Amount |
|---|---|
| **Agency Bills Client** | |
| Magazine space | $100,000 |
| Art and production | 10,000 |
| Markup on art and production @ 17.65% | 1,765 |
| Total billed client | $111,765 |
| **Agency Pays Vendors** | |
| Publication space costs | $100,000 |
| Less: 15% commission | 15,000 |
| Agency pays | 85,000 |
| Art and production costs | 10,000 |
| Total agency payments | $ 95,000 |
| Agency gross income (receivables minus payables) | $ 16,765 |

## Fee System

In the main, direct marketing does not readily lend itself to the commission system of compensation. Work performed in direct marketing bears no relationship to amounts spent in media. Consequently, the fee system is the prevailing method of agency compensation.

Fee systems are based on agency expenditures, primarily for employee time spent on a job. In practice, agencies use the 15 percent commission as a benchmark to assess the reasonableness of any fee. If 15 percent of capitalized sales is taken as a base, an agency can quickly calculate its after-tax profits. It then estimates the fee components—all direct costs, applied overhead, and the margin for normal profits—to arrive at the desired returns for its efforts. Although there are a number of variations in fee arrangements, fee compensation methods can be grouped into two basic categories: fixed fees and cost-plus contracts.

The fixed fee applies to contracts for specific projects. These entail piecework jobs that last for a certain amount of time. Agencies place definite bids for doing a job. In order that both parties understand what fees will be paid for services rendered, project specifications must be fairly clear. Each party must reach a mutual understanding of what the work entails. The agency will demand a fee that covers estimated costs and leaves a "fair" profit. The client must place some value on the finished work so that payments can be evaluated against expected benefits. A prior working relationship is most helpful in fixed fee contracts.

The *cost-plus* agreement is by far the most popular of cost-based methods. Although numerous hybrids exit, fees depend on three factors:

1. Direct costs expended on the account
2. Allocated overhead
3. Markup for profits

**TABLE 2.5. Format for a Hypothetical Fee Proposal.**

| Type of Cost | Amount |
|---|---|
| Estimated direct costs | |
| Salaries, fringe benefits | |
| Direct facility utilization | |
| Out-of-pocket costs | ______ |
| Total direct costs | |
| Allocated overhead | |
| Profit @ *X*% | |
| Total annual fee | ______ |

A fee proposal by an agency might follow the format shown in Table 2-5.

A popular version of the cost-plus method calculates fees on the basis of hourly rates. These usually include overhead and profit factors, which amount to some multiple of wage rates.[10]

Direct labor costs can be figured in several ways. One is the agency team method. This procedure estimates the amount of time an account group would spend according to hours put in by each member of the team. To simplify calculations, most agencies use standard costs, which are later adjusted to actual costs.

A second technique is the composite person method. First, direct labor requirements are estimated for a year. For example, an account executive might be credited as working full-time on the account for a year, a media planner half-time, a copy writer a quarter-time, and so on. The sum yields an annual total. Historical costs would provide costs per person, which would then be updated by anticipated salaries and expenses for the current year. These estimates are reconciled with actual costs each month using standard accounting procedures.

Recent years have seen vast changes in methods of compensating advertising agencies and, by extension, their direct marketing subsidiaries and divisions. From 1986 to 1989 some 38 percent of clients changed their agency compensation methods.[11] Some large advertisers, such as Procter & Gamble and R.J. Reynolds, have raised compensation in hopes of getting better work from their agencies. But most changes in agency compensation have resulted from the desire to cut advertising and direct marketing costs. That has been the prime motive in a move away from fixed commission, which dropped some 40 percent by 1988. Agency profits skidded to less than two-thirds of what they were a decade ago.

10. Association of National Advertisers, *Current Advertiser Practice in Compensating Their Advertising Agencies* (New York: ANA, 1983).

11. David J. Marrow, "Mad. Ave.'s Bargain Hunters," *Marketer* (April 1990), p. 42.

With an almost incessant pressure to reduce operating costs, especially in a highly competitive environment, agency work is increasingly regarded as generic, as a standard set of procedures that can be evaluated in terms of standard costs. This trend is understandable for general advertising, which, despite agency protestations to the contrary, cannot measure the profitability of its work. But direct marketing can do so to a large degree. Then why not reward good results and penalize bad ones? Is it time for clients to compensate direct marketing agencies with a system more in keeping with the realities of the marketplace?

## Financial Audits of Agencies

There are many ways in which companies can evaluate the work of their direct marketing agencies. One way is the financial audit. These examinations spring from the proposition that agencies are clothed with fiduciary responsibilities. They act on behalf of others. They enter into contracts that are legally binding. They disperse funds to media, printers, artists, actors, television production houses, and various suppliers, and they bill their clients for the payments. The financial audit is the chief means of ascertaining whether an agency discharged these obligations in an adequate manner.

Roughly two-thirds of all agreements between advertisers and their agencies allow clients to audit financial records relating to their accounts.[12] These audits apply to direct marketing agencies as well as those in general advertising. Most agencies can expect audits from client companies if substantial sums are involved.

Financial audits usually include verification of costs and expenses, such as the number of hours actually worked on accounts, expenses relating to travel and entertainment, and analysis of payments to media, suppliers, and outside contractors. Financial mismanagement with intent to defraud is rare. According to Price Waterhouse & Co., the greatest problem is a complicated, error-prone billing and payment system. Examples are bills going to clients for costs that were never incurred and payments going to media and suppliers for services that were never rendered. The following practices are a must for all clients:

1. Approve in writing every expenditure made by an agency on its behalf. These expenditures should be approved in advance.
2. Every agreement or approval of an action, including copy, production, and other services, should be in writing and readily accessible for easy reference.

12. Price Waterhouse & Co., *A Guide to Accounting Controls of Advertising Agencies* (New York: Price Waterhouse & Co., 1980).

3. Possible cost overruns should be cleared ahead of time. This will reduce misunderstandings later.
4. Procedures should be carefully monitored to make sure that all parties adhere to terms of contracts.

Clients evaluate direct marketing agencies in other ways besides observing billing methods. Response to advertising is measurable, and clients can thus assess in large measure the bottom line of their agencies' efforts. The ability to measure effectiveness of advertising is one of the greatest assets of direct marketing. Companies have the means to use that asset in more innovative ways than they currently do, such as in devising a system of rewards and punishments based on performance.

# Integrated Marketing

Young & Rubican, a leader of agency trends, began some years ago to promote "the whole egg." Other agencies quickly followed suit with other, similar slogans to set themselves apart from the pack. Omnicom calls it "the networking concept." Leo Burnett pushes the "one team, one voice" idea. Not to be outdone, Grey Advertising touts its "agency without walls." All this sloganeering means the same thing: an agency uniting general advertising, direct marketing, and sales promotion in an integrated marketing plan.

Advertising agencies have diligently increased their rosters of communication services. They have added direct marketing and sales promotion agencies to their corporate structures in the hope of gaining new sources of income. In many instances national advertisers have funneled direct marketing and sales promotion business to their newly integrated agencies. Yet true integration is more slogan than reality.[13] A number of obstacles stand in the way. One is the problem of disparate groups competing with each other for the same business. Different subsidiaries, each an independent profit center, compete for advertising dollars of the same accounts. Each seeks more work for members of its team at the expense of other agency groups. Since fees are not equal, budget control is often disrupted.

In response, several ad agencies terminated their subsidiaries and created "separate but equal" divisions. However, competition between the different parts of the company did not subside. Direct marketers see the world differently from general advertising people, whether working in a subsidiary, a division, or in a general advertising group. As put by Hershell G. Lewis, a direct marketing copywriter, advertising that

13. "The New Advertising," *Agency* (Fall 1990), pp. 28–33.

"amputates salesmanship from attention getting won't last long." To Lewis, it's unscientific "to say a campaign is a success because research showed a 4 percent gain in awareness." The cash register is the only way to keep score.[14] To general advertising, this philosophy is anathema.

Agencies that disbanded their subsidiaries also experienced difficulty in recruiting personnel, who did not want to work for nondescript, no-name divisions. To attract talented people, says Jon Adams, president of FCB/Leber Katz's Integrated Communication Group, "you have to work like hell."[15]

Another problem is that one poorly performing subsidiary can derail an entire marketing campaign. This seemed to be the case with Chiat/Day/Mojo, an agency that eventually closed down its sales promotion subsidiary.

Ad agencies that took on specialties, such as direct marketing and sales promotion functions, often found additional income elusive. More management time was required to coordinate the disparate functions. On the other hand, clients that handed these agencies more business by combining integrated campaigns under one roof clamored for volume discounts.

From a client's point of view, it makes sense to integrate general advertising and direct marketing. From an agency's point of view, however, how well the pieces fall into place depends on who is doing the integrating. General advertisers see direct marketing as supplementary to attention getting. Direct marketers see immediate, traceable sales as the objective of integrated effort. To general advertisers, only long term results count, and those are assiduously built by image creation messages. Direct marketers repeat the famous remark by Keynes about the long run: by then we'll all be dead.

## Summary

Today the structure of the direct marketing industry resembles that of the advertising industry. Since direct marketing is a subgroup of marketing, it can be treated as part of the marketing channel. In direct marketing over the last 25 years there has been a proliferation of facilitating agencies. These include the media companies, direct marketing agencies, telemarketing service bureaus, fulfillment houses, list companies, video production houses, and other suppliers to the industry.

The last 10 years have seen a significant wave of mergers and acquisitions. Advertising agencies have been picking up the smaller direct

14. Hershell G. Lewis, "Let Them Integrate with Us!" *Direct Marketing* (November 1988), pp. 52–55, 110.
15. "The New Advertising," *op. cit.*, p. 31.

marketing firms. This is probably due to a shift from general advertising to sales promotion. Within the agency there has been a separation of direct marketing from advertising because the goals of the two divisions are different. Also, agencies are trying to prevent account conflicts between the two groups. Organizational structure varies depending on the type of company. Agencies are organized by account, somewhat similar to brand managers, but all work is performed by functional departments.

Most agencies are compensated on a fee basis, although the commission system is still being used. This cost-based method relates compensation to work done. Since agencies handle large sums of their clients' money, clients often audit their direct marketing agencies.

Over the last few years agencies have been promoting themselves through slogans. However, slogans do not make a smooth-functioning team. Teamwork takes direction from the top.

---

## REVIEW QUESTIONS

1. What evidence can be mustered to support the proposition that direct marketing is a method of advertising?
2. What major structural changes in the direct marketing industry occurred in the 1980s relative to the 1970s?
3. What are the reasons for the separation of direct marketing from advertising by the agencies?
4. Why do some companies use direct marketing agencies while others do not?
5. **a.** Explain the different organization forms clients use in marketing their products.
   **b.** Draw a product management system organization chart used by clients of large organizations.
6. Explain the different duties of the creative, media, and traffic departments and the account group.
7. Why do direct marketing agencies tend to cluster in certain locations, such as Madison Avenue in New York, Michigan Avenue in Chicago, and Wilshire Boulevard in Los Angeles?
8. Between 1986 and 1989 vast changes in methods of compensating advertising agencies occurred. What were these changes? Why did they occur?
9. **a.** Why do clients conduct financial audits of their agencies?
   **b.** Do clients evaluate their agencies in any other ways? Explain.
10. What is the purpose of the slogans agencies use with respect to their "integrated marketing" services?

## PROJECT

1. You were just hired as a marketing person in the public relations department of a private university. This is your first job after graduating from college. A total of 15,000 undergraduate students and 5,000 graduate students attend this school on two campuses. The university is located in a large city. All of its students commute.

   In the past school year the University has seen a 5 percent drop in enrollment in the business school and an 8 percent drop in the liberal arts school. All other schools have maintained their enrollment.

   Sixty percent of the university's advertising budget went into television, 25 percent was allocated to newspapers, and 15 percent went to miscellaneous media.

   Your supervisor gave you several jobs:

   a. Develop an eight-person organization chart for the public relations department of the university. Define the responsibilities of each position. No names of the people in the department are to be included.
   b. Develop a promotion plan with heavy emphasis on direct marketing. Do not concern yourself with the budget. Suggest how the promotion should be done and why.
   c. State whether or not the university should use an advertising agency. Provide the pros and cons of your recommendation.
   d. Create two pieces for promoting the university. It is fine to work in black and white. If you prefer, you may do it in color. A paste job is also approved. Neatness and clarity count for part of the grade.

CHAPTER 3

# The Social and Legal Environment

## The Firm and Its Environment

Direct marketing, like every other business, operates within a context. It shares an identity with the surroundings in which it exists. It is part of a larger whole, an all-inclusive environment.

Conventional wisdom regards the environment as an "exogenous variable." It is an influence outside the firm, which must reconcile itself with these outside forces to flourish, even to exist.

But environments are not wholly exogenous. They are not given, like immovable objects that cannot be budged or changed in the slightest way. Human beings acting in an organized manner have the capacity to change external conditions, especially in the long run.

Corporations react to, and interact with, their environments. But all outside influences do not affect direct marketing to the same degree. Damage to the physical world, such as pollution, is not a matter of interest to the direct marketing industry. But post office regulations and taxes on out-of-state mail orders are of momentous concern.

This chapter will focus on the social and political environment, for the following reasons:

1. It is not feasible to address all environments in a meaningful way. Because of space limitations, the chapter can only highlight important influences, even if they are limited in number. Social and political factors were chosen because they have the most pervasive impact on direct marketing.
2. Both social and political aspects of business are interrelated with other contexts, as well as with each other. For example, changes in Federal Trade Commission (FTC) regulations can alter how companies conduct business. Ideas of right and wrong spill over into legislation and judicial decisions.
3. Social and political areas present the most important external issues that will face direct marketing in the 1990s.

## The Political Environment

As part of business, direct marketing must run its affairs within the confines of a political environment. These include legislative, regulatory, and judicial functions of government at both federal and state levels. Most laws and regulations apply to business in general and affect direct marketing only in a peripheral way. Examples are antitrust legislation, environmental protection acts, and foreign trade policies. Other government activities impact direct marketing with greater force, such as statutes and regulations governing post office procedures and postage rates, financial services, advertising, and sales promotion. Governmental affairs in these areas mainly cover a wide range of "unfair and deceptive practices."

# Fraud

Although the vast majority of direct marketers conduct business in honest and legitimate ways, the industry attracts significant numbers of scam artists and swindlers. The FTC estimates that dishonest phone operators extract more that $1 billion a year from gullible victims. According to a house commerce subcommittee, the FTC in 1987 received more than 3,700 complaints of telemarketing fraud from businesses and individual consumers.[1]

Since state legislators have closer ties to their citizens than do federal officeholders, states have been most active in strengthening antifraud enforcement. California, New York, and Texas, the three most populous states in the union, have proved the most aggressive in fighting fraud. California makes telemarketers register and submit their sales presentations to appointed officials. The attorney general's office of Texas moved quickly against Advantage Concepts, a Dallas-based direct marketing firm, because of a mailing designed to scare senior citizens into buying supplemental insurance. The firm sent out a letter that was disguised as a governmental document but that in reality was a pitch to generate leads for an insurance company.[2]

State attorney generals find it hard to prosecute fraud, particularly when companies intentionally operate in an illegal manner. Violators move across state lines and change their company names. In these cases, federal agencies are vital to the prevention of crime. On the federal level, the FTC assumes the major responsibility for policing business practices. From 1982 to 1988 the agency obtained $86 million in judgments from 29 cases it brought before the courts.[3]

Art investment has recently become an object of swindles through the use of telemarketing. The Federal Sterling gallery of Arizona was cited for selling bogus Salvador Dali prints. The gallery was asking $900 to $3,500 for items the FTC said were worth roughly $50 each. The FTC went to court and obtained an injunction against the gallery and an order freezing its assets.[4] Other favorite schemes involve travel package deals with large hidden costs, promises of expensive gifts, and prizes that turn out to be throwaways.

Unauthorized billing against credit cards has also assumed serious proportions. To guard against these practices, some banks have even sent warnings to their customers not to give out their card numbers over the phone.

---

1. Mark Kellner and Mark L. Paul, "Renewed Attacks on Telemarketing by Congress and Bankcard Issuers," *DM News* (December 15, 1987), p. 53.
2. David Enscoe, "Crackdown on Fraud," *Target Marketing* (February 1989), p. 10.
3. Cyndee Miller, "Lawmakers Eager to Crack Down on Telemarketing Fraud," *Marketing News* (July 3, 1989), p. 14.
4. *Ibid.*

Mail order is also spotted with fraudulence. In an effort to discourage such practices, Congress in 1983 passed the Mail Order Consumer Protection Amendment. This bill gave greater enforcement powers to the post office, broadening the scope of cease-and-desist orders and providing for civil penalties of up to $10,000 a day for violations. The Postal Service can also require that money collected under false pretenses be returned to buyers, and payments of money orders can be halted by postmasters.[5] In 1988 postal inspectors arrested nearly 1,500 people for criminal mail fraud.[6]

## Advertising and Promotion

Since direct marketing uses paid messages in media, it is subject to all laws and regulations governing general advertising. The FTC was made responsible for regulating "unfair and deceptive" practices by the act that created it in 1914. But it was not until the 1938 Wheeler-Lea Amendment that the FTC acquired authority to act on its own in consumer markets without having to wait for a formal complaint. Subsequent legislation greatly expanded FTC powers.[7] The FTC Improvement Act in particular, coming in 1975, greatly widened the agency's control over trade regulation rules.[8]

A major concern of the FTC is deception in advertising. There are various degrees of falsehood. Some border on outright fraud. Other promotional activity falls within legal bounds but straddles those of unethical conduct. An example of this sort of advertising goes under the name of "puffery," an exaggerated opinion on the part of sellers that has been ruled legal by the courts. Where puffery ends and deception begins, however, is a very fine line of subjective discretion on the part of regulators.

Over the years, the FTC has promulgated a number of rules with respect to truthful advertising. Underlying most of them is the substantive doctrine, from which all guidelines flow. For example:

1. The substantive principle implies that the basis for judging an advertisement is the impression it creates in its entirety. That impression must coincide with the material facts about a product.
2. It logically follows that a printed ad or commercial or mailing piece may contain literal or technical truth yet be judged deceptive. This happens when it fails to disclose a material fact. The omission taints

5. See Guy Adamo, "New Mail Order Law Tightens the Screws on Deceptive Advertising," *Marketing News* (October 26, 1984); and "Mail Order Law Successful in Crackdown of Deceptive Practices," *Marketing News* (August 1985).
6. Enscoe, *op. cit.*, p. 10.
7. See Joe Welch, *Marketing Law* (Tulsa, OK: Petroleum Publishing Co., 1980).
8. "Legal Developments in Marketing," *Journal of Marketing* (January 1977), p. 98.

an ad with falsehood. Hence, advertising must adhere to *affirmative disclosure.*

3. Similarly, an unsubstantiated claim may be unlawful, even if it cannot be proved incorrect. The FTC can request substantiation of any claim made in an ad.
4. Proof must be in hand before, not after, the claim is made. Unless *prior substantiation* exists, the FTC holds, copy was written without adequate evidence. Whether the claim is borne out later is irrelevant. The ad is deceptive.

The FTC in 1984 entered into a consent decree with Commodore Business Machines to stop the company from claiming that certain software could operate on a Z-80 microprocessor. The basis for the suit was the FTC assertion that this piece of equipment was not available for sale when the advertising appeared. Although Commodore's claim may have been true, the firm had no proof of that before such a machine came onto the market.[9]

A question related to the issue of deception is, deceptive to whom? Before 1983 the FTC regarded an ad misunderstood by the most gullible consumer as deceptive. As upheld by the courts, the FTC can insist on advertising so explicit that, in the words of Isaiah, "wayfaring men, though fools, shall not enter therein." According to that decision, the FTC could rule an ad deceptive if it could find one wayfaring fool who did not understand it.

The new definition of deception is the likelihood of misleading "average consumers, acting rationally." This idea is a modern version of "consumer sovereignty," an age-old notion central to explaining demand in classical economics.

The substantiation doctrine also applies to ad agencies and resellers. Department stores and advertising agencies can no longer rely on assurances given them by manufacturers. They must obtain and evaluate information to support any product claims before they make them.[10]

## First Amendment Guarantees

The First Amendment to the Constitution forbids Congress to make laws "abridging the freedom of speech, or the press." Until 1976 this right of free speech did not extend to articles of commerce. Freedom of expression enjoyed by journalists, broadcasters, and politicians was not accorded to purveyors of goods.

9. "FTC Raps Commodore Ad Claims," *Advertising Age* (August 16, 1984), p. 8.
10. Roger L. Jenkins, "Managers Must Develop Tactics to Handle FTC Probes of Ad Claims," *Marketing News* (May 30, 1980), p. 4; "FTC Consent Pacts Set Test, Survey Guides," *Advertising Age* (January 12, 1981), p. 10.

In 1976 commercial speech sneaked into First Amendment coverage through the back door, so to speak, in the famous Virginia Pharmacy case. The Supreme Court struck down a Virginia statute that prohibited pharmacists from advertising or publishing prices of prescription drugs. The law, the Court reasoned, denied information to consumers and prevented them from shopping around for the best price. This precedent-breaking decision accorded marketers the right to be heard.

But it did not decree that marketers can say anything they want. Subsequent cases have established the principle that commercial speech has only partial, not full, First Amendment protection. When the right of firms to communicate runs counter to the public interest, the latter takes precedence. Thus, a U.S. Circuit Court of Appeals in 1977 upheld an FTC order against Warner Lambert for corrective advertising. The court ruled that First Amendment rights did not prevent government from regulating commercial speech if it was deceptive. This ruling became more entrenched over the years. Business has the right to advertise, but not deceptively.

## Endorsements and Testimonials

The endorsement or testimonial is a frequently used copy technique to enhance credibility of the selling message. The FTC makes no distinction between an endorsement and a testimonial. The advertisement presents an opinion that comes not from a product's sponsor but from an outside source—a celebrity, an authority, or a beaming, satisfied consumer.

An expert must by virtue of training and experience possess more knowledge and competence than an ordinary individual. This expertise must be directly related to the advertised product. An actor cannot dress up in a white suit to impersonate a doctor and testify as to the effectiveness of a drug or device alleged to have therapeutic value.

User experience featured in endorsements must be representative of all consumers or users. The testimonial cannot tout a benefit that does not accrue to a representative body of consumers. Any interest the endorser has in the business must be disclosed. Furthermore, the endorser must be an actual, bona fide user of the product. When Bruce Jenner, an Olympics champion, says he ate Wheaties as a boy, he is presumed to be telling the truth. Just to make sure, the FTC asked for affidavits from his parents. A celebrity shown holding up an American Express credit card in some exotic place must, in truth, have been a cardholder before having his or her picture taken.

The substantiation doctrine has slowly been extended to endorsers. The opening wedge came in the late 1970s with the Coogo Moogo decision, in which the FTC established the principle that a testimonial carried personal liability on the part of the endorser. The actor Pat Boone, who endorsed an acne remedy, accepted personal liability when the product did not work as advertised. Boone paid a percentage of the restitution ordered against the manufacturer of the product.[11]

Recently, the Bridges case confirmed endorser liability in a civil suit. The court action was brought by a group of investors who lost money in a real estate venture managed by O.J. Obie & Associates and its parent, Diamond Mortgage, Inc. Both firms went bankrupt in 1986, and two of their executives went to prison for fraud. The plaintiffs charged that contributing to the deception were televised testimonials by actors Lloyd Bridges and George Hamilton. In 1990 the two actors, along with the ad agency that created the commercials, agreed to pay back part of the money investors lost as part of a court-approved settlement. Although no actual trial was held, the judge upheld a celebrity's liability for misrepresenting a product in ruling on a pretrial motion. He said that endorsers must take reasonable steps to ascertain that their statements are true.[12] That opinion expressly forbids celebrities from taking money and doing nothing more than reading scripts. They are now accountable for the integrity of the products they endorse.

Demonstrations are widely used in television advertising to take advantage of the medium's combination of sight, sound, and motion. These commercials, like other advertisements, must adhere rigidly to the principle of substantiality. Legal guidelines include the following:[13]

1. *The element of materiality is vital in a demonstration.*
2. *The demonstration must be related to some aspect of a product's quality.* A Sunoco ad showed a car pulling more than 100 tons, stressing the power of its premium gasoline. The FTC ruled the demonstration was deceptive because the power was no greater than that supplied by other gasolines of a comparable octane rating.
3. *Consumers must see what the commercial purports to show.* The Supreme Court upheld an FTC ruling on a Colgate-Palmolive demonstration that showed shaving cream softening sandpaper. The FTC held that the commercial was deceptive because it used a simulated mock-up and not real sandpaper.[14] Similarly, the FTC rejected a Campbell Soup commercial that used marbles to give the impression of soup rich with vegetables. The FTC claimed that the overall impression was false because consumers do not actually get what was shown on the screen.

11. 92 F. T. C., 310 (1978)
12. "Bridges Case May Chill Use of Celebrities in Ads," *Marketing News* (March 19, 1990), p. 6.
13. Based on Robert J. Posch, *What Every Manager Needs to Know About Marketing and the Law* (New York: McGraw Hill, 1984), pp. 262–265.
14. 380 U.S. 374 (1964).

## Trademarks

Trademarks are valuable assets to makers and sellers of goods. The Lanham Trade-Mark Act (1946) defines a trademark as "any word, name, symbol, device, or combination thereof adopted and used by a manufacturer or merchant to identify the origin of a product and distinguish it from products manufactured or sold by others." It protects its owners from illegal use of their property, and the public from deception in identifying an offering.

In 1989 Congress revised trademark law to make U.S. industry more competitive in international competition.[15] A major change allows a business to register a trademark before using it. In the past, a company could apply for registration only after the trademark had been used in commerce. This provision encouraged "token" or "bogus" use to comply with terms of the law. The 1989 act allows firms to file an intent-to-use application. A formal registration is issued after actual use of the trademark, retroactive to the application filing date, but firms can test new products prior to commercialization without fear of losing development benefits.

A second provision, and one that affects direct marketing, makes false statements in comparative advertising grounds for trademark infringement. This section of the law actually extends various FTC and court decisions stating that false and misleading advertising carries potential liabilities.[16]

Still, the methods for protecting a trademark remain pretty much the same as before the new law. A firm is cautioned to:

1. Monitor markets for possible infringements and insist that violators stop illegal activity that dilutes the value of a trademark. Failure to enforce the exclusive use of a trademark may result in its abandonment.
2. Apply for intent-to-use or register the trademark. Legal protection is better than none at all.
3. Identify the trademark by the appropriate symbol, such as ® to denote that it has been registered. Other symbols are ™, SM, and ©. ™ stands for trademark and serves as a notice that an ® status application is in the works. SM indicates that the product is a service; legally, it is similar to ™. The symbol © is a copyright claim, declaring the sole right of ownership of the entire contents of an advertisement. These symbols put other firms on notice as to legal rights regarding trademarks and are helpful in preventing infringement.[17]

---

15. See Robert J. Posch, Jr., "The New Trademark Law," *Direct Marketing* (August 1989), pp. 80–82.
16. Jeffery A. Tracktenberg, "New Law Adds Risk to Comparative Ads," *Wall Street Journal* (June 1, 1989), p. B6.
17. Richard C. Douglas, "Ad Symbols Warn, Protect, Muddle," *Advertising Age* (March 30, 1981), p. 50.

4. Associate the generic name of a product with the trademark in all promotion, packaging, and advertising. Some examples are Xerox copier, Post-it note pads, and Tabasco pepper sauce. This helps to prevent a brand name from becoming generic, as happens when the brand name comes to represent an entire product class. In that event, the owner of the trademark loses rights to its exclusive use.

### Warranties

Warranties are actual statements by sellers that form the basis of a transaction. Text and illustrations in catalogs thus constitute express warranties and are governed by the uniform commercial code. So are contents of direct mailing pieces and phone solicitations, if they become terms of the bargain in a sale.[18] Indeed, any representation that a buyer relies on in a transaction represents an express warranty.

Some warranties are implied, arising automatically from the sale itself. Such are warranties of title; the mere act of selling implies that the seller owns title to the product and can rightly transfer it. Also implied is the idea that the goods sold have no lien or encumbrance on them. A third implication is that the goods fit the purpose for which they are sold.

A marketer need not give any express warranty. But if a firm chooses to do so, it must conform to the Magnuson-Moss Warranty Act for products costing more than $15. This law sets forth guidelines for written warranties and applies to tangible personal property, not to products distributed for resale. A conspicuous proviso calls for documents to be written in simple, understandable English.

Written warranties must be designated as full or limited. The former includes a promise to fix a defective product free of charge. It need not, however, apply to every part of the warranted product. A warranty for a lawn mower might leave out spark plugs, blades, or the grass-catching bag. A seller who fails to remedy a defect in a product under full warranty after trying a reasonable number of times must give the buyer the option of a refund or a replacement without charge.

The Magnuson-Moss Act does not require the consumer to return a registration card in order to enjoy warranty coverage. The buyer, however, must have proof of the date on which the purchase was made, because a warranty covers a specific period of time.

## Credit Issues

In our consumer economy, direct marketing runs on credit. Credit transactions create debt; they defer payment for goods or services.

18. Ronald A. Anderson et al., *Business Law* (Cincinnati: South-Western, 1984).

The widespread use of credit has extended the government's cloak of consumer protection to consumer finance. A major piece of legislation that impacts direct marketing is the Consumer Credit Protection Act of 1968, popularly known as the truth-in-lending law. A basic feature of this act is that consumers must receive full details about the cost of credit associated with purchases. Firms must disclose in writing such terms as finance charges, annual interest rates, dollar amount of credit costs, down-payment requirements, payment schedules, and other relevant financial information. Billing on open-end credit must occur periodically, and statements must go out at least 14 days before the end of any "free period." The law imposes restrictions on advertising that contains credit terms. The Federal Trade Commission administers the act in areas of consumer finance, retailing, and credit card handling.

The truth-in-lending act has acquired a number of amendments over the years. One is the Fair Credit Billing Act, which became effective in 1975. This law applies to open-end credit plans, such as revolving credit accounts, charge accounts, and lines of credit extended to consumers. The legislation does not cover installment loans, which must be paid in accordance with a fixed schedule. In accordance with the provisions of this law, firms must establish procedures that permit consumers to question or dispute charges on periodic statements.

Another amendment, which became effective the same year, is the Equal Credit Opportunity Act. It forbids discrimination based on race, color, religion, national origin, sex, marital status, or age.

A third important amendment to the original bill of 1968 is the Fair Credit Reporting Act, enacted in 1970. Its purpose was to make consumer credit reports more accurate while guaranteeing consumer fairness and confidentiality. A person about whom a credit report is issued has the right to see the report and correct any misstatements. If a firm denies credit on the basis of such a report, it must inform the applicant of the action and supply the name and address of the reporting agency. Upon written request within 60 days, the firm must disclose the nature of the information that led to credit denial.

The Fair Credit Reporting Act also puts limitations on credit reporting agencies and holds them accountable to certain conduct.[19] A consumer may challenge any information the agency has on file. This must be done in writing. When such a challenge is received, the agency is obligated to investigate and to change the report if the objection turns out to be justified. A consumer who thinks a report is wrong after an investigation may file a statement of dispute, which must be noted in all forthcoming reports. Consumers have the right to sue for damages

19. For a discussion of these limitations, see Robert J. Posch, Jr., "Why Are We Returning to Redlining?" *Direct Marketing* (March 1990), pp. 77–78.

resulting from failure of a reporting agency to comply with provisions of the law.

Finally, adverse information must be deleted from consumer files after seven years, with certain exceptions. Some states mandate shorter periods, such as New York, which requires five years.

Compliance with the act has raised issues of confidentiality and discrimination. The FTC, for example, issued rules prohibiting "alert lists" that do not refer to specific individuals. The FTC regards as illegal reports of credit abuse phrased in general terms, such those relating to neighborhoods, blocks, or households. A credit report must pertain to an individual who is the subject of an inquiry.

Items of information about the creditworthiness of neighborhoods and lifestyles are important considerations in credit decisions. The sale of such data is legal, as long as the reports conform to confidentiality guidelines. Firms that keep records of sales and payments for their own use pose no problems with regard to the Fair Credit Reporting Act. Compliance issues arise when adverse credit reports are sold, rented, or exchanged.

For example, one firm supplied merchants with "alert lists" of buyers who had passed bad checks. The names were assembled randomly and did not relate to specific customers. The FTC held that such lists were illegal because companies did not do business with those people listed. In addition, the reporting agency did not have an adequate system for checking allegations of wrongdoing.[20]

Similarly, the FTC ruled that sales of "credit guides" and "alert lists" collected randomly violates the Fair Credit Reporting Act. No subscriber could conceivably regard every individual listed as being a likely customer.

Rounding out consumer credit legislation are laws dealing with collection. Bad debts present a problem to all direct marketers, influencing choices of marketing targets and media and terms of offers that are made. The basic piece of legislation in this area is the Fair Debt Collection Practices Act of 1978. This law forbids misleading debt collection practices, such as threats to take illegal action or measures not intended to be pursued in the first place. Also prohibited are certain forms of harassment, such as using profane language and making repeated calls that are annoying.[21] The law applies to third-party collecting organizations and excludes in-house collection agencies of firms whose principal business is other than debt collection.[22]

---

20. *Ibid*
21. See Arthur Winston, "Internal Credit and Collection Procedures by Direct Marketers," DMA, *Manual Release* 750 (August 1982).
22. Robert J. Posch, Jr., "Collecting Debts in the 1990s," *Direct Marketing* (February 1990), p. 75.

One method for reducing bad debts is to accept credit cards as a payment option. Total credit card billing for direct marketers runs to considerably more than $100 billion annually.[23] When goods are paid for with plastic money, credit card companies accept the liabilities of bad debts once they approve an order. This benefit, however, must be traded off against the additional fees that have to be paid out to the credit card companies. Furthermore, the authorization system does not protect a direct marketer from fraud. Visa and MasterCard authorizations carry no guarantees that a buyer is a bona fide cardholder and not a thief. If a marketer does not make sure a card is genuine, banks can deduct all money paid out previously from the client's current account. These "charge-backs" are permissable within a year of the sale and need no approval from the seller.

Alternatives to the acceptance of credit cards are internal billing and collection, and doing business on a cash basis. A stringent credit policy, or doing away with credit altogether, may significantly reduce response. Setting up an internal collection department may save money, since collection agencies typically split receipts 50-50 with clients. A firm would incur costs associated with collections but may find it worthwhile if those costs are lower than payments made to outside agencies.

When a collection agency is used, it should be understood that these are independent contractors that sometimes pursue methods that are unethical and illegal. But in its role as principal, a company can insist that its agent obey laws and act ethically. This approach is in a seller's best interest, as collections performed by third parties reflect on a company's reputation for fair dealing.

## Sales Tax Issues

As long as there are governments, there will be taxes—and more and more taxes. The concept of the modern welfare state puts pressure on governments to expand their menu of services. Eventually, these must be paid for; there are no free lunches. So as constituents clamor for more government benefits, legislators are forced into frantic hunts for new revenue, much as oil companies must continually search for new fields in the face of greater demand and fewer resources. Where direct marketing is concerned, tax issues arise primarily at state levels.

When people buy something—whether at a store, by phone, or through the mail—they may be obliged to pay taxes. States that have sales taxes also have use taxes. A consumer who buys from an out-of-state business is liable for a use tax at the same rate as the sales tax in his or her home state. State officials cannot track every transaction that

23. Kevin Hanley, "Credit Card Fraud Alert," *Target Marketing* (October 1986), p. 28.

takes place in another state, so use taxes are seldom collected from out-of-state buyers. Nor do direct marketers have to collect and remit such taxes if they themselves do business in another state.

This principle was established in a 1967 Supreme Court case, *National Bellas Hess* v. *Department of Revenue of the State of Illinois.* National mailed catalogs to consumers in Illinois, accepting and filling orders from Missouri. National had neither stores nor salespeople in Illinois. Under an Illinois statute, National was classified as a retailer and therefore was apparently responsible for collection of sales taxes. The Court set aside the Illinois law as unconstitutional, arguing that it violated the due-process clause of the Constitution and imposed a burden on interstate commerce. Justice Stewart, who wrote the majority opinion, held that state action can only be justified when some benefit is returned for the taxes. Since National had no physical presence in Illinois, it received no benefit whatsoever from state services.[24]

The Advisory Commission on Intergovernmental Relations estimated that the National Bellas Hess decision denied states as much as $1.6 billion a year. Because mail order and electronic sales are growing faster than retail purchases, the amount of tax loss to states is apt to increase, both absolutely and relatively.[25] Also, because many states are being squeezed by budget deficits, lawmakers are prodded into looking for potential sources of revenue.

One possibility is to reverse the consequences of the Bellas Hess decision. A number of states have passed legislation that either directly challenges Bellas Hess or attempts to narrow its scope. So far, the Supreme Court's 1967 ruling has withstood all assaults by its opponents. For example:

- An Oklahoma statute requiring out-of-state companies to collect taxes on products sold by mail in the state was judged unconstitutional by the state attorney general.[26] This opinion confirmed the precedent established by the Bellas Hess decision.
- Likewise, the Pennsylvania and Tennessee tax departments failed to prevail in attempts to have L. L. Bean, a Maine mail order house, held liable for sales taxes in states where the firm has no presence or "nexus."[27]
- Connecticut's aggressive tax collectors were thwarted in their efforts to expand the definition of "physical presence." The state supreme court ruled in favor of a California mail order firm, Cally Curtis, that leased training films in Connecticut. The ownership of property

24. Arthur Winston, "An Analysis of National Bellas Hess," *DM News* (July 15, 1989), pp. 32, 50, 69.
25. Roderick G. W. Chu, "The Catalog Loophole Must Be Closed ," *New York Times* (August 18, 1985).
26. *DM News* (September 1, 1986), p. 14.
27. *DM News* (November 1, 1986), *DM News* (January 29, 1990)

in the state (training films), the Court maintained, did not by itself constitute a physical presence in the state.[28]

In an unrelated ruling the state's superior court rejected Connecticut's contention that Saks/Folio, a mail order house, is an adjunct of Saks Fifth Avenue, a department store in Stanford. Saks/Folio contended that it conducted business independently, having no store sales offices or distribution centers in Connecticut.[29] This decision confirmed the ruling that two separate companies owned by the same parent firm do not automatically create a nexus.

- A Pennsylvania judge held that the state could not subpoena sales records from Bloomingdale's By Mail Ltd., because it operated independently of the Bloomingdale's store in Philadelphia.[30] This decision paralleled the one in Connecticut.
- Land's End on January 1990 filed suit to challenge a California law taxing out-of-state sales charged to credit cards issued by state banks.[31] Court cases move slowly, and a decision will probably not come for several years.

Another line of attack on Bellas Hess is to have Congress rewrite the law. A number of such bills have been introduced in both the House and the Senate, and although none have passed as yet, such attempts are bound to continue.

Business does not speak with a single voice. Although direct marketers have generally opposed national legislation to modify the Bellas Hess decision, retailers have supported it. They have long contended that tax exemptions for out-of-state businesses are a form of unfair competition. Retailers see direct marketers getting a competitive advantage as a result of a discriminatory tax system.

The extent to which consumers purchase by mail to avoid taxes is highly debatable. Much of direct mail sales complement retail operations; they do not feature directly substitutable products. Many popular items sold by direct marketing—magazine subscriptions, tapes and records, financial services, and specialties—do not compete head on with retail stores.[32] Firms such as Sears and Penney pay taxes on catalog sales because their stores are scattered throughout the country. Moreover, several large mail order companies, such as Spiegel and Franklin Mint, collect sales taxes for out-of-state sales. Direct marketing operations that pay taxes on out-of-state purchases have not sacrificed a competitive advantage.

---

28. *DM News* (April 16, 1990).
29. *DM News* (May 7, 1990).
30. *DM News* (January 29, 1990).
31. *Ibid.*
32. See Chapter 1.

No matter what legislators do, there is no way of equalizing costs among all resellers. A national law that imposes out-of-state taxes on mail orders would mean higher costs for direct marketers than for retailers. The reason is that direct marketers face a much wider array of sales taxes, varying among states and types of goods, and this diversity implies larger administrative costs. Whatever the eventual outcome of the controversy, it will be a political solution and not a rational economic one that maximizes the public welfare.

# Social Issues

The pervasive use of direct marketing has given rise to a number of social issues. A direct marketing firm may view its activities as completely economic, but when it works at establishing and maintaining relationships with consumers, such as by the use of databases, there is no way of avoiding social tensions. The most prominent of these are matters of privacy and ethics.

## Privacy

The privacy controversy is not concerned with a single, uniform issue. Rather, it encompasses many different parts.

The types of information that need protection are one aspect of the privacy issue. Computers store vast amounts of data, some of which are considered private. Although opinions differ over what facts should be confidential, personal data remains a sensitive area. Another controversial type of information is financial, such as income and its sources, size of bank accounts and investments, and amounts and types of purchases.

Computer databases today contain voluminous details about individuals, such as those supplied in applications for credit cards, mortgages, and insurance. A *Business Week* cover story asserts that "this information is largely unprotected by rules, laws, or codes of ethics. Instead, it is free to be pored over, analyzed, and sold and perhaps paired with other data to draw an intimate profile based on a person's daily habits."[33]

Many of the abuses occur because of lax controls by credit bureaus and other database compilers. *U.S. News & World Report* investigators rented lists containing actual credit information. This was in clear violation of federal law. [34] TRW, the offending agency, tightened its rental

33. Jeffery Rothfelder et al., "Is Nothing Private?" *Business Week* (September 4, 1989), pp. 74-80.
34. Alice Mundy, "Unwilling Players in the Name Game," *U. S. News & World Report* (May 1, 1989)

procedures. But a number of states have since filed suit charging the company with disseminating reports that contain glaring errors and out-of-date information.

Since direct marketers make widespread use of databases, mail order and telephone selling have borne the brunt of criticism raised in the *Business Week* and *U.S. News* articles. Many practitioners argue that market targeting overcomes privacy violations because commercial messages go only to interested parties, who look forward to such offers. This argument assumes that these "targeted" messages are perfectly matched with people who are happy to get those offers, either by mail or over the phone. This presumption, however, is not supported by the facts. A rather small percentage of mail recipients, perhaps 2 percent on the average, respond to a mailing. The vast majority, the remaining 98 percent, do not. The real world belies the fine spun theories of how databases "target" people who eagerly await the next piece of mail from a friendly banker explaining credit card charges of only 18 percent interest on unpaid balances.

Segmenting lists is anything but a science. People who have reached age 65 do not necessarily want to be solicited by purveyors of health insurance, cemetery plots, retirement communities, and elixirs of youth. Many don't care to divulge their age to strangers. A person who rents an X-rated movie on video may not want to be deluged by offers of pornographic material, erotic literature, or sexually oriented bric-a-brac.

The vital issue is exactly what information about an individual goes public but does not violate his or her privacy. Obviously what is private to one person may not be regarded as such by another. One solution to this dilemma is that advocated by American Express as a program for the direct marketing industry:[35]

- A person should be made aware of the information a company makes available to others.
- An individual should have the option of preventing personal data from being sold or rented against his or her wishes.
- A consumer should have the right to be excluded from any and all lists.
- It is unethical for a firm to collect data for one purpose and rent or sell it for another against the customer's wishes.

Many companies follow these policies. Among them are credit card issuers, publishers, and various list compilers. NDL/Lifestyle Selector reports that only 7 percent of respondents opt to be taken off rented lists when given a choice.

---

35. Quoted in David Enscoe, "Privacy Debate Goes Public," *Target Marketing* (January 1989), p. 36. Also see *Target Marketing* (April 1988), p. 40.

Federal and state laws have also followed this course of action. The Video Privacy Protection Act of 1988, for example, mandates videotape services to provide customers "in a clear and conspicuous manner" an option of not having their names or viewing data disclosed.[36]

A second privacy issue deals with the sheer volume of direct mail and phone calls, particularly the latter. Although First Amendment rights give telemarketers the right to tout their products, consumers need not listen, and many don't want to. They find phone calls an inconvenience or a plain annoyance, and there apparently are enough such people to prod legislators into action. Within the past five years, more than two-thirds of the states have passed laws to regulate unsolicited phone calls. These enactments regulate which consumers can and which cannot be called, when they may be called, and how the calling should be done.

One line of restriction has been against the so-called ADRMPs, an acronym for "automatic dialing recorded message program." These electronic devices can be programmed to dial numbers randomly and deliver a prerecorded sales presentation. ADRMPs dial unlisted numbers, a service for which people pay extra so as not to be bothered by unknown callers.

States have passed a variety of laws to deal with these problems. For example, Wyoming completely bans automated telephone systems for telemarketing. Florida set an asterisk system with fines of up to $10,000 for violations. The telephone company asterisks all names of consumers who do not want telemarketing calls. Texas requires all state lists used for marketing purposes to be matched against a nationally recognized preference service. The Direct Marketing Association maintains lists of people who do not want to be solicited by direct marketers via mail or telephone.[37]

Some states regulate hours of calling. Usually, 9 PM or 10 PM are the cutoff points, but some states are more restrictive. Missouri, for example, prohibits telemarketing calls after 4 PM.[38]

An additional area of regulation deals with the content of telephone messages. A number of states make telemarketing firms register and submit sales presentations. These states include California, Idaho, Massachusetts, Minnesota, Nevada, New Jersey, Oregon, and Wisconsin. The purpose of these disclosures is generally to prevent misrepresentation. The requirements usually call for telemarketers to identify themselves, tell the name of the company they represent, and state the goods or services being offered.

---

36. See Robert J. Posch, Jr., "An Echo Award for Ronald Plesser," *Direct Marketing* (December 1988), p. 86.
37. Lorna D. Christie, "Avoid Legislation with Self-Regulation," *DM News* (February 15, 1988), pp. 39, 49.
38. David Enscoe, "Danger: Automated Junk Calls Threaten Telemarketing," *Target Marketing* (March 1988), pp. 16–18.

## Ethics

To a marketer, strategy and tactics pursued in the course of business are seen as economic activities and judged by the bottom line: revenue minus cost equals profit. But these cost-expending and revenue-generating activities involve ethical considerations, notions of right and wrong.

Ethical issues, of course, are reflected in legislation and law enforcement. But the most difficult ethical problems of direct marketing concern practices that are legal but are seen by customers as distasteful or devious. One such questionable practice is the use of an official-looking envelope to trick people into opening it. Other mailings show what appears to be a check through a window envelope, which turns out to be a rebate contingent on a purchase.

Fund raising for charities has its share of scandals, such as those of TV evangelists Jim Bakker and Jimmy Swaggart, whose sexual transgressions and lavish lifestyles came into the media spotlight. Recently, public attention was directed at charities that allowed direct marketing firms to use their names in promotions. Only a very small percentage of revenue collected actually went to the charities or toward purposes for which these organizations were set up.

No law prescribes how much a charity can spend on fund raising, but some promotions are clearly suspect. One of the worst offenders was was Watson & Hughey, a Virginia-based direct mail firm. It mailed out as many as 50 million sweepstakes pieces to help charities. Some of the charities represented by this firm were spending less than 3 percent of their receipts in nonprofit-related activities.[39] Some states have launched investigations of Watson & Hughey and taken legal action against them. But many other questionable promotions running in the name of charity skirt the edges of legality enough to avoid prosecution.

Restrictive legislation designed to cover a wider range of unethical practices is one way of addressing the problem. However, that solution is not always feasible. In such instances, an alternative is self-regulation. A number of organizations promote standards of ethical conduct and practice self-regulation. Among the more prominent is the Council of Better Business Bureaus (BBB). This organization monitors business communications, handles complaints from both business and consumers, and tries to settle disputes. It publishes semiannually the *Mail Order Report*, which lists the complaint-generating companies. The bureau has consistently found that a small number of companies account for the bulk of all complaints. BBB's Philanthropic Advisory Service keeps files on many national charities, the validity of which can be checked by a phone call to BBB's Washington's office.

The Direct Marketing Association is another organization engaged in promoting higher ethical standards. It works with the FTC in publish-

39. David Enscoe, "Scandals Rock Fund Raising," *Target Marketing* (May 1989), pp. 22–23; "Fund Raising or Profit Making," *Target Marketing* (February 1989), p. 13.

ing consumer information, and its Mail Order Action Line handles complaints, which amount to about 15,000 a year. According to the DMA, about 90 percent of these are resolved to consumers' satisfaction. Its ethical guidelines urge owners and brokers of lists to investigate the intended uses of a list and not to rent it out if they suspect the guidelines will be violated. The DMA *Guidelines for Ethical Business Practices* are reproduced as Appendix B at the end of this chapter.

The accomplishments of the BBB and the DMA have been impressive. Yet self-regulation has its limitations. First, most consumer groups lodge complaints to government agencies, which they feel they can influence. Second, a powerful motive for self-regulation is to prevent government regulation. Industry regulation works best when there is broad agreement on issues. However, when interests are diverse, an industry solution is hardly possible. Third, not all businesses are associated with the BBB or the DMA, especially those most apt to act in unethical ways. Finally, industry boards have no power to enforce compliance. Perhaps cooperation between business, consumer advocates, and government would be a more effective way of treating ethical issues.

## Summary

The marketplace environment contains forces which are uncontrollable. Yet some conditions, such as the social and political environments, can be changed through human effort. Direct marketing is affected by government legislation and regulations.

The majority of direct marketers conduct business in proper ways. Still, significant numbers of scam artists and swindlers are attracted to the industry. The Federal Trade Commission (FTC), the Council of Better Business Bureaus (BBB), and the Direct Marketing Association (DMA) are doing their utmost to protect consumers. To help meet these goals, various laws have been passed over the years at both the federal and the state levels. States have been very active in passing antifraud legislation.

Congress in 1983 passed the Mail Order Consumer Protection Amendment. The Wheeler-Lea Amendment of 1938 gave the FTC the authority to act without having to wait for a formal complaint in "unfair and deceptive" advertising practices. The FTC has been actively pursuing corporations that have strayed outside the laws. The substantiation doctrine has slowly been extended to endorsers. Actors endorsing products must accept personal liability if the product fails. Further, false and misleading advertising carries potential liabilities.

If a firm gives a limited or full warranty, it must conform to the Magnuson-Moss Warranty Act for products costing more that $15. The Consumer Credit Protection Act of 1968, popularly known as the truth-in-lending law, protects the consumer financially from unscrupulous operators. Another law requiring consumer credit reports be made accurate while guaranteeing consumer fairness and confidentiality is the 1970 Fair Credit Reporting Act. The Fair Credit Billing Act of 1975 establishes procedures that permit consumers to question or dispute charges on periodic statements.

Direct marketers selling in another state do not have to collect state sales taxes if they do not have an outlet in that state. This principle was established in a 1967 Supreme Court case, *National Bellas Hess* v. *Department of Revenue of the State of Illinois*. When firms attempt to establish and maintain relationships with consumers, such as by the use of databases, the question of privacy and ethics arises. What information can firms keep on their customers, and which portions of it can be sold to other firms? The Video Privacy Protection Act of 1988, for example, mandates videotapes services to provide customers "in a clear and conspicuous manner" the option of not having their names or viewing data disclosed.

Ethical issues are reflected in legislation and law enforcement. Many of the problems in this area are handled through self-regulation. Among regulatory agencies in the industry are the Direct Marketing Association and the Council of Better Business Bureaus. The *Guidelines for Ethical Business Practices* by the DMA are reproduced as Appendix B at the end of this chapter.

## REVIEW QUESTIONS

1. Explain why this chapter focuses only on the social and political environment. Do you agree with the authors on this focus?
2. California, New York, and Texas, the three most populous states in the union, are the most aggressive in fighting fraud. Explain by citing examples in two of these states.
3. What enforcement powers does the Mail Order Consumer Protection Amendment provide to the post office?
4. State four guidelines for the substantive doctrine.
5. Explain how the FTC ensures that endorsements and testimonials given by an actor or endorser are representative and truthful.
6. How do firms protect their trademarks?
7. Explain the differences between full and limited warranties.
8. What rights accrue to the consumer under the 1970 Fair Credit Reporting Act?
9. Discuss three outcomes in relation to the Bellas Hess decision where states challenged the Supreme Court.
10. Discuss the privacy controversy.

# APPENDIX B

## Direct Marketing Association Guidelines for Ethical Business Practices

The Direct Marketing Association's Guidelines for Ethical Business Practices are intended to provide individuals and organizations involved in direct mail and direct marketing with principles of conduct that are generally accepted nationally and internationally. These guidelines reflect DMA's long-standing policy of high levels of ethics and the responsibility of the Association and direct marketers to the consumer and the community—a relationship that must be based on fair and ethical principles.

What distinguishes the Guidelines, which are self-regulatory in nature, is that all are urged to support them in spirit and not treat their provisions as obstacles to be circumvented by legal ingenuity. The guidelines are intended to be honored in light of their aims and principles.

These guidelines are also the DMA's general philosophy that self-regulatory measures are preferable to governmental mandates whenever possible. Self-regulatory actions are more readily adaptable to changing techniques and economic and social conditions, and they encourage widespread use of sound business practices.

Because it is believed that dishonest, misleading, immoral, salacious, or offensive communications make enemies for all advertising marketing, including direct response marketing, observance of these Guidelines by all concerned is recommended.

---

**WHERE DO DMA'S ETHICAL GUIDELINES COME FROM AND HOW ARE THEY ENFORCED?**

The DMA's Ethical Policy Committee and Committee on Ethical Business Practice jointly work to review and revise the DMA's Ethical Guidelines as necessary to keep them timely, specific, and meaningful in relation to the Association's stated broad objectives.

The *Ethics Policy Committee* was established by the DMA Board of Directors to direct its attention to programs and projects relating to the advancement of the Direct Marketing Association and to strive for the advancement of good ethical practices in the entire direct marketing arena.

Accordingly, the Committee develops programs and practices which will establish in the minds of consumers that direct marketing firms follow good business practices. Its aim is to inform consumers, including business and industrial users, that direct marketing is a good way of doing business. The Committee's goal is to create a positive environment in which to market and to improve the climate for direct marketing.

The DMA Ethics Policy Committee is composed of nine executives from DMA member firms, one of whom serves as liaison to the Board of Directors.

The *DMA Committee on Ethical Business Practice* was established by the Direct Marketing Association to investigate and examine mailings and offerings in relation to the "DMA Guidelines for Ethical Business Practices." The efforts of this Committee are intended to increase good business practices for the direct marketing field and to provide an effective consumer protection mechanism.

During the past 15 years, the Committee has applied the DMA Ethical guidelines concerning privacy, deception, unfair business practices, and other ethics issues to over 600 direct marketing cases. In this way, the Committee works to counter direct marketing techniques that detract from the industry's image.

**THE TERMS OF THE OFFER**

Honesty

*Article 1*

All offers should be clear, honest, and complete so that the consumer may know the exact nature of what is being offered, the price, the terms of payment (including all extra charges), and the commitment involved in the placing of an order. Before publication of an offer, direct marketers should be prepared to substantiate any claims or offers made. Advertisements or specific claims which are untrue, misleading, deceptive, fraudulent, or unjustly disparaging of competitors should not be used.

Clarity
*Article 2*

A simple statement of all the essential points of the offer should be clearly displayed in the promotional material. When an offer illustrates goods which are not included or cost extra, these facts should be made clear.

Print Size
*Article 3*

Print which by its small size, placement, or other visual characteristics is likely to substantially affect the legibility of the offer, or exceptions to it should not be used.

Actual Conditions
*Article 4*

All descriptions and promises should be in accordance with actual conditions, situations, and circumstances existing at the time of the promotion. Claims regarding any limitations (such as time or quantity) should be legitimate.

Disparagement
*Article 5*

Disparagement of any person or group on grounds of race, color, religion, national origin, sex, marital status, or age is unacceptable.

Standards
*Article 6*

Solicitations should not contain vulgar, immoral, profane, or offensive matter nor promote the sale of pornographic material or other matter not acceptable for advertising on moral grounds.

Advertising to Children
*Article 7*

Offers suitable for adults should not be made to children.

Photographs and Artwork
*Article 8*

Photographs, illustrations, artwork, and the situations they represent, should be accurate portrayals and current reproductions of the products, services, or other subjects in all particulars.

Sponsor and Intent
*Article 9*

All direct marketing contacts should disclose the name of the sponsor and each purpose of the contact. No one should make offers or solicitations in the guise of research or a survey when the real intent is to sell products or services or to raise funds.

Identity of Seller
*Article 10*

Every offer and shipment should sufficiently identify the full name and street address of the direct marketer so that the consumer may contact the individual or company by mail or phone.

Solicitation in the Guise of an Invoice
*Article 11*

Offers that are likely to be mistaken for bills or invoices should not be used.

Postage and Handling Charges
*Article 12*

Postage or shipping charges or handling charges, if any, should reflect as accurately as practicable actual costs incurred.

---

**SPECIAL OFFERS**

Use of the Word "Free" and Other Similar Representations
*Article 13*

A product or service which is offered without cost or obligation to the recipient may be unqualifiedly described as "free."

If a product or service is offered as "free," for a nominal cost, or at a greatly reduced price and the offer requires the recipient to purchase some other product or service, all terms and conditions should be clearly and conspicuously disclosed and in close conjunction with the use of the term "free" or other similar phrase. When the term "free" or other similar representations are made (for example, 2-for-1, half price, or 1-cent offers), the product or service required to be purchased should not be increased in price or decreased in quality or quantity.

Negative Option Selling
*Article 14*

All direct marketers should comply with the FTC regulation governing Negative Option Plans. Some of the major requirements of this regulation are listed below:

> Offers which require the consumer to return a notice sent by the seller before each periodic shipment to avoid receiving merchandise should contain all important conditions of the plan including:
>
> a. A full description of the obligation to purchase a minimum number of items and all the charges involved and
> b. The procedures by which the consumer receives the announcements of selections and a statement of their frequency; how the consumer rejects unwanted items, and how to cancel after completing the obligation.

The consumer should be given advance notice of the periodic selection so that the consumer may have a minimum of 10 days to exercise a timely choice. Because of the nature of this kind of offer, special attention should be given to the clarity, completeness, and prominent placement of the terms in the initial offering.

---

## SWEEPSTAKES

Sweepstakes, as defined here, are promotional devices by which items of value (prizes) are awarded to participants by chance without requiring them to render something of value to be eligible to participate (consideration). The coexistence of all three elements—prize, chance, and consideration—in the same promotion constitutes a lottery. It is illegal for any private enterprise to run a lottery.

Where skill replaces chance, the promotion becomes a skill contest. Where gifts (premiums or other items of value) are given to all participants independent of the element of chance, the promotion is not a sweepstakes and should not be held out as such.

Violations of the anti-lottery laws are policed and enforced at the federal level by the United States Postal Service, the Federal Communications Commission where broadcast advertising is involved, and by the Federal Trade Commission. Because sweepstakes are also regulated on a state-by-state basis, and the laws and definitions may vary by state, it is recommended that an attorney familiar with and experienced in the laws of sweepstakes be consulted before a sponsor conducts its promotion.

While this section of the Guidelines may focus on the promotional aspects of running a sweepstakes, it is equally important that the operation and administration of the sweepstakes be in compliance with the ethical standards set forth in other sections as well.

Use of the Term "Sweepstakes'"
*Article 15*

Only those promotional devices which satisfy the definition stated above should be called or held out to be a sweepstakes

No Purchase Option
*Article 16*

The no-purchase option as well as the method for entering without ordering should be clearly disclosed. Response devices used only for entering the sweepstakes should be as visible as those utilized for ordering the product or service.

Prizes
*Article 17*

Sweepstakes prizes should be advertised in a manner that is clear, honest, and complete so that the consumer may know the exact nature of what is being offered. Photographs, illustrations, artwork, and the situations they represent should be accurate portrayals of the prizes listed in the promotion.

No award should be held forth directly or by implication as having substantial monetary value if it is of nominal worth. The value of a prize given should be stated at regular retail value, whether actual cost to the sponsor is greater or less.

Prizes should be delivered without cost to the participant. If there are certain conditions under which a prize or prizes will not be awarded, this fact should be disclosed in a manner that is easy to find and understand.

Premiums
*Article 18*

If a premium gift or item is offered by virtue of a participant's merely entering a sweepstakes without any selection process taking place, it should be clear everyone will receive it.

Chances of Winning
*Article 19*

No sweepstakes promotion, or any of its parts, should state or imply that a recipient has won a prize when this is not the case.

Winners should be selected in a manner that ensures fair application of the laws of chance.

Disclosure of Rules
*Article 20*

All terms and conditions of the sweepstakes, including entry procedures and rules, should be easy to find, read, and understand. The following should be set forth clearly in the rules:

- No purchase of the advertised product or service is required in order to win a prize.
- Procedures for entry.
- If applicable, disclosure that a facsimile of the entry blank or promotional device may be used to enter the sweepstakes.
- The termination date for eligibility in the sweepstakes. The termination date should specify whether it is a date of mailing or receipt of entry deadline.
- The number, retail value, and complete description of all prizes offered, and whether cash may be awarded instead of merchandise. If a cash prize is to be awarded by installment payments, that fact should be clearly disclosed along with the nature and timing of the payments.
- The approximate odds of winning a prize or a statement that such odds depend on number of entrants.
- The method by which winners are selected.
- The geographic area covered by the sweepstakes and those areas in which the offer is void.

- All eligibility requirements, if any.
- Approximate dates when winners will be selected and notified.
- Publicity rights: use of winner's name.
- Taxes are the responsibility of the winner.
- Provision of a mailing address to allow consumers to submit a self-addressed, stamped envelope to receive a list of winners of prizes over $25.00 in value.

Price Comparisons
*Article 21*
Price comparisons may be made two ways:

a. Between one's price and a former, future, or suggested price.
b. Between one's price and the price of a competitor's comparable product.

In all price comparisons, the compared price against which the comparison is made should be fair and accurate.

In each case of comparison to a former, suggested, or competitor's comparable product price, substantial sales should have been made at that price in the recent past.

For comparison, with a future price, there should be a reasonable expectation that the future price will be charged in the foreseeable future.

Guarantees
*Article 22*
If a product or service is offered with a "guarantee" or a "warranty," the terms and conditions should either be set forth in full in the promotion, or the promotion should state how the consumer may obtain a copy. The guarantee should clearly state the name and address of the guarantor and the duration of the guarantee.

Any requests for repair, replacement, or refund under the terms of a "guarantee" or "warranty" should be honored promptly. In an unqualified offer of refund, repair, or replacement, the customer's preference shall prevail.

---

## SPECIAL CLAIMS

Use of Test or Survey Data
*Article 23*
All tests or survey data referred to on advertising should be competent and reliable as to source and methodology, and should support the specific claim for which it is cited. Advertising claims should not distort the test or survey results nor take them out of context.

Testimonials and Endorsements
*Article 24*

Testimonials and endorsements should be used only if they are:

a. Authorized by the person quoted,
b. Genuine and related to the experience of the person giving them, and
c. Not taken out of context so as to distort the endorser's opinion or experience with the product.

---

**THE PRODUCT**

Product Safety
*Article 25*

Products should be safe in normal use and be free of defects likely to cause injury. To that end, they should meet or exceed the current, recognized health and safety norms and be adequately tested, where applicable. Information provided with the product should include proper directions for use and full instructions covering assembly and safety warnings, whenever necessary.

Product Distribution Safety
*Article 26*

Products should be distributed only in a manner that will provide reasonable safeguards against possibilities of injury.

Product Availability
*Article 27*

Direct marketers should only offer merchandise when it is on hand or when there is a reasonable expectations of its receipt.

Direct marketers should not engage in dry testing unless the special nature of that offer is disclosed in the promotion.

---

**FULFILLMENT**

Unordered Merchandise
*Article 28*

Merchandise should not be shipped without having first received the customer's permission. The exceptions are samples or gifts clearly marked as such, and merchandise mailed by charitable organizations soliciting contributions, as long as all items are sent with a clear and conspicuous statement informing the recipient of an unqualified right to treat the product as a gift and to do with it as the recipient sees fit, at no cost or obligation to the recipient.

Shipments
*Article 29*

Direct marketers are reminded that they should abide by the FTC regulation regarding the prompt shipment of prepaid merchandise, the

Mail Order Merchandise (30 Day) Rule. Beyond this regulation, direct marketers are urged to ship all orders as soon as possible.

---

## CREDIT AND DEBT COLLECTION

Equal Credit Opportunity
*Article 30*

A creditor should not discriminate on the basis of race, color, religion, national origin, sex, marital status, or age. If the individual is rejected for credit, the creditor should be prepared to give reasons why.

Debt Collection
*Article 31*

Unfair, misleading, deceptive, or abusive methods should not be used for collecting money. The direct marketer should take reasonable steps to assure that those collecting on the direct marketer's behalf comply with this guideline.

List Rental Prices
*Article 32*

Consumers who provide data that may be rented, sold, or exchanged for direct marketing purposes periodically should be informed of the potential for the rental, sale, or exchange of such data. Marketers should offer an opportunity to have a consumer's name deleted or suppressed upon request.

List compilers should suppress names from lists when requested by the individual.

For each list that is to be rented, sold, or exchanged the DMA Mail Preference Service name-removal list and, where applicable, the Telephone Preference Service name-removal list and, where applicable, the Telephone Preference Service name-removal list should be used. Names found on such suppression lists should not be rented, sold, or exchanged except for suppression purposes.

All persons involved in the rental, sale, or exchange of lists and data should take reasonable steps to ensure that industry members follow these guidelines.

Personal Information
*Article 33*

Direct marketers should be sensitive to the issue of consumer privacy and should limit the combination, collection, rental, sale, exchange, and use of consumer data to only those data which are appropriate for direct marketing purposes.

Information and selection criteria that may be considered to be personal and intimate in nature by all reasonable standards should not provide the basis for lists to be made available for rental, sale, or exchange when there is a reasonable expectation by the consumer that the information would be kept confidential.

Any advertising or promotion for lists being offered for rental, sale, or exchange should reflect the fact that a list is an aggregate collection of marketing data. Such promotions should also reflect a sensitivity for the consumers on those lists.

List Usage Agreements
*Article 34*

List owners, brokers, compilers, and users make every attempt to establish the exact nature of the list's intended usage prior to the sale or rental of the list. Owners, brokers, and compilers should not permit the sale or rental of their lists for an offer that is in violation of any of the Ethical Guidelines of DMA. Promotions should be directed to those segments of the public most likely to be interested in their causes or to have a use for their products or services.

List Abuse
*Article 35*

No list or list data should be used in violation of the lawful rights of the list owner nor the agreement between the parties; any such misuse should be brought to the attention of the lawful owner.

---

**TELEPHONE MARKETING**

(See Articles 9 and 29)

Reasonable Hours
*Article 36*

All telephone contacts should be made during reasonable hours.

Taping of Conversations
*Article 37*

Taping of telephone conversations made for telephone marketing purposes should not be conducted without legal notice to or consent of all parties or the use of a beeping device.

Telephone Name Removal Restricted Contacts
*Article 38*

Telephone marketers should remove the name of any customer from their telephone lists when requested by the individual. Marketers should use the DMA Telephone Preference Service name-removal list and, where applicable, the Mail Preference Service name-removal list. Names found on such suppression lists should not be rented, sold, or exchanged except for suppression purposes.

A telephone marketer should not knowingly call anyone who has an unlisted or unpublished telephone number except in instances where the number was proveded by the customer to that marketer.

Random dialing techniques, whether manual or automated, in which identification of those parties to be called is left to chance, should not be used in sales and marketing solicitations.

Sequential dialing techniques, whether a manual or automated process, in which selection of those parties to be called is based on the location of their telephone number in a sequence of telephone numbers, should not be used.

Disclosure and Tactics
*Article 39*

All telephone solicitations should disclose to the buyer during the conversation the cost of the merchandise, all terms, conditions and the payment plan, and whether there will be postage and handling charges. At not time should "high pressure" tactics be utilized.

Use of Automatic Electronic Equipment
*Article 40*

No telephone marketer should solicit sales using automatic electronic dialing equipment unless the telephone immediately disconnects when the called person hangs up.

---

**FUND RAISING**

(See Article 28)

Commission Prohibition/Authenticity of Organization
*Article 41*

Fund raisers should make no percentage or commission arrangements whereby any person or firm assisting or participating in a fund raising activity is paid a fee proportionate to the funds raised, nor should they solicit for nonfunctioning organizations.

---

**LAWS, CODES, AND REGULATIONS**

*Article 42*

Direct marketers should operate in accordance with the Better Business Bureau's Code of Advertising and be cognizant of and adhere to laws and regulations of the United State Postal Service, the Federal Trade Commission, the Federal Reserve Board, and other applicable federal, state, and local laws governing advertising, marketing practices, and the transaction of business by mail, telephone, and the print and broadcast media.

PART II

# THE PLANNING PROCESS

CHAPTER 4

# Planning for Direct Marketing

## PROFILE

**JEROME W. PICKHOLZ**

**Strategy from the top.** Most decisions in direct marketing are of a tactical nature. But those of Jerome W. Pickholz, chairman and CEO of Ogilvy & Mather Direct, are strategic. They are long-term. And they involve not merely the direction of a brand, but that of an entire business.

A native of New York, Pickholz in 1953 graduated with a BBA in accounting from what later became the Baruch School. Following a stint in the U.S. Navy, he went into public accounting and received his CPA.

Shortly thereafter, he took a job as controller with Hodes Daniel, a direct mail and production company. About four years later, he was appointed general manager and a member of the company's board of directors.

In 1970 the firm was acquired by Cordura Corporation, which envisioned Hodes Daniel as the flagship of a great armada to be launched into direct marketing. Pickholz was appointed president of Hodes Daniel and manager of all Cordura direct mail activities. Thus, in one generation Pickholz went, figuratively speaking, from lieutenant on a navy vessel to admiral of a business enterprise.

But the Cordura ships foundered on the stormy seas of direct marketing. Many units of the corporation were unprofitable and ultimately divested. Hodes Daniel itself became part of Ogilvy & Mather Direct. In 1974, Mr. Pickholz, whose attachment to Hodes Daniel survived its changes of ownership, became president of O&M Direct.

The surging waves of industry growth propelled O&M Direct in two strategic directions. One was domestic expansion, accompanied by new offices in Chicago, San Francisco, Los Angeles, Houston and Atlanta. The second was acquisition in some foreign markets and start-up businesses in others. The New York office, creating tapes, newsletters, and seminars, was used as a training ground for the entire direct marketing network. This strategy succeeded in expanding the firm's markets by adroitly using its excess capacity of intangible assets, namely, direct marketing know-how.

Under Pickholz' leadership, O&M Direct within a decade increased its domestic billings from $25 million to $354.2 million, and its total to $855.2 million. Heading one of the largest direct marketing agencies, Pickholz exemplifies the essence of corporate planning: fitting long-term resources to market situations in order to exploit opportunities. ■

# The Strategy Concept

Within the past two decades, corporations have placed increasing emphasis on formality and strategy in their planning. In part, this emphasis on strategy is a response to the expansion of the firm—in products, in markets, in sheer size of assets. It may take place in small, single-business companies, but it is a central fact in large business complexes.

The term *strategy* was carried over into business from the military. It derives from the Greek expression for "generalship" and concerns the broad strokes of winning a war, not any particular battle. Actions that implement strategy are called tactics. According to this point of view, a strategic plan provides general directions for specific ends—most emphatically, those ends that are substantive and long-term. Although there is little agreement as to the time span, it is usually conceived as running from 3 to 10 years.

Strategy goes on at all levels of a firm—at corporate headquarters, divisional centers of authority, and operational departments. But goals are not the same. Corporate strategy, particularly in large, diversified firms, assesses opportunities of business units and relies on portfolio theory to allocate resources to them. Business-unit strategy is concerned primarily with long-term plans for product-markets. Operational-unit planning embraces narrow product lines and individual products. The hierarchical nature of strategy planning is depicted in Figure 4-1.

Strategic planning in direct marketing involves the same processes as in any other business activity. In fact, direct marketing is only a subfunction of total marketing and therefore shares many aspects with

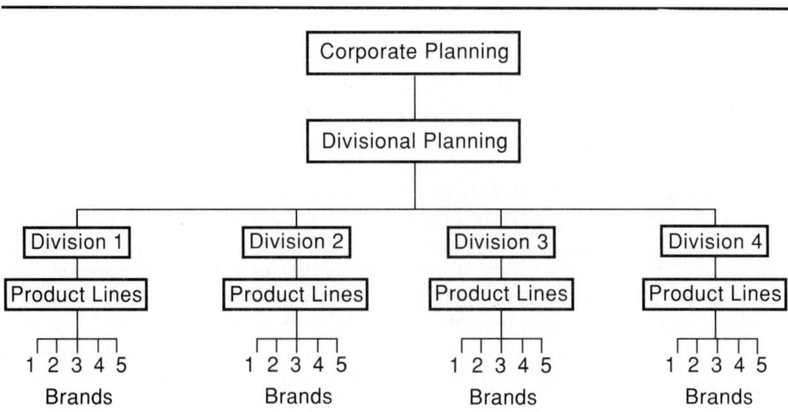


**FIGURE 4-1 Levels of Strategic Planning**

more general practices. But it also has certain unique features. Let us examine how strategic plans affect direct marketing at various levels of the organization.

## Corporate Strategy

Responsibility for strategic planning of a corporation rests with the chief executive officer (CEO). The main concern of strategy at this level relates to strategic business units (SBUs), which roughly correspond to divisions. Ideally, each SBU should be a self-contained profit center, with distinct products and markets. Its decisions should be made with no regard to those of other SBUs.[1]

Only in single-business companies does direct marketing engage top management in strategic planning. For example, strategic plans of L.L. Bean focus on direct marketing because mail order represents about 88 percent of company sales.[2] When mail order makes up such a large chunk of total revenue, the CEO must delve into its operations when putting together the firm's strategic plans. Corporate strategy in single-line businesses is virtually the same as that of SBUs; the SBU is the business of the entire corporation.

In most instances, however, corporate management is largely divorced from direct marketing operations. Top executives of Marks and Spencer, the owner of Brooks Brothers, would pay scant attention to direct marketing in their long-range planning. Their Brooks Brothers division derives some 94 percent of sales from its 50 clothing stores and only 6 percent from direct mail.[3] Here direct marketing is a selling technique that holds small importance to the corporation as a whole. It is thus left to managers at the operational level, separated from the top by several layers of management.

A firm's structure also plays a part in the extent to which direct marketing comes up as a subject of discussion in corporate boardrooms. Does the direct marketing group work as an SBU or as part of a larger entity in the lower structures of the organization?

When existing as divisions or subsidiaries, direct marketing agencies vie with other profit centers for internally allocated funds. As divisions, they can show profits or losses. They set their own policies—subject, of course, to those of the parent organization. They are judged by their profit or cash-generating opportunities and are rewarded or penalized accordingly at budget time.

1. See George S. Day, *Analysis for Strategic Market Decisions* (St. Paul, MN: West Publishing, 1986), pp. 1–26; David Aaker, *Strategic Market Management* (New York: John Wiley & Sons, 1984), pp. 8–9.
2. "Mail Order Top 250+," *Direct Marketing* (July 1990), p. 45.
3. *Ibid.*

When direct marketing does not function as an SBU, it has no claim to corporate resources. Rather, its operations are determined by divisional heads, or even group heads within a division. For example, Leo Burnett, a leading advertising agency, diffuses direct marketing throughout its account groups. As such, direct marketing functions as tasks set by account group heads. Decidedly, it occupies a low position in the corporate hierarchy and would not merit a footnote in any strategic plan written by top corporate officers.

Similarly, direct mail operations at many department stores are submerged in functional departments. They act as a service to merchandise managers who approve budgets for those tasks. Without status as a profit center, direct marketing has no place on the agenda of strategic planning at corporate headquarters. In contrast, J.C. Penney runs catalog operations out of a separate profit center, funded, like all other divisions, by dispensations from the top.

The ideal SBU stands in splendid isolation. However, many profit centers benefit from shared decisions and commonly used facilities. Direct marketing agencies may make use of creative talent and media experts working in other parts of the parent company. Whether organized as a profit center or not, department store catalogers are prone to carry merchandise demanded by the store's credit card customers. In that event, catalog managers and store purchasing departments act in unison with regard to merchandise selection.

Most large diversified corporations employ some form of portfolio analysis in strategic planning, a concept derived from the financial field. Like fund managers in financial houses, corporate management regards SBUs as a portfolio of assets under its care. The idea is to choose the best strategic alternative not for any individual SBU, but for the portfolio in its entirety. Increasing the value of the whole portfolio of businesses is the prime objective of strategic planning at the corporate level.

Probably the best known of these portfolio models is that of the Boston Consulting Group (BCG), developed in the 1960s. This model classifies all of a company's SBUs on a market share–growth rate matrix. Other large companies have developed other systems for categorizing their SBUs as to future opportunities. Figure 4-2 illustrates a BCG grid, with hypothetical SBUs depicted as circles varying in size. Depending on the quadrant in which an SBU falls, the model suggests a general strategy. For example, market leaders in growth industries will throw off excess cash when growth slows, if market share can be maintained. Figure 4-3 indicates the tacit strategies for SBUs in the various quadrants of the BCG grid.

Most large companies, however, use portfolio concepts as decision frameworks; they do not act strictly in accordance with the analytical methods of portfolio theory. Even the Boston Consulting Group, a leader in strategic planning, has pretty much discarded the mathematical

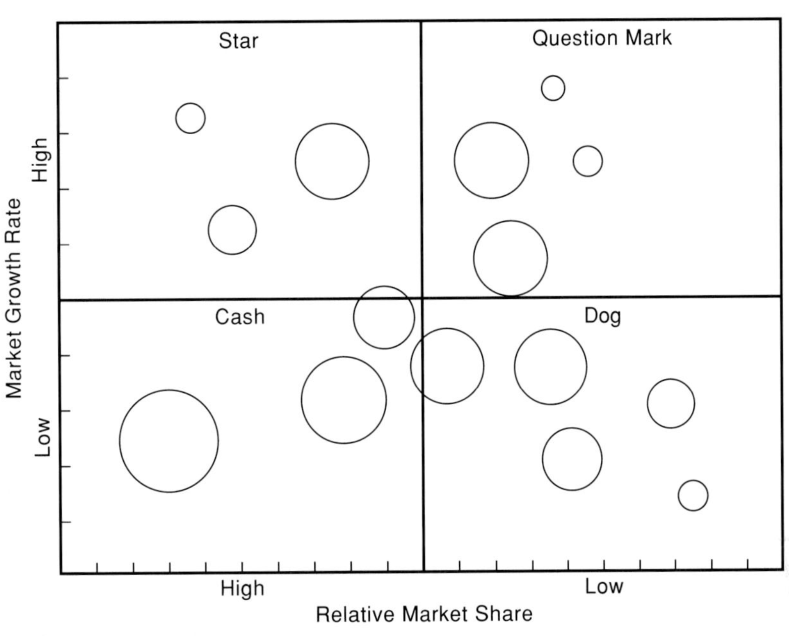


**FIGURE 4-2 Market Share-Growth Rate Matrix**

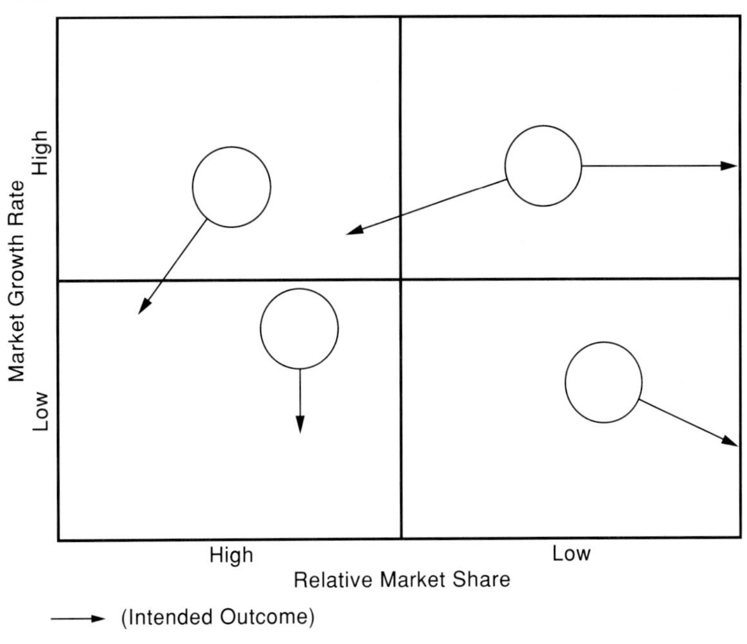


**FIGURE 4-3 Tacit Strategies**

analysis it had developed. Other large companies have acted similarly in deciding how much resources to allocate to their SBUs.

According to George Day, who has written extensively on the subject, portfolio models are used as "diagnostic aids" to derive "natural or generic strategies for SBUs." These broad directions, Day insists, represent only possibilities "dominated by the specifics of the strategic situations."[4] In that sense, the strategic role of any SBU becomes "situational," which covers an enormously wide range of possibilities.

Practically all senior managers would agree with Day if asked point-blank about the basis for their decisions. But they would certainly not admit to blindly following strategies implied by the positions of an SBU on a portfolio chart. Like managers of security portfolios who deny the use of indexing techniques to select stocks, senior corporate executives are paid high salaries for insightful thinking. The key question is reduced to this: To what extent is judgment colored when a corporate planner knows that an SBU falls into a category labeled a cash cow, a dog, or some other descriptive name that connotes performance? Perhaps this question has no answer. But it is especially poignant because top executives in widely diversified companies are unfamiliar with the nitty-gritty of SBU problems. Their decisions seldom, if ever, deal with operational specifics, but the effects of those decisions greatly impact the performance of SBUs.

This fact is well illustrated by Mattel, which in the mid 1980s owned Western Publishing Company, a direct marketer of reading material. Senior corporate executives regarded the division as a cash cow; its main function was to generate cash flow. In accordance with Mattel's directive, Western focused on proven, successful items, such as the Sesame Street Book Club for children and the Knitting Collection for women. Both products were old standbys, and cash flowed in. Later, Western was sold, and the new owner regarded the acquisition as a growth situation. The SBU's objective switched from cash generation to sales building. Western Publishing shifted its efforts to new product development, such as the Scribblers activity program for children, crocheting for women, and a host of new projects for other targeted populations.[5]

## Divisional-Level Strategy

Strategic planning at the divisional level has the same general goals as that at the corporate level. A survey of 53 direct marketing companies conducted by William A. Cohen, a marketing professor, and Steve Kennedy, a marketing manager, found that the principal reasons for

4. *Day, op cit.*, pp. 193–194.
5. Jim Kobs, "Marketing Strategies for Maximum Growth," *Direct Marketing* (May 1987), p. 34.

strategic planning were goal formulation and attainment.[6] At the divisional level, these goals are long-term and relate to product or market development. As corporate strategies give direction to SBUs, divisional strategies give direction to product lines.

For example, Penney's direct marketing division draws up long-term plans for special catalogs aimed at specific population targets. Ultimate Computer Supplies, a division of Ultimate Corporation, a manufacturer of computer systems, was set up in 1985 to market by mail order computer accessories, floppy disks, furniture, storage facilities, and paper products.[7] This division sends out approximately 7 million catalogs a year. Whether divisional management plans for sales growth or profit, it must concern itself with issues such as potential markets and product mix.

Similarly, Tweeds Inc., a merchant of men's and women's apparel, added a new clothing line in late 1989 with its Smythe & Company catalog. Corporate managers had to get involved with merchandising and marketing strategies. The new venture was aimed at young adults—a "horizontal" strategy that sought to enter new markets with new products.[8]

Perhaps best exemplifying divisional strategy is Hanover House Industries, owned by Horn & Hardart Co. In 1988 Hanover adopted a "brand strategy" approach for the 22 catalogs it was publishing at the time. Each catalog carried a loose assortment of related merchandise. Although they went under different names, such as *Colonial Gardens*, *Adam York*, and *International Male*, they had look-alike formats. Under the new dispensation, each catalog was to have its own "brand" identity, like individual brands in a Procter & Gamble product line. Each catalog was to have unique positioning from the standpoint of graphics and merchandise. Divisional management in effect gave a new direction to product and marketing development of all its catalogs, which could be perceived as product lines.[9]

Divisional strategies are "generic." Planning of this type entails three major considerations—markets, products, and technologies—and these correspond to three basic questions:

1. Who is to be served? (markets)
2. What is to be served? (products)
3. How is the product to be served? (technology)

---

6. W. A. Cohen and S. C. Kennedy, "Strategic Planning Trends: The Whos, Whys, and Hows,"*Direct Marketing* (July 1984), pp. 24–32.
7. Jon Boorsteen, "Ultimate Computer Supplies Catalog Sales Are Expected to Top $5 Million," *DM News* (December 1, 1987), p. 30.
8. Joan Gunin, "Tweeds Launches Smythe & Co. with a One-Million-Piece Mailing," *DM News* (January 29, 1990), p. 6.
9. Judith Graham, "Hanover House Recorders Catalogs," *Advertising Age* (July 11, 1988), p. 32.

From a purely conceptual point of view, a firm has many alternatives from which to choose. A mix of three factors, each involving three choices, yields 27 alternatives. This wide range of options prevents a systematic analysis and comparison of all choices, as taught in business schools leaning toward a management-science approach. One popular method of categorizing product-market strategies is to divide them into three broad groups: undifferentiated, differentiated, and concentrated.[10]

An undifferentiated strategy is usually viewed as a business choice that goes after the largest part of the market with a single product. Although the market may be made up of various segments, the different classes of customers are regarded as one inseparable whole. Commonality is seen as greatly outweighing differences. A strategy of this sort is seldom taken in direct marketing, which emphasizes databases and market segments. The objective of dividing markets into smaller parts is to screen out the best prospects.

Therefore, direct marketing pursues either a concentrated or differentiated strategy. Both involve market segmentation. The first alternative defines market boundaries narrowly. It then concentrates on products that are particularly attractive to a specified cluster of customers.

The difference between concentrated and undifferentiated strategies is often one of degree. How large must a market be before it bursts its confines and becomes undifferentiated? Segments also differ in terms of size, and a relatively small cluster of buyers might be called a *niche* market. Direct marketing agencies that specialize in business-to-business mail order basically do niche marketing.

A differentiated strategy has a rather inexact meaning. The traditional view treats differentiation as applied to products. When customers perceive items as set apart from those of competitors, the products are said to be differentiated. The second meaning, and of more recent origin, denotes a firm operating in two or more segments of a market, with products fitted for each group of customers.[11] The Hanover catalogs featuring apparel or fashion goods aimed at various customer groups typifies this meaning.

## Operational Strategies

Planning at the operational level is tactical rather than strategic. The marketing plan forms the basic guide to action and typically spans a one-year period; it is not long-term. It deals chiefly with problems of the moment and how to stimulate response at the moment.

10. W. G. Zikmund and M. F. d'Amico, *Marketing*, 3rd ed. (New York: John Wiley & Sons, 1989), pp. 79–84.
11. Philip Kotler, *Marketing Management*, 7th ed. (Englewood Cliffs, NJ: Prentice Hall, 1991), pp. 283–284.

**TABLE 4.1. Functional Strategies to Increase Sales.**

| Strategy | Examples of Tactics |
|---|---|
| Increase sales with same products in same markets | Increase sales productivity by more frequent mailings to house list, remailing to best customers, phone call follow-ups, etc.<br>Increase order size by upping the minimum order, offering quantity discounts, providing easier credit terms, etc. |
| Extend market with same product | Enter new geographic areas, such as foreign markets.<br>Appealing to new market segments to develop product usage. |
| Modify product mix in same markets | Find new uses for same products<br>Upgrade products so as to offer higher-priced goods<br>Broaden the product line to offer more items |
| Diversify | Combine product development with tactics for market extension |

In many instances, operational tactics and divisional strategies meld, so that the two forms of planning can barely be discerned as separate. Direct marketers are traditionally action-oriented, concerned with immediate results from their efforts. Copywriters and promotional managers dominate the top rungs of executive echelons. Mail order and telemarketing, the two primary fields of direct marketing, are selling methods. They emphasize execution techniques. How do we segment a house list to get a better response? Which headline or cover letter pulled the greatest number of orders? Which premium or inducement resulted in the lowest cost per response?

Even the Hanover House strategy of giving their catalogs individual "brand identities" overlaps into the functional area. Its objective to create easily distinguishable formats is a tactic designed to increase sales now, not at some undetermined time in the future.

Functional strategies to increase sales can thus be phrased in terms of the familiar product-market matrix. If products are held constant, sales increases can come from either deeper market penetration or expansion into new markets. If markets are held constant, revenue can be enhanced by modifying current products or changing the product mix. Developing new product lines might also necessitate going into new markets, which implies diversification. These functional strategies and examples of tactical plans are depicted in Table 4-1.

Diversification can move in several directions and take diverse forms. Growth by diversification can come through concentric, horizontal, or conglomerate strategies.[12] A concentric approach seeks new classes of customers with products that have technological or marketing synergies. Horizontal diversification appeals to current customers with new products that are not technologically related. Finally, a company opting for the conglomerate form of diversification seeks opportunities with products, technologies, and markets that are completely unrelated to existing ones. This type of strategy typically arises at the business unit or corporate level and often results in the creation of a new SBU altogether.

Direct marketing, more so than any other line of distribution, permits the different types of diversification to be accomplished in varying degrees. For example, a catalog can add relatively few new products and expand mailings to new customers by exceedingly small amounts. Most decisions here would be confined to operational managers. On the other hand, the change may be so drastic that a completely new catalog would result, with totally new products going to substantially new markets. Such a decision would fall to divisional management. At the extreme, a firm may decide to penetrate a highly unrelated market, such as keeping consumer catalogs while developing industrial ones. That might necessitate a new division, for both products and markets would be different from existing ones. Responsibility to set up this new venture would rest with corporate management.

## The Offer

Regardless of what functional strategy is adopted, all direct marketing conveys messages to prospects. These messages carry offers or propositions. In this sense, the formulation of messages represent tactics. The offers constitute operational strategies.

A widely held belief among direct marketers is that good offers have the ability to succeed even when embodied in weakly constructed messages. But the most creative execution, practitioners claim, cannot overcome a bad offer. This point of view attests to the strategic importance of the offer.

Actually, there is no universal agreement on what makes an offer. Practically everyone accepts the inclusion of products and transactional terms in the definition,[13] but some authors regard the presentation as being part of the offer itself.[14] We regard the presentation as advertising

12. *Ibid.*, pp. 45–48.
13. See H. E. Brown and R. W. Brucker, "Just What Is a Direct Marketing Offer?" *Direct Marketing* (November 1988), pp. 68–75.
14. M. L. Roberts and P. D. Berger, *Direct Marketing Management* (Englewood Cliffs, NJ: Prentice Hall, 1989), p. 69.

**TABLE 4.2. Main Elements of Offers.**

1. Product
2. Time-related aspects
3. Price
4. Terms of payments
5. Promotional inducements
6. Risk reduction

copy, as just so much "window dressing" that is not an integral part of an offer.

There are many ways to phrase the same product and transactional terms. Separating the presentation from the offer allows the separation of form and content. The content is what is said, the elements that make up an offer. The form is how it is said, the way the offer is dressed up with words, sounds, and illustrations.

This view accords with communication theory. Offers are communicated by signs or symbols, the most important of which is language. But nonverbal codes can support an oral or written message. Psychologists call the ideas conveyed by such signs as *signifieds* and the things to which they refer as *signifiers*. In these terms, direct marketers use signifieds to evoke sets of images about signifiers.

For any message to be understood, the audience must perceive the signs in the way the sender intended. It is the recipients of information who translate the symbols faithfully or misinterpret them, who convert them into something of meaning or disregard them as something of insignificance.[15]

One way of classifying offers is to evaluate them in terms of common features. The most common classification used in direct marketing includes four elements: product, time-related aspects, price, and terms of payment. These four elements appear in virtually all propositions. Two other elements are used frequently enough to warrant a place in any classification system of offers: promotional inducements and risk reduction. The six components are listed in Table 4-2. The first four elements are mandatory: every direct marketing offer must have them. Every offer must specify the nature of the product, how and when it will be delivered, how much it will cost, and how payment can be made. The last two components are optional. They are not necessary to an offer, though they appear quite frequently in direct marketing presentations.

A large number of variations including all six elements are possible. Both offers seeking orders and those seeking inquiries contain the mandatory elements. The optional features are present chiefly in messages designed to get orders. Inducements are unnecessary when peo-

15. Judith Williamson, *Decoding Advertisements* (London: Marian Boyars, 1978), pp. 40–41.

ple ask but don't buy, and risks are never present when only information is sought. Without a commitment, nothing is at stake.

## The Product

The product is what the marketer proposes to sell. It can be a good, a service, or a combination of both. It can be an individual item or a combination of many items. In the case of a good, the product has inherent physical attributes, such as form, design, materials, color, and weight. Services have intangible qualities.

Buyers, however, may not perceive goods in terms of objective physical attributes, especially since products are ordered sight unseen. Product differences may be real or imagined, and benefits may be functional or psychological. A signified displaying dresses on slim models might make a woman think the clothing makes her look thinner. Although the meaning is created by the people who receive direct marketing messages, signifieds in the message do exert an influence as to how the product is perceived.

In the event the message is coded to generate leads, the object of the inquiry becomes the product. That is what is actually offered. It is somewhat like an intermediary product; its function is to beget something else. Information requested, for example, becomes the offer, and selling thus proceeds as a two-step procedure. The information either generates a sale or is followed up with a solicitation.

## Time-Related Aspects

Depending on the terms of purchases and deliveries over time, offers can be either one-shot or continuous. The one-time deal is a stand-alone offer. A pair of shoes bought from a mailing piece carries a one-time commitment. There were no past contracts calling for the purchase, nor are there any obligations to buy something in the future. Although the company may contact the buyer again, there is no obligation to purchase any more merchandise. The vast majority of catalog mailings represent offers of this type.

The continuity offer implies a transaction wherein purchases and deliveries are spread out over time. There are various forms of such offers. The most popular ones are:

- Fixed-term offers
- Automatic shipment plans
- Negative and positive option programs

FIXED-TERM OFFERS. Probably the best known fixed-term offers are those for magazine subscriptions. Buyers contract for a specific number of issues. That number defines when deliveries will be made, for these are governed by publication frequency. A person subscribing for 12 issues of a monthly magazine in effect contracts for monthly deliveries over a full year.

Practically all fixed-term offers designate some minimum number. Monthly publications, for example, may sell half-year subscriptions. Weeklies have shorter time spans for fulfillment but a larger number of issues per period. A half-year subscription order for a weekly specifies 26 issues. The *Wall Street Journal*, coming out five times a week, offers subscriptions for as short as 13 weeks. The minimum is thus 65 units. Like packaged goods, the volume is premeasured and offered in given quantities.

Since a fixed term must come to an end, current customers are solicited with new offers for the future. These "renewal" notices usually begin before the old contract expires.

The key to continuity offers is the product. Satisfied customers ordinarily renew. *National Geographic* magazine, for example, boasts a renewal rate of 82 percent—far above the industry norm, which ranges from 50 percent to 70 percent. The economics of keeping customers satisfied are apparent. For *National Geographic* to maintain its current subscription level, it must replace 18 percent of its subscriber base. Were the renewal rate to fall, more new subscribers would be needed. It costs far less—perhaps one-tenth as much—to keep a current customer than to acquire a new one.

A number of service industries operate in the same way. The most notable is the insurance industry, which alerts customers as to when their fixed-term policies are to expire. Credit card companies go through the same procedure annually, informing those whose term is near expiration that the annual fee will be put on their future invoice. Christmas clubs solicit members to begin putting money aside for the next holiday season.

A variation of the fixed-term proposition is the load-up offer. The program has a fixed term. Intervals between deliveries are constant, but quantities delivered are variable. Three or four single items might be made at periodic intervals at the beginning. After that, deliveries balloon, and the balance of the sale is made in one "load-up" shipment. Ostensibly, this procedure increases volume per customer. The Federal Trade Commission requires all promotional material to clearly specify load-up provisions. Customers are usually apprised in advance of the load-up shipment and have the option of stopping delivery by notifying the seller.

AUTOMATIC SHIPMENTS. An automatic shipment plan calls for the purchaser to take periodic deliveries of some item. Acceptance of the offer sets off a series of automatic shipments. Book publishers and record companies are the most prominent users of such offers, but many other marketers sell products that lend themselves to deliveries at fixed intervals, such as food and cosmetics. These programs tie customers to a source of supply.

Theoretically, deliveries can go on into perpetuity, or as long as the recipient of an item continues to pay for it. Such automatic shipments offers are called "till forbid" offers: they go on until a customer specifically forbids their continuance. A buyer's silence is taken as an authorization for shipment. Only a notification to stop deliveries ends the program, and sometimes a halt can be triggered if a customer returns merchandise.

NEGATIVE AND POSITIVE OPTIONS. Negative and positive option offers are similar to automatic shipment plans, but members are given a clear choice before each shipment. The way these plans work is exemplified by the Book-of-the-Month Club, the outstanding practitioner of the negative option. Members receive an advance bulletin of the club's recommendation or an alternative for the ensuing month. Members can turn down the club's choice or ask that no book be sent that month. As with automatic shipments, a member is not asked to approve each shipment. Silence denotes acquiescence. Failure to reply is taken to mean "yes—send me the club's recommendation."

Another way of forcing members into making a choice is the positive option. Members can send back a card ordering the recommended book, and no shipment is made until that approval is received. Nonreply is taken as a "no." Positive options are rare because they decrease orders. People are forced to exert some effort to reply in the affirmative. In the negative option, no effort at all is required to signal approval.

## Price

Since price is an integral part of a transaction, it is stated somewhere in the offer. Should they decide to order something, customers must know what they have to pay.

The emphasis on price depends on what marketers want and what customers are willing to pay. Many direct marketers that try to differentiate their merchandise have target return objectives. These target returns are expressed as ratios: profits to invested capital or profits to net sales. Prices are usually set to cover all operating expenses plus the desired rate of return. In these instances, customers are not price-sensitive, and selling propositions play up other features. Alfred Oxenfeldt's advice for this situation is well worth heeding: "Don't use price to attain ends that can be obtained more efficiently by other means."[16]

16. Alfred R. Oxenfeldt, *Pricing Strategies* (New York: AMACOM, 1975), p. 12.

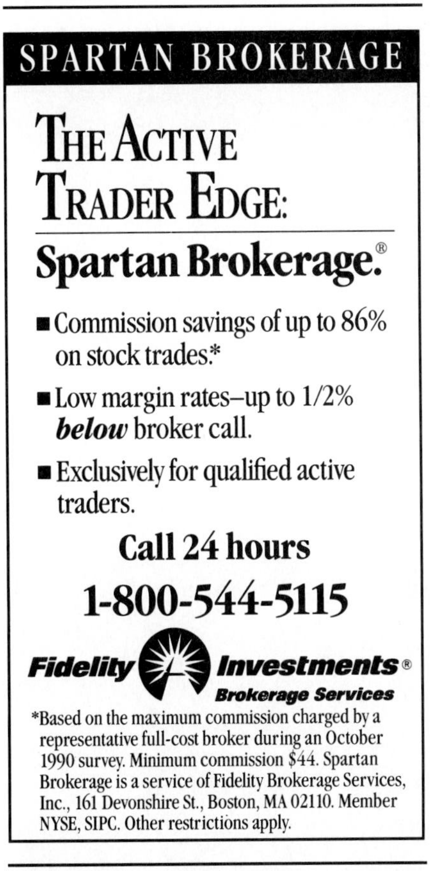

SPARTAN BROKERAGE
THE ACTIVE TRADER EDGE:
Spartan Brokerage.®
■ Commission savings of up to 86% on stock trades.*
■ Low margin rates–up to 1/2% *below* broker call.
■ Exclusively for qualified active traders.
Call 24 hours
1-800-544-5115
Fidelity Investments®
Brokerage Services
*Based on the maximum commission charged by a representative full-cost broker during an October 1990 survey. Minimum commission $44. Spartan Brokerage is a service of Fidelity Brokerage Services, Inc., 161 Devonshire St., Boston, MA 02110. Member NYSE, SIPC. Other restrictions apply.

**FIGURE 4-4 Example of Percent Savings at a Discount Broker**
*Source:* Printed with permission of Fidelity Investments.

Sales volume objectives often suggest a low-price strategy. Such merchandisers usually offer "self-sold" goods, such as name brands and items with well-established price levels. These tactics provide customers with a point of reference for judging the comparative value of an offer. Although prices may be set to generate dollar sales, failure to pull in sufficient revenues could result in reduced profit levels.

Price appeals in direct marketing ads convey the idea of a sale or a bargain, a markdown from some "regular" or customary price level. There are numerous ways of conveying this impression. For example, a discount on a shirt can be heralded by such announcements as "50 percent off regular price," "Originally $20—now $10," "Save $10 on each shirt," or "$20 shirt for half-price." Figure 4-4 shows an advertisement of a discount brokerage house. It phrases its price advantage in terms of a percentage saved on a stock transaction.

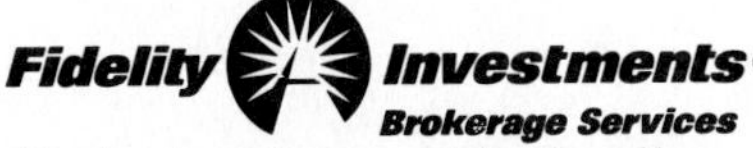

**FIGURE 4-5 Volume Discounts**
*Source:* Reprinted with permission of Spring Hill Nurseries Company.

Figure 4-5 displays a page from the 1991 Spring Hill Nurseries Company catalog. A set of six Calla bulbs cost $23.95, or about $3.91 per unit. An order of one plant goes for $4.99. The purchase of larger quantities results in a discount.

Many catalogs, especially those put out by retailers, make ample use of odd pricing. Prices of $9.95, $17.50, and $38.95 are common (see Figure 4-6).

**FIGURE 4-6 Odd Pricing**
*Source:* Printed with the permission of Spiegel.

## Terms of Payment

Closely linked to price are terms of payment. Easier ways of paying bring higher response. On the other hand, ultra-easy payment terms carry greater risks of bad debts. There are five basic methods of paying for orders: cash, COD, installment, billing, and credit cards. Most offers provide a choice between two or more.

The cash option involves the smallest expenditure of time and cost to the marketer. Recordkeeping for remittances and collections is minimal. Cash payment may appeal to cost-conscious financial people, but not to consumers. Response rates fall. Many people balk at paying for merchandise before they see it, despite money-back guarantees.

The cash on delivery (COD) alternative, like the cash-with-order remittance, eliminates credit extension. A number of drawbacks, however, limit its use. Handling COD orders leads to higher costs and more effort. Because it is now common for both partners in a household to be at work at the time of mail delivery, many packages wind up at the post office and get sent back when addressees don't come to pick them up. Refusal rates of COD shipments also run high.

Installment sales spread out payments over time. These terms usually accompany consumer purchases of high-priced items. This payment plan is a form of credit extension, and if payments due are not charged interest, the marketer in effect marks down the price of the merchandise.

Billing customers directly remains a popular method for arranging payment. Bills normally accompany the merchandise or follow a few days after shipment. This method is relatively simple and straightforward and is used extensively in business-to-business transactions. To implement this option, a firm must possess or establish a billing and collection system for handling credit.

Credit card payment enjoys wide practice in consumer markets. Firms choosing this option must make arrangements with credit card issuers. The two major bank credit cards are Visa and MasterCard. Among the nonbank cards with wide usage are American Express, Diners Club, Carte Blanche, and recently Discover, a Sears entry. When the credit card holder charges purchases to a card, the marketer is free of all risk. Payments are made by the credit card company, less a discount for its services.

## Promotional Inducements

Many direct marketing offers contain promotional overlays—premiums, giveaways, sweepstakes or contests, gifts, or samples. Sales promotions give prospective buyers something extra, something not expected in the normal course of business. These devices, however, seldom make buyers out of nonbuyers. They seldom push nonusers into a buyer category unless they have a genuine interest in the product. Promotions target those with the highest probabilities of accepting an offer, in the hope that something extra will be enough to convert a "highly probable" buyer into an actual one. The direct marketer thus provides an incentive of extra value for responding to an offer.

The main thrust of promotions is the undecided consumer. Interest by itself does not necessarily mean that a purchase will follow. There are always people who are interested but not quite ready to take the plunge. Premiums, sweepstakes, and contests aim primarily at this marginal group. Free gifts and samples may have other objectives.

PREMIUMS. Premiums are used in a great variety of circumstances. They are merchandise given free of charge or at a substantial price reduction in return for purchase of another product. Sometimes they are given simply in return for visiting a store. These are known as *traffic-building premiums.*

Premiums come in many shapes and forms. Some are *self-liquidators.* Consumers pay something for the item, usually an amount that covers premium costs. These are often hard-to-find goods and therefore make good gifts. Cosmetics, for example, are favorite premiums in mailouts of retail stores. These frequently come in the form of "purchase with purchase" and "gift with purchase" programs that build retail traffic.[17]

*Direct premiums* are free gifts that go with a purchase. This offer can come as part of the price, as when an individual buys a certain amount and gets something free. When all is said and done, free merchandise represents a price reduction for the buyer meeting certain conditions. Nurseries, for example, give bonuses of free plants and bulbs for ordering early and buying designated dollar amounts.

Another use of direct premiums is to aid the sales force. This situation arises in business-to-business marketing, where a direct response advertisement attempts to generate leads. Similarly, firms that rely on personal selling to consumers fall back on a variety of gifts to gain entrance into the home—free estimates, surveys, booklets, demonstrations. In general, the more generous the offer, the higher the level of response. The quality of such leads, however, is correspondingly diminished.

*Mail-in premiums* often originate at the point of purchase. Consumers supply proof of purchase to receive free gifts. Calling for extra effort on the part of buyers, this method stirs little enthusiasm among the general public. Retailers do not get involved in processing mail-ins; that is left to the suppliers. Retailers incur no extra cost and so readily accept these types of manufacturer sales promotions.

Yet another type is the *continuity premium.* Gifts in this form depend on the length and degree of customer involvement. Frequent-buyer

17. Dottie Enrico, "GWP and PWP: Pros and Cons," *Stores* (September 1986), pp. 63–68.

programs are a prime example. Customers receive bonus points for each purchase and credit toward additional purchases. Visa, for example, awards cardholders with credit points that can be used to purchase a select number of special items.

SWEEPSTAKES AND CONTESTS. The promotional methods of sweepstakes and contests have grown in use by leaps and bounds in recent years. They are often theme-based programs designed to build sales around special events. Their success depends heavily on how they are joined with other marketing mix elements, but there is great diversity in implementation.

Contests are essentially games of skill. Participants compete in some task, such as naming a new product or completing a puzzle. Winners are judged on their competence in fulfilling the requirements of the contest.

Sweepstakes are simpler than contests. They require no skill and therefore bring higher response. Winners are determined on the basis of chance.

The variety of sweepstakes is endless. The "straight" sweepstakes picks out winners from a bowl or drum that contains thoroughly mixed entries. "Matching" sweepstakes match numbers or symbols to selected winners. The "instant win" allows contestants to see if they won by rubbing or washing off a film covering. "Programed learning" sweepstakes require entrants to return information from a label or package.[18]

In promoting either sweepstakes or contests, marketers must not run afoul of state gambling laws. Sweepstakes must not require a purchase as a condition of entering. Contests, however, may require people to pay in order to enter. The major complaints about sweepstakes fall into three major categories: (1) They are games of chance, not skill. (2) Contestants are not properly advised about their chances of winning. (3) People are told they are tied for first place, but not that they are tied with a million others.[19] Firms running sweepstakes and contests are well advised to make sure in advance that these promotions conform to all relevant laws in markets to which they apply.

## Risk Reduction

Because consumers cannot inspect goods they buy through direct marketing, offers frequently contain risk reduction elements. The major ones are guarantees, warranties, and free-trial proposals.

Guarantees are marketers' policy statements concerning the goods they sell. Some guarantees are very broad. For roughly a century Sears has had a policy of "satisfaction guaranteed or money back." Many

18. Emanual Soshensky, "Contest Firm to Spend $15 million in Face of Risk and Consumer Complaints," *DM News* (August 15, 1983), p. 18.
19. Eileen Norris, "Everyone Will Grab at a Chance to Win," *Advertising Age* (August 22, 1983), p.10.

in the industry believe that such broad-based unconditional guarantees are mandatory in today's environment. Other direct marketers limit their guarantees, for example, to six months from date of purchase.[20]

Free samples are sometimes combined with guarantees for the purpose of encouraging product trial. Magazine publishers occasionally solicit subscriptions by these means. They offer complimentary issues for signing up and the right to cancel if not completely satisfied (see Figure 4-7).

Varying this technique, book publishers and product manufacturers send out examination copies. Recipients of these offers have the right to return the merchandise after a certain period, say 14 days. The free–examination offer also finds favor with publishers selling to professional markets with the use of business reply card decks.

In contrast to guarantees, warranties make specific statements about product quality or performance, and marketers are legally bound to honor these promises. Courts have drawn a fine line between "puffing" and promising. Direct marketers must therefore take care that sales puffery in advertisements does not cross over into the land of legally binding promises.

## A Turnaround

Whether involving portfolios of SBUs or products, all planning models assume that rational choice drives the plan. Controversies are plentiful. Should strategies be handed down from the top or originate from the bottom? What type of portfolio is the best to use? Should strategists stick with hard facts or accept soft data? Should planning proceed sequentially or incrementally? No matter what course of action one adopts, these issues are concerned with techniques for pursuing economic rationalism.

This view sees planning as purposeful, goal-directed, and value-maximizing. Planners make choices after thorough analysis of a situation and evaluation of alternatives. These intellectual activities, highly structured, serve as the basis for choice. Once a strategy is chosen, it is followed by tactics—actions designed to implement strategy. In most instances, end results boil down to acquiring a sustainable advantage in product markets, the primary sources of profits and cash flow.

In recent years stronger and stronger challenges have assaulted this conventional view of economic rationalism.[21] The new theories see goal

---

20. See S. L. Schmidt and J. B. Kerman, "The Many Meanings (and Implications) of 'Satisfaction Guaranteed' " *Journal of Retailing* (Winter 1985), p. 89.

21. See R. M. Cyert and J. G. March, *A Behavioral Theory of the Firm* (Englewood Cliffs, NJ: Prentice-Hall, 1963); Henry Mintzberg, "Organizational Power & Goals: A Skeletal Theory," *Strategic Management*, ed. Schendel and Hofer (Boston: Little Brown, 1979); T. J. Peters and R. H. Waterman, *In Search of Excellence* (New York: Harper & Row, 1982); R. Marris and D. C. Mueller, "The Corporation, Competition, and the Invisible Hand," *Journal of Economic Literature* (March 1980), pp. 32–63.

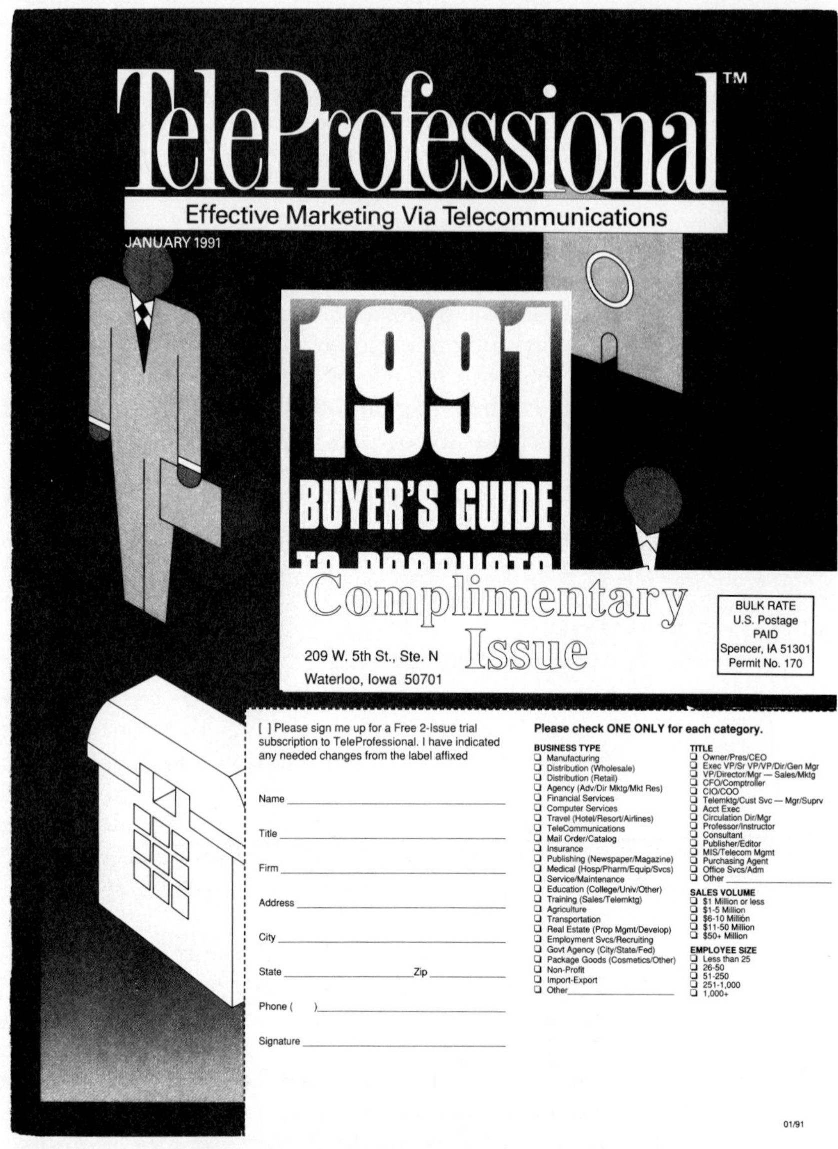


**FIGURE 4-7 Complimentary First Issue**
*Source:* Printed with the permission of TeleProfessional magazine.

setting and conscious choices arising from action rather than from purely intellectual processes. The conventional wisdom regards action as initiated by cognition. The new theories see cognitive processes arising from action.

The modern theories view corporate executives as responders to events. As one firm takes action, it changes the conditions of the market. It alters the options of competitors. As these firms respond, their actions bring forth further counteractions. This endless series of business actions confronts managers with an endless series of situations requiring them to decide what should be done next.[22] The planning process thus turns on itself. Cognition gives meaning to events, but after the fact.

If strategy follows events, the intellectual process supplies reasons for what has happened. When bad things happen, we take measures to counter the effects. When good things happen, we do more of the things that brought these events about. And when good things happen to others, we imitate what they did, hoping the same will happen to us.

This theory implies that strategic planning is an evolutionary process. It proceeds in steps by trial and error. The advocates of this approach, which we will call the behavioral school, are not hostile to analysis. But unlike the rationalists of the management science school of thought, they put their emphasis on doing and on basing decisions about the future on hands-on action. From this perspective, execution becomes strategy.

This controversy between doing and thinking has not eluded the direct marketing industry. But there is a turnabout here. In most other industries, management science is the dominant philosophy. For this reason, the behaviorists are critics of current business practice. In direct marketing, empiricism and trial-and-error rule business life. Management science assumes the role of critic, trumpeting the miracles of "science" and strategic planning taught at leading business schools. So Jim Kobs writes: "Even brilliant execution—using the greatest copy and most attractive graphics—can never save a program that is strategically weak."[23] Paul Hawkes, a principal of Abrams and Hawkes Associates, tells us that "strategic direct marketing" provides "reassurance to clients who have previously suffered at the hands of the inexpert practitioner."[24]

Both schools of thought, with impeccable logic, can claim a plethora of successes. But there are also enough failures to raise doubts. And where there is doubt, there is a reluctance to abandon the old ways. Under these circumstances, direct marketers have ample reason to adhere to the familiar road of empiricism, of test and retest, and close their ears to the sounds of distant trumpets.

---

22. See Thomas V. Bonoma, *The Marketing Edge: Making Strategies Work* (New York: Free Press, 1985); B. Mintz and M. Swartz, *The Power Structure of American Business* (Chicago: University of Chicago Press, 1985).

23. Jim Kobs, "Marketing Strategies for Maximum Growth," *Direct Marketing* (May 1987), p. 32.

24. Paul Hawks, "On Strategy," *Directions* (January/February 1988), pp. 6, 8.

# Summary

The role of direct marketing in a business plan depends on the importance assigned to it. If direct marketing is deemed unimportant, it will be largely ignored by top brass. When the plan depends on direct marketing, it becomes the centerpiece of the business strategy.

Determining strategy goes on at all levels of a firm—at corporate headquarters, divisional centers of authority, and operational departments. The principal reasons for strategic planning at both the corporate and divisional levels are related to goal formulation and attainment. Planning at the operational level is tactical. At this level the concern is with problems of the moment, and how to stimulate response at the moment.

In direct marketing the offers constitute operational strategies. The main elements of offers include:

1. Product
2. Time-related aspects
3. Price
4. Terms of payments
5. Promotional inducements
6. Risk reduction

The first four elements are mandatory. The last two components are optional, although they appear in most direct marketing presentations.

All models of strategic planning assume that rational choice drives the marketing plan. In direct marketing, it appears that business is conducted on the basis of experience and trial and error.

---

**REVIEW QUESTIONS**

**1.** Explain the differences among corporate strategy, business unit strategy, and operational unit planning.

**2.** Explain the difference in strategy between Tweeds Inc. and Horn & Hardart Co. as presented in this chapter.

**3.** **a.** Define each of the following strategies: undifferentiated, differentiated, and concentrated.
   **b.** Which of these strategies is used most often by direct marketers? Why?

**4.** Provide examples of tactics for increasing sales in the following ways:
   **a.** Using the same products in same markets
   **b.** By means of market extension with the same product
   **c.** By modifying product mix in the same markets

5. Explain how growth by diversification can come through a concentric, a horizontal, or a conglomerate strategy.
6. State the main elements of offers.
7. a. Define continuity offers.
   b. Describe the differences among fixed-term offers, automatic shipment plans, and negative and positive option programs.
8. Price appeals in direct marketing ads quite often convey the idea of a sale. Describe three different techniques of how this is done.
9. Describe the five different methods of paying for orders in direct marketing.
10. a. Define a premium
    b. Describe the differences among direct premiums, mail-in premiums, continuity premiums and premiums that aid the sales force.

---

**PROJECT**

1. You are the newly hired corporate vice president of strategic planning for the Cleopatra Hotel and Casino. Cleopatra has been in business in Atlantic City, New Jersey, since 1980. The hotel and casino are filled 110 percent from 4:00 P.M. Friday to 4:00 P.M. Sunday. Thereafter the occupancy rate falls off to 70 percent at night and 50 percent during the day.
   a. State the problem of this case in one sentence.
   b. What type of direct marketing campaign would you consider, if your promotion budget is $500,000? Which people would you go after? Why?
   c. How would you find these people?
   d. What type of response do you expect?
   e. Formulate an offer and design the various promotion pieces that incorporate that offer. It is fine to work in black and white and to use stick figures. A paste job is also approved. However, neatness and clarity count for 10 points.

CHAPTER 5

# Segmentation in Direct Marketing

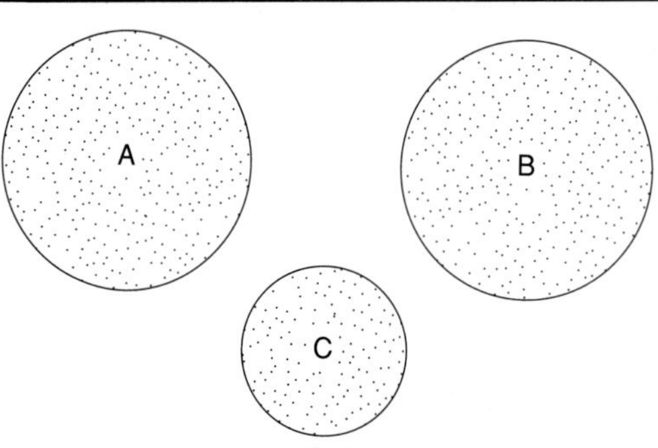


**FIGURE 5-1 Representation of Ideal Marketing Segments**

# What Is Segmentation?

Target marketing, database marketing, relationship marketing, maxi-marketing—these are the latest terms in direct marketing. However industry professionals view these verbalisms—as fads or wonderworks—they all spring from a common underlying idea: market segmentation.

This concept came into vogue in the 1950s[1] and, obviously, means dividing a market into smaller parts. Demand represents unique wants and needs of various groups.[2] These conditions suggest opportunities for products tailor-made for particular segments.

General practice sorts consumers into distinct groups, each behaving similarly with respect to products. Each segment would have a homogeneous demand and is different from all the rest. The art of segmentation dictates chopping up a market so that variation is minimized within customer groups but maximized between them. This concept is illustrated in Figure 5-1, where each segment, designated by a letter, is represented by a circle. Each circle contains certain numbers of customers, depicted as dots. Ideally, the distance between any two units in a circle should be smaller than the distance between two units in different circles.

This clustering principle applies to all marketing. Some authorities insist that truly uniform markets do not exist: they all contain segments that respond to offers differentially.[3] Then what is so special about direct marketing? Isn't the principle of segmentation here the same as everywhere else? Yes and no. Because direct marketing is but one type

1. Wendall Smith, "Product Differentiation and Market Segmentation as Alternative Marketing Strategies," *Journal of Marketing* (July 1956), pp. 3–8.
2. See Philip Kotler, *Marketing Management*, 6th ed. (Englewood Cliffs, NJ: Prentice-Hall, 1988), pp. 281–308.
3. Ibid. Also see G. L. Frazier and R. D. Howell, "Business Definition and Performance," *Journal of Marketing* (Spring 1983), pp. 59–60.

of impersonal promotion, it shares a common body of thought with other forms of marketing and adheres to segmentation principles. Yet these same concepts take on a shape that distinguishes direct marketing from marketing in general.

The key to these differences is media usage. Direct marketing relies heavily on mail and telephone use to communicate with customers. The nature of these media changes the segmentation process to one found nowhere else in the broad field of marketing.

## The Basic Information Unit

Unlike their cousins in general advertising or sales promotion, direct marketers target messages to individuals. Mailing pieces usually bear names and addresses. A package sent to Mr. Smith will not wind up with Mr. Jones. Telephone calls go to specific destinations—homes and organizations. Even when orders come in from general media, delivery must be made to a person at a specific place, and those facts are recorded in computer memories and used for future reference.

Not only is communication targeted at specific individuals, but records are kept for those same customers and prospects. It does not matter whether response turns out high or low. A 1 percent or 5 percent return on a mailing yields information about the behavior of the entire universe to which that mail was addressed. Results tell who responded to an offer and who did not. Obviously, response is highly valued, since that is what a message is usually designed to accomplish. But nonresponse is also important: it indicates unfulfilled opportunities, or perhaps no opportunities at all.

Regardless of how results are interpreted, they are recorded in terms of individuals. A particular human being is the basic unformation unit (BIU), the smallest unit for which information is kept. The small size of the BIU gives direct marketing a high degree of flexibility in handling data. For one thing, data can be aggregated into almost any configuration a marketer desires.

Given the size of a BIU, markets can only be aggregated, never disaggregated. We can combine all individuals in a census block, the smallest geographic unit reported on by the U.S. Census, and then add up all blocks that make up a ZIP code area. But census block information cannot be obtained if BIUs are the larger ZIP code areas. Likewise, it is impossible to obtain individual household information when census blocks are themselves BIUs. In that instance, data would apply to all homes on a block, not to individual households.

BIUs that represent individuals transcend geographic boundaries. A sporting goods chain, for example, can send out flyers to everyone who bought left-handed golf clubs, irrespective of where the buyer lives. An auto manufacturer can target special offers to individuals who own three-year-old vehicles in a certain price range. Department stores send out a specialty catalog depending upon the customer's purchase history.

Flexibility, however, has a price tag. Facts about individuals expand the number of records that must be stored and updated and so increase costs. The amount of information stored in each record presents another cost determinant. Positive trends are the continually falling costs of data processing and the enhanced capability of computers. Small computers today hold as much data and perform much the same functions as the large mainframe machines of the 1960s and 1970s.

However, low unit costs of storing and processing data have caused information to increase geometrically. Many managers apparently hold the mistaken opinion that the goodness of a decision is proportionate to the amount of information acquired. "Let's get all the information we can," they say, "and then we'll figure out what to do with it." The larger the database, the smaller the proportion that is utilized and the more strain placed on the system.[4]

BIU selection also depends on a firm's marketing objectives. Although all promotions target people, campaigns in mass media do not track the behavior of individuals. Such information is neither available nor economically feasible to obtain. A TV advertiser, for example, might order data according to areas of dominant influence (ADIs), an Arbitron designation for television coverage areas. Audiences, reported as TV ratings, are inferences based on surveys. Magazine audience data also come from sample surveys that are projected to a particular universe. These studies define their universe as all U.S. adults, 18 years of age or older. Their statistics are probabilities of how people act as a mass; they do not trace individual behavior.

# Types of Segmentation

Direct marketers use segmentation techniques in two ways. One is to reduce costs by selecting prospects who are supposedly more receptive to an offer. A family without small children would hardly be interested in disposable diapers. Accordingly, Procter & Gamble, maker of Luvs and Pampers, and Kimberly Clark, producer of Huggies, send special offers to mothers of newborn babies. This kind of segmentation technique keeps the product constant but tries to eliminate media waste by targeting the most productive parts of a market. Media waste occurs when commercial messages are transmitted to people who are not prospects of an advertised product.

4. M. L. Roberts and P. D. Berger, *Direct Marketing Management* (Englewood Cliffs, NJ: Prentice-Hall, 1989), p. 155.

**TABLE 5.1. Some Popular Bases for Segmenting Markets.**

| Behavioral | States of Being | States of Mind |
|---|---|---|
| Usage volume frequency | Geographic | Attitudes, opinions |
| Buying volume frequency | Demographic | Personality |
| Brand loyalty | Socioeconomic | Lifestyle |
| Occasion usage | | Benefits sought |
| Distribution outlets | | Images |
| | | Perceptions |

A second approach to segmentation fits products to particular market segments. This route is undertaken by marketers with varied product lines. J.C. Penney and Sears put out specialty catalogs that appeal to different customer groups—presumably, responsive ones.

Some companies pursue both strategies simultaneously; one does not preclude the other. But regardless of what route a firm takes, there are three basic types of segmentation: behavior, states of being, and states of mind. Table 5-1 illustrates the most popular methods of segmenting markets for each of the three basic types.

## Behavior

Differential response is an absolute requirement for segmentation. There must be a clear difference between the responses of people who make up one group and those who compose another. If response to an offer is the same by all types of people, there is no sense in being selective. Markets might as well be treated as though they are uniform.

The ability to segment markets on the basis of actual response gives direct marketing its greatest strength. There are no open ends, no unfilled gaps between marketing action and buyer response; a prospect either said yes or said no to an offer. Trusting in differential response to sort out good and bad customer prospects, direct marketing comes closer to the theoretical ideal than any other aspect of marketing.

Behavioristic criteria for segmenting markets implies a strategy based on heavy usage. For many products, a relatively small percentage of customers accounts for a large portion of total sales. An Ogilvy & Mather study estimated that 23 percent of the population accounted for some 83 percent of total dollars spent through direct marketing.[5] Frequent-flyer programs are based on this same principle, a rather small number of business travelers bring in a disproportionate amount of airline revenue. Banks issue gold cards to high-credit customers because cardholders spend at different rates. Practically everywhere market behavior

5. W. E. Phillip, "The Consumer is Ready. Are You?" Speech at 12th International Direct Marketing symposium, Montreux, Switzerland, April 21, 1980.

denies egalitarian notions and testifies to the fact that some consumers—comparatively few—are more equal than others. Why not concentrate one's effort on where the action is?

Direct marketers employed the heavy-user principle long before the segmentation concept was formalized. Magazine publishers divided their house lists—and they still do—into different classes of customers: active subscribers and expired. Sears Roebuck in the 1930s defined its catalog market in terms of purchase patterns, grading all customers according to recency, frequency, and size of purchase. A customer who did not buy over a period of three years was removed from the catalog mailing list.

Most selection methods today still follow the path marked out by Sears more than a half-century ago.[6] Decisions based on recency-frequency-volume criteria can be unidimensional or two- or three-factored. In any event, segments are relatively few in number and large in size, which raises questions about the extent of homogeneity within a segment.[7] As buying patterns within a segment become more varied, the segment itself loses value. More of its members act contrary to the norm attributed to the whole.

Assigning weights to recency, frequency, and monetary value of a purchase also poses problems. For one thing, such weighting should be related to a particular product mix. Different items have different replacement rates and hence varying buying frequencies. Price variations create changing elasticities of demand and thus fluctuations in buying patterns. (Elasticity refers to the relationship between changes in prices and changes in quantities ordered.)

In practice, many marketers parcel out weights on a purely empirical basis. One popular grading system is to give recency a weight of .50, frequency .35, and dollar value of a purchase .15.[8] The large weight for recency has its rationale in buyer attrition. Some catalogs lose as much as 50 percent of their following within a year. Since catalog houses often use this tripartite factoring to decide whether solicitations should be made or withheld, recency represents a potent screening device.

Critics have pointed out time and again that weightings have no theoretical basis and that arbitrarily derived ratios are too general to apply to individual products. These arguments have validity, yet the recency-frequency-volume scheme of dividing customers and prospects has persisted—and for a very good reason. Firms using it or employ-

---

6. Richard P. Li, "The Hunt for Direct Marketing Success," *Direct Marketing* (March 1987), pp. 38–42; Len Schenker, "Constructing a Database," *DM News* (February 15, 1987), pp. 42, 47.
7. R. C. Blattberg and S. K. Sen, "Marketing Segmentation Using Models of Multidimensional Purchasing Behavior," *Journal of Marketing* (October 1974), pp. 17–28.
8. Bob Stone, *Successful Direct Marketing Methods* (Chicago: Crain Communications, 1979), p. 90.

ing versions of it find that the method works. For example, Higbee's, a Cleveland-based department store chain in Ohio, rated all merchandise groups by recency, frequency, and dollar amount. According to company executives, recency emerged as a key variable in response. For certain specials, customers who bought the promoted items three times a year had a response rate that was 5 times higher than for those who made only one purchase. And highly rated segments had a response 10 times higher than that of the lowest–rated prospects, or nonbuyers within a store's trading area.[9] These results are impressive and not uncommon in the industry.

Another weakness of the heavy-user strategy, critics charge, is that purchase data reveal only past behavior. Because people were attracted to certain products by past promotions does not necessarily make them the best prospects of future promotions. Conceptually, the argument has merit, but it is not supported by empirical evidence.

With the greater use of computers, firms are establishing databases with predictive systems built into them. Statistics clearly show that past behavior is one of the best predictors of future behavior—and it is behavior that direct marketers seek to influence. Given two lists, one with past buyers and one with nonbuyers, the first will almost always outpull the second. This is why responder lists, made up of people who purchased something before, are deemed more valuable than listings in which behavior is an unknown entity. Although forecasts have a long way to go before they reach high degrees of precision, behavior is preferred to other alternatives as the independent variable in predictive equations.

Recency-frequency-volume criteria lend themselves best to frequently purchased products. But what about products bought over long intervals, such as durable goods? In such instances the behavioral measures have to be modified. For example, Buick was able to create a list of 10 million names for its mail promotions based on car ownership. This list was then fine-tuned by applying income, education, occupation—an oft-used measure of social class—and other behavioral measures, such as participation in certain activities and subscriptions to upscale magazines.[10]

## States of Being

States of being refer to characteristics of a particular time. These attributes simply are. They constitue a highly popular means of segment-

9. E. R. Chambers and R. L. Fleischer, "How to Build and Use a Database," *Direct Marketing* (October 1986), pp. 128–134.
10. F. A. Sunderland, "Buick Now Selling up to 800 Autos per Day with DM Sweeps Campaign," *DM News* (July 16, 1990), p. 8.

ing consumer markets, especially for packaged goods, general merchandise, and numerous high-priced durables.

States of being contain two broad categories: geography and demographics. The first represents markets as spatial configurations: counties, census tracts, ZIP codes, census blocks. The second designates markets as people and portrays them in terms of such characteristics as age, gender, place of residence, income, occupation, and education. Demographics and socioeconomic traits are regarded as a single classification. This category is often combined with geography, as well as with other criteria, for purposes of segmenting markets.

GEOGRAPHY. Geography is one of the oldest methods for dividing up markets. Firms have used it to analyze sales territories from the time marketing was in its infancy. Strictly speaking, this is not segmentation unless different geographical areas respond to offerings in different ways. Northern areas, for example, are more apt to buy snowmobiles than places below the Mason-Dixon line.

As far as direct marketing is concerned, the most common geographical units are census tracts and ZIP codes. The U.S. Census greatly stimulated their use in the 1970s, when it provided coded demographics on computer tapes. Instead of dividing customers by city, county, or state, marketers and mailers now could identify population characteristics for areas that coincided with the breakdowns of their mailing lists. Because these ZIP code areas were more homogeneous than the larger geographic designations of former years, they yielded lists of people with similar characteristics. As the 1990 census results become known, the census block as a BIU may achieve the popularity currently enjoyed by the ZIP code.

Information for larger areas, of course, can be obtained by aggregating the smaller ZIP codes, of which there are some 43,000. The travel industry, for instance, contains strong regional biases. Almost three-quarters of travelers to Eastern Europe live on the East coast. These coastal states are also responsible for almost 60 percent of all passenger traffic to Northern Europe. In contrast, three Pacific states account for more than 50 percent of all person-trips to Hawaii.[11] Thus, airlines advertise in regional media. But those that keep information on a neighborhood basis, such as by ZIP code, can better evaluate business from local travel agents and promote on a regional level at the same time.

Geographic segments of greatest concern to direct marketing, however, hinge on small-area analysis. The 1990 Census has included more effective means to build databases with greater selectivity and precision. These data, which combine both geographic and socioeconomic information, cover ZIP code and census block areas.

---

11. Figures based on computer tapes from Census of Travel (1977).

The Census Bureau sells tape files of five-digit ZIP codes within each state. Since mailing lists are often kept in ZIP code sequence, they can be matched to the small geographic areas of the census. That is, census data can be matched with customer lists and product purchases. ZIP code data contain more than 20 different social and economic factors.

Census data apply to areas en masse, not to individuals. When matched to in-house files, they describe individuals by the characteristics of the areas in which they reside. They do not relate directly to particular persons or households.

Block information provides facts about the smallest units of geography kept by the census. There are about 8 million such units on government files, and they include statistics on population gender, race, age, marital status, ethnic origin, and household living arrangements. Block statistics also include housing characteristics, such as length of residence, value of home, and monthly rent.

With the advent of ZIP codes, the Postal Service changed more than the way in which mail is sorted and delivered. It changed ways of doing business by clustering the population into economic and cultural neighborhood types. Marketers were quick to send out mailings for gold credit cards and Caribbean cruises to affluent sections of a city and offers for bargain-basement goods to the less wealthy parts. Today, the census block group, holding an average of about 350 households, identifies smaller, and more uniform, socioeconomic groups. The census block may supplant the ZIP code.

A new wrinkle in the 1990 Census is the use of a laser disk. The type used by the Census Bureau is the "compact disk—read-only memory," or CD-ROM for short. The information is digitally recorded and does not require a large computer to process it. With personal computers capable of accessing the full range of CD-ROM files, census data are open to any small business that can use them.

A major limitation of the decennial census for assessing markets is passage of time. As time from the data collection grows longer, the less accurate information becomes, especially for small geographic areas. A number of private firms will update this information, such as Donnelly Marketing. But these updates are often prepared from large area estimates, such as a census region or metropolitan area, and may contain relatively large errors for small geographic units.

DEMOGRAPHICS. The choice of viable geographic segments links response rates and other states of being into a unified whole. Otherwise, promotions may go out to the public in general or to broad, undifferentiated groups within a region.

The combination of states of being with behavior was first popularized by *Time* magazine in the 1970s under the name of "zip marketing." Using census tapes, a series of *Time* studies joined income and geography as variables in producing a differential response. ZIP codes, which postal authorities define as functional economic units, were crudely ranked by income. All areas were then divided into five parts, each with a roughly equal number of households, and estimates of purchase volume for various products were made for these quintiles.

*Time* conducted more than one hundred studies covering a great variety of products. In almost every case the top 20 percent income bracket was credited with a very large share of consumer spending relative to its incidence in the population. The percentages of buying volume, however, varied substantially from product to product.[12]

More relevant to direct marketing are a number of services that have greatly extended small-area analysis. These systems can perform massive list configuration, sorting practically all addresses in the United States by demographic data. With computer matching, direct marketers can identify specific names with demographic profiles of localities. One of the authors of this book, for example, sorted car registrations by ZIP code and overlaid them with census demographics. The analysis then developed regression equations to forecast market potentials for new car purchases. In turn, these estimates formed the basis for choosing dealership sites. The idea was to pick sites that would draw the greatest number of potential car buyers. The results of this analysis were also used to create and send out mailing pieces to the best prospects in a dealer's trading zone.

There are today a number of such list matching services, such as ACORN, MORE, VISION, PRIZM, and Cluster Plus. These systems are all similar insofar as their databases can generate socioeconomic information for small areas, such as ZIP codes and census tracts. The data do not reach down to individual or household levels. PRIZM, a product of the Claritas Corporation, well illustrates the combination of geography and demographics as a tool for segmentation. PRIZM is an acronym for Potential Rating Index by Zip Marketing. It is a small-area geodemographic system in which neighborhoods are defined by ZIP codes, census tracts, census block groups, postal carrier routes, or some other hybrid contour.

By aggregating data, an analyst can construct demographic summaries of virtually any size and shape. Markets can range from expanses as large as regions, sales territories, and TV coverage areas to areas as small as a two-mile radius around a retail outlet.

PRIZM'S database contains a total of more than 500,000 separate localities. Using multivariate analysis, Claritas grouped these units into 40 unique clusters or lifestyle segments. Persons living in each area are assumed to have similar characteristics and to differ importantly from those in other clusters. Claritas gave each segment a colorful but

12. *Time* Magazine, *Marketing Case Histories* (New York: Time, Inc., 1976); and *A New Approach to Brand Analysis Through Zip Marketing* (New York: Time, Inc., 1976).

expressive nickname, such as Blue Blood Estates, Money & Brains, Blue-Collar Nursery, and Bohemian Mix.

The 40 clusters are further combined into 12 social groups, coded as a two-digit symbol with a letter and a number.[13] Table 5-2 illustrates the PRIZM typology.

To segment markets successfully, a firm must relate demographically constructed clusters to actual buying behavior. Otherwise, it would wind up with a sociological study but not a tool for segmenting markets. A differential response is the essential ingredient. This is what makes these large geodemographic databases so accommodating to direct marketing. A direct response can be tracked back to an advertisement. Each geographic unit is a virtually self-contained entity that can be evaluated in terms of returns, costs, and profitability. For example, socioeconomic databases can be used to:

- Overlay customer and prospect lists with demographic data. The match tells what kinds of neighborhoods these people live in and probably a great deal about their characteristics.
- Target advertising copy at primary markets. In all probability, customer profiles are like those of their neighbors. Copywriters create more appealing ads if they know to whom they are directing their messages.
- Extend customer profiles to newly opened markets. This involves projecting customer demographics to outside lists and broader areas. These extensions rely on the old aphorism about birds of a feather.
- Select targets directly without projecting data from in-house lists. This occurs in two ways. First, the geodemographic database may contain behavioral data, so no in-house file is needed. For example, the U.S. Census carries information about auto ownership, selected household possessions, home value, type of structure, and other consumer attributes. Or the service company database can be merged with outside lists containing purchase information (e.g., Polk auto registration data).
- Plan coupon drops and samples to go where they work best by correlating neighborhood demographic data with retail sales volume.
- Integrate direct marketing with advertising in other media. Some media services have incorporated information from geodemographic databases.

## States of Mind

For many years marketers of consumer goods have espoused psychological measurements in the effort to understand what triggers demand. The psychological school rejects the idea that an association between demographics and purchasing creates a compelling bond between them.

13. *PRIZM* (Alexandria, VA: Claritas L.P., 1986)

**TABLE 5.2. The Prizm Cluster System.**

| Social Groups | | Clusters | | |
|---|---|---|---|---|
| **Code** | **Descriptive Title** | **Percent of U.S. Households** | **Number** | **Nickname** |
| S1 | Educated, affluent executives and professionals in elite metro suburbs | 0.64 | 28 | Blue Blood Estates |
| | | 1.44 | 8 | Money & Brains |
| | | 2.44 | 5 | Furs and Station Wagons |
| | | 4.21 | | |
| S2 | Pre- and post-child families and singles in upscale, white-collar suburbs | 3.28 | 7 | Pools & Patios |
| | | 1.03 | 25 | Two More Rungs |
| | | 3.02 | 20 | Young Influentials |
| | | 7.33 | | |
| S3 | Upper-middle, child-raising families in outlying, owner-occupied suburbs | 5.64 | 24 | Young Suburbia |
| | | 5.19 | 30 | Blue-Chip Blues |
| | | 10.83 | | |
| U1 | Educated, white-collar singles and ethnics in upscale urban areas | 0.45 | 21 | Urban Gold Coast |
| | | 0.81 | 37 | Bohemian Mix |
| | | 1.21 | 31 | Black Enterprise |
| | | 4.77 | 23 | New Beginnings |
| | | 7.25 | | |
| T1 | Educated, young, mobile families in exurban satellites and boom towns | 2.97 | 1 | God's Country |
| | | 5.08 | 17 | New Homesteaders |
| | | 2.18 | 12 | Towns & Gowns |
| | | 10.23 | | |
| S4 | Middle-class, post-child families in aging suburbs and retirement areas | 4.51 | 27 | Levittown, U.S.A. |
| | | 2.26 | 39 | Gray Power |
| | | 1.07 | 2 | Rank & File |
| | | 7.84 | | |
| T2 | Midscale, child-raising blue-collar families in remote suburbs and towns | 1.70 | 40 | Blue-Collar Nursery |
| | | 4.76 | 16 | Middle America |
| | | 2.55 | 29 | Coalburg & Corntown |
| | | 9.01 | | |
| U2 | Midscale families, singles, and elders in dense, urban-row high-rise areas | 1.33 | 3 | New Melting Pot |
| | | 1.80 | 36 | Old Yankee Rows |
| | | 2.07 | 14 | Emergent Minorities |
| | | 2.08 | 26 | Single City Blues |
| | | 7.27 | | |
| R1 | Rural towns and villages amidst farms and ranches across agrarian mid-America | 2.53 | 19 | Shotguns & Pickups |
| | | 4.28 | 34 | Agri-Business |
| | | 1.43 | 35 | Grain Belt |
| | | 8.24 | | |

*(Continued)*

| Social Groups | | Clusters | | |
|---|---|---|---|---|
| Code | Descriptive Title | Percent of U.S. Households | Number | Nickname |
| T3 | Mixed gentry and blue-collar labor in low–mid rustic, mill, and factory towns | 3.06 | 33 | Golden Ponds |
| | | 1.85 | 22 | Mines & Mills |
| | | 2.95 | 13 | Norma Rae–Ville |
| | | 1.95 | 18 | Smalltown Downtown |
| | | 9.81 | | |
| R2 | Landowners, migrants, and rustics in poor rural towns, farms, and uplands | 4.29 | 10 | Back-Country Folks |
| | | 3.65 | 38 | Share Croppers |
| | | 0.96 | 15 | Tobacco Roads |
| | | 1.03 | 6 | Hard Scrabble |
| | | 9.92 | | |
| U3 | Mixed, unskilled service and labor in aging, urban rows and high-rise areas | 1.95 | 4 | Heavy Industry |
| | | 2.30 | 11 | Downtown Dixie-Style |
| | | 1.52 | 9 | Hispanic Mix |
| | | 2.30 | 32 | Public Assistance |
| | | 8.07 | | |
| | Total U.S. | 100 | | |

Its devotees assert that the elements inducing behavior reside in consumers' minds.

For example, the average price of a new automobile is close to $12,000, about half the annual income of the typical American household. It would be logical to conclude that auto purchases are associated with higher-income families. But this concurrence does not mean that income "causes" purchases. A decision to act in a particular manner is an obvious state of mind. Consequently, social psychologists maintain that states of mind are what trigger differential response and are what researchers should examine in segmenting markets.

Several psychological approaches to segmentation have achieved prominence in direct marketing. The most frequently mentioned ones are *benefits sought* and *psychographics*.

BENEFITS SOUGHT. Benefits segmentation, like all psychological research in marketing, rests on the assumption that mental states are precursors of behavior. If that is so, the approach is to search for groups that look for similar benefits in products, and then to adjust offerings to accommodate those preferences.[14]

14. See Russel I. Haley, "The Implications of Market Segmentation," *Conference Board Record* (March 1969), p. 44; Walter Burgi, "What Is Segmentation Anyway?" *Marketing Review* (January–February 1960), pp. 11–12.

The search for benefits that consumers expect is actually an attempt to implement utility theory, which lies at the root of the marketing concept. Consumers are seen as sovereign, rational buyers who maximize their satisfactions. Their buying preferences are supposed to flow from benefits or utilities derived from products. If that is so, variations in benefits consumers seek naturally lead to market divisions or segments.[15]

Researchers resort to various ways of classifying consumers according to the benefits they seek. A common method is the use of sample surveys that ask people about the benefits they ascribe to various articles of commerce. The same survey could also inquire about the benefits inherent in the "ideal" product. The two lines of inquiry yield "gaps" between what consumers want and what they are now getting.[16] Closing these gaps is a task more appropriate to product development than to market development. The firm starts with a market, in this case the survey universe, and tries to find out what benefits customers want. It then tries to create products that possess the qualities for which consumers clamor.

Catalog houses are excellent examples of this approach in direct marketing. They sort a multitude of products to meet obvious customer satisfactions. Another example is the publishing industry. Publications often tailor their material to fit benefits presumably sought by readers. Copywriters for both catalogs and publishers write promotional pieces that emphasize the alleged benefits. A somewhat extreme example is the *Morris Report*, a full-color quarterly for cat owners launched in 1987 by Starkist Foods, the parent company of 9 Lives cat food. Offered by subscription, the magazine contains serious articles about cat health and grooming. It also carries 9 Lives coupons to defray the cost of subscription.[17]

In business-to-business marketing, benefit appeals are common. Purchasing here is supposed to be driven by utilitarian objectives: buyers order goods that can be used advantageously by their companies. Some writers maintain that industrial buyers order not only for company benefits, but for their own. Bob Bly, a freelance writer specializing in business-to-business and direct response advertising, claims that written copy should "not only promise the benefits the prospect desires for his company; it should also speak to the prospect's personal agenda, as well."[18]

---

15. See Russel I. Haley, "Benefit Segmentation: A Decision-Oriented Tool," *Journal of Marketing* (July 1968), pp. 30–35; Daniel Yankelovich, "New Criteria for Market Segmentation," *Harvard Business Review* (March–April 1964), pp. 83–90.
16. Norman N. Barnett, "Beyond Market Segmentation," *Harvard Business Review* (January–February 1969), pp. 152–166.
17. Lynn Folse, " 'Morris Report' Data Base Delivers Direct Dividends" *Advertising Age* (May 16, 1988), pp. S1, S14.
18. Robert Bly, "Business Buyers Are Looking for Personal Benefits," *Direct Marketing* (September 1989), p. 92.

Actually these examples do not represent market segmentation in a conventional sense. They are techniques of appealing to consumers and can be used in any marketing situation. They do not differentiate one market from another. One stumbling block to segmentation by benefits has been the inability to demonstrate a relationship between benefits sought and a differential response. In an age of parity products, a dozen companies will offer similar quality at similar prices if they have evidence that these benefits are strongly demanded. Offers of benefits are more a matter of advertising than of developing products that deliver unique benefits.

And even if people really do seek unique benefits, how does one distinguish them? This leads to what is called the identification problem. Simply knowing that one type of consumer wants benefit X and another wants benefit Y does not give marketers the necessary tools to offer different products to specific markets. Who are the particular buyers? How do we know exactly who is looking for brown shoes and who for black shoes? Are those wanting loud-colored dresses really distinct from people wanting subdued colors? Given a list of names, how do we tell what we should offer to whom? The usual approach has been to relate benefits to demographics. This method lacks discriminating power in segmenting markets because correlations between purchases and benefits are commonly weak. In the absence of any strong relationship, consumers cannot be sorted by common characteristics.

PSYCHOGRAPHICS. Psychographics are also described as lifestyles. This definition is less straightforward than that of benefits, for the term is used in various ways. Some authors talk about lifestyle as if it were synonymous with social class. Others define it in terms of different combinations of demographic elements, such as those of the family life cycle.[19] This measure combines age, marital status, and presence of children in the home. The life cycle approach actually makes databases such as PRIZM and ACORN lifestyle indices.

It is more common, however, to depict lifestyles not by demographics, but by measures of activities, interests, and opinions.[20] These agglomerations are referred to as psychographics by market researchers. Activities suggest behavior; they are things done or acted out. Interest

---

19. W. D. Wells and G. Gruber, "Life Cycle Concepts in Marketing Research," *Journal of Marketing Research* (November 1966), pp. 355–363; P. E. Murphy and W. A. Staples, "A Modernized Family Life Cycle," *Journal of Consumer Research* (June 1979), pp. 12–22; F. W. Derrick and A. E. Linfeld, "The Family Life Cycle: An Alternative Approach," *Journal of Consumer Research*, pp. 214–217.

20. Joseph T. Plummer, "The Concept and Application of Life-Style Segmentation," *Journal of Marketing* (January 1974), p. 34.

and opinions relate to states of mind; they are mental and cannot be observed.[21]

Direct marketers are often able to distinguish between activities and mental states because of their heavy use of lists. Lists are plentiful for activities, such as attendance at tennis matches, golf tournaments, conventions, or trade shows. Other commonly used sources are lists of membership in professional societies, subscriptions to magazines, use of credit cards, and sponsorship of cultural events.

NDL/The Lifestyle Selector, a market research and list firm, includes such characteristics in its database. Firms selling products to upscale markets make frequent use of such information. For example, TRW, a credit information company, combines geodemographic data with financial lifestyle information to assess the creditworthiness of prospects in its in-house lists.[22] Offers to affinity groups have long been a favorite of mailers. AARP members regularly receive association endorsed offers of special health and insurance plans. Banks, insurance companies, and real estate developers presumably find it profitable to key their lists and promotions to lifestyle-related activities. General Motors promotes its high-priced lines to upscale prospects, such as members of country clubs, visitors to auto shows, subscribers to golf and tennis magazines, and buyers of select sports equipment.[23]

Conventional activities-interests-opinions (AIO) measures are derived from sample surveys. Respondents are given batteries of statements with which they are asked to agree or disagree. Consumers may be asked to register their agreement or disagreement on some scale, of which there are numerous versions. The marketing department of Southern Illinois University has accumulated a database of more than 400 psychometric scales published in top marketing journals.[24] Since different constructs may produce dissimilar results, the issue of validity pops up amid the litter of psychological testing methods. If a market takes on varying dimensions depending on survey questionnaire construction, someone must be wrong.

Such measures cannot be matched to customer and prospect lists directly; the relationship can only be inferred. This handicaps the system

---

21. T. P. Hustad and E. A. Pessemier, "The Development and Application of Psychographic Life Style Associated Activity and Attitude Measure," *Life Style and Psychographics,* ed. W. D. Wells (Chicago: American Marketing Association, 1974), pp. 31–70.

22. Dan Bencivenga, "In Search of the Really Rich," *Target Marketing* (September 1989), pp. 28–30.

23. Sunderland, *op. cit.*; Janice Steinberg, "Direct Mail Becoming Hottest Incentive Conduit," *Advertising Age* (July 24, 1989), pp. S4–S6.

24. G. C. Bruner II and P. Hensel, "University Develops Data Base of Psychometric Scales," *Marketing News* (July 23, 1990), p. 10.

with an identification problem. How does one select which individuals fall into which AIO class? AIO measurements may also lack stability. J. Walter Thompson, a leading advertising agency, tested the same 36 lifestyle variables at 12-month intervals. Although that time period was not deemed important as a factor in producing basic changes, the majority of measures showed significant differences from one survey to the next. Agency researchers estimated that questionable classification involved from 15 percent to 45 percent of respondents. Segments derived from later research bore no relation to segments from earlier surveys.[25]

Among the leading syndicated services conducting lifestyle surveys is the Yankelovich Monitor, which has been in existence for more than a decade. This service tracks social trends and reports on "value segments" on an annual basis. In line with the J. Walter Thompson experience, those market segments undergo frequent changes. If the inconstancy reflects social dynamics, it is a valuable tool for forecasting shifts in tastes and values. But if the changing segments are the result of the capricious nature of surveys, the Yankelovich Monitor is one more example of the instability in measurements of the consumer psyche en masse.

A second popular approach to psychographics is VALS, short for values and lifestyles. Developed by Stanford Research Institute, the initial typology was inspired by Abraham Maslow's hierarchy of needs. Stanford researchers divided the population into four basic groups: need-driven, outer-directed, inner-directed, and integrated. These four segments were then subdivided into nine lifestyles. Table 5-3 shows this classification scheme, labeled the VALS I typology, and gives sizes and descriptions of the various segments.

VALS I, like all other psychographic systems, features segments that have no counterparts in population statistics. No statistics are provided by the U.S. Census, or any other agency, on the distribution of introverts and extroverts in our population. This lack of a known universe makes it difficult, if not impossible, to identify customers and prospects outside the original sample. For example, there is no way of saying who in a list is an emulator, an achiever, or a belonger.

A second objection to VALS is that its groupings are weakly correlated with market behavior. As expressed by Peter Kim, director of consumer behavior at J. Walter Thompson, "consumers for a given brand or category rarely fall within VALS' neat groups, nor are the groups readily correlated with buying behavior."[26]

---

25. S. Yuspeh and G. Fein, "Can Segments Be Born Again?" *Journal of Advertising Research* (June–July 1982), pp. 13–21.
26. Judith Graham, "New VALS 2 Takes Psychological Route," *Advertising Age* (February 13, 1989), p. 24.

**TABLE 5.3. VALS I Typology.**

| Group | Percent of Population | Description |
|---|---|---|
| 1. *Need-driven* | 11 | *Share a poverty culture, live apart from cultural mainstream* |
| Survivors | 4 | Least favored of the poor struggling for survival |
| Sustainers | 7 | Poor and distrustful, but hoping their lot will improve |
| 2. *Outer-directed* | 68 | *"Middle America!"* |
| Belongers | 35 | Traditional, middle-class, who want stability and status quo |
| Emulators | 10 | Ambitious, competitive, striving to be achievers |
| Achievers | 23 | At the top, known as "the Establishment," live in comfort |
| 3. *Inner-directed* | 21 | *Led by internal drives and emphasize noneconomic aspects* |
| I-am-me | 5 | Young, individualistic, raised in comfort and affluence |
| Experientials | 7 | Interaction with people, ideas, and events seen as essential |
| Societally conscious | 9 | Successful and mature, concerned with social issues |
| 4. *Integrated* | – | *Combine inner and outer features, are tolerant and self-assured* |

SOURCE: Adapted from Arnold Mitchell, *The Nine American Lifestyles* (New York: Macmillan, 1983).

VALS was seldom used as a true market segmentation device, either by direct marketing or by marketing in general. Its most notable use was in the creation of general advertising. But there is no way of judging the degree of success accruing from its employment.

In 1989 VALS altered its structure, placing greater emphasis upon an individual's psychological makeup. VALS II divides the U.S. population into five major groups with a total of eight lifestyles. Table 5-4 shows the classification of the latest VALS. Edward Flesch, director of the program at SRI, stated publicly, "We needed to make the system more useful to marketing clientele."[27] Only time will tell if this objective is realized, but the big question remains: Are objections to the old system overcome by stressing psychological factors whose relation to purchase behavior is even less demonstrable than those of the earlier typology?

27. *New York Times* (July 21, 1989), p. D18.

**TABLE 5.4. VALS II Classification.**

| Group | Description |
|---|---|
| Actualizers | Successful, sophisticated people with abundant resources; socially conscious |
| Principle-oriented | |
| Fulfilleds | Mature, satisfied, comfortable; amenable to change and new ideas |
| Believers | Conservative, principled; favor proven brands |
| Status-oriented | |
| Achievers | Value safety and eschew risk; career-seeking |
| Strivers | Have fewer resources than achievers; seek careers and approval of others |
| Action-oriented | |
| Experiencers | Young, enthusiastic, impulsive; accept high risks |
| Makers | Self-sufficient, do-it-yourself |
| Strugglers | Concerned with urgent needs of the moment |

SOURCE: Based on *New York Times* (July 21, 1989), p. D18.

# Product Proliferation and Market Fragmentation

As a market matures, it tends to absorb an increased number of products. Brands of low-calorie beer run into the dozens, each vying with the others for a share of the consumer dollar. Apparel lines multiply, and assortments swell the number of brands, models, styles, sizes, and colors. General Motors appeals to new car buyers with well over 200 models. Does this burgeoning output of product forms and styles imply a commensurate increase in marketing segments?

Traditional segmentation theory regards market divisions as arising from divergences in buyers' needs and wants. To implement this concept, analysts sort consumers into mutually exclusive groups. These self-contained clusters of people are separated from all other groupings by a supposedly unique market response.

Real-world markets brazenly defy such neat, structured definitions of consumer behavior. A prime reason is interproduct competition. For example, diet soft drinks are bought by people who prefer good taste as well as low calories. In fact, most users of diet beverages are not on a diet at all.[28] Thus, two distinct segments, dieters and nondieters, are customers of the same product, a diet drink. Moreover, people who drink low-calorie beverages may cross with ease the open boundaries of their segment and consume nondiet soft drinks, such as Coke, Pepsi, and Dr. Pepper. These same people might also substitute tea and coffee for soft drinks, in which case all beverages become interchangeable.

28. "I'm (Not) on a Diet," *Wall Street Journal* (December 11, 1985), p. 35.

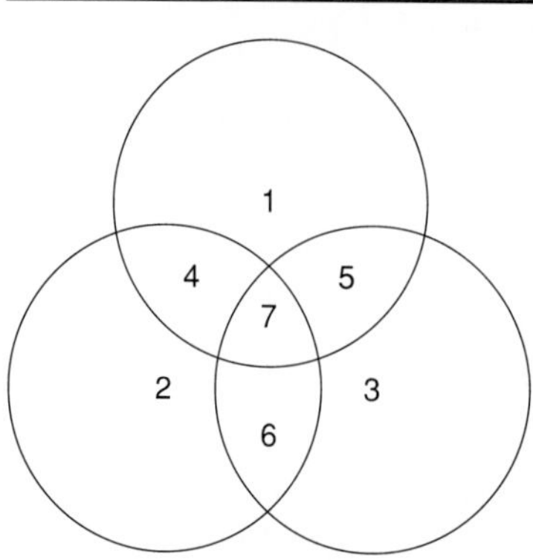


**FIGURE 5-2 Representation of Overlapping Segments**

Most products marketed directly show the same fuzziness in defining segments. Magazines with different editorial policies compete with each other to some degree. Charities as diverse as the Red Cross and local churches scramble for donations from the same people and organizations. NOW and money market accounts at savings banks siphon off balances from passbook and statement savings accounts. Mutual funds constantly contend with shifts of customer balances from one fund to another. A favorable climate for common stocks may entice money away from securities with fixed returns, purportedly a refuge for conservative investors. A contrary condition may make money flow the other way, from equity funds into fixed-rate securities.

Real-world markets contain many cross currents and nonexclusive shopping practices. These come about from two factors: (1) different products competing for the same user segments and (2) multiple usage on the part of customers. The upshot is not the ideal market segmentation depicted in Figure 5-1. Instead, markets may well exhibit overlapping segments, without shape or form. Thus, the true representation might be appropriately called a market fragmentation map, depicted in Figure 5-2.

Do overlapping segments negate the idea of market segmentation? Yes and no. Many markets may have clearly defined segments, such as those with sharp price divisions. Others have ambiguous boundaries that suggest modifying traditional concepts. For direct marketing, such changes present many opportunities, notably by line extensions and "interlacing". These possibilities are best illustrated by catalogs, an important aspect of direct marketing.

## Product Line Extensions

The practice of alternating product usage, often lamented as declining brand loyalty, opened the door to line extensions. These are variations of existing products, such as soaps in different colors, soft drinks of different flavors, or detergents with slightly different formulations. These products use assets jointly and so lead to sizable cost reductions in per-unit outputs. When variety is a factor in buying, line extensions are a convenient way to increase sales among existing customers. Items added to a line have built-in cost advantages and can result in higher margins.

But such additions also run risks. When they are close substitutes to existing items, their contribution to the profits may amount to little or nothing. The incremental products in the line may take sales away from other company offerings. Economists call this a "substitution effect," and marketers refer to it as "cannibalism."

For example, the Sears special catalog *Style* features dozens of women's sweaters throughout its pages, made of different cuts, designs, materials, and colors. A choice of one sweater may here preclude the sale of another. It is also obvious that, at some point, the sheer addition of more styles or varieties will yield no incremental revenue.

However, the substitution effect is offset by multiple usage. Customers may want more than one sweater or might order more than one brand. Therefore, a catalog with too small an assortment might result in lost sales opportunities. Some customers may be looking for a particular style, cut, or color, and too few varieties may lower sales.

A key question posed by line extensions is the extent to which products can be proliferated without hurting margins or net revenue. Traditional segmentation calls for different products for different classes of customers. Line extension strategy eschews the "different strokes for different folks" philosophy: it calls for different strokes for the same folks.

Instead of increasing variety to the same segments, line extensions can expand the customer base by multiplying the number of segments a company serves. For example, sweaters made of acrylic, wool, natural cotton, nylon, rayon, polyester, and various other blends may well represent different segments. In this instance, extending the various product forms combines or aggregates different market segments. This type of targeting does not divide up a market but enlarges it by joining diverse parts; it is countersegmentation.

## Interlacing

Somewhat related to line extensions is what economists refer to as *interlacing*. This practice produces more distant substitutes but through related product lines.[29] Sears' *Style*, for instance, contains lines of men's wear, adding a male segment to that of women. The items range from

29. J. A. Brander and J. Eaton, "Product Line Rivalry," *American Economic Review* (June 1984), pp. 323–334.

suits and shirts for executives to overalls, jeans, and sturdy leather jackets for blue-collar workers, assortments appealing to completely different market segments. The catalog also offers footwear, children's clothing, and furniture.

This catalog specializes in apparel but serves diverse classes of customers. In reality, it stretches product lines with variety and combines different lines in the catalog's product mix. Only by garnering different market segments with a single offer—one catalog—does the firm take advantage of "economies of scope."

In traditional segmentation theory, buyers of individual men's items, women's products, and children's goods are regarded as different market segments. But it is obvious that a person can be in more than one segment at the same time. A women might buy a gift for a man, a male buyer may get something for a female, and both may purchase children's products. The three segments thus give rise to the following seven possibilities:

1. Buys men's items only
2. Buys women's items only
3. Buys children's items only
4. Buys men's and women's items
5. Buys men's and children's items
6. Buys women's and children's items
7. Buys all three types of items

Figure 5-2 shows the seven possibilities, given three segments. When different women's and men's lines are taken into account, such as blouses, coats, and slacks, buying patterns multiply. So do marketing segments when different styles, materials, and brands are added within a line. These overlapping segments create opportunities for cross-selling. That is, a person looking to buy one thing in a catalog can wind up buying several different products. John Stevenson and Associates catch the essence of elastic market segments and loose customer targeting when they write: "The U.S. list business has, in essence, taken 200 million people and exploded them into 4 billion names for rent. In other words, 4 billion individual consumer attributes are now 'addressable' by direct response practitioners."[30]

The same principle of countersegmentation is often employed by publishers. The initial subscription roll for *Traveler* magazine came entirely from its sister publication, *National Geographic* magazine. The travel-oriented segment was part of the *National Geographic* audience. Time, Inc. in 1989 launched a spinoff of its major sports magazine, *Sports Illustrated for Kids*, appealing to a different market segment. Time Warner also extended two other publications into new segments, *Fortune for Students* and *Time for Kids*.

---

30. John Stevenson et al., *The Truth About Database Marketing* (Los Angeles: Krupp/Taylor USA), p. 13.

Countersegmentation does not basically change direct marketing operations. The Sears database has individuals as its basic information unit. But individuals that might be classified into small market segments are combined to form larger mailing targets. Database techniques are not abandoned; they require a higher level of sophistication for arranging marketing targets and determining varieties of offers and cutoff points.

## Summary

The segmentation philosophy is widely practiced in direct marketing as a way of increasing response rates to offers. Market segmentation may be defined as the process of identifying groups of buyers with different desires or requirements. Today most marketing plans include segmentation.

Requirements for segmentation include: differential response, identification, substantiality, stability, and accessibility. Markets can be segmented in a variety of ways, according to three broad criteria: behavioristic, states of being, and states of mind. The criterion most commonly used in direct marketing to segment markets is the behavioristic one of purchase patterns. Records are kept on the recency, frequency, and size of customer purchases.

Demographic and socioeconomic data are also utilized by direct marketers to segment markets. This category is often combined with geography. The 1990 Census offers laser disks providing information on "block groups," the smallest geographic unit, which contain an average of about 350 households.

Several psychological approaches to segmentation have achieved prominence in direct marketing. These include *benefits sought and psychographics.* Line extensions expand the customer base. This type of targeting enlarges the market and results in a type of countersegmentation. It occurs, for example, when a cataloger adds a male segment to that of women in their offerings.

**REVIEW QUESTIONS**

1. In which ways do direct marketers use segmentation techniques?
2. Franklin Mint advertises high-priced collectibles in several mass-circulation magazines, such as *National Geographic* and *Better Homes and Gardens*. Is the firm practicing segmentation?
3. Behavioristic criteria for segmenting markets implies a strategy based on heavy usage. Explain.
4. What are the advantages and disadvantages of the recency, frequency, and monetary value formula?

5. What are some of the main characteristics of products that are employed in geographic segmentation?
6. In 1990 the Census Bureau came out with a laser disk called "Compact Disk–Read Only Memory" (CD-ROM). Discuss the advantages and disadvantages of a small business buying these disks containing specified data.
7. If you were the circulation manager of *Business Week* magazine, how would you go about deciding whether to use PRIZM for subscription offers by mail?
8. How would a company use benefits segmentation in direct-marketing a product on television?
9. How might implementation of a direct marketing program differ when its basis is psychographics stressing activities as opposed to psychographics stressing attitudes and interests?
10. What are the major weaknesses of VALS as related to direct marketing?

---

**PROJECT**

1. King Henry, an English manufacturer of a very popular tea in Europe, is trying to enter the American market. King Henry has been blending tea since 1725. During the 1970s and 1980s various ingredients such as lemon or orange peel, barley malt, anise seeds, rosehips, and green leaves with unusual flavors were combined with herbs into a variety of herbal teas. Herbal teas are caffeine free and are much in demand in the 1990s by the young, affluent, upscale set who believe in distinction, luxury, and natural foods and want to cut down on caffeine.
   a. How would you locate the high-status person or family whom you believe would be your target audience? Which current research techniques would you recommend? Why? Provide supportive materials from research.
   b. State the different media in which King Henry should advertise. Explain. For each medium recommended, provide a minimum of five selections in which you would advertise. Explain your choices. Support your statements by quotes from research.
   c. Write a bibliography by listing sources used in parts *a* and *b* in alphabetical order.
   d. Create at least two promotion pieces to advertise King Henry. It is fine to work in black and white. If you prefer, you may do it in color. A paste job is also approved. Neatness and clarity are part of the grade.

# APPENDIX C

## PRIZM

### The PRIZM System

PRIZM is a geodemographic database that was developed by Claritas Corporation. That is, the system combines demographics and geography. The primary areas are ZIP code regions, census tracts, census block groups, and postal carrier routes.

Because PRIZM captures demographic information for relatively small geographical units, it lends itself to database operations that lie at the heart of direct marketing. Small area units enable the analyst to construct geographic summaries for a wide range of market configurations. This is done by aggregating primary information units into almost any market form. Combinations can be made to construct demographic summaries for larger contiguous areas of various shapes and sizes, such as counties, metro areas, TV coverage areas, states, sales territories, regions, and so forth. On the other hand, PRIZM can disaggregate. For example, it can identify areas with certain demographics and even analyze markets as narrow as a two-mile radius around a specific retail outlet.

PRIZM is one of several services that provide demographic data for small areas such as ZIP code regions. But PRIZM's unique value lies in clustering neighborhoods based on a lifestyle definition, as well as by census-supplied data. This interpretation yields a market-segmented database.

---

Most of this discussion of PRIZM usage is based on J. Chasin and W. S. Sachs, *Marketing Research: A User's Perspective* (Needham Heights, MA: Ginn Press, 1989).

PRIZM's database contains a total of more than 500,000 separate localities. Through statistical analysis, these units are grouped into 40 unique clusters, or "lifestyle" segments. (This classification scheme is illustrated in Table 5-2.) The forty clusters are identified by highly descriptive nicknames, such as Blue Blood Estates, Money & Brains, and Furs & Station Wagons. These 40 units are combined into 12 social categories, coded as R1–R2, S1–S4, T1–T3, and Ul–U3. Each social group has a descriptive title, under which its key characteristics are listed. For example, S1 is made up of educated, affluent executives and professionals living in elite metropolitan suburbs. On the other hand, U3 areas are populated by unskilled service workers and manual laborers residing in deteriorating urban rows and high-rise apartment buildings.

Communities grow and decline, absorb new residents, and are in turn absorbed by others. Whatever the course of change, neighborhoods do not remain constant in character. From 1970 to 1980 eight new cluster arose to replace those that disappeared, and five others received new nicknames to more adequately describe their character.[1] There is little doubt that when the 1990 Census material is released, the PRIZM system will witness more changes.

To segment markets successfully, a firm must relate the lifestyle clusters to buying behavior. Segmentation requires a differential response. In the absence of a relationship between purchase behavior and lifestyle, the analysis can be no more than an interesting sociological study. The following example illustrates a marketer's use of lifestyle segmentation as defined by PRIZM clusters.

## SELECTING TARGET MARKETS

The XYZ Company set out to target buyers of classical records and tapes, but it lacked usage and purchase data on a market-by-market basis. XYZ sought to obtain this information by a survey. Questionnaires were coded and tabulated in accordance with PRIZM lifestyle clusters to relate purchasing information with social groups. Table C-1 shows purchasing profiles for the highest and lowest clusters, as ranked by the level of record and tape sales.

Table C-1 gives unmistakable evidence that buyers of classical records are heavily concentrated in upscale neighborhoods. The buying index shows the Urban Gold Coast segment, in social group U1, as having the largest buying incidence. These areas contain 0.31 percent of all adults but account for almost 2 percent of all classical record and tape purchasers in the nation. The buying index of 628 says that these customers buy more than six times the amount purchased by the average

1. See Michael J. Weiss, *The Clustering of America* (New York: Harper & Row, 1988).

**TABLE C.1.** **Buyers of Classical Records and Tapes (High/low buy indexes for PRIZM clusters).**

| Group | Number | Nickname | Percent of U.S. Adults | Percent of U.S. Buyers | Buyers as as Percent of Segment | Index |
|---|---|---|---|---|---|---|
| U1 | 21 | Urban Gold Coast | 0.31 | 1.94 | 30.5 | 628 |
| U1 | 37 | Bohemian Mix | 0.77 | 3.62 | 22.9 | 471 |
| S1 | 5 | Furs & Station Wagons | 1.68 | 3.84 | 11.1 | 229 |
| S2 | 20 | Young Influentials | 3.35 | 7.60 | 11.0 | 226 |
| S1 | 28 | Blue Blood Estates | 0.60 | 1.24 | 10.0 | 205 |
| ⋮ | ⋮ | ⋮ | ⋮ | ⋮ | ⋮ | ⋮ |
| R2 | 38 | Share Croppers | 4.50 | 0.79 | 0.9 | 18 |
| R1 | 31 | Grain Belt | 1.99 | 0.35 | 0.9 | 17 |
| R2 | 15 | Tobacco Roads | 1.64 | 0.15 | 0.4 | 9 |
| R2 | 6 | Hard Scrabble | 0.10 | — | — | 0 |

customer in the United States. Almost one in three residents of Urban Gold Coast neighborhoods (30.5 percent) are prospects, and it is here that buying probabilities are highest.

The second most ranked segment is Bohemian Mix, also in social group U1. Although purchase probabilities here are lower than for the Gold Coast segment, sales are larger. This is because more people live in Bohemian Mix sections of the country and so offer a bigger market.

At what point are high-buying segments separated from low-buying ones? Ideally, it is where the incremental returns of promotion equal the incremental costs of those efforts. This proposition assumes that promotions can be targeted at each area and that returns from each source can be measured precisely. The potential for such fine tuning is highest with direct marketing, even when mass media is used. Returns from a mass media promotion, however, must be keyed to a source.

To make the marketing program more manageable, the XYZ Company combined segments, reducing their number to eight. These eight segments were relabeled for easy reference and ranked by relative market potential. This summary is shown in Table C-2.

Two of the eight groups, G1 and G2, were designated as primary target markets. They contain only 16 percent of the nation's adult population but account for 34 percent of all buyers in the country. The markets defined as secondary, G3 and G4, add another 29 percent to the buying population. Together, the primary and secondary markets contain almost two thirds of potential buyers. Yet this proportion of the buying public can be reached by contacting only one third of the U.S. population. The firm's strategy is clearly to begin with G1 and G2 as the center of concentration and to move to G3 and G4 if resources are available and margins are satisfactory.

**TABLE C.2. Buyers of Classical Records and Tapes (eight PRIZM groups).**

| Group | Name | Percent of U.S. Adults | Percent of U.S. Buyers | Buyers as Percent of Segment | Index |
|---|---|---|---|---|---|
| G1 | Metro Sophisticates | 8.0 | 20.9 | 12.7 | 261 |
| G2 | Singles & Couples | 8.0 | 13.2 | 8.1 | 156 |
| | Primary targets | 16.0 | 34.1 | 10.4 | 213 |
| G3 | Affluent Suburbs | 9.4 | 13.6 | 7.0 | 144 |
| G4 | Baby Boomers | 11.9 | 15.3 | 6.3 | 129 |
| | Secondary targets | 21.3 | 28.9 | 6.6 | 136 |
| | Total target | 37.3 | 63.0 | 8.2 | 169 |
| G5 | Greenbelt Families | 15.1 | 15.0 | 4.8 | 99 |
| G6 | Urban Melting Pot | 15.2 | 9.8 | 3.1 | 64 |
| G7 | Satellite Towns | 17.5 | 9.1 | 2.5 | 52 |
| G8 | Country Folks | 14.9 | 3.1 | 1.0 | 20 |
| | All other targets | 62.7 | 37.0 | 2.9 | 59 |
| | Total U.S. | 100.0 | 100.0 | 4.9 | 100 |

Like other systems based on small area analysis, PRIZM is best used to identify markets when:

- A firm possesses a customer file or a detailed profile of customers that can be integrated with a geodemographic database. Such firms include financial institutions, retailers, catalog houses, issuers of credit cards and charge accounts, travel companies, publishers with subscriber lists, and other marketers with proprietary information about customers.
- A firm distributes through a system of retail outlets or dealers, such as auto companies, major appliance manufacturers, and vendors of clothing.
- A firm caters to markets representing unique targets that can clearly be characterized by geodemography.
- A firm sells products that are inadequately measured by syndicated research. These usually have singular distribution patterns, either in terms of usage, purchases, or media habits of buyers.

## SELECTING A PROMOTIONAL MIX

Following the definition of target markets, the next step is to select a promotional mix. One issue that confronts marketers using PRIZM relates to efficiency in transmitting commercial messages to target markets. In part, this depends on how the XYZ Company is going about the task now. For example, if the firm markets from a database, the company can code its list according to PRIZM criteria. It can then observe whether its database matches well with that of PRIZM. That is, are customers concentrated in primary markets? In addition, sales are seldom equal in all niches of a primary sales area. Are some areas in the primary sector not covered or inadequately penetrated? In that event, the company may wish to promote in the underrepresented sectors. Alternatively, it may wish to put proportionately more weight in those primary areas where sales are already above average, on the grounds that buying incidence is greater. Market coverage by itself does not dictate how to apportion media weight. The same procedures apply to secondary markets, as defined by the XYZ Company.

Even if the XYZ company uses a database, it must still go outside its own lists to promote its offerings. All databases deteriorate over time and must be constantly replenished. XYZ has many options to go that route. It can go to direct mail and telephone, the two most important media used by direct marketers. It can veer toward mass media, the preferred method of general advertisers. Either way, it must confront the issue of media waste. This is incurred when messages are transmitted to people who have no interest in using a product. They are simply not in the market.

The more mass the medium, the more general the nature of the audience. But whether mass or class, outside media must incur some waste. Promoting classical records to just the primary market implies a buyer proportion of roughly 10 percent; 90 percent is wasted promotional expenditures. How much waste must a company accept? There are no precise rules.

PRIZM codes have been incorporated into a number of media studies and promotional databases. Some available direct mail and telephone lists contain PRIZM codes, such as those of National Compiled Lists, Advo Metromail, and R.L. Polk. However, PRIZM can be overlaid over almost any list, and names can be selected that match markets. Selection is by area, and individuals will not necessarily have the average characteristics of the area. Selecting individuals to contact by phone entails matching exchanges to PRIZM segments. As with matching of mailing lists, telephone matching applies to area, not individual, characteristics.

Advertisments in most mass media, with the possible exception of newspapers, are bought on the basis of audience. General advertisers and their agencies usually buy on that basis, utilizing reader estimates for print media and viewer and listener estimates for broadcast media.

Two audience services that measure newspaper readership, Scarsborough Research and Simmons Market Research Bureau (SMRB), have PRIZM codes available. But newspapers are a local medium, and most space buying is done on the basis of circulation. Large metropolitan papers make local editions available to advertisers. Since the XYZ Company has its major markets in metro centers, it need only match the circulation of various editions to its primary markets to select the best promotional areas of newspapers.

Magazines have two major services measuring audiences: SMRB and MRI. Both are notorious for issuing faulty figures of low-quality data. Audience estimates may vary widely for the same magazines measured at the same time. However, magazines with high proportions of subscribers can estimate circulation distribution by ZIP codes. These counts can be aggregated to select the regional editions that best fit a company's markets.

Local TV markets are nonselective, and local ratings are not of much help in selecting PRIZM clusters. A TV coverage area which defines a station's signal, can extend to two or more metropolitan areas. Both Arbitron and A.C. Nielsen have PRIZM codes available, but their ratings may be as questionable as those of print audiences. In any event, direct marketers usually judge their purchases on a cost per response basis and proceed on a trial and error basis.

PART III

# IMPLEMENTATION

PROFILES

CHAPTER 6

# Database Marketing

## PROFILE

**LEO R. YOCHIM**

**Innocent Instigator of Innumberable Innovations.** From Leo Yochim's first exposure to the (then) new world of computers, as a U.S. Marine in 1949, to his present position as CEO of Printronic Corporation of America, he has been "instigating innovations" in electronic data processing.

As early as 1954, he established one of the nation's first computerized pension plan costing and analysis systems. At the age of 27, he was managing one of General Electric Company's first EDP Departments. In 1958, he installed the Columbia Broadcasting System's first computer and, as corporate systems manager, ran a data processing department that served all eight operating divisions of the company, plus the corporate staff. 1960 found him putting his accumulated experience to work for Price Waterhouse & Co., advising the firm's clients on their computer installations and EDP Systems.

Leo then tailored his extensive knowledge of computer hardware and software to the special needs of direct mailers. In 1964 he established the first independent EDP service bureau for the direct mail field. He devised computer programs and techniques never before attempted in mass mailing operations: the transfer of mailing lists to computer and the first commercial use of the "computer letter."

Mr. Yochim has conducted seminars in all phases of EDP applications for direct mail in many countries. He is a member of the U.S. Direct Marketing Association, the European Direct Marketing Association, the American Management Association, and the Direct Mail Idea Exchange. A former president of the Direct Marketing Computer Association, Mr. Yochim is a board member of the World Direct Trade Council and of the U.S. Direct Marketing Association and chairman of the New York Direct Marketing Day Educational Committee.

Recently he was named "Man of the Year" by the Mail Advertising Service Association of the United States, the first non-member of that group to be so honored. In January 1988 he received the Maxwell Sackheim Award from the Direct Marketing Creative Guild which is given to "recognize and honor genuine marketplace innovations in the direct response industry." ■

# What Is a Database?

Database marketing is increasingly linked with direct marketing, and the two expressions are sometimes used synonymously. The term implies marketing practices that revolve around a database. That is, a database is manipulated to perform certain marketing functions.

Although the word *database* is widely used, there is no exact agreement as to its meaning. In the most elementary sense, it is a mailing list.[1] Certainly, the concept of database marketing evolved from mail order operations. But a database is more than just a list. Several dozen names can make up a list but would hardly qualify as a database.

First, most lists today are kept on computers. The use of a computer in itself suggests a list of some minimum size. However, when a list becomes a database is anybody's guess. Second, there is a qualitative difference. The old lists kept on metal plates and used to print out labels are not considered databases. Some of them were quite large, such as those of large-circulation magazines. But they were not flexible. Publishers were not able to change names or sequences of records except with great difficulty. Modern computerized lists are easily manipulated to accomplish marketing tasks. According to McFadden and Hoffer, "a database is a shared collection of interrelated data designed to meet the varied information needs of an organization."[2]

The kinds of information kept in databases range widely. The simplest system holds records of names, addresses, and ZIP codes. At the other extreme, a database may store information about corporate communications and responses, transactions and payments, personal facts, demographic and psychological profiles, and neighborhood evaluations. What is common to all databases is that the information contained therein can be rearranged to meet a variety of purposes. Whether simple or complex, a database defined as a list comes in two basic kinds: internal and external. The internal type is compiled by the company itself; data are gathered primarily through company efforts. Every inquiry and order adds to the existing company's lists. External databases are either house lists of other firms or lists developed by outside compilers.

# Database Marketing

No matter what kind of list it represents—internal or external, large or small, simple or complex—a database is related to business objectives. It is not constructed for its own sake. It is a means of performing corporate

1. Edward Nash, "Avoiding Database Disasters," *Marketing Insights: Premium Issue*, pp. 120–124.
2. Fred R. McFadden and Jeffrey A. Hoffer, *Data Base Management* (Menlo Park, CA: Benjamin/Cummins, 1985), p. 3.

functions—in the case of direct marketing, those relating to transactions by the use of communication in media.

These objectives are twofold: order getting and order filling. The first entails tasks designed to create transactions. The second involves fulfilling the obligations or terms of transactions. A catalog house must deliver items ordered and paid for by cash or credit. A magazine must send subscribers a given number of issues periodically, as contracted for in a sales agreement. In all such instances, the database acts as a customer-servicing mechanism. It should also handle financial work, such as accounts receivables, for no company can afford to neglect money inflows.

Marketers, however, concern themselves primarily with order getting. Selling methods are partially determined by what is sold. Industrial goods marketers put heavy emphasis on personal selling, so databases become means of generating leads for the sales force. Supermarkets serve as busy conduits for packaged goods, and databases here are used as promotion devices to spark in-store sales. This leads to the definition of database marketing as the storage of up-to-date information in computers on customers and their buying patterns.

With a zeal approaching a fetish, direct marketers hunt for ways to create transactions by "target marketing." This process calls for distinguishing major market segments and building programs to appeal to one or more of them.[3] From this perspective, database marketing is the implementation of target marketing.

# Uses of Databases

Like any marketing tool, a database cannot do everything. It lends itself more readily to some tasks than to others. The principal tasks facilitated by a database are:

- Improving the selection of market segments
- increasing repeat purchases
- enhancing cross-selling

## Selection of Market Segments

If databases are implementation devices for target marketing, an important role pertains to segmentation. Does the database increase marketing productivity by lowering costs of selecting market segments?

Lowering costs in this regard is usually accomplished by mailing to more responsive segments and avoiding groups whose response pat-

3. Philip Kotler, *Marketing Management*, 6th ed. (Englewood Cliffs, NJ: Prentice-Hall, 1988), pp. 280, 298–302.

terns do not justify outlays of time and money. For example, Higbee's department store found that the rate of response of "recent" buyers to certain special promotions was about 10 times more than that of noncustomers. For other mailings, differential responses ranged from 3:1 to 5:1.[4] After modeling its client's list, a management consulting firm estimated that profit contributions came from only 50 percent of prospects; the lower half yielded a net loss. Eliminating the bottom 50 percent increased profits and cut operating costs at the same time.[5]

## Repeat Purchases

Databases facilitate repeat purchases in a large variety of situations. These arise especially with respect to continuity offers, where some form of assent is necessary for a customer to continue receiving a good or a service. Book clubs, magazine subscriptions, insurance, and credit cards are prime examples of continuity built into an offer.

For example, publishers seek to renew magazine subscriptions when their terms expire. Simply keeping records of expiration dates and sending out renewal notices are old practices, indeed, done years before computers and databases came into existence. Because manual systems were not as efficient as today's electronic wonders, they were replaced. Computers make it easier to keep subscription records and also reduce the cost. But do they increase renewal rates? Performing an old function more efficiently makes the new systems vital for doing business but does not necessarily bring in more business. How does a database increase revenue by enhancing the rate of repeat purchases?

Computerized systems provide a more effective means of control for dealing with present customers. *Better Homes and Gardens* (BH&G), for example, mails more than 25 million letters a year to encourage renewals. Each name on the subscriber list—totaling more than 6 million—bears dates as to when direct mail notices were sent out. After several mailings, the company may contact the reluctant expiree by telephone, which might bring in a higher response than another mailing piece.

Based on purchase history and other information, each name is assigned a repeat purchase probability. Higher-probability names get different offers from those going to subscribers with lower likelihoods of repurchase. The company tracks some 27 different types of subscribers, who are classified by how they were acquired as customers in the first place. If they signed up to receive the magazine from a sweepstakes, they receive a sweepstakes offer at renewal time. If they initially sub-

---

4. E. R. Chambers and R. L. Fleischer, "How to Build and Use a Database," *Direct Marketing* (October 1986), pp. 128–134.
5. Richard J. Courtheoux, "Database Modeling: Maximizing the Benefits," *Direct Marketing* (March 1987), pp. 44–51.

scribed as a result of a promotional tie-in with a nonprofit organization, renewal efforts might take the same tack, proposing to give a certain percentage of the price to a school or to some other worthy cause.

BH&G employs computer modeling to maintain its monthly circulation base of 8 million copies. If that amount is exceeded, the publisher incurs extra costs. Advertisers pay for 8 million copies only; bonus circulation is gratis. If the publication does not meet its circulation guarantee—8 million in this case—the publisher must give refunds. A forecast of circulation tells the publisher how many renewals and new subscriptions he needs to maintain his advertising rate base. The firm knows when to offer prospects generous incentives and when to lower or raise prices to get new or repeat sales.[6]

## Cross-Selling

BH&G is but 1 of 13 magazines owned by the same company, Meredith Corporation. The parent firm maintains a massive house list of some 33 million unduplicated names, to which it markets various magazines, books, and special editions spun off as line extensions.

Other publishing houses operate in much the same way. Books offered by Time, Inc. draw on the appeal and reputation of its magazines, such as *Time, Sports Illustrated,* and *People*. On the other hand, publications benefit from book sales by having more receptive prospects for subscription promotions. consequently, both books and magazines enjoy more sales from a synergistic relationship. Synergy exists when the combined effect is greater than the total of the separate parts. At the same time, unit costs fall because the firm uses its assets more intensively. Economists refer to cost reductions accruing from the joint use of assets as *economies of scope*.

The National Geographic Society similarly enjoys opportunities for cross-selling that arise from synergy. It sells calendars, globes, tapes, books, and maps to subscribers of its magazines. Catalog houses put together merchandise so that the goods will have the widest appeal to specially selected audiences, whose purchase histories are kept in computer memories.

# The Value of a Database

The decision whether or not to construct a database involves more than just its use. Building a database often entails substantial investments, even if the company possesses centralized computer facilities and uses

6. Ruth Podems, "Serving Families for 77 Years," *Target Marketing* (September 1989), pp. 18–22.

them for such activities as physical distribution, accounts receivable, and customer service. The firm may still have to add equipment, particularly when users are physically separated from the central computer. Outlays for systems design, programs, and continuing operations further elevate costs. For these reasons, databases require careful advance planning, in which the costs of usage are weighed against the benefits that will result.

Since database marketing is essentially a means of carrying out better targeting of prospective customers, benefits boil down to improvements in marketing practices. Eliminating marginal buyers reduces misdirected promotional messages and so lowers costs. Communicating with the best prospects, given a budget, raises sales regardless of sources of additional revenue, new customers, or repeat buyers. Whether costs are reduced or revenue enhanced, the bottom line is an increase in marketing productivity.

For example, several magazines offer advertisers "high-income" editions. The usual method of putting together these editions calls for a two-step procedure. Services such as PRIZM, ACORN, or Donnelley Marketing maintain data on household income for the 43,000 or so ZIP codes in the United States. The first step extracts all high-income neighborhoods from the main file. Second, all subscriber names in the selected ZIP code areas, are combined into a single list. The entire analysis is relatively inexpensive.

*Time* magazine, however, does it a different way. The publication sends out questionnaires to all subscribers asking them about their line of work and their total household income. With a circulation of more than 4 million subscribers and a comparatively high turnover rate (this cannot be figured because *Time* does not report its renewal rate), costs of gathering and processing this information could run up a substantial bill. By the questionnaire method, *Time* picks up high-income subscribers who do not live in high-income areas. By the same token, however, *Time* loses low-income subscribers living in affluent ZIP code areas. Presumably, circulation gains exceed losses among those who answer the survey.

But a significant number of subscribers, both wealthy and poor, do not return questionnaires. For these reluctant readers, no information about income is available. The question is are the incremental benefits worth the extra costs of querying individual subscribers? Although figures for carrying out such a cost-benefit analysis are not public, *Time's* answer is apparently positive.

The point is not which method is best. Results show that there is more than one way of getting the same thing. The means are situational, or company-specific.

Nevertheless, database marketing performs best under certain conditions. One condition is if the additional cost of database usage is less than the incremental net revenue produced by some new feature. To illustrate, suppose a firm mails out an offer to 1 million people. The cost of the mailing is $300 per thousand, or $300,000 in total. The mailing piece produces a response of 2.7 percent. If each responder buys one unit, total sales come to 27,000 items (1,000,000×.027). If the firm makes $15 profit on each item sold, not counting the cost of the mailing, the net profit would amount to $105,000. This profit calculation is quite straightforward. Sales of 27,000 units, each bringing in $15 over its costs, would yield $405,000 ($27,000 \times \$15 = $ $405,000). Let's call this figure "marginal contribution." From this total we must deduct the $300,000 for mailing costs. Returns thus net out at $105,000 ($\$405,000 - \$300,000$).

Now suppose the company's management approves a project to build into the database a sophisticated forecasting system that assigns each name on the list a probability of buying. The names are ranked in accordance with these buying probabilities, and the ranked list is divided into 10 equal parts, each amounting to 100,000 names. The purchase probability of a decile is assigned to each group of 100,000. Given group buying probabilities, a table of purchases and marginal contributions can be constructed for the various segments. Table 6-1 presents these calculations.

The bottom line summarizes the results for the overall 1,000,000 mailing. The response for the total mailing is 2.7 percent, shown in column 2. This would produce sales of 27,000 items. At $15 profit per item, exclusive of mailing costs, the marginal contribution would total $405,000, as displayed in column 4 and in the cumulative total in column 5.

If the 10 groups have differential buying probabilities, they will all yield different results in terms of purchases. These are also indicated in Table 6-1. For example, the top decile has a purchase likelihood of 8.0

**TABLE 6.1. Hypothetical Example of Database Value.**

| Decile | Probability of Buying | Items Bought | Marginal Contribution* | Cumulative |
|---|---|---|---|---|
| 1 | .080 | 8,000 | $120,000 | $120,000 |
| 2 | .060 | 6,000 | 90,000 | 210,000 |
| 3 | .040 | 4,000 | 60,000 | 270,000 |
| 4 | .030 | 3,000 | 45,000 | 315,000 |
| 5 | .020 | 2,000 | 30,000 | 345,000 |
| 6 | .015 | 1,500 | 22,500 | 367,500 |
| 7 | .010 | 1,000 | 15,000 | 382,500 |
| 8 | .007 | 700 | 10,500 | 393,000 |
| 9 | .005 | 500 | 7,500 | 400,500 |
| 10 | .003 | 300 | 4,500 | 405,000 |
| Total | .027 | 27,000 | 405,000 | |

*Marginal contribution is assumed to be $15 per item.

percent and would account for 8,000 salable items ($100,000 \times .080 = 8,000$ items). At $15 per item, the marginal contribution for this group would total $120,000. Similar calculations are used for all other deciles.

Table 6-1 makes it obvious that some groups are profitable and some are not, provided mailing costs are constant. If the unprofitable segments can be eliminated, then (1) mailings will be reduced and (2) profits will be increased.

This is demonstrated by the following example. Suppose a response rate of 2 percent represents the breakeven point. That is, the marginal contribution less mailing costs equals zero. There is no net profit at this response level. This is apparent from Table 6-1. At a .020 buying probability, 2,000 items would be sold, with the marginal contribution totaling $30,000. That is exactly the mailing cost for the 100,000 batch deposited at the post office.

Table 6-2 converts the marginal contributions into net profits. This is done by deducting mailing costs from the marginal contribution of each group of 100,000. The company really ends up with the result of that calculation. Table 6-2 again shows that the segment with a buying probability of .02 represents the breakeven point for the mailout. Its gross margin of $30,000 exactly covers the mail costs, leaving a net profit of zero. Mailing to less responsive segments simply loses money, reducing total profits from the maximum of $195,000. This maximum would occur if the company mailed to only 500,000, the upper half of the list (see column 4). Indeed, mailing to half the list would actually bring in $90,000 more profit than sending out pieces to the entire one million names in the file.

Would the predictive system increase marketing productivity? That depends on the cost of incorporating the system into the present framework. If the cost is less than $90,000, the difference between selecting the profitable part of the list and mailing to the whole list, the answer is yes. If not, the nos have it.

**TABLE 6.2. Net Profit for Segments.**

| Decile | Purchase Probability | Net Profit | Cumulative Profit | |
|---|---|---|---|---|
| 1 | .080 | $90,000 | $ 90,000 | |
| 2 | .060 | 60,000 | 150,000 | |
| 3 | .040 | 30,000 | 180,000 | |
| 4 | .030 | 15,000 | 195,000 | |
| 5 | 0.20 | 0 | 195,000 | |
| ---------- | ---------- | ---------- | ---------- | Cutoff point |
| 6 | .015 | (7,500) | 187,500 | |
| 7 | .010 | (15,000) | 172,500 | |
| 8 | .008 | (19,500) | 153,000 | |
| 9 | .005 | (22,500) | 130,500 | |
| 10 | .003 | (25,500) | 105,000 | |

This hypothetical example just illustrates the basic principle. In actual practice, the decision is far more complicated. It would require figuring out the returns of many promotions and the total costs added on to the new system. In economic terms, the net revenue gained from introducing the system must, at the very minimum, equal the costs associated with the system. Estimating these amounts is easier said than done. How can individual probabilities of responding be figured before promotions are actually sent out? In many instances, a company would have to spend its entire developmental budget before it could fit people into various groups and predict how they will respond to mailings. A probability is a long-term frequency, representing a response from an infinite number of mailings.

Predictions of consumer behavior still must go far to attain the accuracy of pure science. Marketing models contain large elements of subjectivity—gut feelings, hunches, and guesses, some educated and some not—rationalized as subjective probabilities by statisticians with Bayesian leanings.

Another grisly fact is that mistakes often cannot be easily corrected. Once a system is built, a portion of the costs—in most cases, a sizable one—is fixed. Such costs are not proportional to variations in revenue. Salaries of programers, operators, and maintenance people, for example, remain fairly constant despite fluctuations in sales. The investment in a database also is a sunken cost. The money is spent and cannot be retrieved like data. If a company borrows to install a system, interest and principal must be paid no matter how the system works.

Computer systems grow at a much faster rate than businesses.[7] One reason is rooted in the economics of computer installation. When assets are fixed, or cannot be retrieved by stopping an operation, the system encourages people to look for new applications. "Since we have it, let's look for things to do with it." Under these circumstances, economies come about that were not originally planned. However, it would not be prudent to anticipate such benefits when making investment decisions.

Because database is essentially a tool for implementing segmentation strategies, it works well when market segments have clear-cut differentials in profitability. It pays off best when the following conditions hold:[8]

1. *Gross margins are relatively small.* What if the marginal contribution per item in the previous example were $37.50 instead of $15? In that case, the breakeven point would drop to eight-tenths of a 1 percent response (see Table 6-3). Only mail to the bottom two segments on the list would be unprofitable. The savings that would result

7. J. Daniel Couger, "E Pluribus Computum," *Harvard Business Review* (September–October 1986), p. 88.
8. For example, see Fred D. Wiersema, "Advanced Segmentation's Practical Parameters," *Direct Marketing* (March 1987), pp. 31–37.

**TABLE 6.3. Net Profit Under Different Conditions.**

| Decile | Buying Probability | Marginal Contribution of $37.50/unit* | Mailing Cost of $120 per Thousand** |
|---|---|---|---|
| 1 | .080 | $270,000 | $108,000 |
| 2 | .060 | 195,000 | 78,000 |
| 3 | .040 | 120,000 | 48,000 |
| 4 | .030 | 82,500 | 33,000 |
| 5 | .020 | 45,000 | 18,000 |
| 6 | .015 | 26,250 | 10,500 |
| 7 | .010 | 7,500 | 3,000 |
| 8 | .008 | 0 | 0 |
| ------- | ------- | ------- | ------- Cutoff point |
| 9 | .005 | (11,250) | (4,500) |
| 10 | .003 | (18,750) | (7,500) |

*Assumes mailing costs are $30 per thousand.
**Assumes marginal contribution of $15 per unit.

by eliminating the loser segments would come to only $30,000 (the addition of the net losses for segments 9 and 10 in Table 6-3). The investment for building the database, however, would be the same as if savings were $90,000.

2. *Mailing costs are relatively low.* What if the firm could reduce mailing costs to $120 per thousand from $300 per thousand, with marginal contribution remaining at $15 per unit? As shown in Table 6-3, the outcome is similar to the case of increased marginal revenue. Worse prospects become more profitable. Segments 6–8, losing propositions at a mailing cost of $300 per thousand, are profitable at $120 a thousand. Savings by eliminating unprofitable segments amount to a paltry $12,000 (total of deciles 9 and 10).
3. *Overall response is comparatively low.* A low response rate leaves a large unprofitable potential. If the database can eliminate a good part of that, this would exert pressure on the company to computerize its selection process.
4. *Underlying conditions favor segmenting markets.* Market segments must be distinct, with little ambiguity and overlap. Frequent flyers are excellent prototypes. Those who put on thousands of air miles are readily identifiable and easily accessible to appealing offers.

Another condition is that the database be capable of making a significant contribution to marketing performance. This is doubtful if direct marketing constitutes a minor activity in a company's marketing mix.

# Building a Database

Most companies that engage in direct marketing already have the essential information to start a database. To fill an order, a firm must know to whom a shipment goes, the place to which it is sent, and, if payment is not in cash, who gets the bill. Therefore, a customer file is the best place to start building a database.

The accounting department normally possesses such a file. If this is the case, a company will begin constructing a customer list from files in the accounting section.[9] The accounting system, however, is highly specialized. Its purpose relates to financial functions, such as accounts receivable and accounts payable. Often financial management spills over into inventory and production control. The manager of an accounting department, usually the comptroller, reports to the chief financial officer and has no responsibilities whatsoever to marketing.

Marketers also want to do things that go well beyond the functions of a financial system. A marketing database should therefore be separated from an accounting file and made to operate on its own. Transactional data might be sorely needed for the database to operate well, but such information can be obtained, batched, and entered periodically—monthly, weekly, or daily.

## The Basic Elements

Any ongoing business that does direct marketing produces a name-and-address list of buyers. Every order contains transactional data, such as products bought, price, and payment methods. When these items are grouped into a file, a customer's record thus comprises:

- Customer name
- Account number
- Street address
- City, state, ZIP code
- Product data(e.g., product description, catalog or item number, date of purchase, delivery date)
- Method of payment

This information represents a record, a unit of storage information that relates to an individual. A mailing list is an accumulation of such records.

Every database must be product-specific. Whereas records of individuals are usually compiled by a consumer products firm, business-to-business marketers keep records of the company from which orders came. The file of an industrial marketer might thus be modified to reflect the following kinds of information:[10]

- Name and title of the person who ordered
- Billing to individual or company

9. John Stevenson, "The Few Elements You'll Want Most for Database Construction," *Direct Marketing* (January 1988), p. 78.
10. See Mary Ann Kleinfelter, "B-to-B Database Marketing: Today's Challenge," *Directions* (May/June 1989), pp. 1–2, 14–15.

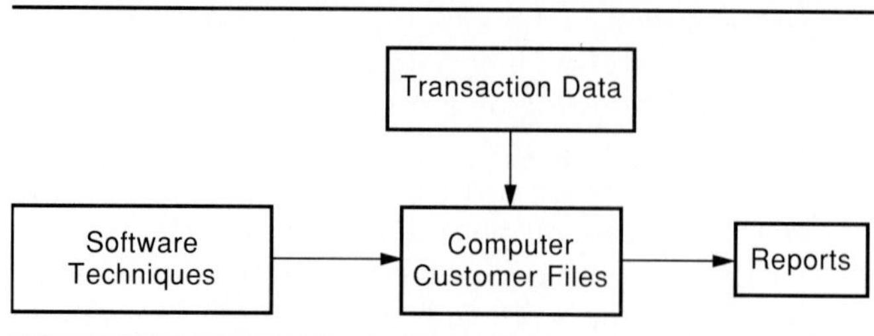


**FIGURE 6-1 Components of a Database**

- Mailing address of individual or company
- Buyer or user of the product
- Standard Industrial Classification (SIC code)

What is collected or coded in a database must relate to the purpose of the direct marketer. Business-to-business promotions often are aimed at generating leads or inquiries. Similarly, promotions for many services and high-ticket consumer items have the same goals. In these instances, a database should record follow-up results, such as qualifications and conversions. Qualifications indicate whether those responding to an offer for information were serious buyers, coupon clippers, or just plain curious. Conversions tell how effective follow-up efforts were. How many sales did they produce?

Whether marketing is directed to consumers or businesses, other basic information can easily and cheaply be added to customer files. If orders are recorded over time, the computer becomes the bearer of purchase histories. These are invaluable in estimating the worth of different customers in terms of average sales, number of purchases, profitability, payments made, or any other measure of performance a company deems important.[11] Other easily collectable data are source of order, dates and types of promotional material transmitted, complaints, returns, and service calls.

A database system can then be depicted as in Figure 6-1. The center of the database is the computer, which contains the customer file. A vital adjunct of the computer is software, which comprises programs instructing the computer in what to do. Software costs depend on the complexity of the programs and whether they can be obtained from outside or must be developed in-house. Sophisticated techniques and specialized applications are more expensive, for they are not as readily available as off-the-shelf items.

Information from outside sources constantly enters the computer and modifies the database in the process. Orders and inquiries are input regularly as they arrive. These add data to the customer file or create

11. Courtheoux, *op. cit.*

new records. Other types of information come from outside suppliers, such as commercial services and public agencies. These enhance the basic elements of the database and are discretionary on the part of management. Their addition hinges on costs and the improvements expected.

Reports are computer outputs. They tell how marketing performed and indicate possible ways of improving marketing results.

## Enhanced Databases

Although a database may have come into being from a company's accounting files, it becomes detached from the financial records. It also changes constantly as it accepts data from the outside. The outside information falls into several important categories: purchases and ownership, demographics, psychographics, and inferential data.

The prominent kind of purchase information concerns automobiles and is gathered by R. L. Polk. This research firm collects auto registration data and supplies names of car owners sorted by car year and model and by geographic regions that range from state and county to ZIP code area and census tract. Several states, however, do not permit Polk to sell names and addresses of auto owners. Warranty lists denote other purchases, normally of durable goods. These lists can be bought from outside sources and overlaid on a firm's customer list. Since past behavior is the best predictor of future behavior, purchase and ownership records are extremely valuable for targeting specific segments among both customers and prospects.

The U.S. Department of Commerce is the prime outside source of population demographics. The Bureau of the Census, a part of the Commerce Department, carries out periodic surveys to update its counts of the entire population every 10 years. To safeguard privacy, the Census Bureau does not release information about particular individuals. When census-based information is incorporated into customer records, it is inferred.

Psychographic data come primarily from surveys or responder lists. Data generated from sample surveys cannot modify a customer list directly. Samples make up but a fraction of the population, and chances of matching names to customer files are extremely small. Psychographic surveys are used mainly to develop a profile of marketing targets. But implementation is difficult because both inside and outside databases are seldom coded psychographically. For example, VALS is a psychographic classification system based on consumer surveys, but there is no way of categorizing individuals on a customer list by whether they are principle-oriented, status-oriented, or action oriented.

Responder lists indicate activities only; they cannot reveal interests or opinions. Such records may contain names of those who bought tickets to tennis matches, theater performances, music recitals, golf tournaments, and other functions. In this sense, they reflect behavior only. States of mind must be inferred. Activities, however, may be weakly related to product purchases, so data on activities may not improve marketing performance very much.[12] When activities are entered into a database, it is vital to establish a close relationship between lifestyle and market behavior. Attending a professional football game does not make a person a good prospect for football gear. On the other hand, an individual who regularly goes to operas may well be a prospective buyer of video disks or tapes of operatic performances.

Inferential data are not specific to an individual. They are deduced, usually by statistical analysis. For example, a marketing survey may find purchases correlated with certain demographics. In that case, those demographics are indicators of market demand. Direct marketers make wide use of correlation analysis to establish linkages for segmenting markets and evaluating outside lists and specialized media.

Consider this supposition: A financial house needs to forecast the potential market for securities that it handles. It conducts a sample survey of the universe that, in the opinion of key executives, constitutes its market. The study finds that high-income households are more likely to own stocks, bonds, and mutual funds than low-income homes—a not-unexpected conclusion. The next logical step would be for the marketing manager to go to census reports or to services that update census data and, using the survey statistics, select groups of upscale areas in which to promote the company's offerings. He or she might even rate each of the selected areas and alter both offers and advertising frequencies in accordance with the groups' respective scores.

The forecast for each individual is actually that of the geographic area. It is a probability, not a certainty. All people living in an affluent town do not share the wealth equally. Some of the richest areas have among their residents domestic servants, tradesman, artisans, and schoolteachers—all necessary to the economic life of the community. Some scions of wealthy families may have assets tied up in ventures other than liquid securities. Yes, promotions based on such segmentation will be better than those that disregard neighborhood quality. But "better" does not mean that the effort is worthwhile.

Analyses of this sort are usually multivariate: two or more variables are analyzed simultaneously. These techniques are quite common in marketing, especially for purposes of analyzing markets, planning programs, selecting targets, estimating sales potential, forecasting demand, and scanning environments for marketing opportunities. Such statistical analyses do not require databases.

---

12. See Chapter 5.

If data from outside sources, such as census reports and syndicated services, are overlaid on customer or prospect files, only factors that really count should be entered. A marketer can add literally dozens of attributes to a database: demographics, psychological factors, lifestyle, and others. Incorporating information, however, does not lead to better decisions and can be just as wasteful as advertising in mass media whose audience contains high proportions of nonprospects.

Studies of population characteristics often reveal what statisticians call collinearity. This means that several "causal" factors are interrelated, in which case one cannot tell which factor triggers the action. For example, income, multiple car ownership, and home value are all correlated with new car purchases. But high income is highly correlated with multiple car ownership, and both are closely associated with home value. If one of these is known, so are the other two. Then are all three characteristics needed to forecast demand? Marketing experience indicates that two variables are the maximum. Additions beyond this seldom produce more meaningful forecasts.

## Negative Screening

Negative elements are present in all databases. These are things that must be changed.

One common change is address. In consumer markets, address changes are extensive. According to the Bureau of the Census, about 20 percent of all households change residence each year. Deaths, marriages, and normal changes in household formation add to the attrition of any list.

Mail to a wrong address is not delivered. Calls to an out-of-service phone number do not get through. Customer files should be meticulously updated, for an unaddressable or uncallable name is a "no-name." Updating lists of rented names can also be cost-effective, especially for large mailers. There are several techniques for doing so, such as ZIP code correction and NCOA processing.

Business-to-business marketing also encounters frequent changes in name-address files. People change jobs. They are transferred to different departments and cities. They quit jobs and hop to other companies. They get fired and are rehired elsewhere. They quit the hassle of business altogether and retire. The most popular methods of keeping abreast of such changes are telephone calls or mailings designed to verify an individual's status, and call reports by sales personnel.

Another negative element is a late payment or an overdue account. Sales are not credited by an accounting system until they are paid. Databases should also code names for DMA mail or telephone preference requests to be excluded from solicitations. A person who does not want a mailing piece or phone call and takes special measures to put these wishes in writing is not a good prospect.

# Managing a Database

Even small databases or simple name-and-address lists today are stored on computers. These records may be kept on tape or disk. Any list on a tape or cartridge is stored and retrieved sequentially, in some order. The most common way of storing names and addresses is in ZIP-code order. A computer operator must go through every preceding record before a specific entry can be retrieved. For that reason, tape operations are usually handled in a batch mode. For example, all labels are printed at the same time, and all insertions and deletions in the main file are handled as one operation.

A strong advantage of tape storage is that it is relatively inexpensive, especially for routine and regularly scheduled work, such as a monthly magazine that must run off address labels or update its subscriber files each month. A disadvantage of tape storage is that different people cannot use the database for varied applications at the same time.

Disk storage provides more options in the way records are kept. Data can be stored sequentially, as on tape, or files can be stored in a database management system. With the latter format, users have direct access to any record. Multiple uses can occur concurrently. This feature assumes importance in customer service and telemarketing operations, where many people need to access the same files. There are several types of database management systems, but a discussion of these is beyond the scope of this book.

Managing a database requires technical knowledge, and the job usually falls to system professionals. These are staff personnel highly specialized in statistics, programing, or electronics. These technicians often do not understand the jargon of marketing people who use the information that computers generate. On the other hand, users on the marketing side have little understanding of computers. They can make sense out of TV ratings, publishers' statements, and cost-per-thousand computations, but not strange terms such as *byte, closed loop, CPU time, on-line, off-line,* and *digital coding*.

Because database managers are divorced from users, computer outputs do not always do the things they can or should do for marketers. By the same token, marketers are not always sure what to ask for, and they often state their needs in broad, ambiguous terms.

The standard recommendation of management consultants is for all parties involved to develop closer coordination. The buzzword is *integration*. Marketing and computer personnel, advisors say, should develop a better "interface." This advice is sound but difficult to follow.

John Stevenson and Associates, affiliated with Foote, Cone, and Belding, an advertising agency, write that "database marketing is too important to leave to the MIS technicians." They hold that database marketing should not be viewed as a "systems issue." They also admit that database management should not be left to the marketing staff, which holds "a narrow, tactical view of what database marketing is all about." According to these authors, the proper role of a database is to provide "strategic, proprietary information to the senior management of a firm."[13]

Top management involvement means financial support for a project. But would top managers get involved with a database? Should they?

Usually not. A typical large company has a management information system (MIS), of which the database is a part. Unless database marketing provides a differential advantage that materially affects the corporation, top managers are not prone to take a personal interest. There is no question about the importance of a database in direct marketing. But whether that makes a vital difference in corporate performance is doubtful, especially among large companies with extensive MIS systems. When something is common, possessed by everyone, it is unlikely to generate a differential advantage.

Although possession of a database may not give a firm an edge on the competition, lack of one puts it at a disadvantage. Like Alice in Wonderland, modern management must run faster just to stay in place. It's as though managers from many companies were on the same treadmill. Under these circumstances, users and operators of a company database will have to "interface" with each other and have no choice but to muddle through.

## Summary

According to McFadden and Hoffer, "a database is a shared collection of interrelated data designed to meet the varied information needs of an organization." Information kept in databases ranges from customer addresses to demographic and psychological client profiles to corporate transactions.

Database marketing may be defined as the storage of up-to-date information in computers on customers and their buying patterns. The principal uses of database are to:

1. Improve the selection of market segments
2. Increase repeat business
3. Enhance cross-selling

Database marketing is essentially a means of carrying out better targeting of prospective customers. This results in benefits leading to improvements in marketing practices. Eliminating marginal buyers reduces misdirected promotional messages and so lowers cost.

---

13. John Stevenson et al., *The Truth About Database Marketing* (New York: Krupp/Taylor USA, 1989), pp. 29–30.

The best place to start building a database is with a customer file. This should include the buyer's name and address, product purchase, date of purchase, delivery date, price, method of payment, and monetary value. Other basic information can easily be added to customer files.

Every database must be product-specific. Data collected should relate to what direct marketers want to accomplish. Only information that will be used should be stored in the computer.

Databases are enhanced from data that come from outside the firm. The Census Bureau can provide population demographics. Psychographic data comes primarily from surveys and responder lists.

Negative elements are those items that need to be changed. These pertain to address changes of personnel, late payments, stock inventory, and prices.

---

## REVIEW QUESTIONS

1. Discuss the range of information kept in databases.
2. Explain the differences between internal and external lists.
3. What are the objectives of databases as related to business?
4. Explain how using databases:
   a. Improves the selection of market segments
   b. Increases repeat purchases
5. a. How does the National Geographic Society enjoy opportunities for cross-selling?
   b. How does *Time* magazine enjoy opportunities for cross-selling?
6. The Yen Company mails out an offer to 2 million people. The cost of the mailing is $350 per thousand. The offer has a response rate of 2.4 percent.
   a. If the Yen Company makes $12 profit on each item, what is its profit or loss?
   b. If the Yen Company makes $22 profit on each item, what is its profit or loss?
7. What are the problems of installing sophisticated in-house forecasting systems?
8. Discuss the components of a database.
9. a. What purchase information does the R.L. Polk Company collect?
   b. Can the firm sell the information in all 50 states? Explain.
10. Discuss the problem of negative screening.

CHAPTER 7

# Financial Aspects of Direct Marketing Programs

# Nature of Budgets

Regardless of where business plans are made in a corporation, they represent proposed actions and expected benefits. Corporate budgets include both of these elements. The proposed actions are explicitly translated into costs and expenses. The benefits of carrying out action programs are converted into monetary units, which may be positive or negative.

The budgeting process reduces plans and consequences to simple numbers. The conversion of all activity into dollars and cents allows management to control both planning and implementation without getting bogged down in a morass of small details. Budgets thus answer two basic questions:

1. How much will it cost to do something?
2. How much will the action program bring in?

The difference between net returns and outlays is profit. The residual is an overriding concern of any business.

Profits are time-related. Short-term profits usually cover one year by conventional accounting standards. Since most marketing plans cover a one-year period, they symbolize short-term inflows and outflows of funds. These monetary flows are monitored and reviewed at monthly, quarterly, or semiannual intervals. The exact timing depends on the operating procedures of particular companies.

Profits can also be long-term, which means that an outlay produces revenue over a period longer than a year. Such expenditures are called investments. Because revenues from investments may come in for many years, these outlays are accounted for in corporate balance sheets.

A chart of accounts is vital in preparing any company's financial statement. This document classifies all budget items under various headings, identifying each item by a code number. This system facilitates financial control of expenditures and makes analysis easier. However, charts of accounts in the corporate world are highly diverse. Seldom do two companies put the same items under the same heading. Despite these incongruities, the profit concept is strikingly similar from company to company. It doesn't matter much where individual items are pigeonholed. Revenue and expenditure aggregations over a sufficient period of time minimize discordant elements. When all costs and expenses are subtracted from total revenue, the bottom-line calculation is pretty much the same.

# Profitability

Profitability is a basic concept in financial analysis. At the most elementary level, it calls for calculating money inflows occasioned by specific expenditures. These estimates are pivotal to subsequent appraisals of cash flows and investment yields. The unit of analysis may vary, but the fundamentals remain the same. Profitability is profitability, without regard to what the estimates are for—an entire division, particular product lines, individual catalogs, or any other level of activity.

Profitability of any operation requires in advance a profit-and-loss statement (P&L statement). This calculation is often referred to as a *pro forma P&L*; it is an economic forecast. To illustrate the procedure in simple terms, Table 7-1 shows a P&L worksheet for a one-shot offer using direct mail. Exact costs in this worksheet pertain to a particular mailing,

**TABLE 7.1. Detailed P&L Worksheet for Direct Promotion (100,000 packages costing $250 per M., 3.2% response, or 3,200 orders).**

| | | Unit Value | Number of Units | Total Dollars |
|---|---|---|---|---|
| 1. | Cash selling price | 29.95 | 3,200 | 95,840 |
| 2. | Deferred payment price | — | — | — |
| 3. | + Shipping/handling | 1.75 | 3,200 | 5,600 |
| 4. | Ave. gross order value | 31.70 | 3,200 | 101,440 |
| 5. | − Returns (10%) | 31.70 | 320 | 10,144 |
| 6. | Ave. net sale | 31.70 | 2,880 | 91,296 |
| 7. | Cost of goods per sale | 7.49 | 2,880 | 21,571 |
| 8. | • Per unrefurbished return | 7.49 | 64 | 479 |
| 9. | Order receipt & processing | | | |
| 10. | • Business reply postage | 0.18 | 3,200 | 576 |
| 11. | • Order process & customer setup | 1.50 | 3,200 | 4,800 |
| 12. | • Credit card fee (3½%) | 1.11 | 1,600 | 1,776 |
| 13. | • Credit check | 0.75 | — | — |
| 14. | • Installment billing | — | — | — |
| 15. | • Customer service | 7.50 | 160 | 1,200 |
| 16. | Shipping & handling | 1.75 | 3,200 | 5,600 |
| 17. | Returns postage | 1.50 | 320 | 480 |
| 18. | Returns handling | 0.50 | 320 | 160 |
| 18A. | Returns refurbishing | 0.75 | 256 | 192 |
| 19. | Bad debt (3%) | 31.70 | 86 | 2,726 |
| 20. | • Collection effort | 1.00 | 86 | 86 |
| 21. | Premium | 1.00 | 3,200 | 3,200 |
| 22. | Promotion (CPO) | 7.81 | 3,200 | 25,000 |
| 23. | Overhead | 3.80 | 2,880 | 10,956 |
| 24. | Total expenses | | | 78,802 |
| 25. | Profit before taxes | | 2,880 | 12,494 |
| 26. | Profit % to net sales | | | 13.7% |

SOURCE: Pierre A. Passavant, "Direct Marketing Economics and Budgeting," DMMA, *Manual Release 600.1* (October 1979), p. 1. Reprinted with permission of the Direct Marketing Association.

but the same procedure applies to other direct marketing programs. The form is the same, perhaps with minor adjustments.

Most items in Table 7-1 are self-explanatory. A few, however, may need clarification:

> *Item 1. Cash selling price.* All items sell for $29.95 regardless of quantity ordered.
>
> *Item 7. Cost of goods per sale.* This is defined as the cost of goods delivered to the shipping point. If the seller is a manufacturer, the figure would represent unit production cost. If the mailer is a reseller, the cost of goods per sale would be the firm's unit purchase price.
>
> *Item 8. Cost per unrefurbished return.* This item assumes that 20 percent of returns cannot be refurbished. Thus, 20 percent of 320 returns (item 5) equals 64 units. At a cost of $7.49 per unit, total costs of unrefurbished returns amount to $479 (320 × .2 × $7.49).
>
> *Item 11. Order process & customer setup.* These costs include mail openings, credit checks, shipping labels, and other data processing.
>
> *Item 12. Cost of credit card fee.* This estimate assumes a credit card fee will apply to 50 percent of all orders placed, or to 1,600 orders.
>
> *Item 15. Cost of customer service.* The estimate of total costs assumes that 5 percent of all orders will result in complaints, inquiries, and special requests at $7.50 per unit. Thus, (3,200)(.05)($7.50) = $1,200.
>
> *Item 18A. Returns refurbishing.* The worksheet assumes that 80 percent of returns can be refurbished and put back into inventory. This is figured as (320)(.8)($0.75) = $192.
>
> *Item 21. Premium.* The mailing offers a $1 premium to buyers. We presume that customers will keep the $1 even if they return the merchandise.
>
> *Item 23. Overhead.* This estimate covers all expenses not accounted for in items 7–22, made up of expenses allocated to the mail promotion. This assumes what in accounting is called "full costing." A further assumption is that two-thirds of the overhead is being charged to plant and warehouse.

The worksheet shown in Table 7-1 is rather cumbersome, especially when financial planning includes a large number of individual projects. A simplified version of the worksheet is shown in Table 7-2. Revenues and costs are grouped into larger categories and summarized.

**TABLE 7.2. Pro Forma Profit-and-Loss Statement.**

| | |
|---|---|
| Net sales | $91,296 |
| Less cost of goods sold | 44,175 |
| Gross profit | 47,121 |
| Less selling expenses | 34,627 |
| Net profit | $12,494 |

SOURCE: Based on data from Pierre A. Passavant, "Direct Marketing Economics and Budgeting," DMMA, *Manual Release* 600.1 (October 1979), p. 1.

The format of any budget document depends upon how it is to be used. For example, the worksheet in Table 7-1 is rather detailed but is necessary for operating managers. Estimates of returns and their costs are meaningful to operating managers because the amounts involved are largely determined by operations. On the other hand, financial managers have less interest in these minute operating details. They normally assume that operating personnel know their jobs and would minimize customer returns of merchandise. If returns should turn out excessive, they would show up as a significant variance in cost accounting analysis after the promotion had been run.

Table 7-2 treats order processing, shipping, handling, and returns—items 9–18A—as inventory costs. From an accounting standpoint, these items are reflected in the cost of goods sold.

A cost accounting system takes goods out of inventory whenever a sale is made and registers them as costs in P&L statements. That is, finished goods inventories are diminished, and charges accrue to cost of goods sold. This procedure is in keeping with the generally accepted accounting principle of matching costs with revenue.

The most controversial part of the pro forma statement in Table 7-1 is allocated overhead, part of which resides in the cost of goods sold and part in selling expenses. The practice of assigning overhead costs to operations is called *absorption* or *full costing*. Accountants defend the practice on the grounds that each operation must bear its fair portion of total costs. These include charges directly traceable to the project as well as those shared with other company activities.

Although full costing enjoys universal application, it has been criticized on many counts. The most serious charge is that it fails to aid managerial decision making. Operational managers, its critics hold, are burdened with expenditures that they do not authorize and over which they have no control.[1] Detractors also point out that allocated costs are arbitrary under the best of circumstances.

An alternative to full costing is *direct costing*. This system omits indirect charges from operating costs and expenses. The Accounting Principles Board of the American Institute of Certified Public Accountants has not sanctioned direct costing for purposes of financial reporting. As a consequence, this method is not used to report financial results to the general public or government agencies. It is, however, used internally to guide managerial decisions.

Corporate practice thus displays two bases of profitability analysis. One uses full costing, which allocates overhead to all units. The second method states results in terms of direct costs and attaches no overhead

---

1. See Sanford R. Simon, *Managing Marketing Profitability* (New York: American Management Association, 1969), pp. 27–28; Sam R. Goodman, *Financial Analysis for Marketing Decisions* (Homewood, IL: Dow Jones-Irwin, 1972), pp. 139-140.

charges to costs. The excess of revenue over costs, however, is regarded as a contribution to overhead and profits.

# Profit Optimization

The pro forma P&L statement in Table 7-2 estimates a pretax profit of $12,494 for mailing out 100,000 pieces. With sales totaling $91,296, this means that 13.7 cents out of every sales dollar goes toward profit. A return of that size is no mean achievement.

However, this 13.7 percent profit-to-sales ratio is not the end of the subject. A number of other questions intrude. If the company's offer was that profitable, why stop at a mailing of 100,000? Direct mail is an expandable medium. Why not send out more mailings—another 10,000, 100,000, or 200,000? A related question is, where should the company stop? These questions do have answers. From the standpoint of theory, one must relate the operating plan to a sales response curve.

## Sales Response Curve

A sales response curve reveals how prospective buyers react to different levels of marketing expenditures. For the moment assume that, except for the number of mailings, all factors remain constant—price, quality of merchandise, transaction terms, warranties, guarantees, and all incentives. In other words, this hypothetical construct assumes static market conditions. Yet even under such restrictive circumstances, a sales response curve can take many shapes. Possibilities depend on products and markets. To illustrate the principle of how to maximize profits, let us assume a response curve with a convex shape, as shown in Figure 7-1.

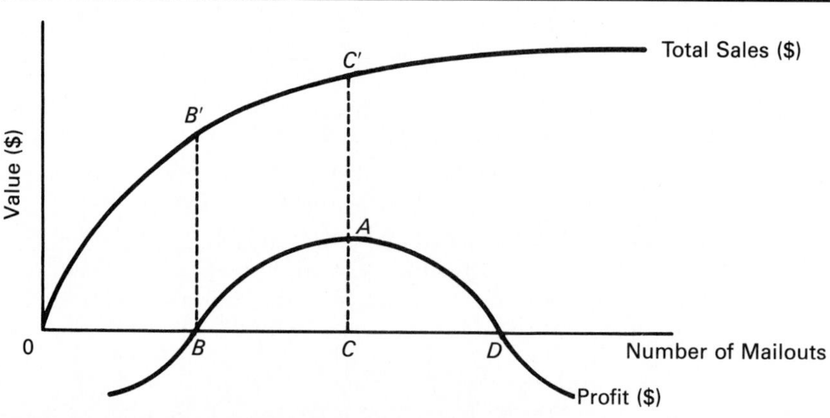


**FIGURE 7-1 Illustration of a Convex Sales Response Curve**

The sales response curve depicted in Figure 7-1 represents an exponential function. Sales rise as the number of mailings gets larger, but the increase proceeds at an ever-decreasing rate. Mathematically, the sales function is described as a second-degree polynomial: $S$ (sales) $= a \log M$ (mailings), with the symbol $a$ denoting the intercept on the graph. The value of $a$ for this chart is close to zero, meaning that there can be no sales without mailings, and you don't need many mailings to make a sale.

The slowing rise of the sales curve implies a differential response among potential buyers. Early recipients of the mailing have higher buying rates than later ones. It follows that the company can somehow discriminate in sending out offers to groups of customers, mailing first to the best prospects, next to the second best, next to the third best, and so forth.

The firm may mail out successive increments of the same offer or different mailing packages to different groups. Regardless of the technique, the company gets progressively lower response rates as it continues mailing more pieces; later solicitations go to less likely buyers. This explains why total sales rise with more mailouts but at a diminishing rate.

These suppositions coincide with the theories of database marketing. Their fundamental propositions are as follows:

1. Demand is not uniform but varies by individuals.
2. Databases can be constructed to forecast individual probabilities of buying.
3. When prospects are grouped by these probabilities, the marketer develops classes of customers with different response rates.
4. A company will communicate first with the best customers and work down progressively to less-likely buyers.

## Profit Maximization

A sales response curve serves as a guidepost to profits. Seldom, if ever, is maximum profit achieved, for business operates in an environment of change and uncertainty. But the profit-maximizing concept is a direction toward better profitability. It provides no explanation for the unfolding of economic events, but it is a useful guide to financial decision making. Firms can achieve great success without knowing exactly why things happen, but they must know how things happen.

Figure 7-1 shows that if the basic propositions of database marketing are fully met, profits are maximized when the number of mailings add up to the quantity *OC*. If that number were 100,000, then revenue of $91,296 would yield maximum profit. That revenue is designated by the line *CC'*. Profit would total $12,494, represented by the line *CA*.

This relationship clearly suggests that, given a cash selling price of $29.95 per unit and costs as stated in Table 7-2, profits cannot be improved by increased mailings. Any quantity beyond *OC* would bring in more revenue but less profit.

The chart also shows the mailing threshold, or the minimum level that must be reached before any profits accrue. That mailing quantity is *OB* and represents the breakeven point. In terms of dollar sales, breakeven is reached when revenue comes to *BB'*.

Note that breakeven is also encountered at quantity *OD*. If a company keeps mailing in excess of *AC*, it will encounter losses from each unit, and profits will eventually shrivel to nothing. On the surface, such behavior appears irrational. Marketing decisions, however, are situational, and many situations demand unprofitable solicitations.

One such situation occurs when products complement each other. For example, many magazine publishers mail out subscription offers to people with low probabilities of buying. They lose money on these operations, hoping to make up the losses by getting more advertising revenue. In turn, that depends on the size of a magazine's circulation. Distribution of more copies means higher prices for space units, which in turn, affects total revenue.

The model represented in Figure 7-1 is one in which price remains constant but promotional efficiency declines as volume expands. This model, then, seeks to identify the point at which the additional cost of continued mailings equals the additional revenue that is generated. That point is where total profits reach their maximum. This principle is illustrated in the upper diagram of Figure 7-2, which merely reproduces the section in Figure 7-1 where profits are positive.

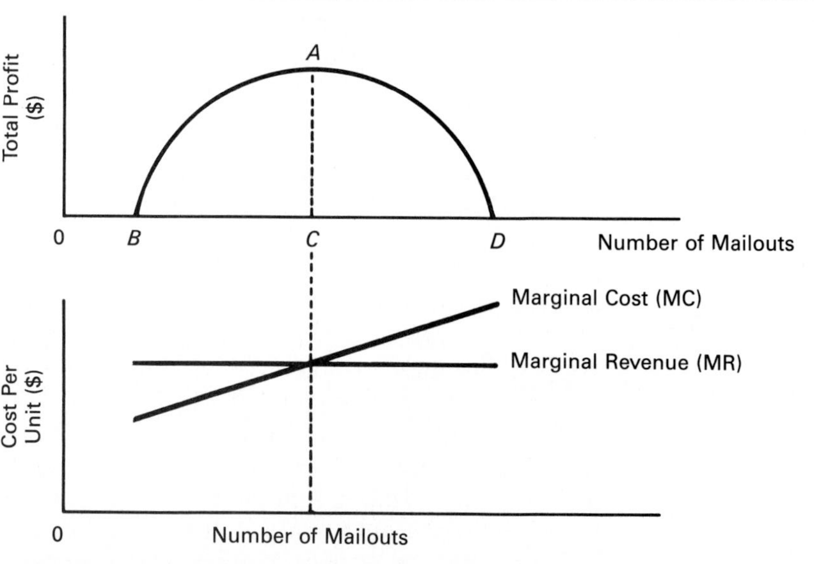


**FIGURE 7-2 Illustration of the Marginal Principle with Constant Unit Prices**

Positive total profits occur for any quantity of mailouts falling within the range *BD*. The highest level of profits, however, is obtained when the number of mailing pieces reaches point *C*. The crux of the analysis is to determine the quantity corresponding to point *C*. How many pieces of mail should go out so as to produce the most profits?

This is illustrated in the lower part of Figure 7-2. The vertical axis represents marginal revenue and marginal cost per unit of output. The term *marginal* refers to the cost and revenue associated with the last unit of outgoing mail. The horizontal axis signifies the number of mailing pieces sent out. Since each successive unit sells for the same price, $31.70, marginal revenue takes the form of a straight line. Because additional mailings bring less response, incremental units are burdened with higher unit costs. Thus, the marginal cost curve slopes upward.

The marginal decision rule states that additional revenue (MR) should equal or exceed marginal cost (MC). Whenever this occurs, the last mailing unit makes a profit. Because MR is horizontal while MC climbs upward, the two curves must eventually meet. At that intersection, where MR = MC, the last mailing returns a dollar of revenue for every dollar of cost. No more profit can be squeezed out by more mailings, for then MC will exceed MR. Total profit here is at the maximum and corresponds with point *A* in the upper part of Figure 7-2.

The marginal approach suggests how a firm should adjust its inputs. However, reality inhibits pinpoint accuracy. The intersection of marginal revenue and marginal cost can only be approximated. There are several techniques for accomplishing this. One of the most widely used is breakeven analysis.

## Breakeven Analysis

Breakeven analysis approaches profitability through the use of marginal concepts. To illustrate how breakeven analysis works, let us take the pro forma P&L statement of Table 7-2 as our starting point. We will then rearrange it in accordance with breakeven directives. The new version is shown in Table 7-3.

Converting the pro forma P&L to a summary for use in breakeven analysis entails taking all costs and dividing them into variable and fixed components. A variable cost is one that is proportional to sales. Each unit sold bears a commensurate production and distribution cost. Fixed costs are not consistently related to sales.

The rearrangement of costs is fairly straightforward. Because two-thirds of the $10,956 overhead was allocated to plant and warehouse, $7,341 was taken out of cost of goods sold and put into fixed costs as factory overhead. The remaining $3,615 was deducted from variable selling expenses and shifted into selling overhead.

**TABLE 7.3. Pro Forma P&L Summary Prepared for Breakeven Analysis.**

| | |
|---|---|
| Net sales | $91,296 |
| Less variable costs | |
| Cost of goods sold | 36,834 |
| Selling expenses | 31,012 |
| Total variable costs | 67,846 |
| Marginal contribution | 23,450 |
| Less fixed costs | |
| Factory overhead | 7,341 |
| Selling overhead | 3,615 |
| Total fixed costs | 10,956 |
| Profits | $12,494 |

SOURCE: Based on data from Pierre A. Passavant, "Direct Marketing Economics and Budgeting," DMMA, *Manual Release* 600.1 (October 1979), p. 1.

Some of these so-called fixed costs are not constant, irrespective of volume. They can be altered and are often referred to as "programmed costs." Anything programmed can be unprogrammed. For purposes of breakeven analysis, all costs not proportional to sales were lumped together in the fixed cost category. Cost of goods sold is treated as a variable cost, though some components may act contrarily under various conditions of inventory valuation.

The analysis does make some bold assumptions. For example, revenue is shown as a net figure to make it consistent with the pro forma statement of Table 7-2. The summary thus ignores a deduction of $10,144 for 10 percent returns. By doing so, the breakeven analysis makes an implicit assumption that returns are proportional to changes in sales volume. This is probably contrary to fact, especially when mailings expand to customers with lower propensities to buy. The same result would have occurred if the charge of $10,144 for returns were added to net revenue and charged to variable costs. The bottom line would remain unaltered, but the assumption of proportionality of returns to sales would be made explicit.

A similar problem arises with the 3 percent estimate for bad debts, which is a part of variable selling costs. As mailings go to less-likely customers, the rate of bad debt probably edges upward. The format of Table 7-3 must then be regarded as a first approximation.

In this problem, 2,880 units were expected to change hands at a price of $31.70 each. Total net sales would thus amount to $91,296. Each unit here bears a variable cost of $23.56 ($67,846/2,880). Thus, the difference between a unit's revenue and variable cost is $8.14. The difference is known as the marginal contribution per unit. It signifies that $8.14 out of every sale goes toward fixed costs and profits.

Since variable costs are defined as being proportional to revenue, every sale has the same variable cost. It also follows that each unit sold yields the same marginal contribution. If one unit adds $8.14, two add $16.28, and so on. When the additions fall below total fixed costs of

$10,956, the activity results in a loss. When the total marginal contribution equals fixed costs, profits are zero; that is the breakeven point. Total revenue exactly covers total costs, both variable and fixed. When marginal contribution begins to exceed fixed costs, the project begins to show a profit.

In terms of dollar volume, the breakeven point can be figured by the formula

$$\begin{aligned} \text{BE} &= F/(1 - V/R), \text{ where} \\ \text{BE} &= \text{Breakeven point} \\ F &= \text{Total fixed cost} \\ V &= \text{Total variable cost} \\ R &= \text{Total revenue} \end{aligned}$$

Using this formula and substituting the appropriate values from Table 7-3, the breakeven point for this project comes to $42,630. The calculation is as follows:

$$\text{BE} = \$10,956/(1 - \$67,846/\$91,296) = \$42,630$$

At a price of $31.70 per unit, the direct mail program would have to sell approximately 1,345 units to cover all costs ($\$42,630/\$31.70 = 1,345$).

Breakeven in terms of unit volume can be calculated by the formula $\text{BE} = F/\text{MC}$, where MC stands for marginal contribution per unit. For this project, $\$10,956/\$8.14 = 1,345$ units.

Breakeven analysis can be presented to managers in the form of simple charts. These show cost-profit-volume relationships. The calculations for breakeven used in this example are illustrated in Figure 7-3.

In keeping with the preceding analysis, this chart shows that the company must sell 1,345 units, amounting to $42,630, before the mailing program becomes profitable. Lower sales will result in a loss. Sales above the breakeven point become profitable, with each additional unit contributing $8.14 to profits. Since all fixed costs are met, the entire marginal contribution after the breakeven point represents profit.

Breakeven analysis provides numerous advantages to direct marketers. It is a quick, uncomplicated way of figuring by how much sales can be off before operating losses show up. If sales forecasts are higher than the breakeven point, the analysis indicates how much deviation exists between profits and no profits. This amount is one measure of risk. In our promotional mailing, sales were estimated at 2,880 units. Actual sales would have had to deviate by more than 50 percent from budget forecasts for expected profits to actually result in nonprofits. In short, the mailing would really have had to be ineffective.

Breakeven analysis also indicates the extra profits that will result if sales should happen to rise above budget forecasts. Each additional

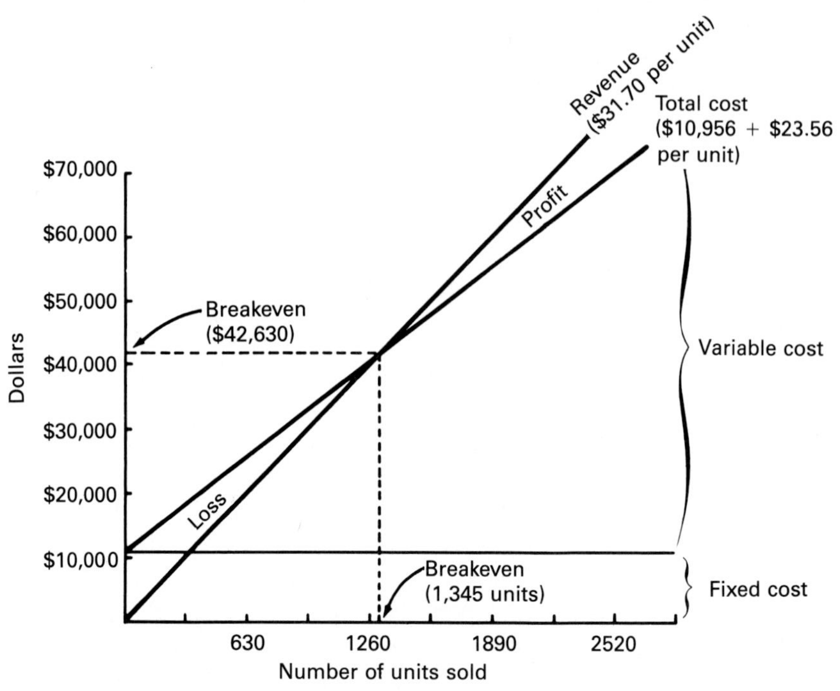


**FIGURE 7-3 Illustration of a Breakeven Chart**

sale increases profits by $8.14, the marginal contribution per unit. This figure indicates the profit expectation for each sale once the breakeven point is passed.

Breakeven analysis, however, is not without its problems. One drawback pertains to fixed costs. These are presumed to remain constant over an infinite range. However, that presumption is flawed. The expenditures have limits, and when they reach the outer boundaries, they rise in jumps. Consequently, limitations to current capacity must be taken into account in calculating nonvariable costs.

Another problem is the conventional assumption of linearity. For example, the revenue line in Figure 7-3 runs at a 45° angle. This is accurate if all recipients to a mailing are offered the item at the same price. But variable costs are also portrayed as a straight line. In reality, variable costs also hold for a limited range of volume, and proposals to stretch operations beyond those limits must make compensating adjustments.

Inventory valuation can also create difficulties for breakeven analysis. Ongoing operations add costs to the value of inventory, which shows up on a balance sheet. Figure 7-3 made the implicit assumption that sales were the same as production volume for a manufacturer, or purchasing volume for a reseller, and that costs are applied to the units sold. But with inventories, costs may be carried forward from prior pe-

**TABLE 7.4. Breakeven Points for Three Alternatives.**

| | A | B | C |
|---|---|---|---|
| Sales volume | 1,000 | 1,345 | 2,000 |
| Unit price | $34.52 | $31.70 | $29.04 |
| Revenue | 34,520 | 42,637 | 58,080 |
| Total variable cost | 23,560 | 31,688 | 47,120 |
| Marginal contribution | 10,960 | 10,949 | 10,960 |
| Fixed cost | 10.956 | 10,956 | 10,956 |
| Profit | 4 | (7) | 4 |

riods and show up with values that differ from their original worth. It is feasible to segregate production costs from marketing costs and confine the analysis to the latter. Some authors do this, though for reasons other than avoiding difficulties brought on by inventory valuation issues.[2]

Finally, breakeven analysis grows exceedingly complex with marketing activities that involve multiple products. Prime examples are catalogs. Each item in a catalog has a different variable cost and profit-to-volume ratio. But a catalog using breakeven analysis would average all elements carried by the publication. A number of unprofitable items would then be included in the average. Eliminating losers calls for an item-by-item analysis.

## Possible Breakeven Points

The model used for breakeven analysis assumed that everything remained the same, except for the number of mailings. The response rate from these mailings thus determined both breakeven and profits. But suppose all things were not constant. For example, firms have some leverage in pricing, particularly for goods sold through direct marketing.

The projection was that a mailing of 100,000 would sell 2,880 units for $31.70 each. At that price, the breakeven came to about 1,345 units. But suppose the price were changed to $34.52 per unit. Costs are the same. What would the breakeven levels be for a 100,000 mailing using these new prices?

A change in price would change the sales response curve. That is, more or less of the product will be demanded according to the price a marketer sets. Higher prices usually reduce sales; lower prices increase them. But this does not hinder the calculation of breakeven points for various prices, under the assumption of constant costs. Table 7-4 shows the results of calculating breakeven for three pricing points: the original proposed price of $31.70, a lower one of $29.04, and a higher price

2. Martin Baier, *Elements of Direct Marketing* (New York: McGraw-Hill, 1983), pp. 36–39.

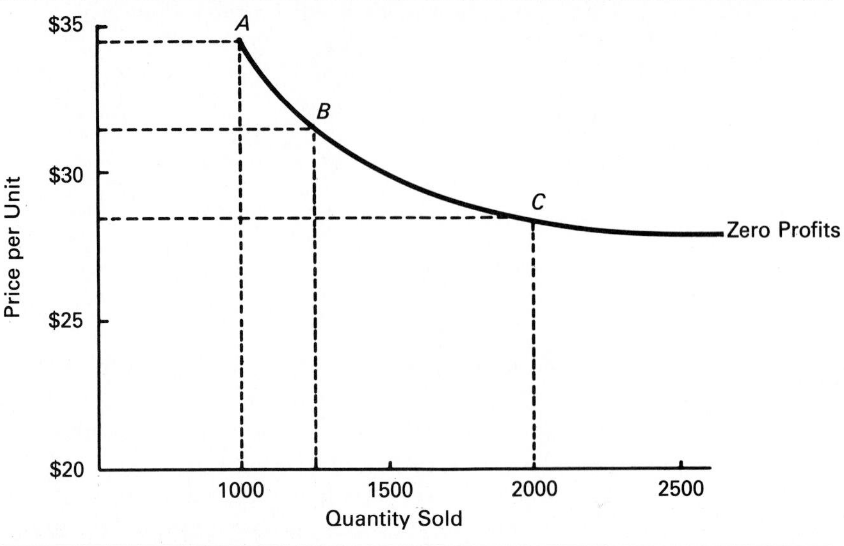


**FIGURE 7-4 Zero Isoprofit Curve**

of $34.52. At $34.52 only 1,000 units need be sold for the mailing to break even. At the lowest price, $29.04, sales must reach 2,000 units. A price of $31.70 yields a breakeven point of 1,345 units. Which is most profitable, alternative A, B, or C?

The existence of different breakeven points for the same mailing suggests different price-quantity-profit relationships. These relationships are depicted graphically in Figure 7-4.

The rectangles formed by the dotted lines represent total revenue for each price-volume combination.

- *Price.* The horizontal lines that extend from points *A*, *B*, and *C* to the vertical axis indicate unit price. Proposal A prices the offer at $34.52 per unit, B at $31.70, and C at $29.04.
- *Volume.* Verticle lines from each point to the horizontal axis signify quantity or sales volume. These quantities are 1,000 units for alternative A, 1,345 units for B, and 2,000 units for C.

If the price-volume couplings, designated as points *A*, *B*, and *C*, are joined, the connecting line traces what is called an *isoprofit curve*. Profit for every point on that line is zero, described by the equation $0 = R - (F + V)$.

Calculations for the breakeven points were made only for expository purposes. By themselves they serve no useful end. Breaking even is seldom a desirable goal for a business. Then why do such mental doodling? Because if a zero-profit curve has many alternatives, so do positive-profit curves. Isoprofit curves, derived by breakeven analysis, have great value as a device for considering profit alternatives.

## Isoprofit Curves

Isoprofit curves permit planners to answer "what if" questions. At a given volume, what price must a firm charge to make a given profit? Conversely, if price is given, how many items must a firm sell to meet its desired profit goal? What price-quantity combinations will yield other feasible profit levels? What changes can a manager make that would affect price-profit-volume relationships?

The approach has the earmarks of *satisficing,* a term coined by Herbert Simon.[3] What is satisfactory varies from company to company, and so does the choice of alternatives. A telemarketing agency might reduce profits by using a "softer" sell to reduce complaints to local authorities. A direct marketing agency may turn down a larger account and stay with a smaller but faithful client.

To illustrate how isoprofit curves work, let's assume a manager thinks that profit levels of roughly $12,500 and $15,000 are good performance levels for a mailing. Now let's consider the alternative prices of $34.52, $31.70, and $29.04. The question becomes: What quantities must we sell at these prices to attain a profit of about $12,500? How much more need we sell at these prices to make a profit of $15,000?

The answer to these questions can be derived from the equation

$$Q = \frac{F + P}{p - v}, \text{ where}$$

$Q$ = Quantity that needs to be sold
$F$ = Fixed costs
$P$ = Profit goal
$p$ = Unit price
$v$ = Variable cost per unit

If we want a profit of about $12,500 and price the product at $31.70, the answer is as follows:

$$Q = \frac{\$10,956 + \$12,500}{\$31.70 - \$23.56} = 2,882 \text{ units}$$

We can do the same for all other price alternatives and profit goals. The results of these calculations are depicted in Figure 7-5.

Figure 7-5 shows six possible quantities needed to reach certain profit levels, given three alternative prices. The chart does not tell which price to use or what sales volume would actually come about at either of these prices. The analysis merely represents a range of feasible options. Direct marketers usually test the most promising alternatives before launching a program. For example, the two price levels can be tested and

3. Herbert Simon, "Theories of Decision-Making in Economics and Behavioral Science," *American Economic Review* (June 1959), pp. 253–283.

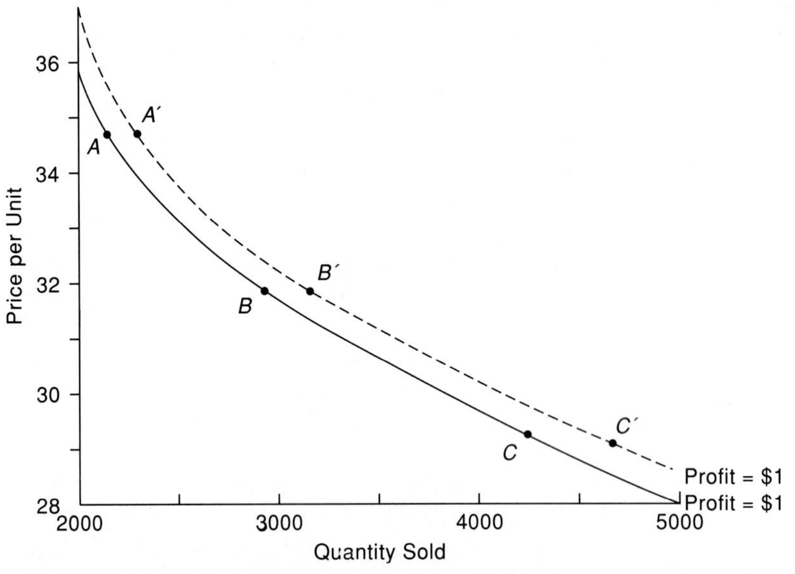


**FIGURE 7-5 Isoprofit Curves**

final choices made on the basis of test results. From this standpoint, analysis using isoprofit curves narrows the range of choices and so aids planning and testing processes. The key values shown in Figure 7-5 are reproduced in tabular form in Table 7-5.

Products distributed in continuous offers sometimes have highly inelastic demands. In those instances, quantity is relatively fixed—within given bounds, of course. The marketer then has a certain amount of leverage in setting prices. The question in this case might be: To obtain a profit of $12,500, assuming a quantity of 2,140 units, what price must be charged for the product?

Using the breakeven approach, the answer can be derived from the formula

$$p = \frac{P}{Q} + \frac{F}{Q} + v$$

**TABLE 7.5. Quantity-Price-Profit Relationships.**

| | Quantity Needed to Attain Profit of: | |
|---|---|---|
| **Price per Unit** | **$12,500** | **$15,000** |
| $34.52 | 2,140 | 2,368 |
| 31.70 | 2,882 | 3,189 |
| 29.04 | 4,280 | 4,736 |

Substituting the appropriate values, we get

$$\frac{\$12,500}{2,140} + \frac{\$10,956}{2,140} + \$23.56 = \$34.52$$

Like quantity estimates, pricing points are guidelines. They are educated guesses about possibilities. The actual decision should be made on the basis of a sales test.

## Probabilistic Breakeven

Conventional breakeven analysis allows a change of only one variable at a time. If we want to change price, cost-volume relationships are assumed to be constant. But more often than not, several variables must be altered simultaneously. Reduced prices may increase volume. More sales may affect operating economies and so lower costs. Large purchases may produce bigger volume discounts and lower order costs.

One way of approaching problems of this type is through probabilistic breakeven.[4] Like its isoprofit cousin, this form of breakeven analysis considers price-cost-volume relationships, but values of each variable are assigned probabilities. This procedure allows different quantities to have different unit costs.

The probability inputs are supplied by company managers. They are subjective but supposedly are based on experience. An analysis usually contains several approaches to a problem, with variables changing simultaneously. These approaches are represented as sets of probability distributions.

The analysis requires a computer-tabulated solution to handle the large number of calculations, usually in the form of probability density functions. These data lend themselves to computer simulation programs, such as Monte Carlo. These computations produce probable breakeven and profit points from randomly selected values of assigned probabilities. The final output comes after a series of iterations that are deemed statistically reliable. This results in a distribution of outcomes, with a calculable risk attached to each.

An advantage of probabilistic breakeven analysis is that relevant variables are not viewed as linear. Nor are they seen as deterministic. Managers can ask such questions as: What are the odds of a promotion producing a certain sales volume? These risk considerations can be extended to a number of other factors—profit levels, prices, and quantities. Whether these complicated procedures are worth pursuing depends on the overall commitment and the risk involved.

---

4. T. F. Anthony and H. J. Watson, "Probabilistic Breakeven Analysis," *Management Planning* (November/December 1976), pp. 12–19.

## Continuity Programs

Determining profitability of continuity programs is an extension of the approach used for one-time offers. For example, suppose the 100,000 mailing example used earlier in this chapter (Table 7-1) elicited 2,880 net sales. Terms of each item remain the same, but the offer calls for six shipments, one per month, instead of just one.

The costs and revenue of the first shipment will be the same as for the one-time offer. Profit before taxes will amount to $12,494, or 13.7 percent of net sales. Evaluating profitability of the next five shipments will take the same form. We can create a P&L statement for each shipment, but the figures change. For example, all time periods after the first mailing involve no costs of acquiring customers. Only the first mailing totaled 100,000 pieces at $250 per thousand. Subsequent months are free of that expense. They might also exclude the premium that was offered in the initial mailing.

Other costs would change as well, such as returns and debts. Profitability of the program is calculated by adding up all transactions during the six months. Total sales would be higher, as would pretax profits. This assumes that the firm spends the same amount of money in the initial mailing to acquire customers and that the response to this mailing is the same as for the one-shot offer. The portion of the marginal contribution going to profits would also be higher, since one-time costs do not appear in subsequent months.

## Multistage Operations

Not all direct marketing efforts are one-step programs, such as sending out a mailing designed to get immediate sales. Many programs are multistage; that is, a return to a solicitation is only a preliminary step toward a sale.

Direct marketing makes extensive use of multistage selling. Books are sometimes offered on approval. Customers can examine a book's contents and then decide to buy it or return it. Similarly, magazine publishers offer trial subscriptions. Those who respond to such promotions may cancel after receiving one or more free issues.

In other instances, direct marketing combines mailings with personal selling. Offers of free literature and brochures are commonplace as lead generators in industry and are followed up by personal visits from salespeople. Insurance companies and financial houses also solicit inquiries and requests for literature and follow them up with sales calls or with further selling mailouts.

Budgets for all these situations must be based on the total cost of the marketing program. In fact, the initial cost of a response may be a minor part of the entire selling process. Under these conditions, it is customary to budget each stage separately. In this way, the individual parts can be appraised and better controlled. Initial response serves only as a sort of screening device. The stage in which a transaction occurs determines the conversion rate of subsequent stages.

For example, suppose a mailing of 5,000 pieces to company managers elicits 400 inquiries. The response rate is 8 percent, and the firm evaluates the results in terms of cost per inquiry. Suppose follow-up calls by sales personnel result in 80 sales. The conversion rate would be 20 percent (80/400). But only 1.6 percent of the initial mailing (80/5,000) resulted in a sale.

The cost per sale is based on both the mailing and follow-ups. To evaluate each step, total costs must be divided into two parts: costs of the initial mailing and costs of personal selling. This twin-phased cost can then be described by the following equation:

$$\mathrm{TC} = \left(\frac{\mathrm{Cm}}{\mathrm{Rm}}\right)\mathrm{CR} + \frac{\mathrm{Cs}}{S}, \text{ where}$$

TC = Total cost per sale

Cm = Costs of a mailing

Rm = Returns from the mailing

CR = Conversion rate, or sales as a percentage of returns

Cs = Cost of selling

$S$ = Number of sales

The first expression in the equation, (Cm/Rm)CR, refers to the cost per sale of the initial mailing. The second part of the equation, (Cs/$S$), denotes the unit costs of personal selling.

This equation reflects the common practice of assessing each part of a multistage program as though each stage were independent. In reality, however, there may be interaction between stages. Each may exert an influence on the other. For example, a mailing may solicit a large number of inquiries from coupon clippers or curious readers. If all these leads are followed up, costs of personal selling may sharply rise. Similarly, telephone solicitors paid bonuses for leads are encouraged to increase the number of potential buyers. But these prospects may be of poor quality, and selling efforts may incur high costs.

A firm might do well to regard multistage operations from a systems perspective. A part that optimizes its own actions may not necessarily contribute to the efficiency of the whole. Since interaction exists, it must be evaluated. It is the total budget that must be optimized, not any particular part.

# Lifetime Value of a Customer

Most businesses are continuous, long-term propositions. No matter what techniques they use to market their products, many businesses are highly dependent on repeat buying; they cannot survive without it. Even mass marketers would not last long if customers stopped shopping at their stores after one trip. The emphasis retailers place on customer service reflects the value placed on shopper loyalty. It is almost a truism that when customers keep coming back, profits from repeat sales are higher than potential earnings from the original sale. It is for this reason that businesses "buy" into a market and are willing to lose money in getting an initial sale in order to make profits on subsequent sales from the new customers acquired.

Perhaps direct marketers are more mindful of customer loyalty because many databases track purchases. These computer systems permit firms to estimate how much they have paid to acquire customers and how much they have gotten back. Such databases have fostered the recent application of forecasting a customer's lifetime value, often referred to as LTV.

Although this concept applies to almost any database that records transactions on an individual basis, its primary use has been in continuity programs, such as those of magazines, catalogs, insurance companies, book and records clubs, and credit card issuers. These businesses sell goods and services at periodic intervals.

Continuity programs are of various types, but they all have certain features in common. One is the maintenance of front-end and back-end operations. *Front end* describes action taken to acquire new customers. *Back end* relates to company action from the time a prospect enters the database as a buyer. Most concern with LTV has been with the front end. How much can a firm afford to spend on customer acquisition, given the lifetime value of a customer? In effect, this perspective regards customers as long-term assets. Since they are bought by front-end spending, acquisition of customers is regarded as an investment. It is a means of building assets that generate income in the long run.

Conventional accounting treats promotion as an operating expense. Outlays are charged to the period in which they are incurred, and benefits arising from those expenditures are presumed to be used up in the current accounting period. Accounting practice, however, does not preclude a company from separating its internal analysis from public reporting. In this way, operating control is not constricted by an accounting straitjacket devised for tax purposes and custodial reporting.

Direct marketers commonly acquire new customers at a loss. Prices of introductory offers frequently do not cover costs. Premiums, discounts, generous credit policies, and special offers may push returns from an initial mailing into the red. When promotion is treated as an investment, it is necessary to know how long, and in what amounts, income will continue beyond the current period, which is conventionally accepted as one year.

Spiegel was a pioneer among catalogers in developing logarithms to calculate LTV.[5] A number of insurance companies have also modeled the worth of policyholders in the long run.[6] A *Catalog Age* survey among catalogers in 1988 found just 18 percent doing studies to estimate the lifetime value of customers.[7] But roughly one-third of respondents claimed to calculate how much they could afford to spend per prospect, although they did not reveal their methods. This percentage rose to 50 percent in 1989 but declined to 46 percent the next year. Catalogers of books, records, and videos chalked up the highest percentage, 65 percent.[8]

There are many ways of calculating the lifetime value of a customer, but the most common is a two-step procedure. The first step is to examine the historical record to analyze what has happened in the past. The next step is to extrapolate those events into the future, predicting what will happen if the series of tomorrows is similar to all bygone yesterdays. To illustrate:

Suppose a sample of 10,000 customers a magazine publisher acquired some time ago is extracted from a database. The cost of customer acquisition came to $30,000, or $3 per customer. In addition, suppose that the effective life of that $30,000 investment is thought to be five years. This publisher used the customer list to sell additional items to subscribers, such as books, records, videos, and other published materials. Table 7-6 shows projected total revenue and costs for that investment over five periods, with each period equal to one year.

Are the anticipated returns of $60,000 worth the $30,000 investment in new customers? A widely used practice to handle problems of this sort employs present value concepts. This idea, first propounded by Irving Fisher, sees the future value of an investment growing because the cash it generates accumulates at compound interest.[9] Money makes money. The basic question then boils down to: How much is the $30,000 today worth five years hence? The customary way of evaluating a future sum is to discount expected profits to the present time and compare the results with today's outlay.

5. Ernest H. Schell, "Lifetime Value of a Customer," *Marketing Insights* (Fall 1990), p. 87.
6. Donald Jackson, "Determining a Customer's Lifetime Value," *Direct Marketing* (March, May 1989).
7. *The Catalog Age Report*, 1988.
8. *Ibid.*, 1990.
9. See Irving Fisher, *The Rate of Interest* (New York: Macmillan, 1907) and *The Theory of Interest* (New York: Macmillan, 1930).

**TABLE 7.6. Profits from 10,000 New Customers in a Continuity Program.**

| Period | Number of Customers* | Total Revenue | Total Cost | After-Tax Profits** |
|---|---|---|---|---|
| 0 | 10,000 | — | $30,000 | — |
| 1 | 6,000 | $120,000 | 84,000 | $21,600 |
| 2 | 3,600 | 72,000 | 48,000 | 14,400 |
| 3 | 2,160 | 46,000 | 26,000 | 12,000 |
| 4 | 1,296 | 30,000 | 17,000 | 7,800 |
| 5 | 778 | 16,000 | 9,000 | 4,200 |
| | | | Total profits | 60,000 |

*Customers remaining at the end of the period.
**Assuming a combined tax rate of federal, state, and local governments of 40 percent, with no tax loss carryforwards.

To do this, the firm must choose a discount rate. Among the alternatives are:

1. Take the prevailing rate on the money market as the cost of capital.
2. Estimate current earnings on invested capital, which is an opportunity cost.

Suppose the firm assumes a 14 percent cost of capital and uses present value tables to make the calculations. The results are presented in Table 7-7.

Some firms estimate cash flow, on the assumption that incoming cash supplies the means of carrying out corporate policies. These calculations must add back depreciation. If no depreciation is involved—as might be in evaluating a selling technique—profit and cash flow calculations are identical.

Since the present value in Table 7-7 is larger than the initial investment of $30,000, costs of acquiring new customers have met the firm's capital cost requirement. Stated another way, the present value (PV) ratio is more than 1.0 ($45,149/$30,000 = 1.5). How much can a firm afford to spend for a new customer, given present value? Answer: $4.51 ($45,149/10,000 = $4.51).

**TABLE 7.7. Present Value Estimates.**

| Year | Net Profit Inflow | Discount Factor at 14%* | Present Value |
|---|---|---|---|
| 1 | $21,600 | .915 | $19,764 |
| 2 | 14,400 | .776 | 11,174 |
| 3 | 12,000 | .657 | 7,884 |
| 4 | 7,800 | .557 | 4,345 |
| 5 | 4,200 | .472 | 1,982 |
| Total | 60,000 | | 45,149 |

*Assumes monthly payments

The LTV concept is not applicable to every direct marketing project. On the marketing side, LTV lends itself better to projects that cross-sell or introduce product enhancements. The calculation also assumes that the future will be exactly like the past, an assumption that departs more and more from reality as time passes. On the financial side, the basic formulation of present value makes no allowance for reinvestment or replacement of the capital initially procured.[10] The manner of choosing an expected interest rate also affects operating decisions.[11]

LTV calculations contain a built-in bias that attributes to front-end operations the entire profit over the life of a project. But repeat buying is affected by many factors, such as product quality and pricing. A magazine that upgrades the quality of its editorial content may lower customer attrition rates and even increase sales of related items. Better customer service, such as product guarantees by American Express, can do the same thing. To regard customer acquisition as a long-term expense without according similar treatment to the long-term benefits produced by back-end expenditures leads to inefficient allocation of resources.

To represent customer value only in terms of front-end performance obscures an important point. In large part, front-end performance depends on back-end performance. For example, when back-end operations enhance cash flow, promotion people think that this means the company can afford to spend more for a new customer.[12] But it is just as logical to say the firm now needs less funds for new customers, since the member retention rate may have improved. A magazine that raises its subscription renewal rate needs fewer new subscribers to maintain its circulation. Consumers may be offered more value for their money; therefore, new customers should be able to be acquired at lower costs.

When back- and front-end operations are regarded as an interconnected system, management is furnished with more productive alternatives from which to choose. It is presented with more meaningful tradeoffs and priorities. The emphasis shifts away from forecasting methods that take past attrition rates, revenues, and costs as unchanging and that project them onto a changing future. The alternative is an integrated approach that centers on a relevant set of organization aspects. A program's success depends not on a right forecast but on doing the right thing in a right manner.

---

10. Robert Dorfman, "The Meaning of Internal Rates of Return," *Journal of Finance* (December 1981), pp. 1011–1021. For a contrary view, see F. M. Fisher and J. J. McGowan, "On the Misuse of Accounting Rates of Return to Infer Monopoly Profits," *American Economic Review* (March 1983), pp. 80–97.
11. See H. Bierman, Jr., and J. E. Haas, "Are High Cut-off Rates a Fallacy?" *Financial Executive* (July 1973), pp. 88–91; E. J. Elton and M. J. Gruber, "Valuation and Asset Selection Under Alternative Investment Opportunities," *Journal of Finance* (May 1976), pp. 525–543.
12. Jackson, *op. cit.* (May 1989), p. 24.

# Summary

Since a budget is an operating plan converted into financial terms, the direct marketing budget is usually of a one-year duration. However, it is monitored or reviewed periodically, either monthly, quarterly, or semiannually.

An important consideration in budgeting is profitability. To analyze profitability normally requires a pro forma P&L statement.

One possible objective of a firm is to optimize profits. To do so, the firm must know the values represented in the sales response curve. The decision rule for maximizing profits is to alter inputs in such a way that marginal revenue equals marginal costs. But that end can seldom be accomplished with precision.

A popular application of marginal theory is breakeven analysis. Decisions with respect to possible profit alternatives can be made by the use of isoprofit curves. Another approach, which is computer-based, is probabilistic breakeven.

In continuous programs, firms may acquire customers at a loss in the hope of recouping profits later. This practice leads to questions of an investment nature. There are basically three kinds of investment criteria: payback, rate of return, and present value. Although each method has limitations, a fundamental question pertains to the interdependency of front-end and back-end operations.

## REVIEW QUESTIONS

1. What are the uses of a pro forma P&L statement for particular projects?
2. What is the difference between a cost and an expense?
3. If firms do not in fact maximize profits, does it make sense to use profit maximization models?
4. What is the difference between a fixed cost and a programmed cost? Since breakeven analysis lumps both together, is the distinction of practical consequence?
5. What assumptions are made in breakeven analysis?
6. What are the major advantages of breakeven analysis?
7. What modifications to standard breakeven analysis are introduced by probabilistic breakeven?
8. What are the arguments against evaluating separately each stage of a two-step marketing program?
9. Criticize the concept of payback. Despite its shortcomings, is it a useful tool in decisions concerning investments?
10. What are the assumptions in using a return-on-investment model to set spending levels for front-end operations?

CHAPTER 8

# The Role of Marketing Research

## PROFILE

**ARTHUR BLUMENFIELD**

**Computer Specialist.** Arthur Blumenfield is president of Blumenfield Marketing Inc. of Stamford, Conn., and has been involved in the computer field since 1954. He began his career at the Standard Oil Company (now Exxon) and has since worked or consulted for many leading companies and nonprofit organizations in the United States and Europe.

His expertise is the creative use of computers to effectively solve business problems. He is regarded as an authority in the use of computers within the direct marketing industry, where he has implemented many innovative and effective solutions. Among these are the development of the "mathematical equivalent analysis" method of identifying duplicate names on mailing lists and the invention of personalized children's books ("Me Books").

He is the author of numerous articles regarding the use of computers in direct marketing, including chapters in various McGraw-Hill books. He also authored the Direct Marketing Association's "Standards for Computerized Mailing Lists" and served as consultant to that organization.

He is a frequent speaker at industry seminars throughout the United States and Europe and has repeatedly addressed the International Direct Marketing Symposium in Switzerland and the Pan-Pacific D.M. Symposium in Australia.

Mr. Blumenfield serves as a director of Direct Marketing Day in New York, a nonprofit foundation dedicated to providing scholarship funds and seminars for professors and students of marketing. ■

# Functions of Marketing Research

Direct marketing has many things in common with other aspects of marketing. One is the use of information to make decisions.

In the broadest possible sense, marketing research has two prime tasks: planning and monitoring. Since direct marketing can trace results to some action, the industry has less need for research that measures performance. The transactional process embraces monitoring; response is part of operational functions.

Direct marketing always gets feedback on what it is doing. This is inherent in its operating procedures. As response comes in, it is traced to its source and compared with original expectations. Are sales in line with initial goals? Did a campaign accomplish what it set out to do? Most research in direct marketing thus deals with planning rather than monitoring.

Marketing research is pragmatic, especially for planning. It is meant to assist business managers in making business decisions. At one time marketing research was regarded as an applied science—and many authors of marketing research books still regard it as such. In 1987 the American Marketing Association revised this definition, stressing information rather than "scientific method." This new "official" version now reads:

> Marketing research is the function which links consumer, customer, and public to the marketer through information—used to identify marketing opportunities and problems; generate, refine, and evaluate marketing actions; monitor marketing performance; and improve understanding of marketing as a process. Marketing research specifies the information required to address these issues; designs the method for collecting information; manages and implements the data collection process; analyzes the results; and communicates the findings and their implications.[1]

In what specific areas of planning do direct marketers call on marketing research for assistance? Most writers use the general areas of the four *Ps*—product, price, promotion, and place—to categorize marketing functions. This categorization is extremely broad and, even worse, does not emphasize the variables most important to direct marketers. William A. Cohen, professor of Marketing at UCLA, has proposed the planning functions of merchandising, message, and media.[2] Merchandising includes the offer—the product and terms of the transaction. The message is the creative presentation, including copy, graphics, and layout of the advertisement. Media refers to carriers of messages and their selection. We would propose adding another *M* to the planning stage: markets. Messages in media are meant to present merchandise to buyers, who make up markets.

---

1. "New Marketing Research Definition Approved," *Marketing News* (January 2, 1987), p.1.
2. William A. Cohen, "Rather then Heed Four Ps, Direct Marketers Should Follow Four Ms," *Marketing News* (December 21, 1984), p. 14

# Markets and Merchandising

The basis for any marketing program is an estimation of market potential and an analysis of the characteristics of that potential. Direct marketers make extensive use of the geodemographic information to segment markets—a key practice of the industry. They use both census information and data supplied by research houses that syndicate their services. This aspect of direct marketing was discussed at some length in Chapter 5.

As an example of demographic usage, Table 8-1 displays a proposed coop program by Carol Wright, providing a demographic profile of the

**TABLE 8.1. Demographics of a Carol Wright Co-op Program.**

| | Total U.S. Households | Total Co-op | Index | Younger Families | Index | Established Families | Index |
|---|---|---|---|---|---|---|---|
| Household Size | | | | | | | |
| 1–2 | 55.2% | 31.0% | 56 | 27.8% | 50 | 35.2% | 64 |
| 3 or more | 44.8 | 69.0 | 154 | 72.2 | 161 | 64.8 | 145 |
| Average persons | 2.6 | 3.3 | 127 | 3.4 | 130 | 3.2 | 122 |
| Head of household age | | | | | | | |
| 18–24 | 6.2% | 3.0% | 48 | 4.0% | 65 | 1.6% | 26 |
| 25–34 | 23.0 | 33.5 | 141 | 51.6 | 224 | 7.6 | 33 |
| 35–49 | 28.0 | 43.5 | 155 | 35.5 | 127 | 54.1 | 193 |
| 50–64 | 21.7 | 18.5 | 85 | 7.1 | 33 | 33.5 | 154 |
| 65 and over | 21.1 | 2.4 | 11 | 1.8 | 9 | 3.2 | 15 |
| Median age | 45.3 | 38.1 | 84 | 33.3 | 74 | 46.4 | 102 |
| Household income | | | | | | | |
| $40,000+ | 24.6% | 39.8% | 162 | 35.0% | 143 | 45.9% | 187 |
| $25,000–$39,999 | 23.9 | 32.0 | 134 | 34.0 | 142 | 29.3 | 123 |
| Under $25,000 | 51.5 | 28.3 | 55 | 30.9 | 60 | 24.8 | 48 |
| Median income | $24,271 | $35,049 | 144 | $33,232 | 137 | $37,908 | 156 |
| Average income | $29,294 | $38,955 | 133 | $36,670 | 125 | $41,943 | 143 |
| Education | | | | | | | |
| Not H.S. Graduate | 26.6% | 13.3% | 50 | 12.7% | 48 | 14.1% | 53 |
| H.S. Graduate | 35.3 | 35.1 | 99 | 35.7 | 101 | 34.3 | 97 |
| Some college/ college grad | 38.1 | 51.6 | 135 | 51.6 | 135 | 51.5 | 135 |
| Marital status | | | | | | | |
| Married | 58.6% | 78.2% | 133 | 79.2% | 135 | 76.9% | 131 |
| Children under age 18 | | | | | | | |
| None | 61.7% | 37.2% | 60 | 28.5% | 46 | 48.5% | 79 |
| 1 | 16.1 | 22.5 | 140 | 21.8 | 135 | 23.3 | 145 |
| 2 | 14.2 | 25.7 | 181 | 31.5 | 222 | 18.0 | 127 |
| 3 or more | 8.1 | 14.7 | 181 | 18.2 | 225 | 10.2 | 126 |
| Average children | 0.7 | 1.2 | 171 | 1.5 | 203 | 0.9 | 131 |
| Presence of children | | | | | | | |
| Children under 6 | 18.6% | 31.3% | 168 | 45.1% | 242 | 13.4% | 72 |
| Children 6–11 | 17.9 | 31.7 | 177 | 39.3 | 220 | 21.8 | 122 |
| Children 12–17 | 16.7 | 26.9 | 161 | 20.7 | 124 | 35.1 | 210 |

SOURCE: Reprinted with permission of Donnelly Marketing, Inc.

30 million households selected as a target market for the mailing. Estimates were apparently derived by fitting mailing lists to census-based data.

Demographic data are used most frequently to define and understand target markets. When linked with purchases, this information readily applies to a defined universe. Direct marketers can project their inferences to a target of a given size and implement their decisions by selecting lists based on identical criteria. Carol Wright's list selection in Table 8-1 shows precisely the types of households to which mailings will go. A firm's managers can easily see if the demographic profiles of mailing recipients fit their marketing targets.

Many industry practitioners, especially those at direct marketing agencies, think consumers can be better understood if psychological factors are joined with the basic demographic information. Research of this kind is used sparingly because consumer mental states are intangible. In instances when mental measures are used for segmentation purposes, psychographics probably ranks among the leading methods. Psychographics requires a consumer survey that, in its most popular form, asks about activities, interests, and opinions (AIO). This is done by giving respondents a long list of questions and asking them to indicate the extent to which they agree or disagree with each one. Table 8-2 reproduces a page from an AIO questionnaire. The research technique then clusters consumers into groups with similar response patterns.

So far, most psychological research has been used for developing creative ideas with respect to offers and messages. The big drawback with respect to market analysis is the lack of established relationships between any psychological segments and purchase behavior.

## Idea Generation

Any offer or presentation must start with a concept of its eventual form. Although presentations are seldom so novel that they have no resemblance to anything else, they are nevertheless discrete and unique. One offer is not exactly the same as another. One ad is not an exact replica of another, or it would constitute a violation of copyright. In that sense, every offer and every presentation of that offer represent something new, an innovation.

Offers include both products and terms of exchange. Product innovations imply new products, and many direct marketing firms either concentrate on product development, if producers, or search for new products to resell, if resellers. Transactional terms are market innovations. Both product and market innovations span a wide range of possibilities. They can resemble what already exists or be vastly different. But no matter what the extent of novelty, ideas must precede implementation. The same holds true for advertisements or sales pro-

**TABLE 8.2. A Page of an AIO Study.**

Please indicate to what extent you agree or disagree with each of the following statements. For each statement, circle the symbol (explained below) that comes closest to expressing how you feel.

Agree strongly ++
Agree somewhat +
Neither agree nor disagree ○
Disagree somewhat –
Disagree strongly – –

| Statement | No. | Disagree strongly | Disagree somewhat | Neither agree nor disagree | Agree somewhat | Agree strongly |
|---|---|---|---|---|---|---|
| Day to day, it's a hum-drum life. | 1. | – – | – | ○ | + | ++ |
| It is important to be accepted into an organization that accepts successful individuals only. | 2. | – – | – | ○ | + | ++ |
| If it was good enough for my parents, it's usually good enough for me. | 3. | – – | – | ○ | + | ++ |
| Classical music is more interesting than popular music. | 4. | – – | – | ○ | + | ++ |
| I would rather spend a year traveling in the United States than in England or France. | 5. | – – | – | ○ | + | ++ |
| I should do more to improve my physical shape. | 6. | – – | – | ○ | + | ++ |
| It's important that a house be clean. | 7. | – – | – | ○ | + | ++ |
| Members of a family should be close. | 8. | – – | – | ○ | + | ++ |
| It is not necessary that things be perfect for a person to be happy. | 9. | – – | – | ○ | + | ++ |
| When other people can do certain things better than I can, I am willing to pay for their service. | 10. | – – | – | ○ | + | ++ |
| In general, one should try to have a thing fixed before it is replaced. | 11. | – – | – | ○ | + | ++ |
| A product guarantee means more to me than price. | 12. | – – | – | ○ | + | ++ |
| The kitchen is the most important room in my home. | 13. | – – | – | ○ | + | ++ |
| Children should be brought up by their mothers. | 14. | – – | – | ○ | + | ++ |
| College sports are turning into a business. | 15. | – – | – | ○ | + | ++ |
| There is no substitute for experience. | 16. | – – | – | ○ | + | ++ |
| To get anywhere in the real world, you need more than a college degree. | 17. | – – | – | ○ | + | ++ |
| It's not what you know, but who you know that counts. | 18. | – – | – | ○ | + | ++ |
| Insurance companies charge excessive rates for car insurance. | 19. | – – | – | ○ | + | ++ |
| Nothing is worth getting upset about. | 20. | – – | – | ○ | + | ++ |
| Money isn't everything. | 21. | – – | – | ○ | + | ++ |
| Using credit is the last resort. | 22. | – – | – | ○ | + | ++ |
| The activities of married women are best confined to the home and family. | 23. | – – | – | ○ | + | ++ |
| A person can save a lot of money by shopping around for bargains. | 24. | – – | – | ○ | + | ++ |

SOURCE: Reprinted with the permission of Drs. Joe Chasin and Martin Schlissel, St. John's University.

motions, which are marketing innovations. The thought precedes the deed.

The common ingredient to all innovative ideas is commercial value. What is their worth in the marketplace? No matter how novel an idea is, it is useless if it cannot be translated into something of value arising from market transactions.

Although ideas can come from any stratum of a corporation, in direct marketing the main sources are managers and "creative" personnel, those concerned with developing ways of presenting an offer. The best way to generate ideas is for a company to hire creative people and build an environment in which they can achieve their full potential. This is also probably the most difficult way because it encounters almost insurmountable obstacles. There is no way to have foreknowledge of a person's creativity; the only means of judgement is what he or she produces. In addition, organizational structure has many barriers that discourage creativity. In the absence of an ideal environment, firms often attempt to stimulate creativity by somewhat formal research methods. These can be divided into group techniques, individual methods, and sample surveys.

## Group Techniques

Companies use a number of group techniques to stimulate creative ideas, such as brainstorming, focus groups, synectics, and Delphi. In the course of time, these methods became formalized and were incorporated into marketing research. The most common ones employed by direct marketers are brainstorming and focus groups. Synectics and Delphi call for expert opinions, often technical in nature, and most problems in direct marketing do not warrant those approaches.

Although marketing researchers carry out idea-generating group sessions, their findings act only as guides. Research has never put together an offer or written an ad. Only people do, usually those directly involved in operations to create transactions.

BRAINSTORMING. Brainstorming is an old technique, dating back to advertising agencies in the 1930s. Copywriters used to sit around and "rap" with each other to develop creative ideas. The technique was formalized in the 1950s and adopted to various lines of business. A pioneer in popularizing group research was Alex Osborne of BBD&O, a leading advertising agency.[3] The main applications of brainstorming methods have taken place in consumer product categories.

Although it has numerous variations, brainstorming exhibits highly uniform features.[4] It calls for working sessions with small groups of employees, ranging from 5 to 10 people. These participants are recruited from different parts of the company so that they can bring diverse points

3. Alex F. Osborne, *Applied Imagination: Principles and Procedures of Creative Thinking* (New York: Charles Scribner & Sons, 1953).

4. Charles H. Clark, *Brainstorming: The Dynamic Way to Create Successful Ideas* (Garden City, NY: Doubleday, 1958).

of view to the sessions. However, it is recommended that groups be made up of people in roughly similar positions. For example, a vice president and a secretary should not attend the same meeting. Rank not only has its privileges but commands deference. The odds are that the secretary will act meek and say little while the officer expounds on everything.

The key figure in a brainstorming session is the group leader or moderator. He or she must guide the discussion, keeping interest high and ideas flowing. The moderator must maintain an easygoing atmosphere so that participants feel relaxed.

The best practice emphasizes adherence to "deferral of judgment." That is, the moderator must discourage one member of the group from criticizing the comments of another, no matter how mild or justified the criticism. This taboo supposedly prevents inhibitions. If people fear they will be ridiculed for what they say, they will tend to keep their mouths shut.

The objective of a brainstorming session is to elicit as many ideas as possible, regardless of relevancy or quality. Ideas will be screened and evaluated later. But there will be none to consider if they aren't brought up in the first place.

Brainstorming, like other group methods, rests on the assumption that people are more creative in a group than as individuals. The surroundings, proponents of group techniques claim, are contagious and cause people to exert themselves to contribute to the discussions. This claim, however, has been disputed by a number of authorities.[5]

Some firms use a variant called "reverse brainstorming." Instead of attempting to generate new ideas, the method dwells on negatives. It tries to draw out what went wrong or what problems group participants encountered with offers or advertisements. These negatives might then be used to improve current operations.

The main advantage of brainstorming is that it produces ideas cheaply and quickly. But the quality of these ideas is often berated. Brainstorming produces simple, "single-node" solutions to business problems. The technique cannot handle complex issues that require logical, sequential thinking. The results are "top-of-the-head" thoughts, shallow and often trivial. Critics have attacked brainstorming as a device that substitutes perfunctory action for competency in solving business problems.[6]

It is true that group research yields a low percentage of usable ideas. The same can be said of most other methods, but that is not the point. These sessions are meant to trigger the creative thinking

5. T. J. Bouchard, "Personality, Problem Solving, and Performance in Small Groups," *Journal of Applied Psychology* (February 1969), pp. 1–29.

6. See E. P. McGuire, *Generating New Product Ideas* (New York: The Conference Board, 1972), p. 15; Arthur Gerstenfeld, *Effective Management of Research and Development* (Reading, MA: Addison-Wesley, 1970), p. 100.

of those charged with that task. If brainstorming opens vistas of the mind, stimulates the imagination, and ignites the fires of creativity, it should be used. If group sessions aid in the formulation of new ideas, showmanship and play acting do not matter. The role played is positive.

FOCUS GROUPS. The genesis of focus groups followed World War II, when Robert Merton adopted them to study wartime propaganda. Afterwards focus groups drifted into social psychology and then entered marketing research.[7] Focus group sessions are highly similar to those of brainstorming. The procedures are unstructured. A moderator is used to keep the discussion on track and to make people interact with each other. The biggest departure from brainstorming is that focus group members are consumers, not company employees.

Working sessions are small, usually ranging from 7 to 11 persons. A group of fewer than 7 is deemed too small for sufficient interaction among participants. More than 11 makes the group too large to control and encourages everyone to participate equally. Unlike brainstorming sessions, focus groups are recruited by a marketing research house. They are sometimes run in front of one-way mirrors so that creative personnel and clients can observe. These devices are often installed to impress clients and to heighten their involvement. But mirrors add little or nothing to the ideas generated by a focus group.

Focus groups are highly popular with advertising agencies. This type of research focuses mainly on three areas:

1. *Evaluate problems.* These call for assessing alternative courses of action, such as adopting different strategies, offers, or positionings.
2. *Search problems.* These seek to answer questions about what variables account for consumer choices. They often involve the same issues as those addressed by motivation research.
3. *Idea generation.* This area deals with creative issues. In direct marketing, it includes both offers and the manner in which they are presented (advertisements).

The first and second applications are most controversial. The answers that are sought require research findings to be generalized or projected to a finite population. But groups are small and not chosen by probability methods. Since probabilities of selection are not known, estimating sampling error is impossible. In addition, the data represent answers of a group, not of individuals completely free of group and moderator influences.[8]

---

7. David L. Morgan, *Focus Groups and Qualitative Research* (Beverly Hills, CA: Sage Publications, 1988).

8. See *ibid.*; Danny Bellenger, *Qualitative Research in Marketing* (Chicago; University of Chicago Press, 1976); Gilbert Churchill, *Marketing Research* (New York: Holt, Rinehart & Winston, 1987), pp. 235–236; and D. K. Johnson, "Validity of Focus Group Findings," *Journal of Advertising Research* (June 1978), p. 21.

Illustrative of both the strengths and the weaknesses of focus groups is the experience of a small publishing company that decided to create a series of juvenile mystery books. These were later translated into a syndicated comic strip. The first step in planning the project was running focus group interviews. Their purpose, in the words of the company's president, was "to find out what kids liked and disliked about mystery books that already existed in the marketplace." A number of subsequent focus groups followed to develop fictitious characters and personalities.[9]

It is obvious that the children recruited for focus groups were not representative of all children. The likes and dislikes of the children's universe concerning mystery books could not have been inferred from the focus groups. Quantitative research, with samples projectable to a defined population, was not done. Only quantitative research is capable of describing what children read and what they like to read, and focus group data are qualitative.

The fact that the books were successful is beside the point. Success had nothing to do with the findings concerning likes and dislikes. Success might come about for the wrong reasons, or the right reasons might be coincidental. At any rate, a focus group cannot confirm conclusions about the behavior or attitudes of any market segment.

It is also obvious that books and comic strips are created by artists and writers, not by focus groups. If these creative personnel draw inspiration, hunches, and ideas by listening to groups of children, well and good. There is nothing wrong with managers basing decisions on subjective and intuitive judgments; that is what they are paid to do. And if focus groups helped in that successful endeavor, they made a positive contribution to the project.

To sum up, focus groups are often misused or are used for purposes that are irrelevant. On the other hand, they bring managers and creative personnel in contact with actual consumers. Copywriters can listen to how would-be buyers talk and feel and thus understand how customers go about buying products. These contacts can trigger ideas and align marketing action more closely with that of buyers.

## Individual Methods

There is some question whether individual methods should be classified as forms of marketing research. Many ideas come about informally such as through reading trade magazines, internal reports, and newspapers or through talking to dealers, salespeople, or engineers. Or an idea may simply come out of the blue.

9. B. G. Yovovich, "Creativity Put in Focus (Group)," *Advertising Age* (October 15, 1984), p. 76.

Most of the formal techniques go under the name of morphology. This term implies that some common structure exists. Morphological methods postulate creativity as made up of known components arranged in a unique way, or related to each other in different combinations. Given this premise, the generation of ideas becomes a job of deducing all possible combinations from a set of relevant parameters. This formal process entails two steps:

1. Identifying all relevant factors
2. Developing all combinations of these variables and then choosing the combinations with the best potentials of being translated into market value

Morophological methods have been applied mostly to developing new products rather than transactional devices. One form of morphology is attribute listing, often used in product design. From a complete catalog of product attributes, the designer generates grids representing possible combinations. The difficult part is choosing the most promising ones from alternatives that can run into the millions. This is done mainly by rules of thumb based on experience.[10]

Among the advantages of this method is that it produces many alternatives in a systematic fashion. However, a knowledge of all relevant variables must be present. The outputs, like those of group techniques, serve only as cues to the creative person, who still must convert word sets or concepts to practical ideas.

A variant of this method is forced relationships. It begins, like attribute listing, by enumerating the relevant variables. The creator must then associate each factor with as many possible alternatives as he or she can imagine. The last step links the alternatives by iteration so that the most feasible ones can be chosen for consideration.

Somewhat related to this technique is product-matrix charting. For example, let's say a cataloger wants to create a publication featuring certain types of apparel. One axis might represent many different products. The second axis can be made up of product forms, colors, materials, styles, and other aspects. The idea is to combine the various products with combinations of various product attributes. An example of a product matrix is Table 8-3, which uses two variables: men's apparel types and possible materials. Any number of variables can be added to the columns that indicate material, such as color, style, and degree of formality. As variables are added, the number of possibilities increases geometrically.

10. Edward M. Tauber, "HIT: Heuristic Ideation Technique—A Systematic Procedure for New Product Search," *Journal of Marketing* (January 1972), pp.58–64.

**TABLE 8.3. Product Type–Product Materials Matrix.**

| Apparel Type | Apparel Material | | | | | |
|---|---|---|---|---|---|---|
| | Cotton | Wool | Gabardine | Polyester | Mixed | ... |
| Sweater | | | | | | |
| Shirts | | | | | | |
| Slacks | | | | | | |
| Socks | | | | | | |
| ⋮ | | | | | | |

## Sample Surveys

Sample surveys have many applications to idea generation. There are a great variety of approaches. Some of the more prominent ones are motivation research and synthetic methods.

*Motivation research* was brought into marketing research by Freudian psychologists, such as Ernest Dichter and Hans Zeisel. They believed people cannot truly say why they act the way they do, and that the real answer often lies below the level of consciousness, buried deep in the psyche. These motivation researchers sought to apply clinical techniques to consumers *en masse* to find out what triggers purchases. One such device was the nondirective interview which is associated with free response. Although the true depth interview, falls in the domain of psychiatry, marketing research uses a watered-down version of this technique, putting American consumers, figuratively speaking, on a couch.

*Projective* techniques go hand in hand with nondirective interviews. The idea is to present a person with an ambiguous cue, such as a picture or statement. In interpreting it, the respondent is supposed to reveal the "true inner self." Other projective techniques include such old standbys as word association, sentence completion, and indirect questions.

Motivation research has waned considerably since the halcyon days of the 1950s, but vestiges of the practice remain. The best known is the focus group interview, a counterpart of the group therapy session. Semantic differential scales used in "brand image" studies require respondents to project their feelings by relating a scale's labels to a brand or product.

Another class of surveys, called *synthetic procedures*, explore consumer needs and problems. These use such well-known methods as quadrant analysis, magnitude estimation, and market gap analysis. Although employed mainly in product research, synthetic procedures also have transactional and advertising applications.

*Quadrant analysis* asks consumers to rate attributes according to perceived importance and degree of satisfaction. For each attribute, the

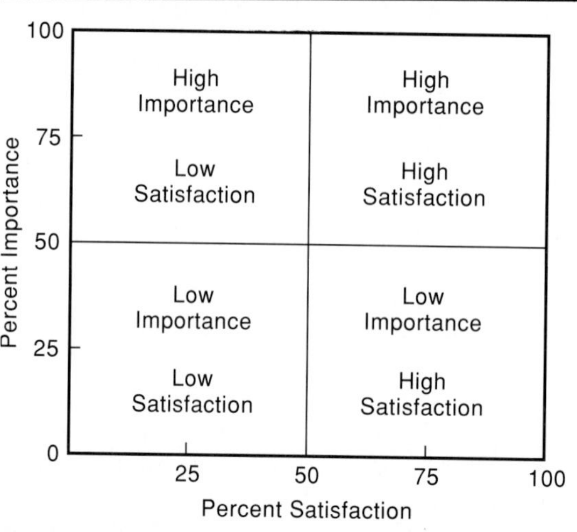


**FIGURE 8-1 An Example of Quadrant Analysis**

level of importance is plotted against the level of satisfaction. This yields a grid that is generally simplified to a four-cell matrix. An example of such a matrix is shown in Figure 8-1.

The high importance–low satisfaction quandrant is the key cell. It supposedly reveals where consumers are dissatisfied in areas they deem important.

Another version of importance-satisfaction rating is magnitude estimation. The same information used in quadrant analysis can be transformed into a magnitude estimation chart. A hypothetical example is the form in Table 8-4.

The table indicates that consumers regard attribute A as more important than B, C, or D and that they are moderately satisfied with the attribute's offer. Attributes can refer to product features or to transactional factors, such as price. Attribute B is also considered important, but consumers are dissatisfied with it. If an offer can overcome that problem, the product might become a strong competitor in the marketplace.

**TABLE 8.4. An Illustration of Magnitude Estimation.**

| Attribute | Importance Rating | × | Percent Dissatisfaction | = | Dissatisfied Score |
|---|---|---|---|---|---|
| A | 80 | | .20 | | 16 |
| B | 70 | | .50 | | 35 |
| C | 60 | | .30 | | 18 |
| D | 40 | | .10 | | 4 |

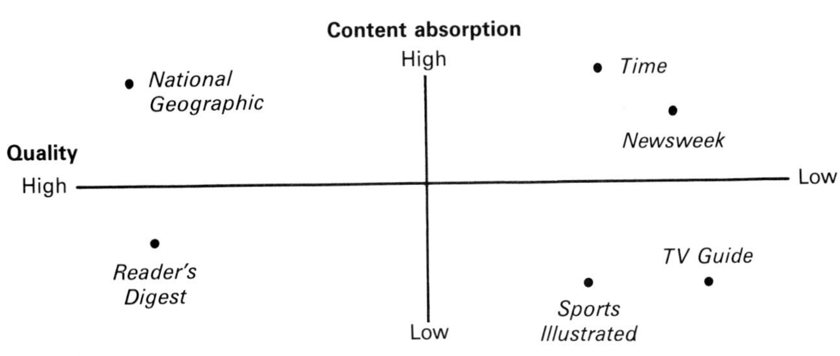


**FIGURE 8-2 Perception Map of Magazines**
*Source:* William S. Sachs and George Benson, *Product Planning and Management* (Tulsa, OK: Pennwell, 1981), p. 392. Reprinted with permission from W. S. Sachs.

*Market gap analysis* is used primarily for developing new products or offers, especially positioning. From that standpoint, it is a form of psychological segmentation. The techniques seek gaps in existing markets with respect to consumer perceptions, benefits, or any other relevant measure of buyer attitudes.

One popular class of research methodology used in market gap analysis is multidimensional scaling. This is a computer-based method that transforms attitudinal data into a set of points in space. Products, perceptions, or attitudes are mapped in certain dimensions. The points on such a map represent psychological distances existing in people's minds. Items falling closest to each other are regarded as similar. This model makes an implicit assumption that products near each other on a space map are substitutable and are therefore highly competitive.

The logic points to developing offers that lie in market gaps or holes as they exist in consumers' minds. A key issue is the potential size of a gap. For example, an offer created to fill a gap may not find a sufficient number of customers who desire certain benefits. Figure 8-2 depicts on a two-dimensional map consumer perceptions of different magazines developed from preference rankings.

# Message-Media Testing

A prominent trait of direct marketers is their penchant to test, test, and retest. The practice rests on the well-founded notion that business decisions should be undertaken with minimum risk.

Direct marketing is admirably suited for testing programs in advance to reduce risks. First, small-scale tests can be run under real market conditions. These tests can measure the actual market response that results from an action. Second, the costs of testing are relatively low.

Since tests produce actual response, they yield revenue; they are never a total loss. There is payback, and successful tests may even cover all out-of-pocket costs.

Testing covers two main elements of a marketing program: copy and media. *Copy* refers to the presentation of the offer or the advertising message. It includes both content and form, what is said and how it is said. *Media* refers to that which carries the commercial message.

Whether marketers test copy or media, estimates are of two kinds: relative and absolute. A relative estimate evaluates one ad in terms of another. Which ad worked best? Often, a test ad is run against a "control," an ad known to generate a highly satisfactory response. In like manner, one media vehicle may be compared with another. The same advertisement can be run in both media and ad response recorded. Since the ad content is held constant, the medium with the stronger pull is the one preferred.

The absolute estimate is a determination of the number of returns an ad will pull and whether it will result in a payout. A winning ad may be the best of a bad lot. It is thus necessary to project response to some known universe, such as mailing lists of a certain size, magazines with a given circulation, or cable television stations with known potentials.

## Message Testing

Testing the effects of a message placed in media is called a *copy test*. These research projects can address the effects of a whole ad or some component. Since the objective of the test is to reduce risk, the subject to be tested must involve a substantive difference in response. It is hardly worthwhile to test the effect of some trivial feature, such as a postage stamp on a mailing envelope. Changing an entire ad represents a larger variation in pull than altering some component. Likewise, testing entire mailing packages involves greater differences than testing smaller parts.

Regardless of what is being tested, the criterion for evaluation is actual response. Unlike copy tests of general advertising, awareness, recall, and attitudes are ignored. Measurement is in terms of orders.

Direct marketing tests can be described by their basic designs. They almost all fall into a class of designs called *experimental*, in which the idea is to manipulate one or more variables while holding all other things constant. Any effect can then be attributed to the tested variables.

THE SINGLE TEST. The simplest test, although not necessarily the most common, is the single-variable, one-time test. Exemplifying this situation is the firm developing a mailing piece for the first time. The manager wishes to know whether the mailing will pay off. A test of this nature can be symbolically represented as follows:

$$X \quad O$$

The symbol X denotes a mailing piece going to a test group, usually a probability sample drawn from a possible list. The symbol O signifies the response of that group to the mailing. Something (X) is presented to people in the sample, and their reactions are measured (O). If the sample is large enough, the mailer may reasonably predict the advertisement's performance and decide whether to go ahead with the mailing on a larger scale.

However, some questions exist as to whether the single-test design constitutes a true experiment. Control over extraneous variables is weak. The timing of the test may affect results, and if no other information were available except test response, predictions of payouts would be hazardous. This test includes the effects of both copy and media.

This model is low-cost, easy to conduct, and can be efficient when the product or offer is wholly new. A key assumption of this model is that the value of O prior to the test is zero. The test must start out without anyone using or being familiar with the product. No one should have seen any advertising for the product. In short, prior consumption levels and knowledge of the product must be nil.

ONE-TIME COMPARISONS. A better way of testing is to compare alternatives. The most elementary example is a test of two different formats of a mailing piece. This can be represented as:

$$\begin{array}{lll} EG: & X_1 & O_1 \\ EG: & X_2 & O_2 \end{array}$$

In this design, two formats are tested with matched experimental groups (EG). These groups are drawn from the same universe so as to be statistically identical. Mailing formats are keyed so that an analyst can trace returns to each message.

Because of seasonal variations, timing can affect the outcome of the test. Another weakness of the straight comparison is that neither format may yield a satisfactory response. To overcome these deficiencies, most tests use a control, a proven alternative. If a control ad is added to the two formats, the test diagram becomes

$$\begin{array}{lll} EG: & X_1 & O_1 \\ EG: & X_2 & O_2 \\ CG: & X_3 & O_3 \end{array}$$

Major extraneous factors are assumed to affect all groups alike, which cancels out their impact. Since the result of the control is known, all other presentations can be assessed against a "winning" program. Theoretically, the comparison test with or without a control can be extended to any number of alternatives.

A/B SPLITS. One form of the posttest in print is the A/B split, in which alternate messages go into every other copy. This method produces two identical samples or matched groups, with each exposed to a different advertisement. Since media effects are held constant by statistical matching, differences in pull can be ascribed to the advertisement.

Many magazines, however, do not offer A/B splits, and newspapers seldom do, except for inserts. When these facilities are available, they are usually limited to two alternatives.

The A/B split applies only to results of a particular issue of a publication. Nevertheless, the test can be generalized to other media on the basis of past experience.

## Issues of Estimating Returns

Since copy and media tests employ samples, estimations contain chance errors. Because response rates are low in direct marketing—a few percentage points—reliable estimates require large samples. Table 8-5 shows sampling errors based on sample size and level of response. These errors are calculated at the 95 percent level of confidence, which reflects the perceived risk. The *absolute error* is expressed as a percentage of the response level. The *relative error* represents the ratio of absolute error to the response level. Given a sample size, absolute error rises as the response level increases. But the corresponding relative error falls. Consequently, promotions that expect higher rates of return can test wi.h smaller samples.

**TABLE 8.5. Sampling Errors at the 95 Percent Confidence Level.**

| | Response Level (%) | | | | |
|---|---|---|---|---|---|
| **Sample Size** | **1.0** | **2.0** | **3.0** | **4.0** | **5.0** |
| | | **Absolute Error** | | | |
| 750 | .70 | 1.00 | 1.22 | 1.04 | 1.56 |
| 1,000 | .61 | .87 | 1.06 | 1.21 | 1.35 |
| 3,000 | .36 | .50 | .61 | .70 | .78 |
| 5,000 | .27 | .39 | .47 | .54 | .60 |
| 7,000 | .23 | .33 | .40 | .46 | .51 |
| 10,000 | .19 | .27 | .33 | .38 | .42 |
| | | **Relative Error (%)** | | | |
| 750 | 70 | 50 | 41 | 35 | 31 |
| 1,000 | 61 | 44 | 35 | 30 | 27 |
| 3,000 | 36 | 25 | 20 | 18 | 16 |
| 5,000 | 27 | 20 | 16 | 14 | 12 |
| 7,000 | 23 | 17 | 13 | 12 | 10 |
| 10,000 | 19 | 14 | 11 | 10 | 8 |

Given a level of response, both absolute and relative error decline as sample size increases. Tests anticipating incremental improvements can reduce sample error only by raising sample size. But the increase in sample size, and consequently in cost, is not proportional to the reduction of sample error. For example, a response rate of 2 percent based on a sample of 750 will have an error of 1 percent. That might be considered large, as it is 50 percent of the estimate. To reduce that error by half, to 0.5 percent, requires a sample of 3,000, four times as large as the original sample.

Sampling error has emerged as the main culprit when programs put into execution never quite achieve their test results. A number of other reasons have been advanced, such as biased lists and name duplication, but the most commonly accepted explanation is that sampling causes a "regression toward the mean."

The argument runs as follows. Suppose a direct marketer tests six lists of equal response value but has to pick only three for the actual marketing campaign. Although all lists should yield the same response rate, sample estimates will not be equal because they contain sampling error. Some tests will show up with higher-than-expected returns. Some lists will test below their true values. The marketer chooses the three lists with the highest test returns, although when these lists are used in their entirety, the return will fall below that suggested by the test on the basis of statistical probability.

This explanation was tested empirically by Raab Associates using 11 years' data of a well-known magazine. The information encompassed 475 mailings to 12.7 million names spread over 188 lists. The author of this analysis concluded that the "regression toward the mean" theory explains only a small part of why actual results fall below those of tests. According to the analysis, the actual drop in response was much greater than predicted, and sample estimates were greatly overstated. Raab therefore recommends much larger samples—about five times larger than those currently used—to achieve desired confidence levels. He also suggests that marketers explore alternative evaluation methods.[11]

A second factor is the inconstancy of media vehicles. This proposition is illustrated here with regard to magazines. Table 8-6 shows summary information for three leading magazines used by direct marketers: *McCall's*, *People*, and *Time*. The table shows average paid circulations as of December 31, 1989, and calculations of ranges and standard deviations for issues during a six-month period.[12]

It is readily apparent that variation exists among magazines and among different issues of the same magazine. For example, *People* issues ranged in circulation from a low of 2.9 million copies to more than

11. David M. Raab, "List Tests: Less Reliable than You Think," *Direct Marketing* (March 1990), pp. 70–74, 95.
12. Figures are based on publishers' statements.

**TABLE 8.6. Circulation Summary.**

| | McCall's | People | Time |
|---|---|---|---|
| Average paid circulation (000) | 3,200 | 3,271 | 4,339 |
| Percent subscriptions | 93 | 46 | 95 |
| Range (000) | 7,892–8,139 | 2,901–4,257 | 4,242–4,442 |
| Standard deviation (000) | 78 | 279 | 46 |

4.2 million copies. Suppose a firm ran a test in the issue of *People* with the highest circulation but just by chance advertised nationally in the one with the lowest circulation. That firm's ad would appear in 1,355,000 fewer copies than projected! And response would certainly fall far below any forecast. Of course, the situation may be reversed. A marketer might test in a low-circulation issue, advertise in a high-circulation issue, and experience exhilarating results. But forecasts based on testing would still contain a certain degree of inaccuracy, even if sampling error were zero.

Knowledge of the standard deviation allows the calculation of various probabilities of change in circulation from issue to issue. These estimates are shown in Table 8-7. Continuing with *People* as an example, Table 8-7 indicates that circulation will differ between test issues and issues carrying the national ad by 190,000 about half the time. Approximately one out of every three tests—a probability of .68—will miss its mark by more than 279,000 copies. The marketer must accept the fact that actual circulation may deviate from that of the test issue by 279,000 copies with a risk factor of 2 to 1. A marketer who wants a better chance of being right must sacrifice predictive accuracy. For example, at odds of 9 to 1, a probability of .90, the deviation between the test issue and the advertised issue is 460,000 copies. *McCall's* and *Time* yield much smaller deviations.

The analysis of normal variations in the media universe leads to the following conclusions as to why forecasts are less accurate than they are thought to be. Although the analysis applies to magazines, it offers insights about tests in other media.

- Because circulation varies from issue to issue, tested ads will result in different numbers of buyers than actual ads placed in national issues.

**TABLE 8.7. Variation in Issue-to-Issue Circulation (000).**

| Probability | McCall's | People | Time |
|---|---|---|---|
| .50 | 53 | 190 | 31 |
| .68 | 78 | 279 | 46 |
| .90 | 129 | 460 | 76 |
| .95 | 153 | 547 | 90 |

- Forecasts will be more accurate if tests are done in magazines that have small issue-to-issue variations. A high percentage of subscription copies seems to reduce fluctuations of individual issues (see Table 8-6). But that implies that actual campaigns will be carried out in the same magazines used for testing. The choice of media should not be determined by research feasibility.
- Forecasts can be either too high or too low according to probability theory. A nagging question is, why do marketers overestimate results more often than not? The answer is that a low response discourages an ad from appearing at all, whereas a high response is positive. Consequently, ads tested in issues with below average circulation have a lesser chance of appearing. There is still a "regression toward the mean," but not because of sampling. The media universe itself is in constant flux.
- The same thing applies to many lists, especially those rented by publishers. Subscribers at one time are nonsubscribers at another time. A publisher must replace from 30 to 50 percent of subscribers annually. Replacement raises more questions about tests. For example, even if new subscribers replace the expired so that circulation is kept at an even level, is the universe the same? Put another way, is the behavior of new subscribers the same as those who were replaced?
- Telescopic tests compound issue-to-issue fluctuations. The coefficient of variation is greater for a region than for an entire edition.

Another issue is long-term effects. A test can only measure immediate response. Does this offer beat the control? Does this ad outdraw the others? Many attractive inducements elicit a high response. But these bargain hunters may not be repeat purchasers, and the short-term euphoria of a high response may give way to a sobering reality.[13] But how can one test an event that takes place in the future? Patience and experience seem to be the only reliable guides.

## Summary

The value of marketing research is its guidance toward better decisions. These decisions involve both planning and monitoring. Since monitoring in direct marketing is part of fulfillment, the chapter focuses on the role of marketing research in the planning process.

Research design can be descriptive or experimental. The main types of descriptive research used in direct marketing are group sessions and surveys conducted with individuals or households. Experimental research primarily entails copy testing and media evaluations.

Descriptive surveys are used to define market parameters. An important source is the Bureau of the Census. Population characteristics are

13. Paul Hawkes, "Offer Testing," *Directions* (January/February 1988), pp. 6, 8.

also described by large list houses, media studies, and private surveys. The last group includes attitude studies, the main purpose of which is to help in the formulation of marketing strategy. The most popular group technique is the focus group interview. These studies are used mainly to stimulate ideas of creative personnel, such as copywriters and art directors.

There are two major types of experiments carried out in direct marketing: copy tests and media tests. The former assumes primacy because copy decisions are always under the control of management. Decisions related to media involve solutions to selection or allocation problems.

The most common type of copy test compares alternatives at the same point in time. Usually a "control" device is used in these tests. Testing is easiest to conduct using the telephone or direct mail. But response rates are generally low, and the need for large samples leads to considerations of cost.

---

## REVIEW QUESTIONS

1. In what main ways does marketing research in direct marketing differ from that of general marketing? In what ways is it similar?
2. What is the purpose of the proposed co-op program by Carol Wright?
3. Why would a direct marketing bother with attitude research when exact figures of response are available for each commercial message?
4. What is the purpose of brainstorming? What are its advantages and disadvantages?
5. Discuss the application of focus groups to direct marketing.
6. Discuss whether motivation research is used in marketing today. Look up and explain such techniques as word association, sentence completion, and indirect questioning.
7. What factors militate against testing response for different components of an advertising message?
8. An advertiser runs an ad in a regional edition of a particular magazine to determine whether that magazine should be used in a national schedule. Comment on the validity of that test.
9. Explain the A/ B split. Is it a true test?
10. Are telescopic tests true experiments?

## PROJECT

1. Jose Lockhart, the current owner of 15 Jose Partes de Automovil de Calidad stores in Mexico, wants to open Jose Quality Auto Parts stores in Spanish communities in the United States. His stores in Mexico are known for selling a quality product at fair prices and for giving excellent service.

   Jose, an MBA graduate of the St. John's University Graduate School, learned that it is very important to develop marketing programs that address the population as a set of distinct market segments. One needs accurate demographic information to make the appropriate decision concerning where to locate one's stores and how to spend one's advertising dollars. Further, ethnic groups are very responsive to promotional programs that emphasize their cultural background.

   **a.** List the 10 largest Hispanic communities (towns or cities) in the United States and give Hispanic population figures. Provide the most current data with the source(s) and pages.

   **b.** Interview three local auto parts store owners or managers as to the different types of customers they have. Provide the type, percentages, and sources for each. (Type refers to either retail or wholesale.)

   **c.** List and discuss three direct marketing methods for promoting Jose Quality Auto Parts stores.

   **d.** Design two promotion pieces to promote the auto parts stores. A promotion piece here is a type of advertising the intent of which is to get the prospect to buy the product or to go to the store. It is fine to work in black and white and to use stick figures. If you prefer, you may do it in color. A paste job is also approved. Neatness and clarity count as part of the grade.

CHAPTER 9

# Fulfillment and Customer Service

## PROFILE

**LEE EPSTEIN**

**Direct Marketing Expert.** Lee Epstein is president and founder of MAILMEN INC., a volume mailing and computer service company located in Hauppauge, Long Island. Well known in the direct marketing industry, he has been honored for his dedication to sharing his knowledge of postal affairs to educate members of the advertising community.

He has served as industry chairman and is currently a member of the Postmaster General's Technical Advisory Committee (MTAC). Lee is a board member and a former chairman of the board of the Third Class Mail Association. He is founder, board member, and a past president of the Direct Marketing Club of New York. In 1984, they named him Direct Marketer of the Year and, in 1986, made him a recipient of their coveted Silver Apple Award. He serves as treasurer and member of the board of the John Caples International Awards (Direct Marketing Creative Guild).

The Long Island Direct Marketing Association named him Man of the Year in 1982. In 1984, the Direct Marketing Association List Council presented him with their List Leader of the Year Award for his contribution to the industry. In 1985, the Direct Marketing Computer Association gave him their Lifetime Membership Award.

A sought-after speaker at national postal forums and direct marketing clubs, he has also written many articles and chapters for direct mail and marketing books, including *Direct Mail Advertising and Selling for Retailers*, for the National Retail Merchants Association; *The Direct Marketing Handbook*, published by McGraw-Hill; and the DMA Fulfillment Monograph.

He has represented the industry before congressional committees and the Postal Rate Commission on postal matters, and is the recipient of the U.S. Postal Service's Distinguished Service Award. An expert in mass marketing, he provides the necessary technical knowledge and support needed by this industry.

Lee is president and chairman of the board of Direct Marketing Day in New York. It is a nonprofit corporation that sponsors direct marketing educational activities in the New York area. To date, the board has spent funds for education in excess of $1,000,000. ■

# What Is Fulfillment?

The term *fulfillment* is used in the trade literature in a bewildering variety of ways. It means different things to different people. Under the fulfillment heading, authors have included such things as list maintenance, promotional mailings, customer relations, form design, mailing pieces, and back-end operations. To say that there is no agreement among marketers as to what constitutes fulfillment is an understatement.

One reason for the absence of any agreement on meaning is that different industries operate in different modes and hence give different definitions to fulfillment. Another reason is that practically all direct marketing functions—promotion, customer service, and fulfillment—run off a database. This necessitates computer processing, which becomes the stepping stone for practically all operations. Managers from various parts of a company become intertwined with computer and database personnel. In those circumstances, database management overlaps promotional, fulfillment, and customer relations. Often there is no strict dividing line between these functions, since their performance is partially dependent on database and computers.

Direct marketing can be divided into three broad functional areas: promotion, physical distribution, and customer service. Promotion includes activities meant to create transactions. Physical distribution is concerned with the movement of goods and constitutes the heart of fulfillment. Customer service handles such diverse functions as requests for information, complaints, returns of merchandise, and nondeliveries of orders.

Not all companies use databases for all three functions. Some firms employ databases for promotion only. For example, Kimberly-Clark sends new mothers coupons for Huggies, which are redeemed at retail outlets. The company also follows up these coupon drops with mailouts of literature about baby growth and child development. Ukrops Super Markets of Virginia maintains an on-line database that allows shoppers to present identification cards at checkout counters to get coupon rebates and volume discounts.[1] Auto dealerships use databases to send out promotional literature to customers and prospects. In all these instances, companies do not engage in physical distribution. No goods are sold away from the store and delivered afterward. Consequently, there is no direct marketing fulfillment.

Only when items are shipped as a result of orders does direct marketing involve physical distribution. The company fulfills a request for goods on terms previously agreed on. This activity is actually something that happens after the sale is made, and it is therefore a posttransactional undertaking. It generates no revenue; it only incurs costs.

---

1. Lynn G. Coleman, "Data-Base Masters Become King of the Marketplace," *Marketing News* (February 18, 1991), p. 13.

The division between promotion and physical distribution, however, is not always neat and clean. Order taking, conventionally regarded as a part of physical distribution, might entail personal selling. For example, telephone operators frequently try to sell other items when taking an order, especially any items related to the order.

Nevertheless, firms engaged in physical distribution do not perform the same fulfillment functions. A major element in shaping fulfillment operations is the nature of demand.

For example, a magazine publisher assigns responsibility for delivery of subscription copies to its circulation department. This section also manages the database. Among its tasks is the preparation of labels, batched according to postal carrier routes and affixed to subscriber copies at the printing plant. The tasks here are no different from those of promotional mailings. The circulation department also scans computer records continuously to send out renewal notices to customers well before subscriptions expire.

Fulfillment in publishing houses thus centers on computer processing and takes on revenue-producing tasks. Getting magazines ready for delivery is more or less a routine function of a circulation department, since demand is known long in advance. Far more important is the ability to control demand; expirees must be balanced against new subscribers to maintain circulation at desired levels. This function entails promotion, not fulfillment.

In contrast, catalog fulfillment involves much greater complexity of operations. There is no single product sent out at fixed intervals in known quantities. Rather, there are many products, kept in inventory and demanded at varying intervals at varying rates. Fulfillment encompasses the full span of physical distribution functions: entering orders, controlling inventory, warehousing, and shipping out orders. In other words, fulfillment covers everything that happens from the receipt of an order to the shipment of the product to the customer or subscriber.

Many catalog houses relate delivery to customer service. Some firms place customer service and order filling in separate departments. Others combine them into one.

Because consumers buy goods blindly, as it were, there are bound to be disappointments and complaints. The Better Business Bureaus record more consumer complaints about direct marketing than any other business activity.[2] Stanley J. Fenvessey, a management consultant, describes customer service as the last step in the fulfillment cycle.[3] His concept of fulfillment relationships is instructive and is reproduced in Figure 9-1.

---

2. Kevin Higgins, "Mail Order Industry Is Fighting the Old, Sleazy Image on Several Fronts," *Marketing News* (July 8, 1983), pp. 1,12.
3. See Edward L. Nash, *Direct Marketing* (New York: McGraw-Hill, 1982), pp. 372–373; Stanley J. Fenvessey, "Introduction to Fulfillment," *DMA Release* 500.1 (October 1979); Carol Faumenhaft, "Fulfillment Order Processing Suggestions," *DMA Release* 500.1d (October 1979).

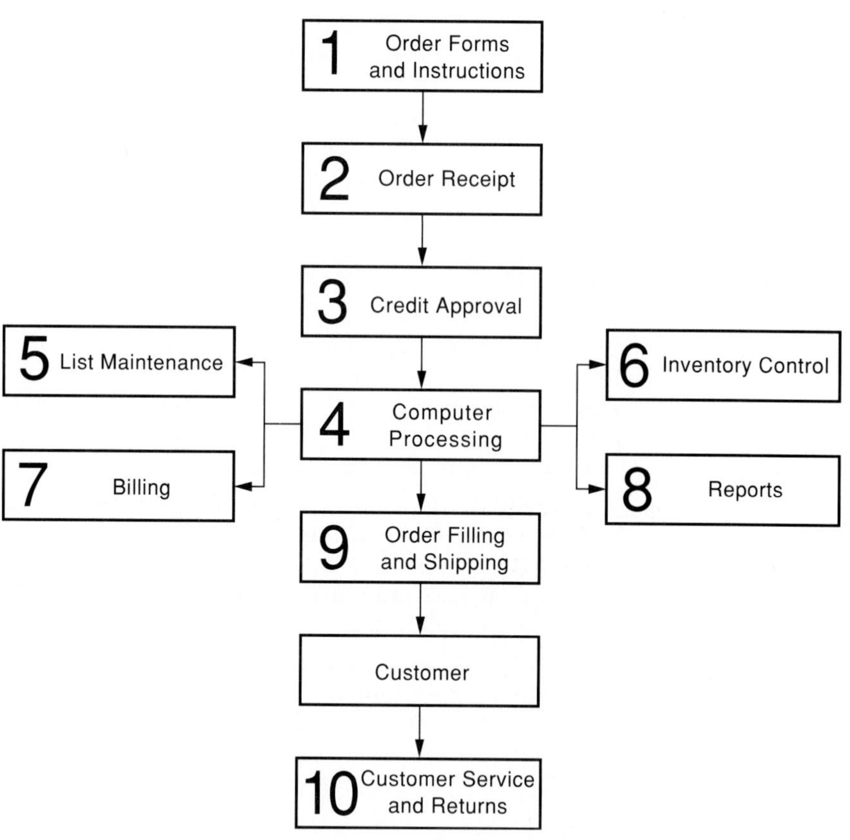


**FIGURE 9-1 Ten Steps in the Fulfillment Cycle**
*Source*: Stanley J. Fenvessey, *Fenvessey on Fulfillment* (Stamford, CT: Catalog Age, 1988), p. 3.

In Figure 9-1, functions 1, 2, 3, 4, 9, and 10 clearly involve physical distribution and constitute the main body of fulfillment functions. Items 6 and 8 are integral parts of order-filling activities, though many direct marketing firms do not carry on these tasks. Function 5 is more closely associated with revenue-generating actions, such as selling and promotion. Function 7, billing, properly belongs in the accounts receivable department. Invoices are consequences of transactions, though these documents are usually made up when goods are shipped.

Figure 9-1 also shows computer processing at the center of all steps in the fulfillment cycle-order filling, customer service, inventory control, list maintenance, and accounts receivable. Since companies do not operate uniformly, the fulfillment mix varies from company to company. Some use computer processing primarily for order getting, whereas others employ computers mainly for order-filling tasks.

# Physical Distribution

Though the computer ties promotion and fulfillment to each other in some respects, the two functions can be separated. The distinguishing feature is the relationship of tasks to transactions. Promotional and selling activities attempt to create transactions. Fulfillment is concerned with carrying out the terms of the transaction, such as delivering to customers the goods they ordered. In that sense, fulfillment takes on physical distribution characteristics. It relates to posttransactional activities. It acts as a cost center, not an income generator.

The identification of fulfillment with data processing has been a source of confusion, the effect of which has been to mix physical distribution with selling.[4] Insurance companies, for example, have sophisticated record-keeping systems for servicing and renewing customer contracts. But because they do not deliver tangible products, there is no physical distribution and, hence, no fulfillment in the traditional sense. Likewise, a number of other service organizations—real estate brokers and financial houses, to name a few—sell products through direct marketing techniques, but they service accounts without physical distribution. A brokerage house may execute an order, such as buying or selling certain securities. But nothing is delivered except a confirmation of the trade and a settling of balances afterward. Except for possibly a stock certificate, no physical item is transferred from one place to another.

Defining fulfillment in the narrow sense of physical distribution, we can outline its major aspects without ambiguity. Every system designed to deliver goods to customers has four main parts: order entry and communication, inventory, warehousing, and transportation.

## Order Entry

Physical distribution begins with receipt of an order. The order form facilitates entering an order, especially when products are many and highly diverse. Simple, clearly marked choices reduce errors in encoding and processing an order.

The heart of order processing is the computer. To cut down on clerical work—and clerical errors as well—order forms are often preaddressed. Direct marketers use a number of other devices to ensure that vital delivery information is accurately input. For example, providing boxes for single numbers and letters encourages printing of names and addresses. These forms ostensibly give clerks fewer problems with interpreting bad handwriting. Orders can be entered into a computer di-

4. *Ibid.*

rectly, or they may be batched and entered later. This holds for both mail and telephone.

Orders coming in by telephone, however, present a different set of problems from those of mail. For many catalogs, more than 50 percent of all orders come in by phone. For goods featured in electronic media, almost 100 percent are ordered by telephone. Telephone operators record the purchase while the caller is still on the phone, either into the computer or onto a log from which the information is transferred later. A telephone order taking system requires that operators be trained to communicate with the person on the other end and to record orders accurately.

A major problem in order taking by telephone relates to sharp peak levels of incoming calls.[5] Customers often are made to wait, and they may abandon their attempts to place orders. It is widely recommended that abandonment rates not exceed 5 percent, with 2 percent considered optimal.[6]

Fenvessey argues that interactive voice response "is certain to have a major place in the future of direct marketing" because it can streamline order taking.[7] With this process, a customer can enter an order and ascertain if an item is out-of-stock or available, without the intervention of a live operator. The system works as follows:

1. On calling, the customer receives a prerecorded message that initiates the transaction.
2. The caller can respond to certain prompts by pressing touch-tone keys on the telephone.
3. Each touch-tone entry is confirmed orally over the phone by a computer.

Banks and brokerage houses employ this technique to let customers complete transactions. Airlines, financial houses, and large corporations use the system for various purposes, such as passing callers to appropriate extensions or providing information on account balances and interest rates. Although interactive voice response has potential, Fenvessey's prediction has yet to come true—if it does.

Credit approval and payment verification are part of any order entry system. Dollar amounts and prepaid orders must be cross-checked. When payments by check run to large amounts, orders may be sent to a holding file until bank verification arrives. In the case of credit, computers examine customers' previous purchases, payments, and balances. Computers can also initiate outside credit checks for new customers,

---

5. "Customer Service: More than a Necessary Evil," *Target Marketing* (September 1989), pp. 91–92.
6. *Ibid*.
7. Stanley J. Fenvessey, "New Forums of Business Communication," *DM News* (January 1, 1989), pp. 23, 52.

especially when orders involve large dollar amounts. Exact credit limits and cutoff points depend on policies adopted by individual companies.

Order processing also involves billing. Sellers do want to get paid for their merchandise. This step is necessary no matter how payment is made—by time payments, open account, credit cards, or other means. Direct marketers have three billing approaches available to them: prebilling, postbilling, and a combination of the two.

PREBILLING. Most direct marketers employ the prebilling system, in which the computer prepares an invoice before the merchandise is assembled. This approach works best when shipping and handling charges are predetermined and the computer contains complete, up-to-date information on inventories.

In this situation, the computer sends invoices along with order selection and shipping instructions. At the warehouse, invoices are adjusted for out-of-stock items. When a perpetual inventory exists, a sophisticated computer systems can readily ascertain whether specific items are at hand. This check obviates most adjustments.

POSTBILLING. Postbilling is frequently used in fulfilling orders from businesses. A major reason is that the company wants to inform its customers which carriers will be transporting the goods and on which dates.

This approach returns copies of order selection and shipping documents, with any adjustments, for keying into the computer. In some operations, a separate invoice is prepared at the shipping point and mailed to the customer.

COMBINATION. Some companies prebill cash customers and postbill those who buy through credit. This method applies to consumer purchases.[8]

## Inventory

General inventory concepts are the same for all products, whether consumer or industrial goods, whether products of resellers or of manufacturers. Resellers have relatively wide assortments in their warehouses. In general, manufacturers have fewer varieties of individual items but different types of inventories, such as raw materials and work-in-process inventories. Whether it involves a reseller or a manufacturer, direct marketing is concerned primarily with finished goods. These may be intermediate or end products. The former go to industrial firms, the latter to consumers.

8. Stanley J. Fenvessey, *Fenvessey on Fulfillment* (Stamford CT: Catalog Age, 1988).

A number of physical distribution texts deal with inventory policy in great detail.[9] Students interested in that subject should consult these books. The purpose of this section is not to recount every nuance of that topic. Rather, it is to highlight fulfillment practices in direct marketing as they relate to physical distribution.

Customer demand determines the outflow rate; sales govern the speed at which goods go out of inventory and are sent to buyers. Physical distribution controls only the replenishment and base level of inventories. An order that cannot be filled because a product is unavailable is called a *stockout*. An efficient inventory policy seeks to replace goods so that stockouts and excess supplies are minimal. These objectives raise two fundamental questions:

1. How often should goods be ordered?
2. In what quantities should they be ordered?

These two questions are answered by the *economic order quantity* model, widely referred to as EOQ.

THE EOQ MODEL. The EOQ model is a basic concept of inventory management. It answers the two prime questions by balancing out conflicting costs between order frequency and order quantity.

If goods are ordered at frequent intervals, order costs rise. These costs are "fixed" in the sense that they are not proportional to the size of an order. They include such elements as office work, order processing and transmission, loading and unloading at the dock, and transportation.

A second set of costs arise from carrying inventories. These charges are variable; they correspond to the volume of goods on hand. Carrying cost include such items as warehouse space, depreciation, insurance, taxes, obsolescence, and capital costs tied up in inventory.

Orders for large quantities of goods increase average carrying costs. Conversely, orders for small quantities lessen carrying costs but increase ordering costs. Given a demand, reducing the size of orders increases the frequency of orders. An EOQ model calculates the quantity that will minimize total costs—the combination of ordering and carrying costs. An example of an EOQ model is shown in Figure 9-2.

As can be seen in the figure, order costs fall as the quantity ordered increases. The larger the quantity per order, the fewer orders must be placed. On the other hand, carrying costs rise in proportion to the size of an order. Lowest total costs correspond to the quantity at which the two curves intersect. In Figure 9-2, the minimum total cost of inventory equals an annualized amount of $142,000. The optimal order quantity is roughly 283,000 units. The average amount of stock in inventory would

9. See Donald Bowersox, *Logistical Management*, 3rd ed. (New York: Macmillan, 1986); D. M. Lambert and J. R. Stock, *Strategic Physical Distribution Management* (Homewood, IL: Richard D. Irwin, 1982).

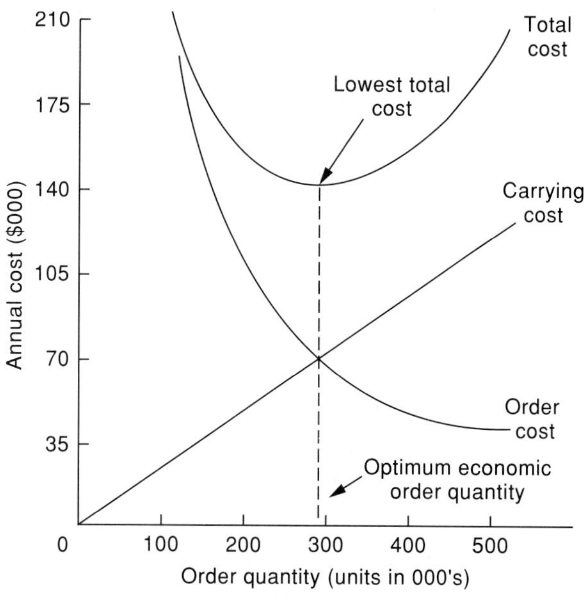


**FIGURE 9-2 An Example of an EOQ Model**

be 141,500 units, calculated as half the economic order quantity. For accounting purposes, its value would be 141,500 times the unit cost of the product.

The EOQ model assumes a constant sales rate. If the entire order runs out in 52 days, average daily sales would amount to 5,442 units. By the end of the 52-day period, the base inventory is assumed to fall to zero. If sales of this item are to continue, inventory will have to be replenished. A model of this sort is depicted in Figure 9-3.

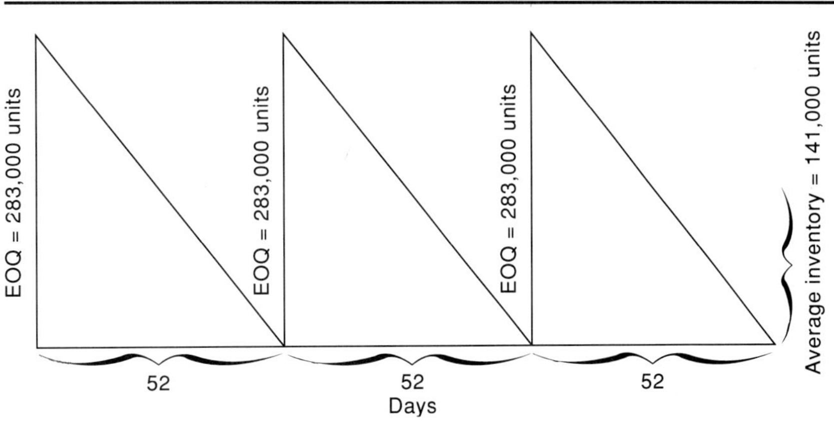


**FIGURE 9-3 Inventory with Constant Demand**

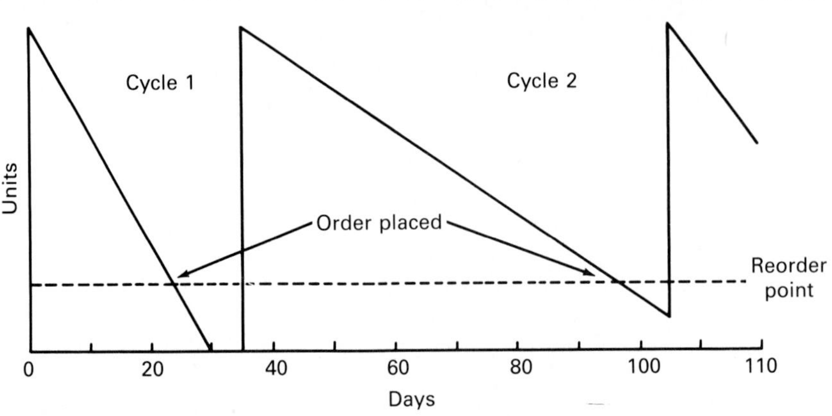


**FIGURE 9-4 Q System for Base Stock**

EOQ VARIATIONS. Few firms can use the basic EOQ model unaltered because of its inherent limitations. Its assumptions violate the flux and uncertainty of the real world. Retailers in particular work in an environment where sales fluctuate from day to day, month to month, and season to season. Deliveries do not always arrive with pinpoint precision exactly when base inventories reach zero.

The EOQ concept has many modifications. The two basic ones are the P and Q systems. The P system calls for orders placed at fixed intervals, as in Figure 9-2. However, the quantity varies depending on the sales rate. Higher sales in a period trigger larger orders. Slower sales lead to smaller orders. The estimation of lead time—how long it takes for an order to arrive from the time it was placed—must be figured into the order quantity that brings stocks up to a given level.

The Q system varies the time of ordering but keeps the order quantity fixed. Orders are placed when stocks fall to a predetermined level, the reorder point. Timing is usually set by the sales rate and the replenishment cycle. In this system, higher sales occasion more frequent orders. Slower sales mean less frequent placement of orders. Figure 9-4 depicts a Q system.

Note that cycle 1 in the diagram indicates robust sales and, consequently, a rapid decline of inventories. The reorder point is reached in 25 days. Cycle 2 stretches to some 60 days after the last shipment, indicating a period of slow sales.

As can be inferred from Figure 9-4, the Q system is more responsive to variations in sales. In cycle 1, for example, the Q system reduces the deficiency, that is, stock falling below the base level, compared to that under a P system. On the other hand, when sales slow, the Q system delays the reorder of goods. Because of their greater flexibility, Q systems tend to reduce safety stocks and, hence, carrying costs. But they must be monitored more carefully and are therefore best applied to higher-priced goods.

SAFETY STOCK. Reorder points and Q systems may ameliorate the effects of stockouts, but they do not prevent them. Protection against stockouts is assigned to safety stock. These supplies are additions to base inventories.

One type of uncertainty resulting in a stockout is a higher-than-expected sales rate. There are two methods for setting up safety stock levels. One is to estimate stockout costs and balance them against costs of keeping buffer items. This route to a shelter against uncertainty is hazardous. The more common method is to specify a desired level of protection and then set safety stock accordingly. This is done by applying statistical probability. A frequency distribution of average daily sales is derived by sampling past data. The standard deviation around the average of this distribution provides the basis for calculating the amount of protection needed.

How does this work? Suppose we took such a sample and found the distribution followed a normal curve, as illustrated in Figure 9-5. Further, suppose we want enough safety stock to fill 90 percent of all incoming orders during a 10-day period. Direct marketers call this the *fill ratio.* At least 90 percent of catalog orders for staple items are completed. Fashion-oriented goods have much lower percentages—many less than 80 percent.[10]

Knowing average daily sales and its standard deviates allows the analyst to estimate safety stock at any desired level of protection. Figure 9-5 shows that if we want to be in stock 90 percent of the time, we would have to maintain stock representing 1.3 normal standard deviation, the area under the curve that would encompass 90 percent of daily sales. The safety stock could then be estimated by the formula.

$SS = PL(SD)\sqrt{LT}$, where
$SS$ = Safety stock
$PL$ = Protection level, expressed in normal standard deviation
$SD$ = Standard deviation of average daily sales
$LT$ = Lead time, expressed in days

Suppose we found the standard deviation of average daily sales to be 1,000 units, and the lead time is 10 days. Then the solution to the equation would be

$$SS = 1.3(1,000)\sqrt{10} = 4,110 \text{ (rounded)}$$

10. *Fenvessey on Fulfillment, op. cit.,* p. 8.

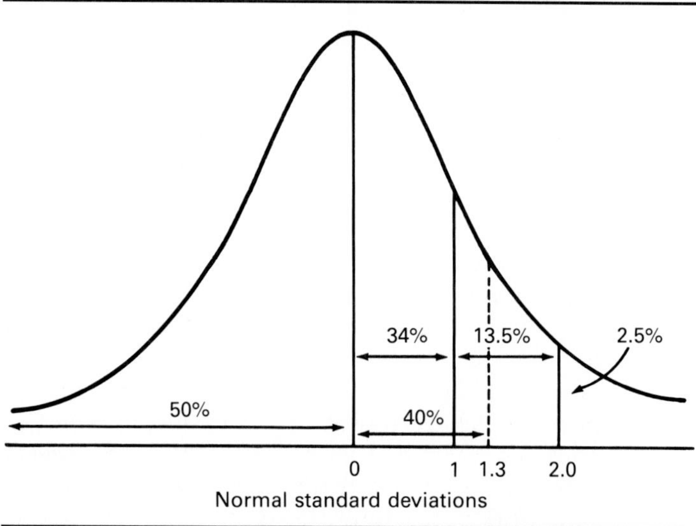


**FIGURE 9-5 Normal Distribution of Average Daily Sales**

This solution protects against one type of contingency—sales variation. But there are other kinds of departures from expectations, such as delayed deliveries. To safeguard against late shipments, the same probability approach is used. To protect against both types of uncertainties at the same time, the marketer must combine two frequency distributions and estimate the standard deviation of the combination. Estimations can be derived by formula when distributions are normal or Poisson. If they assume different shapes, the analyst must fall back on computer simulation.

ZERO BACKLOGS. Many of the most efficient fulfillment operations have adopted the concept of *zero backlogs*.[11] This technique adopts a currency operating goal. A small amount of unfilled orders from the previous day are left over and filled in the morning; after that, incoming orders are processed the same day. Its proponents claim that adherence to this schedule can increase productivity by as much as 40 percent. To do so, the firm must be able to forecast incoming orders accurately and establish efficient work schedules.

This technique is akin to the Japanese technique of *kanban*, in which supplies arrive at manufacturing plants immediately as they are needed. Fulfillment centers using this method must provide a high level of service, for they work with no allowable backlogs. Among direct marketers relying on zero backlog approaches are Quill Corporation, In-

11. *Ibid.*, pp. 259–260.

mac, Brookstone, and General Nutrition. Each firm ships 75 percent of its orders on the day of receipt.

FASHION GOODS. Some consumer goods sold through direct marketing are one-time purchases. Requiring little or no reordering, these goods stand in stark contrast to stock with a relatively stable demand. To handle orders of this type, firms forecast demand for a given period, and this estimate determines the stock on hand. Inventory stocking of such one-time orders is often referred to as *open-to-buy planning.*

Fashion merchandise and highly seasonal items may use one-time ordering for inventory. Not expecting demand to stretch beyond a specific point in time, purchasing agents are reluctant to plan for reordering. They have no plans to replenish inventories once goods run out.

Nevertheless, a single-order policy may foreclose opportunities, especially if demand for some items is stronger than expected. Buyers are entrapped by one-order commitments, yet they will not accept liability for reorders. Firms that have buying leverage can escape this dilemma by pressuring suppliers to keep reorder lines open for them. The channel policies of large department stores and catalog houses shift risks of holding inventory onto suppliers. These direct marketers pursue policies of "postponement," but suppliers are forced to undertake practices of "speculation."

## Warehousing

Warehousing encompasses everything done with goods from the time they are acquired for inventory to the time they are shipped out to customers. Most direct marketers are unfamiliar with warehousing, primarily because efficient warehouse operations are more closely allied with industrial engineering than with marketing techniques.

A firm doing direct marketing can fill orders in two basic ways: in-house or out-of-house. Fulfillment from private warehouses provides greater control and generally lower costs. The outside fulfillment house calculates a certain margin for profits, money that the private operator is able to save. The greatest obstacles to marketers having their own warehouses are sales volume and financial resources. Both must be adequate. This is why large direct marketing operations do their own fulfillment and small operations seek services from the outside.

A warehouse involves a long-term investment spread over a period running from 20 to 40 years. A large sales volume is necessary to justify such investments. Outlays for warehouses represent fixed costs in plant and equipment, and operating units must generate sufficient revenue to cover the overhead. Variable unit costs of a warehouse have a U-shaped curve, reaching their lowest point at somewhere between 70 percent and 85 percent of capacity. This cost pattern presents another cogent reason for a large, steady volume. If sales are low or highly variable, the warehouse will not run at an economical level.

Warehouses are built with customized designs to take advantage of a firm's unique products, and these special features make warehouses difficult to sell in the event of adversity. When all factors are brought together, a decision to build a private warehouse is reserved for companies that can afford all the risks.

Many retailers selling identical products through store and nonstore outlets can use the same facilities for keeping inventories. Common warehouses offer economies of scope. In some instances, however, companies selling through different channels keep separate inventories. This synergistic violation is more apt to happen in consumer fields than in industrial areas. General merchandisers such as Saks Fifth Avenue and Bloomingdale's have special warehouses for direct marketing. Stores are supplied by different centers.[12] Apparently, the requirements for direct marketing are large enough, and sufficiently different from those of retailing, to warrant special inventories and fulfillment centers.

Warehouse functions fall into two basic categories: movement and storage. Since direct marketing handles finished goods primarily, warehouse operations in this regard are geared toward movement. The structures housing goods are essentially distribution centers that concentrate on receiving and shipping out goods for fulfillment of orders.

Movement is related to the rearrangement of products into customer-specified assortments. The heart of the process is order picking. Movement functions also include packing and preparing orders for shipping, which involves weighing, metering, and manifesting.

Storage includes receiving, inspecting, and holding goods. It can be either "temporary" or "permanent." Temporary storage refers to holding items in base inventory and is therefore intimately related to movement.

Warehouses handle goods either by manual or automated systems. The most common method is still manual, with the forklift as its centerpiece. These systems have used palletization principles for some 40 years. In recent years, however, a number of electronic devices have come into use that have resulted in automation in picking, weighing, metering, manifesting, packing, stacking, and retrieval.

## Transportation

Transportation is the last stage of the physical distribution process. Warehouse control ceases when goods leave the dock for their final destinations.

---

12. Don Abramson, "What Retailers Must Learn About Fulfillment," *DM News* (June 1, 1984), p. 28.

Most goods sold by direct marketers, especially to consumers, go out in packages weighing less than 50 pounds. These light shipments are often referred to as parcels. The most popular delivery method is the United Parcel Service (UPS), which accounts for about 94 percent of all mail order shipments.[13] The U. S. Postal Service (USPS) and Federal Express are also capable of small parcel deliveries.

Direct marketers selling to businesses usually ship larger quantities than those dealing with consumers. Small shipments to businesses are almost always sent out on trucks. Whether private or common carriers are more efficient depends on a number of factors, such as volume of shipments, distance, and return hauls.

Shipping and handling costs of consumer goods have inched up every year, and more and more companies have been passing those charges on to customers. The ratio of those charges to the value of orders has also been going up. A number of traffic departments have recently made efforts to reduce outbound transportation costs. There are five main approaches available to direct marketers to reduce costs of shipping.[14]

- *Package weight reduction.* A number of package engineering devices can reduce shipping costs. Among them are elimination of overpacking, use of lighter packing material, and use of bags instead of boxes when possible.
- *Delivery expenses study.* This type of study compares the actual method used with alternative forms. UPS provides customers with delivery expense analysis free of charge. The study is objective and includes delivery modes other than UPS.
- *USPS third-class bulk.* In some instances, shippers can employ third-class bulk mail if they have shipments of at least 50 pounds or 200 parcels, each weighing under $15\frac{1}{2}$ ounces. These parcels must be sorted into bags according to mail centers or ZIP codes. If a firm can use this method for its delivery service, it can achieve substantial savings.
- *Drop shipments.* Parcels may be shipped to a distant UPS or USPS distribution center, from which it is delivered locally. The shipment can be made either by private or contract carrier. This method is feasible if a shipper has a sufficiently large volume to fill a trailer with a certain frequency.
- *Alternative delivery systems.* Recently, a number of independent delivery systems have sprung up to compete with UPS and USPS. However, routes are limited, and service may also have certain limitations.

---

13. *Fenvessey on Fulfillment, op. cit.*, pp. 265–267.
14. *Ibid.*

# Customer Service

Customer service means different things to different companies. Some companies equate customer service with public relations. Financial houses render their customers service by providing them with data on stock prices, company operations, security issues, forecasts on industry trends, account balances, and other matters of concern. Other industries emphasize after-sale activities and product support. Our discussion will focus on customer service related to fulfillment.

Fulfillment raises three main issues with respect to customer service.[15] These relate to:

1. Timing of deliveries
2. Product availability
3. Quality of delivery

## Timing of Deliveries

The issue of timing primarily concerns the speed with which customers receive the goods they order. Many sales are impelled by impulse. However, the initial ardor of impulse buyers cools quickly when delivery is slow, leading to cancellations and returns. Certain goods must be delivered in season, such as nursery stock and garden supplies. But for most merchandise, consumers prefer fast deliveries.

Another force that encourages timely delivery is government. The FTC 30-day rule, with certain exceptions, stipulates that firms must complete orders within 30 days. If shipment cannot be made within that time, the company must notify customers of that fact and give them the option of getting their money back (see Figure 9-6).[16]

The timing of shipments to business customers raises different considerations. These firms are evidently ordering goods for their own warehouses, and speedier deliveries shorten their inventory performance cycles. Quicker shipments also allow business customers to lower average inventories. Many industrial firms insist on consistency as well as speed in shipment. Both speed and consistency are cornerstones for building an effective delivery system.

---

15. See James L. Heskett *et al.*, *Business Logistics*, 2nd ed. (New York: Ronald Press, 1973); Bert Rosenbloom, "Using Physical Distribution Strategy for Better Channel Management," *Journal of Academy of Marketing Science* (Winter/Spring 1979), pp. 61–99; Peter Gilmour, "Customer Service: Differentiating by Market Segment," *International Journal of Physical Distribution and Materials Management*, vol. 12, no. 3 (1982), p. 38.

16. See Chapter 2.

Dear Customer:

The merchandise you have ordered is temporarily out of stock. A new supply is expected, and we will process your order as soon as possible.

Please use this pre-paid postcard. Space is provided for instructions regarding your order.

**If we do not receive this card** within 30 days, and have not shipped your order, a refund or cancellation will be issued.

We are sorry for any inconvenience this may have caused.

MAIL ORDER DEPARTMENT
THE METROPOLITAN MUSEUM OF ART

☐ HOLD MY ORDER AND SHIP AS SOON AS POSSIBLE

☐ CANCEL MY ORDER

☐ I WOULD LIKE TO CHANGE MY ORDER TO: ____________________

**FIGURE 9-6 FTC 30-Day Notification**
*Source*: Reproduced from Stanley J. Fenvessey, *Fenvessey on Fulfillment* (Stamford, CT: Catalog Age, 1988), p. 70.

## Product Availability

Product availability refers to ordered items being in stock. Stockouts cause lost sales. The cost of protection against stockouts is high relative to the benefits afforded. A policy of zero stockouts is neither practical nor affordable. Under these circumstances, how much shortage in stock should a company abide?

Company managers hold conflicting views about stockout policies. One issue is cash flow. A reduction of inventories increases cash flow by having fewer goods tied up in storage. But lower inventories also cause stockouts, which in turn lower sales and cash inflows. Where is the cutoff point?

Consumers who order items not in stock have numerous courses of action open to them. First, they can substitute another item for the one not in stock. This new item can bear a higher, lower, or similar price. The choice of a substitute product can cause sales volume to increase, decrease, or stay constant. Second, some customers may agree to wait until the out-of-stock item is replenished at the warehouse. In this event, the company incurs the additional cost of a back order and possibly that of expedited shipment. Third, customers may cancel their orders, choosing not to wait. This choice creates a lost sale. Finally, customers may be so miffed that they will not order again. Here the company loses customers and the revenue connected with their potential future purchases.

Unfortunately, the costs of these various outcomes are almost impossible to measure accurately. Instead, they are commonly estimated in a general way, and differences of opinion are bound to exist. But judgement decisions must be made in formulating stockout policies.

FROM:

*Thank You for shopping with* Williams-Sonoma . . . *Your satisfaction is very important to us.*

*Our goal, in both our catalog and our stores, is to present the best quality cooking and serving equipment available. If, at any time, you have received an item from* Williams-Sonoma *that you feel does not measure up to this standard, please return it to us for a replacement or a refund. We stand behind our products.*

*Sincerely,*

PLEASE PRINT

clip here

TO: WILLIAMS-SONOMA
CUSTOMER RETURNS DEPT.
4300 Concorde Road
Memphis, TN 38118

clip here

1. **NAME** ____ Day Time Telephone ( ) ____
2. **THIS ITEM WAS:** ☐ Purchased by me ☐ A Gift to me
3. **TO RETURN MERCHANDISE WHICH IS NOT DAMAGED:**
   — Please enclose this packing slip and all related correspondence in your package. A letter sent separately may cause a delay.
   — Address your package with the label above. — Insure your package and save the receipt.
   • **WHAT IS BEING RETURNED?**
   ITEM NO. ____ QTY. ____ / ITEM NO. ____ QTY. ____
   • **REASON FOR RETURN:** ☐ Defective ☐ Wrong Item in box ☐ Not as Expected ☐ Too Late ☐ Wrong Item on Packing Slip ☐ Item Ordered Not in Box
   Comments: ____
   • **ACTION YOU WISH:** ☐ Please Exchange for ITEM NO. ____ QTY. ____
   ☐ Replace ☐ Refund ☐ Merchandise Voucher ☐ Credit ☐ M/C ☐ Visa ☐ Am. Express ☐ Other
   Card Number ____ Name on Charge Card ____ Expiration Date ____
4. **IF AN ITEM ARRIVES DAMAGED:**
   —Call us at (415) 421-4555 or write to: WILLIAMS-SONOMA, Customer Service Department
   100 North Point, San Francisco, California 94133.
   — Be sure to enclose this packing slip with your letter. We will advise you as to what to do with the damaged merchandise.

**FIGURE 9-7 An Example of a Merchandise Return Instruction Form**
*Source*: Stanley J. Fenvessey, *Fenvessey on Fulfillment* (Stamford, CT: Catalog Age, 1988), p. 178.

## Delivery Quality

Two considerations relate to delivery. One is the fidelity of order entry. Did the customer get exactly what was ordered? Also, did the goods arrive at their destination in perfect condition? Errors in either of these activities result in return of merchandise.

A company that does not make it easy for people to return goods invites customer dissatisfaction. Some firms include instructions about how to return goods with the package (see Figure 9-7). Others have toll-free numbers that customers can call regarding unsatisfactory deliveries. Although toll-free telephone numbers encourage complaints, not having such hookups encourage dissatisfied customers to stop dealing with the company.

Some firms make pick-up services available for returning merchandise. Others send return labels with their deliveries. UPS has a merchandise return service that picks up the goods at customers' homes and charges the company for both pickup and return.

Dissatisfaction with merchandise may also come about because buying is done at a distance. In the case of apparel, for example, customers don't get a chance to try things on. A size 14 dress of one company is not exactly the same as a size 14 dress of another manufacturer.

Different styles may grace the same body in different, and sometimes unpleasant, ways. Pictures in brochures may look different to buyers than the items they visualize when ordering. In any event, a company must expect a certain amount of returns and dissatisfaction as part of its ongoing business. The issue of customer service concerns how these complaints are handled.

# Summary

Fulfillment means different things to different companies. But practically all agree that fulfillment includes delivery of goods, or physical distribution. Fulfillment covers everything that happens from the receipt of an order to the shipment of the product to the customer or subscriber.

Fulfillment operations are normally separated from transactional processes. The two activities are inherently different. One is a profit center, the other a cost center.

Physical distribution management has adopted a systems approach. This orientation focuses on the system as a whole, acknowledging that any part need not function optimally for the entire operation to perform efficiently.

The major goal of a physical distribution system is minimal cost, at a given level of customer service. The latter concerns three aspects: timing of deliveries, product availability, and delivery quality.

An important aspect of product availability is inventory control. A useful concept is the EOQ model. But that is only the beginning, for most companies use EOQ variations.

Warehousing includes everything done with inventories from the time they are acquired to the time they leave the warehouse. One warehousing decision is whether to fulfill orders in-house or from the outside. If done in-house, another major choice is whether the warehouse is to be manual or automated.

The last phase of fulfillment is transportation. Consumer goods rely on specialized services of the U. S. Postal Service or United Parcel Service. Direct marketers of industrial products ship larger quantities to customers and depend on motor transportation, supplied by common carriers, contract carriers, or private ones.

**REVIEW QUESTIONS**

1. If you were in charge of a book club, what tasks would you expect to accomplish by using a database?
2. Is the database of a brokerage house used for fulfillment?

3. State the 10 steps in the fulfillment cycle. Discuss which functions fall into physical distribution and order-filling activities.
4. In what major ways does physical distribution differ in nature from transactions?
5. What are the weaknesses of the basic EOQ model?
6. Explain the Japanese technique *kanban*.
7. How does open-to-buy planning shift risks from buyers to sellers?
8. Discuss why some retailers use the same warehouse for store and nonstore outlets and others use separate warehouses.
9. Discuss four approaches available to direct marketers to reduce shipping costs.
10. Explain the importance of timing of deliveries to the consumer, government, and business.

PART IV

# USES OF MEDIA

PROFILES

CHAPTER 10

# Direct Mail to Consumers

## PROFILE

**JOHN CAPLES**

**Dean of Mail-Order Copywriting.** A member of the Copywriters Hall of Fame, John Caples began his career as a mail order copywriter at Ruthrauff & Ryan in 1925. Two months into his job, he created the now-classic ad tor the U.S. School of Music, with the headline "They laughed when I sat down at the piano. But when I started to play!" This success was soon followed by another for the Hugo French School: "They grinned when the waiter spoke to me in French—but their laughter turned to amazement at my reply."

In 1927 Mr. Caples brought his mail order skills to BBDO as a writer and account executive. He was elected a vice president in 1941. Over the years he supervised advertising copy tests for many of the agency's most important clients.

*The 100 Greatest Advertisements* by Julian Watkins contains two of John Caples' creations. One is his "piano" ad. The other is an ad created for Phoenix Mutual headlined "To Men who want to quit work some day."

Caples' strong advocacy of copy testing grew with his creative reputation. Formulas for creating effective advertising plus his research on scientific methods for testing advertising effectiveness were set down in a number of his books.

Mr. Caples made his transition to advertising at the age of 25, having earned a B.S. degree in engineering at the U.S. Naval Academy. He has since received numerous awards from the advertising industry, among them the annual award of the National Association of Direct Mail Writers in 1969 and the Leadership Award of the Hundred Million Club in 1972.

Reflecting on his long career, Caples as a septuagenarian said, "My earliest ambition was to make enough money so I could retire at 40... Now in my seventies I never want to retire." John Caples passed away in 1990 and up to then continued writing books and articles, imparting to the present generation a wisdom that, like his advertising classics, has seemingly withstood the test of time. ■

# The Direct Mail Medium

Direct mail is one of the oldest ways used by marketers to communicate with buyers. The beginnings of modern mail order as a business is often attributed to Aaron Montgomery Ward, who in 1892 sent out his first catalog. Today direct mail remains the heartbeat of the direct marketing industry. Most contemporary managers first learned their trade by mailing out the printed word.

Though direct marketing today embraces many more media than in its early days, mail has maintained its important position. Telemarketing expenditures exceed those of direct mail, but a large portion of phone calls—perhaps as much as half—are incoming, having originated from mail solicitations.[1] Mail is still the main vehicle for accomplishing the major purposes of direct marketing: generating immediate sales and leads.[2] Total spending by American business on direct mail for 1990 exceeded $22 billion.[3]

Mail order accounted for about $137 billion of product sales in 1989. Of that total, some $87 billion was credited to consumers.[4] Though consumers spent a modest portion of their total expenditures on mail order, some 2.8 percent, the total is significant. Approximately one-third of U.S. adults say they order something each year through the mails.[5]

The greatest growth in post office deliveries has been in third-class mail, which amounts to roughly 40 percent of the total number of pieces in the mail.[6] According to the U.S. Postal Service, the average American household receives almost 10 pieces of third-class mail per week, or more than 500 pieces a year.[7]

Most commonly, mailers resort to third-class mail to cut costs. Pieces may be mailed singly or in bulk. The latter course is cheaper, about half the cost of first-class mail, but users need a post office permit. All mailing pieces going third class must be identical, sorted by ZIP code, and bundled. A company mailing this way pays extra if it desires to have undelivered mail returned. Third-class mail is slow and uneven but offers substantial cost advantages over first class for sending out millions of pieces of promotional literature.

---

1. See *Direct Marketing* (July 1990), p. 2.
2. *DMA Statistical Fact Book*, (New York: DMA, 1989), p. 19.
3. Based on Robert J. Coen, "Estimated Annual U.S. Advertising Expenditures," prepared for McCann-Erickson, Inc.
4. "Mail Order Top 250+," *Direct Marketing* (July 1990), p. 27.
5. *DMA Statistical Fact Book, op. cit.*, p. 45.
6. Based on DMA, *Third Class Mail* (New York: DMA 1987); and *Direct Marketing* (January 1989, July 1990).
7. Quoted in *DMA Statistical Fact Book, op. cit.*, p. 59.

Although there are various types of mailings, this chapter excludes catalogs. These have become such an important part of mail order that the subject is discussed in a separate chapter.[8]

# Advantages of Direct Mail

The most eloquent testimony to the effectiveness of direct mail is the vast volume going out to consumers and organizations. The persistence of mail as a major selling medium evinces an advantage over alternative channels. The most commonly cited advantages are: selectivity, personalization, flexibility, isolation, and response rates.

## Selectivity

Consumer markets can be segmented in more ways and in greater detail by direct mail than by any other medium. Database marketing, a child of the information age, permits firms to fit mailouts to almost any configuration. In terms of geography, mail can be sent to units as small as a city block. Small geographic areas, such as ZIP code regions and census blocks, can be selected in accordance with numerous demographic and lifestyle factors.

The ideal of database marketing is to communicate directly with individuals. In that respect, the U.S. Postal Service will bring that goal closer by creating a national address list, a project slated for completion in 1991. The directory will contain about 85 million addresses out of a total approximating 100 million. At present, the post office plans to license the computerized list to private database companies, permitting mailers to achieve a closer match of products to markets.[9]

The selection process of direct mail differs markedly from that of most other media transcending geographic boundaries. Most TV or radio broadcasts deliver audiences on an all-or-nothing basis; an advertiser must accept all viewers or listeners of a particular broadcast. Print media such as magazines and newspapers are bound by their circulations. An auto manufacturer, for example, cannot say that a commercial or an advertisement should be seen by car owners only. A company cannot send messages in print or through the air to people of a certain age, income, or marital status. Even smaller regional or metropolitan editions of magazines and newspapers require advertisements in all copies going to a given geographical area.

8. See Chapter 12.
9. Michael W. Miller, "Post Office's Planned Address List Prices Raises Privacy Jitters," *Wall Street Journal* (December 13, 1990), pp. B1, B4.

In contrast, mailers overcome the constraints of time and distance. They can send mail to people with known buying habits, no matter where they live. They can eliminate poor prospects by judicious selection of mailing lists. Selectivity reduces media waste, defined as communicating with disinterested individuals.

There is, however, a tradeoff between media efficiency and effectiveness. A mailing list of good buyers, for example, will yield a lower cost per order than a commercial on evening television. Any nightly program will be watched by many people—in most instances, a large majority—who have no interest in buying the advertised product. A decision to forgo the telecast will therefore cut media waste. But those same programs may have larger potentials than a mailing list. They may reach bona fide customers that cannot be contacted by direct mail. Though not as efficient as mail, TV advertising may be effective as a means of reaching potential customers. Decisions to use a medium must consider not merely efficiency, such as cost per order; they must also consider total audience reach and whether it is worthwhile to appeal to that audience despite higher costs.

The same reasoning holds for direct mail, which has various degrees of selectivity. As lists are compiled from the general population, they become larger and less selective. When selection is too restrictive, it rejects less profitable segments and thus imposes limits on profitable sales. On the other hand, indiscriminate mailings tip the balance the other way. The test of good management is to find that balance to obtain the greatest possible returns from company efforts.

## Personalization

To some extent good copy can make messages seem personal in any medium. One such example is Max Sackheim's classic advertisement that ran for many years and kept pulling responses. Headlined "Do You Make These Mistakes in English?" this ad for the Sherwin Cody correspondence school exploited to the utmost personal feelings about self-improvement. Those who felt that their use of English was a barrier to advancement could empathize with the message and take it personally. A sensitive reader might regard the common mistakes listed in the ad as being made solely by him or her.

In general, however, direct mail is more conducive to personalization than any other medium. Mail is private; it is directed to a particular person. Even envelopes addressed "To Resident" imply that the mailing piece belongs to the occupant of a particular dwelling. It is not just for anyone.

Computer technology today mass-produces personalized mail. Computer letters fill in data from a computer-stored memory and tailor personal insertions to specific readers. The letter can open with "Dear

Mr./Mrs. X." High-speed printers make the letter look like it was typed separately.

The personal touch is extended by referring to other known facts about an individual in the body of the letter itself. Figure 10-1 exhibits such a computer-coded message. Every letter has the same elements

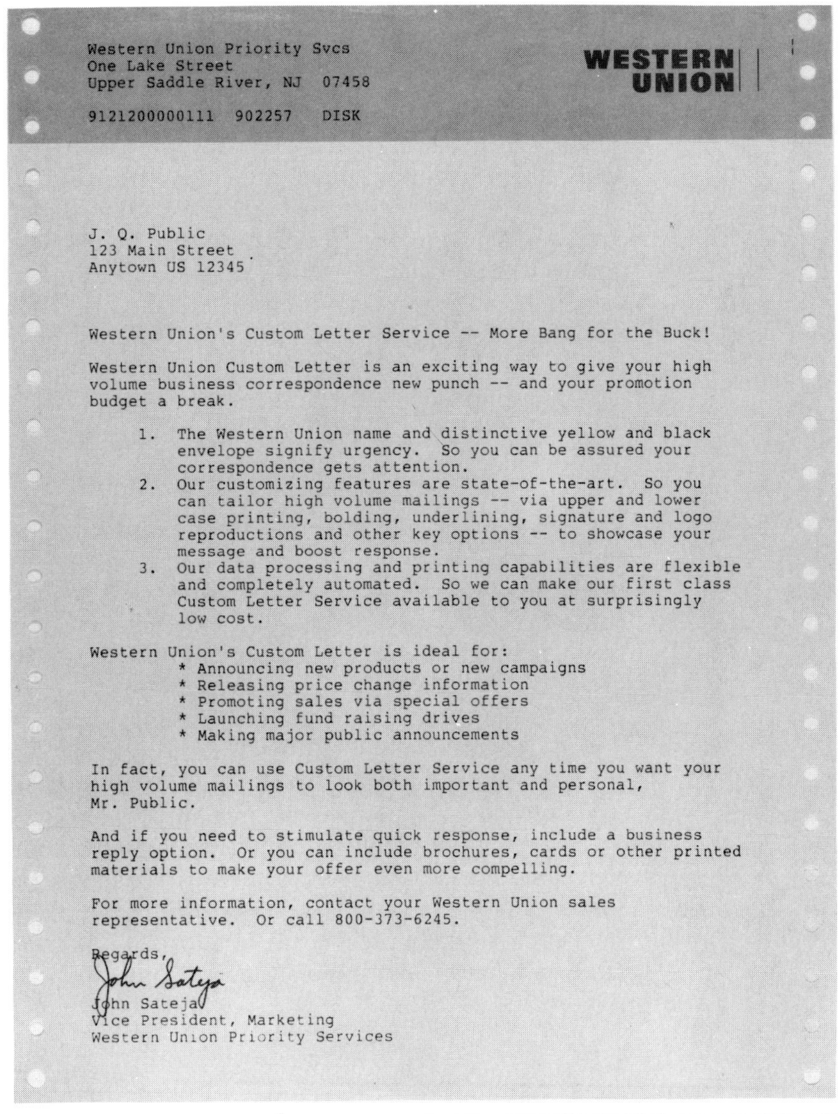

Western Union Priority Svcs
One Lake Street
Upper Saddle River, NJ 07458

9121200000111 902257 DISK

WESTERN UNION

J. Q. Public
123 Main Street
Anytown US 12345

Western Union's Custom Letter Service -- More Bang for the Buck!

Western Union Custom Letter is an exciting way to give your high volume business correspondence new punch -- and your promotion budget a break.

1. The Western Union name and distinctive yellow and black envelope signify urgency. So you can be assured your correspondence gets attention.
2. Our customizing features are state-of-the-art. So you can tailor high volume mailings -- via upper and lower case printing, bolding, underlining, signature and logo reproductions and other key options -- to showcase your message and boost response.
3. Our data processing and printing capabilities are flexible and completely automated. So we can make our first class Custom Letter Service available to you at surprisingly low cost.

Western Union's Custom Letter is ideal for:

* Announcing new products or new campaigns
* Releasing price change information
* Promoting sales via special offers
* Launching fund raising drives
* Making major public announcements

In fact, you can use Custom Letter Service any time you want your high volume mailings to look both important and personal, Mr. Public.

And if you need to stimulate quick response, include a business reply option. Or you can include brochures, cards or other printed materials to make your offer even more compelling.

For more information, contact your Western Union sales representative. Or call 800-373-6245.

Regards,

John Sateja

John Sateja
Vice President, Marketing
Western Union Priority Services

**FIGURE 10-1 A Computer Letter with Name in Salutation**
*Source:* Customer Letter is a service mark of New Valley Corporation and a service of its Western Union Priority Services Division.

slotted into the same designated places, but it still gives an appearance of having been written specially to the mail recipient.

Letters from financial houses can give the exact balance in an account. They can also tell how much certain investments have yielded. Such information, when connected with personal data, provokes a rise in reader interest.

The popularity of the more costly computer letters stems from the increase in response. This greater response must be weighed against the higher costs.

## Flexibility

Direct mail is an extremely flexible device in terms of both media and copy elements. As a medium, it has no fixed audience parameters. Unlike television, magazines, or newspapers, direct mail has no defined audiences. There are no ratings. There is no level of circulation, as in print, that a mailer must work with. Instead firms can determine how large or small they want their mailings to be. A company can send out as many messages as it wishes—running into the millions or narrowed to as small a number as one.

Determination of the audience rests not with the medium but with marketers. Mailers need not adjust their plans to fit circulation patterns or audience characteristics. As a medium, direct mail adapts to fit marketing plans. The user calculates how many people are to be reached. By determining the quantities of mail sent out, the firm determines audience size.

In terms of copy elements, creative personnel enjoy a wide variety of forms from which to choose. They must produce their outputs on a two-dimensional surface. But beyond that, they have few restrictions. They can make their mailings as simple or as complex as they desire.

They can use a conventional mailing format, which has an outer envelope. Its contents can vary widely, from simple letters and circulars to bulging brochures, coupon books, or records and tapes. The only limit to those variations is the imagination of their creators.

Another alternative is the self-mailer, which does not have an outer envelope. These, too, have numerous variations, ranging from a single-folded sheet to a complex package with multiple items. Since the self-mailer comes off a press ready to address, it is cheaper to produce than conventional mailing pieces. An example of a self-mailer is shown in Figure 10-2.

## Isolation

Direct mail stands in splendid isolation. It has no editorial environment. The commercial message is not read "involuntarily," as in an advertisement in a magazine. It is not watched as something incidental, like a

## Maybe there is a substitute for experience.

At The Wall Street Journal, we recognize that business experience is something you don't start earning until after you graduate. But while you're waiting, we can provide some of the same competitive advantages that experience brings. For instance, our wide-ranging news coverage gives you a clearer understanding of business in general. Our feature reporting prepares you for more specific ambitions–whether in management, accounting, finance, technology, marketing or small business. And our in-depth analysis helps you formulate your ideas in a sharper more persuasive way.

# THE WALL STREET JOURNAL.



What's News—

Aluminum Production

The Outlook

*A Little-Noted Rise to Growth*

## Save over 45%

Subscribe to The Wall Street Journal now, and you'll enjoy student savings of over 45% off the regular subscription price.

Plus, a **FREE ADDED BONUS**,

you'll receive a complimentary copy of the latest edition of

**"Managing Your Career,"**

over 50 pages of solid and valuable guidance for you on career decisions and job hunting.

That's a pretty generous offer. Especially when you consider what it actually represents. **Tuition for the real world.**

☎ 1-800-634-0992

**Call toll-free or mail this postage-free card.**

❑ Send me one year of The Wall Street Journal for $74.50–*a savings of over 45% off the regular subscription price.* I understand I will also receive a complimentary copy of "Managing Your Career." †(Offer also applies to 15 week term).

❑ Send me 15 weeks for $27. ❑ Bill me later ❑ Payment enclosed

❑ Charge my ❑ VISA ❑ MasterCard

Card no. ____________________

Exp. Date ____________ Signature ____________

Name ____________________

Address ____________ Room/Apt# ______

City ____________ State ____________ Zip ______

School ____________ Major ____________

Student I.D.# ____________ Phone ____________

Graduation Month/Year ____________________

These prices are valid for a limited time *for students only* in the continental U.S. By placing your order, you authorize The Wall Street Journal to verify the enrollment information supplied above.

 †Offer good while supplies last.

**FIGURE 10-2 A Self-Mailer**

*Source:* Reprinted with permission of Dow Jones & Company, Inc.

commercial that is seen because the viewer happens to be watching the show on which the ad appears. Direct mail is the medium, and to again quote Marshall McLuhan, "the medium is the message."

The rub, however, is the degree of volition, the desire of receivers to read their mail. Many people regard unsolicited mail as "junk," something that is not wanted. According to an annual survey of the U.S. Postal Service, 15 percent of third-class mail was discarded without being opened. Another 9 percent drew a "don't know" reply when people were asked what they had done with it.[10] If people didn't know whether they read or discarded a piece of mail, it couldn't have made a meaningful impression. The USPS household diary study collects information from a national sample of more than 5,000 households each year. Householders keep diaries of the pieces of mail they receive and send during a sample week.

According to the study, only 41 percent of all third-class mail to consumers was opened and read. This percentage has fallen continuously over the years, sliding from a 63 percent readership in 1972. The decline in attentiveness has averaged more than 1 percent per annum during a span of nearly two decades.

Less attention to third-class mail is the outcome of a mounting assault on American mailboxes. Volume of mail received per household rose by more than 200 percent from 1972 to 1988, from 3.0 to 9.7 mail pieces per week.[11] As direct mail has swollen in volume, a larger portion has gone into trash cans.

The key to reader attention is the existence of a relationship between sender and recipient of a mailing piece. This is apparent from the findings of the USPS household diary study, shown in Table 10-1. The results demonstrate that direct mail is most effective when recipients are already doing business with senders. Present customers getting third-class mail read it much more frequently than noncustomers—58 percent versus 30 percent for organizations with which noncustomers are familiar. When the organization is not known, only 24 percent of its mail is read; a much larger proportion is discarded or quickly forgotten.

A similar situation exists with respect to attitudes about mailings. Some 62 percent of all direct mail pieces going to current customers were said to be "useful." Though their names were known to recipients, organizations sending mail to noncustomers received only a 23 percent usefulness score for their efforts. A meager 15 percent of pieces by unknown organizations were deemed useful.

---

10. Quoted in *DMA Statistical Fact Book, op. cit.*, p. 27.
11. *Ibid.*, p. 59.

**TABLE 10.1. Treatment of Third-Class Mail.**

| Treatment | Homes Doing Business with Organization | Mail to Noncustomers: Organization Known | Mail to Noncustomers: Organization Not Known | All Mail Pieces |
|---|---|---|---|---|
| Read | 58.2% | 30.2% | 23.9% | 41.1% |
| Looked at/ put aside | 33.8 | 45.4 | 41.1 | 35.0 |
| Discarded/ didn't know | 8.0 | 24.5 | 35.1 | 23.8 |
| Total mail | 100.0% | 100.0% | 100.0% | 100.0% |
| Deemed useful | 62.1% | 23.4% | 15.8% | 40.2% |

NOTE: Percentages based on total pieces received.
SOURCE: Based on Direct Marketing Association, *1989 Statistical Fact Book,* (New York: DMA, 1989).

These USPS findings underscore rather vital implications for direct mail:

- Since the amount of third-class mail per household is expected to increase, there is bound to be further deterioration of communication effectiveness. Relatively less direct mail will be read, and more will be discarded.
- Whether better creative ads can reverse this trend is problematical. It hasn't so far.
- Differentials in readership and attitudes between customers and noncustomers emphatically support heightened concern with customer service. Hard-won customers are too valuable to ignore.
- Costs of acquiring new customers must rise as this segment becomes less and less receptive to direct mail solicitations. Deteriorating communication coupled with ever-climbing postal rates may impose severe limits on corporate growth.
- The declining productivity of direct mail leads to a search for cost-saving technologies and more innovative uses of media.

## Response Rates

The greatest advantage of direct mail lies in its payoff. It pulls a higher response than other media used for direct marketing. But it is also the costliest. For direct mail to justify its costs, it must have enough pulling power to bring costs per order below those obtained by other media. The ratio of cost to response is used as a rough measure of media efficiency. These ratios, however, are not uniform. They vary in accordance with three elements: the product offered, markets served, and media used. Depending upon the particular combination of those elements, each situation will have its own unique efficiency rating.

# The Direct Mail Package

The direct mail package stands as the conventional format. It is by far the most popular and accounts for the overwhelming majority of all direct mail.[12] This package consists of four main elements:

1. Outer envelope
2. Letter
3. Brochure
4. Order form

Not every direct mail package contains all four items, but they appear frequently.

## Outer Envelope

The outer envelope is the first contact with mail recipients. The envelope must create a favorable impression, because people don't open every piece of mail, especially mail that might be considered unwanted or useless. The envelope must entice enough for people to want to open it. Unless an envelope is opened, the piece cannot be read. If the piece is not read, it cannot make a sale.

Copywriters and designers have a number of techniques at their fingertips to make mail desirable. Several of the most prominent follow:

- The headline or main selling proposition is put right on the envelope. This technique works well with low-involvement products offered to those with strong dispositions to buy.[13]
- An extension of the headline is a notation that the package contains information requested. This option may be used to follow up inquiries.
- The envelope carries teaser copy to arouse reader curiosity (see Figure 10-3). This method makes use of innuendo rather than an outright declaration.
- The envelope is personalized with an indication that "the package is just for you" (see Figure 10-4).
- The envelope is designed with a peek-in window displaying some prominent portion of the offer inside, enticing the recipient to open it to see the whole thing (see Figure 10-5). It should isolate the things that are important in the offer.
- A show-through envelope is used; the entire envelope is one large window. A good design will highlight pictures, headlines, offers, or other desirable features to induce a person to open and read further.

---

12. DMMA, *Manual Release* 310.1 (May 1979).
13. Guy L. Yolton, "Direct Response Copy Techniques for Consumer Direct Mail," DMMA *Manual Release* 300.1 (May 1979).

**FIGURE 10-3 An Envelope with Teaser Copy**
*Source:* Reprinted with permission of New Process Company.

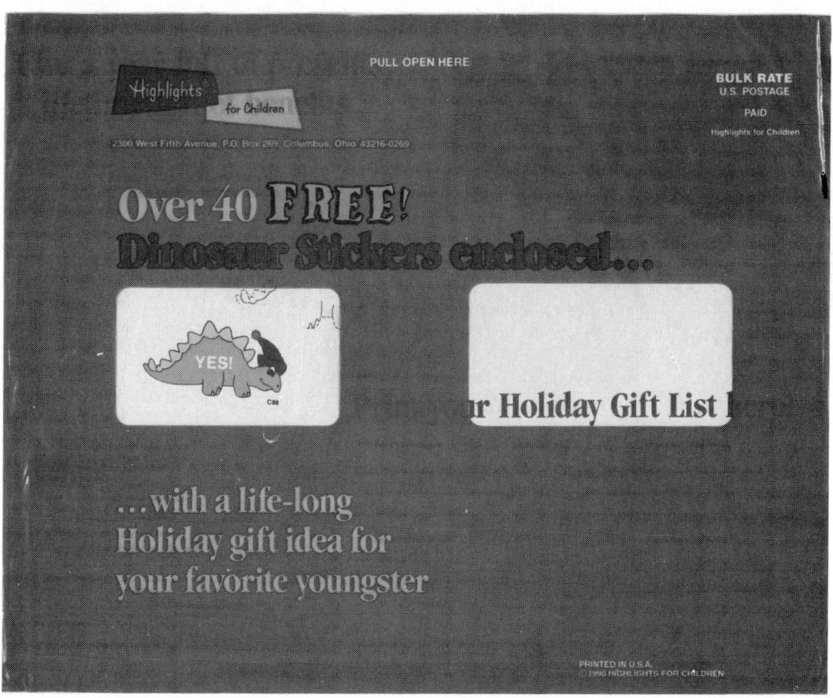


**FIGURE 10-4 An Envelope Showing a Feature of the Offer Through a Plastic Window**
*Source:* Reprinted with permission of Highlights for Children.

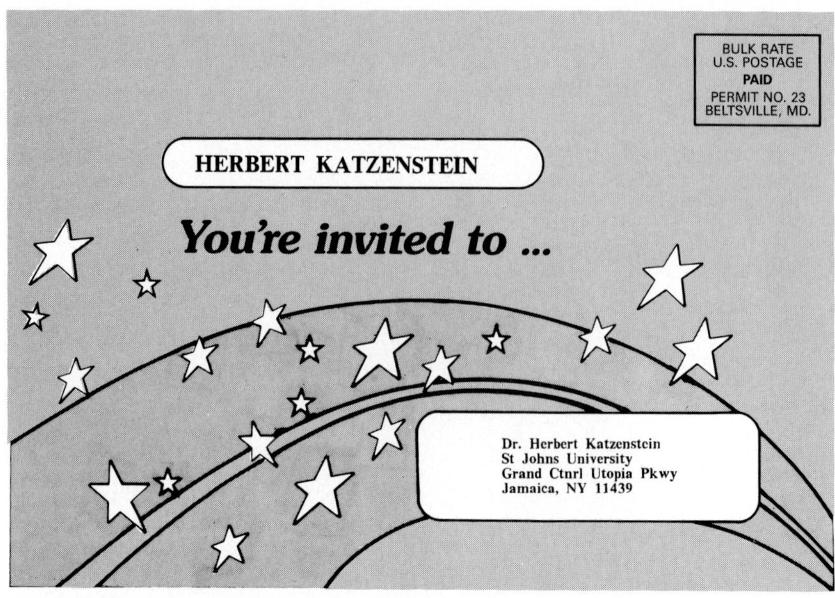


**FIGURE 10-5 An Example of Personalization of an Envelope**
*Source:* Reprinted with permission of Direct Marketing Association of Washington.

- Stock quality may be a consideration. Financial services may use valuable-looking stock to convey security and financial strength. Glossy stock may be appropriate for gourmet food.[14]
- Some mailings use official-looking envelopes or windows showing items that look like little checks. These may not be illegal, but they are considered unethical by many practitioners in the industry.

Some companies go to extremes to add personalization to an envelope, paying extra to have it addressed by hand. Gene C. Wunder, a marketing professor at Ball State University, found that consumers pay as much attention to computer-printed labels as to hand-addressed envelopes. According to his test using a mailout by a health care organization, the response rate was about the same.[15]

Envelopes are all subject to various constraints. One is cost. More elaborate envelopes bear higher costs. Will the enhanced presentation justify enhanced costs? More complex designs may also create printing and production problems. For example, heavy or infrequently used stock may be hard to produce in very large quantities and may upset tight mailing schedules.

Other restraints come from post office regulations. The post office sets limits on envelope size. Postal authorities might also forbid odd-

14. *Marketing News* (February 29, 1988), p. 21.
15. Dave Wilkinson, "The Envelope," *Direct Marketing* (March 1987), p. 66.

shaped envelopes. Also, envelopes have weight limitations, and mailers must pay monetary penalties for exceeding those limits.

## The Letter

The most important part of the direct mail package is the letter. Its main job is to present the selling proposition to mail recipients. It gives details on such things as benefits, product descriptions, terms of the sale, and guarantees. Brochures can often be eliminated without lowering response, but not letters. Letters can be sent out alone or combined with other elements.

The importance of the written word elevates the copywriter to king in the domain of direct mail letters. A strong consensus holds that the personal tone is essential to a successful letter. A letter is meant to convey a message from one person to another, and it is supposed to look and sound that way in direct mail as well. If not addressed to an individual by a computer, a letter will have a salutation such as "Dear Friend" or Dear Customer." Right at the outset, the idea is to create a bond of familiarity between sender and receiver.

The length of the letter is a matter of some debate. A common rule of thumb is that the letter should be long enough to do the selling job but not so long as to erode reader interest. But how long is that? Letters generally run from two to four pages. Some copywriters favor long messages, provided they fit in with the proposition, and a few advocate six- to eight-page letters.[16]

A letter's opening paragraph gets the most reading. It should introduce the main theme and create a desire to continue to read. Most writers advocate opening with the promise of some benefit. Like headlines in a printed advertisement, the beginning of the letter qualifies readers by weeding out those not interested in the offer. The body of the letter can then enlarge upon the subject, present data to support the selling proposition, and urge the reader to take immediate action. Some letters actually carry headlines. They are said to act as good attention getters when they are succinct, catchy, and to the point. A brochure recommends running headlines flush left, not centering them above the body copy.[17]

A tactic that resembles a headline is the *Johnson box*. It consists of a sentence or two above the salutation that summarizes the main points of the proposition. This summary highlights the offer right at the beginning. Most copywriters usually agree that benefits of an offer should not be buried in body copy.[18]

---

16. DMMA, *Manual Release* 310.1 (May 1979).
17. DMMA, *Manual Release* 300.2 (May 1979).
18. See Joan Throckmorton, *Winning Direct Response Advertising* (Englewood Cliffs, NJ: Prentice-Hall, 1986), p. 77.

The end of the letter usually goes back to the beginning and repeats the main benefits and selling points. Poscripts often encapsulate the offer further.

The idea of placing emphasis at the beginning and end came from eye camera tests. The laboratory findings plotted people's perceptions of visual material. Technicians found that in perusing a letter, readers' eye movements wandered all over a page in a haphazard pattern and alighted with high frequency on the postscript at the bottom. This supports the psychological principles of primacy and recency: the first and last impressions are remembered best. But more to the point, mailing tests indicated that letters with postscripts obtained higher returns than letters without them.[19]

The postscript idea is extended by the *extra slip* or *memo*. These devices go by several other names, such as *second letter*, *publisher's letter*, or *lift letter*. This addition stands by itself and can come as a separately folded letter. Sometimes it is even placed in a special envelope.

A common practice is to preface this second letter with a warning, such as: "Read this letter only if you have decided not to respond to this offer." The letter might than start off with such a copy as: "To be honest with you, I am puzzled. I can't understand your decision not to accept our offer." The letter would then go on to regurgitate the major reasons for saying yes to the proposition. An example of such a letter is shown in Figure 10-6.

When it was first used, the second letter apparently got some marginal buyers to change their minds. But as the extra letter gained acceptance as an effective pulling device and came into wider use, response rates fell off. Today many copywriters claim that lift letters are grossly overused and add little or nothing to response.

## The Brochure

Whereas the letter rests on the power of the written word, the brochure creates its effects through the ingenuity of art, drawings, photographs, and color. It usually runs from four to six pages and folds into #10 or 6 × 9–inch envelopes.

The primary purpose of a brochure is to support the offer set forth in the letter. It can dramatize in pictures what was conveyed with words. It can illustrate the key features of a product. Most brochures prefer photographs to drawings because they convey impressions that are more realistic. However, drawings prevail when the product is complex, such as industrial machinery, where technical features must be illustrated.

Whether a brochure goes into a mailing depends on the product. Financial services, charities, and social causes are difficult to visualize,

19. Maxwell C. Ross, "Direct Mail Letter Copy: Fundamentals," DMMA *Manual Release* 310.2 (May 1979).

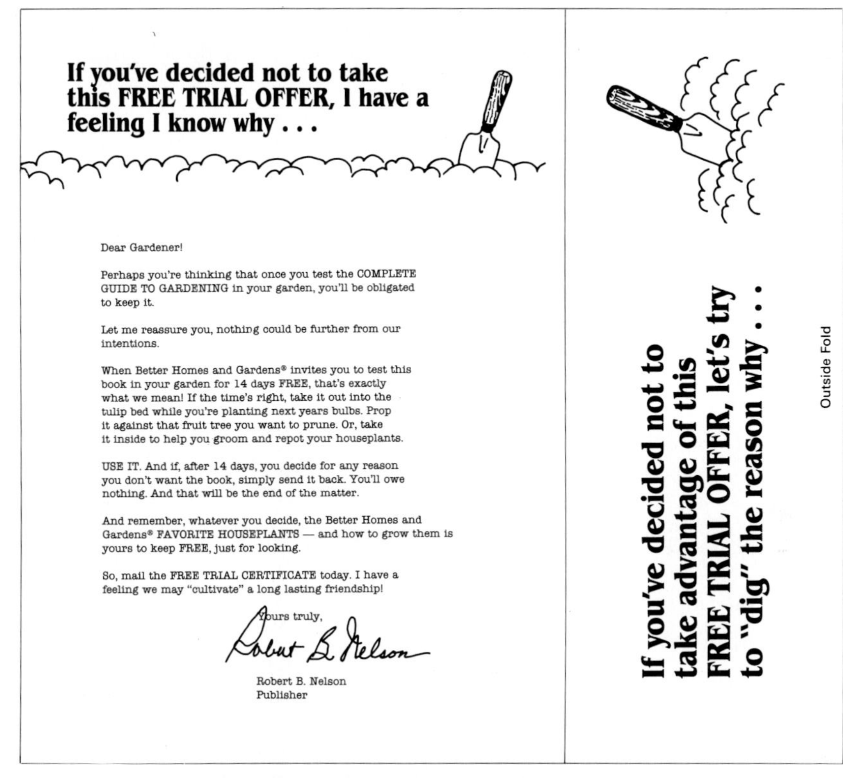

**If you've decided not to take this FREE TRIAL OFFER, I have a feeling I know why . . .**

Dear Gardener!

Perhaps you're thinking that once you test the COMPLETE GUIDE TO GARDENING in your garden, you'll be obligated to keep it.

Let me reassure you, nothing could be further from our intentions.

When Better Homes and Gardens® invites you to test this book in your garden for 14 days FREE, that's exactly what we mean! If the time's right, take it out into the tulip bed while you're planting next years bulbs. Prop it against that fruit tree you want to prune. Or, take it inside to help you groom and repot your houseplants.

USE IT. And if, after 14 days, you decide for any reason you don't want the book, simply send it back. You'll owe nothing. And that will be the end of the matter.

And remember, whatever you decide, the Better Homes and Gardens® FAVORITE HOUSEPLANTS — and how to grow them is yours to keep FREE, just for looking.

So, mail the FREE TRIAL CERTIFICATE today. I have a feeling we may "cultivate" a long lasting friendship!

Yours truly,

Robert B. Nelson
Publisher

**If you've decided not to take advantage of this FREE TRIAL OFFER, let's try to "dig" the reason why . . .**

Outside Fold

**FIGURE 10-6 Publisher's Letter**
*Source:* Better Homes & Gardens. Reprinted with permission of Meredith Corporation.

and their benefits are not always possible to demonstrate in art form. In these instances, a sample newsletter may be more effective than a poorly done brochure. Business-to-business direct mail frequently has little need for brochures. John Graham, president of a direct marketing agency, claims that close to 90 percent of all brochures to business to businesses are irrelevant.[20]

A mailing piece may include other inserts that take the place of brochures. The most popular are folders, broadsides, booklets, and circulars.

- *Folders* are used for short, compact messages that present an idea quickly. They often go with letters but can be sent alone.
- *Broadsides* are large folders that can be likened to spectaculars. They are used to produce deep visual impressions. Usually, they are reserved for special occasions, such as the kickoff of a campaign or a special announcement.

20. John R. Graham, "Resist That Urge to Do Another Boring Brochure," *Marketing News* (July 31, 1981), pp. 9, 11.

- *Booklets* consist of eight or more pages bound together with staples or glue. They are often designed for thorough reading or didactic purposes, especially when the product is complex and requires a lengthy explanation.
- *Circulars,* also called *flyers,* can get across a message at low cost. They come in either color or black and white.

## The Order Form

The response form is the last link in the chain of a direct mail package. All other elements—envelope, letter, brochure—are designed to get the reader to complete the response form. Everything in the package is meant to make readers take specific action—make a purchase, request information, visit a store, or make a donation to a charity.

The return of the order form is the bottom line of direct mail. A package is judged by its response in relation to cost. The order form normally contains the terms and conditions of an offer. A returned form evidences that the customer agrees to the terms of an offer, whether it be a sale or a request for free literature. When this return is processed, it sets off a chain of activities within a fulfillment system.

Order forms come in various formats. They can be separate or part of a folder, broadside, or brochure. Reply forms can appear as self-mailers or made to fit into envelopes. Postage for both return cards and envelopes can be prepaid. In most instances, additional postal costs for a postage-paid or business-reply envelope are more than warranted by higher returns. Costs are incurred only if the prepaid mailing devices are returned.

Two different views exists about the design of order forms. Some practitioners recommend "busy-looking" order or request forms.[21] Other busy work advocates suggest forms that involve customers in things like putting a token into a "yes" or a "no" slot, punching out tokens and gluing them to designated parts of the order form, affixing stickers to reserve spaces, or tearing off stubs with guarantees on them. The involvement philosophy holds that people like to do things. When given things to do, they are more prone to respond to the ad.

The second view holds that order forms should be kept simple. If customers cannot figure out how to respond, no orders will be forthcoming. If they are given too many options, too many obstacles block the path to filling out order forms.[22] The keep-it-simple theory tries to make ordering so easy that readers have to spend little time doing it. This gives them no reason to procrastinate.

---

21. Bob Stone, *Successful Direct Marketing Methods*, 4th ed. (Lincolnwood, IL: NTC Business Books, 1988), p. 344.
22. Charles Greenberg, "The Basics Are Basic Because They Still Work," *Marketing News* (June 11, 1990), p. 11.

Individual names and addresses can be preprinted on order forms. An advantage of preaddressed forms is that they can be used as a mailing label if the return envelope has a window. In addition, preaddressed order forms help in updating information contained in a database. These labels carry identification codes, such as a customer's account number and billing status.

# Creative Approaches

Copy approaches for direct mail have much in common with those of general advertising. Yet direct mail also has its unique features. One is that the mail package must perform all selling functions. It must attract prospects. It has to stimulate interest and desire. It has to get readers to take some sort of action.

The types of appeals are almost endless. The reason given for taking action, however, follows general lines of strategy. The most important ones deal with degrees of rationality, product attributes, positive or negative appeals, and sense of urgency.

## Degrees of Rationality

One method of persuasion is appeal to reason. Direct marketing copy can run from being highly rational to extremely emotional. Commonly accepted criteria for judging the rationality of a selling argument includes relevancy, clarity, timeliness, truthfulness, and completeness.[23]

The rational message supports the offer with objective, factual data. The argument is intellectually defensible. Messages of this nature are referred to in the industry as *reason-why copy*. The irrational argument resorts to devices that violate logic, such as appeals to feelings, emotions, and prejudices.

Which type of argument to use depends on a seller's perception of what motivates buyers. Messages directed to industrial markets, for example, take on a rational appearance. Catalogs to business often contain listings and specifications to facilitate ordering. Buyers are thought to be experts who know what they want and who order to satisfy company requirements. Yet many copywriters insist that business buyers are human beings and are frequently swayed by appeals to the heart rather than to the head.

Mail to consumers uses a good deal of irrational appeals, especially when buyers are considered irrational. In many instances, less information is used. When prospects are nondeliberative, irrational messages prevail.

---

23. See J. A. Howard and J. Hulbert, *Advertising and the Public Interest* (Chicago: Crain Communication, 1973), pp. 80–87.

Product type is also a factor. Different products lend themselves to different kinds of appeals. Products such as stamps, coins, and technical and professional literature are usually sold using rational appeals. These are specialties, and buyers are knowledgeable about the subject. Messages for financial services take the same approach, partly because of government regulations and partly because of buyer deliberation. But even here there are differences among copywriters. On the other hand, irrational arguments are frequent with respect to products such as gifts, apparel, perfumes, cosmetics, and foods. Solicitations for charities and causes are mostly nonrational. Self-interest does not apply—except for requests for political contributions, where, unlike charitable do-goodings, altruism doesn't cloud the brain.

## Product Features versus Personal Benefits

Almost all communication in direct marketing is product-related. It conveys meanings about goods or services. But it can focus attention on different aspects of experience with the product.

At one end of the spectrum are messages that deal entirely with product attributes. These include such elements as design, function, shape, package, color, and price. This approach makes the assumption that product attributes are the main reason people buy. Copy that hews this line is often called the "product as hero" message. An example is shown in Figure 10-7.

The more popular method, especially for consumer direct mail, is to highlight personal benefits. If personalization is highly regarded in direct mail, then telling prospects what they gain can be very effective. In its extreme form, an emphasis on benefits may completely ignore product characteristics, saying practically nothing about the product except the minimum necessary to complete the transaction. This type of copy assumes that readers know everything about the product or that the product is so standardized than no explanation is necessary.

Most direct mail copy falls somewhere between the two poles of product features and benefits. Greater weight may be assigned to one or the other, and sometimes it is difficult to ascertain where the emphasis lies. Services in particular cannot separate what is rendered from the benefit. Joan Throckmorton, a well-known copywriter, holds that when the product is hazy, benefits are not clear. And, says Throckmorton, "No amount of fine writing will help."[24]

There is a tendency for the product-oriented ad to take a more rational approach than the benefits-oriented message. Yet a product emphasis is not always rational. It may appeal to features that have little

24. Throckmorton, *op. cit.*, p. 35.

**THERE'S NO OTHER COPIER ON EARTH LIKE IT.**

The Minolta Beta 450Z has features no copier ever had before.

Like auto magnification. Which allows the 450Z, with its automatic document feeder, to take a stack of different size originals and automatically reduce or enlarge them to uniform size copies.

If you simply want to make copies of that stack of originals, the 450Z will automatically select the correct paper size for each one.

The 450Z has a unique variable magnification zooming lens that gives you a virtually limitless range of copy sizes. From almost 50% larger than the original to 50% smaller.

If you don't need reduction, enlargement or auto magnification, ask your dealer about the Beta 450 (without the Z).

Both make copies that are out of this world.

**Call your Minolta dealer for a demonstration. Look in the Yellow Pages under the Minolta trademark. Or call toll free 800-526-5256. In New Jersey call 201-342-6707.**

MINOLTA

☐ Please have my dealer contact me for a demonstration of the new Minolta Beta 450Z.
☐ Please send me more information.

Name________
Title________
Company________
Address________
City________ State________
Zip________ Telephone________

Mail to Minolta Corporation
Business Equipment Division
101 Williams Drive
Ramsey, N.J. 07446.

BETA

© 1983 Minolta Corporation

**FIGURE 10-7 A Message Focusing on Product Attributes**
*Source:* Reprinted with permission of the Minolta Corporation.

relevancy. An example would be a message that follows the advice of Elmer Wheeler, a promotion executive in the 1930s: "Don't sell the steak, sell the sizzle."

On the other hand, a benefits appeal can run along strictly rational lines. Personal advantages touted by a financial house can often be translated into hard facts of interest, dividends, and returns on investment.

An emphasis on product features is appropriate when a product enjoys a physical advantage or a unique feature valued by buyers. When a product's advantages are obvious, customers can usually infer the benefits.[25]

## Positive versus Negative Appeals

Any argument can be phrased positively or negatively. A negative approach by a financial service may read: "Don't invest until you have read about our new bond offering!" The same thing can be said in a positive way: "Invest only after you have read about our new bond offering!"

Either approach can be effective in particular situations. However, most companies avoid the negative. They don't want their products associated with negative feelings, as though consumers bought them out of fear. They want their products preferred because of favorable qualities.[26]

There are goods and services that evoke unpleasant images. People usually don't like going to a doctor or dentist, or even to a lawyer. For them to do so, something must be wrong. For example, proprietary drugs are taken to alleviate discomfort. In such cases, copy can dramatize the negative side. Though it may show a happy ending with people enjoying themselves after being liberated from pain, readers are given a headache before they are shown how to get rid of one.

An extreme case of negativism is insurance advertising, which makes up a major category of direct mail. Its messages are notorious for themes of impending disaster. Health insurance paints pictures of normally vigorous individuals being struck by sudden illness. Bills mount, mortgages are foreclosed, and families are plunged into poverty. Some life insurance ads virtually back the hearse right up to the door. The scenario portrays hapless widows bereft of hope and sad-faced orphans deprived of their cherished dreams—all because the head of the household failed to carry life insurance. Home insurers show trees falling on parked cars and roofs carried away by high winds, causing huge dents in families' hard-earned savings (and in their cars, too).

25. Philip W. Burton, *Advertising Copywriting* (Columbus, OH: Grid Publishing, 1978), p. 10. Also see Mike Pavlish, "The Harder, the Better Works Best in Direct Mail," *Marketing News* (August 28, 1989).

26. Herschell G. Lewis, "The Positive Aspects of Negatives," *Direct Marketing* (September 1989), pp.34–40.

Such appeals are scare tactics, playing on motives of fear. Yet protection against calamities—or, rather, against their financial consequences—is the main reason to buy insurance. Many insurance firms do use positive appeals. But the fear motive has been exploited for a long time and is successful, as evidenced by its persistence.

## Soft versus Hard Sell

The soft sell is prevalent in general advertising. It is distinguished from the hard sell in that it sets no time limit on action; when to take action is left to the consumer. It is like a salesperson extolling the virtues of a product on every call but never quite asking for the order. It adopts the principle that commercial messages represent a learning experience that leads to action at some later time. Soft-sell messages aim at keeping the brand in people's minds until they have occasion to take action.

In contrast, the hard sell is typical of retail advertising. It tries to create a sense of urgency. Take action now! Sale ends tomorrow! Supplies limited!

Insofar as direct mail attempts to make a sale "now," it uses the hard sell. Mailers commonly hold that a message should get a consumer to respond in a matter of minutes. Every delay is detrimental to response. A reader who does not take immediate action is most likely lost. For that reason, copy is usually written for prospects who presumably have a high interest in the product. Techniques for making it easy to answer are numerous: bind-in or blow-in cards, flaps, tip-ons, computerized reply forms, and toll-free 800 numbers.

The conventional wisdom in direct mail holds that effectiveness of copy is judged by the quickness and quantity of returns. As put by Jain and Migliaro in an American Management brochure, "Cumulative effect, recall, and other measures of advertising effectiveness have no place in the direct marketer's lexicon. The only thing that counts is the number of orders generated by each individual ad."[27]

Recent years have witnessed some voices of protest against this hard-sell, "bird-in-the-hand" attitude. Edward Nash, head of a leading direct marketing agency, argued that emphasis on immediate response is shortsighted because it concentrates on core markets. It generates sales now but fails to build for the future. According to Nash, concentrating on a small percentage of responders ignores the larger portion of the audience that did not respond. On that basis, Nash favors consideration of long-term, attitude-building techniques.[28]

---

27. C. L. Jain and A. Magliaro, *An Introduction to Direct Marketing* (New York: AMACOM, 1978), p. 25.
28. Edward Nash, *Direct Marketing* (New York: McGraw-Hill, 1986), p. 24.

## Putting It Together

A single creative approach can have a wide variety of different appeals. Many writers have compiled lists of such appeals—greed, fear, pleasure, and so forth. These are not of much help in putting together a direct mail package because no one determines the best time to use particular appeals. If one wants a blueprint, perhaps the best solution is Bob Stone's simple, seven-step formula for writing a successful letter:[29]

1. *Promise a benefit in the headline or in the first paragraph.* In case of doubt, you can get a strong lead or opening with this approach. Most people won't read an unsolicited letter unless they see a clear benefit.
2. *Enlarge on the most important benefit.* If the lead is relevant, you can build interest without reader diversion.
3. *Give details about basic product features.* If you expect readers to take action, they must know what they are getting.
4. *Support your statements with proof.* You can dispel the normal reader's skepticism if you can support your claims with demonstrable facts.
5. *Tell readers why they should act.* By introducing a sense of urgency, you can put the readers in a receptive frame of mind before you get to the close.
6. *Rephrase prominent benefits in your close.* By summing up the main benefits, you reinforce preferences built previously.
7. *End with a call for action.* Use a strong, urgent close. This is your moment of truth.

# Direct Mail for Store Traffic

An increasing amount of direct mail today is meant not to get an order or an inquiry, but to bring customers into a store. The emphasis in this instance falls on conventional retailing. Like other forms of general advertising and promotion, direct mail is used to get customers to visit the premises of the seller.

For many years auto dealers have targeted car owners from Polk lists to get them to visit dealerships. Many department store catalogs—perhaps a majority—have store traffic as their main goal. Monthly statements to regular customers are stuffed with notices of special events and fantastic sales.

Somewhat related to direct mail for building store traffic are frequent-user programs. Neiman Marcus uses the mails to keep in touch with heavy buyers in its well-known In Circle Program. Customers have to charge at least $3,000 in any calendar year to quality for the In Circle membership. These big spenders receive a number of benefits, such as

29. Stone, *op. cit.*, pp. 334–335

special treatment when shopping in the store, free gifts, and discounts for special events, such as New Year's Eve balls and black-tie dinners. The Hyatt hotel chain relies on its Gold Passport to reward frequent patrons.[30]

For these programs to run successfully, customers must have a continuous need for the product. Business travelers, for example, have a frequent need for travel reservations, hotel rooms, and car rentals. A second requirement is that the gain in sales must be large enough to pay for incremental costs, which can be high.

The great jump in direct mail that promotes store traffic has come from national and local advertisers. Premiums, sweepstakes, coupons, cash refunds, and samples have been the major devices.

Direct mail has ridden on the sales promotional bandwagon. In the early 1970s media advertising accounted for about two-thirds of all promotional dollars. Today, about two-thirds go to sales promotion, and one-third is spent on media advertising.[31] Surprisingly, the largest portion of direct mail ads comes from national advertisers, who account for 40 percent. Some 25 percent originate with local advertisers, and only 20 percent are for mail order goods. The remaining 15 percent of direct mail ads come from mass merchandise, such as Sears and J.C. Penney.[32]

According to Donnelley Marketing, couponing consumers direct is the most popular method.[33] Most coupons are distributed as freestanding inserts in newspapers, but the amounts going through the mails have been growing. The top users of price-off coupons are packaged goods manufacturers. They reimburse retailers for the face value of coupons plus a handling charge after the number redeemed is processed by a clearinghouse.

There are two types of direct mail coupons: single and multiple. Both forms come as self-mailers or in envelopes accompanied by advertisements. Firms doing multiple couponing may include several of their own brands or noncompetitive items to help defray the cost of promotion.

Multiproduct couponing is usually carried out by promotional organizations, which plan the mailing and then solicit participation by different firms. The largest such mailer is Carol Wright. Its schedule for co-op mailings in 1991 include 2 mailings of 40.3 million pieces and 8 mailouts of 30.3 million. The vast majority of coupon promotions require extensive mailings from mass-produced lists. The products themselves must have high purchase frequency and intensive distribution.[34] A product bought often increases the opportunities for coupon redemption;

30. David Scholes, "Targeting Frequent Users," *Direct Marketing* (March 1989), pp. 56–58.
31. Donnelley Marketing, *12th Annual Survey of Promotional Practices.*
32. *Wall Street Journal* (November 2, 1987), p. 31.
33. Donnelley Marketing, *op. cit.*
34. John C. Hoyt, "Direct Mail Couponing," DMMA, *Manual Release* 230.2 (April 1979).

the buyer is always in the market. When distribution is intensive, there is little waste in circulation. When a product is available everywhere, redeemers have no difficulty in finding outlets that carry the merchandise.

A recent development is electronic retail promotion (ERP). This form allows supermarkets to bypass local newspapers to distribute coupons. Consumers that present UPC bar-coded cards at the checkout counter are credited with existing coupons. Through these cards, computers track the buying habits of each cardholder, allowing supermarkets to initiate frequent-shopper programs.

Singing the praises of ERPs, some pundits have already predicted a significant decline in the number of coupons placed in newspapers and sent by mail.[35] Citicorp took the lead in 1989 by enlisting 13 supermarkets around the country to participate in an ERP program called "Reward America." The program, however, was not profitable and was terminated at the end of 1990.[36] It demonstrated technical feasibility but little else. One drawback was that relatively few stores at the present time have ERP installations. Perhaps one day ERP will cut into the volume of conventional coupons. But for now, electronic coupons are still in the experimental stage.

# Summary

Direct mail is the heart of the direct marketing industry. It is the third largest advertising medium, next to newspapers and television. The expansion of direct mail is due to certain advantages it has over other media. The most important ones are selectivity, personalization, flexibility, isolation, and response rates.

A factor in the growth of direct mail has been advances in computer technology, which have enabled marketers to select a greater variety of targets more efficiently. It has also been a major force in the personalization of advertising through the computer letter. These advances have helped direct mail maintain the highest response rates of any direct marketing medium.

The most popular format is the direct mail package. It consists of four main elements: an outer envelope, a letter, a brochure, and an order form. The most important part of the direct mail package is the letter. Its main job is to present the selling proposition and secure the desired agreement or purchase from the prospect. The brochure dramatizes the content and main points of the letter by using illustrations.

35. Jan Larson, "Farewell to Coupons?" *American Demographics* (February 1990), pp. 14–17.
36. Fred R. Blakley, "Citicorp Operation in Marketing Data Is Laying off 174," *Wall Street Journal* (November 30, 1990), p. A4.

Appeals can be rational or irrational. The type used generally depends upon seller's perceptions of how customers go about buying the product. An appeal can also stress a benefit or a product attribute. Most messages combine both approaches in varying proportions.

Since the direct marketing message aims at creating sales now, it is a hard sell. However, the objective of short-range results is to some extent being modified by a greater concern for attitude-building factors.

---

## REVIEW QUESTIONS

1. What evidence points to direct mail as the primary medium of direct marketing?
2. What is the case for direct mail involving less media waste than television or magazines?
3. Discuss uses and misuses of computer letters.
4. What are the main functions of an outer envelope in a direct mail package?
5. What objectives does the beginning of a direct mail letter seek to accomplish?
6. When would you recommend or not recommend the use of a brochure?
7. What is the justification for long copy in direct marketing, when it is generally shunned by general advertising?
8. Why do charity solicitations usually use irrational appeals?
9. Are benefits-oriented messages more rational than product-oriented messages?
10. Direct marketing thrives on the hard sell. Explain.

---

## PROJECT

1. You are the newly hired corporate vice president of advertising and sales promotions for Bueno Supermarkets. The organization expects to open its store in Kansas City, Missouri, near the University of Missouri, in four months. Your research department has given you a report on the customers within the 10-mile trading area of the new store, which includes major competitors such as two Kroger stores, a Safeway store, an A&P, and a major cooperative.
   a. What promotion plans would you consider if funds are limited to direct marketing strategies? Explain. In addition to the usual techniques, include some creative ideas.

b. List the results you expect to achieve from your promotion plans. State the results in terms of a percentage projection. Substantiate your recommendations.
c. Indicate what further information you would want, why it is needed, how it can be obtained, and how it can be used. State the sources for this information.
d. Create two promotion pieces to advertise the new Bueno Supermarket. It is fine to work in black and white. If you prefer you may do it in color. A paste job is also approved. Neatness and clarity count as part of the grade.

CHAPTER 11

# List Management

It is almost axiomatic among direct marketers that mailings sent to the wrong people invariably end up as failures. In a speech before a college student group, Malcolm Dunn, president of a prominent list management house, claimed that list selection can change direct mail results by 1,000 percent.[1] Perhaps Dunn was a bit carried away by the force of his own rhetoric, but one thing is certain. Unless a mailer addresses an envelope properly, it will not get to its destination. What gasoline is to a car, lists are to direct mail; the industry cannot run without them.

There are many ways of classifying lists. All such methods involve sorting names into meaningful categories. One way to begin is to break lists into two broad groupings: consumer lists and business lists. Consumer records refer to data on individuals and households. Business lists consist of organizations. These two types of lists have little in common. Practitioners work in either consumer or business fields, rarely in both.

Whether consumer or business, lists can be further divided into internal and external. The internal list is known as the *house list*. A company generates this list from internal records, such as sales, credit reports, inquiries, and promotions. External lists come from outside the company and make up the list market. These lists are available for use through various arrangements with their owners, most commonly by rental.

## The House List

The house list is the fulcrum of a company's direct mail program. Whether used for solo mailings or continuous programs, direct mail packages or catalogs, the house list is basic. Because it is built from internal records of corporate activities, it differs from firm to firm. In general, however, house lists comprise three distinct entities: customers, prospects, and former customers.

Customers are buying units that deal with the company. They are the basic category of any house list. The other two elements, prospects and former customers, need not be included. Though these names may be kept in a computer file, they do not produce transactions that require record keeping. It is the customer component that is a firm's most valuable asset. The list of these buying units creates opportunities for a company to do business.

Definitions of a customer vary widely. Some mailers keep inactive customer names in their active files several years. Others remove inactive customers fairly soon. Magazine publishers, for example, do not carry expires for more than three months. They may continue sending them

1. Malcolm Dunn, speech at St. John's University, October 14, 1983.

subscription offers, but they are officially considered noncustomers. No matter what the definition, all firms seek to maintain their customers' loyalty and to increase their purchases.

The customer is king and is largely responsible for house lists outpulling outside lists by a wide margin. A 1989 survey among direct mail houses found minimum threshold rates of response averaging 3.25 percent for house lists compared with 1.85 percent for external ones.[2]

Prospects are names accumulated from a wide array of promotional activities. People sending in inquiries, joining sweepstakes, leaving their names at trade show booths, and participating in numerous other activities might be grouped into a "prospect" file. The rate at which this motley group converts to customers depends on product interest and company follow-up.

Former customers are those who once dealt with the company but have stopped buying. The definition of a customer also determines that of a noncustomer.

## What Goes into a Customer List?

Computer technology permits almost any amount of data to be stored in customer records. Because data processing costs are continually declining, the demand for additional facts about customers has been incessant. A popular attitude holds that the more we know about a customer, the more effective list utilization will be. But knowledge has both costs and limits. Simply knowing that a person is left-handed does nothing to increase the sales of a book, unless the book is about problems of left-handed people. Knowing that a woman buys red meat is no help to a firm selling apparel. Try this one, an actual recommendation from a creative director: Place an ad offering a free booklet on insomnia to get response from people interested in mattresses.[3] Why not a booklet on sex?

What should go into a customer list is relevant data. But what is relevant? The most important factors determining relevancy are the size of the list, the markets to be served, and the uses to which the list will be put.

When a list is small, it does not pay to try to enhance it. The mailer would find no advantage in segmenting such a list. The same holds true for lists oriented to narrow, vertical markets, such as surgeons, accountants, and computer programmers.

Because business markets employ macrosegmentation only, business lists lack detailed selection codes. The most common ID codes are those

2. Quoted in DMA Direct Marketing Association, *Statistical Fact Book* (New York: DMA, 1989).
3. "10 Tips for Generating Fresh Names," *Target Marketing* (April 1988), p. 60.

of Standard Industrial Classification (SIC), a four- or five- digit government system that groups all companies into like industries.

Consumer lists are larger and encompass more varied buying behavior than lists pertaining to business. All customers are not equal. If a list pulls 4 percent on average, some groups may respond at a 2 percent rate and some at 6 percent. Differential response patterns imply that some names have a greater sales potential than others. Separating the good customers from the poor ones necessitates adding codes to profile constituents of the in-house list. These additions were discussed in Chapter 6 on database marketing.

The last factor determining what goes into a house list is its anticipated use. Some companies are protective about their lists, using them strictly for internal purposes. In those cases, companies will profile their list members in accordance with their own needs. Customer codes will relate to company operations.

On the other hand, some firms pursue peripheral profits from customer files. One popular method is through list rental. Some firms have found this avenue quite lucrative, experiencing strong demand for their lists by mailers of noncompetitive products. Another form is the package insert. With each shipment to customers, the firm inserts promotional literature of other mail order sellers, and gets paid for doing so. A variation of this form is the co-op mailing.

When a firm anticipates using its list to get outside revenue, it must code its in-house file to meet the needs of the list market. This step often involves "list enhancement," in which various types of data from a master control list are transferred to the house list. At a minimum, the list owner must offer demographic selection. Purchase-related information would increase opportunities of attracting rentals.

## List Maintenance

Like any tangible thing, a house list cannot remain intact over time; it deteriorates. To stop lists from getting run down, a firm must engage in preventive maintenance. The process is mainly a matter of repairing damage from wear and tear.

One source of deterioration is attrition owing to customer inactivity. Magazines, for example, often lose between 30 percent and 50 percent of home deliveries by customers' failure to renew their subscriptions. To maintain the customer file at a predesignated level, the publisher must replace the losses with new names. There are a number of ways in which fresh names can be generated:

- Advertise in mass media, such as magazines and television. Ironically, media waste is encouraged by the necessity to maintain a medium devoted to target marketing.
- Institute a referral program. Some catalog houses run "send a friend

**TABLE 11.1. Types of External Lists.**

| Type of List | Consumer | Business |
|---|---|---|
| Response | Individual | Company |
| Compiled: | | |
| Occupant | Occupant/Resident | Occupant/Position/Title |
| Name and address | Name and address | Name and address |

SOURCE: "List Industry Overview," *Direct Marketing* (August 1990), p. 75.

a catalog" campaigns. They solicit current customers for names of their friends who may want a catalog. Financial houses and real estate developers resort to the same tactic in communicating with customers.

- Regenerate old names. Large mailers have millions of old names stored in computers. Some of them make special efforts to renovate files that had been left to gather dust.

Another cause of attrition is change of address. Our nation is highly mobile, with about one-fifth of the population changing residence each year. Some parts of the country, such as California, have much higher mobility rates.[4] This constant shifting of addresses makes it mandatory for a firm to "clean" its lists, or else it will be paying for a large amount of undelivered mail. The post office does not forward bulk third-class mail. But the postal authorities will, for a fee, return undeliverable items, known as "nixies."

The frequency of cleaning depends on the cost of a mailing package and the value placed on a customer. If unit sales are high, a firm might do best to clean at short intervals. For low-cost mailings and low-margin merchandise, cleaning can be done at longer intervals. But if the firm seeks to rent its list, it must update it more frequently.

# External Lists

Whether consumer or business, there are two basic kinds of external lists: *response* and *compiled*. Compiled lists may be addressed in two ways: either by name or by "occupant" or "resident." These alternatives are shown in Table 11-1.

## Response Lists

The consumer list market puts the greatest value on response lists. This type of list is a house list that can be rented. In other words, someone's house list is another firm's response list. These lists are made up of

4. U.S. Bureau of the Census, *CPC Reports*.

people who have bought something by mail, since experience suggests that people who buy one thing by mail have a higher likelihood of buying something else than do nonmail purchasers. Because responder names obtain the largest returns on mailings, these names command the highest prices.

Nevertheless, there should be some relationship between customers on a response list and products offered by the renter company. The customer list of an art gallery selling expensive paintings may not be an appropriate vehicle for a mailer offering low-priced apparel. On the other hand, catalog lists have recently been much in demand for fundraisers, credit card companies, publishers, and insurance firms.[5]

The owner has the right to approve or disapprove every rental order, regardless of whether the deal is struck by an agent. This permits list owners to refuse to rent to direct competitors.

If the list is large enough, mailers can rent portions of it and omit the rest. This is essentially a segmentation technique. By selecting segments, marketers can choose portions of the population that presumably have higher probabilities of responding to an offer. According to the Third Annual Survey of List Practices, conducted by Donnelley Marketing, the most popular segmentation method was geographic. But the most successful technique for increasing response rates was list profiling. Remailing to duplicated names ranked second. Geographic segmentation ranked fourth out of five common methods. Donnelley concluded that geographic segmentation is the most overrated tool among the more popular techniques.[6]

## Compiled Lists

Compiled lists are "manufactured" by list production houses. These compilations are put together from numerous sources. There are the large, extensive lists derived from sources such as telephone directories, voter lists, and auto registrations. There are other, smaller lists having some common characteristic, such as newlyweds, new homeowners, and families with babies.

Unlike response lists, compiled names do not represent mail order buyers. Supposedly, compiled lists are not responsive to mail solicitations. Then what is their attraction? Compiled lists may be admirably suited to mass mailers who want broad penetration of a market. If a marketer wants to reach large numbers across the country but does not deem it advisable to pay high rates for television, compiled lists are one answer.

5. "List Snapshots," *Target Marketing* (August 1989), pp. 23–24.
6. Donnelley Marketing, *Third Annual Survey of List Practices, 1989.*

**TABLE 11.2. List Usage Volume.**

| Type of List | Sales (millions) | Number of Names (billions) | Rates (per M) |
|---|---|---|---|
| Business compiled | $136 | 4,000 | $34 |
| Consumer compiled | 210 | 8,400 | 25 |
| Occupant/Address | 94 | 13,000 | 7 |
| Response lists | 789 | 10,800 | 73 |

SOURCE: "List Industry Overview," *Direct Marketing* (August 1990), p. 75.

Higher mailing costs in recent years have caused marketers to cut down on saturation mailings. Compilers of large, extensive lists have added numerous "enhancements," such as demographic and lifestyle data. Marketers are increasingly going into compiled lists and selecting names that match the profiles of their customers. Compilers argue that these lists offer selectivity that response lists cannot parallel. These "higher-quality" names can also come in large quantities because of the enormous size of the overall list.

Smaller lists do not have the enhancements found in the larger ones. But they work well for marketers selling certain lifestyle-oriented goods or services. For example, new homeowners make excellent prospects for lawn care services, insurance, security systems, and interior decorating services.

The major compilers are Donnelley Marketing, Metromail, and R.L. Polk. These three firms account for more than 90 percent of all compiled list sales. Usage and rates of various classes of lists are shown in Table 11-2. The category of business lists in Table 11-2 combines compiled and response lists but is made up primarily of compiled names. Response lists are relatively insignificant in business-to-business marketing, and their premiums over compiled lists are not large as in consumer markets.

The most extensive information on lists is furnished by the Standard Rate and Data Service (SR&D). It issues a directory, *Direct Mail Lists Rates and Data.* This assemblage excludes lists that organizations keep for private use. A page from the SR&D directory is presented in Figure 11-1.

## List Rentals and Brokers

List compilers usually have full control in maintaining, promoting, and scheduling their lists. Response lists can be rented from their owners. The large majority of them, however, are obtained through list brokerage firms.

The broker is an intermediary in a channel of distribution. These middlemen bring buyers and sellers together, doing all the contact work

| | Total Number | Price per/M |
|---|---|---|
| Lumber, wood products, pulp & paper industries executives (No. G9511) | 9,200 | * |
| Metalworking industry executives (No. G9508) | 39,000 | * |
| Printing & publishing executives (No. G9523) | 10,000 | * |
| Textile & apparel manufacturing (No. G9519) | 9,000 | * |
| Oil industry executives (No. E9529) | 7,400 | * |
| Producing, drilling & refining cos. | 3,500 | * |
| Supply cos. | 2,200 | * |
| Gas producers & processors | 1,400 | * |
| Electrical & electronics industry executives (No. E9536) | 4,400 | * |
| Transportation equip. manufacturing executives (No. E9537) | 3,500 | * |

Selections: telephone numbers, 5.00/M extra.
Minimum order 3,000.

### CANADIAN MAILING LISTS/TRADE ASSOCIATION MEMBERS

**Media Code 3 045 2750 0.00** **Mid 025521-042**
Member: D.M.A.
Research Projects Corp.
Pomperaug Ave., Woodbury, CT 06798. Phone 203-263-0100, toll free, 800-243-4360.
**NOTE: For basic information on the following numbered listing segments 1, 3, 5, 6, 7, 8, 9, 10, 11, see Research Projects Corp. listing in this classification.**

**2. DESCRIPTION**
Individuals who are active members of business, trade and professional associations in Canada. Includes business executives, engineers, lawyers, accountants, and architects.
ZIP Coded in numerical sequence 100%.
Selections available: key coding, province, postal code.

**4. QUANTITY AND RENTAL RATES**
Rec'd January, 1985.

| | Total Number | Price per/M |
|---|---|---|
| Total list (No. C9512) | 140,000 | 35.00 |

Minimum order 5,000.

## Canadian Master Business Index

ALVIN B.
ZELLER

**Media Code 3 045 2756 7.00** **Mid 024316-036**
Member: D.M.A.
Alvin B. Zeller, Inc.
475 Park Ave., South, New York, NY 10016. Phone 212-689-4900, Toll free, 800-223-0814.
**NOTE: For basic information on the following numbered listing segments 1, 5, 6, 7, 8, 9, 10, 11, see Alvin B. Zeller, Inc. listing under classification No. 46.**

**2. DESCRIPTION**
Canadian businesses and executives; postal coded.

**3. LIST SOURCE**
Business directories.

**4. QUANTITY AND RENTAL RATES**
Rec'd July, 1984.

| Selections by employee strength: | Total No. — Companies | Total No. — Exec. | Price per/M |
|---|---|---|---|
| Under 10 employees | 14,000 | 20,000 | 35.00 |
| 10 to 49 employees | 14,500 | 33,000 | * |
| 50 to 99 employees | 4,000 | 12,000 | 40.00 |
| 100 to 499 employees | 8,000 | 24,000 | * |
| 500 to 999 employees | 1,000 | 3,800 | 65.00 |
| 1,000 & over employees | 900 | 2,400 | * |

| Executives by job function: | Total Number | Price per/M |
|---|---|---|
| Presidents or top man-each plant | 40,000 | 35.00 |
| Vice-presidents | 25,000 | * |
| Financial executives | 22,000 | * |
| Production and plant executives | 25,000 | * |
| Advertising & sales executives | 8,000 | * |
| Office managers & personnel executives | 6,100 | * |
| Purchasing executives | 5,800 | * |
| Canadian manufacturers | 36,000 | * |
| Top executives at each plant | 35,000 | * |
| Vice president & senior management under the top man | 18,000 | * |
| Finance executives | 17,000 | * |
| Production & plant managers | 25,000 | * |
| Advertising & sales executives | 8,700 | * |
| Personnel & office managers | 5,500 | * |
| Purchasing executives | 5,000 | * |
| Highest rated Canadian companies with president | 17,000 | * |
| Canadian metalworking firms and their executives: | | |
| Metalworking firms | 9,000 | * |
| Metalworking executives | 31,000 | * |

Selections by SIC, employee size, province, 2.50/M extra; city, 5.00/M extra.

## Canasus Business Magazines Canadian Subscribers

**Media Code 3 045 2774 0.00** **Mid 035063-000**
Canasus Communications Inc.
874-330 Graham Ave., Winnipeg, Man., CN R3C 4A5. Phone 204-944-1441, Telex, 07-55675.

**1. PERSONNEL**
Circulation Manager—Tracy Karr.
**Branch Office**
Vancouver, B.C. Canada V6C 1S4—50-200 Granville St. Phone 604-669-1721.
**Broker and/or Authorized Agent**
All recognized brokers.

**2. DESCRIPTION**
Canadian subscribers and expires to Atlantic Business, Manitoba Business, Saskatchewan Business, Alberta Business and BC Business.
Postal coded in numerical sequence 100%; by province 100%.
List is computerized.

**3. LIST SOURCE**
Direct mail and circulation records.

**4. QUANTITY AND RENTAL RATES**
Rec'd January, 1985.

| | Total Number | Price per/M |
|---|---|---|
| Total list | 91,923 | *78.00 |
| Subscribers | 68,653 | *85.00 |
| Atlantic Business | 14,079 | * |
| Manitoba Business | 6,674 | * |
| Saskatchewan Business | 7,376 | * |
| Alberta Business | 17,385 | * |
| BC Business | 23,139 | * |
| Expires | 23,270 | *65.00 |
| Montreal names, English (1984) | 16,312 | * |
| Atlantic Business (1984) | 1,426 | * |
| BC Business (1984) | 5,532 | * |

(*) Canadian funds.
Selections: province, FSA, postal code, SIC Code, 5.00/M extra; key coding, 2.50/M extra.
Minimum order 5,000.

**5. COMMISSION, CREDIT POLICY**
20% commission to recognized brokers and ad agencies. 5% discount for payment with order. Orders cancelled before mail date invoiced for running and work-in-progress charges; after mail date, full price charged. Terms: 2% 10 days; net 30 days after list sent, for gross names shipped.

**6. METHOD OF ADDRESSING**
4-up Cheshire labels. 4-up pressure sensitive labels, 10.00/M extra. Magnetic tape (9T 1600 BPI), 50.00 refundable deposit.

**7. DELIVERY SCHEDULE**
Ten working days.

**8. RESTRICTIONS**
Sample mailing piece required for approval. One-time use only. No copies or reuse of list to be made.

**9. TEST ARRANGEMENT**
Random cross-section; record kept of names furnished; no extra charge. Minimum 5,000.

**11. MAINTENANCE**
Updated monthly and bimonthly.

## CareerTrack Seminar Attendees

**Media Code 3 045 2780 7.00** **Mid 031082-000**
CareerTrack Media.
1800 38th St., Boulder, CO 80301. Phone 303-447-2323.

**1. PERSONNEL**
List Manager—Constance Howard.

**2. DESCRIPTION**
Managers, supervisors and administrative personnel who have attended CareerTrack's seminars, including Image & Self-Projection, Power Communication Skills, People Skills, Stress Management For Professionals, etc. 90% women; 80% at business address.
Average unit of sale 95.00.
ZIP Coded in numerical sequence 100%.
List is computerized.
Selections available: state, SCF, sex, Nth name.

**3. LIST SOURCE**
Brochure mailings.

**4. QUANTITY AND RENTAL RATES**
Rec'd March, 1985.

| | Total Number | Price per/M |
|---|---|---|
| Total list (1983-85) | 175,000 | 65.00 |
| Inquiries & referrals | 35,000 | 50.00 |
| Hotline (last 90 days) | 40,000 | 75.00 |

Selections: keying, 2.50/M extra.
Minimum order 5,000.

**5. COMMISSION, CREDIT POLICY**
20% to recognized brokers. Net 30 days.

**6. METHOD OF ADDRESSING**
4-up Cheshire. Pressure sensitive labels, 10.00/M extra. Magnetic tape; 25.00 flat fee.

**7. DELIVERY SCHEDULE**
Two weeks after receipt of order.

**8. RESTRICTIONS**
Sample mailing piece required for approval.

**10. LETTER SHOP SERVICES**
Printing, inserting, Cheshire labeling available.

**11. MAINTENANCE**
Updated weekly.

(D-C2)

## Career Women Association Members

JAMI

(This is a paid duplicate of the listing under classification No. 518.)
**Media Code 3 045 2786 4.00** **Mid 018443-000**
Career Women Association Members.

**1. PERSONNEL**
**List Manager**
JAMI, Inc., Two Executive Dr., Fort Lee, NJ 07024. Phone 201-461-8868.
All recognized brokers.

**2. DESCRIPTION**
Working women who belong to one or more of over 50 working womens' associations and clubs.
ZIP Coded in numerical sequence 100%.

**3. LIST SOURCE**
Membership rosters.

**4. QUANTITY AND RENTAL RATES**
Rec'd April, 1985.

| | Total Number | Price per/M |
|---|---|---|
| Total list | 240,417 | 50.00 |
| Professionals | 37,373 | * |
| Finance | 12,483 | * |
| Real estate | 34,947 | * |
| Personnel | 19,899 | * |
| All other executives | 135,715 | * |

Selections: state, SCF, 3.00/M extra; ZIP Code, 6.00/M extra; keying, 2.00/M extra; category, 10.00/M extra.
Minimum order 5,000.

**5. COMMISSION, CREDIT POLICY**
20% commission to all recognized brokers.

**6. METHOD OF ADDRESSING**
4-up Cheshire. Pressure sensitive labels, 6.00/M extra. Magnetic tape (9T 1600).

**8. RESTRICTIONS**
Sample mailing piece required.

(D-B)

Names & Addresses, Inc.
presents
CASHFLOW

### CASHFLOW MAGAZINE SUBSCRIBERS

**Media Code 3 045 2799 7.00** **Mid 024044-000**
Coordinated Capital Resources, Inc.

**1. PERSONNEL**
**List Manager**
Names & Addresses, Inc., 3605 Woodhead Dr., Suite 101, Northbrook, IL 60062. Phone 312-272-7933.

**2. DESCRIPTION**
Executives with money-management and treasury responsibilities who subscribe to Cashflow Magazine. Mostly male.
Average unit of sale 50.00.
ZIP Coded in numerical sequence 100%.
List is computerized.

**3. LIST SOURCE**
Direct mail.

**4. QUANTITY AND RENTAL RATES**
Rec'd March, 1985.

| | Total Number | Price per/M |
|---|---|---|
| Total list | 30,017 | 95.00 |

Selections: state, ZIP Code, SCF, 3.00/M extra; key coding, 1.00/M extra.
Minimum order 5,000.

**5. COMMISSION, CREDIT POLICY**
20% commission to all recognized brokers.

**6. METHOD OF ADDRESSING**
4-up Cheshire. Pressure sensitive labels, 5.00/M extra. Magnetic tape (9T 1600 BPI), 25.00 non-refundable fee.

**8. RESTRICTIONS**
Two sample mailing pieces required for approval.

(D-C)

### CENTER FOR MANAGEMENT DEVELOPMENT

**Media Code 3 045 2819 3.00** **Mid 028322-000**
Center For Management Development.

**1. PERSONNEL**
**List Manager**
The Direct Media Group, Business List Management Div., 70 Riverdale Ave., P.O. Box 4565, Greenwich, CT 06830. Phone 203-531-1091.

**2. DESCRIPTION**
Participants in one-to-three day self-improvement workshops and management seminars on time management, developing leadership skills, quality circles, labor relations and secretary as a manager; 96% located in the northeast; 50% 5-line addresses; 30% 4-line.

**3. LIST SOURCE**
Direct mail.

**4. QUANTITY AND RENTAL RATES**
Rec'd March, 1985.

| | Total Number | Price per/M |
|---|---|---|
| Total list (1983-84) | 12,369 | 50.00 |

Selections: state, SCF, ZIP Code, 3, 4 or 5-line address, sex, 2.00/M extra; key coding (to 11 digits), 1.00/M extra.
Minimum order 5,000.

**5. COMMISSION, CREDIT POLICY**
20% commission to all recognized list brokers.

**6. METHOD OF ADDRESSING**
4-up Cheshire. Pressure sensitive labels, 5.00/M extra. Magnetic tape (9T 1600 BPI).

**7. DELIVERY SCHEDULE**
Ten working days.

**8. RESTRICTIONS**
Sample mailing piece required for approval.

**11. MAINTENANCE**
Updated quarterly.

**FIGURE 11-1 Sample Page from *Direct Mail Lists Rates and Data***
*Source*: Reprinted with permission by Standard Rate and Data Service, Inc.

to effect a transaction. Because there are thousands of response lists for rent, brokers increase efficiency by minimizing transactional effort. Buyers need not expend energy in searching out specific lists.

Brokers are list specialists. In the course of doing business, they have acquired a deep knowledge of lists suitable to certain products. A mailer can often use that experience to advantage in list selection.

But control over selections must rest with the mailer. A SR&D study cosponsored by the American List Council found that 53 percent of mailers interviewed made substitutions or additions to brokers' list recommendations.[7] These modifications reflected not only differences over marketing matters, but conflicts of interest as well. Whether a broker can act as an agent of a seller and service a buyer at the same time is debatable. An ironclad rule of agency is that an agent cannot serve two masters.

BROKERS. In most instances, the brokerage firm is an agent of the seller, not the buyer. Some brokerage houses do act as consultants and are paid by mailers for special assignments, such as doing intensive list searches and analyses.[8] But in the main, brokerage compensation comes from selling lists, not from earning service fees from list renters.

As in real estate, a broker authorized by a listing acts on behalf of a principal. Owners can either list their rental properties as exclusive or deal with many brokers. Some list owners are reluctant to employ a broker who handles competing lists. Other owners don't care. They see a brokerage firm that handles similar lists as having more contacts in the industry and more prestige among firms wishing to rent.

A broker who rents a list usually receives a 20 percent commission from the owner. Brokers present list information to potential renters on data cards, which show list prices and key facts about list characteristics. A customer might be given a number of these cards from which to choose the lists desired. These data cards are similar to media rate cards and serve much the same purposes. Figure 11-2 illustrates a data card.

Data cards do not, however, contain all information a mailer might desire. For example, the cards do not indicate when, or how often, a list is cleaned. A widely used rule of thumb is four times a year. But some lists are cleaned perhaps once a year. Mailers who buy such lists may encounter low response or a large percentage of undeliverables.

Another issue is an owner's definition of a responder. Some mailers may keep names in their files for years despite the fact that orders were not forthcoming. These are somewhat like church membership lists, which leave people on their rolls though they never show up. A

7. "Most Mailers Turn to Brokers for List Rentals, SRDS Study Finds," *DM News* (June 1, 1986).
8. "My Dream Broker," *Target Marketing* (May 1990), p. 34.

**BUSINESS WEEK SUBSCRIBERS (A McGRAW-HILL PUBLICATION)**

MAL DUNN/GSC

100% paid subscribers to the leading general business management magazine. Key executives in small, medium, and large firms. Their purchasing power makes them prime targets for a variety of business and consumer offers. This list provides the most affluent corporate leaders available on the list rental market. Target these men and women for quality offers ranging from investment products and services, recreation and leisure activities, self improvement programs, travel related items and a variety of high ticket consumer and business products and services.

Average Household Income - $79,400 84% Travel On Business
81% Own Home Average Age - 44
88% Invest; 76% In Stock Market

Minimum Order: U.S. & Canada $550, International $950
$20/M Maximum Select Charge
Computer Run Counts In Advance $14/M - Minimum $140
10% Discount for Non-Political Fund Raisers

| | | |
|---|---|---|
| 738,945 | U.S. Subs | $ 97/M |
| 29,251 | Canadian Subs | $ 97/M |
| 64,391 | International Subs | $220/M |
| 480,641 | Home Address | $107/M |
| 225,174 | Business Address | $107/M |

STATE COUNTS

| | | | | | |
|---|---|---|---|---|---|
| AL | 6,152 | KY | 5,286 | ND | 1,201 |
| AK | 1,954 | LA | 5,612 | OH | 30,180 |
| AZ | 10,436 | ME | 2,716 | OK | 5,355 |
| AR | 3,015 | MD | 15,777 | OR | 7,434 |
| CA | 105,951 | MA | 30,444 | PA | 35,100 |
| CO | 12,473 | MI | 23,707 | RI | 2,870 |
| CT | 19,995 | MN | 15,125 | SC | 6,043 |
| DE | 2,339 | MS | 2,351 | SD | 1,127 |
| DC | 4,850 | MO | 11,955 | TN | 8,948 |
| FL | 30,775 | MT | 1,628 | TX | 41,848 |
| GA | 17,287 | NE | 3,687 | UT | 3,601 |
| HI | 4,730 | NV | 2,690 | VT | 1,619 |
| ID | 2,014 | NH | 4,495 | VA | 19,391 |
| IL | 42,462 | NJ | 38,111 | WA | 14,251 |
| IN | 11,472 | NM | 2,774 | WV | 2,019 |
| IA | 5,398 | NY | 74,961 | WI | 13,536 |
| KS | 5,638 | NC | 15,331 | WY | 831 |

**For more information call or write**
**MAL DUNN ASSOCIATES**

**Hardscrabble Road**
**Croton Falls, NY 10591**
**(914) 277-5558**

**622 Hungerford Drive**
**Rockville, MD 20850**
**(301) 424-4201**

| | |
|---|---|
| Size | 738,945 |
| Price | $97/M |
| Unit of Sale | $40.00 |
| Male | 91% |
| List No. | A10101 |

Selects Available

| | |
|---|---|
| Nth Name | No Charge |
| State/SCF | $10.00/M |
| Industry SIC | $10.00/M |
| Home/Business | $10.00/M |
| Job Function | $10.00/M |
| Company Size | $10.00/M |
| Slug Title | $10.00/M |

Services

| | |
|---|---|
| 4-UP Cheshire | No Charge |
| Magnetic Tape | $25.00 |
| Pressure Sensitive | $12.00/M |
| Key Coding | $3.00/M |
| Running Charges | $14.00/M |

List Updated Weekly

**Terms and Conditions**

1. We believe the information concerning this list to be accurate but we cannot guarantee its accuracy or the outcome of the mailing.
2. Stated prices are for one-time use only. Multiple and unlimited use arrangements are available.
3. Net name arrangements are available on large orders for many lists.
4. Commissions are paid to recognized brokers and advertising agencies at standard industry rates.
5. Names will be shipped only to a bonded mailhouse or service bureau.
6. Purchase orders are required. Mal Dunn/GSC reserves the right to require prepayment on any order.
7. Payment in full is required within 30 days of our invoice.
8. Cancellations must be in writing and accompanied by the returned names and are subject to running charges. Orders cancelled after mail date on purchase order will be charged full price.
9. We are not liable for any damages or loss sustained through use of this list, nor for any special or consequential damages, and in no event shall our liability exceed the price of the list.

7101 Wisconsin Ave (301) 986-0840
Suite 1001 (800) 873-5478
Bethesda MD 20814 FAX (301) 656-1254

Hardscrabble Road (914) 277-5558
Croton Falls NY 10519 (800) 677-5478
FAX (914) 277-5636

129 Newbury Street (617) 247-2608
Boston MA 02116 (800) 366-3866
FAX (617) 247-3584

**FIGURE 11-2 Illustration of a Data Card**
*Source*: Reprinted with permission by Mal Dunn/GSC.

recency–frequency–monetary value (RFM) selection would obviate that problem.

A third fact not on data cards pertains to frequency of mailing. How many times was a list mailed, and when? An overused list frequently leads to a decline in response rates. A sophisticated mailer asks these questions rather than simply choosing a set of lists from data cards.

What does a list broker do to earn that commission? The following is a description of the main functions:

- *Negotiates all terms, including price, with the firm renting the list.* The final agreement, however, is subject to approval by the principal.
- *Assumes responsibility for getting materials to and from a client.* These materials include file tapes and a sample of what goes into the mailing package.
- *Develops markets for client lists by means of personal calls on prospects, space advertising, and sending out data cards.* Some brokerage houses publish newsletters.
- *Works with prospects on details of a mailing, such as insert programs, pac on pacs, postcards, and piggy-back programs.*
- *Submits mailing contents before a rental contract is consummated.* An owner has the right to reject any mailing piece, regardless of the reason.
- *Bills and remits on behalf of the principal.* Payments fall due within 30 days.

LIST RATES AND RENTAL TERMS. On average, response lists in 1990 went for about $70 per thousand names. But there is great variation around this average. The more select the list, the higher the price. Such hard-to-get names as those of foreign investors; owners of yachts, airplanes, and Rolls Royces; and foreign-currency buyers can sell for three to four times the average.

Another set of names that command premium prices are *hotline names.* That designation was coined by Jim Knox of Computer Directions Corporation to describe new names received from a mailing. These names were made available almost immediately upon receipt for an extra charge. The term *hotline* today has an expanded meaning. Names can be from one month to one year old, depending on how an owner classifies them.[9]

Rentals conventionally cover a one-time usage at a specific mailing date. Prices and terms, however, are quite complicated because of "selection" factors. As with media rate cards, listed prices are only asking prices. They denote what a seller wants, but they are often negotiable. A major reason is that mailers usually do not use an entire list. Unless concessions are made, a mailer would probably find many rental lists unprofitable to use at all.

A major reason for not using entire lists is name duplication. A firm renting several lists is bound to find multiple listings of the same

9. Annette Brodsky, "List Brokers' Compensation: 'So Where's the Broker?' " *Directions* (January-February 1989), p.6.

names. To send these people identical mailings at the same time is wasteful. Outside lists also carry names found in internal customer lists. No publisher, for example, would care to send an introductory offer to present subscribers, especially if that offer carries a discount from the regular renewal price.

Duplication between a rented list and a mailer's house list increases the true cost of a mailing. If the house list, for example, overlaps the rented list by one-third, the cost per name of the rental in effect rises by 50 percent. The duplication factor is particularly difficult for companies sending out high-cost packages, such as catalogs or brochures printed on expensive paper. Since most lists are available on magnetic tape, it is simple matter to eliminate name duplication. Two lists are run in parallel, and matched records are eliminated. This procedure is known as *merge-purge.*

But should the mailer pay for names that are unused? A standard arrangement is the *85 percent net name* agreement. A firm obligates itself to pay for at least 85 percent of the total list, even if the usable proportion falls below 85 percent. For very large quantities—one million or more names—renters can swing deals that reduce cutoff points to as low as 70 percent.

A recent rental form is the *net* agreement. Here there is no minimum quantity that a renter must pay for. Instead, mailers pay only for the names they use. This arrangement is probably the most economical for mailers.

The kind of deal negotiated depends on the size of the order and the mailer's bargaining acuteness. Renters who give large orders or contract for lists on an annual basis can wring greater concessions from owners.

Some industry observers believe that eventually the entire industry will be on a *net-net* basis, with practically every list rental contract the outcome of dealing.[10] A large number of list agreements, whether net-net, net 70 percent, or net 80 percent, carry extra charges and deductions of various kinds. List selections by demographics, overlays, RFM, and a host of other factors carry additional charges because they involve extra costs.

Merge-purge operations identify not only active names that appear on two lists, but also names with undesirable characteristics. This action is known as *list suppression*. What is suppressed, or removed from a rented mailing list, depends on what a mailer deems undesirable. Some managers want to eliminate "bad-pay" prospects. Others insist on overlays with lists of people who requested that their names be removed from mailing lists. Banks and financial institutions want to suppress poor credit risks. Some firms in the financial community set criteria for

---

10. See "Major Trends in List Usage," *Direct Marketing* (August 1986), pp. 38–48, 114.

good credit so high that two-thirds of a list's names do not qualify for a mailing. As mailing requirements become more varied and idiosyncratic, list rental rates become less standardized.

LIST ABUSES. In any rental agreement, only the names of people who responded to the offer belong to the mailer. The remaining names are the property of the owner who rented the list. With the use of computers, the issue of list security has become more complex.

List owners, for various reasons, have always "seeded" lists as protection against name theft or unlawful use. They scatter decoys or dummy names across their lists, and when one of these "seeds" arrives with an unauthorized mailing, it is a signal to investigate.

Outright theft, however, is probably the least common abuse. Ed Burnett, head of a leading brokerage house, cites a cumulative volume of 180,000 orders for close to 2 billion names. In all that experience, he was involved in only three known cases of outright theft.[11]

Most of the claimed abuses are computer-related. In fact, there are questions about whether these so-called abuses are trespasses at all. Computer usage has raised a whole new set of issues (or as some in the industry put it, has opened a new can of worms). Here are a few examples.[12]

- A merge-purge of three outside lists finds a number of duplicates. Which list gets its total number of names reduced?
- A company matches its house list against an outsider list. It mails to duplicates a second time on the grounds that these names represent good prospects. Does the client have to pay the list owner for those duplicated names? These names are house list names, but the mailer would not have known that had there been no merge-purge against the outside list.
- A house list and outside list are matched for duplication. The outside list has data on customer age. Can the client add that information to duplicates? In effect, this means a transfer of information from the rented list to the house list.
- A firm sends out mail to a merged list (devoid of duplicates) with the note "address correction requested." Who owns the name with the corrected addresses? The mailer paid for the corrections but has no right to the name unless it represented a response.
- A firm rents a list and then pays an outside source to append phone numbers to that list. Who owns the records with phone numbers? Can the renter follow up the mailing with a phone call without paying the owner of the rented list?

11. Ed Burnett, "How to Cope with List Problems and Abuses," *Directions* (March/April 1988), p.1.

12. *Ibid.*, pp. 1–16.

Most of these questions have no ready answers. As computers get used more and more to enhance list response, more such questions will arise. There is little doubt that the rules for list rentals will be rewritten.

## Merge-Purge

A merge-purge combines records from a number of different sources after eliminating duplicate names. Its main purpose is to prevent multiple mailing packages being sent to the same individuals. The lists normally merged for a direct mail promotion include house lists, outside rental lists, and suppression lists.

A promotion using rental lists reduces mailing costs by not mailing multiple packages to a firm's own customers. The mailer can also distinguish customers and prospects and send different solicitations to each. A side benefit of duplications is that a mailer gets to know which customers appear on other lists. Evidently, the more lists a customer appears on, the more things he or she buys by mail. A firm can also segment its lists into heavy and light mail buyers by classifying the extent to which its customers appear on other lists. It might then make special efforts to promote to the "mail junkies."

THE DUPLICATION UNIT. How a company defines a duplicated unit depends on the purpose of its actions. Most firms prefer the household as the relevant unit when sending out promotional literature. Catalog houses usually want to mail no more than one catalog per household. On the other hand, some companies don't object to sending mail to individuals sharing the same household. A number of companies have varied aims. Financial houses may send out multiple newsletters and brochures when individuals in the same home have separate accounts. However, a firm might deem one mailing per home sufficient when soliciting business from noncustomers.

The duplication issue in business-to-business direct mail presents problems wholly different from those of consumer markets. Mail to a company can go to corporate headquarters, divisions, locations, departments, individuals, or titles. Many company units have more than one address and post office box. The same executive may hold several titles. In addition, business lists contain a good deal of inaccuracies because of high personnel turnover and changes in job titles. For these reasons, the techniques of merge-purge dealing for business mail bears little resemblance to that for consumer mail. Because merge-purge systems are used much more extensively in consumer markets, the discussion of the subject will be confined to the consumer area.

MEASURING DUPLICATION.[13] The first step in any merge-purge is editing, especially if several lists are being compared. Lists represent unique records, and information is often entered in different ways. Lists are compared by using a standardized format. That is the main job of editing.

A variety of software programs perform merge-purge. Some use simple match codes. These might, for example, employ a zip code, a fixed number of digits taken from the address, and a fixed number of consonants in the person's name and street of residence. Other kinds of software use every element in the records to determine whether names match. Some programs use phonetics rather than spelling, and others use complicated scoring formulas to judge if two records are for the same individual or household. No matter what the system, all contain certain amounts of error. Following are two hypothetical examples of possible name matches.

| | | |
|---|---|---|
| Example 1 | John DeFazio<br>72 Baldwin-Orchard<br>Cranston, RI 02920 | John DeFazio<br>72 Baldwin-Orchard<br>Cranston, RI 02920 |
| Example 2 | Jane Wright<br>19 Crown St.<br>Worcester, MA 01609 | Jane Steward<br>19 Crown St.<br>Worcester, MA 01609 |

All merge-purge programs would pick example 1 as a duplicate. Yet the names may be of two separate individuals, such as father and son. Few programs would tab the second example as a match. Yet the two names may well be of the same person. For example, a married woman may keep her maiden name in business and use her married name at home. No system is 100 percent foolproof.

Although error is unavoidable, the relevant question is the amount of error that occurs. Kestnbaum & Co. studied 25 merge-purge programs and found a wide range in the quality of performance. Variation in quality is only partly attributable to computer programming. Another part of the problem is the poor condition of the lists themselves. Compiled lists in particular are highly variable, since they are put together from different sources with different degrees of care.

All merge-purge programs have two kinds of error: overestimation and underestimation of duplicated names. When too many rental names are identified as overlapping a house list, response lists contract in volume. In general, this shrinkage increases rental costs. When the number of duplicated names is underestimated, mailing costs increase. First,

13. This discussion is based on a series of articles by James Wheaton and Cynthia Baughan, "What to Look for When Evaluating Merge/Purge Systems," *Direct Marketing* (July–December 1987).

customers receive multiple mailing pieces. Redundancy might increase total response, but it is not proportional to the increase in cost. Second, mail is sent to names that should have been suppressed, which increases bad debt.

A merge-purge sorts all names into three basic groups:

1. Names duplicated with those of the house list or suppression lists.
2. Names duplicated between rented lists.
3. Exclusive names available for mailing.

Duplicates from rented lists can be handled in several ways. One method is to allocate duplicated names randomly among lists. If list 1 has 500 names also found in list 2, each list can be credited with 250 names. Costs of each list are reduced by the same amount, provided agreements with the two list owners are the same.

A second method is hierarchical. The main reason for assigning priorities is to reduce rental charges. For example, suppose list A is rented for $50 per thousand names on a net-net arrangement. List B rents for $80 per thousand on the same terms. The renter will pay less if all duplicates are assigned to list A.

A third way is to lump all duplicates together, regardless of source. Under these conditions, a response from any outside list represents that of an exclusive buyer. Since duplicated names are expected to yield higher returns, all lists will have depressed response rates. Because each list has a different percentage of duplication, response deflation will penalize the list unequally. This will distort list comparisons.

## List Management

A number of list management houses have arisen in recent years. List management firms offer a wealth of experience, and often more expertise than a small company can muster on its own. In-house list management in small companies often diverts the staff from more important functions, as maintaining a specialized staff may be too costly.

Some list brokers manage lists as a way of adding revenue to the proceeds from their brokerage activity. But a list owner can separate brokerage and list management. The two functions need not be combined in a single firm.

Large firms usually manage their own lists. Doubleday & Company, for example, has managed its customer list in-house since 1974. Staff and equipment are already there—accounting, computer services, creative, credit, and collections. In these circumstances, an outside management firm could add little to performance, and costs would be higher.[14]

---

14. Kevin Hanley, "Two Views on List Management," *Target Marketing* (August 1987), p. 45.

Should a company decide to use an outside manager, it must decide on a number of criteria. Some of these are:

- *Experience.* One way of evaluating a firm is to examine its past and present accounts. Among the issues to be addressed are the kinds of accounts handled and how well this new one would fit into the whole operation. For example, are the accounts competitive or complementary? Are they mass lists or quality lists?
- *The size of lists the management house handles.* A company has a choice of being a dominant client in a small operation or a small part of a large operation. The big firm usually has adequate expertise available but may pay scant attention to a small account. On the other hand, a small service company may give more attention to the account but possess less depth of staff. In any event, the choice of whether to use a list management firm must be made after a firm has realistically assessed its own needs.[15]

## Summary

An important component of direct marketing is lists. These can be divided into consumer lists and business lists. Consumer records refer to data on individuals and households. Business lists consists of organizations. Lists can be further divided into internal and external. Internal lists are house lists. External lists come from outside the company.

House lists are made up of customers, former customers, and prospects. The strongest pull comes from house lists. Customer lists include such data as recency of purchase, frequency, dollar volume, and items bought. Lists must be kept up to date. People move, stop ordering, or pass away.

There are two basic types of external lists: response lists and compiled lists. A response list is someone's house list and can be rented provided the owner approves. Compiled lists are derived from such sources as telephone directories, auto registrations, catering halls, and voter lists.

Brokers are list specialists. They can provide response lists on all types of buyers. Response lists went for about $70 per thousand names, on the average, in 1990. Rentals conventionally apply to a one-time usage at a specific mailing date.

Merge-purge is a procedure for combining addresses and eliminating duplicates or keeping just duplicates. The rationale for focusing on duplicates is that people who appear on several lists are probably good prospects.

15. *Ibid.*, pp. 30–31; Bob Karl, "Finding the Right List Manager," *Direct Marketing* (March 1987), pp. 90–96.

List purchases can only keep the names of people who responded to their offer. The remaining names are the property of the owner who rented the list. Large firms usually manage their own lists. Small firms might not have the necessary staff.

---

## REVIEW QUESTIONS

1. Why do house lists pull better than responder lists?
2. What are the uses of lists?
3. Why do firms that rent lists engage in preventive maintenance?
4. How are new names generated for a customer file?
5. What are the drawbacks of compiled lists? When is it best to use them?
6. What questions should a mailer ask before selecting a set of lists from data cards? Explain each one.
7. What services do list brokers provide?
8. What can list owners do to protect their lists from unlawful use?
9. What are three uses of the merge-purge technique?
10. What are some of the list problems involved in mailing to a business?

---

## PROJECT

1. Doug Merriam, a junior at the College of Business Administration of St. John's University, decided to put his education toward entrepreneurship in his senior year. He was thinking of selling T-shirts displaying a picture of a boxer (a short-haired dog with brownish coat and a square-jawed muzzle).
   **a.** State three target sources that would be likely to buy a quantity of T-shirts with a picture of a boxer. Explain.
   **b.** State a minimum of three direct marketing techniques of selling these T-shirts. List the pros and cons of each technique.
2. **a.** How would you determine if there is a demand for these T-shirts?
   **b.** State the procedure of developing a list of prospective customers among the target sources chosen.
3. Create two direct marketing promotion pieces to sell the T-shirts. It is fine to work in black and white. If you prefer, you may do it in color. A paste job is also approved. Neatness and clarity count as part of the grade.

CHAPTER 12

# Catalogs

# The Catalog Market

Catalogs are a special branch of direct mail. The catalog gets into buyers' hands through the mail, though they can be promoted through other media. Orders resulting from catalogs are most commonly fulfilled by mail.

*Webster's New Collegiate Dictionary* defines a *catalog* as a list or register with descriptive details. In the instance of direct marketing, the items are articles of commerce that form a shopping list. Some lists are short; others are long, stretching into many pages. Buyers traverse the pages of listed articles as they would the aisles of a retail store, seeking specific goods, browsing through assortments, and making some unplanned purchases because particular items caught their fancy. Shoppers who leaf through these lists or registers make up the catalog market.

Like many estimates of market size, those of the catalog market are extremely rough. In the consumer sector, approximately 40 percent of all U.S. adults buy some merchandise from catalogs in a given year. Projected nationally, this market embraces some 71 million shoppers. The typical buyer places three orders per year from one or more catalogs. The highest incidence of ordering comes from middle-aged, white-collar individuals in upper-income households.[1]

Catalog sales have been increasing at a greater rate than store retailing. Since 1980 the number of catalogs sent out annually has more than doubled, rising from about 5.8 billion to more than 12.5 billion copies. That averages to roughly 147 catalogs per U.S. household. Nevertheless, growth has slowed significantly in recent years. At the beginning of the 1980s, sales growth raced along at a two-digit pace.[2] Toward the end of the decade, after adjustment for inflation, this heady rate fell to low single-digit numbers.

All signs indicate that the catalog mode of distribution has entered a mature stage. New customers are no longer coming in droves to the catalog market. Almost all catalog marketers have experienced increasing difficulties in getting new names for mailing lists.[3] There are only so many people who will purchase by mail, and more and more catalogers have entered the field to court the same customers. Individual companies face market saturation because the industry is approaching its peak. It has reached the largest amount of possible sales from the

1. *DMA Statistical Fact Book* (New York: DMA, 1989), pp. 66–67.
2. "Catalogue Cornucopia," *Time* (November 8, 1982), p. 72.
3. Holly Klokis, "Open up to In-Store Sales," *Chain Store Age Executive* (April 1986), pp. 18–20.

maximum efforts of all firms. The marketplace seems to be flooded with catalogs. Competition is more intense. Corporate management places more emphasis on cost efficiency and has reduced its investment in growth strategies.

According to Don Schultz, Associate Dean of Medill School of Journalism at Northwestern University, firms in a mature market tend to retreat to strategies that led to their initial success. Such "refinements of past strategies," argues Schultz, "are not the way to enter the 1990s." Instead, he advocates innovation, new approaches to cataloging.[4] A firm cannot compete in a dynamic market by standing pat. But innovation is a two-edged sword, cutting in opposite directions. Its costs may yield no differential advantage if the innovation can be easily imitated.

Some direct marketers took innovative measures, such as launching electronic catalogs. Of greater consequence, however, at least from the perspective of investment flows, was the shift of catalog houses into retailing. This trend caught up several nationally recognized catalogers, such as Eddie Bauer, Williams-Sonona, Banana Republic, Talbots, Sharper Image, and Lillian Vernon. A number of retailers, such as Bloomingdale's and Marshall Fields, went the other way, putting more resources into catalogs. In both instances, retailers and catalogers adopted each other's distribution methods to use existing assets to open new markets. These retail–mail order businesses have extreme distribution mixes. At one end stands L.L. Bean, with 90 percent of total revenue coming from mail order. At the other extreme are companies such as Brooks Brothers, for which 85 percent of revenues are based on sales rung up at its stores.[5]

Rebecca Jewett, marketing vice president at Talbots, advises that retail-catalog businesses maximize results by creating synergy between the two types of activities. She argues that such synergy is profitable when the store and catalog reach the same kind of customer, those with "similar decision-making processes." For example, Talbots' store displays emulate catalog offerings. When customers cannot find a particular item in the store, they can get it via red-line sales. A red phone set up in the store allows customers to order the merchandise, which is sent to their homes without shipping and handling charges.[6]

Joint use of resources, however, can take many forms. Some retailers issue catalogs that feature merchandise not displayed in the store. As much as 40 percent of items in Neiman-Marcus catalogs are not carried by the stores. Whatever the format, both retail and catalog distribution channels are becoming increasingly hybridized.

---

4. "Catalogers: Look out for the Plight of the 90s," *Direct Marketing* (July 1987), p. 120.
5. "Mail Order's Top 250+," *Direct Marketing* (July 1989), p. 82.
6. "Catalogers," *op. cit.*, pp. 120, 127.

**TABLE 12.1. Catalog Buyers in the Last 12 Months (1988).**

| Cataloger | Adult Buyers (000) | Percent of Population |
|---|---|---|
| Sears, Roebuck | 27,575 | 15.6 |
| J.C. Penney | 24,254 | 13.8 |
| L.L. Bean | 6,003 | 3.4 |
| Spiegel | 5,665 | 3.2 |
| Lillian Vernon | 5,326 | 3.0 |
| Hanover House | 4,109 | 2.3 |
| Lands' End | 3,822 | 2.2 |
| Royal Silk | 1,643 | 0.9 |
| Talbots | 1,502 | 0.9 |
| Horchow | 1,209 | 0.7 |

Base = 176,250 adults

SOURCE: Adopted from Simmons Market Research Bureau, quoted in DMA *Statistical Fact Book* (New York: DMA, 1989).

# Differences Among Catalogs

Catalogs can be classified according to the markets for which they are intended. A first classification is between catalogs meant for consumers and those destined for business organizations. Consumer and business catalogs circulate in completely different domains, as though they were in worlds apart. What are the differences?

For one thing, the two types of catalogs operate on vastly different scales. In terms of sheer numbers, business catalogs have low circulations. Compared with consumer markets, customers in business markets are few. Among the top 50 catalogs listed by Standard Rate & Data Service, using 12-month buyers as the measurement of size, there is not a single business-to-business entry. Table 12-1 shows the 10 most popular catalogs and the number of customers they garner during a year.

In many instances, top catalogers issue multiple catalogs. For example, Hanover House issues 23 different catalogs with varying circulations. At the high end is the Hanover House catalog that sells general merchandise. At the low end is *Men America*, credited with only 22,000-plus buyers in 1989, a customer base equal to that of many successful business publications.[7]

The disparity between consumer and business segments is immense. Compared to the large-scale operators shown in Table 12-1, business-to-business catalogs operate in pygmy-sized markets. If a firm selling in an

7. "Catalogers of the Year," *Target Marketing* (October 1989), pp. 17–24.

organizational market could obtain one-twentieth as many customers as the smallest consumer giant, it would be considered large by any standard in the business universe. The business catalog, however, pulls a larger order size as well as more frequent orders. Exact figures—or even approximate ones—are not available and so must be inferred. One indication are estimates of the lifetime value of a customer. A large number of consumer firms, 47.6 percent, estimate customer worth at less than $200. In contrast, two-thirds of business-to-business catalogers value customers at more than $200. [8]

However, the number of orders from business catalogs is much smaller than those generated by personal selling. This suggests that business customers use catalogs to order standard, off-the-shelf items that are relatively inexpensive. The higher frequency of mailings to businesses also suggests that orders represent routine buying. A related factor is that house lists in the business sector yield higher response rates than those in consumer markets.

Primary business catalogs are more likely to come in a standard $8^3/_8 \times 10^7/_8$ format, indicating greater functionalism in design. This accords with routine buying behavior. Some 80 percent of primary business catalogs adhere to the standard size, as opposed to only 52 percent of consumer catalogs. [9]

Larger production runs give consumer catalogers lower per-unit costs compared to business catalogers for publications of equal paper quality. But larger orders give business catalogers better gross margins. Consequently, they pursue leads with greater intensity. A typical business marketer sends out about five catalogs before mailings are halted because of no orders. The comparable number to consumers is approximately three. One-third of industrial marketers send out more than six books, as compared with less than 10 percent of consumer catalogers. Some 86 percent of mailers to industrial markets do not charge for their catalogs. This compares with only 44 percent of consumer catalogs. Many of these consumer publications, however, offer rebates with purchases.[10]

Few house lists, in either consumer or business markets, remain intact over a long period of time. They deteriorate and must be replenished with new names if a business is to grow and prosper. Not many catalogers, however, break even when prospecting for new customers. Because a business customer has a greater long-term value, catalogers in organizational markets can afford to spend more to convert prospects into customers. To estimate what is affordable, a company must track

8. *The Catalog Age Report* (1989).
9. *Ibid.*
10. *Ibid.*

**TABLE 12.2. A Two-Step Procedure in Catalog Marketing.**

| Objective | Criterion for Evaluation |
|---|---|
| **Customer Acquisition** | |
| Solicit inquiries | Cost per inquiry |
| Generate leads | Cost per lead |
| Convert inquiries and leads to customers | Cost per conversion |
| Build prospect file | Cost of file building |
| **Customer Service** | |
| Convert one-time buyers into regular customers | Rate of conversion |
| Optimize mailings | Sales by mailing frequency, by segments |
| Profitability | Returns on investment, returns on sales |

the behavior of first-time buyers, measuring their orders over a number of years.[11] Yet less than one-fifth of catalog houses in consumer and industrial fields have made studies to estimate the lifetime value of their customers, according to the *Catalog Age Report*.

When firms divide mailings into those sent to prospects versus those sent to customers, operations separate into two distinct parts. The first step deals with customer acquisition, the second with customer service. Each function entails different objectives and, consequently, different ways of evaluating the results of efforts. Table 12-2 summarizes these differences. According to this scheme, companies should integrate customer acquisition with customer service. The first step organizes prospect-seeking activities to attain a firm's highest potential. The second step concentrates on maximizing sales and profits from the potential customers or new buyers resulting from prospecting effort.

# Consumer Catalogs

Catalogs can be defined in various ways: by the articles they carry, by the markets they aim to reach, and by the quality of their production and artistic design. The first two are the most common ways of classification. Using these criteria, consumer catalogs can be classified based on whether they carry general or specialized merchandise and whether their issuers are store or nonstore operators. The second criterion is a determinant of the items a catalog features and the marketing objectives it tries to achieve. These two factors yield four generic groups of consumer catalogs, shown in Figure 12-1.

11. See Jack Schmid, "Front End vs. Back End," *Target Marketing* (October 1989), p. 37.

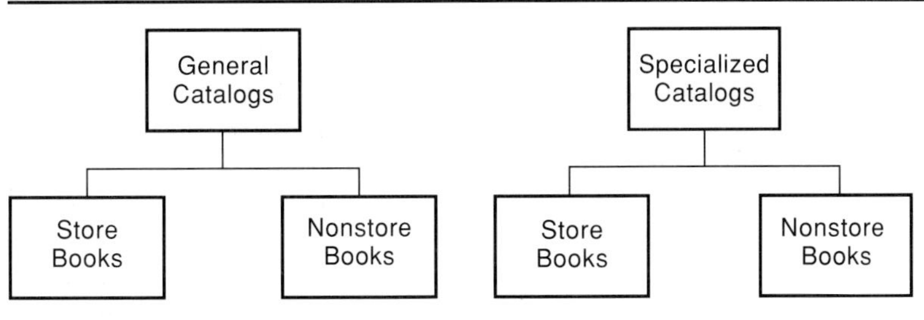


**FIGURE 12-1 Four Generic Types of Consumer Catalogs**

## General and Specialty Catalogs

Whether store or nonstore, specialty catalogs have recorded the strongest growth in recent years. Their offerings cater to particular tastes and interests, associated mainly with upscale economic segments of American society. Examples are publications featuring gourmet foods, cookware, gifts, plants of both indoor and outdoor varieties, hobbies, electronic gadgets, and the latest fads and fashions.

The move to specialty catalogs has paralleled the strong trend toward specialty retailing.[12] For one thing, general merchandisers do not carry broad selections. They cannot afford to assign valuable shelf space to slower-moving items. Nor can they afford to keep large inventories for goods whose demand is driven by specialized interests. Rather, they concentrate on the most popular merchandise. In contrast, specialty shops can focus on a wide selection of a narrow field by drastic reduction in the number of product lines carried.

These same influences prevail in catalogs. Both general merchandise and specialty catalogers must carry inventories, and the more lines a catalog carries, the less able it is to offer a wide variety in any particular line. As items are added, inventory costs per unit rise. But the same principle holds for both types of catalogs, general and specialized. Then why are speciality catalogs able to take on more items in a line? General catalogs appeal to audiences with diverse tastes, so that each product line, in effect, lacks a large demand. Specialty catalogs go to buyers interested in few product categories, so that it becomes economical to offer a wider selection within each group. About 80 percent of all catalogs today are specialized, and the proportion is still growing.

Publishers Clearing House catalogs, for example, offer a wider range of magazines than can be found anywhere else. They also offer combinations of magazines at cheaper prices than buyers can get from individual publishers or outlets for single copy sales. Specialty catalogs, however, must take care that their target markets are easily identifiable

12. Jeb Brown, "What's Happening to Department Stores," *Retail Weekly* (January 10, 1989).

and not too small. For example, it would be extremely difficult to obtain a sufficient number of names of people demanding left-handed golfing equipment or videos of Italian operas.

The decline of the general catalog reached a dramatic moment when Montgomery Ward discontinued its century-old catalog at the end of 1986. It was the nation's first mail order catalog, started in 1872, and through the years had eased the dreary isolation of rural families. At the turn of the century if offered mechanical washing machines for $2.75 and fur jackets for less than $10. By the 1980s this general catalog was badly out of date, and out of step with American shopping habits. Like the dinosaur, this huge multiproduct catalog geared to an undifferentiated audience could draw no sustenance in an environment swarming with niche marketers offering limited assortments of greater depth and breadth. Ward's decision to exit the catalog business signaled a piece of Americana disappearing from the social scene. After an absence of six years, Ward in 1991 decided to get back in the catalog business, but with small, specialty books.

Among marketers who were more successful in making the transition from all-purpose to specialty retailing by mail, Spiegel is the outstanding example. Like Montgomery Ward, Spiegel is an old-line cataloger. It began its American career in 1904 selling inexpensive furniture and household supplies to working-class homes out of its Chicago headquarters. Customers were allowed to pay for their purchases with modest down payments and monthly installments ranging from $0.50 to $7.00. By the 1970s, markets had changed. The firm was still selling lackluster merchandise to the low-income end of the market. But traditional blue-collar families were shrinking in number and the new waves of immigrants read little English and did little catalog shopping. Mass merchandisers and discounters made deep inroads in those markets, and Spiegel completely and irrevocably lost its differential advantage.

To revitalize its ailing catalog sales, Spiegel redirected its efforts. It dropped hundreds of items: bulky ones that had to be freighted, fitted ones that required extensive processing, and replaceable ones that called for large inventories. The new catalogs were specialties, totaling two dozen. They emphasized style and quality. They were tastefully designed and expensively printed, taking on a lavish appearance (see Figures 12-2 and 12-3). Their apparel bore names of such top designers as Norma Kamali, Liz Claiborne, Allen Tracy, and Yves St. Laurent. Home furnishing catalogs sported such glittering names as Fieldcrest, Laura Ashley, Henredon, and St. Cruset. Mailings were reduced but were tightly targeted to upscale audiences. From 1976 to 1982, catalog response rose from 2 to 4 percent. Today, orders from Spiegel customers are among the highest of all catalogs, averaging more than $100 each.[13]

---

13. *DMA Statistical Fact Book, op. cit.*, p. 80.

**FIGURE 12-2 Changing the Design to Keep up with the Times**
*Source*: Spiegel. Reprinted with permission.

**FIGURE 12-3 Promoting Elegance and Quality**
*Source*: Spiegel. Reprinted with permission.

Besides the big, glossy publication Spiegel mails out twice a year, the company issues more than 20 specialty catalogs, called *specialogs*.[14] Some of these the firm created internally; some it acquired.[15] Gross sales in 1988 reached $1.3 billion, ranking Spiegel among the top four catalog retailers. Company executives credit a large part of this growth to customer acquisition. Whether other firms can take Spiegel's road to success and attain similar results is not clear. Spiegel benefited immensely from the deep pockets of Otto-Versand, a German corporation that acquired the catalog house in 1982.

The proposition of whether other catalogers can match Spiegel's turnaround may be tested with respect to the huge Sears, Roebuck catalog, which goes back more than 100 years. In the mid-1970s, five companies dominated the catalog business: Aldens, Penney, Sears, Spiegel, and Ward, all competing directly in the general merchandise field. Aldens stopped publishing catalogs in 1982, and Ward followed in 1985. Spiegel changed its direction to upscale segments, while Penney went into specialties and drastically cut its assortments. By the end of the 1980s, Sears stood alone as publisher of the general merchandise catalog.

But Sears has already split the Big Book's 1,000+ pages into two volumes—one a seasonal issue carrying apparel and home fashions, and the other an annual issue featuring appliances, home improvements, automotive supplies and recreational goods. The catalog's problems are the same as those that have plagued all other large general merchandisers. The product mix remains broad and unfocused, while swarms of specialty catalogs, like piranhas, bite away at their victim with sharp offers of variety and breadth in specific product lines. Sears' large book incurs heavy production and mailing charges, but customers shop it selectively, and many pages show up without productive yields.[16]

Will Sears go the way of other general catalogs? The company already has more than a dozen small, specialty catalogs, covering such diverse fields as hunting and fishing, apparel, and lawn and garden. A number of scenarios are possible. The Big Book can be remodeled, even after being sliced in half. Or it can be cut up into specialty components and issued as specialogs. The 1990s will determine the fate of this surviving dinosaur.

Specialty catalogs are usually built around some theme. This gives the catalog a definite direction. Apparel for outdoor activities, such as hunting or fishing, naturally goes with boots and camping equipment.

---

14. Kate Fitzgerald, "Spiegel Writes the Primer on Catalog Sales," *Advertising Age* (August 1, 1988), pp. S-1, S-12.
15. "Mail Order's Top 250+," *op. cit.*, p. 38.
16. "Sears' Big Book: Dinosaur or Phoenix?" *Direct Marketing* (July 1986), pp. 71–74; David Snyder, "Last Chapter for the Big Catalog," *Advertising Age* (July 18, 1988), p. 26.

A catalog featuring sporting goods would have a somewhat broader appeal and might also include cycling, tennis, golf, skiing, and physical fitness equipment. Products should be related to the central theme of the catalog. If not, individual items will meet with disinterested readers. A catalog devoted to hardware would not necessarily entice its readers to buy collectibles. An electronics catalog would not be read by many gourmet cooks, even if it sold microwave ovens. The focus of any catalog defines its market. The width of this focus depends on the selection of related or complementary products. If the scope is too broad, a specialty catalog loses focus. Many gift and gadget catalogs went out of business for this reason: products were spread thinly over a wide range, and too many pages lacked readership involvement.

## Store and Nonstore Catalogs

Whether specialty or general, catalogs can be separated into those put out by stores and those issued by nonstore operators. In consumer markets, retailers such as Sears and Penney have the most extensive catalog operations (see Table 12-1). Other prominent retailers also run catalog operations that are important adjuncts to their stores. Among them are Bloomingdale's, Neiman-Marcus, Eddie Bauer, Brooks Brothers, Bryland, Carroll Reed, Spencer Gifts, Talbots, and Williams-Sonoma. In industrial fields, nonstore catalogs are put out by manufacturers or distributors.

NONSTORE CATALOGS. In consumer markets, nonstore publications act as stand-alone businesses. They represent an alternative to retail or personal selling, and authorities often regard them as a "pure" form of cataloging.

The cataloger is in effect a merchant wholesaler who takes on retail functions. This firm usually buys goods from manufacturers or their agents for the purpose of reselling, but directly to consumers.

Many of these middlemen, like retailers, put out products under their own labels. Most of these products are acquired through contract manufacturing. Some firms are actually manufacturers that market their products directly to consumers. *Catalog Age* credits the L'Eggs catalog, a part of the Hanes group, with more than 1.8 million people who bought something over the span of a year.[17] Pfaltzgraff, a maker of dinnerware items since the early nineteenth century, issues catalogs for people who cannot find its goods in retail outlets.[18] Patagonia catalogs carry lines of outdoor clothing the company makes itself, and lists its dealers on

---

17. Quoted in DMA, *Statistical Fact Book*, *op. cit.*, p. 80.
18. "Manufacturer Complements Retail with Mail Order," *Direct Marketing* (September 1983), pp. 72–77.

**TABLE 12.3. Catalog Cost Ranges (60# coated stock).**

| Finished Size | Leaves/Pages | Colors/Sides | Cost per Thousand | | |
|---|---|---|---|---|---|
| | | | 50M | 100M | 300M |
| $8\frac{1}{2}'' \times 11''$ | 16/32 | 2/2 | 206.50 | 179.55 | 160.75 |
| $8\frac{1}{2}'' \times 11''$ | 16/32 | 4/2 | 287.05 | 233.35 | 197.70 |
| $8\frac{1}{2}'' \times 11''$ | 24/48 | 2/2 | 303.00 | 267.40 | 243.25 |
| $8\frac{1}{2}'' \times 11''$ | 24/48 | 4/2 | 395.50 | 328.60 | 283.10 |
| $8\frac{1}{2}'' \times 11''$ | 32/64 | 2/2 | 392.80 | 344.55 | 309.80 |
| $8\frac{1}{2}'' \times 11''$ | 32/64 | 4/2 | 497.25 | 417.25 | 362.85 |
| $8\frac{1}{2}'' \times 11''$ | 48/96 | 2/2 | 561.60 | 491.80 | 447.90 |
| $8\frac{1}{2}'' \times 11''$ | 48/96 | 4/2 | 684.86 | 573.50 | 503.70 |
| $5\frac{1}{2}'' \times 8\frac{1}{2}''$ | 16/32 | 2/2 | 134.20 | 116.70 | 104.80 |
| $5\frac{1}{2}'' \times 8\frac{1}{2}''$ | 16/32 | 4/2 | 185.85 | 152.15 | 127.90 |
| $5\frac{1}{2}'' \times 8\frac{1}{2}''$ | 24/48 | 2/2 | 197.55 | 174.87 | 158.42 |
| $5\frac{1}{2}'' \times 8\frac{1}{2}''$ | 24/48 | 4/2 | 255.25 | 213.35 | 184.20 |
| $5\frac{1}{2}'' \times 8\frac{1}{2}''$ | 32/64 | 2/2 | 285.95 | 253.75 | 229.55 |
| $5\frac{1}{2}'' \times 8\frac{1}{2}''$ | 32/64 | 4/2 | 372.50 | 308.50 | 264.65 |

NOTE: All are self-cover, saddle-stitched; prices do not include bound-in order cards/forms/envelopes.

SOURCE: Shell Alpert, Alpert O'Neil Tigre & Co., June 1987; Direct Marketing Association, *1989 Statistical Fact Book* (New York: DMA, 1989), p. 72.

the catalog order form to encourage traffic at distributor retail outlets.[19] Catalogs by producers must have enough items to make the catalog worthwhile.

Catalogs operating as stand-alone businesses must be judged on their own financial results. They are liberated from high rentals; they do not need choice locations. Customer traffic and prestigious quarters are of no concern. Catalogers can accept and fulfill orders out of low-cost warehouses, and they can limit other overhead expenses, such as salaries, losses by theft, insurance rates for dealing with the public, and daily maintenance to accommodate streams of visitors and shoppers.

The nonstore enterprise, however, incurs several expenses that stores do not. Some important costs are those of promotion and list rentals. These are at least double, and often triple, those faced by average general merchandisers. Costs of producing and mailing catalogs are usually higher for the nonstore firm. Because these firms operate as independent profit centers, their demand is not enhanced by in-store operations, and costs do not benefit from volume-related economies. Nor are their costs shared by synergistic operating units. Table 12-3 indicates how paper costs decline with greater volume. These costs average some 40 percent of total printing costs.[20]

19. Michele Whitney, "Patagonia Pulls a 10% Response on Mailing off Its Spring Catalog; Average Order $100," *DM News* (June 1, 1986), p. 27.

20. See *DMA Statistical Fact Book, op. cit.*, p. 75.

A somewhat troubling aspect of the nonstore catalog is inventory. If a retail store does not have goods on hand, it does not put them on the shelf. A cataloger cannot do this. This firm must order merchandise well in advance of the book's publication. If goods are overstocked, stores can sell their excess at a clearance sale. Catalogers can get rid of their overstocked goods only by selling leftovers to remainder merchants at 10 percent to 20 percent of their initial value. If goods sell faster than predicted, a store can stock its shelves with other items. A cataloger who does not deliver goods that are advertised can alienate customers. Back orders push up costs by increasing employee time and shipping charges and may decrease customer satisfaction despite greater effort to fulfill orders.

Catalog success stories abound in the trade press because they are eagerly sought by the media as newsworthy. Most of them are true, but the truth is only partial. There is a darker side to the business. The history of recent catalog ventures is littered with shattered dreams and costly failures. About half of all new catalog ventures fold within two years.[21] Catalogs that have lasted and, for the most part, maintained their dominance possess two prime characteristics: long experience and adequate resources. Among them are such familiar titles as Spiegel, Fingerhut, and Hanover House.

Steve Warsaw, a well-respected authority on catalogs, estimates that a moderate-sized start-up program requires a 450,000 mailing at minimum, and that that volume would yield returns nowhere near break-even. Paper and printing costs for that volume plus mailing and list rental would come to more than $420,000. This assumes a 48-page catalog, standard $8\frac{1}{2} \times 11$, with 60# coated stock (see Table 12-3). When administrative expenses are added, start-up costs would, according to Warsaw's estimate, run into the "mid six digits."[22] This start-up figure is a marketing cost only. It does not include cost of merchandise, which requires keeping at least a 30-day supply of stock on hand. Fast-moving items need a somewhat larger amount of transit inventory. A cataloger might regard these outlays as investments. Though inventory fluctuates, it always remains in some degree until a business is liquidated. No matter how one looks at the business, catalog costs run to substantial amounts, and new entrants assume high risks.

Business-to-business catalogs can make out on much smaller volumes. The reason is that they commonly replace costly personal selling functions, either in part or in whole. Distributors in industrial photography, office supplies, computer accessories, printing, and publishing commonly sell low-priced products through catalogs. Their strictly

---

21. Steve Greene, "A Boutique in Your Living Room," *Forbes* (May 7, 1984), pp. 86–88.
22. Steve Warsaw, *Successful Catalogs* (New York: Retail Reporting Corp., 1989), pp. 221–222.

functional "no frills" formats keep production costs low. They usually provide 800 numbers, and operators staff those phones during working hours. Still, costs of these product catalogs are well within the range of savings engendered by eliminating or reducing personal visits. These savings set the upper margin for efficient catalog operations.

Besides the popular product catalog, which is geared to getting orders, the business field includes incentive and dealer catalogs. The incentive catalog is linked with motivational programs for a sales force. It typically consists of a core of widely popular items, such as television sets and vacation offers, surrounded by some luxury items, such as mink coats, expensive cars, and trips to exotic places with or without a companion. At other times goods are offered, such as clothing or household items (see Figure 12-4).

Dealer catalogs are promotional publications that are mailed to stores or dealers. Their objective is to get the cooperation and support of channel members. They spend more on artwork, type, mechanicals, photography, and color separations. Production costs run higher, as they use better-grade paper. Expensive four-color photographs are duplicated and made available to retailers, furnishing them with promotional material at practically no expense to themselves.

Both incentive and dealer catalogs cannot be evaluated on the basis of their returns. They are parts of larger programs and constitute a cost of doing business. They act as aids in a sales-directed program. Their contribution is not direct and cannot be isolated from the whole.

STORE CATALOGS. The largest catalog producers are retail stores—Sears, Penney, Bloomingdale's, and the like. The volume of their catalogs dwarfs the output of the largest nonstore catalogers.

Store catalogs have emerged from two sources. The largest has been the movement of retailers into cataloging. The top store catalog operators initially ran retail establishments and gradually moved into catalogs. Some, such as Sears, have issued store catalogs for many years, but only recently have they increased their catalog operations manifold by cultivating specialty marketing. For example, Commonwealth Trading, Inc., running a chain of some 400 Hit and Miss stores, went into mail order with the same merchandise by founding Chadwick's of Boston, an off-price women's apparel catalog house. On the other side, some catalog houses moved into retailing and opened stores. Among them are well-recognized catalogers such as Sharper Image, Eddie Bauer, Horchow, and Lillian Vernon, although the last two just got their feet wet.[23] No matter what the source, the result is a catalog associated with a retail establishment. This combination creates a dual channel of distribution.

23. See Ronnie Gunnerson, "Retail and Mail Order—A Marriage Made in Heaven," *Target Marketing* (September 1986), pp. 10–12.

**FIGURE 12-4 An Incentive Catalog**
*Source*: Reprinted with permission by the Van Heusen Corporate Markets Company.

The store-catalog union offers a company certain operating advantages. Among the most cited are the following:[24]

- Some part of the inventory, if not the entire stock, may be held in common. This decreases overall inventory in relation to sales.

24. See Freeman F. Gosden, Jr., *Direct Marketing Success* (New York: John Wiley & Sons, 1986), pp. 49–51.

**FIGURE 12-4** ***(continued)***

Horchow Mail Order, a catalog house, opened retail stores in Dallas to handle inventories more efficiently.

- Since goods are common, they can be ordered from the same suppliers. Larger order quantities may result in better service and bigger discounts.
- Marketing through two channels provides more knowledge of consumer demand. Sales in one channel may guide merchandise selection in the other. Firms can also experiment with certain products in one channel before making large commitments.
- A reputation established in one channel helps sales in another. Bloomingdale's by Mail benefited greatly from the image created by the store.
- Remnants from catalog merchandise can be sold in the store. This cuts waste owing to normal errors in forecasting demand.
- Dual distribution gives customers alternative shopping methods. A marketer can appeal to those who prefer to shop at home as well as to those who would never buy from a catalog.

- The density of mail order customers can indicate where to locate a store. Or the characteristics of a customer list might, through corollary methods, provide valuable insights into the choice of retail sites.

Because store catalogs have widely different sales patterns, they vary in objectives. At one end, they seek to increase store traffic. At the other, they try to sell merchandise by mail, like the stand-alone catalog. Many store-catalog merchandisers espouse dual functions, sometimes using a single catalog and sometimes with separate ones. Saks Fifth Avenue, Bloomingdale's, and Neiman-Marcus publish two kinds of catalogs, one to pursue mail order and a second to increase store traffic.

Traffic-building catalogs go out four to eight times a year, showing merchandise that is displayed at stores. Mailings are geared to event promotions, such as Christmas, Easter, Mother's Day, and back-to-school.

These catalogs are sent to charge account customers or to residents in a store's trading area. Though these catalogs do draw response by mail or phone, orders from a distance are not encouraged. Facilities to receive mail or phone calls are not well developed. To discourage such orders, Louis, an upscale clothing store, omits prices altogether in its catalog and provides no order form. The store will fill orders, however, if customers call.[25]

Some catalogs are distributed to shoppers in the store. This device gives customers a chance to shop the store's merchandise at their leisure. It is not uncommon for consumers to overlook goods they might want in the crowded, busy environment of the store's floor. A related technique is one of cross-selling. For example, a woman looking for a dress may not think of visiting a shoe department to round out her wardrobe. Giving customers a catalog, either in the store or through the mail, extends consumer awareness of goods.

At the other end of the spectrum is the mail order catalog owned and operated by a retailer. Bloomingdale's by Mail, established in 1982, is a prime example of a store catalog seeking direct sales. Merchandise for catalogs is managed separately, and product selection leans toward mail order, not in-store selling. Publications carry many products not found in stores, in accordance with their pulling power. The amount of space allocated to them in a catalog must be commensurate with returns. The database used for mailouts has no relation to store trading areas. Mailouts are based on net order volume, and criteria for targeting prospects hinge on response to mailings. The glittering image of Bloomingdale's as a trendsetter has drawn orders from customers all over the United States, customers who have never entered a Bloomingdale's store.[26]

---

25. Marlene Nadle, "Upscale Boston Clothing Store Uses Catalog to Build Customer Traffic," *DM News* (September 15, 1986), p. 16.
26. Gary Ostrager, "One Retailer's Infatuation With Direct Response Marketing," *Directions* (Jan/Feb 1986), pp. 6–12.

Such catalogs are not event-driven. Rather, they include products to flatten out the peaks and valleys of seasonal demand. Telephones and desks for receiving incoming mail are well staffed and set up to process orders. These catalog divisions are self-funding; they stand on their own feet as separate profit centers.

Sales from nonstore shoppers are incremental; they would not have occurred had there been no catalog. These additional transactions must then be evaluated in terms of incremental costs. Are they sufficiently covered by new sales to leave a sufficient profit?

Many catalogs are designed to fulfill a dual function: building store traffic and pulling mail orders. These catalogs may carry goods not available in the store, especially slow-moving items. Mailings go to segments of a house list or to charge account customers, as well as to selective households outside store trading areas. These supposedly best address consumers' interests.

It has been argued that traffic-building and dual-purpose catalogs cannot achieve the success of "pure" mail order publications.[27] This may be so if success is judged from the standpoint of direct response from a mailing. But if an objective is in-store sales, then the effects of the catalog must be judged by how much business it brings in. It is the net returns that count, whatever the source, mail or shopping in the store. Though measurements of additional store sales might not be as precise, the use of incremental returns as a yardstick for judging effectiveness still holds.

However, dual-purpose catalogs may face difficulties in attaining common goals. First, customers must perceive that they are dealing with one company, with one policy, whether they shop in the store or by mail. Products that sell by mail do not neccessarily do well in retail settings, and vice versa. Each function requires its own exercise. Nevertheless, a store with different managers still requires them to cooperate with each other. Though each may have a different merchandising point of view, corporate management should have the same policies and a single overall strategy. Product and section managers cannot be allowed to maximize their own operations at the expense of others.

## Creating a Catalog Image

The growth of specialty catalogs brought with it greater concern for design and image. This strong interest involves *positioning,* the act of establishing a viable competitive stance in consumer minds. With more and more specialty catalogs entering the market, each publisher seeks to create an image that sets it apart from the crowd.

27. Bob Stone, *Successful Direct Marketing Methods* (Chicago: Crane Books, 1979), pp. 227–229; John A. Scharff, "More Advice for Retail Catalogers," *DM News* (November 1, 1985), pp. 54–57.

These vague, perhaps undefined, impressions lodged in people's heads cannot be dissociated from the merchandise that is offered. An image must convey the message of the sort of goods a catalog carries as compared to its competitiors. An image implies something about the merchandise consumers expect to find between the covers of the catalog. But the same goods can be presented in various ways. Image creation thus relies on copy techniques to convey the desired impressions.

Some catalogs have discarded the traditional, down-to-earth look for more artistic, institutional-type advertising. Although these techniques are difficult to describe, the underlying trend in these image-creating efforts is the "soft sell."[28] This philosophy is especially favored by art directors and catalog designers and is most strongly embraced by prestigious store catalogs.

Abercrombie & Fitch, for example, has over many years built up a reputation of authority in the world of sports. Such famous persons as Teddy Roosevelt, Amelia Earhart, and Ernest Hemingway, all advocates of the active outdoor life, were publicized as regular customers. To preserve its sports authority image, the firm's catalogs try to capture a mood of elegance and adventure. They present products with backgrounds of rustic scenes, water-blue skies, and stately mansions. Models appear to be well-bred, mature individuals who command respect.[29]

The soft-sell approach has also extended to mixing illustrations with an editorial style of copy. San Francisco–based Esprit catalogs give little product information, focusing more on the models in a stream-of-consciousness type of approach. Esprit's "real people" campaign, begun in 1984, profiles these individuals using short sections of novel-like prose. Specialty retailers such as CITY of Chicago and Louis of Boston display only one item per page to preserve their upscale image. Some catalogs mimic a magazine's format, interspersing articles and "advertorials" among their displays. These are sometimes called *magalogs*. An example is shown in Figure 12-5. Lands' End sometimes runs short stories that have nothing to do with the products its catalogs carry.

In keeping with the magazine concept, some catalogs carry paid advertising. These are usually for noncompetitive products that match customer demographics. Practically, the fact that they pay part of the printing and mailing costs has more to do with their inclusion than what they add to the "magazine look."

But creating a catalog image does not necessarily mean abandoning the mail order style and the hard sell. In fact, most catalogs adhere to the Lillian Vernon or Hanover House approach. As put by Joan Throckmorton, president of a direct marketing agency, copy that "merely in-

28. Anita M. Basch, "Tailoring Catalogs to Fit Corporate Personality," *Advertising Age* (October 27, 1989), pp. S-21–S-23.

29. Kevin Hanley, "Marketing Through Catalogs," *Zip Target Marketing* (July 1985), pp. 23–24.

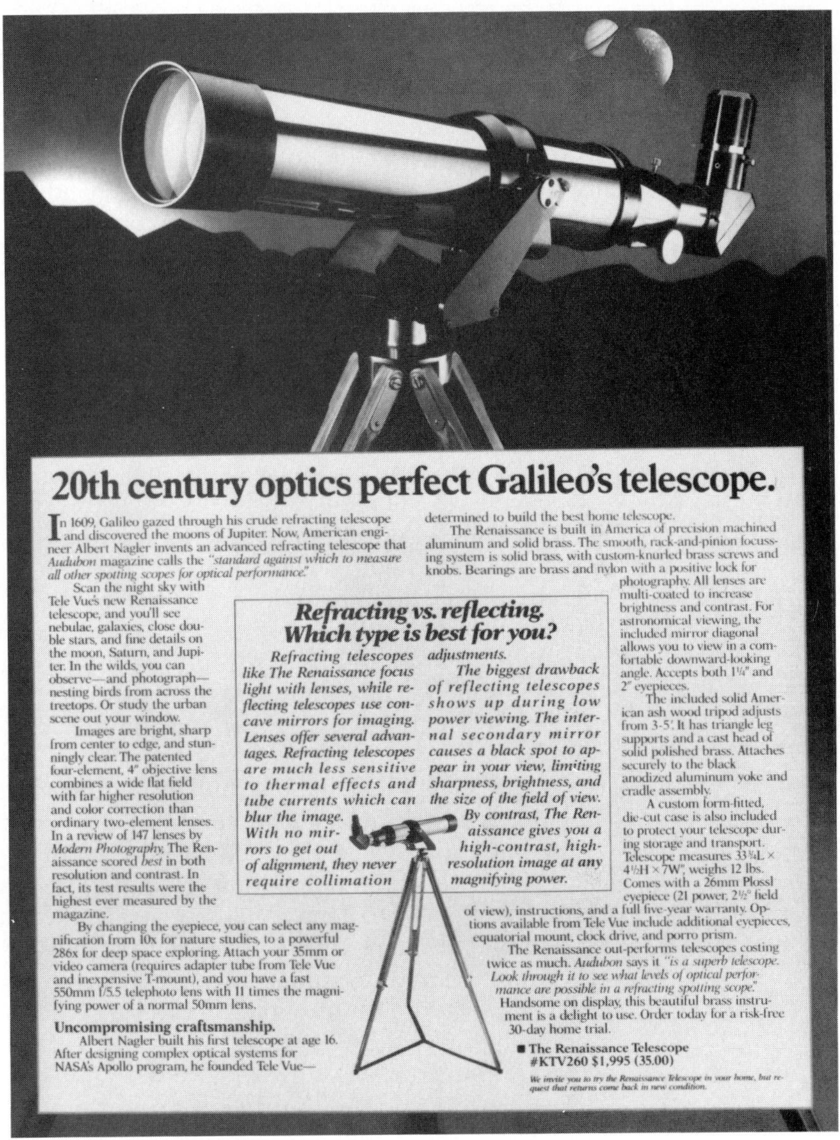


**FIGURE 12-5 Mimicking a Magazine's Format**
*Source*: Reprinted with permission from the Sharper Image.

fluences" is not for direct marketers. A catalog image must have credibility.[30] This attribute is not incompatible with the "workhorse ad" that sells right from its pages or brings customers into a store.

30. Joan Throckmorton, *Winning Direct Response Advertising* (Englewood Cliffs, NJ: Prentice-Hall, 1986), pp. 6, 342.

Most catalogs identify themselves with the company, whether it be a retailer or a mail order house. Specialogs from Sears, Penney, and Bloomingdale's associate themselves with their respective stores. Spiegel, Fingerhut, and Breck's market their goods under their corporate insignias. Recently, Hanover House announced catalogs with "brand identities." These will be devoted to common product categories. Unlike Spiegel or Fingerhut, Hanover expects to advertise its catalogs individually, like multiple-brand marketers of packaged goods. Each brand stands alone, with no perceived affiliation with other brands in the same company.

## Catalog Layout

Catalogs have often been likened to a retail store delivered to one's home. Buyers shop these pages as they would the aisles of a retail establishment. The similarities between stores and catalogs extend to other activities. As retailers base value on floor space, commonly by sales per square foot, catalogers base value on page space, most frequently by sales per square inch.[31] Other analogies are: the order form is the counterpart of the checkout counter; the index, the store directory; and the front and back covers, the store display windows. Brent Bissell, a catalog consultant, suggests that the mixing and placement of items in catalogs can benefit from principles of retail floor planning.[32]

As in retailing, merchandise must be arranged in some sort of order so that it is easy for consumers to find things. A popular arrangement consigns all items in a product category to the same section of the catalog. This scheme assumes that consumers first decide on a category, or some related set of items, and then go about choosing a specific one. For example, Penney's catalog of home furnishings divides sections into living room furniture, dining sets, beds and mattresses, ceiling fans and lighting fixtures, and so on. Breck's fall bulb catalog, with narrower product lines, divides its sections into displays of tulips, daffodils, irises, crocuses, and so forth.

A second method is the mixed product arrangement, which combines items from different product categories. Its proponents claim that this mixture attains a better through-the-book readership than the product category form. An example of this format appears in Figure 12-6.

Whether a catalog employs product categories, mixed products, or some hybrid form of both methods, the assortments must be ordered. One type of composition is order by popularity. The most appealing

31. See DMA, *1989 Statistical Fact Book, op. cit.*, p. 75.
32. Brent J. Bissell, "Catalog Merchandise Floor Planning," *Direct Marketing* (March 1987), pp. 78–82.

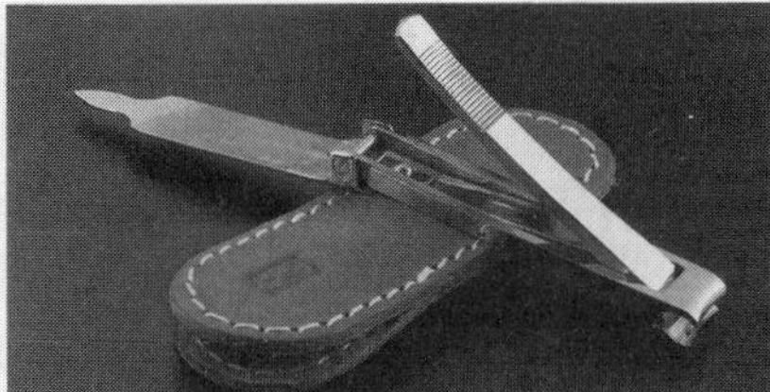

**MARCOVICI NAIL NIPPER.** Made in France for Marcovici Designs, this nail care instrument is one of the finest hand care devices you can own. Crafted from stainless steel that is forged, ground and polished by hand, it combines nail clipper, cuticle pusher, file and cleaner functions into a precise tool that folds into a sleek and compact, 3½" long shape. Includes an Italian leather carrying case.
43602W ........................................ $24.95

**CUSTOM-FIT DEERSKIN GLOVES.** These gloves are custom-cut and sewn to your hand size by a group of skilled craftsmen—one at a time and mostly by hand. They are individually table cut to an outline of your hand to ensure an exact fit. Supple, long-fiber deerskin leather stretches to conform to your hand like a second skin yet breathes better than ordinary leather. With elasticized wrist and Velcro® closure. Black with embossed logo. After your order is placed, you will receive a gift certificate and a return measuring kit for supplying a hand outline to the manufacturer. Allow 3-4 weeks for delivery.
42913W ........................................ $64.95

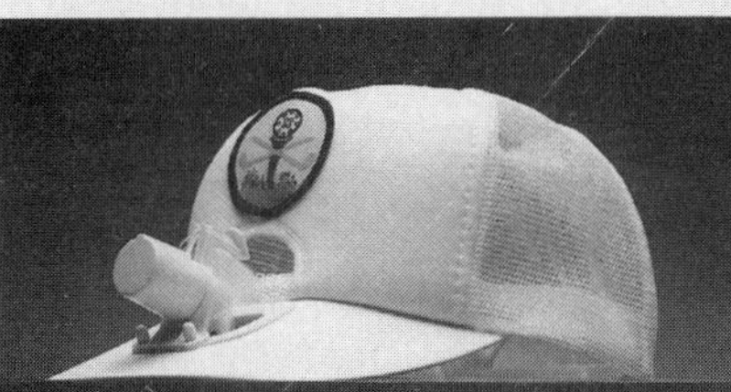

**THE SOLAR-POWERED VENTILATED GOLF CAP.** Offered exclusively by Hammacher Schlemmer, this is the only golf cap with a built-in solar-powered fan which directs a constant breeze toward your forehead to cool you. The motor is powered by six ½-volt solar cells for daytime use and by two AA batteries (included) for nighttime. Made of nylon mesh with nylon front; adjustable plastic strip fits hat sizes 6⅞ to 7⅝. 4.8 oz.
37022W ........................................ $29.95

**RAY-BAN® FOLDING WAYFARER® SUNGLASSES.** Ray-Ban® Wayfarers® combine modern sensibility with classic American styling. Folding to a compact 3 x 2½ x 1½ inches they take up half the space of conventional sunglasses. Their matte black frame is flexible yet resilient and has three hinges where the glasses fold, one on each temple and one above the nosebridge, that are unnoticeable when the glasses are being worn. Their Bausch & Lomb® impact-resistant optical glass lenses provide 100% protection against UVA, UVC and UVB rays.
42753W ........................................ $79.95

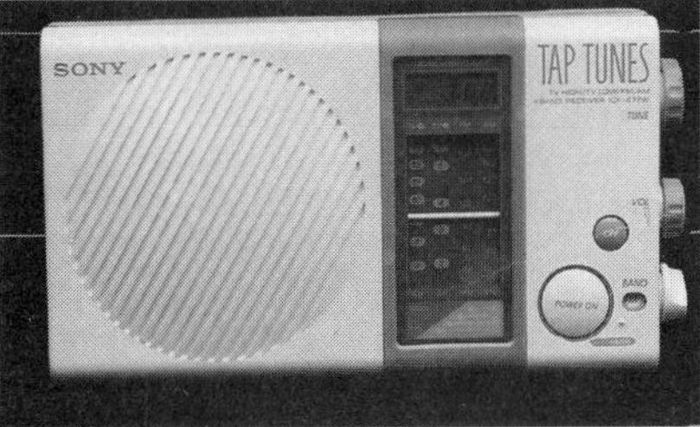


**THE SHOWER CLOCK/TV BAND RADIO.** This shower clock/radio has two TV bands so that it can receive the audio portion of VHF television broadcasts as well as AM and FM radio broadcasts. It uses a digital quartz clock that turns the radio off after 15, 30, 45 or 60 minutes. The unit can be used safely in showers, spas or saunas. Two built-in antennas ensure strong reception and the speaker is loud and clear even above shower noise. Includes one AA and three C batteries. ABS housing. 5¼" H. x 2" D. x 9¼" L.
35206W ........................................ $69.95

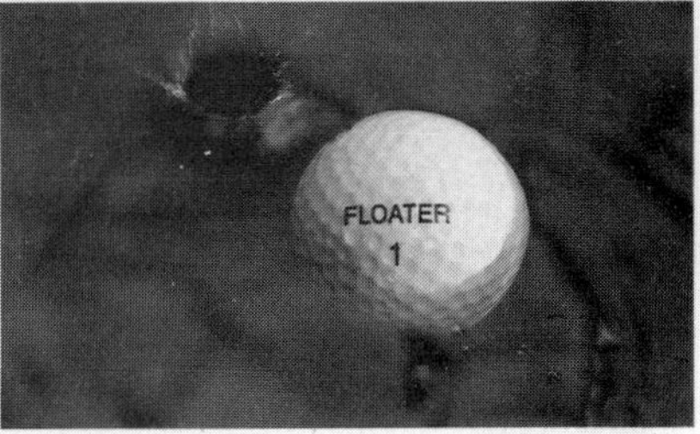


**FLOATING GOLF BALLS.** Designed to give golfers greater confidence around water hazards, these golf balls float. Their 2-piece construction includes a patented inner core that has a specific gravity lighter than water to provide exceptional buoyancy. Rated at 80 compression, they have the same "carry" as standard golf balls and their Surlyn® cover is cut- and scuff-resistant.
37049W Set of Twelve ........................................ $24.95

**FIGURE 12-6 A Mixed Product Arrangement**
*Source*: Reprinted with permission from Hammacher Schlemmer.

product sets are placed first, the next best-selling product mixes are placed second, and so forth. This assumes that a catalog is read from cover to cover, with readership highest near the front and diminishing as the reader proceeds toward the back.

However, catalogs do not have a strict front-to-back readership. Inside and outside covers, centerspreads, and pages surrounding order forms receive the highest reader traffic. The proper merchandise mix should, like retail floor layouts, put impulse and commodity items in high-traffic areas. Shopping goods, usually located in stores' low-traffic areas, such as at the back of the store or on the top floors, should be placed in low-readership spaces of catalogs.

Whatever the choice of products and their arrangement, they also must be presented using some kind of graphic design. Free-form designs are the hallmark of upscale, stylish catalogs done with artistic elegance. More common, however, is the blocked form or layout. These graphic forms can be symmetrical or asymmertrical (see Figures 12-7 and 12-8), but generally achieve a balance pleasing to the eye. Most catalogs use more than one graphic design or layout to avoid monotony.

The use of formal layouts facilitates product evaluation. Assigning products to given space units attaches to each item a cost that is proportional to the amount of space it takes up. Costs are easily adjustable through unequal treatment of items, such as the use of color versus black and white. Response for each item can then be compared with its unit space costs.

**FIGURE 12-7 A Symmetrical Layout**
*Source*: Reprinted with permission of Austin Street Market.

**FIGURE 12-8 An Asymmetrical Layout**
*Source*: Reprinted with permission of Lillian Vernon.

Most catalog copy is rather short, crisp, and to the point. Space is limited, so copy must meet rigid length requirements. Copy thus focuses on the essentials: catalog number, size, color, weight, and price. Illustrations work with copy to convey an unambiguous message of what is offered.

Many catalogs have copy blocks featuring products or groups of items with their own headlines. One type is the label headline, which identifies the product. It has been argued that label headlines are a waste of space because items are recognizable from the illustration.[33] However, labels do clarify pictures in certain instances.

Catalog copy typically uses an inverted pyramid style. The most important point is at the beginning, in accordance with journalistic prin-

33. Don Kanter, "Direct Response Copy Catalogs," DMMA, *Manual Release 310.3* (May 1979).

ciples. Other features follow in order of their importance. This form of writing presents a catalog's merchandise in the most effective manner.

## Summary

Catalogs are an important branch of direct mail. They can be classified according to two criteria: whether they are tied to retail stores or to nonstore operations, and whether they carry general or specialized merchandise.

The nonstore catalogs have scored their greatest gains with specialty offerings. The underlying cause of this upsurge is income growth. These catalogs are designed for particular groups or market segments, and they pursue focus strategies. By definition, their product lines are limited but possess great depth. This provides them with an advantage over retail establishments, which cannot be expected to allocate valuable floor space to items with small local demand.

Consumer and business catalogs circulate in different spheres. Consumer catalogs are mailed out in the millions, whereas business catalogs have circulations in the thousands. The business catalog pulls a larger order size than the consumer catalog.

Catalogs issued by stores have the largest volume. The two primary objectives of store catalogs are to enhance sales in a store's trading area and to expand sales outside the retail trading area.

The growth of specialty catalogs has brought greater concern for design and image. Some catalogs use more artistic, institutional-type advertising.

Catalogs have two basic types of merchandise arrangements. First, they can be ordered by product category. Second, products can be mixed. Either way, a popular sequence is that of showing the best-selling items first and the worst-selling last. But this sequence is often modified by placing best sellers in catalog areas with the highest reader traffic.

**REVIEW QUESTIONS**

1. Compare catalog sales with retailing sales over the period 1980 to the present.
2. What are the advantages of running a nonstore catalog operation?
3. Why have several nationally recognized catalogers opened up retail stores?
4. Discuss some of the differences between consumer catalogs and business catalogs.

5. Why do many catalogs devoted to specialty merchandise carry a mixed assortment?
6. What are the objectives of customer acquisition and customer servicing?
7. Why would a department store send catalogs to customers who usually shop at the retailer's location?
8. In what ways can catalogs supplement retail sales?
9. What are the pros and cons of a product category arrangement, as compared with a mixed-type catalog?
10. Why and how did Spiegel make the transition from an all-purpose to a specialty catalog?

CHAPTER 13

# Telemarketing

## PROFILE

**MURRAY ROMAN**

**Telemarketing Pioneer** Murray Roman was noted for his innovations in telemarketing. Before his death in 1984 he dominated the field and provided a training ground for many who struck out on their own. The techniques he pioneered have been adopted by virtually all practitioners today.

Roman was born in Russia in 1920 and arrived in America as a child. His career began in the 1940s after he served as a bombardier in World War II. He worked at a number of fundraising and public relations positions, and in the 1950s he experimented with using the telephone to solicit funds. But his first serious involvement in telemarketing came in the 1960s when, while working for Communicator Networks, Inc., he ran a campaign for the Ford Motor Company that resulted in some 20 million telephone calls to American consumers.

It was during that gigantic Ford campaign that Roman developed assembly line methods for standardizing and controlling internal operating procedures. He also brought to fruition the taped message using well-known personalities in telephone solicitations.

Roman acted as a consultant to both the Republican and Democratic National Committees for electioneering and raising funds by telephone. In 1968 Edwin Newman of NBC featured Murray Roman and his wife Eva, in a documentary on the American political process. Word of Roman's accomplishments spread quickly, and by the end of the year his recently founded company, Campaign Communications Institute (CCI), was handling more than 60 percent of the political fundraising campaigns in the United States. As of December 1983 CCI employed some 700 communicators at its New York headquarters and its operations had spread into Europe and Australia.

Roman's widely emulated approach to telemarketing is set forth in his books *Telephone Marketing: How to Build Your Business by Telephone* (1976) and *Telemarketing Campaigns That Work!* (1983). ■

# The Scope of Telemarketing

We have all known the telephone from birth and use it routinely in our daily lives. It is so pervasive that we take it for granted and never give a thought to how much we depend on it. Our homes and businesses are wired in a complicated telephone network that stretches around the world. American firms spend more on telephone-based marketing than they do on any other medium. In 1989 such expenditures reached the lofty sum of some $55 billion.[1]

Telemarketing, the application of the telephone to marketing, has been in common use for many years in real estate, insurance, and brokerage businesses. As early as the 1920s, financial houses gave investors market updates by phone. The years during World War II witnessed shortages of male-dominated sales staffs, and rather than hire women, many companies began selling by phone. Led by Time, Inc., publishers turned to the telephone in increasing numbers during the 1950s to renew expiries and acquire new subscribers.[2]

Yet modern telemarketing is relatively new. In fact, the word *telemarketing* first appeared on a printed page in 1967.[3] The early efforts were small-scale and unsystematic. The distinguishing features of current efforts are the mass application of the telephone to marketing tasks and its integration with market planning. In describing the state of the art, Stone and Wyman correctly see telemarketing as "the integrated and systematic application of telecommunications and information processing technologies and management systems.[4]

The total value of all goods and services resulting from telemarketing sales in the United States is estimated at more than $41 billion.[5] An AT&T shopper survey in 1987 calculated that out of more than 81 million telephone households, some 35 percent, or 28.5 million homes, shopped by phone. Another 19 million, or 23 percent, according to the survey, were judged as receptive to telephone shopping.[6] On that basis, the overall consumer potential of telemarketing adds up to an astounding 47.5 million households.

Though business establishments are less numerous than households, their potential is larger in terms of dollar volume. But business-to-

---

1. *Direct Marketing* (April 1990), p. 4.
2. *Telemarketing Today: The Right Connection* (New York: Direct Marketing Association, undated), p. 2.
3. *Ibid.*, p. 3.
4. Bob Stone and John Wyman, *Successful Telemarketing* (Lincolnwood, IL: NTC Business Books, 1986), p. 5.
5. Eugene M. Johnson and William J. Meiners, "Telemarketing: Trends, Issues, and Opportunities," *Journal of Personal Selling & Sales Management* (November 1987), p. 65.
6. AT&T Telephone Shopper Study, 1987.

business marketing requires different functions in the use of telephones. For one thing, the business marketplace demands greater emphasis on lead generation. As a lead-getting device, telemarketing acts as a salesperson's helper. Its uses include taking inquiries, qualifying leads, and making appointments for the sales force.

# Forms of Telemarketing

Telemarketing is carried out in-house and by outside service bureaus. Though outside agencies often compete with internal operations, the two supplement each other as well.

A second factor that determines how telephone marketing is conducted is whether telephone calls are incoming or outgoing. Incoming calls are made at the initiative of customers or prospects. Plans or practices that generate these customer-to-seller phone calls go under the name of *inbound telemarketing*. The directing of calls from salespeople or solicitors to would-be buyers is referred to as *outbound telemarketing*. The exact scale of inbound or outbound telemarketing is not known. The Telemarketing Association, however, splits the total $55 billion telephone bill for marketing 50-50, half for inbound and half for outbound.

## Inbound Telemarketing

Inbound telemarketing usually relies on a toll-free 800 number. Its main applications are taking orders, receiving requests for literature, and servicing customers. Order processing and customer service frequently involve cross-selling or upgrading initial sales. For example, a six-month subscription might be extended for a full year by offering a price break for the additional six months. A buyer might agree to purchase an additional garment at a cut rate.

Not so long ago the 800 number stood out as an exception. Today it is ubiquitous. AT&T offers directories of these toll-free numbers for both consumers and businesses, and its operators provide assistance in looking up 800 numbers. The business directory alone contains more than 180,000 listings in better than 100 business fields.

ORDER TAKING BY 800 NUMBERS. The 800 number has become a common method for ordering goods and services. People frequently use these toll-free numbers to make travel reservations. The Omaha telephone center of Marriott Hotels handled more than 10.7 million calls in 1988 and took almost 3.5 million reservations. Marriot's 800-number system links its numerous hotels to travel agents and airlines so that customers can have immediate information on room availability. The Hertz telephone facility at Oklahoma City receives approximately 20 million calls annually, virtually all of them via an 800 number.[7] American Airlines created a new business out of its incoming phone system. In 1984 it formed a subsidiary, American Airlines Direct Marketing Corporation, to offer its telemarketing services to other firms. Within four years this AA offshoot brought in more than $100 million in operating revenue.[8]

THE 900 NUMBER. Though still limited, the use of 900 numbers has undergone a meteoric rise in the past three years. Unlike 800 numbers, the 900 group requires callers to pay for the service.

Until recently, 900 numbers were used for promotions and "dial-it" services. The 900 number came into being when NBC adopted it to conduct instant polls of the Carter-Reagan presidential debates in 1980. Gradually, a number of dial-it services sprang up, ranging from sports results and stock quotations to short stories from characters such as Woody Woodpecker and Dinosaur Buddy. The typical promotion featuring a 900 number is made via television. Dick Clark's "30 years of Rock 'n Roll" drew 1.8 million calls in a single day as people voted for their favorite songs.[9]

Recently corporations began using 900 numbers to generate leads, especially in selling to businesses. Eugene Kordahl, president of National Telemarketing, Inc., argues that 900 numbers qualify callers better than 800 numbers because spending "a little money really shows that they're interested."[10] One version of the 900 number business-to-business effort gives callers an option of talking to a service representative or ordering various products through a designated 800 number.

MEDIA INTEGRATION. Inbound telemarketing, whether toll-free or pay-call, depends on other media. The most successful incoming call programs are generated by catalogs and television.

There are two prime sources of response to any offer on television: mail and phone. The telephone is the preferred route. Buyers expend less effort in picking up a phone than in writing a letter. Sellers do not wait very long for their results. Orders start coming in right away, about 5 to 10 minutes after the commercial is shown. ("Call this free 800 number now. Operators are standing by to receive your call.")

Television viewing proceeds largely at the pace set by the broadcaster. Practically all viewers see a commercial at the same time, despite

---

7. Michael J. Major, "800 Number: Once a Specialty, It's Now Almost a Necessity," *Marketing News* (May 28, 1990), p. 6.
8. Dennis B. Crosby, "Telemarketing Comes of Age," *Directions* (March–April 1988), p. 9.
9. N. R. Kleinfeld, "Business Dials 1-900-Profits," *New York Times* (May 8, 1988), sec. 3, p. 4.
10. "Get on the Phone," *Target Marketing* (November 1989), p. 45.

**TABLE 13.1. Percent of Orders Placed by Phone versus Mail.**

| Type of Catalog | Phone | Mail |
|---|---|---|
| Consumer | 36.6 | 54.4 |
| Business | 60.6 | 30.2 |

SOURCE: Based on Direct Marketing Association, *Statistical Fact Book,* (New York: DMA, 1989), p. 69.

VCRs, and calls are therefore bunched up. Direct marketers using TV need more phone lines than those using print, since reading is spread out over time and calls come in driblets. TV viewing brings a volume of calls at peak hours that may exceed the capacity of even the largest telemarketing agencies. One way of handling this overload is by delayed announcement recordings, advising callers to stay on the line until a representative is available.

Most telephone orders generated by television are for "low-priced" products, usually under $30. The rejection ratio of these phone orders varies widely in accordance with the type of offer and the audience watching at the time. A commercial on a children's program, for example, will normally yield a higher proportion of items that cannot be delivered, for one reason or another, than a commercial shown to an adult audience.[11] Shipping and handling costs are incurred for all products sent, regardless of whether they are accepted by addressees. In view of the wide differences among products, the Direct Marketing Association recommends thorough testing before rolling out a campaign in mass media.[12]

An 800 number appended to a catalog or other mail order piece increases response significantly—as much as 60 to 80 percent, some companies claim. However, this does not hold for all products. Again, marketers are advised to heed the sound judgment of the DMA to test. Does the additional response justify the cost of inbound WATS lines?

Business catalogs have a higher proportion of orders placed by phone than consumer catalogs. This is the conclusion of a major survey conducted by *Catalog Age.* Table 13-1 presents the key findings for the consumer-business comparison, based on 356 survey respondents.

One reason for the difference in phone orders between consumer and business catalogs is the incidence of 800-number listings. It is more common for business catalogs to carry 800 numbers. The *Catalog Age* survey indicates that some 51 percent of consumer catalogers use toll-free order numbers, as contrasted with 74 percent for business catalogs.[13]

11. Direct Marketing Association, *Manual Release* 250.2 (July 1985).
12. *Ibid.*
13. Quoted in *DMA Statistical Fact Book,* (New York: DMA, 1989), p. 88.

Many department stores issue catalogs to increase store traffic. In that event, an 800 number would not support the strategy of the catalog. Consumer catalogers' reluctance to use toll-free numbers is also occasioned by sales volume. Unless a catalog pulls a large response, the costs of a toll-free number may not be justified. On the other hand, orders placed from business catalogs are for larger quantities than those placed by consumers, which makes more funds available for inbound phone calls.

Direct mail and printed advertisements also produce phone calls, especially from industrial purchasers and would-be buyers of financial services. These are primarily inquiries that direct marketers solicit in multiple-step selling procedures. Business leads are usually qualified and then funneled to the sales force for follow-up. In this way, expensive personal visits are scheduled for the best prospects.

Handling leads for financial services involves more varied procedures. Insurance companies, banks, and security dealers follow up such leads with further mailings or outgoing phone calls. The method used depends on the price of the service and the expected conversion percentage. The expectation that a small percentage of leads will be converted to sales triggers a mail follow-up. The prospect is sent the literature requested, and perhaps future promotional mailings. If the expected conversion ratio is high or potential sales volume large, more expensive personal calls may be warranted.

H&R Block, for example, established a tax hotline in 1990 for answering questions on tax issues. Afterward, Block mailed all callers discount coupons for tax preparation, hoping thereby to increase walk-in traffic at its tax centers.[14]

Customer service is another form of inbound telemarketing that is dependent on other media. This application of the telephone encourages customers to call for product information and to voice complaints. The objective of offering service is not to increase revenue directly. Instead, it is a guarantee of performance; for example, a hotline may be set up to answer questions of software buyers on how to run their computer programs. Perhaps such applications should be considered as a cost of doing business.

An outstanding example of a telephone service center is that of GE, established in 1981. A year later it was handling more than 1.4 million calls, providing consumers information about thousands of products. Recently, GE opened a second information center for business customers.

Many firms service customers by phone. A large number of them combine order processing with customer service, such as AT&T. Finan-

---

14. Alica Orr, "Telemarketing Gets down to Business," *Target Marketing* (May 1990), pp. 24–25.

cial houses in particular, even large ones such as Merrill Lynch and Fidelity Investment, use this format. Fidelity has special 800 numbers customers can use to find out prices of its various funds. But some services are so melded with order processing that the two cannot be considered apart. Is a funds transfer an order, a service, or a shift of money from one fund to another? A similar service-order activity is the offer of management expertise to maximize financial returns, such as calculations on the best withdrawal strategies for clients with IRAs, Keoghs, and retirement accounts. Many department stores handle customer service in a like manner, though by regular phone numbers at stores, because their business is local.

Customer service by regular or 800 numbers in business-to-business marketing is extremely widespread, especially for products that require technical support. Burroughs, for example, possesses a dozen telephone service centers that customers can call for assistance. But most industrial marketers render service—give information and resolve complaints—through regular phone numbers. When they lack sufficient volume to justify a toll-free number, they may arrange for customers to call collect.

The popularity of customer service by incoming telephone calls is also growing among manufacturers of consumer goods. Several auto manufacturers have set up WATS telephone lines to take consumer complaints. Whirlpool has carried 800 numbers pertaining to its appliances since the early 1980s and estimates that this service reduces unnecessary repair visits by some $500,000 a year.[15] When goods are still under warranty, a knowledgeable service representative can often clear up a problem over the phone. Taking care of a problem in this way is a good deal cheaper than fixing an appliance at a customers' home or bringing the item to the shop. Even sellers of low-priced convenience goods have adopted toll-free numbers to cement customer relations. Procter & Gamble puts 800 numbers on all of its packages so that customers can ask for product information and lodge complaints. General Mills prints an 800 number on every box of Bisquick. A customer whose biscuits don't rise can call the service center for help.[16]

## Outbound Telemarketing

Outbound telemarketing involves contacting customers and prospects by telephone. Outgoing calls may be integrated with other commercial messages in print and electronic media. The most common applications of outbound telemarketing are direct selling, sales support, and total account management. The last two applications are prevalent in business-to-business marketing.

---

15. Stone and Wyman, *op. cit.*, p. 8.
16. *The Van Vechten Report* (August 1988).

DIRECT SELLING. A distinct advantage of outgoing telephone marketing is speed. Customers are reached instantly. There is little time lag between the transmission of a commercial message and the response to it.

Outbound telemarketing also excels in other areas. For one thing, the telephone is the only medium that can be used at various stages of a sale. It can be used to presell, sell, and postsell. A telephone representative can arouse interest in buying, call again to confirm a sale, and follow up with an inquiry about the buyers' satisfaction. Another plus is personal contact with customers, particularly in consumer markets.[17]

Outbound telemarketing has a wide variety of direct selling objectives:

- Reactivating customers, such as renewing subscriptions
- Obtaining new orders or new customers
- Working in conjunction with other direct marketing programs
- Increasing orders of current customers
- Presenting a viable option to personal selling, particularly in organization markets

Most abuses, perceived or real, take place in consumer markets by firms using telephone canvassing techniques. These involve "cold calls" designed to produce short-run profits through one-time sales.[18] A recent survey of telemarketing service bureaus revealed that the average firm makes about 1.5 million calls a year, with roughly one-third being "cold." The current U.S. 900 number marketplace reels in some 225 million phone calls a year and about $450 million in revenues.[19]

The importance of order getting by telephone in business-to-business marketing is underscored by the rising costs of personal selling. In 1987 McGraw-Hill Research calculated that a typical company had to shell out more than $250 for a single call on a client. Since it takes about 5.5 visits to close a sale, total costs are reckoned at slightly above $1,375. The past decade has witnessed in-person visit costs rising at least 15 percent per annum, and the spiral is continuing. Unless an order is substantial, it will not cover selling expenses.

In contrast, costs of outgoing telephone calls range from $7 to $15. A sales representative can see about five customers a day, but a telephone operator can make as many contacts in an hour.[20] Outbound calls have become highly popular with financial houses, which place thousands

17. Edward Blank, "Telemarketing: The Key Element of the Direct Marketing Mix," *Telemarketing* (April 1984), pp. 46–48.
18. "Telemarketing Canvassing Not the Same," *Marketing News* (October 11, 1985), p. 14.
19. Robert Ingenito, "It's your Call: 900 Numbers," *Direct Marketing* (September 1990); pp. 49–53, 83.
20. Joel Dreyfuss, "Reach out and Sell Something," *Fortune* (November 26, 1984) p. 127–132; *Telemarketing Today, op. cit.*

of calls to sell IRAs just before the April deadline for income tax filing. Is it any wonder that telephones have replaced personal visits in many areas?

The greatest use of outgoing phone calls has been in selling to small, marginal accounts. A. B. Dick, for example, realizes orders for supplies running to some $50 each.[21] Personal visits in such circumstances are clearly uneconomical. Dupont resuscitated its flagging sales for educational material and related seminars by shifting from field sales to outbound telemarketing.[22]

LEAD GENERATION AND QUALIFICATION. Telemarketing today takes on a dual function: to generate leads and to qualify leads coming from other media. In both instances, the telephone works together with personal selling to upgrade the probability of a sales representative closing a sale.

In one instance, calls are used to screen interested prospects from a general list and then schedule appointments for personal visits. Insurance agents, brokerage houses, and funds managers favor this technique as do businesses selling to other businesses.

For example, an operator, either human or mechanical, may solicit prospects with short messages lasting a minute or so. The telephone then acts as a lead-generating device. A representative then attempts to schedule appointments with prospects who show an interest in the offer. These meetings can be arranged right away, while the person is on the phone, or later, by a follow-up call. Either way, sales productivity improves because personal visits are made with the most interested prospects. Paul A. Gilpin, an independent insurance agent in Massachusetts, estimates that about 6 to 8 percent of people who listen to his entire telephone message agree to a face-to-face meeting. Gilpin claims that this response is "far greater than a mailing would have been."[23]

Another common use of the telephone in business-to-business marketing is lead qualification. Such inquiries and requests for literature usually come in from other media. Rather than have sales personnel chasing every lead, the telephone is used to screen the most productive.

Qualifying inquiries entails a multistep procedure, though companies do not follow each step every time. First, outgoing calls are used to verify the position or function of the inquirer. Is the person an in-

---

21. Stone & Wyman, *op. cit.*, p. 9.
22. Jim Emerson, "Double-Digit Growth Rate Continues," *DM News* (March 15, 1986), pp. 44–45.
23. "Computer Telemarketing Brings Sales in from Cold," *Marketing News* (March 14, 1986), p. 33.

fluencer, a decider, or a gatekeeper? Often, a number of people are involved in a buying decision.

Using a script as a guide, the telemarketer then seeks to obtain all relevant data related to the inquiry. These calls may cover such items as products or services a prospective firm is considering, current purchases and the likelihood of future change, and the degree of interest in the offer.

The final step presents the telemarketing firm with several options. It may decide to send out the literature and use a follow-up call to close the sale, particularly if the potential is not large enough to merit a personal visit. Or the lead may be passed on to the sales department, allowing it to make the determination. The prospective buyer may then be contacted directly by a sales representative seeking to set up an appointment or demonstration.

MEDIA INTEGRATION. Like inbound calls, outbound telemarketing enjoys a synergy with other media. That is, response to a media combination will be greater than if a promotion were to allocate the same amount of money to one medium only. One reason is that people do not respond in the same way to messages in different media vehicles. A printed ad, frozen in words or pictures on a two-dimensional surface, does not convey the same set of images that a human voice elicits on a telephone. These differences argue for use of a media mix to create more varied yet mutually reinforcing impressions.[24]

A direct mail piece followed by a phone call confers a number of advantages. People don't sit down and answer a mail solicitation the moment they read it, even if they decide to place an order. Many put the material away, delay the order, and sometimes forget about it. A phone call can evoke immediate action and shorten response time. A quick decision is especially important when time is of the essence, as with promotions during the Christmas season.

Telephone follow-ups can also clarify information when mailings deal with complicated or complex products. They can determine if a mail piece went to the wrong person and needs to be rerouted.

Richard L. Bencin, a telemarketing authority, sings the praises of integrated marketing programs that combine mail, telephone, and video brochures. He calls this media package "telefocus marketing."[25]

Advantages of videotaped messages are that they are less expensive than television advertising and they are not limited to the short time

24. For example, see Joseph C. Fisher, "Getting the Most out of Telemarketing," *Direct Marketing* (June 1987), pp. 34–37; Telemarketing Co., "The Combined Punch of Mail & Phone," *Profits By Phone* (undated).

25. Richard L. Bencin, "Telefocus Marketing," *Direct Marketing* (December 1987), pp. 32–40.

of on-air commercials. Video brochures have been used successfully by several prominent companies, such as Cadillac, Mercedes Benz, Air France, and Royal Silk. The Bauer Corporation, a ladder manufacturer, issued a 18-minute video on safety targeted to production executives.

Video technology is still developing, and costs are falling. For example, Datavision Technologies, a tiny San Francisco company, recently brought out video presentations that act as personalized form letters. This new technology codes message segments and stores them on video players that hook up to a computer. A company can punch in data relating to a prospective customer. The computer then selects the appropriate message for a customer and transfers it to a videocassette ready for mailing. An assembly of clips for a variety of 10-minute video messages can cost as little as $50,000, though a six-figure charge is more common. American Express has used this technique for a promotion to cardholders.[26]

According to Bencin, telefocus marketing can be most effective for:

- High-priced goods and services
- Upscale prospects
- Complicated products
- Products not easily portable but needing demonstration
- Prospects not readily accessible

Since a media mix is product- and market-specific, the proper one will vary in accordance with products, markets, and company objectives. It is therefore prudent for a firm to test its programs before committing large sums to full-blown campaigns.

# Delivering the Message

The ultimate goal of telemarketing, like almost all marketing tactics, is to consummate transactions. The message structure thus depends on whether telephone operators are acting as order getters or order takers. Order getting mandates placing outgoing calls for the purpose of selling products. In that sense, the delivery of the message is a process for getting orders. Order taking involves handling incoming calls; orders come in from the outside. Though not completely routine, the job is somewhat like order entry. Large discount brokerage firms, for example, have representatives receiving and confirming orders to execute trades. In a number of instances, however, firms do have opportunities to "upgrade" the initial order, or to cross-sell when a company markets complementary products. A customer may decide to add a three-year

26. *Business Week* (October 8, 1990), p. 83.

warranty to the purchase of an air conditioner. A caller might buy a belt with the purchase of slacks, if reminded of that option.

The elements of telemarketing are similar to those of personal selling. Although the telephone rules out face-to-face contact, it compels a one-on-one encounter. One person communicates with another, and words pass between them. The more natural the conversation between them, the more effective the telephone message.

Seeking a direct sale, the outgoing message takes the form of a sales presentation. Its components can be described as follows: the approach, qualifying prospects, presentation, handling objections, and closing the sale. These parts do not always come in the same order. Some may be left out, and sometimes they will overlap. But these five elements are present in the vast majority of order-getting messages.[27]

## The Approach

Direct marketers think of the approach as an introduction to the prospect. It is the first step of any telephone conversation. The caller tells the person at the other end of the line who is calling, the company represented, and the nature of the call: "I am Mr./Ms. Jones of the XYZ Company. I am calling to let you know about. . . ." It is an axiom that the opening lines be positive and pleasant, for first impressions are important. Once a rapport is established, the operator can move on to other parts of the message.

## Qualifying Prospect

*Qualifying* means determining whether the prospect is truly a potential customer. In turn, that issue depends how a company defines its potential buyers. Do they have to be actual users of the product, or can they be logical prospects? For example, a home with a new refrigerator is a user but would not be in the market for a refrigerator for 10 years or more.

Another question is the role of the "prospect" in the decision process. In joint decisions involving consumer items, one partner may be dominant. In industrial markets, several people may be involved. Even the "decider," granted the phone operator finds out who this is, may not act independently. Selling to businesses is a much more complex process, and qualifying procedures requires more training of telephone operators. In any event, the qualification step is a screening device to avoid spending valuable time on the phone with those not likely to take favorable action.

---

27. Richard L. Bencin, "What's My Line," *Direct Marketing* (June 1987), pp.94–101.

When the objective of phone calls is lead generation, results may not be immediately obvious. The lead generation rate may not change, but quality might deteriorate. This happens in consumer fields where leads are followed up by sales calls, as in direct selling of annuities, insurance, home improvements, custom-made furnishings, and small appliances. Telephone solicitors are usually paid by the hour and given an incentive for every appointment they make. There is therefore motivation to make appointments, regardless of whether some minimum qualifying standard is met. A company should evaluate its lead generation program by comparing the proportion of sales closing to contacts.

## Presentation

The presentation is the heart of the telephone message. It contains the proposition and the data that support it. It tells the product story and gives reasons for taking action. To be effective, product features or benefits—whichever is stressed—should be delivered in terms that are meaningful to would-be customers.

If a canned presentation is used, all telephone solicitors render identical presentations, almost word for word. Most cold canvassing follows this approach. Telephone solicitors are not permitted much leeway in deviating from the prepared script. The advantage is control in a situation where solicitors are not called on to display great skills, as with low-priced, simple offers. The strict adherence to script also prevails when knowledge about the product is not required, such as in getting leads that are qualified later.

Some presentations give phone operators more flexibility in presenting the sales message. However, the approach is still structured. Certain points must be covered. But it is not as rigid as the undeviating, canned presentation. If customers indicate an interest, operators can talk to them on their own terms. This approach is most commonly used for calling known customers or prospects for complicated products, such as investment packages, insurance, and real estate. Operators must receive more training to deliver this sort of presentation.

## Handling Objections

Practically every sales presentation elicits a number of questions and reservations. Few phone calls asking for a commitment bring an enthusiastic, unqualified yes. It is normal for prospects at the other end of the line to offer resistance, hesitation, or misgivings with respect to a solicitor's proposition. Since these negative inclinations exist, no matter what is being promoted, most sales managers deem it desirable to bring them out into the open. In this way, a salesperson has a chance to correct misunderstandings and overcome doubts. There is nothing more discouraging when a prospect listens in silence and, without explanation, says, "I'm sorry, no. Have a nice day." Then a click and a low, monotonous dial tone.

Besides suggesting points for counterpoints, objections have other values. They often provide cues or signals as to how far two parties are from a transaction. A well-trained salesperson might at a certain juncture attempt a trial close. This is usually done by making the implicit assumption that a prospect will buy and asking an innocent question that implies a sale. "Would you like the item in red or black." "Would you prefer us to bill you direct, or do you prefer us to accept your credit card?"

## Closing the Sale

Closing entails asking for the order. In the case of following up on a lead, a close ends with a definite appointment. If the telephone conversation indicates that both buyer and seller are reasonably near a meeting of minds, the solicitor might try to close even before a presentation has run its course.

There are many closing techniques, and these are well detailed in books on selling. The most common ones are as follows:

1. *The direct close.* The seller asks for the order in a simple, straightforward manner.
2. *The assumptive close.* The seller implies that an agreement has been reached, and the only thing left is to iron out minor details. The salesperson then asks about the buyer's preferences with respect to the product and terms of the transaction.
3. *The most-likely-alternative close.* The seller narrows options to the most likely alternatives. The salesperson then asks which the prospect wants, A or B. In the event of closing on leads, the query would take a form something like: "Would you prefer the appointment for Tuesday or Wednesday?" If another date is mentioned, well and good. The close is made.
4. *The "standing room only" close.* The salesperson attempts to create a sense of urgency. Customers are told that supplies are limited, and that unless they order now, the item will not be available at the same price.
5. *The extra-inducement close.* This is an extension of the "standing room only" close. The solicitor offers a special price, a free gift, or a premium for ordering now. Later, these specials will not be available.
6. *The emotional close.* The salesperson appeals to some kind of psychological drive—fear, ego, flattery, or other motivation.
7. *The summative close.* The salesperson summarizes the potential benefits in the presentation and asks for the order (see Figure 13-1).

| | |
|---|---|
| WIFE: | Jack. Why are you wearing an ice pack on your head? |
| HUSBAND: | I'm conducting an experiment Helen. You see, the faster I cool down, the sooner I turn off that air conditioner. |
| WIFE: | Uh huh. |
| HUSBAND: | And the more money we save on electricity. |
| WIFE: | But Jack. What about me? |
| HUSBAND: | Not to worry Helen. I've got an ice pack for you too. |
| WIFE: | Oh good. |
| HUSBAND: | Look, it's pink. |
| WIFE: | Terrific. |
| VO: | If summer air conditioning is driving your electric bill up, call FPL for a free "Summer Energy Diet" kit. It's full of sensible ways to keep your electric bill down with things like window tinting or insulation. FPL even offers rebates for energy-saving improvements like these. So in the summertime, you don't have to turn your air conditioner off. Or, take any other drastic measures. |
| WIFE: | Jack, If your ice pack idea is so great, why are you still sweating? |
| HUSBAND: | I'm not sweating, Helen. |
| WIFE: | Well, what's all the moisture on your forehead? |
| HUSBAND: | Oh no, my ice pack's leaking. (Voice trailing off) |
| WIFE: | I'll say. |
| HUSBAND: | Boy, that's the last time I buy something second-hand. |
| WIFE: | Uh huh. |
| HUSBAND: | Didn't even get a warranty. |
| WIFE: | Terrific. |
| VO: | Call FPL at 1-800-DIA-FPL for your "Summer Energy Diet" kit. That's 1-800-DIAL-FPL. |

**FIGURE 13-1. TV Script Written for Florida Power & Light Company Demonstrating the Summative Close**
*Source*: Reprinted with the permission of Florida Power & Light Company.

# Talking Computers

Voice response systems represent a new and developing technology that marries the telephone to the computer. The human voice is digitalized, stored in memory, and activated by an appropriate signal to a computer program. These systems reduce the number of telephone operators and consequently lower operating costs.

Voice response technologies are used both for incoming and for outgoing telephone calls. On incoming 800 numbers, they direct calls to the proper locations for fulfilling orders and providing personal and general information. In the forefront of this technology, AT&T has developed these systems for a variety of specialized uses.[28] Among them are:

- College registration, where students employ identification numbers to select courses and sections. Choices are automatically confirmed and may be billed to a major credit card.
- Order entry, where customers place orders for direct mail or catalog items. A related application allows retail stores to order direct from wholesalers.
- Health insurance, where doctors and pharmacies enter a patient's Social Security number. The system responds with the status for insurance benefits and calculates any copayment that is required.
- Shipping information, where the system provides freight rate quotations and tracks shipments from numbers on bills of lading.
- Banking information, where customers can transfer funds, order checks, and get the latest interest rates and account balances.

A call to an 800 number of a financial house with many departments and services might evoke a verbal message such as the following:

> Thank you for calling XYZ investments. Please choose one of the following five options. For mutual fund prices and yields, press 1. For account balances, press 2. For making redemptions or exchanges between funds, press 3. For information and assistance on purchasing funds, press 4. For other services, press 5. If you don't have a touch-tone phone, stay on the line and a representative will be with you in a moment.

On outgoing calls, talking computers perform various functions, from customer service to cold calling. These systems are known as ADRMPs, short for automatic-dialing recorded-message players. Sears and J.C. Penney, for example, enhance customer service with recorded messages to alert customers of when catalog orders were shipped.

In order-getting activity, ADRMPs come in two main versions: with operator assistance and with no human intervention whatsoever. In the first instance, an operator asks the prospect to listen to a recorded message, usually delivered by a celebrity or well-known authority. The recording may contain interviews with satisfied customers, but the message is most often a testimonial by the presenter, users, or both. When the presentation is over, the operator gets back on the line to complete the selling process.

The completely automated message requires no operators. ADRMPs can dial all telephone numbers sequentially within a telephone exchange area. When the prospect picks up the phone, a recording is automatically activated. It delivers the sales presentation and asks for the order at the end.

---

28. See Nina Aversano "The Telephone as Computer," *Review of Business* (Fall 1989), pp. 5–8.

Prerecorded messages can boast of a number of successful endeavors, but they have also stirred heated controversies. Most telemarketers are lukewarm to the idea because automated calls lack intimacy. Sequential dialing enters calls into homes with unlisted numbers and violates what many phone customers consider their right to privacy. More than a dozen states have restricted the use of ADRMPs or have outlawed them entirely. The DMA has come out squarely against random or sequential dialing for solicitation purposes, and recommends that a live operator ask permission to play a recorded message.[29]

## In-House or Service Bureau?

A firm engaged in telemarketing can carry it out in several ways: in-house, via service bureaus, or by both methods. The eventual choice depends on two factors: the nature of the telemarketing program and the firm's resources.

Most service bureaus work on a contractual basis. They calculate rates by the number and length of calls. Agreements include a low setup fee and minimum monthly charges. If the volume of business does not reach the minimum, clients are liable for the difference. But these minimum levels are low.

Service bureaus are typically larger than in-house operations. A 1987 survey sponsored by *Telemarketing Intelligence* magazine found the median number of company workstations was 11. A little more than one-third of all companies had fewer than five workstations. In contrast, the 64 service bureaus studied had a median number of 99 workstations, and some 29 percent possessed more than 200. Service bureaus also gave employees better formal training and did extensive monitoring of phone calls. In-house operations pursued a learning-on-the-job approach and were less likely to monitor work in the phone room.[30]

Because of their larger size, service bureaus offer lower costs than in-house facilities. Telemarketing is a labor-intensive industry. A greater volume reduces expenses of labor and telephones which make up as much as 80 percent of total costs. Unless a company can count on a large volume of calls, it cannot set up a telemarketing program more cheaply or quickly than a service bureau.

Farming out telephone operations can drastically cut expenses and capital outlays. The process is called *outsourcing*. Its popularity derives from operating economies, which free corporate resources for more im-

29. *Telemarketing Today, op. cit.*, p. 9.
30. Jim Emerson, "Telemarketing Research Findings High-lighted at ATA Meeting," *DM News* (December 15, 1987).

portant projects. Even though telemarketing may be critical to a business, it may not be so critical that the business does it itself.

A firm can derive advantages from outsourcing when:

- Incoming calls come in sudden bursts, as from direct response messages on television. Perhaps two-thirds or more of all inbound calls arrive within five minutes of when a commercial is telecast. Since direct response commercials are mostly aired in fringe time, swelling numbers of calls stream in at off-working hours. In-house facilities are seldom equipped to handle these peak loads.
- Test and development programs are uncertain and do not justify investment outlays in telemarketing. Service bureaus can set up test programs inexpensively because facilities, personnel, and experience are already there. If the test proves unsuccessful, the proposed undertaking can be dropped without incurring sunken costs. If successful, the marketer has time to determine whether an investment in an in-house telemarketing center would be worthwhile.
- Short-term promotions do not warrant facilities and equipment that would remain idle after the promotion is ended. Service bureaus can adequately fill that gap.
- Small firms with limited resources are strapped for investment funds. By using a service bureau, a larger percentage of expenditures become variable rather than fixed.

On the other hand, the greatest asset of an in-house center is control. The firm hires, trains, and supervises the telephone staff in accordance with company policy. Accumulated experience contributes to the firm's knowhow, not to that of an outside agency. The firm models its facilities and work schedules to fit its own needs, and it alone reaps the rewards of learning by doing.

In-house operations are particularly suited to incoming calls when operators work with computer terminals and CRT equipment. Technical and customer service calls are best handled in-house, for company personnel are more familiar with company products, policies, inventories, and out-of-stock situations. They have access to the company's database and are most qualified to solve problems that arise. Outside agencies cannot be expected to possess the same expertise as company personnel.

A major determinant of going in-house versus out-of-house is the expected pattern of incoming calls. Those induced by print media are spread out in time and can be accommodated without great difficulty. But these calls can come at almost any time of the day or night, and phones might have had to be staffed outside of normal business hours. Advertising in broadcast, however, results in different response patterns. Orders come in spurts, depending on the time of broadcasts, and are difficult to process efficiently. Many companies therefore assign broadcast response to outside agencies.

**TABLE 13.2. Inbound Telemarketing Applications.**

| Application | Service Bureau | In-house Operation |
|---|---|---|
| Order taking | 81% | 87% |
| Customer service | 67 | 88 |
| Handling questions/problems | 42 | 97 |
| Upgrading orders | 81 | 68 |
| Account management service | 56 | 49 |
| Handling complaints | 58 | 90 |
| Dealer locator | 69 | 40 |
| Total | 100% | 100% |

NOTE: Total adds up to more than 100 percent because of multiple applications.
SOURCE: Direct Marketing Association, *1989 Statistical Fact Book* (New York: DMA, 1989).

The greatest obstacle to an in-house center is lack of management capability. The work force differs radically from those in other marketing fields. Many operators are part-timers, working for little more than minimum wage. Work hours run into the night, and employees come and go at odd times. Employee turnover runs high, and work flows often involve production line techniques that fall outside the ken of marketing management.

A comparison of in-house and service bureau functions indicates a clear cleavage between the two. Table 13-2 shows telephone usage for inbound phone calls by in-house and by service bureau applications. The figures are based on a survey of 707 companies and 64 outside services.

In-house centers do proportionately more order taking and customer servicing. The figures, however, do not tell what kinds of orders are handled. For example, orders that are highly bunched fall to outside agencies, whereas steady, slow-moving orders go right to the company. Complaints also seem to be concentrated in-house, since outside agencies are not as familiar with customers or have access to their records.

For outgoing phone calls, Table 13-3 compares applications of in-house centers and service bureaus, using the same samples as Table 13-2. The prime functions of service bureaus are direct selling in consumer markets, and screening leads and making appointments in business-to-business markets. In-house applications of outgoing calls are direct selling and screening leads, particularly in business-to-business markets. But in-house operations seem exclusively apt in opening new accounts and servicing small and geographically remote accounts. This indicates that telemarketing has replaced much of personal selling because of rising costs of sales calls.

**TABLE 13.3. Outbound Telemarketing Applications.**

| Application | Service Bureau | In-house Operation |
|---|---|---|
| Direct selling | 86% | 86% |
| Screen/Qualify leads | 67 | 72 |
| Setting appointments | 77 | 40 |
| Full account management service | 50 | 45 |
| Opening new accounts | — | 72 |
| Handling small accounts | — | 67 |
| Geographic remote accounts | — | 62 |
| Credit checks | 20 | 23 |
| Collections | 19 | 24 |
| Total | 100% | 100% |

NOTE: Total adds up to more than 100 percent because of multiple applications.
SOURCE: Direct Marketing Association, *1989 Statistical Fact Book* (New York: DMA, 1989).

## Picking a Service Bureau

The decision to employ a service bureau is only the first step. The second is to decide which one to employ. The choice of agency involves several considerations.[31] One is experience. Service bureaus tend to specialize in certain products and markets. Campaign Communications Institute, one of the oldest service bureaus, concentrates on outbound telemarketing and unsolicited cold calls to sell products in consumer markets. Other firms specialize in business-to-business telemarketing. The service bureau's specialty should be related to the client's operation.

If the client's program calls for outbound calls, evaluation should be based on back-end results. The criterion should not be the number of orders or leads obtained, but their quality—how many leads were converted to sales, or how many recorded sales on the telephone resulted in paid orders. It is always a good idea to ask the agency for references and to check out the agency with present or former customers.

Another consideration is financial condition. Telephone service bureaus have a high mortality, since many firms get into the business on a shoestring. Steven Granat, president of Electronic Marketing Associates, Inc., says that "a lot of companies don't even have a street address. They're working out of a post office box."[32] No firm likes to start a campaign and suddenly find itself unable to take orders because

31. Stone and Wyman, *op. cit.*, p. 197. However, cf. Paul Streibig, "In-house Telemarketing May Be Better than an Outside Agency," *Marketing News* (February 29, 1988).
32. Telemarketing's Inside Line," *Target Marketing* (May 1988), p. 49; "Service Bureau Shakeout," *Ibid.* (August 1986), p. 12.

its agency could not pay the phone bills. Before hiring an outside agent, the client should run a credit check and get a Dun & Bradstreet report on all firms under consideration.

The size of a bureau is also important, especially if the media plan calls for a television schedule. There must be enough lines to handle sudden order peaks.

A related question concerns busy signals. A service bureau runs efficiently by allowing a certain proportion of busy signals for incoming calls. Admittedly, an error-free phone system without busy signals or waiting lines is not affordable. But there may be disagreements as to where to draw the line on the level of service. This problem may become aggravated when a service bureau has two or more clients in television, and orders peak at the same time, overloading lines. Clients should ask to examine busy reports, kept by almost all service bureaus.

Finally, costs must remain an important factor. But consideration of costs alone is not the entire story; they must be related to performance. For example, costs can vary from $30 per phone hour to as much as $60 per hour. Yet the $60/hour charge can be cheaper if the expensive firm makes more than twice as many contacts or generates more than twice as many leads. Measures of quantity must be tempered with assessments of quality service for an effective operation.

# Summary

Modern technology is distinguished by the mass of application of the telephone to marketing activity and its integration with planning. The main factor that impelled telephone usage along this road was telephone penetration among 47.5 million households.

Telemarketing is carried out in-house and by outside service bureaus. Inbound telemarketing usually depends on a toll-free 800 number. Its main uses are taking orders, receiving requests for literature, and servicing customers. Recently firms began using 900 numbers to generate leads or to receive information on weather, travel, or sports. With 900 numbers, the caller has to pay for the service. Outgoing calls are mainly undertaken for the purpose of order getting.

A firm has the option of conducting telemarketing in-house, out-of-house, or by a combination of the two methods. The great advantages of out-of-house service bureaus are their low costs and ability to handle large surges in calls. Firms planning test and development programs and short-term promotions are well advised to use service bureaus. The greatest advantage of the in-house center is that the marketing firm has control of the operation. But in-house telemarketing requires considerable management skills in supervising and planning work flows, as well as comparatively large investments in facilities.

## REVIEW QUESTIONS

1. The 800 number has become a common method for ordering goods and services. Explain and provide two examples.
2. Michigan State University usually solicits endowment funds by a telephone follow-up to a mailing. What are the advantages of this approach?
3. Consumer surveys indicate that more than any other medium, telemarketing is likely to be associated with invasion of privacy. Why?
4. When is the structured approach for a telephone sales presentation preferred over an unstructured one?
5. Despite its lower costs, the automated, prerecorded message is not in great favor with direct marketers. Why?
6. Voice response technology is used for incoming telephone calls. Provide four examples. State the benefits of this system.
7. Explain the acronym ADRMPs. Provide two examples.
8. Explain the term *outsourcing*. Provide two examples.
9. What are the advantages of using a service bureau when a company has an in-house telemarketing operation?
10. What are some of the considerations for choosing a service bureau?

# APPENDIX D

## Direct Marketing Association Guidelines for Marketing by Telephone

The structured use of the telephone to purchase or sell products or services, or to obtain or give information to businesses and residences, is known as telemarketing. "Inbound" telemarketing programs enable customers to call companies to place orders or to receive product and service information. "Outbound" telemarketing programs are those in which companies call customers, and potential customers, to inform them of offers that may be of interest and to provide service information.

For the purpose of these guidelines, all telephone calls made for marketing purposes will be referred to as contacts. Those persons who are called will be referred to as customers.

More and more businesses today are using telemarketing to meet the needs of their customers. Telemarketing is a people oriented marketing medium that enables companies to target their products and services to customers who would be most interested in them.

The Direct Marketing Association's Guidelines for Marketing by Telephone are intended to provide individuals and organizations involved in direct telephone marketing with accepted principles of conduct that are consistent with the ethical guidelines recommended for other marketing media. These specific guidelines reflect the responsibilities of DMA and telephone marketers to the consumer, the community, and industry. Telephone marketers should also be aware of DMA's Guidelines for Ethical Business Practices, the more comprehensive Guidelines for all direct marketing.

---

Used with permission of the Direct Marketing Association.

The Guidelines are self-regulatory in nature. Telephone marketers are urged to honor them in spirit and in letter.

The Guidelines are also part of DMA's general philosophy that self-regulatory measures are preferable to governmental mandates whenever possible. Self-regulatory actions are more readily adaptable to changing technologies and economic and social conditions. Further, self-regulation encourages widespread use of sound business practices.

Special recognition should be given to the Telephone Marketing Council, which worked with the DMA Ethical Committees in writing and approving these Guidelines.

Prompt Disclosure/Identity of Seller
*Article 1*

When speaking with a customer, telephone marketers should promptly disclose the name of the sponsor, the name of the individual caller, and the primary purposes of the contact.

All documents relating to a telephone marketing offer and shipment should sufficiently identify the full name and street address of the seller so that the customer may contact the seller by mail or by telephone.

Honesty
*Article 2*

All offers should be clear, honest, and complete so that the recipient of the call will know the exact nature of what is being offered and the commitment involved in the placing of an order. Before making an offer, direct marketers should be prepared to substantiate any claims or offers made. Advertisements or specific claims which are untrue, misleading, deceptive, fraudulent, or unjustly disparaging of competitors should not be used.

No one should make offers or solicitations in the guise of research or a survey when the real intent is to sell products or services or to raise funds.

Terms of the Offer
*Article 3*

Prior to commitments by customers, telephone marketers should disclose the cost of the merchandise or service, all terms, and conditions, including payment plans, refund policies and the amount or existence of any extra charges such as shipping and handling and insurance.

Reasonable Hours
*Article 4*

Telephone marketers should avoid making contacts during hours which are unreasonable to the recipients of the calls.

Use of Automatic Equipment

*Article 5*

When using automatic dialing equipment, telephone marketers should only use equipment which allows the telephone immediately to release the line when the called party disconnects.

ADRMPs (Automatic Recorded Message Players) and pre-recorded messages should only be used in accordance with tariffs, state and local laws, and these guidelines. When a telephone marketer places a call to a customer for solicitation purposes, and desires to deliver a recorded message, permission should be obtained from the customer by a live "operator" before the recorded message is delivered.

Taping of Conversations

*Article 6*

Taping of telephone conversations made for telephone marketing purposes should not be conducted without legal notice to or consent of all parties or the use of a beeping device.

Name Removal

*Article 7*

Telephone marketers should remove the name of any individual from their telephone lists when requested directly to do so by the customer, by use of the DMA Telephone Preference Service name-removal list and, where applicable, the DMA Mail Preference Service name-removal list.

Minors

*Article 8*

Because minors are generally less experienced in their rights as consumers, telephone marketers should be especially sensitive to the obligations and responsibilities involved when dealing with them. Offers suitable only for adults should not be made to children.

Monitoring

*Article 9*

Monitoring of telephone marketing and customer relations conversations should be conducted only after employees have been informed of the practice.

Prompt Delivery

*Article 10*

Telephone marketers should abide by the FTC's Mail Order Merchandise (30 Day) Rule when shipping prepaid merchandise. As a normal business procedure, telephone marketers are urged to ship all orders as soon as practical.

Cooling-Off Period
*Article 11*

Telephone marketers should honor cancellation requests which originate within three days of sales agreement.

Restricted Contacts
*Article 12*

Telephone marketers should remove the name of any customer from their telephone lists when requested by the individual. Marketers should use the DMA Telephone Preference Service name-removal list and, where applicable, the Mail Preference Service name-removal list. Names found on such suppression lists should not be rented, sold, or exchanged except for suppression purposes.

A telephone marketer should not knowingly call anyone who has an unlisted or unpublished telephone number except in instances where the number was provided by the customer to that marketer.

Random dialing techniques, whether manual or automated, in which identification of those parties to be called is left to chance, should not be used in sales and marketing solicitations.

Sequential dialing techniques, whether a manual or automated process, where selection of those parties to be called is based on the location of their telephone number in a sequence of telephone numbers, should not be used.

Transfer of Data
*Article 13*

Telephone marketers who receive or collect customer data as a result of a telephone marketing contact and who intend to rent, sell, or exchange those data for direct marketing purposes should inform the customer. Customer requests regarding restrictions on the collection, rental, sale, or exchange of data relating to them should be honored.

Names on the DMA Telephone Service name-removal list should not be transferred except for suppression purposes.

Laws, Codes, and Regulations
*Article 14*

Telephone marketers should operate in accordance with the laws and regulations of the United States Postal Service, the Federal Communications Commission, the Federal Trade Commission, the Federal Reserve Board, and other applicable federal, state, and local laws governing advertising, marketing practices, and the transaction of business by mail, telephone, and the print and broadcast media.

CHAPTER 14

# Consumer Publications

The two leading print media directed to consumers are magazines and newspapers. Together they account for about $38 billion, or about 30 percent of all U.S. advertising expenditures.[1] However, only a small percentage of that total represents direct marketing.

Both magazines and newspapers are primarily vehicles of general advertising, not direct marketing. These media are not personal; they are not directed to specific individuals. Rather, they are mass media, written and circulated to large segments of the general public.

Unlike direct mail or telephone promotions, ads in print media are encased in an editorial environment. Reading of ads is in varying degrees involuntary. Readers happen upon ads while going through editorial matter. Though many people "shop" the pages of newspapers, they generally do not buy newspapers to read advertisements. This is even more true of magazines.

Newspapers and magazines share some features with direct mail insofar as messages are conveyed on printed pages. The principles of writing and graphic design apply to all advertising, general and direct. The notion of a cost-benefit trade-off is also common to virtually all types of promotion. But the nature of media imposes certain restrictions on the form of commercial messages. Advertisements carried by newspapers and magazines must conform to paper size and production requirements of each medium. Advertising coverage is determined by media circulation patterns, and not by marketers' specifications. To reach potential customers, advertisers must match media to their markets.

Despite characteristics that lend themselves to general advertising, newspapers and magazines are important to direct marketers. First, they perform certain functions efficiently. If they did not, they would not be used. Second, they supplement other direct marketing efforts by extending media reach. For example, any mailing list or combination of lists has its limits. Many prospects cannot be reached efficiently because their names do not appear on any list a firm uses. But these people might respond to ads they see in magazines and newspapers. Third, a media mix can convey different and more varied impressions than one medium alone.

## Newspapers

Newspapers are essentially local media. Advertising expenditures for newspapers during 1989 totaled about $32.4 billion. Of that total, $28.6 billion, or 88 percent, was local.[2] There are several national newspapers,

1. Robert J. Coen, "Estimated Annual U.S. Advertising Expenditures," prepared for *Advertising Age*.
2. *Ibid*.

**TABLE 14.1. Circulation of Daily and Sunday Newspapers 1990.**

| Type | Number of Newspapers | Circulation (millions) |
|---|---|---|
| Daily | 1,626 | 62.7 |
| Morning | 530 | 40.8 |
| Evening | 1,125 | 21.9 |
| Sunday | 847 | 62.0 |

SOURCE: Newspaper Advertising Bureau. Reprinted with permission.

the most prominent of which are *USA Today* and *Wall Street Journal*. These are the exceptions, however.

In total, there were roughly 1,626 daily newspapers in 1990. Evening papers outnumbered morning dailies by about 2 to 1—1,125 versus 530. But in terms of circulation, morning daily newspapers dominated by a wide margin, about 2 to 1. Sunday newspapers had a combined circulation of some 62 million. Both dailies and Sunday newspapers reach approximately two-thirds of all U.S. households.[3] The circulation statistics are reproduced in Table 14-1.

The outstanding trait of newspapers is their ability to blanket local markets. Approximately three-fourths of all readers get their daily papers by in-home delivery. Subscriptions to Sunday newspapers account for about 68 percent of all reader acquisitions.[4]

The biggest advantage of newspapers is high penetration of retail trading zones and local markets. Most newspapers today offer programs built around total market coverage, referred to as TMC. The classic TMC program calls for a daily paper to publish a weekly—the format can vary enormously—and send it out free of charge to all residents that do not subscribe to the daily. A direct response advertisement in both publications would thus reach close to 100 percent of households in a market.

## Direct Marketing Applications in Newspapers

Newspaper advertising space can be bought in three basic ways: ROP, Sunday supplements, and preprints.

ROP. ROP stands for *run of press;* buyer does not specify a section or position in the paper when ordering space. The advertiser does not know where the ad will end up in the paper. This is dictated by editorial requirements. However, layout people usually try to place an ad near related editorial material. For example, an ad for sporting goods

3. Newspaper Advertising Bureau.
4. See publishers' statements.

would be placed in the sports section. A movie ad would be placed near entertainment material.

National advertisers use ROP in direct response advertising when their programs are tied to those of local retailers. These activities are primarily promotions funded by cooperative programs, in which the national advertisers share costs with local retailers. Although national brands are featured in the advertising, the prime objective is to generate store traffic.

Aside from retail-oriented advertising, national advertisers do not make great use of ROP. Compared with magazines and television, newspapers have high costs per thousand contacts. To get nationwide coverage, a marketer must connect hundreds of local newspapers, which is done through newspaper representatives. But space costs for national advertisers are roughly double those of local establishments.

In terms of local advertising, the most popular forms of direct advertising using ROP are carried out by local organizations, mainly in small-space advertisements. Other applications are special events and announcements by retailers and neighborhood services. Among the latter are promotions by entertainment places and movie houses, seminars by stock brokerage houses that elicit advance registration, and open-house events by real estate companies.

SUNDAY SUPPLEMENTS. Sunday supplements are actually magazines distributed by newspapers. Because they offer four-color reproduction or calendered stock, they appeal to national advertisers. These firms prefer supplements with large circulations when they employ direct marketing techniques. Leaders in the quest for national advertising dollars are *Parade, Sunday Magazine Network,* and *USA Weekend*. *Parade* is the largest, with a rate base of 35.1 million as of December 1990. (The rate base is the average issue circulation that a publisher guarantees to advertisers.) *Parade* also offers the most extensive national distribution; it is carried by newspapers in practically all top markets. *Sunday Magazine Network* is the next largest syndicated supplement, with a rate base of 18.9 million. These supplements are distributed mainly in the leading metropolitan areas. *USA Weekend* guarantees a circulation of 15.3 million. Copies of these supplements are carried by many small-city newspapers and have the largest circulations in C and D counties.[5]

More than half the ads carried by these supplements are mail order. Companies using these large-circulation publications for direct marketing are attracted by their mass coverage. As compared with other magazines, supplements offer lower-cost circulation, thinner issues, and smaller editorial-to-advertisement ratios. But the products advertised

---

5. *Ibid.*

**TABLE 14.2. Supplemental Page Rates.**

| Supplement | Rate Base (000) | One-Time Page Rate ($) Four-Color | Black and White | Effective Date |
|---|---|---|---|---|
| *Parade* | 35,092 | 422,200 | 341,800 | 7/90 |
| *Sunday Magazine Network* | 18,948 | 230,163 | 186,441 | 1/90 |
| *USA Weekend* | 15,300 | 179,775 | 156,060 | 10/90 |

SOURCE: *Adweek's Marketer's Guide to Media* (October–December 1990), pp. 93–94.

must have larger popular demand and wide distribution. While the cost per thousand circulation is low compared with magazines, total page costs run high because of large circulation size. For example, a one-time, four-color page in *Parade* costs a hefty $422,200. Rate bases and page costs for the three supplements are shown in Table 14-2.

Four-color page costs on a per thousand basis are lowest for *USA Weekend* and highest for *Sunday Magazine Network.* The price differential is probably due to demand rather than cost factors. Since *Sunday Magazine Network* circulates in the largest markets, it holds greater attraction for large national advertisers. These firms are also most apt to use the four-color format. *USA Weekend* concentrates on small cities. Large firms that distribute products in major metropolitan complexes also do business in smaller areas. But smaller markets are not as important to them and not worth paying premiums to advertise.

Supplements are also published by newspapers, and these circulate in local markets. The prominent ones appear in the magazine sections of the *New York Times, New York News, Chicago Tribune,* and *Los Angeles Times*. These publications offer excellent reproduction in four colors and attract local retailers. They do not fit into plans of national advertisers because of their restricted geographic coverage.

PREPRINTS. Preprints have become the most popular direct advertising device in newspapers. Sometimes called free-standing inserts, or FSIs, they are printed by advertisers and shipped to newspapers for insertion. Newspapers then act as carriers for advertiser-printed inserts.

Most of the time, these inserts are left loose, but sometimes they are tipped (glued) in. These inserts come in many formats: cutout coupons, reply postcards, pops-ups, and others. Though many companies use FSIs, the prime users are large national advertisers and chain store retailers, such as major department stores, book publishers, record clubs, and packaged goods manufacturers. These firms market many products and can allocate costs of printing and binding among different items. Some firms also join with other marketers in sharing space and production costs.

**TABLE 14.3. Insert Volume in Daily and Sunday Newspapers.**

| Year | Circulation (billions) | Revenue ($ billions)* |
|---|---|---|
| 1980 | 27.7 | $2.0 |
| 1981 | 28.7 | 2.3 |
| 1982 | 30.0 | 2.5 |
| 1983 | 35.7 | 3.1 |
| 1984 | 41.3 | 3.7 |
| 1985 | 45.4 | 4.2 |
| 1986 | 51.5 | 4.9 |
| 1987 | 54.8 | 5.4 |
| 1988 | 56.4 | 5.9 |
| 1989 | 59.8 | 6.3 |

* Based on a 12-page tabloid including printing and inserting.

SOURCE: Newspaper Advertising Bureau. Reprinted with permission.

There are two specialized firms—News America and Valassis—that sell participation in FSIs. News America was formed in 1988, when Rupert Murdock purchased the second and third largest suppliers of FSIs and combined them into a division that is now larger than Valassis, the former top supplier of FSIs. These companies in 1989 accounted for almost 89 percent of all print media couponing. These FSI "syndicators" take responsibility for all planning, production, and distribution.

The programs of FSI suppliers are especially attractive to firms having narrow product lines, which would normally not find it cost-efficient to produce FSIs on their own. But many large multiproduct marketers also use these companies in conjunction with their own FSI programs. A third form of competition are retailers, some of whom have launched FSI programs and signed up manufacturers to participate.

Use of free-standing inserts has increased enormously. From 1980 to 1988 the number of FSIs has more than doubled. The rate of annual growth was close to 9 percent compounded. In terms of revenue, compounded annual growth amounted to about 13 percent, part of which is attributable to inflation. Data for FSI volume in daily and Sunday newspapers are displayed in Table 14-3.

Retailers and national advertisers tend to differ in their preprint usage patterns. Retailers seem to divide their preprint advertising more evenly between daily and Sunday papers. National advertisers lean heavily toward Sunday. They also use full-run insets to a greater extent than retailers. Retailers' greater use of less-than-full-run inserts reflects their more scattered, less intensive distribution compared with manufacturers using FSIs.

Retailers and manufacturers also use FSIs for different objectives. Retail inserts are meant mainly to increase store traffic. Sales volume increases because FSIs bring more shoppers into a store. These preprints emphasize traditional retail incentives of discounts and special deals.

The FSIs of national advertisers aim to strengthen sales of particular brands. Store traffic may increase, but that is incidental. Manufacturer FSIs emphasize promotional techniques associated with direct response advertising, such as self-liquidators, premiums, coupons, sweepstakes, and contests.

## Coupons

The 1980s can truly be called the age of the cents-off coupon. Their numbers increased spectacularly during that decade, rising from a little over 102 billion in 1980 to some 265 billion in 1989.[6] In 1990, perhaps because of the recession,the number of coupons vaulted to more than 300 billion. Coupons have not only proliferated but have expanded their scope to more products, including low-volume items such as laxatives and medications. Another factor in the coupon upsurge is that copywriters are squeezing more coupons into their ads (see Figure 14-1).

Coupons have a number of purposes. The main ones are to:

- Gain market share or improve competitive position in a market.
- Move surplus inventories from shelves, warehouses, and store rooms.
- Encourage stocking at retail and get better shelf space by stimulating product demand. Retailers are paid extra for each coupon redeemed, and sometimes they run their own promotions using tie-ins with manufacturers' coupon drops.
- Speed up adoption of a new product by incorporating an incentive to an introduction.
- Develop a new class of users for a product already on the market.

Many advertisers who disavow direct marketing are some of the heaviest users of couponing. Do coupons then fall within the domain of direct marketing?

Bob Stone, chairman emeritus of Stone & Adler, Inc., argues in the affirmative. This is probably the majority opinion within the industry. His reasons are that coupons meet the three requirements of a direct marketing offer:

1. They present a definite offer—in this case, a discount off the price of a product.
2. They provide all information necessary for prospects to make a decision.
3. They represent response devices when presented at checkout counters. These responses can be traced directly to an offer by keying the coupon.

6. "FSIs Still Dominate Coupon Delivery System," *Promo* (July 1990), p. 19.

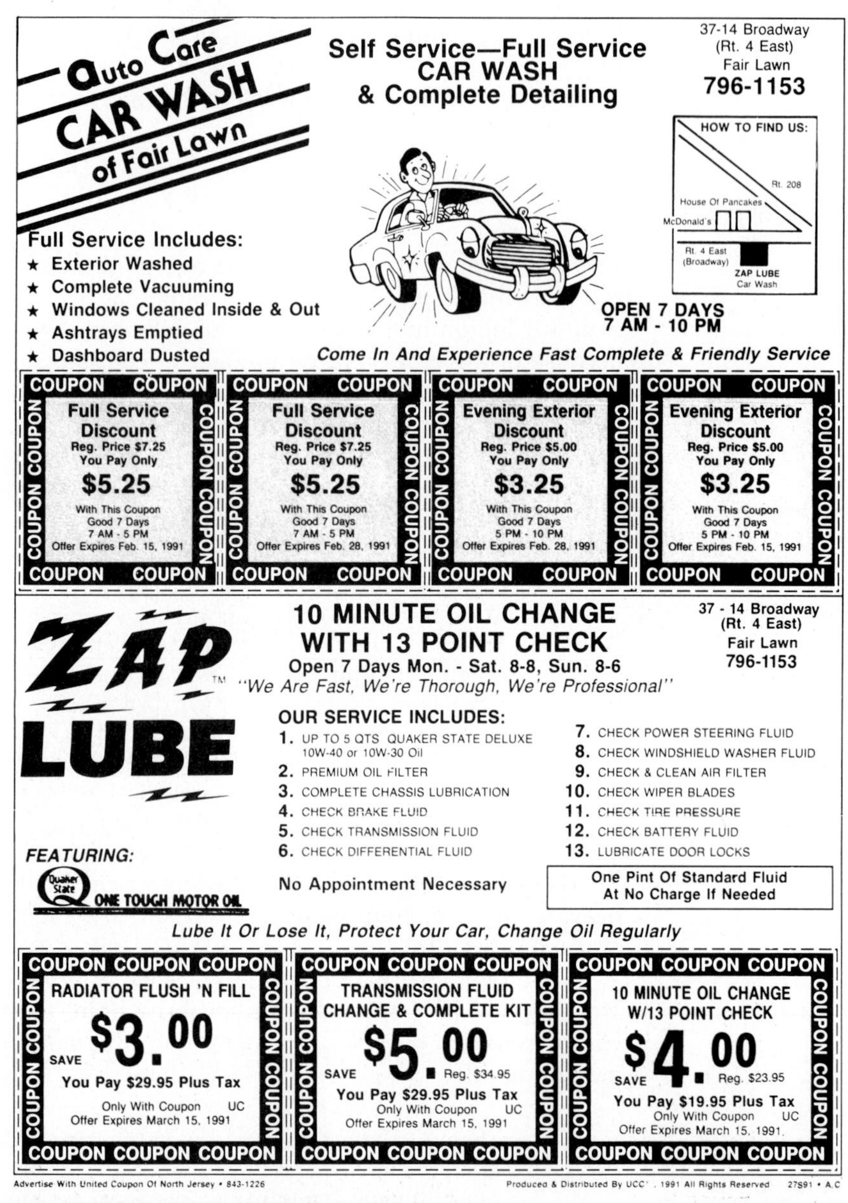


**FIGURE 14-1 Ad with Multiple Coupons**
*Source:* Reprinted with the permission of the Auto Care Car Wash of Fair Lawn.

Nevertheless, there are differences in response patterns between coupons in general media and those in direct mail. In both instances, response is traceable to a coupon but not to an individual. However, a customer redeeming a coupon at a supermarket is unknown, whereas a consumer redeeming a mail coupon creates a name and address that

**TABLE 14.4. Trends in Coupon Distribution.**

| Medium | 1985 | 1986 | 1987 | 1988 | 1989 |
|---|---|---|---|---|---|
| FSIs | 59.9% | 68.0% | 72.7% | 77.3% | 79.7% |
| Newspaper/ROP | 12.2 | 7.4 | 5.9 | 5.4 | 4.8 |
| Newspaper/Coop. | 8.0 | 7.1 | 4.6 | 2.4 | 1.6 |
| Direct mail | 4.4 | 4.0 | 5.3 | 5.0 | 4.3 |
| In/On package | 4.8 | 5.8 | 5.3 | 5.2 | 3.9 |
| Magazines | 8.6 | 6.5 | 3.7 | 2.4 | 3.3 |
| Other | 2.1 | 1.2 | 2.5 | 2.3 | 2.4 |
| Total coupons (billions) | 179.8 | 202.6 | 215.2 | 221.7 | 265.0 |

SOURCE: Based on *DMA 1989 Statistical Fact Book* (New York: DMA, 1989), pp. 136, 138; and *DMA 1990/91 Statistical Fact Book* (New York: DMA, 1990), pp. 153–155.

enters a database. In the former instance, couponing is properly media advertising that uses direct marketing techniques. Retailing serves as the channel of distribution. In the latter case, there are no store visits, and direct marketing itself is the distribution channel.

Free-standing inserts are the major means by which coupons are distributed. This medium in 1989 accounted for about 80 percent of all coupons, and the proportion was rising. Newspaper ROP was a distant second, representing only some 5 percent, and was losing ground. These trends are shown in Table 14-4.

According to a M/ A/ R/ C study, consumers used multiple outlets to redeem coupons. For those who shop with coupons, the most popular place to redeem them is at supermarkets. Drug stores were next, with some 52 percent of coupon users bringing their cents-off cutouts to drug outlets. Discount stores were used by about 47 percent.[7] The incidence of redemption is related to how often people shop at the various outlets. The huge lead of supermarkets and drug stores as favorite redemption centers suggests that most coupons are for packaged goods.

COUPONING ISSUES. The massive use of coupons today has understandably raised a number of issues. One is rather long-standing—misredemption. Coupons not properly redeemed run from about 15 to 20 percent. When a coupon's value is greater than the cost of the newspaper, people are most likely to misredeem.

Most marketers are not very concerned with shoppers who get credit for coupons without buying the designated brands. Their greatest concern is with organized crime, which siphons off millions of dollars each year through misredemptions. Electronic data processing seems about the only way of detecting possible fraud by comparing the number of redemptions with the number of brand purchases.

7. "Consumers O.K. Cents-off Coupons," *Promo* (May 1990), p. 1.

A second issue is "coupon clutter." As the number of cents-off coupons has skyrocketed, response rates have fallen off. In 1988 the redemption rate fell by one percentage point, to 3.2 percent. This compares with about 4.9 percent for direct mail coupons. But in relation to costs, the differential does not warrant a switch to mail. So far, no alternative coupon delivery system has emerged to challenge FSIs.[8]

Other longstanding criticisms come from the advertising industry. Ad agencies in particular have raised objections to coupons on various counts:

- *Coupons are untargeted.* They are not sent to specific individuals. But does that matter if they generate sales?

  Most coupons are for low-priced products selling in self-service outlets. These are convenience goods, used by almost everyone. Why target? The market is an integrated one.
- *Coupons do not build "brand franchises" or "brand loyalty."* This point of view expresses what is called the "brand-image erosion theory." It argues that by emphasizing discounts, coupons present brands in a bargain-basement atmosphere and destroy consumer preferences based on quality.

  A recent M/ A/ R/ C study, conducted with a national sample of 1,356 grocery shoppers, found that consumers have positive attitudes toward coupons. Some 85 percent thought they saved them money, and almost the same percentage said that coupons promote products of the highest quality.[9]

  Are consumers telling the truth or rationalizing their actions to save money? A number of studies involving private labels, sold as price-off brands in stores, have come up with similar results. Consumers say they choose those brands because of product quality, not price.

  Yet product differences among convenience goods are minute and imperceptible. Can one really tell which detergent cleans white and which cleans whiter than white? Which brand of toilet paper is softer, White Cloud or Charmin? How can one tell which coffee tastes richer when the two top brands formulate a flavor that appeals to the mainstream of the market? They cannot be distinguished except by those with the acutest of tastes.

  Perhaps advertising no longer has the power it did in a non-video age, when media were few and television had not yet dulled consumer senses with constant repetition of outworn, meaningless reasons why Brand A is better than Brand B. The fact is that consumers neither hate nor love advertising; they are apathetic. Consumers neither thrill to advertising nor denounce it as a fraud; they ignore it. Perhaps many in the advertising industry are still living in the past, hoping to create an explosive impact. But what if con-

8. See Julie L. Erickson, "FSI Boom to Go Bust," *Advertising Age* (May 1, 1989), pp. 1, 82.
9. "Consumer O.K. Cents-Off Coupons," *op. cit.*, p. 34.

sumers are looking for quality? If brands are seen as being much the same, consumers are acting rationally when they pick the one that is cheaper.

- *Coupons are used by consumers who would have brought the brand anyhow.* Even the M/ A/ R/ C study concluded that 7 of 10 shoppers use coupons to stock up on products they usually buy.[10] A corollary to this argument is that new customers gotten by couponing are the most apt to switch when a competitive coupon appears.

These assertions ring true. Yet a firm that fails to issue coupons stands a good chance of seeing its market share lost to competitors who market with coupons. A firm must go this route strictly in self-defense. Coupons are here to stay because they have become an accepted way of doing business.

Can advertising act as a counteractive force against the couponing storm? This is what the brand-image erosion theory postulates. That presumption is most doubtful. Every brand has a hard core of users, but every brand also has a larger "soft core" of users who try to save money when they shop. A decision to avoid coupons alienates this large segment of customers and virtually seals a brand's fate to suffer a lower market share.

To date, advertising has not been able to increase brand loyalty in the face of cents-off competition. The 265 billion coupons issued in 1989 attest to why advertising is not up to the task of stopping brand share erosion in the face of the coupon avalanche.

## Consumer Magazines

As an advertising medium, magazines differ from newspapers in many important ways. A number of publications circulate in small or regional geographic areas. However, most magazines aspire to national distribution, though in many instances circulation is thin. Compared with newspapers consumer magazines cover a wider area, but they do so with less intensity. The large-circulation magazines offer regional editions, but their coverage of local markets remains relatively low.

Consumer magazines are essentially a national medium. That is, they are used by producers rather than resellers. Yet of the hundreds of publications in existence, exclusive of supplements, only three can boast U.S. circulations that exceed 15 million: *Modern Maturity, Reader's Digest, and TV Guide*. Major consumer magazines penetrate less than 10 percent of the nation's households. This pattern of dispersion puts magazines at a disadvantage in competing with television for mass, nationwide audiences. The cost of ads placed in magazines during the 1989

10. *Ibid.*

amounted to \$6.7 million, or about 5 percent of the nation's advertising expenditures.

The great advantage of magazines is selectivity. The day of the general mass-circulation magazine as a leading carrier of advertising messages is long gone. *Crowell-Collier, Saturday Evening Post, Life,* and *Look* are half-forgotten relics of American journalism. They fell from grace because advertisers shifted their patronage to television to reach the vast numbers that make up middle America. The publications that survived and prospered despite the onslaught of television were those that succeeded in achieving selectivity.

Two kinds of selectivity are germane to advertising, and often these are blended in the same publication. One type pertains to an editorial approach, the other to reaching a particular segment of the population.

A magazine's editorial content supposedly binds readers with similar interests. Readers of travel magazines, for example, are apparently attracted to far-away places and tourism. Outdoor publications cater to people who love to hunt, fish, and explore the great outdoors. Garden books appeal to amateur gardeners, plant growers, and botany devotees. The more specialized the editorial direction, the more homogeneous are the interests of a magazine's readers. Less intense specialization attracts readers with more varied interests.

Selectivity based on interest creates a favorable climate for product advertising. A food recipe would enjoy higher readership in a publication featuring culinary arts than in a news weekly. Ads for cameras, film, and photographic equipment get better reception in photography magazines.

The other kind of selectivity, based on reader characteristics, is associated with editorial policy. Publications that focus on business and investment, such as *Fortune, Forbes,* and *Business Week*, draw readership from business executives. These audiences are bound to be upscale. *Modern Maturity*, with a circulation of more than 22 million, goes primarily to older Americans. Though the "seven sisters" (a common industry term for the women's periodicals *Redbook, McCall's, Woman's Day, Ladies Home Journal, Better Homes & Gardens, Family Circle,* and *Good Housekeeping*) sport large circulations, their readers are predominantly female.

Reader characteristics are in part determined by circulation policies. Publications with similar editorial content may have different reader or subscriber profiles.

Advertising decisions usually consider both editorial and readership factors. The first consideration suggests synergism between an editorial environment and an advertised product. The second factor indicates the market potential offered by a publication. This editorial-market mix can be visualized, simply but crudely, by a $2 \times 2$ matrix, illustrated in Figure 14-2.

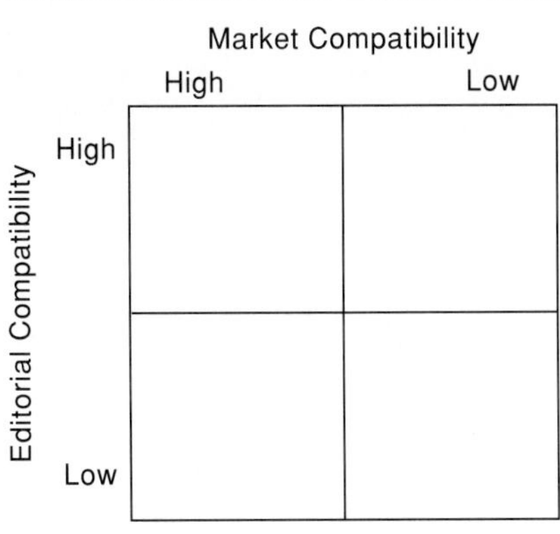


**FIGURE 14-2 Editorial-Reader Characteristics Matrix**

The editorial-marketing relationship is a concept widely accepted by media planners. An example of an ad displaying editorial affinity is shown in Figure 14-3, taken from *Vogue* magazine. Nevertheless, there is no hard evidence demonstrating that advertisements related to editorial content are more effective than those that are unrelated, given the same market potential. Franklin Mint, one of the largest users of magazines for direct marketing, enjoys little or no editorial affinity for its products. When editorial content is neutral with respect to a product, the marketer must select media vehicles on the basis of external criteria. Most frequently these are circulation and reader characteristics.

## Direct Marketing in Consumer Magazines

According to Leading National Advertisers (LNA), an organization that compiles data on advertising space and expenditures, direct response advertising in consumer magazines accounted for almost $644 million in 1988. This sum amounted to about 10.5 percent of total advertising in consumer magazines.[11] This percentage is probably an upper limit. It is often difficult to classify a direct response ad when a toll-free number is slapped on an otherwise general advertisement.

Direct response advertising in consumer magazines is weighted heavily toward collectibles, books, and music. In terms of dollar volume, the top 10 direct response advertisers in consumer magazines for 1988 are

11. Based on Coen, *op. cit.*

**FIGURE 14-3 An Example of Editorial Affinity**
*Source:* Fortunoff, Inc. Reprinted with permission.

**TABLE 14.5. Top 10 Direct Response Advertisers in Magazines, 1988.**

| Company | Advertising Expenditures | Pages |
|---|---:|---:|
| Franklin Mint | $78,983,404 | 1,830 |
| Sony Corporation | 46,488,942 | 676 |
| National Paragon Corp. | 41,363,299 | 80 |
| Time, Inc | 33,516,197 | 685 |
| Bertelsmann AG | 32,576,154 | 495 |
| MBI, Inc. | 17,577,482 | 629 |
| Hamilton Collection | 11,752,457 | 152 |
| Primerica Corp. | 9,394,050 | 91 |
| Brown-Forman Co. | 9,083,722 | 179 |
| Hachette SA | 7,800,991 | 250 |

SOURCE: Larry Peters, "Space Advertising: A Source of New Customers," *Directions* (July/August 1989), p. 11.

shown in Table 14-5. These 10 companies were responsible for almost half—45 percent, to be exact—of total direct response advertising placed in consumer publications.

## Uses of Magazine Space

How would a direct marketer benefit from the use of space in consumer magazines compared with other alternatives? That depends on how well the usage fits a firm's objectives. The main reasons cited for using magazine space are as follows:[12]

- *Customer acquisition.* The acquisition of new customers seems to be a major reason for using space. Many catalog companies place ads in magazines as alternatives to prospecting by cold mail or telemarketing. These catalog houses often qualify prospects by requiring a nominal payment for the catalog. Financial services also find receptive audiences for offers of literature. These requests are often followed up by direct mail or telephone. Large-circulation magazines especially make large numbers of potential customers available at reasonable costs.
- *Sales.* Generation of direct sales is another important reason for buying magazine space. When firms commit large budgets to magazine advertising, they usually seek direct revenue for their expenditures. This is evident from the figures for the leading direct response advertisers shown in Table 14-5. Big players such as Franklin Mint, Lenox Collection, Bradford Exchange, and Time, Inc. invariably judge their efforts by the sales results.

12. See Florence Peloquin, "Speaking of Space," *Direct Marketing* (September 1989), pp. 42–45; Kathleen Harnett, "Space Ads Pay off," *Target Marketing* (January 1988), p. 18; "Special Feauture Section," *Direct Marketing News* (January 1, 1989.)

Firms with sales objectives often look for editorial affinity to enhance reader interest in their products. Small-budget advertisers may use magazines with mail order sections. Advertisers in these publications can lower costs by buying fractional pages, yet communicate with readers who are mail order buyers.

- *Tests*. The testing of offers and creative ideas is frequently cited as an advantage of using magazine space. Many magazines offer split runs and regional editions, where several versions of copy can be tested. But the decision to use publications is made before the test. It is most unlikely that a firm would test an offer in magazines if it intended to advertise full-scale in direct mail, or any medium other than publications.

Magazines can be classified by their editorial content and the nature of their readership. These features indicate the type of audience a magazine intends to reach and, thus, the appropriateness of advertising aimed at a particular group. For example, Figure 14-4 shows an ad intended to appeal to women, taken from *Woman's Day* magazine. While most editorial matter leans toward selectivity, some magazines are apparently used more than others for direct response advertising. Table 14-6 shows the top 10 magazines ranked by 1988 direct response expenditures.

Except for *Muscle & Fitness*, a highly specialized book aimed at young men interested in body building and physical fitness, the leading carriers of direct response ads are also among the top general-advertising vehicles. All offer circulations of 2.5 million or more copies per issue. Though these magazines feature specialized editorial matter, their ads go out to mass audiences. Women, for example, make up the prime readership of *Better Homes & Gardens*. But with a rate base of 8 million, *BH&G* cannot deliver a homogeneous female readership.

Media selection turns on several factors, notably costs of advertising and benefits accruing from that advertising. These criteria hold for both general and direct response advertisers. But "benefits" are defined differently, and all media selection decisions do not follow the same set of rules.

## Advertising Rates

Magazines set forth their advertising prices on rate cards, which are compiled by Standard Rate & Data Service for user convenience. These rates should be viewed as asking prices, or a starting point for negotiating. More and more publishers today are willing to follow practices in television markets and to make deals.

The one-page ad is the most common and therefore serves as the standard unit. Fractional pages go for less money, and multiple pages carry higher price tags. The standard one-page ad covers space within a border that matches the margins of a page.

**See how much you can save on Cannon's® pretty bath linens!**

CHOOSE GOLD, PINK OR BLUE FOR YOUR 30-DAY FREE HOME TRIAL — you won't find a better time to brighten your bath decor. Especially at this delightfully low direct mail price! CANNON'S BUTTERFLY DESIGN IS A JOY ANY SEASON OF THE YEAR. Bright and lively butterfly print coordinates beautifully with bold solid colors in a complete 20-piece ensemble. ALL ARE LUSCIOUSLY SOFT AND ABSORBENT — the kind of towels you'll love wrapping up in after a shower or bath. And Cannon's cotton/polyester blend keeps these lovely linens bright and soft as new, washing after washing. PICK YOUR FAVORITE COLOR and send for your Free Trial set today.

Choose from 3 decorator colors

**20-Pc. Set includes:**

- 4-Bath Towels (22" x 42") (2 print, 2 solid)
- 4 Hand Towels (15" x 24") (2 print, 2 solid)
- 4 Solid Guest Towels (11" x 18")
- 8 Wash Cloths (12" square) (4 print, 4 solid)

We reserve the right to substitute similar merchandise of equal or better quality If substituted merchandise is not acceptable, you can return it postpaid during your free trial period without further obligation. Offer good in USA only.

**Complete 20-Pc. Ensemble**

just By Mail Only **$24.99** plus shipping and handling

**Try the Set, Free, for 30 days!** (with credit approval)

Just one of the many fine products available from Fingerhut.

5-058604-000 ©Fingerhut

**Plus...2 FREE GIFTS TO KEEP!** JUST FOR TRYING THE TOWEL SET.

A special Surprise Gift!

**7-Piece Kitchen Utensil Set.**
In mellow, walnut-finished hardwood. Made in Taiwan or the People's Republic of China or Philippines. Some assembly required.

**NO-RISK COUPON** Fingerhut Corporation, P.O. Box 2500, St. Cloud, MN 56395

Please send me the 20-Pc. Butterfly Bath Ensemble in the color indicated below. Cash price is $24.99 plus shipping and handling. I agree to pay the total cash price of $29.97 in 3 monthly installments of $9.99 each. **No finance chrges will be added.** Sales or use tax will be added to my purchase where applicable. I understand that I may return the Bath Ensemble at my expense and owe nothing if I am not completely satisfied after my 30-day Home Trial. The Free Gift merchandise is mine to keep in either case. (This order is subject to approval of my credit by Fingerhut.)

| CHECK (✓) YOUR COLOR CHOICE: | Gold (A1) | Blue (A2) | Pink (A3) |
|---|---|---|---|
| | ☐ | ☐ | ☐ |

662387

Print Name ______
Address ______ Apt. No. ______
City ______ State ______ Zip ______
Area Code ______ Phone ______ Date ______
Please Sign Your Name ✓ ______

*CLIP AND MAIL TODAY FOR PROMPT SHIPMENT!*

**FIGURE 14-4 An Advertisement Directed to Women**
*Source:* Fingerhut Corporation. Reprinted with permission.

**TABLE 14.6. Leading Magazines Carrying Direct Response Ads.**

| Magazine | Expenditures (millions) |
|---|---|
| *TV Guide* | 56.1 |
| *Cosmopolitan* | 14.6 |
| *Family Circle* | 13.4 |
| *Better Homes & Gardens* | 12.8 |
| *Good Housekeeping* | 12.4 |
| *Woman's Day* | 11.6 |
| *Muscle & Fitness* | 11.4 |
| *Time* | 11.4 |
| *People* | 10.8 |
| *McCall's* | 9.0 |

SOURCE: Larry Peters, "Space Advertising: A Source of New Customers," *Directions* (July/August 1988) p. 2.

A *bleed ad* extends beyond the border to the very edge of a page. Since bleed ads take up more space, their costs are often quoted at a premium over the cost of a standard page. But some publications charge the same for both sizes, bleed and standard. Advertising practitioners differ as to whether a bleed is worth the extra cost. In direct marketing, experience is the only reliable guide.

Rates also depend on the use of color. More colors bring higher charges, because printing presses must run for longer times. Color reproduction is one of the major advantages of magazines, and many products benefit from being shown in natural tones. Among them are fashion items, food, cosmetics, and automobiles. But for both black-and-white ads, and color ads costs display no uniformity, as they depend on printing equipment, stock, color, and the size of print runs. Table 14-7 compares black-and-white and four-color costs for a select number of leading magazines in various classifications.

Among the dual-audience magazines, the highest color surcharges are those for newsweeklies—*Time, Newsweek,* and *U.S. News & World Report*. These publications are directly competitive. Magazines in the women's category have fairly uniform color premiums, with the exception of *Redbook, Cosmopolitan,* and *Glamour,* which compete for the same business and charge higher premiums for color than the remaining female-dominated publications. These comparisons suggest factors other than production cost differentials in advertising rates.

Practically all large-circulation magazines have special, less-than-full-run editions. Some are distributed geographically, some demographically. *Time* has a host of special editions, such as those going to high-income homes and to subscribers in professional and managerial occupations. *Newsweek* sports an edition going to business executives. Both magazines break up circulation by metropolitan area, state, and television market. But these editions are priced at higher rates than full runs.

TABLE 14.7. **Black-and-White versus Four-Color Page Rates.**

| | One-Time Rate ($000) | | Percent Increase of Four-Color Rates |
|---|---|---|---|
| | Black and White | Four-Color | |
| **Dual Readership** | | | |
| *Modern Maturity* | 185.0 | 205.0 | 11 |
| *National Geographic* | 107.1 | 139.3 | 30 |
| *Newsweek* | 63.1 | 101.0 | 60 |
| *People* | 64.8 | 83.5 | 29 |
| *Reader's Digest* | 103.7 | 124.7 | 20 |
| *Smithsonian* | 33.7 | 50.6 | 50 |
| *Time* | 77.0 | 120.1 | 56 |
| *TV Guide* | 95.9 | 112.9 | 18 |
| *U.S. News and World Report* | 45.0 | 67.1 | 49 |
| **Female Readership** | | | |
| *Better Homes & Gardens* | 104.6 | 126.5 | 21 |
| *Cosmopolitan* | 43.4 | 58.4 | 35 |
| *Family Circle* | 70.4 | 83.8 | 19 |
| *Glamour* | 39.2 | 55.3 | 41 |
| *Good Housekeeping* | 82.2 | 103.2 | 26 |
| *Ladies' Home Journal* | 65.7 | 78.2 | 19 |
| *McCall's* | 65.4 | 77.1 | 18 |
| *Redbook* | 54.1 | 71.5 | 32 |
| *Woman's Day* | 61.0 | 73.1 | 20 |

SOURCE: Based on *Adweek's Marketer's Guide to Media.*

Costs are usually expressed in terms of cost-per-thousand (CPM) of audience or circulation. General advertisers use audience as the base for calculating efficiency. Since they strive to create images or mental impressions, readers represent their marketing potential. Media dollars buy so many readers, and lower reader costs thus yield greater efficiencies. This way of thinking leads to the conclusion that knowing the audience makes the circulation level irrelevant. After all, the number of copies in circulation is only a means of obtaining readers.

Though this logic stands on firm ground, in practice the audience concept rests on quicksand. The act of reading is an abstract, intangible quality that is extremely difficult to measure. Two firms dominate the audience measurement field in print: Simmons Market Research Bureau (SMRB) and Mediamark Reasearch, Inc. (MRI). Though using different methods, the two services purport to measure average issue audience with large national probability samples. But their research results are strangely at odds. Table 14-8 shows the audiences reported by these services for the same magazines.

In the dual-readership category SMRB and MRI are not too far apart on weeklies. But MRI reports monthly magazines as having substantially larger audiences than those credited by SMRB. Since survey results are projected to the total adult population, small percentages rep-

**TABLE 14.8. Audience Estimates of SMRB and MRI.**

| | SMRB (millions) | MRI (millions) | MRI as a Percent of SMRB |
|---|---|---|---|
| **Dual Audience** | | | |
| *National Geographic* | 23.0 | 29.6 | 129 |
| *Newsweek* | 18.0 | 18.4 | 102 |
| *People* | 29.5 | 30.4 | 103 |
| *Reader's Digest* | 35.5 | 47.5 | 134 |
| *Smithsonian* | 6.0 | 8.3 | 138 |
| *Time* | 21.4 | 20.6 | 96 |
| *TV Guide* | 39.3 | 44.8 | 114 |
| *U.S. News & World Report* | 12.2 | 11.1 | 91 |
| **Female Audience** | | | |
| *Better Homes & Gardens* | 22.3 | 31.4 | 141 |
| *Family Circle* | 17.1 | 24.6 | 144 |
| *Good Housekeeping* | 19.8 | 34.4 | 174 |
| *Ladies' Home Journal* | 15.0 | 18.4 | 123 |
| *McCall's* | 14.4 | 17.3 | 120 |
| *Redbook* | 10.4 | 13.0 | 125 |
| *Woman's Day* | 14.5 | 21.8 | 150 |

SOURCE: *Adweek's Marketer's Guide to Media* (November–December 1990).

resent large numbers. For example, MRI reports 14 percent more *TV Guide* readers as compared with SMRB. But that 14 percent represents a difference of 5.5 million readers!

Female audiences in Table 14-8 are shown for the magazines known as the "seven sisters." They compete for the same ad budgets. Not only does MRI report generally higher audiences, but differences between the two measurement services range widely—from 74 percent for *Good Housekeeping* to only 20 percent for *McCall's*.

Since SMRB and MRI claim to measure the same thing—the audience of an average issue—it is obvious that both services cannot be right. Yet no one can say with any degree of certainty which survey is more accurate. Readership reports cannot be verified against any objective measure of reading. General advertisers base their choice of service on subjective evaluation, and they defend the figures they use on the proposition that something is better than nothing. There is no way of telling which set of statistics, SMRB's or MRI's, yields greater benefits for media expenditures.

Direct marketers, however, judge their efforts by tangible, measureable benefits: direct sales, inquiries, store traffic. They ignore audience; they have yet to find any relationship between readership statistics and response. Media selection decisions depend very much on what statistical base is used to compare costs. Table 14-9 shows CPM calculations using circulation and audience.

**TABLE 14.9. Cost Per Thousand ($).**

| | Circulation | Audience | |
|---|---|---|---|
| | | SMRB | MRI |
| **Dual Readership** | | | |
| *National Geographic* | 17.12 | 6.06 | 4.70 |
| *Newsweek* | 32.29 | 5.57 | 5.43 |
| *People* | 24.96 | 2.84 | 2.74 |
| *Reader's Digest* | 7.67 | 3.51 | 2.62 |
| *Smithsonian* | 24.10 | 8.42 | 6.13 |
| *Time* | 30.03 | 5.61 | 5.83 |
| *TV Guide* | 7.15 | 2.87 | 2.52 |
| *U.S. News & World Report* | 31.21 | 5.49 | 6.09 |
| **Female Audience** | | | |
| *Better Homes & Gardens* | 15.81 | 7.13 | 5.31 |
| *Family Circle* | 15.65 | 5.42 | 3.93 |
| *Good Housekeeping* | 20.64 | 5.87 | 4.89 |
| *Ladies' Home Journal* | 13.12 | 4.71 | 3.94 |
| *McCall's* | 15.42 | 5.81 | 5.00 |
| *Redbook* | 18.82 | 7.57 | 6.16 |
| *Woman's Day* | 15.89 | 5.36 | 3.66 |

SOURCE: *Adweek's Marketer's Guide to Media* (November–December 1990); Standard Rate & Date Service (1990).

NOTE: Costs are based on one-page, four-color rates, rounded to the nearest $100. Readers and copies are rounded to the nearest 1,000.

Table 14-9 gives clear evidence that evaluations of efficiency vary according to the set of figures used: circulation, SMRB audience, or MRI readership. If audience figures are used, the costliest dual-readership magazines in terms of circulation fall into lower cost brackets. Indeed, *Newsweek* and *Time* wind up with lower reader CPM than *National Geographic* or *Smithsonian*. And SMRB raises *People*, a high-cost vehicle in terms of circulation, to the most efficient.

With respect to women's magazines, *Good Housekeeping* has the highest circulation CPM. But MRI gives this publication a favorable position. *Woman's Day*, with a somewhat average cost per copy, emerges as the most efficient advertising vehicle according to MRI. Costs for *Better Homes & Gardens* appear average with respect to circulation but much higher than most of its sister publications according to SMRB.

Direct marketers use cost per response as the criterion for media selection. But that requires past experience, and even then, the results of any ad can differ radically from those of the past. Direct marketers frequently test their ads in various media, but predictions are still far from perfect. Under these circumstances, direct marketers fall back on circulation estimates. The rate base is what magazines guarantee, and paid copies are audited by the Audit Bureau of Circulations (ABC).

Circulation counts should serve only as a first step in assessing a magazine's potential. A publisher's statement contains many valuable facts that allow an advertiser to judge the quality of circulation. This subject is discussed in Appendix E, at the end of this chapter.

## Hybrid Advertising

In recent years, more and more general advertisers have become involved in aspects of direct marketing. This trend has brought the techniques of image creation and awareness together with the action-generating methods of direct marketing. This unlikely melding of disparate philosophies is now called *integrated marketing*.

General advertisers did not abandon their old ways. Rather, they sought to integrate elements of direct marketing into their ongoing programs. This mixing of direct response with general advertising has resulted in hybrid forms. Ads carry 800 numbers and reply formats of mail order, yet maintain their general-advertising appearance and message. The ads attempt to obtain the best of two possible worlds: image building and direct action.

A large number of product advertisements today build image and invite response. Among them are ads for travel and hotels, banks, automobiles, and cameras. Such advertisements blur the once-clear distinctions between general advertising and direct marketing. Figure 14-5 illustrates an ad that would convey the standard soft sell and reinforcing image of general advertising were an 800 number not included.

Combined general and direct response advertising, however, does create a number of problems for creative personnel. One weakness is that advertising becomes neither fish nor foul. The Marriott ad tacks an 800 number onto the copy but gives no reason why anyone should call. That number might well have been pasted onto any ad. Even when graphic designers work directly with direct response copywriters, illustration and copy may not be coordinated. Direct response advertisers have criticized much of the hybrid advertising because the call to action, either to dial an 800 number or to fill out a coupon, is not related to the rest of the ad.[13] But then, marketing is constantly changing, merging and mixing new elements. As new programs appear, so do new sets of problems that, in time, work themselves out.

# Summary

Newspapers and magazines are mass media of an impersonal nature. The commercial message does not stand by itself but is imbedded in an

13. Carol Nelson "The Coupon Dilemma," *Direct Marketing* (June 1989), pp. 51–51, 103.

A POSH HOTEL ROOM
ISN'T MUCH COMFORT
WHEN YOUR BREAKFAST
IS LATE.

Mornings are so much better when it's
the coffee and eggs that are steaming instead of you.
That's why we at Marriott make this promise:
if your breakfast doesn't show up on time, it won't
show up on your bill. This commitment is one reason
business travelers rate Marriott their first
choice. Our rooms are quite tasteful, but service
is what our guests really hunger for.

SERVICE.
THE ULTIMATE LUXURY.®

Marriott.
HOTELS · RESORTS · SUITES

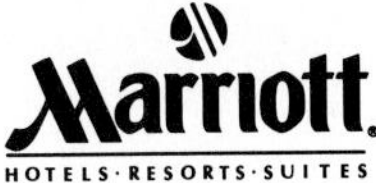

It begins the moment you call 1-800-MARRIOTT.
Or call your Travel Agent. Go USA!

**FIGURE 14-5 Hybid Advertisement by Marriott Hotel**
*Source:* Marriott Corporation Reprinted with permission.

editorial environment. However, they supplement other direct marketing efforts, performing functions that other direct marketing vehicles cannot do as efficiently.

Newspapers are a local medium. Their outstanding characteristic is that they offer high penetration in local markets. The most popular direct marketing device using newspapers today is the preprint, or freestanding insert. Retail users split their preprint circulation almost evenly between Sunday and daily, whereas national advertisers make the most use of Sunday papers.

Coupons constitute a growing use of direct response devices in newspapers. Coupons are actually a promotional technique. A major problem with coupons is misredemption.

Consumer magazines are primarily a national medium. Unlike newspapers, magazines offer selectivity. For direct marketing there are two kinds of selectivity; one depends on editorial policy and the other on circulation policy.

Advertising rates include premiums for color and space. Magazines offer discounts for volume and frequency. An advertiser can purchase space for less-than-full-run editions, but it must pay a premium for the privilege.

General advertisers evaluate magazines on the basis of audience. But direct marketers have leaned heavily in the direction of circulation, mainly because of critical differences between primary and pass-along readership.

As more large companies have taken up direct marketing, they have blended it into their usual method of operation. This has resulted in a hybrid type of advertising, which contains elements of both direct marketing and image-building objectives.

## REVIEW QUESTIONS

1. What is the greatest advantage offered by newspapers to direct marketers?
2. In what ways do direct marketers use supplements?
3. Why do national advertisers favor preprints in Sunday newspapers rather than dailies?
4. Many authorities maintain that coupons do not enhance a consumer franchise. Evaluate this statement.
5. State four purposes of using coupons.
6. What forms of selectivity do magazines offer?
7. Are large-circulation magazines suitable media vehicles for direct response advertisements featuring specialty products?

8. Does a copy decision to use color affect a media decision to use particular magazines? Why or Why not?
9. Is the advertiser completely protected by a magazine's circulation guarantee?
10. Why do many direct marketers refuse to base their media decisions on the total audience concept?

---

**PROJECT**

1. Kenneth Burkhardt decided to go into business selling fun rooms. Ever since Ken converted the top of his garage into a playroom, his friends have been urging him to manufacture prefabricated playrooms. It took him 18 months to design and construct his own game room. Ken helped to construct seven such rooms for his friends. It took four skilled craftsmen just 18 working days to set up the last playroom. This did not include the time of getting the various building permits.

   Ken's friends invested $250,000 in the business. This was to cover the downpayment on the building and property, equipment, materials, labor costs, the promotion, and overhead. Fortunately, Kenneth had 11 orders for his fun rooms when he started. Five were contracted for $24,000, two for $30,000, and four others for $36,000. A deposit of 20 percent was required. These were contracted for completion over the next 20 months.

   a. What type of direct marketing campaign would you recommend and over what time period? Why?
   b. What results do you expect? Why?
   c. Design the various promotion pieces you would recommend. It is fine to work in black and white and to use stick figures. If you prefer, you may do it in color. A paste job is also approved. Neatness and clarity count as part of the grade.

# APPENDIX E

## Circulation Analysis

Alex MacRae, Director of Marketing & Sales Development, National Geographic Society

---

### WHY IS CIRCULATION IMPORTANT?

Most media users are national advertisers who have their ad agencies grinding out audience figures put out by Simmons Marketing Research Bureau (SMRB) and Mediamark Research, Inc. (MRI). These audience statistics form the basis of reader CPM, reach, frequency, demographics, buying patterns, lifestyles, and other measures. For national advertising, such calculations are primary to media decision making. If the audience is the criterion, why should anyone bother with circulation?

Even for national advertising, audience statistics leave much to be desired, SMRB and MRI are miles apart, and decisions vary greatly depending on whose measurements one accepts. Second, audience measurements makes no distinction as to the quality of readership. Though their figures show substantial differences, both SMRB and MRI define readers by some minimal exposure standard. If a survey respondent claims to have glanced at a single page in an issue, that individual is counted as a magazine reader.

It doesn't matter if the exposure was of short or long duration. It doesn't matter how much content was involved. It doesn't matter what a "reader" absorbed. It doesn't matter whether that issue was read intensely or casually. All exposures are equal. An exposure is an exposure is an exposure, and that makes a reader.

But how do circulation figures change this picture? Circulation represents inert copies, not actual people who respond to editorial fare and buy articles of commerce offered for sale.

Audited circulation statistics provide evidence that allows national advertisers to make inferences about the quality of audiences. Despite their penchant for audience statistics, media buyers at general-advertising agencies can gain better insights about reader interests and loyalties to various publications by examining circulation figures of the Audit Bureau of Circulations (ABC).

For direct marketers, this is particularly important. Indeed, it is circulation, not audience, that holds center stage. The number defines the amount of printed messages transmitted. Since direct marketers are thus fed back a measurable response, they can calculate the percentage of magazine recipients—subscribers or buyers of single copies—who took action as a result of an offer. Direct marketers have long learned that readership figures from a survey are less reliable than circulation statistics as an indicator of cost per response. General advertisers could well take a lesson from direct marketing experience, even though they cannot ascertain what counts. Circulation patterns affect response because they impact the quality of readership.

But what about passalong readers? Circulation does not measure that.

We know from experience that passalong readers do not respond to direct mail offers, or at most account for a very minor part of total response. How do we know? Practically 100 percent of *National Geographic's* circulation is via subscription. Most response to direct marketing ads in *National Geographic* comes in during the first 10 days of the issue date—long before the magazine has had time to circulate among many pass-along readers. Indeed, subscribers usually receive copies at or before the time issues go onto stands at retail. A secondary layer of readership cannot reverse the fortunes of an ad that fails to make an impact on primary readers.

Success depends heavily on the response of primary audience, defined as subscribers or single-copy purchases. Knowledge of ABC reports, almost lost pieces of intelligence among general advertisers, gives its possessors an undeniable edge in buying space. What do these reports contain, and where does one look?

## TYPES OF ABC REPORTS

ABC issues two types of reports: pink sheets and white sheets. The first contains circulation estimates of the publishers. ABC brings out these publishers' statements every six months. The white sheets are audited figures for the entire year.

If ABC does actual audits, why should it distribute sets of estimates made by publishers? The reason is timing. It is not uncommon for ABC audited reports to come out 18 months after the period in question. This lag is too long for effective decision making. Advertisers prefer the most recent data available to use in space buying. They are thus willing to trade off estimates for audits in order to get more up-to-date information. Besides, estimates of large-circulation magazines have experienced only minor and immaterial differences from audited statistics.

So let's turn to the pink sheets and see what they can possibly tell us about readers. Figure E-1 shows a publishers's statement of *National Geographic* magazine, for the six months ending December 31, 1990.

---

## SECTION 1: AVERAGE PAID CIRCULATION

Section 1 of a publisher's statement shows the average paid circulation for a six-month period. This circulation is divided into subscription and single-copy sales. It also shows a subgroup titled "average total nonpaid distribution" for a six-month period.

Magazines usually have widely varying proportions of subscriptions and single-copy sales. Practically the entire circulation of some magazines is made up of single-copy sales, for example, *Family Circle* and *Woman's Day*. Others distribute their copies wholly by subscription. *National Geographic's* paid circulation, for example, is more than 99 percent subscription.

Whether one or the other is more desirable in terms of response depends on many factors, and this is usually determined on the basis of experience. But certain reader patterns can be acurately inferred. A circulation heavy on subscription will enjoy greater continuity in readership; the same people read the publication from issue to issue. Conversely, single-copy sales have higher reader turnover.

Analysis of how magazines distribute their copies helps in setting media schedules that consider reach and frequency. These calculations are vital in spacing advertisements within selected media. A continuity objective might stress subscriber circulation. A reach objective would put greater emphasis on circulation turnover.

Section 1 ends with nonpaid distribution. Some of the nonpaid issues represent complimentary copies to advertisers. The major part comes from subscribers who have not paid their bills.

For most magazines, the proportion of nonpaid circulation is relatively small. But small percentages translate into large numbers for large-circulation magazines. Therefore, both the number and percent should be inspected by a potential advertiser, because the figures indicate the extent to which quality is diluted. Nonpayment for subscriptions suggests a lack of interest in a magazine.

# NATIONAL GEOGRAPHIC MAGAZINE

CLASS, INDUSTRY OR FIELD SERVED: Travel, customs of people, products and related human interest, subject to geographical and sociological nature.

## 1. AVERAGE PAID CIRCULATION FOR 6 MONTHS ENDED DECEMBER 31, 1990

| | | | |
|---|---|---|---|
| Subscriptions: Individual | | 244,161 | |
| Association, See Pars. 11(a) & 11(b) | | 9,857,255 | |
| Total Subscriptions | | | 10,101,416 |
| Single Copy Sales: through retail outlets | | 85,075 | |
| Bulk and all other, See Par. 11(c) | | 3,212 | |
| Total Single Copy Sales | | | 88,287 |
| AVERAGE TOTAL PAID CIRCULATION | | | 10,189,703 |
| Advertising Rate Base | | | 10,125,000 |
| Average Total Non-Paid Distribution | 66,421 | | |

## 1a. AVERAGE PAID CIRCULATION of Regional, Metro and Demographic Editions

| Edition & number of issues | | Rate Base | Edition & number of issues | | Rate Base | Edition & number of issues | | Rate Base |
|---|---|---|---|---|---|---|---|---|
| Northeast (6) | 2,116,200 | 2,165,000 | Europe (6) | 807,945 | 690,000 | Florida (6) | 389,973 | 400,000 |
| Southeast (6) | 1,033,428 | 1,055,000 | United States (6) | 7,957,274 | 8,135,000 | Texas (6) | 465,040 | 480,000 |
| East Central (6) | 1,535,643 | 1,580,000 | North America (6) | 8,788,566 | 8,930,000 | New England (6) | 519,904 | 530,000 |
| South Central (6) | 688,825 | 700,000 | Canada (6) | 831,037 | None | Pacific N.W. (6) | 563,409 | 570,000 |
| West Central (6) | 644,667 | 660,000 | Middle East & Africa (6) | 72,578 | 60,000 | Pacific S.W. (6) | 1,373,684 | 1,405,000 |
| Western (6) | 1,937,093 | 1,975,000 | Washington D.C. | | | Big G 15 (6) | 3,377,673 | 3,485,000 |
| Atlantic (6) | 881,014 | 750,000 | Metro (6) | 210,526 | 210,000 | Big G 25 (6) | 4,358,011 | 4,500,000 |
| Pacific (6) | 407,015 | 350,000 | New York Metro (6) | 459,132 | 470,000 | Big G 36 (6) | 5,011,350 | 5,185,000 |
| Latin America (6) | 103,168 | 95,000 | Chicago Metro (6) | 253,735 | 260,000 | Asia (6) | 131,155 | 100,000 |
| Non-Regional (6) | 11,613 | None | L.A. Metro (6) | 501,586 | 510,000 | Australia/New Zealand (6) | 275,310 | 250,000 |
| British Isles (6) | 329,113 | 290,000 | S.F. Metro (6) | 311,288 | 305,000 | | | |
| Continental Europe (6) | 478,833 | 400,000 | California (6) | 1,106,033 | 1,125,000 | | | |

See Par. 11(d)

## 2. PAID CIRCULATION by Issues

| Issue | Subscriptions | Single Copy Sales | Total Paid | Issue | Subscriptions | Single Copy Sales | Total Paid |
|---|---|---|---|---|---|---|---|
| July | 10,094,355 | 89,346 | 10,183,701 | Oct. | 10,115,363 | 85,358 | 10,200,721 |
| Aug. | 10,093,495 | 93,791 | 10,187,286 | Nov. | 10,109,444 | 85,033 | 10,194,477 |
| Sept. | 10,093,156 | 87,292 | 10,180,448 | Dec. | 10,102,680 | 88,905 | 10,191,585 |

## ANALYSIS OF TOTAL NEW AND RENEWAL SUBSCRIPTIONS

Sold during 6 Month Period Ended December 31, 1990

### 3. AUTHORIZED PRICES:

| | |
|---|---|
| (a) Basic Prices: Single Copy: $2.65. Subscriptions: See Par. 11(e) | 12,576 |
| (b) Higher than basic prices: U.S., 1 yr. $22.50; Canada, 1 yr. $31.95; Foreign, 1 yr. $32.80 | 129,686 |
| (c) Lower than basic prices: 2 yrs. $39.00 | 5,183 |
| (d) Association subscription prices: See Par. 11(a) | 7,592,435 |
| Total Subscriptions Sold in Period | 7,739,880 |

### 4. DURATION OF SUBSCRIPTIONS SOLD:

| | |
|---|---|
| (a) One to six months (1 to 6 issues) | 1,877 |
| (b) Seven to twelve months (7 to 12 issues) | 7,666,048 |
| (c) Thirteen to twenty-four months | 70,089 |
| (d) Twenty-five to thirty-six months | 1,220 |
| (e) Thirty-seven to forty-eight months | 74 |
| (f) Forty-nine months and more | 572 |
| Total Subscriptions Sold in Period | 7,739,880 |

### 5. CHANNELS OF SUBSCRIPTION SALES:

| | |
|---|---|
| (a) Ordered by mail and/or direct request | 70,392 |
| (b) Ordered through salespeople: | |
| 1. Catalog agencies and individual agents | 45,038 |
| 2. Publisher's own and other publishers' salespeople | 398 |
| 3. Independent agencies' salespeople | 31,106 |
| 4. Newspaper agencies | 511 |
| 5. Members of schools, churches, fraternal and similar organizations | None |
| (c) Association memberships, See Par. 11(a) | 7,592,435 |
| (d) All other channels | None |
| Total Subscriptions Sold in Period | 7,739,880 |

**FIGURE E-1 Publisher's Statement**
*Source: National Geographic Publisher's Statement,* Six Months Ended December 31, 1989. Reprinted with permission.

6. USE OF PREMIUMS:

| | |
|---|---|
| (a) Ordered without premium | 7,739,754 |
| (b) Ordered with material reprinted from this publication | None |
| (c) Ordered with other premiums, See Par. 11(f) | 126 |
| Total Subscriptions Sold in Period | 7,739,880 |

## ADDITIONAL CIRCULATION INFORMATION

7. POST EXPIRATION COPIES INCLUDED IN PAID CIRCULATION (PAR. 1):

(a) Average number of copies served on subscriptions not more than three months after expiration ........ 188

8. COLLECTION STIMULANTS: ........ None

9. BASIS ON WHICH COPIES WERE SOLD TO RETAIL OUTLETS:

Nonreturnable ........ 100.00%

## 10. U.S. PAID CIRCULATION BY ABCD COUNTY SIZE for the December, 1990 Issue

June, 1988 issue used in establishing percentages for subscription circulation.
Total paid circulation of this issue was 0.02% greater than average total paid circulation for period.

| County Size | No. of Counties | % of U.S. Population | Subscription Circulation | | Single Copy Circulation | | Total Circulation | |
|---|---|---|---|---|---|---|---|---|
| | | | Copies | % Total | Copies | % Total | Copies | % Total |
| A | 177 | 41% | 3,373,080 | 42.95 | 1,967 | 42.95 | 3,375,047 | 42.95 |
| B | 408 | 30% | 2,447,937 | 31.17 | 1,428 | 31.18 | 2,449,365 | 31.17 |
| C | 496 | 15% | 1,168,601 | 14.88 | 681 | 14.87 | 1,169,282 | 14.88 |
| D | 1,993 | 14% | 863,886 | 11.00 | 504 | 11.00 | 864,390 | 11.00 |
| | 3,074 | 100% | 7,853,504 | 100.00 | 4,580 | 100.00 | 7,858,084 | 100.00 |
| Alaska-Hawaii Unclassified | 27 | | 82,581 | | 10 | | 82,591 | |
| TOTAL U.S. | 3,101 | | 7,936,085 | | 4,590 | | 7,940,675 | |

COUNTY SIZE GROUP DEFINITIONS BY THE A.C. NIELSEN COMPANY

A—All counties belonging as of June 19, 1981 to the 25 largest SCSAs or SMSAs according to the 1980 Census of Population.

B—All counties not included under A that are either over 150,000 population or in SCSAs or SMSAs over 150,000 population according to the 1980 Census of Population.

C—All counties not included under A or B that are either over 40,000 population or in SMSAs over 40,000 population according to the 1980 Census of Population.

D—All remaining counties.

11. EXPLANATORY:

Latest Released Audit Report Issued for 12 months ended June 30, 1990
Variation from Publisher's Statements

| Audit Period Ended | Rate Base | Audit Report | Publisher's Statements | Difference | Percentage of Difference |
|---|---|---|---|---|---|
| 06-30-90 | (a) | 10,536,785 | 10,536,785 | 0 | |
| 06-30-89 | (b) | 10,711,174 | 10,701,946 | 9,228 | 0.09 |
| 06-30-88 | (c) | 10,507,715 | 10,507,715 | 0 | |
| 06-30-87 | 10,200,000 | 10,618,724 | 10,613,168 | 5,556 | 0.05 |
| 06-30-86 | (d) | 10,620,031 | 10,620,031 | 0 | |

(a) Effective 01/01/90 changed from 10,481,000 to 10,125,000
(b) Effective 01/01/89 changed from 10,280,000 to 10,481,000
(c) Effective 01/01/88 changed from 10,200,000 to 10,280,000
(d) Effective 01/01/86 changed from 10,150,000 to 10,200,000

(a) Pars. 1, 3(d) & 5(c): Association subscriptions, averaging 9,857,255 copies per issue, represent copies served to members of the National Geographic Society. 80% of dues is allocated for a 1 yr. subscription to this publication and is non-deductible from dues.

It is the publisher's policy to start all member subscriptions with the January issue and run the calendar year. Consequently, a number of back copies for each issue are mailed from one to nine months after publication date. Individual and Bulk Subscriptions receive back copies only on request. New members have the option of starting with the July issue if they pay a full 1-1/2 years fee, or the October issue if they pay 1-1/4 years fee.

In Association subscriptions is an average of 10,868 copies per issue, in Individual Subscriptions, an average of 3,958 copies per issue and in Bulk Subscriptions, an average of 289 copies per issue, representing back copies which did not date back more than three months from date of order. Back copies which dated back more than three months prior to date of sale have been included in Unpaid Distribution.

Included in Association subscriptions is an average of 30,010 copies per issue, served to Life Members.

"The National Geographic Society" is a non-profit membership corporation organized under the laws of the District of Columbia for the increase and diffusion of geographic knowledge. Members are of two classes, annual and life. Annual dues are $21.00 in the United States, $30.45 in Canada and $31.30 elsewhere.

(b) Par. 1: A statement by the National Geographic Society that the renewal percentages of Society members to the NATIONAL GEOGRAPHIC MAGAZINE for the calendar year 1990 was 81.84% referred to member renewals only (See Par. 1 for proportion of member subscriptions to total paid circulation). Records requested by ABC are not available to substantiate any claim by NATIONAL GEOGRAPHIC MAGAZINE of percentage of renewals by non-members of the National Geographic Society.

(c) Par. 1: Single Copy Sales, Bulk and all other, averaging 88,287 copies per issue, consist of an average of 85,075 copies sold in quantities of 1 to 10 and an average of 3,212 copies sold to individuals, business concerns, schools, libraries, hospitals, etc., in quantities of 11 to 1,000 at $1.40 to $2.65 each, distribution by purchasers.

(d) Par. 1a: National Geographic Magazine publishes identical editorial content in all its editions worldwide. Advertising is accepted in 32 editions: six basic editions, twelve domestic regions, five domestic metro markets and nine foreign regions.

(e) Par. 3(a): Basic Prices: Subscriptions: To new members and educational subscriptions in U.S., 1 yr. $21.00; Canada, 1 yr. $30.45; Foreign, 1 yr. $31.30.

The educational subscription price applies to educational and religious institutions, governmental branches, hospitals, military units, embassies, airlines, railroads and museums, if the subscription is received direct.

(f) Par. 6(c): The following premiums were offered during this statement period:

A copy of the February, 1988 issue of the National Geographic Magazine, with a value of $2.65, was offered to New Members residing in Australia at prices shown in Par. 3.

A world map and framing prints, with no advertised or stated value, was offered with some subscriptions at prices shown in Par. 3

332(a)

**FIGURE E-1** ***(Continued)***

## 12. GEOGRAPHIC ANALYSIS OF TOTAL PAID CIRCULATION for the December, 1990 Issue

Total paid circulation of this issue was 0.02% greater than average total paid circulation for period.

| STATE | Subs. | Single Copy Sales | TOTAL | % of Circ. | % of Pop. |
|---|---|---|---|---|---|
| Maine | 59,834 | 4 | 59,838 | | |
| New Hampshire | 55,790 | 21 | 55,811 | | |
| Vermont | 30,378 | 4 | 30,382 | | |
| Massachusetts | 234,661 | 37 | 234,698 | | |
| Rhode Island | 31,071 | 8 | 31,079 | | |
| Connecticut | 133,560 | 40 | 133,600 | | |
| **NEW ENGLAND** | **545,294** | **114** | **545,408** | **6.87** | **5.45** |
| New York | 479,074 | 266 | 479,340 | | |
| New Jersey | 233,568 | 858 | 234,426 | | |
| Pennsylvania | 352,402 | 143 | 352,545 | | |
| **MIDDLE ATLANTIC** | **1,065,044** | **1,267** | **1,066,311** | **13.43** | **16.24** |
| Ohio | 308,510 | 50 | 308,560 | | |
| Indiana | 152,095 | 15 | 152,110 | | |
| Illinois | 342,022 | 64 | 342,086 | | |
| Michigan | 289,123 | 34 | 289,157 | | |
| Wisconsin | 162,815 | 15 | 162,830 | | |
| **EAST N. CENTRAL** | **1,254,565** | **178** | **1,254,743** | **15.80** | **18.40** |
| Minnesota | 176,389 | 23 | 176,412 | | |
| Iowa | 83,094 | 6 | 83,100 | | |
| Missouri | 155,151 | 21 | 155,172 | | |
| North Dakota | 22,246 | 6 | 22,252 | | |
| South Dakota | 22,160 | 4 | 22,164 | | |
| Nebraska | 52,470 | 5 | 52,475 | | |
| Kansas | 89,213 | 12 | 89,225 | | |
| **WEST N. CENTRAL** | **600,723** | **77** | **600,800** | **7.56** | **7.59** |
| Delaware | 24,764 | 1 | 24,765 | | |
| Maryland | 172,119 | 42 | 172,161 | | |
| District of Columbia | 18,036 | 240 | 18,276 | | |
| Virginia | 226,164 | 55 | 226,219 | | |
| West Virginia | 34,348 | | 34,348 | | |
| North Carolina | 162,638 | 18 | 162,656 | | |
| South Carolina | 72,336 | 12 | 72,348 | | |
| Georgia | 165,884 | 24 | 165,908 | | |
| Florida | 398,208 | 76 | 398,284 | | |
| **SOUTH ATLANTIC** | **1,274,497** | **468** | **1,274,965** | **16.06** | **16.31** |
| Kentucky | 73,293 | 17 | 73,310 | | |
| Tennessee | 117,367 | 13 | 117,380 | | |
| Alabama | 83,085 | 18 | 83,103 | | |
| Mississippi | 42,880 | 4 | 42,884 | | |
| **EAST S. CENTRAL** | **316,625** | **52** | **316,677** | **3.99** | **6.47** |
| Arkansas | 50,407 | 6 | 50,413 | | |
| Louisiana | 84,612 | 11 | 84,623 | | |
| Oklahoma | 88,757 | 13 | 88,770 | | |
| Texas | 465,971 | 76 | 466,047 | | |
| **WEST S. CENTRAL** | **689,747** | **106** | **689,853** | **8.69** | **10.48** |
| Montana | 44,092 | 12 | 44,104 | | |
| Idaho | 48,745 | 4 | 48,749 | | |
| Wyoming | 23,919 | 1 | 23,920 | | |
| Colorado | 179,982 | 26 | 180,008 | | |
| New Mexico | 53,553 | 14 | 53,567 | | |
| Arizona | 122,619 | 18 | 122,637 | | |
| Utah | 71,138 | 6 | 71,144 | | |
| Nevada | 45,312 | 3 | 45,315 | | |
| **MOUNTAIN** | **589,360** | **84** | **589,444** | **7.42** | **5.02** |

| STATE | Subs. | Single Copy Sales | TOTAL | % of Circ. | % of Pop. |
|---|---|---|---|---|---|
| Alaska | 34,143 | 4 | 34,147 | | |
| Washington | 262,265 | 33 | 262,298 | | |
| Oregon | 149,573 | 16 | 149,589 | | |
| California | 1,105,811 | 2,185 | 1,107,996 | | |
| Hawaii | 48,438 | 6 | 48,444 | | |
| **PACIFIC** | **1,600,230** | **2,244** | **1,602,474** | **20.18** | **14.04** |
| Miscellaneous | | | | | |
| Unclassified | | | | | |
| **UNITED STATES** | **7,936,085** | **4,590** | **7,940,675** | **100.00** | **100.00** |
| U.S. Circ. Percent of Grand Total | | | | **77.91** | |
| Poss. & Other Areas | 20,110 | 5 | 20,115 | 0.20 | |
| **U.S. & POSS., etc.** | **7,956,195** | **4,595** | **7,960,790** | **78.11** | |
| **Canada** | | | | | |
| Newfoundland | 9,018 | | 9,018 | 1.08 | 2.25 |
| Nova Scotia | 28,411 | 9 | 28,420 | 3.41 | 3.45 |
| Prince Edward Island | 3,185 | | 3,185 | 0.38 | 0.50 |
| New Brunswick | 16,983 | 1 | 16,984 | 2.04 | 2.80 |
| Quebec | 90,004 | 13 | 90,017 | 10.80 | 25.81 |
| Ontario | 354,922 | 43 | 354,965 | 42.58 | 35.96 |
| Manitoba | 34,875 | 2 | 34,877 | 4.18 | 4.20 |
| Saskatchewan | 31,981 | 4 | 31,985 | 3.84 | 3.99 |
| Alberta | 118,686 | 12 | 118,698 | 14.24 | 9.35 |
| British Columbia | 141,632 | 27 | 141,659 | 16.99 | 11.39 |
| Northwest Territories | 2,042 | 1 | 2,043 | 0.25 | 0.09 |
| Yukon Territory | 1,722 | 1 | 1,723 | 0.21 | 0.21 |
| **CANADA** | **833,461** | **113** | **833,574** | **100.00** | **100.00** |
| Canadian Circ. Percent of Grand Total | | | | **8.18** | |
| Foreign | 1,281,915 | 81,183 | 1,363,098 | 13.37 | |
| Unclassified | | | | | |
| Military or Civilian Personnel Overseas | 31,109 | 3,014 | 34,123 | 0.34 | |
| **GRAND TOTAL** | **10,102,680** | **88,905** | **10,191,585** | **100.00** | |

10a. CANADIAN PAID CIRCULATION BY ABCD COUNTY SIZE for the December, 1990 Issue

June, 1990 issue used in establishing percentages for subscription circulation.

| County Size | No. of Counties | % of Canadian Population | Subscription Circulation Copies | Subscription Circulation % Total | Single Copy Circulation Copies | Single Copy Circulation % Total | Total Circulation Copies | Total Circulation % Total |
|---|---|---|---|---|---|---|---|---|
| A | 68 | 66% | 573,088 | 68.76 | 78 | 69.03 | 573,166 | 68.76 |
| B | 64 | 18% | 152,607 | 18.31 | 21 | 18.58 | 152,628 | 18.31 |
| C | 38 | 6% | 44,840 | 5.38 | 6 | 5.31 | 44,846 | 5.38 |
| D | 96 | 10% | 62,926 | 7.55 | 8 | 7.08 | 62,934 | 7.55 |
| | 266 | 100% | 833,461 | 100.00 | 113 | 100.00 | 833,574 | 100.00 |
| Unclassified | | | | | | | | |
| TOTAL CANADA | 266 | | 833,461 | | 113 | | 833,574 | |

EXPLANATION OF ABCD COUNTY SIZE

A—All counties which are, in whole or in part, within the boundaries of Census Metropolitan Areas.

B—All remaining counties which are, in whole or in part, within the boundaries of Census Agglomerations of 25,000 population or over and other counties containing a place of 25,000 or more population not officially designated as Census Agglomerations.

C—All remaining counties which are, in whole or in part, within the boundaries of Census Agglomerations of less than 25,000 population and other counties containing a place of 10,000 or more population.

D—All remaining counties.

We certify that to the best of our knowledge all data set forth in this Publisher's Statement are true and report circulation in accordance with Audit Bureau of Circulations' Bylaws and Rules. 04-0750-0

NATIONAL GEOGRAPHIC MAGAZINE, published by National Geographic Society, 1147 - 17th Street N.W., Washington, District of Columbia 20036

DOROTHY M. WAGNER — Manager, Cashiers Division

OWEN R. ANDERSON — Executive Vice President

Date Signed, January 29, 1991



**FIGURE E-1** ***(Continued)***

Section 1a of a publisher's statement shows average paid circulation of various editions. These statistics are often used by media planners to adjust schedules for less-than-full-run buys. When markets are segmented geographically or demographically, they must be matched to the appropriate circulation patterns of media. Costs-per-thousand circulation and costs per response can then be calculated.

---

**SECTION 2: PAID CIRCULATION BY ISSUE**

Section 2 displays paid circulation by issue, broken down by subscriptions and single-copy sales. The importance of issue-by-issue circulation stems from the fact that publishers are accountable if copies fall below the rate base. The rate base is not actually a guarantee of a fixed number, but advertisers expect rebates if publishers deliver fewer copies than specified in the rate base.

A second factor is variability from issue to issue. In general, magazines with higher subscriber proportions have relatively low variation from issue to issue. Magazines with high single-copy sales have greater variability. This confirms the earlier conclusion that, all other things being equal, magazines dependent on subscribers will have more consistency of readership. On the other hand, magazines relying on single-copy sales will have higher reader turnover.

Another factor in issue-by-issue variability is frequency of publication. Weeklies come out more often than monthlies and consequently have higher reader turnover. For example, weeklies must sell more subscriptions than monthlies for the same circulation. They thus have more expirations and must solicit renewals and new subscribers more frequently. These circulation patterns increase issue turnover.

---

**SECTIONS 3–6: NEW SUBSCRIPTION AND RENEWALS**

Sections 3 to 6 of a publisher's statement yield data about the quality of subscriptions, for example, are subscriptions sold at basic prices? A large proportion sold at less than the basic price indicates a reluctance to buy a magazine unless it can be gotten at a bargain. Whether buyers at regular prices and at discounted ones respond differently, however, is not known. It is commonly surmised that they do.

Another consideration is duration of subscriptions sold during a reporting period. A large number of subscribers sold for a term of less than one year is regarded as an indication of low buyer interest. The question of whether this translates into lower readership or lower response to advertising is still open.

There is also a difference between weeklies and monthlies with respect to the duration of a subscription. For a one-year term, a weekly must obtain a commitment for 52 issues, as compared with only 12 for a monthly. Because the price of a one-year subscription to a weekly is much higher, a higher percentage of sales are made for less than a year. Consequently, weeklies have proportionately more expirations and higher subscriber turnover.

Section 6 shows the amount of subscriptions sold with and without the use of premiums. This is closely related to the discount issue. Heavy premium sales are thought to lower readership quality, as many buy the magazine for the premium rather than for its intrinsic content.

There is enormous variation among publishers in the way they sell their magazines to the public. There is quite a bit of discounting, even among large-circulation magazines. There are also large variations in continuity and turnover, which in turn depend partly on publication frequency. If these elements are important to direct marketers, then ABC reports are necessary for setting media schedules.

A vital figure in estimating subscriber turnover is the number of renewals. The statistic is reported in Section 11, called "explanatory." Unfortunately, publishers are not obligated to report renewal figures under ABC rules. As of now, very few ABC-audited magazines report renewal rates. The reason is because renewals run from 50 percent to 70 percent for most magazines. Like the repurchase rate for many other product, renewals are powerful indicators of consumer loyalty, and publishers are not prone to make their "reader disloyalty" rates public.

There is actually no way to estimate a renewal rate if a publisher wishes to withhold that information. Some agencies use an indirect method of assessing renewals by calculating a "turnover rate." The method is not sensitive, and the results may actually be misleading. The ABC bylaws prohibit a publisher from claiming a renewal rate unless it appears on the pink sheet. This is in accordance with the spirit of ABC rules, which imply that any claims should not be hearsay, but be made in print.

Arrears represent magazines sent to people whose subscriptions have expired. This information is given in Section 7. Under ABC rules, a magazine can carry expiries for three months and include them in paid circulation totals. The greatest complaint about arrears is that unscrupulous publishers sometimes use them to bring paid circulation up to meet a rate base.

The number of arrears reported by large-circulation magazines are relatively small. They seldom run more than 1 percent of a magazine's total paid circulation. Nevertheless, even 1 percent can translate to substantial numbers when circulation is large.

**SECTION 10: COUNTY SIZE**

Section 10 of a pink sheet shows circulation broken down by "ABCD" county size. The letters indicate size, running from the largest, designated as A, to the smallest, designated as D. The top counties, A and B, are urban and belong to the more populous metropolitan areas. The exact definitions are given in the ABC report.

County size estimates are based on the circulation of a single issue. Advertisers usually apply the proportions of the studied issue to a magazine's average issue.

This section shows the number of counties in each of the four groups and the percentage of both circulation and U.S. population contained in each. Subscriptions and single-copy sales are also reported for each grouping.

More circulation in A and B counties generally means a more upscale and urban readership. Circulation mix according to county size is meaningful to advertisers whose target markets are defined by the same demographics.

**SECTION 12: GEOGRAPHIC ANALYSIS**

Section 12 shows paid circulation for each state. Like county size figures, these states counts are based on a single issue. Because a particular issue may deviate from the average, the percentages are used to adjust circulation patterns.

General advertisers match state estimates to product distribution. No advertiser wants to place insertions where products are not available. Direct marketers are not bound by geography, for delivery can be anywhere. But some types of goods do have geographic biases. In that event, firms arrange state figures to select geographical editions that best correspond with sales potentials.

CHAPTER 15

# Direct Response in Electronic Media

## PROFILE

**NICHOLAS DAVATZES**

**A Cable TV Wizard.** Nicholas Davatzes is president and chief executive officer of the Arts & Entertainment Network (A&E). A&E is a joint venture of the Hearst Corporation, ABC Video Enterprises, Inc., and NBC. The network's 24-hour-a-day schedule features performing arts, drama, comedy, and documentaries. Since A&E began in 1984, its quality programming has received more Awards for Cable Excellence (ACE) than any other basic cable network. Under Mr. Davatzes's leadership, the network has grown to reach 50 million households in the United States and Canada via 5,600 cable systems.

Before joining A&E in December 1983, Mr. Davatzes was senior vice president and group executive for Warner Amex Cable Communications, Inc., where he was responsible for four Qube Cable operating companies. He joined Warner Amex as senior vice president, administration and human resources. In 1981 he was promoted to group executive.

Prior to joining Warner Amex, Mr. Davatzes was president of Intext Communications Systems, a diversified information services, publishing, and technical training organization.

From 1965 to 1977, Mr. Davatzes was with the Xerox Corporation in various executive positions at the corporate and field operating levels, and he was promoted to vice president of sales and marketing in 1975 for the Learning System Division.

Mr. Davatzes, a U.S. Marine Corps veteran, is the recipient of the Marine Corps Historical Foundation Heritage Award for his support to the foundation. Mr. Davatzes is a director of the Cable Advertising Bureau (CAB) and the National Academy of Cable Programming. He is on the board of directors of the International Radio and Television Society Foundation (IRTS) and serves on the advisory board for St. John's University College of Business Administration (CBA).

Mr. Davatzes received a B.A. degree in economics and a master's degree from St. John's University.

Mr. Davatzes is a founder of the Connecticut Foundation for Childhood Leukemia. ■

# Parameters of Broadcasting

Broadcasting is the dominant form of electronic media, especially television broadcasting. Television provides advertisers with wide coverage and high penetration within markets. The Television Bureau of Advertising (TVB) research department estimates that television advertising in 1990 will amount to roughly 22 percent of total U.S. ad expenditures.[1] The total volume of advertising carried by television that year came to almost $30 billion.

The huge expenditures for television largely reflect the number of potential customers delivered by the medium. Television is virtually everywhere. This is evidenced by the following statistics: [2]

- Ninety-eight percent of the nation's households own a television set.
- The number of TV sets per household averaged 2.0 for the first time in 1990.
- Close to 98 percent of television households have color sets.
- TV usage per home during the first half of 1990 averaged 6 hours and 56 minutes.
- The typical adult spends more than 4½ hours a day in front of a TV set. The average American is more occupied with television than anything else, except working and sleeping.

## Patterns of TV Viewing

Two elements affect TV viewing: season of the year and time of day. These factors govern the rise and ebb of audiences. These overall trends are displayed in Table 15-1, which shows average ratings by season of the year and by time of day.

**TABLE 15.1. Average Home TV Ratings, by Time of Day (1990).**

| | Quarter | | | |
|---|---|---|---|---|
| | 1 | 2 | 3 | 4 |
| Daytime (M–F 10 A.M.–4:30 P.M.) | 5.6 | 5.1 | 5.0 | 5.1 |
| Early news (M–F 6:30–7:30 P.M.) | 11.9 | 10.3 | 9.9 | 11.3 |
| Prime time (M–S 8–11 P.M.) | 15.1 | 12.5 | 9.4 | 12.9 |
| Late evening (M–F 11:30 P.M.–1 A.M.) | 4.5 | 4.3 | 4.5 | 4.5 |

SOURCE: Adweek, *Marketer's Guide to Media* (October–December 1990).

1. TVB, *Trends in GNP. Ad Volume. TV Ad Volume.* (August 1990).
2. TVB, *Trends in Television* (April 1990), and *Trends in Viewing* (July 1990).

The season of the year has a marked effect on television viewing. The greatest amount of TV viewing is done in the first and fourth quarters of the year. The lowest amount takes place in the third quarter, which coincides with the summer months.

The parts of the viewing day most affected by seasonality are early news and prime time. People spend more time outdoors in summer months, and even the best shows will not bring them indoors. As viewing falls, broadcasters hold down costs by putting on reruns. When colder weather sets in and days get shorter, people come indoors during early evening and prime time. Television viewing goes up, for no other reason than that people have nothing else to do. They flick on their sets to be entertained or simply to pass the time during the dull winter evenings.

Programing has little effect on overall viewing levels. Excellent programs do not increase the total size of television audiences, either in winter or summer. Programing is a device by which broadcasters vie for a larger share of an already-existing number of homes watching television. Since 1983 the amount of viewing per home per day has remained virtually constant, with only minor seasonal changes from year to year. It thus appears that TV viewing is approaching saturation, if it has not already done so. Future changes will involve shifts in industry components, such as audience growth in cable and national syndications and a commensurate decline in the viewing of major network shows and traditional TV fare.

Time of day is the other element that regulates ratings. Irrespective of season, audiences build up gradually from early morning, reaching their zenith in prime time, defined as 8:00 P.M. to 11:00 P.M., Eastern Standard Time. From 11:00 P.M. onward, TV ratings head downward. Every season shows this same pattern.

## Advertising Trends

Advertising trends parallel those of TV viewing. Since advertisers use media as communication vehicles, the mutual relationship makes sense.

Like TV viewing itself, the share of advertising for television has remained quite stable. Since 1983 television has garnered roughly 22 percent of total advertising expenditures. Figure 15-1 shows the trend in television advertising, in terms of market share. Television's share of advertising volume rose continuously until 1984, when its relative importance reached an all-time high. From that point on, television's share of the advertising market stabilized or declined slightly. From 1985 to 1989 that figure did not change by more than one-half of one percentage point. Though the proportion of total advertising going into television did not change much, dollar volume increased as total advertising volume continued to grow.

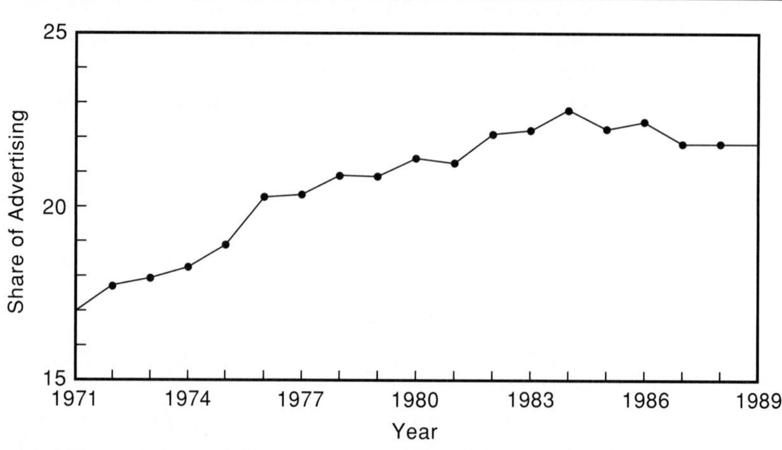


**FIGURE 15-1 TV Advertising as a Percent of Total**

Though ad expenditures in electronic media maintained their relative position for most of the 1980s, significant changes took place within the television industry. The most important ones were as follows:

- Network TV experienced a declining share of the market. From 1980 to 1989 networks' share of total television volume fell from 44.7 percent to 33.9 percent, a substantial shrinkage.
- Nonnetwork TV maintained its share of total television volume at approximately 56 percent.
- National syndication climbed from virtually zero in 1980 (0.4 percent) to 4.8 percent in 1989.
- Cable television made the greatest gains, in terms of both dollar volume and share of market. Its ad revenue soared from $45 million in 1980 to $1.5 billion in 1989, an increase of some 3,200 percent! Though still growing, cable television in 1989 accounted for 5.7 percent of all television advertising. Of the cable TV total, 82 percent of the $1.5 billion revenue went to cable networks.

Table 15-2 indicates the trends in market share for various parts of the television industry. Networks take in roughly one-third of all

**TABLE 15.2. Percent of Total Television Advertising Volume.**

| | 1980 | 1985 | 1989 |
|---|---|---|---|
| Network TV | 44.7 | 38.3 | 33.9 |
| Nonnetwork TV* | 54.4 | 55.8 | 55.6 |
| National syndication | 0.4 | 2.5 | 4.8 |
| Cable TV | 0.5 | 3.4 | 5.7 |
| Total | 100.0 | 100.0 | 100.0 |

*Spot and local TV combined.

SOURCE: TVB.

money spent on advertising in television. But its portion is declining. Spot and local television together account for some 55 percent, splitting this sum almost evenly. National syndication and cable television are the fastest-growing parts of the television industry, in 1989 accounting for a combined 10.5 percent share of total dollars.

# Uses of Television in Direct Marketing

Direct marketing uses two different advertising formats on television. One is the direct response commercial, which solicits sales or inquiries. These commercials make up a large majority of marketing efforts on television. The other format is the support commercial, which aims at enhancing response to advertisements in media other than television. Support commercials automatically lead to multimedia usage. But direct response commercials may also be part of a multimedia mix. This is becoming more and more common as integrated marketing takes stronger hold of direct marketing practices.

The most frequently displayed items on television are those with mass appeal. This is in keeping with the nature of the medium. Popular books, well-known magazines, records, tapes, and household products lend themselves best to television advertising. Products destined for narrow or specialized markets incur large amounts of media waste; firms transmit more messages to nonprospects. It was no accident that one of the first marketing successes in television was the campaign for Ginsu knives. Almost every viewing household was a potential customer.

## Television as a Support Medium

The support commercial makes no attempt to sell directly. Rather, it seeks to increase response to an offer carried by another medium, usually direct mail, newspapers, or magazines. Its major goal is to create awareness of the offer, to draw attention to the printed advertisement. It provides no phone number or address. The conventional 30-second commercial is sufficient for a supportive role, because no extra time is necessary to explain why and how viewers should take action.[3]

The support commercial received impetus from what is called a *transfer device*. It is attributed to Les Wunderman, founder of Wunderman, Ricotta & Kline, and has spread widely to support commercials.[4] A transfer device offers extra premiums to responders who give some indication that they have seen the commercial. For example, viewers might be asked to circle a picture on the reply card, check some box, or

3. Leonard F. Materna, "Direct Marketing Support Television," DMA, *Manual Release* 260.1.
4. Edward L. Nash, *Direct Marketing* (New York: McGraw-Hill, 1982), p. 160.

write in a secret code that is not so secret. Whatever the request, the technique is said to increase response.

An example of a support commercial featured Ed McMahon, host of NBC's "Tonight Show." This commercial, run in the waning days of 1990 and early in 1991, exhorted viewers to respond immediately to the multimillion-dollar sweepstakes of American Family Publishers. *Reader's Digest* and Publishers Clearing House have for years spent vast sums on television to inform people that they can become millionaires by opening their sweepstakes mailing piece and returning the reply card.

Support commercials are most effective when the mailing covers a large portion of a market, because the commercial can influence only the viewers who received the mail package. For example, suppose a mailing goes out to 50 percent of the market, and the TV schedule carrying the support commercial reaches 30 percent of all homes. Assuming that the mail recipients have the same TV viewing habits as the population in general, the commercial will support the mailout in 15 percent of total households ($.50 \times .30$).

It is readily apparent that a given television rating for a support commercial has an elastic audience potential. What makes it so is the coverage of the mailing. For the sake of argument, say the mailing goes to 70 percent of the market. In that eventuality, the same TV schedule, seen by 30 percent of the audience, would reach 21 percent of the homes that received the mailing ($.70 \times .30$). If the combination of TV and direct response is more effective than direct response alone, the costs per response depend heavily on the extent to which the primary medium, print or mail, covers the television reception area.

The support commercial has also found valuable uses by direct marketers employing a two-step process. Television offers that contain many choices necessitate that sort of approach. To sell a continuity program, for example, a record club might offer recordings at nominal prices from a long list. In that case, the record company would have to send buyers a list of titles from which to choose. The two-step sale also comes about whenever the buyer must append a signature to verify a commitment, such as for an insurance policy. Time delays of follow-up mailings greatly decrease final conversions.[5]

An example of how support commercials reduce time in two-step transactional processes is the case of the Columbia Record Club. Columbia ran its regular print program in the Sunday newspaper. A 30-second commercial sought to reinforce the print advertising by calling viewers' attention to the newspaper insertion.

Total advertising costs of a support program should represent a lower percentage of total sales than advertising without TV support. That calculation always poses the key question: "How do we know?

5. Al Eicoff, "Support Advertising," *Directions* (January–February 1988), pp. 9–12.

How do we compare a TV-supported program with a nonsupported one?" Most consultants recommend test markets as the way to go, though they, too, encounter problems.[6]

A recent development has been the combination of cable television and direct mail. This technique sends direct mail to subscribers of local cable systems. Mailing monthly statements to subscribers, a cable operator knows who potential viewers are and where they live. The idea of this support advertising is to have the broadcast medium presell offers going to viewers' mailboxes.[7]

Areas wired for cable are well defined. Cable penetration often reaches 60 or 70 percent of all homes, making this target market highly desirable to banks and other local business units. The reach of the cable TV schedule is here the determining factor in dual-media efficiency. For example, if a mailing goes to all hooked-up homes and a schedule reaches only 50 percent of subscribers, two-media messages work on only 50 percent of the target market. One-half gets only the mailing, not supported by the commercial.

## Direct Response Television

Direct marketing in television is primarily direct response advertising—a sale or an inquiry. Unlike support commercials, direct response television must generate sales or requests from their own messages. The entire transactional process takes place within a self-contained channel of distribution.

Television lends itself to some offers better than to others. One-shot products, sales of which are closed with a credit card or "bill me" payment, have high failure rates. Orders for these products must cover all costs and profits from a one-time sale. There have been successes for one-shot deals, but the ratio is not high.

Continuity programs have a better record of performance. These feature products unavailable or not easily obtainable at retail outlets. Magazine subscriptions, insurance policies, and membership in book and record clubs, for example, are popular items on television. Complicated items or services are often difficult to explain within the time frame of a commercial.

Price is another component that affects the use of direct response television. A great deal of TV buying is impulsive, and high-priced products present risks that inhibit spur-of-the-moment decisions. Many of the most popular products touted on television go for $19.95. With goods selling at roughly five times their acquisition costs, the range of

6. See Chapter 6.
7. Robert Kweller, "Cable TV & Direct Mail: A Powerful Duo," *Target Marketing* (January 1988), pp. 28–29.

products offered in this medium is limited. The advertised item must be obtained at a cost of about $4.

Direct response operation also involves the choice of television vehicles. This aspect of media selection depends largely on time costs and availabilities.

## Media Vehicles

The objective of all media buying is to obtain the most benefits at the lowest costs. To general advertisers, benefits mean audiences, and costs are based on measures of viewing. Though network viewership has eroded in recent years, the networks still command the highest ratings. Network affiliates in 1989 won a 58 percent share of total household viewing hours. Comparable figures were 23 percent for independent stations and 14 percent for basic cable. [8] Having the largest audiences, networks are able to charge the highest prices for time. A 30–second commercial on network prime time, for example, averaged roughly $116,000. [9] Such princely sums go far beyond the relatively small allotments of most direct marketing budgets. Nor can these high media costs be justified by the returns that advertising is expected to bring. For this reason, direct response advertising makes little or no use of network television.

The second impediment to the use of network television is the length of a direct response commercial. The usual message designed to obtain sales runs from 90 to 120 seconds. Unlike awareness advertising, direct response needs more time to sell the product and explain transactional terms. Joseph Shain, president of a direct marketing agency, advances the premise that "direct response TV is not advertising but the sales part of a direct channel of distribution."[10] Commercials designed to generate inquiries have less information to convey and normally run from 60 to 90 seconds. Either way the cost barrier of network television is virtually insurmountable. In practical terms, the greater commercial length means that media expenses can rise from two to four times those for a standard 30-second commercial. In 1989 only 2.2 percent of all commercials appearing on network television were 60 seconds or more in length.[11]

High costs and lack of long time availabilities have confined direct response advertising to nonnetwork TV sources. These encompass spot markets and cable television.

---

8. Grey Advertising, Inc., *1989 Media Modules*, p. 31.
9. *Ibid.*
10. Joseph Shain, "TV Tactics," *Direct Marketing* (September 1989), p. 21.
11. TVB, *Trends in Television*, *op. cit.*, p. 13.

**TABLE 15.3. Ratings Efficiency of Spot TV by Market Group.**

| Market Group | Percent of U.S. Population | Average ADI Rating* | | | Average CPM (30 seconds) | | |
|---|---|---|---|---|---|---|---|
| | | Day | Fringe | Prime | Day | Fringe | Prime |
| Top 10 | 31 | 4.8% | 4.7% | 10.8% | $3.55 | $4.91 | $13.82 |
| Top 50 | 67 | 4.9 | 4.5 | 10.9 | 3.76 | 5.42 | 12.97 |
| Top 100 | 86 | 5.0 | 4.3 | 11.0 | 3.71 | 5.81 | 12.28 |
| U.S. | 100 | 5.2 | 4.3 | 11.1 | 4.13 | 5.81 | 12.67 |

*ADI = Area of dominant influence

SOURCE: Gray Advertising, Inc., *1989 Media Modules*, p. 56.

# Spot Markets

Spot television implies a market-by-market approach. Two factors dominate direct response advertising in this environment: buying time at low cost and carefully monitoring response rates to control budgets. Low-cost time is dictated by low budgeted costs per response, referred to as its *allowable*. In turn, the search for low-cost time pushes direct response TV into fringe time slots.

Although ratings determine TV prices, the main criterion in direct response television is cost per order or cost per lead. The reason is that ratings are not highly correlated with response. Bob Stone cautions that "the more attentive viewers are to a show, the less likely they are to respond immediately." He thus recommends reruns, talk shows, and old movies as the best vehicles for direct response advertising.[12]

Many writers have commented on the apparent lack of correlation between ratings and costs per response. This behavior, however, may be more a consequence of stations' pricing structures than attentiveness to shows. Advertisers must pay higher prices per viewer in larger markets and for higher-rated shows. This higher cost per viewer increases the cost per response. As long as advertisers pay more per viewer, they must have higher costs per response even if audiences respond uniformly. Stone and other authors who see proportionately less response in higher-rated shows make no allowance for the price differential.

Table 15-3 shows cost-per-thousand (CPM) calculations for home viewing by time of broadcast day and market group. As can be inferred from the data, all viewers are not regarded as equal. Prime-time viewers in the 10 largest markets are considered more valuable than viewers in fringe time and smaller markets. For example, viewers in prime time would need response rates roughly 2½ to 3 times higher than viewers of other day parts to produce the same cost per order.

12. Bob Stone, *Successful Direct Marketing Methods*, 4th ed. (Lincolnwood, IL: NTC Business Books, 1988), p. 254.

The boundaries of a spot market are defined by the strength of a station's signal. A widely used concept of defining TV markets is that of ADI, which stands for *area of dominant influence.* Table 15-3 classifies spot markets in this way. The ADI designation is one of Arbitron, a supplier of local ratings. According to Arbitron, an ADI consists of all counties that obtain a major share of viewing from a home station. This classification avoids overlapping markets, making each ADI a mutually exclusive geographic unit.

Regardless of the reason for cost-per-order differences, direct marketers cannot compete with national advertisers and retailers for prime time. Returns do not justify paying premiums for these audiences. The reruns, talk shows, and old movies engaged by direct marketers appear on nonprime time.

A vital question for direct marketers is how does one assess cost per response unless commercials are actually run and response rates monitored? Testing seems to be a pat answer. However, the most common tests compare one commercial with another. Tests of returns by media sources yield only rough estimates. Primary reliance is a on a "rollout" trial-and-error method that requires close monitoring.

In general, direct marketers are attracted to media with highly discounted rate structures. A common practice is buying time segments that are "preemptible." The discount rises as the time of prior notice decreases; a one-week notice for preemption carries a higher discount than a two-week notice. A discount of as much as 50 percent is given for a preemptible position.

A preemptible buy permits a station to "bump" a purchaser if a better buyer comes along. In periods of strong television demand, such as the pre-Christmas season, companies with free funds are apt to overbid preemptibles. Since availabilities at such times are tight, stations find it difficult to provide preempted spots with suitable alternative time slots. For that reason, many direct marketing firms order more time than they need, figuring that a good portion of the spots for which they contract will be lost.

Low-cost spots can also be bought in package deals. One avenue that has proved popular with direct marketers is the run-of-station (ROS) buy, in which a station charges low rates but gives no guarantees as to when a commercial will be run. Scheduling is entirely at the discretion of the station. If advertisers do not require their commercials to run at preferred hours, they can usually get bargain-basement rates through ROS.

Though special rates fall within budget allowables, the commercials are viewed by relatively small audiences. Poor-quality programs and inattentive viewing may also decrease response. Media planners must therefore schedule a large number of showings to generate a given volume of orders.

Another severe limitation in the use of spot television is that long commercials have become a rarity. According to TVB's research department, commercials of 60 seconds or more in 1989 amounted to a meager 7 percent of all commercials shown on nonnetwork television. About 83 percent were of 30-second duration.[13] This trend toward shorter commercials tends to push direct response advertisers out of spot markets. Another effect is more combinations of direct response with general advertising in so-called integrated commercials. As with print, most of these commercials are general image–type advertising with an 800 number tagged on.

## Cable Television

Direct marketing is a prominent player in cable television. Timebuying practices parallel those in spot markets. Cable's greatest attractions to direct marketers are relatively low advertising rates and available time slots that accommodate long commercials, those lasting at least two minutes. Direct marketers get discounts because they buy unsold inventory, with no rating guarantee or assigned time slot.

Another feature appealing to direct marketers is the option of buying time on a per-order basis. Cable operators with unsold time on their hands and strapped for cash are willing to sell commercial time on a per-order basis. This sort of "commission selling" makes media costs variable to direct marketers. They take no risks, paying only when a sale is generated. Large cable systems are more cautious in negotiating such deals, selecting products with good selling prospects from well-known companies.[14]

But these conditions are changing rapidly. In the early stages of cable television, the direct marketing industry was a major source of broadcast revenue. Today cable TV has reached a mature status, penetrating almost 60 percent of homes with television sets. Little by little cable has nibbled away at broadcast network audiences, attaining a combined prime time and late-night audience share of 21 percent at the start of the 1990–1991 TV season.[15]

Audience increases begat advertising cost increases. From 1987 to 1989 advertising volume in cable television rose by some 50 percent, reaching almost $1.5 billion.[16] This rising volume occurred largely because national advertisers came into cable television. They brought

13. TVB, *Trends in Television, op. cit.*, p. 13.
14. Roger Rowland, "Shaky Reception Follows Cable Marriage," *Advertising Age* (January 17, 1983), p. M-34.
15. Kevin Goldman, "Cable TV's Ratings and Ad Revenue Grow," *Wall Street Journal* (November 5, 1990), p. 11.
16. TVB, *Trends in Television, op. cit.*, p. 11.

**TABLE 15.4. Select Cable Network Ratings.**

| Network | Household Rating* | Early Fringe | Prime Time | Late Night | Weekend 1–4:30 P.M. |
|---|---|---|---|---|---|
| WTBS | 0.8 | 1.1 | 1.4 | 0.8 | 1.2 |
| USA | 0.6 | 0.7 | 1.1 | 0.5 | 0.8 |
| CNN Headline News | 0.5 | 0.6 | 0.7 | 0.3 | 0.3 |
| ESPN | 0.5 | 0.5 | 1.1 | 0.5 | 0.7 |
| Nickelodeon | 0.4 | 0.6 | — | — | 0.7 |

*Monday–Sunday 24-hour total.

NOTE: Missing data indicate that the network did not telecast during entire period.

SOURCE: Grey Advertising, Inc., *1989 Media Modules,* p. 52.

strong up-front buying into the cable television industry. *Up-front sales* involve nonpreemptible time that is bought before the fall TV season begins. Up-front buying for the 1990–1991 basic cable schedule reached some $750 million, according to Cabletelevision Advertising Bureau. Automotive companies along with packaged good firms were in the forefront of this buying splurge.[17]

The move of national advertisers into basic cable is not so much due to viewers switching to cable as to audience delivery at lower prices. Audience gains made by the cable industry must be apportioned over some 55 cable networks. Table 15-4 indicates ratings of the leading cable networks.

As can be seen in the table, the leading basic cable networks have comparatively low viewing levels. Ratings amount to a fraction of those enjoyed by networks, and they are about one-fifth of spot TV audience levels. The highest ratings are achieved by WTBS, actually an independent superstation that carries the same broad-based shows as broadcast stations. USA features reruns of hour-long shows, such as "Miami Vice" and "L.A. Law," syndications that had their day years ago in many spot markets.

Nevertheless, national advertisers' continuing pervasion of basic cable television leaves less room for direct marketers. As more time is sold to higher paying customers, cable broadcasters have less time available for the traditional 1½- and 2-minute commercials of direct response advertising. The latter is already scarce, especially in the second and fourth quarters.

Many cable networks are currently rejecting longer spots in prime time and weekend day-time periods. Two-minute inventories are still available, but they are in great demand. Direct marketers who seek

17. See Goldman, *op. cit.*; John McManus, "Strong Upfront Helps Cable, Barter Markets," *Adweek* (July 17, 1989), p. 5.

frequency are under mounting pressure to shorten their commercials. If current trends continue, the typical 90-second and 120-second spots could be headed for extinction.[18] And if they go, so will contracting for airtime, with payments based on the number of orders that are generated.

## Media Control and Back-end Operations

Since television shows that carry direct response commercials have low ratings, a campaign might use hundreds of time slots and stations to generate an adequate number of orders. The focus on reruns, movies, and anthology series engenders high variation in viewing and response because such shows do not build program loyalty. Showing a different movie each week provides for no continuity in viewer interest. This makes it necessary to closely monitor the performance of the numerous spots and stations used in the advertising schedule. With the increasing use of computers, media planners can assess response patterns almost on a daily basis. Depending on the results of those ongoing evaluations, they can expand or cancel television schedules in a short time, even on only three days' notice.[19]

Another vital part of television direct response pertains to back-end or support operations. These and phone costs often run from 10 percent to 15 percent of expenditures. Telephone answering services must be able to handle the incoming calls with dispatch. An experienced service can hold costs down by taking orders quickly. Calls come in waves or bunches, and a telephone answering service should be able to handle sudden spurts in volume without too many busy signals or without having to put callers on hold, listening to music for lengthy intervals.

Most TV-generated orders are not for goods that consumers had been thinking about buying. Response is "impulsive"; callers probably never before considered purchasing the item. Unless the order is taken promptly and goods delivered within two days, buyer enthusiasm cools. Above all, buyers do not tolerate back orders.

Return rates average about 8 percent, and they go up with longer delivery time. Returns also depend on how much a commercial deliberately exaggerates a product's benefits. Heightened expectations increase response, but returns multiply when expectations are not met; in extreme cases they can be as high as 40 percent.[20]

---

18. Allison Fahey, "Cable Too Hot for Direct Response," *Advertising Week* (October 30, 1989).
19. Joseph Shain, "TV Tactics," *Direct Marketing* (November 1989), pp. 74–75.
20. "Catalogers: Look out for the Plight of the 90s," *Direct Marketing* (July 1987), p. 120.

Lead generation on television is affected by the same things as order generation. Four factors are paramount: market size, product, advertising message, and nature of the medium.[21]

First, markets cannot be too narrow. Though direct marketers can get cable time at a discount, remnant buying will soon run out. Even now TV time is not cheap, since buying a spot represents an addition to the usual selling costs. TV commercials have an extremely wide production range, from as low as $10,000 to a high of $200,000. The more commercials are made to conform to the "image" of a company, the more they will cost. The proper measure of effectiveness is not cost per inquiry, but cost per sale. The lead is a means of getting a sale.

Second, the cost of the product sold should be high enough to yield a sufficient margin. Advertised catalogs, for example, should carry products that cost at least as much as other items sold on television.

Third, a commercial should prompt viewers to request whatever is offered. As a means of generating leads, the commercial should focus on the object of the lead, and not on the merchandise or the service. Since selling is not an objective, lead-getting commercials can be of shorter duration than order-soliciting messages.

Fourth, the nature of the medium is highly related to the content of the commercial. Television audiences are not selective, even those watching cable. Telecasts often bring in people who are not serious about buying. If telephone lines are not to be flooded with "browsers" rather than buyers, there should be some way to qualify requests. For example, many catalog offers charge a fee and apply it to the customer's first purchase. The direct response commercial should also not give a wrong impression of what it is that viewers are asked to request. When creatives give in to temptations to expand inquiries by puffery, results will show high inquiry rates but low sales. Unlike direct orders, callers don't have to go through the hassle of returning any merchandise. They don't order at all.

## Innovations in Electronics

Like other aspects of consumer and industrial electronics, media is dynamic. New technologies appear with frequency and vie with older methods in communicating with audiences. Innovations here follow the same general patterns as those in other fields. Some are radical, but most are extensions of current ways of doing things. Some reach their potential early in their product life cycle, but most are diffused slowly over time. And in almost every instance, the old and the new exist side by side for some undetermined period of time.

21. See Rick Sangerman, "Television as a Catalog Marketing Tool," *DM News* (March 15, 1986), p. 20.

Among the main innovations in electronic media are VCRs and interactive systems. Both of these have been adopted by direct marketers, but as of now, they are still in a formative stage. As with every innovation, there is no way to predict how they will develop or to apply a timetable to the process.

## Videocassettes

The development of videocassettes has had two main effects on direct response advertising. The first relates to changes in television viewing habits. The second pertains to how firms use videocassettes as a direct marketing medium.

Despite the dire predictions of industry gurus, VCRs have had a surprisingly minor impact on TV viewing. In 1990 about 70 percent of all U.S. homes had VCRs. Yet viewing habits are the same as they always were. Only 1.5 hours of programing per week is recorded for later viewing. This represents about 3 percent of total TV usage. Interestingly, this activity has declined as VCR home penetration increased. When only 20 percent of households owned VCRs, in 1985, 2.1 hours of programing per week was recorded for later viewing.

Has there been a shift from watching television to watching videocassettes? Based on Nielsen data, the media department of Ogilvy & Mather estimates that the average VCR-equipped household spends less than three hours a week watching videocassettes. If video rental activity is added to broadcast and cable viewing, the typical American household spends 51 hours a week in front of the TV set—5 hours more than in 1980, when only 1 percent of homes had a VCR! [22]

As a direct marketing medium, videocassettes have been used sparingly in special circumstances. Videologs are used in business-to-business marketing to demonstrate new products. These are usually lead-generating devices, followed up by sales calls. The business market generally entails order sizes large enough to carry video costs. Similarly, some auto companies send videocassettes to select customers to promote expensive models.

Several catalogers of consumer products have also used videologs. Results of these efforts were mixed and are not precisely known. Royal Silk in 1987 shipped some 15,000 30-minute cassettes showing silk in action. Customers were charged $5.95, which could be deducted from orders of more than $60. Company spokesmen credited the video with higher sales per order compared with the regular catalog. But it is also obvious that people who took the catalog were the company's better customers.

---

22. Ogilvy & Mather, "VCRs: Separating Fact from Fiction," *Changing Media* (September 1990).

Soloflex in 1987 credited its videolog with "dramatic" increases in sales of its home fitness center, which sold for $1,050. Yet the company discontinued the cassettes to buy time on cable TV instead. A company spokesman was reported to say that the $6.95 mailing charge made videocassettes prohibitive—an incredible statement with respect to a $1,000 item![23]

Videocassettes allow marketers as much time as they want to get their story across. But production costs run high and, depending on content, can soar to several hundred thousand dollars. Joyce K. Reynolds, president of Retail Advertising Video Enterprises, believes videocassettes should be used in conjunction with print programs, never by themselves. She also holds that although the ideal videocassette may contain videologs, the successful product informs, motivates, educates, and entertains. It is not one continuous sales pitch.

An example is Spiegel's "Just For You Fashion Video Journal." This cassette went to large-sized women. It was an educational tape, showing big women how to choose clothes to improve their self image.

Other suggestions by Ms. Reynolds include:[24]

- A seller of home furnishings might present products in a "how to decorate your home" program.
- A purveyor of baby products might produce a tape for first-time mothers on how to care for their infants.
- A manufacturer of PCs might put step-by-step instructions on a video.

So far, experience with vidoecassettes indicates rather special uses in niche markets. It also suggests that videocassettes have been used as supporting media within a marketing mix.

## Interactive Media

Videotex as an interactive system was first developed in Europe, and its diffusion was spurred by governments that never sought a return on their investments. The development was an extension of computer technology. It allows individuals to gain access to a voluminous databank and select whatever information they want.

Videotex is used in four areas: the retail store, public places, businesses, and the home. An example of retail videotex is the electronic kiosk. This in-store site offers shoppers a semiprivate place from which to examine products. An example of a public kiosk is one produced under the auspices of the state of Connecticut. It lists local hotels, restau-

23. Cora S. Trager, "Video Catalogs: A Moving Experience," *Advertising Age* (October 26, 1987), pp. S-8–S-9.
24. Joyce K. Reynolds, "The VCR: Very Critical Resource," *Direct Marketing* (November 1989), pp. 51–53.

rants, museums, parks, and maps, and it provides printouts of selected pages. Corporate videotex links mainframe computers to PCs, such as TVS 5000, a product by Telesystemes of France.[25]

Videotex's biggest potential, as well as its greatest challenge, is in the home. Since the early 1980s a number of home videotex systems have made their appearance in this country. Most of them ended in failure. The most notable ones were Viewtron and Gateway.

Viewtron was a creature of Knight-Ridder, which ran small-scale tests in south Florida. After two years of testing, the newspaper chain announced with great fanfare that the service was being extended nationwide. Its sales manager claimed that more than 20,000 starter kits were to be shipped before year's end. Shortly thereafter, the service was terminated for lack of support and lack of profits.[26]

Gateway was a Times-Mirror project that, with 350 volunteers, began testing in Mission Viejo and Rancho Palos Verdes, California. The system was meant to give consumers a means to shop, bank, purchase theater tickets, read newspapers, check restaurant menus, browse through catalogs, and communicate with businesses via electronic mail. Videotex terminals were connected by telephone to Gateway's computer in Santa Ana, and subscribers could call up the desired information on their TV sets. This service, too, went down the drain after the company had proclaimed its test a huge success and had announced plans to build a national network of videotex systems.[27] Volunteers for the initial test were apparently not representative of all consumers. The vast majority of people were not quite ready to convert their domiciles into electronic cottages from which to transact their affairs.

The most serious project to date is Prodigy, a joint venture of Sears and IBM. After four years of planning and testing, in 1988 it was initiated in three cities. In September 1990 the service was expanded to every state in the country except Alaska. At that time it boasted some 460,000 subscribers and set goals for reaching 1,000,000 by the end of 1991.

Its greatest appeal is to computer buffs. Marketing the service to computer owners lowers costs of equipment that users need and appeals to a segment already familiar with computer applications. However, the potential market was substantially narrowed from earlier plans, which called for selling the service to all homes that had TV sets. About 10 million homes are estimated to have computers that are compatible with the service. Since its beginning, Prodigy was capitalized at $700 million, but it has yet to turn a profit. Up to 1991 the bulk of its rev-

25. Jim Mammarella, "Hello, PC; Later, TV," *Direct Marketing* (February 1986), pp. 74–77.
26. *Ibid.*
27. Barry L. Parr, "Gateway Begins Full-Scale Operations in California," *Direct Marketing* (February 1985), pp. 24–30.

enue had come from advertising and commissions on product sales. Whether this project will pay out is much in doubt, for even giant corporations grow impatient when investments bear no returns.

## Home Shopping

The most successful new services in electronic media were not born of technological innovation. Rather, they resulted from creative programing in conventional television. These are the home shopping shows. A telephone and a credit card is all a viewer needs to place an order.

The pioneer in this new field was Home Shopping Network (HSN) of Clearwater, Florida. It started up in 1985 with around-the-clock, 24-hour commercials on cable television. Since then a large number of imitators have entered the field, and mass merchandisers have joined the circus-like atmosphere of television selling.[28]

As in most new industries, a "shake-out" was not long in coming. Among the most prominent casualties was J.C. Penney's Telaction, an interactive home shopping service begun in 1987 in the Chicago area. Unlike live shopping shows, Telaction let shoppers choose merchandise at times convenient to them. Customers needed only to flip on the TV channel and punch in designated code numbers on pushbutton phones.[29] The demise of Telaction reinforced the conclusion that purchases on television are largely impulsive decisions spurred by showmanship.

By the beginning of 1991, almost 10 years after television home shopping first appeared, the industry had settled into a stable pattern. Retailers discarded their early fears that this form of selling would cut deeply into store shopping. Dollar value of shop-at-home television amounted to roughly $1.8 billion, a small fraction of total retail sales. Most television shopping shows ran on cable, appealing to limited audiences, and pushed low-priced, bargain-basement goods. Two shopping networks dominated the industry: HSN, the first-on-the-scene network, and QVC/CVN, with an exclusive contract to merchandise Sears products. With channel use approaching capacity and cable penetration of U.S. homes rapidly approaching saturation, any future growth can only be modest.[30]

---

28. Scott Ticer, "The Guys Who Started It All Go on a Shopping Spree," *Business Week* (December 15, 1986). Also see "Home Shopping Shows Are Now a Major Force in the Marketplace," *DM News* (January 1, 1987), pp. 31, 35; Leslie Wood, "Home Shopping," *Target Marketing* (March 1987), pp. 16–17.
29. Diane Schneidman, "Consumer-controlled TV shopping," *Marketing News* (October 9, 1987), pp. 1, 10; Robin Schatz, "Penney Introduces System for TV Home Shopping," *Newsday* (February 19, 1987), p. 45; Rebecca Fannin, "QVC and the Sears Connection," *Market and Media Decisions* (February 1987), p. 4.
30. Howard Schlossberg, "Picture Still Looks Bright for TV Shopping Networks," *Marketing News* (October 23, 1989), p. 8.

# Summary

Television is the dominant broadcast medium for direct marketing. But it still receives a small portion of total media expenditures for direct marketing. One reason is that television is a mass medium with little selectivity.

Television is used in two ways by direct marketing: to sell products by direct response commercials and to support a program in another medium. The first is the more important.

Because of its massive dimensions, low selectivity, and high cost, network television is seldom used by direct marketers. The large majority of direct marketing commercials are run in spot television, particularly in fringe time. Consequently, time must be negotiated on a station-by-station basis. Direct marketing commercials tend to be longer than the typical announcement of 30-second duration. Popular in spot-time buying is the concept of gross rating points.

Television spots are bought and evaluated on the basis of ratings. There are two services that supply ratings to the industry: Nielsen Station Index and Arbitron. Most markets are rated four times a year, based on viewer diaries. The infrequent measurements, as well as inherent flaws in measuring techniques, create serious problems of testing and evaluation.

In recent years, as more large companies have begun using direct marketing techniques, more consideration has been given to image building. But image-type direct marketing commercials are still the exception rather than the rule.

Direct marketers have moved into cable TV because it offers selectivity and spot availabilities. During 1990–1991, cable TV penetrated almost 60 percent of homes with television sets.

VCRs have had a minor impact on TV viewing as of 1990. Home shopping shows, a new service, have recently made their appearance on cable television.

**REVIEW QUESTIONS**

1. State at least four reasons why companies spend so much of their advertising dollars on television.
2. Why are there relatively few direct response commercials on network television?
3. In general, television yields audience demographics that direct marketers find undesirable. Comment.
4. The media efficiency of a support commercial depends not only on its cost per thousand, but on the size of the audience in the primary medium. Explain.

5. Why do support commercials usually have higher costs per thousand than direct response commercials, even when commercial length is held constant?
6. Should a television buyer be given sole discretion over media spending?
7. What kinds of products seem most suitable to direct response advertising on television?
8. Are direct marketing agencies justified in weighing spot television audiences by demographics to achieve better marketing targets?
9. The Ginsu knives commercial has often been characterized as being in bad taste. Comment.
10. Is image building compatible with direct response commercials?

---

**PROJECT**

1. a. You are to study commercials of different television programs for eight hours. Specifically, you are to watch two hours each in the morning, afternoon, prime time, and late fringe time (after 11:00 P.M.). Further, you are to divide your viewing between network television (ABC, CBS, or NBC), independent stations (WGN, WOR, WTBS, WNYW, or WPIX), cable networks (A&E, Lifetime, MTV, or Discovery), and sports stations (ESPN, MSG, or SC). List the different types of commercials (consumer products, specific services, promotions for movies and television programs) seen on each show. Do you note any patterns in the commercials? Explain.

   b. How many of the advertisements you have seen apply direct marketing techniques? Explain.

   c. What is the difference between the direct marketing commercials and the general marketing advertisements? Explain.

   d. Create two direct marketing television ads. It is fine to work in black and white. If you prefer, you may do it in color. A paste job is also approved. Neatness and clarity count as part of the grade.

   Further, if you prefer, you may produce a direct marketing videotape commercial in place of the ads.

PART V

# DIRECT MARKETING IN DIFFERENT MARKETS

CHAPTER 16

# Business-to-Business Marketing

The business-to-business field displays a far greater sales volume than the consumers market. Because production is roundabout, transactions are forged together in a long chain that stretches from raw materials to finished goods. The combined value of se transactions outweighs that of final outputs.

The business-to-business market extends beyond business firms to nonprofit and public organizations, such as schools, churches, and government agencies. For that reason, business-to-business marketing is often described as organizational marketing.[1] Sales comprise intermediate products, which are goods and services devoted to making some other product. Regardless of customer types, business-to-business marketing carries out activities to achieve nonconsumer transactions.

Yet there are many similarities between marketing to organizations and marketing to consumers. The tasks in the two fields run parallel. The major objectives in both cases are direct sales and lead generation. Most direct marketing expenditures flow into media. The message-carrying devices to organizations and to consumers are generally the same: telephone, direct mail, publications, and broadcast media. Then what are the differences between organization and consumer orientation? Can firms apply the techniques of one area to another?

There are two schools of thought on this subject. One regards buyers as buyers, no matter what they buy. Proponents of this view advocate consumer-type promotions to business personnel, such as special offers, sweepstakes, and coupons.[2] A contrary opinion regards motives and decision-making processes in organizational markets as basically different from those in consumer markets. Though direct marketing has a common look between the two applications, this view argues, the similarity is superficial. The content differs radically.[3] Which point of view merits adoption, the focus on similarities or the emphasis on differences? This chapter leans toward the latter position. If the two forms of direct marketing were essentially the same, there would be no need for this chapter at all.

Direct marketing in business fields has experienced rapid sales growth in recent years. According to Arnold Fishman, total mail order sales for business products in 1989 amounted to some $50 billion. Of

---

1. Philip Kotler, *Marketing Management*, 7th ed. (Englewood Cliffs, NJ: Prentice-Hall, 1991), pp. 195–217.
2. Jim Roberts, "It's Time for Industrial Marketers to Use Consumer-type Promotions," *Marketing News* (October 28, 1983), p. 6.
3. See R. M. Gaedeke and D. M. Tootelian, *Marketing: Principles and Applications* (St. Paul, MN: West Publishing, 1983), p. 137; Lester Wunderman, "Business-to-Business Marketing," *Direct Marketing* (July 1983), pp. 32–44.

this total, supplies and services were the fastest-growing sectors, reaching some $14.5 billion. The smallest of the specialty marketers, and the slowest-growing, was the industrial sector. This segment, made up of industry-specific producers and industrial maintenance and medical marketers, recorded total sales of about $3.6 billion.[4]

But the largest amount of sales was registered by "generalized marketing," firms that use multiple distribution channels and do not specialize in mail order selling. This group of companies were credited with roughly $32.3 billion in sales, or 64 percent of total mail order sales made to business.[5] This indicates the widespread use and functional diversity of direct marketing in business areas.

# Functions of Direct Marketing to Organizations

The use of direct marketing in business-to-business sales depends heavily on trends in other distribution channels. A major factor is relative costs. Industrial sales costs have risen constantly over the last decade, now amounting to more than $250 per visit. About four calls are needed to close a sale, pushing selling costs into four figures per order. As a percent of sales, personal selling expenses have risen higher and higher. For low-priced products or those ordered in small quantities, face-to-face selling has become a money-losing proposition. It is no wonder that direct marketing of business supplies and services has grown by leaps and bounds.

A second factor is the emerging small-business markets, especially in office supplies and equipment. Japanese electronic firms introduced miniaturized equipment, such as computers and copying machines, that were ideal for small offices. American suppliers of business machines and forms suddenly found a bulging demand in the once-neglected small business markets. But these customers are dispersed and hard to reach. The media used for reaching these buyers are mainly telephone, direct mail, and catalogs.[6]

The bulk of office supply sales, for example, is achieved through direct marketing. Almost 50 percent of all office supplies are sold by that method.[7]

4. Arnold Fishman, "1989 Mail Order Overview," *Direct Marketing* (September 1990), pp. 41–44.
5. *Ibid.*
6. C. R. Hartman, "Why Direct Marketing Is Hot," *D&B Reports* (September/October 1987), pp. 40–41.
7. "What's New at the Office," *Direct Marketing* (January 1989), p. 41.

Telemarketing in particular has been an attractive method for reaching small business customers. These programs use highly trained people to solicit new business and maintain reorders. Firms have also set up inbound 800 numbers to accept customer orders and requests for literature and information. Many of these inbound systems are tied to automated order-entry systems and periodic mailings and catalogs.[8]

Direct marketing is not merely a substitute for personal selling; it often complements face-to-face sales. It generates and qualifies sales leads, so that selling personnel make more efficient use of their time.

A third task of direct marketing to business is customer service. This function takes on many forms. Some buyers are hooked up to suppliers' computers so they can get updated order status reports. In the placing of orders, product support comes from telemarketing centers. Only those problems that cannot be handled over the phone are transferred to personal visits.

## National Account Management

Though direct marketing has replaced personal selling in handling small accounts, it has complemented personal selling in managing large accounts. The recent wave of mergers and acquisitions has resulted in more centralized purchasing and standardization of suppliers. To meet these changing demands, many industrial firms have adopted national account management.

The practice of dividing the sales force according to customer size has been in existence for many years. IBM, for example, had a national accounts division handling its largest customers, while a traditional sales force served the rest of potential buyers. Sales representatives often fell back on direct marketing when smaller accounts were not capable of supporting personal visits. But the more recent national management systems are organized in teams made up of sales, service, and technical personnel. National account managers operate in much the same way as product managers. Like product managers, they have wide responsibilities but limited authority, and they must rely on persuasive skills to get cooperation from line personnel. Telemarketing often supports and supplements the activities of national accounts.[9] Consequently, cooperation between telemarketing departments and national accounts are vital in the performance of marketing functions to a firm's best customers.

Some companies include both national account management and telemarketing management under the newly created position of general

8. R. Cardozo and S. Shipp, "New Selling Methods Are Changing Industrial Sales Management," *Business Horizons* (September–October 1987), pp. 23–28.
9. *Ibid.*

**TABLE 16.1. SIC Classification of Industry.**

| | Division | Major Groups |
|---|---|---|
| A. | Agriculture, forestry, fisheries | 01–09 |
| B. | Mining | 10–14 |
| C. | Contract construction | 15–17 |
| D. | Manufacturing | 20–39 |
| E. | Transportation, communication, electric, gas, and sanitary services | 40–49 |
| F. | Wholesale | 50–51 |
| G. | Retail | 52–59 |
| H. | Finance, insurance, real estate | 60–67 |
| I. | Services | 70–89 |
| J. | Public administration | 91–97 |
| K. | Nonclassifiable | 99 |

SOURCE: U.S. Census Bureau.

sales manager. In that situation, this executive oversees and coordinates the tasks of both national accounts and telemarketing. Whatever an organization's structure, modern direct marketing assumes more importance in generating business transactions.[10]

# Standard Industrial Classification

Business markets and direct marketing databases in the business-to-business area are often described by a government code called *Standard Industrial Classification* (SIC). Since government statistics of business activities are compiled and arranged by SIC codes, businesses find it helpful to keep their records in the same way to facilitate comparisons. Classifying businesses by SIC codes has often been compared with classifying consumers according to demographics.

The SIC system begins by describing the nation's economic activities in terms of 10 broad divisions. These divisions are in turn subdivided using two digits, three digits, and so forth. As a code takes on more digits, with eight the maximum to describe industries, establishments in a classification become more and more homogeneous. For example, D designates all manufacturing industries (See Table 16-1). SIC 20 denotes food and kindred products. The group labeled SIC 202 consists of all establishments producing dairy products. SIC 2023 refers to units devoted to condensed and evaporated milk.

Mailers to businesses frequently select lists on the basis of SIC codes. Figure 16-1 displays a page from a catalog that specializes in mailing lists for direct marketers.

10. F. E. Webster, Jr., and Y. Wind, *Organizational Buying Behavior* (Englewood Cliffs, NJ: Prentice-Hall, 1972), pp. 78–80.

# S.I.C. 2599

## TOBACCO

| SIC CODE | | NATIONAL QUANTITY |
|---|---|---|
| 2111 | Cigarette Mfrs. | 20 |
| 2121 | Cigar Mfrs. | 40 |
| 2131 | Tobacco Processors—Chewing, Smoking & Snuff | 240 |
| 2141 | Tobacco Processors—Stemming & Drying | 20 |

## TEXTILE PRODUCTS

| SIC CODE | | NATIONAL QUANTITY |
|---|---|---|
| 2211 | Cotton Fabric Mills | 640 |
| 2221 | Synthetic Fabric Mills | 460 |
| 2231 | Wool Fabric Mills | 210 |
| 2241 | Smallware Fabric Mills | 420 |
| 2251 | Hosiery (Full & Knee Length) Mills—Women's | 220 |
| 2252 | Hosiery Mills—(Ex. Women Full & Knee Length) | 330 |
| 2253 | Knit Outerwear Mills | 1,030 |
| 2254 | Knit Underwear Mills | 100 |
| 2257 | Knit Fabric Mills—Circular | 180 |
| 2258 | Knit Fabric Mills—Warp | 140 |
| 2259 | Knitting Mills, n.e.c. | 80 |
| 2261 | Coton Fabric Finishing Plants | 280 |
| 2262 | Synthetic Fabric Finishing Plants | 180 |
| 2269 | Fabric Finishing Plants, n.e.c. | 180 |
| 2271 | Carpet & Rug Mills—Woven | 130 |
| 2272 | Carpet & Rug Mills—Tufted | 400 |
| 2279 | Carpet & Rug Mills, n.e.c. | 50 |
| 2281 | Yarn Spinning Mills—(Except Wool) | 350 |
| 2282 | Yarn Mills—Texturizing, Throwing & Winding | 90 |
| 2283 | Yarn Mills—Wool | 110 |
| 2284 | Thread Mills | 100 |
| 2291 | Felt Goods Mfrs.—(Except Belts & Hats) | 90 |
| 2292 | Lace Goods Mfrs. | 80 |
| 2293 | Padding & Upholstery Filling Mfrs. | 100 |
| 2294 | Textile Mill Products—Processed Waste | 110 |
| 2295 | Fabric Mfrs.—Coated, Not Rubberized | 160 |
| 2296 | Tire Cord & Fabric Mfrs. | 20 |
| 2297 | Fabric Mills—Nonwoven | 20 |
| 2298 | Cordage & Twine Mfrs. | 170 |
| 2299 | Textile Goods Mills, n.e.c. | 220 |

## APPAREL

| SIC CODE | | NATIONAL QUANTITY |
|---|---|---|
| 2311 | Suit & Coat Mfrs.—Men's & Boys' | 630 |
| 2321 | Shirt & Nightwear Mfrs.—Men's & Boys' | 790 |
| 2322 | Underwear Mfrs.—Men's & Boys' | 70 |
| 2323 | Neckwear Mfrs.—Men's & Boys' | 210 |
| 2327 | Separate Trouser Mfrs.—Men's & Boys' | 450 |
| 2328 | Work Clothing Mfrs.—Men's & Boys' | 360 |
| 2329 | Clothing Mfrs. (Men's & Boys'), n.e.c. | 1,060 |
| 2331 | Blouse & Waist Mfrs.—Ladies | 1,150 |
| 2335 | Dress Mfrs.—Ladies | 2,510 |
| 2337 | Suit, Coat & Skirt Mfrs.—Ladies | 880 |
| 2339 | Outerwear Mfrs. (Ladies), n.e.c. | 2,340 |
| 2341 | Underwear & Nightwear Mfrs.—Ladies, Girls | 560 |
| 2342 | Brassiere & Girdle, etc. Mfrs. | 160 |
| 2351 | Millinery Mfrs. | 90 |
| 2352 | Hat & Cap Mfrs.—(Except Millinery) | 260 |
| 2361 | Dress & Blouse Mfrs.—Girls', Children's & Infants | 380 |
| 2363 | Coat & Suit Mfrs.—Girls', Children's & Infants | 80 |
| 2369 | Outerwear Mfrs. (Girls', Children's & Infants') | 340 |
| 2371 | Fur Goods Mfrs. | 480 |
| 2381 | Glove (Dress & Work) Mfrs.—Ex. Knit & Leather | 100 |
| 2384 | Robe & Dressing Gown Mfrs. | 120 |
| 2385 | Outer Garment Mfrs.—Waterproof | 150 |
| 2386 | Leather & Sheep Lined Clothing Mfrs. | 200 |
| 2387 | Belt Mfrs. | 240 |
| 2389 | Apparel & Accessory Mfrs., n.e.c. | 220 |
| 2391 | Curtain & Drapery Mfrs. | 1,540 |
| 2392 | Housefurnishing Mfrs.—Ex. Curtains & Draperies | 890 |
| 2393 | Bag Mfrs.—Textile | 200 |
| 2394 | Canvas & Related Products Mfrs. | 1,080 |
| 2395 | Pleaters & Stitchers for the Trade | 470 |
| 2396 | Trimming Mfrs.—Automotive & Apparel | 410 |
| 2397 | Embroidery Mfrs.—Schiffli Machine | 150 |
| 2399 | Textile Mfrs. (Fabricated Products), n.e.c. | 2,980 |
| 2399A | Sewing Contractors | 2,310 |

## LUMBER

| SIC CODE | | NATIONAL QUANTITY |
|---|---|---|
| 2411 | Logging Camps & Logging Contractors | 2,330 |
| 2421 | Sawmills & Planing Mills—General | 3,380 |
| 2426 | Hardwood Dimension & Flooring Mills | 540 |
| 2429 | Sawmills (Special Products), n.e.c. | 300 |
| 2431 | Millwork Plants | 2,700 |
| 2434 | Kitchen Cabinet Mfrs.—Wood | 3,270 |
| 2435 | Veneer & Plywood Mfrs.—Hardwood | 300 |
| 2436 | Veneer & Plywood Mfrs.—Softwood | 140 |
| 2439 | Structural Wood Members Mfrs., n.e.c. | 640 |
| 2441 | Box Mfrs.—Nailed Wood & Lock Corner | 370 |
| 2448 | Wood Pallet & Skid Mfrs. | 940 |
| 2449 | Container Mfrs. (Wood), n.e.c. | 250 |
| 2451 | Mobile Home Mfrs. | 340 |
| 2452 | Building Mfrs.—Prefabricated Wood & Component | 710 |
| 2491 | Wood Preserving Plants | 380 |
| 2492 | Particleboard Plants | 20 |
| 2499 | Wood Products Mfrs., n.e.c. | 3,180 |

## FURNITURE

| SIC CODE | | NATIONAL QUANTITY |
|---|---|---|
| 2511 | Household Furniture Mfrs.—Wood | 2,540 |
| 2512 | Household Furniture Mfrs.—Upholstered | 1,740 |
| 2514 | Household Furniture Mfrs.—Metal | 450 |
| 2515 | Mattress & Bedspring Mfrs. | 920 |
| 2517 | Radio & TV Cabinet Mfrs.—Wood | 60 |
| 2519 | Household Furniture Mfrs., n.e.c. | 5,540 |
| 2521 | Office Furniture Mfrs.—Wood | 470 |
| 2522 | Office Furniture Mfrs.—Metal | 330 |
| 2531 | Public Building & Related Furniture Mfrs. | 370 |
| 2541 | Partition & Fixture Mfrs.—Wood | 1,380 |
| 2542 | Partition & Fixture Mfrs.—Metal | 580 |
| 2591 | Drapery Hardware & Blind & Shade Mfrs. | 620 |
| 2599 | Furniture & Fixture Mfrs., n.e.c. | 500 |

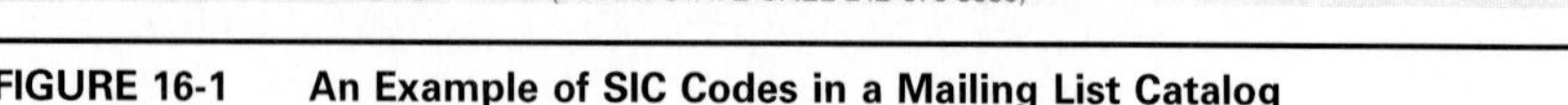


**FIGURE 16-1 An Example of SIC Codes in a Mailing List Catalog**
*Source:* Ed Burnett Consultants, Inc. A Database America Company. Reprinted with permission.

Many business publications also use SIC codes to define their circulations. They show how many copies go to particular industries. Magazines tailored for specific industries are called *vertical publications*. The practice of classifying circulation by SIC codes permits advertisers to target their audiences with greater precision.

Some publications are more interested in job titles than in SIC codes. The *Journal of Accountancy*, for example, is more concerned with the professional status of recipients than the industries in which they are employed. Accounting is used by all businesses, regardless of the goods or services they sell, and all practitioners share a set of professional norms. Print media devoted to occupations that cross into many industries are described as *horizontal publications*. For purposes of targeting prospects, all media can be categorized in terms of job titles, SIC codes, or both. The choice depends on how a firm conceives of its markets—vertical, horizontal, or a blend of the two.

# The Buying Center

Unlike consumer markets, the buying decision process involves many individuals. The exact number depends on the inner workings of a company and the nature of the product. The more complex and costlier the product, the more people are brought into the decision-making process.

Buying centers handling different products have various numbers of participants, even within the same company. These individuals do not have an equal voice; some talk louder than others. Regardless of how much weight a person carries, all personnel who have some say in what should be purchased make up a *buying center*.

The players in a buying center are traditionally seen as performing in six capacities, though some individuals may function in more than one. These six roles are:[11]

- *Users* of the product or process
- *Influencers,* who often draw up specifications and evaluate alternatives
- *Deciders,* whose decisions are used to select the products to be purchased and the suppliers from whom to purchase
- *Approvers,* who authorize the proposals of buyers

11. For example, see Bob Stone, *Successful Direct Marketing Methods*, 4th ed. (Lincolnwood, IL: NTC Business Books, 1988), pp. 125–129.

- *Buyers,* who negotiate with vendors and send in the order
- *Gatekeepers,* who control the flow of information to the buying center

When a buying center includes many managers, marketers have great difficulty reaching all of them. This is especially so when communication must be made from a distance, via faceless media. In that event, direct marketers usually seek the decision makers or individuals who influence buying in major ways.[12]

Nevertheless, the search for decision makers presents a number of problems. Buying centers do not have the same compositions. They vary from company to company, even for the same products. Chief decision makers are therefore difficult to identify, which is a prime requisite for direct marketing. How else can one communicate with them at a distance?

One way of overcoming this problem is to address these personnel by their titles. Some promotions lend themselves to an approach that contacts traditional titles, such as comptroller, head of auditing, or office manager. But many products are bought by businesses whose decision makers have titles unique to each company. People with different titles might buy the same products. Those with the same title may take on different buying functions, and some of them may not be involved in company purchases at all.[13]

Another problem in compiling a list of key decision makers is frequent job changes, especially among lower-echelon personnel. Company presidents are often not the most responsive recipients of direct marketing messages. Middle managers are most prone to change positions, titles, and companies. These changes play havoc with business-to-business databases.

Business lists are also subject to variations in name compilations. There are today at least seven primary sources of business names: American Business Lists, Compilers Plus, Dun & Bradstreet, Edward Burnett, International Business Lists, TRW, and Trinet. At a panel of the Direct Marketing Association in 1990, each of these firms presented counts for Standard Industrial Classification (SIC) codes in specific industries. Some 40 SIC codes were compared. Not once did two compilers match counts. In certain instances, compilers used different SIC numbers for the same industrial category. The general conclusion of the panel was that different compilers were offering direct marketers products and pursuing different approaches to list compilation.[14]

---

12. *Ibid.*, p. 512.
13. Maxim C. Bartko, "Look Closer: Look-Alike Databases Aren't Identical," *DM News* (September 10, 1990), p. 33.
14. See Ronald Friedman, "Tracking Better Leads," *Zip Target Marketing* (June 1986), pp. 33–34.

# Lead Generation

One of the most important activities in business-to-business direct marketing is lead generation. No firm can conduct business only by dealing with its current customers, unless it has a virtual monopoly position. But very few businesses have such favored status. Customer databases erode in time, and firms must always be on the lookout for new customers in order to grow, or even to survive. The prospective buyers can be found in a firm's existing markets or in new ones.

A lead generation program is one way to develop new customers. The method assumes that more than one contact is necessary to make a sale or to start a business relationship. A multistep sales approach further presumes that buying is a deliberative process, with information serving as a necessary prelude to decisions. This view accords with the realities of buying centers.

A common problem in acquiring new business are the costs of contacting potential buyers—costs that run high in relation to expected returns. In that case, an efficient lead generation program makes the initial contact at low cost, weeds out the less likely buyers, and concentrates its efforts on the best prospects.

Leads can be generated in many ways. The most popular media for lead acquisitions are telephone, mail, and the business press. Regardless of media, commercial messages can elicit leads "tightly" or "loosely." A "tight" approach aims to discourage marginal buyers or prospects with low purchase probabilities. A "loose" approach seeks quantity, with less regard for quality. Both methods involve tradeoffs. The tight lead results in a lower volume of inquiries but a higher sales closing rate. The loose lead produces a high volume of inquiries and, thus, a more complete coverage of prospective buyers. But it also garners more prospects with low buying interest and hence has a lower sales rate.

How many leads should a firm generate, and at what rate? It all depends on a firm's resources and its follow up plans. If inquiries are to be followed up by mail or phone solicitations, then returns from these efforts must be considered in the lead generation program. For example, if a firm intends to sell through catalogs, its follow-up program must evaluate catalog sales that come from lead generation efforts. The vital statistic is not the cost per lead but the cost per order resulting from that lead.

If follow-up contacts are made by personal visits, the number of leads must be attuned to operations of the sales force. Sales personnel usually call on firms when offers involve complex products. The number and timing of incoming leads must be determined by the workload of the sales force. Leads must be followed up with dispatch, for they cannot be put in inventory and drawn upon at discretion. Hot leads turn cold in a short time. If the lead supply is too large to handle adequately, marketing effort is wasted. On the other hand, leads that number less than a firm's follow-up capability imply foregone opportunities.

A program based on personal selling requires far fewer leads than one based on impersonal selling. But reliance on the sales force also calls for better-quality leads. Though personal visits are the most effective selling tools, they incur the highest costs.

Most large companies employ a combination of personal and impersonal methods to follow up leads. They give the best leads to the sales force and communicate with less likely prospects by impersonal means. This approach implies the presence of a lead qualification program. Good leads must be sorted out from the bad and the not-so-good leads.

# Lead Follow-up Programs

In the early days of direct marketing, the emphasis was on quantity. The idea was to get as many inquiries as possible. But it was soon realized that not all inquiries were equal. Most direct marketers today eschew this "shotgun" approach for more precise targeting. Yet a lead is a lead, and brings in no revenue by itself. It must be followed up with selling efforts. To justify its costs, lead generation must be converted to sales generation. These undertakings seek to turn prospects into buyers.

A lead follow-up program usually consists of three parts: lead qualification, lead fulfillment, and lead tracking. Not all companies place the same emphasis on each part. But in one way or another, all three components are usually present in company efforts to follow up inquiries, requests for literature, or other leads generated.

## Lead Qualification

The purpose of qualification is to screen out bad leads or nonserious prospects. The screening process covers a wide range of options. It can simply disqualify bad leads or grade them according to some sales criteria. The extent to which leads are qualified depends on how a company sells its products. When sales are made entirely by mail, a firm may have no need to qualify leads. When a firm sells by personal contact, qualification is an efficient marketing tool. By identifying promising prospects, lead screening permits highly paid sales personnel to spend their time calling on the most likely buyers.[15]

15. Nancy Dobrozdravic, "Computerized Lead-Tracking Analysis Makes Direct Marketing More Effective," *Marketing News* (May 22, 1989), pp. 27–28.

Qualification is done primarily by phone. Sometimes, the use of the telephone to evaluate the quality of leads is known as "telequalifying." The objective is to get information about a prospect, and not to sell anything.

If the lead-generating message contains an 800 number, qualification is done by the answering telephone operator. A few simple questions during the phone conversation are enough to classify callers into good, mediocre, and bad prospects. When inquiries come in by mail, qualification must be made by outgoing telephone calls. "Hot" leads are forwarded immediately to field sales offices. Since companies do not buy impulsively, a "good" lead is a firm that intends to purchase the advertised product within six to eight months. Whatever qualification system is used, it should result in leads yielding more sales than the number of conversions without the use of lead qualification.

## Lead Fulfillment

A lead is actually a request of some kind—an inquiry, a request for literature, a response to a sales promotion. Like actual orders, these requests must be fulfilled, and time is often of the essence. Most authorities recommend that a request be fulfilled within 48 hours.

The marketer has a number of options in fulfilling the request, based on the lead's qualification. Bona fide leads with good buying probabilities are sent literature concurrent with the name and address of the prospect being sent to the sales office. If the lead has a below-average buying probability, the firm can send out less elaborate literature. Many companies believe that all inquiries should be answered, even nonqualified leads. Consequently, these firms make up different packages for different groups of prospects.

## Lead Tracking

A modern development stemming from computer technology is the lead-tracking program, sometimes called an *inquiry management system.* Lead-tracking systems visualize the entire lead program as an integrated whole and seek to trace all steps from beginning to end. They start with lead generation and end with transactional activity.

A tracking system has many functions. Among its more important objectives are:

- Prospecting for new customers
- Improving lead qualification before names of prospects go to fulfillment and sales offices
- Determining costs and revenue per lead with greater accuracy

- Evaluating sources of leads so that a company can plan for more efficient lead programs
- Producing timely reports of activities to improve day-to-day operations

Companies can either develop a computerized tracking system internally or contract for outside services. These systems can be as simple or as complex as a company wishes. Irrespective of the exact design, all tracking systems have common features.

The first step is tallying the number of inquiries that come in and identifying them by source. Mail returns can be coded by source and date of mailing. Telephone inquiries should carry the same information. But because people often forget where they saw a particular ad, different phone numbers can be assigned to different sources. For example, the SPSS phone tracking system links by computer unique phone numbers to various printed advertisements and mailing pieces. This system records the number dialed, the date, and the time of the incoming call.[16] Dating inquiries provides insights on response times to ads and mailing pieces. It also provides data for timing promotions to better fit selling schedules.

The SPSS program uses different database sets to perform complicated statistical analyses for predicting prospects' buying probabilities.[17] Not all lead tracking systems are so elaborate, but practically all marry lead information to some sort of database. And all systems track prospects from the time they made an inquiry to their final status as customers or noncustomers. At the very minimum, relevant facts recorded about respondents include:

- Name and address of respondent
- Company size
- Source of lead
- Level of interest
- Time frame for purchasing the product in question

The final stage of lead tracking is the generation of a series of reports. These outputs vary from company to company. Some of the most common reports are:[18]

- Weekly source analysis, which shows total leads produced each week by source
- Inquiry summary report, which exhibits results of each source in terms of costs and revenue
- Inquiries, broken down by product, sales territory, department, and other relevant categories

---

16. *Ibid.*
17. Friedman, *op. cit.*
18. Bill Kelley, "Is There Anything that Can't Be Sold by Phone?" *Sales & Marketing Management* (April 1989), p. 61.

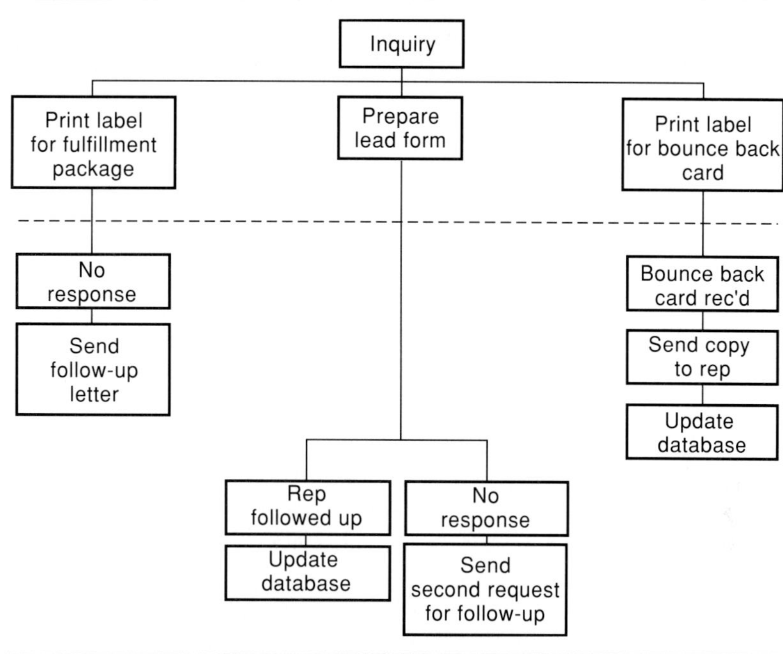


**FIGURE 16-2 A Flowchart of SIPS Tracking System**

Figure 16-2 presents a flowchart of SIPS, a computerized lead inquiry system developed by Rachlin Enterprises of East Northport, New York. The flowchart clearly shows that a lead-tracking system requires input from the sales force. But salespeople are not in love with paperwork and are often wary of bureaucrats who issue commands from behind desks. Sales personnel believe they should spend their time selling, not doing clerical work.

Getting the sales force to cooperate in implementing a lead-tracking system is difficult under any circumstances. There are many approaches to achieving this result, especially when the sales personnel are employees of the company. But when selling is done by outside agencies, such as distributors and commission agents, a firm may be in no position to impose nonselling jobs on sales representatives. Such realities strongly argue for designing tracking systems with simplicity and minimal information.

# Media Usage

Business-to-business direct marketing uses the same media as consumer goods sellers. The most popular media in the business area are telephone, mail, and magazines. But there are aspects of business marketing that make it different from consumer marketing. This section focuses only on media elements that are unique to business-to-business direct marketing.

## Telemarketing

The telephone is widely used in the conduct of business and is therefore the most popular medium in marketing directly to business firms. It is estimated that more than $115 billion of advertised products, ranging from paper clips to highly complex items, are marketed by telephone.[19]

As previously noted, the telephone is the chief method of qualifiying leads. It is also an important adjunct in selling to national accounts, and it provides a major means of selling to small accounts where face-to-face selling would not be profitable. For example, the telemarketing center of B.F. Goodrich supplements personal visits with calls to high-volume accounts, and it sells direct to smaller firms.

Another use of the phone is to revive low-volume and dormant accounts. For example, Goodall Rubber's Kansas City office found that some 68 percent of its accounts contributed only 6 percent of total business. These accounts averaged less than $3,000 in sales, a figure that did not cover costs of personal visits. The telemarketing center was able to sell to these accounts at a profit by replacing personal visits with lower-cost selling. The cost of telemarketing can be as little as one-tenth that of personal selling. In the event that sales to low-producing accounts increased to certain designated levels, Goodall gave responsibility for selling back to the sales force.[20]

Finally, small businesses can put the phone to good use. Many small firms do not have the resources to establish a sales force. In other instances, customers may be too scattered to justify a company sales department. Though the phone is not as effective as personal selling, it can be an efficient alternative.

One problem with telemarketing in business is personnel qualification. Some businesses require salespeople with college degrees or technical competence. A representative of a drug company calling on doctors must have some knowledge of pharmacy. A person representing technical products may need an engineering degree. These credentials are often hard to find among people looking for telephone work. Nor is it easy to transfer outside sales personnel to telemarketing centers.

---

19. *Ibid.*
20. David Enscoe, "The Mail Stops Here!" *Target Marketing* (September 1989), pp. 12–14.

Many do not have the temperament to sit at a desk and make phone calls. In addition, pay scales for telemarketers are lower than those for outside salespeople, and overqualified employees will not stay at those jobs.

## Direct Mail

Direct mail to businesses is essentially the same as that going to consumers. The leading devices are direct mail pieces and catalogs. Standardized, off-the-shelf products lend themselves best to direct selling by mail.

Product catalogs to industrial customers are seldom graced with handsome illustrations, clever copy, elegant design, or sparkling color. Items are described in language common to the trade, and pages are replete with order numbers and prices. The design is usually stark and devoid of sales trappings. There is little need for salesmanship. Buyers are supposed to be experts, knowing exactly what they want and purchasing it on a rational basis. The catalog achieves efficiency by conforming to routinized purchase behavior.

There are notable exceptions, however. These occur when the buying center is composed of generalists or the product is customized. Catalogs to business services of this nature take on characteristics of those sent to consumers.

A problem that surfaced several years ago is that some of the largest U.S. corporations stopped delivering bulk mail to employees. General Motors, for example, does not distribute third-class mail or controlled-circulation magazines at its plants. Many other large corporations have followed suit. These policies stem from efforts to cut costs, and one place to trim overhead is in the mailroom.[21]

The Direct Marketing Association in 1989 established a task force to help mailers cope with the situation. The effects of hostile mailrooms on the direct marketing industry, however, are somewhat hazy. The greatest impact seems to have fallen on catalogers and trade publications.

Direct marketers are trying various stratagems to circumvent mailroom gatekeepers. Some suggest putting a person's name on the first line and title on the second. Others say that blind title lists work better.[22] The most effective way is the costliest: first-class mail. However, this method is prohibitive for sending magazines. Another way of avoid-

21. "Telemarketing's Role Grows in Business-to-Business," *Target Marketing* (November 1989), p. 34.
22. "Lists Needed for Card Packs," *Target Marketing* (August 1986), p. 29.

ing the obstacles of the mailroom is to contact prospects directly by telephone.

A new device whose usage has grown significantly in direct mail is the card pack. In the past, card packs were used primarily by publishers catering to professional and technical audiences. Today, card packs are broadening their scope to other markets. The educational market in particular has been an expanding application. Computer-related areas have also been a fertile field for card packs, and some claim that the market is already saturated. Despite their recent expansion, card packs face a limited potential.

## Magazines

An important role in business-to-business direct marketing is assumed by the business press. There are three main types of business publications: trade, vertical, and professional.

Trade publications are merchandising vehicles. They go mainly to distributors and other intermediaries. Large companies are less dependent on resellers than small ones, moving goods directly to customers. Direct shipments with no intermediaries account for perhaps half of all industrial goods.

Vertical magazines seek audiences affiliated with an industry, irrespective of position. Direct marketers who aim to cover an industry can achieve high penetration by advertising in one or two vertical publications.

Professional magazines cover a multitude of occupations. These cut across industries, with audiences such as computer engineers and programers, doctors and laboratory technicians, and copywriters and marketing specialists. These publications can be thought of as "horizontal" because they cross industry lines. Somewhat akin to professional publications are broad-based management publications, such as *Business Week, Forbes,* and *Fortune*. These horizontal magazines are edited for generalists and have much wider scopes than publications dealing with more structured occupations.

The type of copy depends strongly on the type of audience. Large, horizontal-type magazines will normally draw advertisements aimed at generalists. Copy may resemble that found in consumer magazines. Advertisements will be phrased in simple, easily understood language, prominent illustrations to feature the product. However, the descriptions will use rational, *reason-why* copy. Emotional appeals are deemphasized. An example of an ad aimed at a horizontal market is shown in Figure 16-3.

Ads in more specialized magazines, vertical or horizontal, use copy specific to an industry or occupation. These ads may contain technical details and industry jargon, understandable only to a highly professional or technical audience.

Most business publications have small circulations, averaging around 50,000. Yet such a modest circulation can cover a narrow segment quite thoroughly. Several magazines maintain paid subscriptions, and direct marketers have ABC-audited figures to guide them in buying space. The majority of publications, however, are of the controlled-circulation type. Free copies are sent to qualified persons who request them. This method of distribution yields high levels of market coverage. Controlled-circulation publications are also audited by several organizations, including ABC. Other organizations are Business Publications Audit of Circulation (BPA) and Verified Audit Circulation Corporation (VAC). But roughly half of all business magazines remain unaudited. Most of these do not carry advertising.

The business press is an important source of leads. Its reader service is a unique feature that invites inquiries to both advertisements and editorials. These magazines carry reader service cards, sometimes referred to as "bingo cards." Such a card appears in Figure 16-4. The magazine numbers all advertisements and articles and provides readers with postage-free cards containing matching numbers. Requests for information about editorial items or advertised offers are made by checking or circling the number corresponding to a particular ad or article.

Opinions as to the effectiveness of reader service cards vary. Producers of installations and capital equipment normally pay scant attention to bingo cards. These goods involve large expenditures and long, drawn-out negotiations. Buyers usually conduct an active search for suppliers and are in contact with representative of seller organizations.

Other companies indifferent to reader service are those that sell commodity-type products in large quantities. These firms usually have large sales staffs that cover the leading buyers in a market. Small accounts can be solicited more economically by telemarketing centers than by printed advertisements in the trade press.

Nevertheless, the business press remains an important vehicle for direct marketers, for generating both direct sales and inquiries. These magazines provide good industry coverage at a reasonable cost.

## Summary

The business-to-business field has a greater sales volume than the consumer market. The scope of the nonconsumer segment is expanded if government and nonprofit organizations are included. The techniques

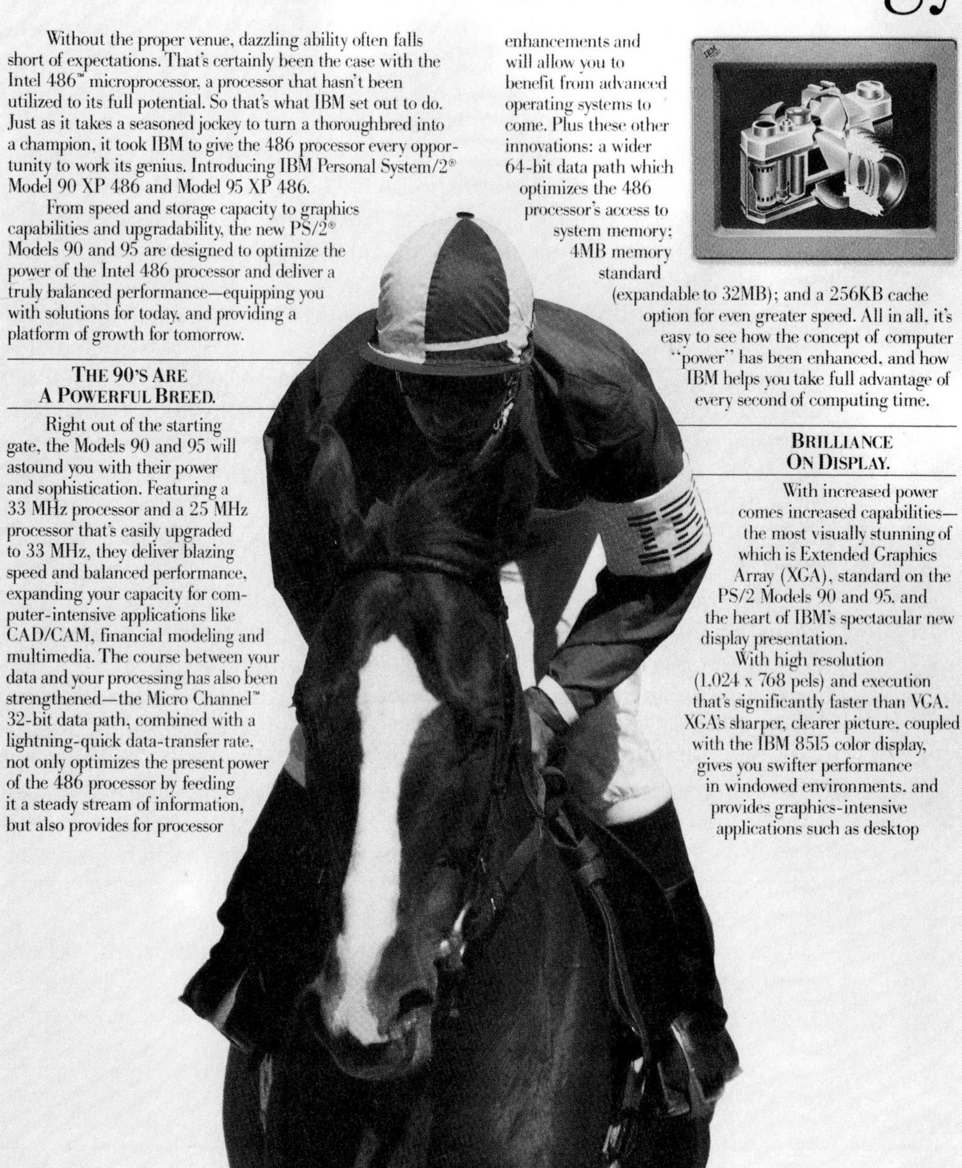


**FIGURE 16-3  A Copier Advertisement for Horizontal Markets**
*Source:* IBM Corporation. Reprinted with permission.

# horses run.
# realizes its full potential.

publishing, image processing and engineering design with a stunning new look.

| Features | IBM PS/2 Model 90 | IBM PS/2 Model 95 |
|---|---|---|
| **Microprocessor** | | |
| Standard | 80486 | 80486 |
| Clock speed | 25-33 MHZ | 25-33 MHZ |
| Optional upgrade | 33 MHZ | 33 MHZ |
| **Memory** | | |
| Standard | 4MB (70ns) | 4MB (70ns) |
| Maximum | 32MB | 32MB |
| **Integrated Functions** | Extended Graphics Array (XGA) and display port, dual DMA serial ports, DMA parallel port, pointing device port, keyboard port, diskette controller support for three drives, SCSI adapter with Cache. | |
| **Fixed Disk Storage** | | |
| Standard | 80-320MB | 160MB-320MB |
| **Display Modes** | | |
| APA Modes | XGA (includes all VGA modes) 640 x 480 x 256 colors/ 64 gray shades; 1024 x 768 x 16 colors/gray shades; hardware support for 132 column text mode; 16-bit direct color mode at 640 x 480 x 64K colors | |
| **Available Expansion Slots** | three 32-bit | six 32-bit |
| **Bus Architecture** | | |
| Data path | MCA 32-bit | MCA 32-bit |

## Fast Times Are In Store.

To satisfy even the most demanding storage needs, from LAN systems to data base management to numeric-intensive applications like financial analysis and modeling, IBM has one of the most advanced solutions available. IBM's super-fast SCSI hard disks are pure state-of-the-art performers. With additional hardfile expansion bays, the PS/2 Models 90 and 95 have enormous storage potential—up to .96 Gigabytes on the Model 90 and up to 1.6GB on the Model 95. And with the PS/2 External Storage Enclosures, the Models 90 and 95 can provide 8.96GB and more.

We've also augmented the computing power by adding more flexibility to resident memory—our new 1.3 version of OS/2® requires as little as 2MB on your system. With this streamlined version you not only get more room for applications, but some users will experience a substantial performance increase in system functions as well. So when you need to make great strides with your computing power, you can count on IBM to give you terrific storage capability wherever you may need it.

## Designed To Keep You Out In Front.

For the turns and hurdles ahead, you'll need technology that has foresight built in. Through a unique design, the Expandable Processor (XP) allows for an architected family of upgradable processor enhancements that can extend the life of your system. With Micro Channel busmaster adapters, you can incorporate multiple processors—like adding "computers" to your computer. And coupled with the industry-standard Small Computer System Interface (SCSI), you'll be able to support new applications and continue to build on your system as your needs become more varied and complex.

With optimized performance in balance, power, speed and adaptability, the new PS/2 Models 90 and 95 are designed to keep you ahead of the pack. To find out more about the new leader in 486 computing, contact your IBM Authorized Remarketer or IBM marketing representative. For a remarketer near you, call 1 800 272-3438.

How're you going to do it?

PS/2 it!

IBM

IBM, Personal System 2, PS/2 and OS/2 are registered trademarks and Micro Channel is a trademark of International Business Machines Corporation. 486 is a trademark of Intel Corp. Technical illustration created using Micrografx Designer and provided courtesy of Micrografx, Inc., Richardson, Texas. © 1990 IBM Corp.

9107

**Graphic Arts Monthly**

**July 1991** **FAX (303) 470-4589**

**This card expires October 15, 1991**
**After this date contact advertiser directly**

Reader Inquiry Card
**Please Print All Information**

**FOR FASTER SERVICE**
**Use Peel Off Mailer Label**

Name__________ Title__________

Firm__________ Div.__________

Address__________

City__________ State__________

Telephone__________ Zip__________

**Is This Your Personal Copy?** ☐ Yes 999 ☐ No

**1. Type(s) of Graphic Arts Operations:**

01 ☐ Commercial Printing
02 ☐ In-Plant Printing
03 ☐ Newspaper
04 ☐ Publications Printing
05 ☐ Book Printing
06 ☐ Business Forms
07 ☐ Specialty Printing
08 ☐ Paper Box/Pkg/Converter
09 ☐ Trade Service
10 ☐ Manufacturer/Dealer
11 ☐ Quick Printing
12 ☐ Other

**2. Annual Sales Volume At This Location:**

13 ☐ Less than $500,000
14 ☐ $500,000 to $1 Million
15 ☐ $1 Million to $3 Million
16 ☐ $3 Million to $10 Million
17 ☐ $10 Million to $20 Million
18 ☐ Over $20 Million

**3. Number of Employees:**

Private Plants CheckNumber in Printing Department Only

19 ☐ Less than 10
20 ☐ 10-19
21 ☐ 20-49
22 ☐ 50-99
23 ☐ 100-Over

**4. We Plan to Purchase the Following Equipment:**

35 ☐ Sheetfed offset presses up to 21"
36 ☐ Sheetfed offset presses 22" or larger
45 ☐ Multi station auto-collators
46 ☐ Saddle stitchers
47 ☐ Power paper cutters 38" or larger
48 ☐ Data collection systems
49 ☐ Registration systems
43 ☐ Color electronic prepress systems
54 ☐ Automatic ink color control systems
55 ☐ Sheetfed coaters

**5. We Plan to Purchase This Equipment:**

50 ☐ Immediately
51 ☐ 3 months
52 ☐ 6 months
53 ☐ 12 months

| 1 | 2 | 3 | 4 | 5 | 6 | 7 | 8 | 9 | 10 | 11 | 12 | 13 | 14 | 15 | 16 | 17 | 18 | 19 | 20 |
|---|---|---|---|---|---|---|---|---|---|---|---|---|---|---|---|---|---|---|---|
| 21 | 22 | 23 | 24 | 25 | 26 | 27 | 28 | 29 | 30 | 31 | 32 | 33 | 34 | 35 | 36 | 37 | 38 | 39 | 40 |
| 41 | 42 | 43 | 44 | 45 | 46 | 47 | 48 | 49 | 50 | 51 | 52 | 53 | 54 | 55 | 56 | 57 | 58 | 59 | 60 |
| 61 | 62 | 63 | 64 | 65 | 66 | 67 | 68 | 69 | 70 | 71 | 72 | 73 | 74 | 75 | 76 | 77 | 78 | 79 | 80 |
| 81 | 82 | 83 | 84 | 85 | 86 | 87 | 88 | 89 | 90 | 91 | 92 | 93 | 94 | 95 | 96 | 97 | 98 | 99 | 100 |
| 101 | 102 | 103 | 104 | 105 | 106 | 107 | 108 | 109 | 110 | 111 | 112 | 113 | 114 | 115 | 116 | 117 | 118 | 119 | 120 |
| 121 | 122 | 123 | 124 | 125 | 126 | 127 | 128 | 129 | 130 | 131 | 132 | 133 | 134 | 135 | 136 | 137 | 138 | 139 | 140 |
| 141 | 142 | 143 | 144 | 145 | 146 | 147 | 148 | 149 | 150 | 151 | 152 | 153 | 154 | 155 | 156 | 157 | 158 | 159 | 160 |
| 161 | 162 | 163 | 164 | 165 | 166 | 167 | 168 | 169 | 170 | 171 | 172 | 173 | 174 | 175 | 176 | 177 | 178 | 179 | 180 |
| 181 | 182 | 183 | 184 | 185 | 186 | 187 | 188 | 189 | 190 | 191 | 192 | 193 | 194 | 195 | 196 | 197 | 198 | 199 | 200 |
| 201 | 202 | 203 | 204 | 205 | 206 | 207 | 208 | 209 | 210 | 211 | 212 | 213 | 214 | 215 | 216 | 217 | 218 | 219 | 220 |
| 221 | 222 | 223 | 224 | 225 | 226 | 227 | 228 | 229 | 230 | 231 | 232 | 233 | 234 | 235 | 236 | 237 | 238 | 239 | 240 |
| 241 | 242 | 243 | 244 | 245 | 246 | 247 | 248 | 249 | 250 | 251 | 252 | 253 | 254 | 255 | 256 | 257 | 258 | 259 | 260 |
| 261 | 262 | 263 | 264 | 265 | 266 | 267 | 268 | 269 | 270 | 271 | 272 | 273 | 274 | 275 | 276 | 277 | 278 | 279 | 280 |
| 281 | 282 | 283 | 284 | 285 | 286 | 287 | 288 | 289 | 290 | 291 | 292 | 293 | 294 | 295 | 296 | 297 | 298 | 299 | 300 |
| 301 | 302 | 303 | 304 | 305 | 306 | 307 | 308 | 309 | 310 | 311 | 312 | 313 | 314 | 315 | 316 | 317 | 318 | 319 | 320 |
| 321 | 322 | 323 | 324 | 325 | 326 | 327 | 328 | 329 | 330 | 331 | 332 | 333 | 334 | 335 | 336 | 337 | 338 | 339 | 340 |
| 341 | 342 | 343 | 344 | 345 | 346 | 347 | 348 | 349 | 350 | 351 | 352 | 353 | 354 | 355 | 356 | 357 | 358 | 359 | 360 |
| 361 | 362 | 363 | 364 | 365 | 366 | 367 | 368 | 369 | 370 | 371 | 372 | 373 | 374 | 375 | 376 | 377 | 378 | 379 | 380 |
| 381 | 382 | 383 | 384 | 385 | 386 | 387 | 388 | 389 | 390 | 391 | 392 | 393 | 394 | 395 | 396 | 397 | 398 | 399 | 400 |

**FIGURE 16-4 An Example of a Reader Service Card**
*Source:* Graphic Arts Monthly. Reprinted with permission.

of business-to-business direct marketing depend on three major factors: relative costs, emerging small-business markets, and consumer service. Modern direct marketing is assuming more importance in generating business.

A widespread system for classifying markets is the government's Standard Industrial Classification. Direct mail lists and circulations of business publications are often qualified by SIC codes.

Industrial buying centers include all individuals who participate in a buying decision. The more complex and costly the product, the more people a buying center is apt to contain. Inexpensive products may be bought by low-level managers.

Products that lend themselves to direct marketing are standardized, relatively low-priced, and ordered in small lots from ongoing inventories. Direct marketing in these instances acts as a substitute for personal calls.

Industrial markets are small compared with consumer markets. Goods and services produced for horizontal markets are more apt to use direct marketing methods than those for vertical markets. Direct marketing copy usually is "reason-why," proceeding along rational lines.

Copy made for "straight buys," such as that used in catalogs, has few frills and promotional aspects.

A modern development stemming from computer technology is the lead-tracking program. It determines the success of a firm's prospecting efforts and results in a report of the prospects' buying behavior.

One of the major uses of the business press is lead generation. An important method is the reader service card, also called the "bingo card." If such a card is used, the leads generated must be qualified and followed up. Qualifications are done primarily by phone.

---

## REVIEW QUESTIONS

1. Explain why business-to-business marketing is often described as organizational marketing.
2. Can the direct marketing techniques used by savings banks be used as effectively by investment banks?
3. The company manufacturing Nutrasweet embarked on a direct marketing campaign to stimulate demand. Would a semiconductor manufacturer benefit as much by using the same methods to enhance demand for computers containing the firm's components?
4. When is direct marketing to organizations a substitute for personal selling?
5. What are the advantages and limitations of a database that classifies firms by SIC codes?
6. Describe the duties of each of the following: influencers, deciders, approvers, buyers, and gatekeepers.
7. **a.** Explain the difference between tightly and loosely elicited leads.
   **b.** How many leads should a firm generate and at what rate?
8. State the important objectives of a tracking system.
9. Since business publications have relatively small circulations, they are not capable of covering a market effectively. Comment.
10. Why would small business be more prone to favor reader service cards than large firms?

---

## PROJECT

1. You are the marketing director of the Goldmark Gasket Company of Detroit, Michigan. They have approximately 10,000 current customers (large and small firms) in the manufacturing business.

A gasket is a ring or disk of packing to make a joint or closure watertight or gastight. It is made out of metal, rubber, or plastic. The firm spends around $50,000 per year for advertising. Two salespeople are usually on the road throughout the year seeing their best customers. In addition, five in-house salespeople keep in contact by telephone with customers.

**a.** Name five different options open to the firm for promoting and selling gaskets. List the advantages and disadvantages of each. Remember, all of your customers are large and small manufacturing firms located throughout the United States.

**b.** What types of lists would you secure and why?

**c.** What is your advertising plan for the year? State the sequence of activities you plan to conduct.

**d.** What type of results do you expect?

**e.** Create two promotion pieces, at the minimum, that you would recommend to promote the Goldmark gaskets. It is fine to work in black and white. If you prefer, you may do it in color. A paste job is also approved. Neatness and clarity count as part of the grade.

CHAPTER 17

# International Direct Marketing

> We are in an unprecedented period of accelerated change, perhaps the most breathtaking of which is the swiftness of our rush to all the world's becoming a single economy. Already it may be said that there is no such thing as a U.S. economy, so enmeshed is it in all the other economies of the world. There won't be any such thing as a European economy or Japanese economy or Soviet-bloc economy or Third World economy either.
>
> U.S. companies create and sell $81 billion in goods and services in Japan. Is that part of the U.S. economy or the Japanese economy? Are Korean stocks purchased in London by a Turk part of the Korean, British, or Turkish economy? Of course, they are all part of one economy, the new global economy, and that economy is on a booming course as it races toward the year 2000. . . .
>
> As we turn to the next century, we will witness the linkup of North America, Europe, and Japan to form a golden triangle of free trade.[1]

International direct marketing offers enormous opportunities for business firms. Asian and European marketers are far behind the United States in exploiting this field. According to Arnold L. Fishman, U.S. mail order sales in 1989 were estimated to be $183.30 billion.[2] Table 17-1 shows that Otto Versand has replaced Sears, Roebuck as the top mail order firm as of 1989. Other foreign firms are moving up in the ranking.

Table 17-2 lists U.S. firms marketing abroad and non-U.S. firms marketing in the United States. It appears that financial services, information, education, and collectibles companies operate overseas. Books

**TABLE 17.1. Ten Leading Mail Order Companies Worldwide.**

| Rank | Company Name | Country | Year of Data | Sales ($ millions) | Type of Merchandise |
|---|---|---|---|---|---|
| 1. | Otto Versand* | West Germany | 1988 | 6,600 | General |
| 2. | Quelle | West Germany | 1989 | 5,338 | General |
| 3. | Sears, Roebuck & Co. | United States | 1989 | 3,280 | General, insurance |
| 4. | J.C. Penney | United States | 1989 | 3,170 | General, insurance |
| 5. | United Automobile Association Services | United States | 1989 | 2,738 | Insurance |
| 6. | Time Warner | United States | 1989 | 2,636 | Cable, publishing |
| 7. | Great Universal Stores | United Kingdom | 1989 | 2,173 | General |
| 8. | Bertelsmann | West Germany | 1989 | 1,600 | Publishing |
| 9. | Reader's Digest Association | United States | 1989 | 1,584 | Publishing |
| 10. | Associated Communications | United States | 1989 | 1,546 | Cable |

*Includes Spiegel data.

SOURCE: Arnold L. Fishman, "International Mail Order Guide," *Direct Marketing*, (October 1990), p. 48. Reprinted with permission of Hoke Communications.

1. John Naisbitt and Patricia Aburdene, *Megatrends 2000* (New York: William Morrow & Co., 1990), pp. 19, 23.
2. Arnold L. Fishman, "Mail Order Top 250+," *Direct Marketing* (July 1990), p. 27.

TABLE 17.2. **Global Direct Marketing By U.S. Firms and Non-U.S. Firms.**

| U.S. Direct Marketing Firms Selling Abroad | Non-U.S. Direct Marketing Firms Selling in the United States |
|---|---|
| American Express | Aer Rianta |
| Avon | Bertelsmann |
| Citibank | Jelmoli |
| CBS | Moore Ltd. |
| Encyclopedia Britannica | Patrimonium |
| Franklin Mint | Quelle |
| Grolier | Otto Versand |
| Reader's Digest | |
| Time Warner | |

SOURCE: Arnold L. Fishman, "International Mail Order Guide," *Direct Marketing,* (October 1990), p. 51. Reprinted with permission of Hoke Communications.

and magazines also seem to be very much in demand. In the United States, foreign apparel, foods, drinks, and crafts are strongly sought after, whereas U.S. goods of this nature are not in demand overseas. Foreign cultures are well established in the United States, which probably causes the demand for goods from the home country. Further, the high discretionary income of Americans and the large population result in the desire for foreign goods.

What Table 17-2 does not show is that the United States was the world's largest exporter in 1989, valued at $364.4 billion. There were tens of thousands of small and medium-size companies that sold via direct mail to foreign countries. The Japanese have an affluent middle class that want American goods. L.L. Bean fulfills from the United States all over the world. DenMat sends their dental supply brochure to a market of over 150,000 dentists in three countries. "Shop the World by Mail," a listing of foreign catalogs written in English, was mailed to 200,000 names worldwide in 1991. The four-page piece is sent to the Middle East, the Far East, Europe, and South America. In the United States, Shop by Mail distributes a 40-page catalog of foreign catalogs. See Figure 17-1.

# Benefits of International Business

According to Naisbitt and Aburdene, the world is becoming a single economy. Today there are many enterprises that view the world as their local sphere of activity. This implies that products and services are directed to global wants and needs. There is emphasis on value-enhancing distinction. Also, consumers around the world prefer fewer choices if this results in a lower price. The firm derives many benefits from globalization and standardization.

# Shop the World by Mail

PURCHASE DIRECT AT OUTSTANDING SAVINGS FROM FACTORIES & RETAIL SHOPS AROUND THE WORLD.

FABULOUS FOREIGN CATALOGS IN ENGLISH!

**ENGLAND**

**1. Glorafilia**: England's foremost needlepoint collection. Stunning range of needlepoint and embroidery kits in mouth-watering colors to delight all lovers of this fine craft. Color catalog $4.

**GERMANY**

**2. Willi Geck**: Magnificent 112 page color catalog offers all the best in tableware, collectibles and giftware from Europe's most famous manufacturers. Seventeen shops offer unrivalled savings and selection. $5 refundable.

Shop the World by Mail

**3. Catalogs and Merchandise from around the world!** The fabulous *new 1990 collection* of catalogs from over 25 countries, plus wonderful merchandise from some of your favorite catalogers. Purchase china, crystal, clothing, furniture, handicrafts, jewelry, linens, perfumes, etc. at considerable savings direct from more than 100 factories and retail shops in Canada, Europe and the Orient. Color catalog $4.

**ENGLAND**

**4. Historical Collections**: Gift items from every period of English history. Celtic jewelry to Victorian toys—many are copies of museum pieces; all are authentic replicas. Reasonable prices. 48 page color catalog $4.

**HONG KONG**

**5. Prince Fashions**: Fabulous prices on jewelry, women's clothing, watches and gift items from the largest mail order company in Hong Kong. This is the kind of source one thinks of when equating Hong Kong with wonderful bargains. Color catalog $3.

**THAILAND**

Johny's Gems

**6. Johny's Gems:** Thailand is THE place to buy jewelry and embassy wives in Bangkok highly recommended this shop for unbeatable selection, great prices and incomparable service. Rings, bracelets and necklaces set with every imaginable kind of precious and semi-precious stone. Color catalog. $4.

**ENGLAND**

**7. British Museum:** Authentic museum replicas reproduced from our finest and most unusual treasures. Unique, reasonably priced pieces include jewelry, sculptures, gifts, etc. NEW Color catalog AVAILABLE AUG. 1ST. $4.

**IRELAND**

**8. Blarney Gift Catalog:** Experience the delights of shopping in Ireland! Waterford and Galway crystal, Belleek, Dresden, Irish jewelry, wool knits, blankets, rugs—at duty-free export prices. $4.

**HONG KONG**

A. ANDREWS & CO.

**9. A. Andrews:** THE mail order source for diplomatic personnel for over 20 years. Incredible *380 page* catalog offers china, crystal, clothing, jewelry, furniture, giftware, cameras, and more at low Hong Kong prices. Color catalog $10 refundable.

**ENGLAND**

**10. Naturally British**: High quality originals hand-made in Great Britain by skilled craftspeople. Exclusive range of merchandise. Furniture, keepsakes, clothing, jewelry, pottery and toys. Color catalog $4.

**ENGLAND**

THE NATIONAL TRUST

**11. The National Trust:** England's most famous historical country homes inspire this collection of traditional foods, exclusive knitwear, unique china and porcelain, unusual stationery and quality reproductions. Color catalog $4.

**HONG KONG**

**12. Handart Embroideries:** Great, great values on the finest hand-embroidered tablecloths, placemats, blouses, handkerchiefs—all at bargain Hong Kong prices. Illus. price list $3.

**SCOTLAND**

**13. Stockwell China Bazaar:** An unsurpassed collection of fine china and porcelain, crystal, silver and gifts from the most famous manufacturers in England and Europe at fantastic Scottish prices. Splendid color catalog. $4.

**GERMANY**

**14. Hummel:** For the collector or the investor, a sweeping selection of the enchanting figurines first created by Sister M.I. Hummel. Priceless miniatures at very affordable prices. Collector's catalog $4.

**THAILAND**

**15. Venus Jewelry:** Precious gems handcrafted into stunning rings by one of Bangkok's leading manufacturers/retailers. We have supplied U.S. military personnel for many years and guarantee that our prices are a fraction of the U.S. cost. Color catalog $4.

**HONG KONG**

MAJESTIC FURNITURE CO. LTD.

**16. Majestic Furniture:** Handcarved rosewood and teakwood tables, ornate Coromandel screens inlaid with mother-of-pearl, chairs, desks, buffets, cabinets, etc. Unusual pieces to accent any home all at famous Hong Kong savings. Color catalog $3.

**ITALY**

**17. Leather School**: A monastery school offering exceptional values on fine Florentine leather goods, leather bags, luggage, desk sets, albums, wallets, etc. Color catalog $5 refundable.

**HONG KONG**

**18. Amazing Grace Elephant Company**: Wonderfully different gift catalog offering Asian handicrafts, antiques, jewelry and clothing—an extravaganza of unique gifts at non-extravagant prices. Delightful color catalog. $4.

**ENGLAND**

**19. Royal Academy of Arts:** Innovative museum shop with many original items designed or decorated by Academy members. Exciting collection includes china, crystal, pottery, clothing, toys, posters and more. Color catalog $4.

**HONG KONG**

**20. Banyan Tree:** Wonderful source for exotic home furnishings! The best, old and new, gathered from China, Thailand and India. An Aladdin's Cave of endless delights. Color catalog $4.

**ENGLAND**

**21. The National Gallery:** One of England's most popular museums since 1824 offers this reasonably priced selection of gifts including cards, calendars, paperweights, desk accessories, games, prints, videos, etc. $4.

**HONG KONG**

**22. Wilco:** A shopper's paradise of handmade items from Hong Kong and mainland China. Jewelry, cloisonne, table linens, and more—all at very affordable Hong Kong prices. Color catalog. $4.

Catalogs come directly from overseas. Allow up to 12 weeks for delivery. When charging an order of $25 or more, call (919)467-3165. To request your catalogs circle the proper numbers, fill in the information below and enclose payment.

| | | | |
|---|---|---|---|
| 1 | $ 4.00 | 12 | $3.00 |
| 2 | 5.00 | 13 | 4.00 |
| 3 | 4.00 | 14 | 4.00 |
| 4 | 4.00 | 15 | 4.00 |
| 5 | 3.00 | 16 | 3.00 |
| 6 | 4.00 | 17 | 5.00 |
| 7 | 4.00 | 18 | 4.00 |
| 8 | 4.00 | 19 | 4.00 |
| 9 | 10.00 | 20 | 4.00 |
| 10 | 4.00 | 21 | 4.00 |
| 11 | 4.00 | 22 | 4.00 |

**Total Catalogs:** ______ (How Many)

**Total Cost of Catalogs Circled:** $______

**Overseas Handling Fee:** $ 2.00

**Total Amount Enclosed:** $______

(PLEASE PRINT)

For information on our **Shop The World Club** and fabulous 1990 shopping journeys, check here ____ and add $1 to your order.

NAME ______

ADDRESS ______

CITY ______

STATE ______ ZIP ______

*MAIL TO:* **Shop The World By Mail** Box 5549, Dept. AG0, Cary, N.C. 27511

**FIGURE 17-1 "Shop the World by Mail" Ad**
*Source*: Reprinted with permission by Shop the World by Mail.

## Profits

Overseas markets open up new opportunities for a firm. Economies of scale in production and marketing usually result in extra profits. Standardization leads to cost reduction. Excess capacity can now result in extra net earnings by sending abroad the supply of unsold goods. Many companies today depend on foreign markets for more than half of their sales. A silver craftsman with a business in Tel Aviv sells his figures in the United States and England via a catalog. An 800 number is provided for customers to call the business abroad and place orders.

## Growth

American firms that want to expand find the U.S. market saturated. So why not go to countries with people that have the necessary purchasing power? Japan presents a golden opportunity. Direct marketing has grown there at an average annual rate of 16 percent during the 1980s according to the Japan Direct Marketing Association. They estimated gross sales of 1.4 trillion yen (approximately $10 billion) in 1989. Among those already having joint venture arrangements are Spiegel and The Sharper Image. Others researching the Japanese market include L.L. Bean, Lands' End, and Williams-Sonoma.

## Survival

Most businesses look to overseas markets to survive. Other countries are not as blessed as the United States in terms of discretionary income, large population and market size, relative political and economic stability, and a high level of consumption. This leads foreign firms to swamp U.S. households with direct mail. An unbelievable number of Hong Kong custom tailors provide mail order services. Tailors from Hong Kong Panee's Clothiers, for example, travel throughout the United States year-round. They are in Nanuet, New York, on Friday; in Montvale, New Jersey, on Saturday and Sunday; and in Morristown, New Jersey, on Monday. House calls are made by appointment. Delivery normally takes 7 to 10 weeks, but orders can be expedited. Their suits start at $299. U.S. magazines such as *Readers Digest, Business Week, Time, Newsweek*, and *National Geographic* are in great demand in Europe. In the United Kingdom magazines are bought at stands, but in many of the other countries they are bought by subscription.

## Diversification

Overseas sales can help to stabilize risk and revenue fluctuations due to cyclical factors, technology changes, economic conditions, and seasonality. Microbits is a Canadian cataloger that markets microcomputer supplies in Canada. To enter the European and Far East markets they entered into a merger with Misco, a British cataloger active in the overseas market. This venture diversified Microbits' markets.

Day-Timers reportedly sends "millions of pieces of mail" to U.S. executives each month and mails their catalogs to middle and upper level managers in the United Kingdom. In order to diversify, Day-Timers has also been mailing to Australia about three times a year over the past two years.

Direct marketing campaigns flow in both directions. For example, Fukutake Publishing of Japan dropped 300,000 pieces in its second U.S. direct marketing campaign, targeting parents and grandparents for its Challenge Plus educational products. The direct mail campaign was supplemented with direct response advertising in such magazines as *Parade* and *Parents*. Direct response television advertising is also being considered. Challenge Plus is a continuity club based on one used in Japan for the last 20 years. It teaches children math and science at a cost of $192 per year.

## Improved Technology

The quest for global information and knowledge will continue to drive the improvements in telecommunications and computers. As many as 8,000 conversations can be carried on a single fiber-optic cable compared to 48 for a copper cable. Advancements here lead to cost and time savings to business. "We are laying the foundations for an international information highway system. . . . We are moving toward the capability to communicate anything to anyone, anywhere, by any form—voice, data, text, or image at the speed of light."[3]

Today, one can place an international toll-free call to a hotel such as the Elbow Beach in Bermuda for reservations. One can find out room availability and costs immediately. Long & Foster, a real estate firm based in Fairfax, Virginia, established international toll-free service in February 1986 from West Germany to their office to supply housing information in the United States. Corporate and military personnel could call the United States if they were planning to move here.

Some direct marketers such as Otto Versand (Germany) and Quelle (Germany) have found favorable results from the videolog, a shop-at-home video catalog. Royal Silk found that orders through video catalogs averaged around $100, compared to $70 for print catalog orders in 1987. Computers today track such factors of customer purchases as recency, frequency and monetary value, lifestyles, attitudes, and interests. Today, sharp business people know their customers' wants and needs.

---

3. Naisbitt and Aburdene, *op. cit.*, p. 23.

### Economies of Scale in Production and Marketing

The Black & Decker Manufacturing Company gained significant production cost savings when they instituted a global strategy. The firm was able to reduce the number of motor sizes for the European market from 250 to 8 and to downsize 15 models to 8. The Colgate-Palmolive Company introduced its Colgate tartar control toothpaste in over 40 countries, each of which chose one of two ads. By running the same commercial in different countries, the company saved millions in advertising costs.[4] Such a campaign helps brand-name recognition as well as offering a uniform global image.

## Foreign-Market Entry Strategies

A company must choose an entry strategy when it makes the commitment to go international. This decision must be based on an analysis of company resources, the degree of management commitment, and an analysis of market potential. There are six foreign-market entry strategies:

1. *Exporting.* A company sells its products from its home base without any organization personnel overseas.
2. *Licensing.* A licensor allows a foreign firm to manufacture or service a product or service for sale in the licensee's country.
3. *Joint venture.* An enterprise is formed by two or more investors for conducting a business by sharing ownership and control.
4. *Contract manufacturing.* A company contracts a local manufacturer to produce goods for them.
5. *Direct investment.* A company acquires an existing company or builds a new company from the ground up.
6. *Management contracting.* A contract is signed with local foreign people or the foreign government to manage the business.

### Exporting

L. L. Bean, a mail order company located in Freeport, Maine, fulfills its orders from the United States all over the world. The Arctic Trading Company located in Churchill, Canada, probably the northernmost trading post in North America, sells 75 percent of its products to U.S. customers and receives orders from Germany, Sweden, and Saudi Arabia. Artic Trading built its mail list from a $5,000 ad in the *New Yorker* and free advertising in the form of media coverage.[5]

---

4. John Marcom, Jr., "Cable and Satellites Are Opening Europe to TV Commercials," *Wall Street Journal* (December 27, 1987), p. 1.
5. Lucille de Saint Andre, "Arctic Trading Co. Gets Most of Its $500,000 Business from U.S.," *DM News* (November 15, 1986), p. 69.

Exporting is used by first-timers in the international marketplace. It helps to clear excess product capacity and stabilize revenue fluctuations due to seasonality, economic conditions, and technological changes. Companies wishing to get information and help in selling their products overseas should contact the U.S. Department of Commerce (DOC), which sponsors local exporting seminars, overseas trade fairs, and trade missions. They provide extensive published information about foreign marketing opportunities and business practices. Other sources of help include Angela Draper-Singh, Director, International Operations, Direct Marketing Association, Inc.; international direct marketing agencies such as Ogilvy & Mather Direct Response, Inc., Wunderman Worldwide, and Dillon, Agnew & Morton, an international list broker. There is danger in moving into foreign markets without thorough analysis. U.S. firms have trouble in mailing to Western Europe due to a variety of government and postal regulations.

Legal restrictions against direct mail are tighter in most countries than in the United States. British, U.S., and Dutch direct marketers are worried about proposals for a Pan-European data protection commission, which they fear could restrict database activity in 1992. The law, which applies to both direct marketing and all computerized use of personal information, requires that consumers have access on demand to any data being held on them. Further, it provides for fines and criminal penalties for failure to register such data with the data protection registrar.

## Licensing

Licensing is similar to franchising in that locals are authorized to manufacture or sell products. The right to use a patent or trademark is granted to a foreign company under a license agreement. The Sharper Image has licensing agreements in Germany, Japan, and Switzerland "wherein local firms produce and mail out catalogs in the respective native languages."[6] *Penthouse* magazine licenses Germany, Italy, Spain, Japan, and other countries to put out their own editions. Licensing is the only way to tap into the markets in Communist countries. It is a good alternative to foreign production in an environment where there is inflation, increasing government regulation, and skilled labor shortages. Licensing royalties are guaranteed as a percentage of sales, whereas income from investments fluctuate and are risky. Disadvantages include licensors' lack of control, limited royalty rates, and possible future competition by the licensee.

---

6. Paul Miller, "Border Crossings," *Catalog Age* (April 1990), pp. 67–69.

## Joint Venture

Companies recognize that marketing alliances with a foreign company can provide easy access to a foreign market, circumvent tariffs and quotas, offer rapid growth and market coverage, and open opportunities for a company in a market that prohibits wholly owned enterprises. The joint venture of Microbits and Misco led to Microbits having greater resources and outlets for its products relative to its competition. Both companies gained in that each was a specialist in different areas. The Sharper Image has worked out a cooperative venture with catalogers in Germany and Switzerland. Recreational Equipment Inc. (REI) and Austad's (a golf supply cataloger) mailed their catalogs together to names on both of their Japanese lists.

## Contract Manufacturing

Companies have goods manufactured abroad since it allows quick entry into the target country, avoids local ownership problems, offers tax incentives to take advantage of lower labor costs, and satisfies laws requiring the product to be manufactured locally for it to be sold in that country. For example, firms contract manufacturing in Japan to produce and distribute their goods there through loyal and established channels.

## Direct Investment

Otto Versand, a company based in Germany, has become the largest mail order company in the world probably by buying existing companies or building new ones. In 1982, the firm bought Spiegel of Chicago; in 1987 they entered into a joint venture with Sumitomo to set up Otto Sumisho, and they have a 51 percent interest in the new company. Otto Versand owns mail order companies or is part owner of direct marketing firms in Belgium, France, Italy, Japan, the United States, and Spain.

R.R. Donnelley & Sons expanded into the European market by buying four printing plants in the United Kingdom over the years. In October 1990 the Chicago-based printer purchased Business Mail Data Services Ltd. of Branford, England, to enter the European database management industry.

## Management Contracting

Day-Timers, a firm located in East Texas, Pennsylvania, sends millions of pieces of mail to U.S. executives each month. To sell to executives in the United Kingdom, Canada, and Australia, the firm opened offices there because "we need to have people who know the culture and can take incoming calls." Mary Ann Kleinfelder added, "There are cultural differences in even seemingly very similar countries like America, the United Kingdom, and Canada."[7] Ogilvy & Mather Direct has been setting up offices throughout the world while hiring local talent in such places as Germany, Holland, France, Thailand, New Zealand, and the U.S.S.R.

# Direct Marketing in Specific Countries

A spirit of free trade is sweeping the world, with the mail order market providing many attractive opportunities. Business firms and private consumers are seeking additional values such as exclusivity, uniqueness, information, and quality service. A firm has to be able to demonstrate superior reliability, ease of repair and supply, cost savings, improvement in process, and possession of the necessary data to advise customers.

Table 17-3 shows the export and import activities conducted by the United States with its major trading partners. In addition, it specifies the international mail order dollar value by country. For example, Canada, which has been and still is America's biggest trading partner, did a $6.6 billion international mail order business in 1989.

## Canada

The U.S.–Canada Free Trade Agreement signed in January 1989, phases out tariffs between the two nations by 1998 and thereby provides a new opening for doing business. Canada has a population of 26.7 million affluent and middle-class people, 75 percent of whom speak English and are quite similar to their U.S. neighbors. Canadians love our goods and oversized mailings. People there enjoy answering surveys. Canadian list brokers and letter shops do a first-class job.

Day-Timers mails between 3 million and 4 million catalogs to Canada, doing about 10 percent of its business there. Inmac, a computer supplies and accessories cataloger, maintains headquarters there as well as in other foreign countries, publishing specific catalogs for each country. Recreational Equipment Inc. (REI) has been successful in Canada, drawing both response rates and average orders that are 50 percent higher than those from U.S. buyers.[8] The direct mail business is well established in Canada. Approximately 130 U.S. catalogers presently do mail order business there.[9]

---

7. Terry Brennan, "Day-Timers Makes Foray Into U.K. With First 100,000-Piece Mail Test," *DM News* (November 15, 1989), p.14.
8. Paul Miller, "Border Crossings" *Catalog Age* (April 1990), pp. 67–68.
9. Susan Bass, "Guide on Foreign MO" *Catalog Business* (April 1, 1989) pp. 18–19.

**Table 17.3. International Markets Statistics.**

| Country | 1990 Population (millions) | 1989 Exports by U.S. (billions) | 1989 Imports by U.S. (billions) | International Mail Order (billions) | Year |
|---|---|---|---|---|---|
| **Europe** | | | | | |
| Belgium | 9.9 | 8.7 | 4.6 | 0.629 | 1988 |
| France | 56.0 | 11.6 | 13.0 | 6.019 | 1989 |
| Germany | 79.5 | 17.0 | 25.0 | 13.512* | 1989 |
| Italy | 58.0 | 7.2 | 11.9 | 1.239 | 1989 |
| Netherlands | 14.9 | 11.4 | 4.8 | 0.840 | 1988 |
| Norway | 4.2 | | | 0.448 | 1988 |
| Spain | 39.0 | 4.8 | 3.3 | 0.346 | 1989 |
| Sweden | 8.5 | 3.1 | 4.9 | 1.077 | 1989 |
| Switzerland | 6.7 | 4.9 | 4.7 | 1.039 | 1989 |
| United Kingdom | 57.0 | 20.9 | 18.2 | 6.360 | 1989 |
| **Non-Europe** | | | | | |
| Canada | 26.7 | 78.6 | 88.2 | 6.600 | 1989 |
| Japan | 123.6 | 44.6 | 93.6 | 11.443 | 1989 |
| **United States** | 250.0 | 364.4 | 472.9 | 137.39 | 1989 |

* West Germany

SOURCES: Population: *1991 Information Please Almanac*, 1990 World Population Information Sheet, Washington, D.C.: Publications Reference Bureau.

Exports/Imports: Joanne Tucker, "Favorable Trends in U.S. Trade Expected to continue in 1990," *Business America*, (April 23, 1990), p. 5.

International Mail Order/Year: Arnold Fishman, "International Mail Order Guide," *Direct Marketing* (October 1990), p. 48.

There are some problems involved with direct mail to Canada. Approximately 25 percent of the people speak and read only French. Further, many still write the King's English, which includes such variant spellings as *colour, flavour,* and *cheque*. Thus, if the direct mail package is done in America, the people who read it may focus on the word rather than the message.[10] In addition, there are many small ethnic groups for which few mailing lists exist. Also, toll-free telephone numbers, WATS, and first and third-class mail cost quite a bit more there than in the United States.

## United Kingdom

The number of British direct marketing agencies has risen to 50. As Table 17-3 indicates, the United Kingdom did $6.36 billion in the international mail order business in 1989. The expertise of the direct marketing people is unmatched in the rest of Europe. Agencies such as Ogilvy & Mather Direct Worldwide, whose organization is shown in Figure 17-2, are well established in Great Britain as well as in 32 other foreign countries.

10. Lois K. Geller, "Direct Marketing, Canadian Style" *Target Marketing* (May 1990), p. 52.

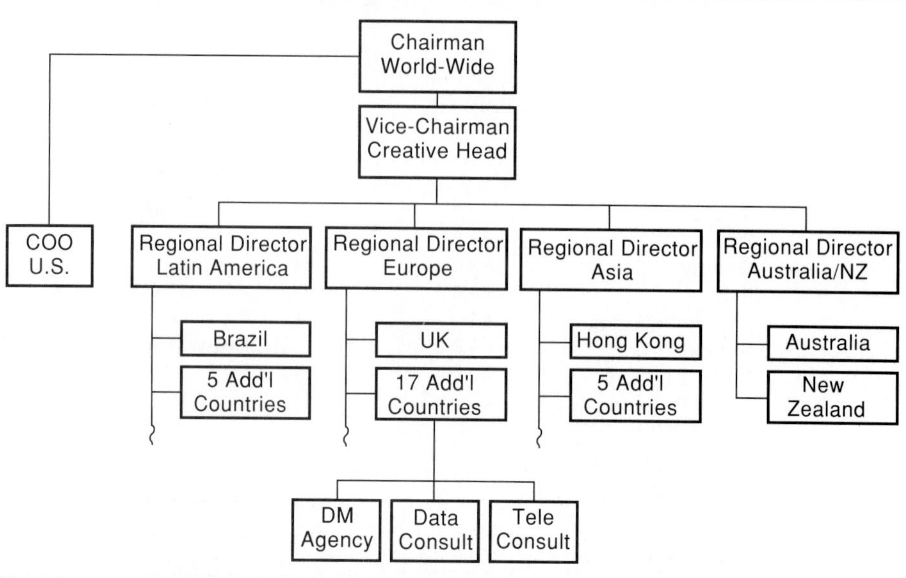


**FIGURE 17-2 Ogilvy & Mather Direct Worldwide**
*Source*: Reprinted with permission of Ogilvy & Mather Direct Worldwide.

It is of the utmost importance that corporations in foreign countries hire local people and have local marketing teams or local offices in place. Due to different cultures and languages, the needs and buying behaviors are significantly different in other nations. American Express's business is built around global strategies that are locally relevant, and services are locally delivered. According to Thomas S. Cash, senior vice president of worldwide marketing, American Express Travel Related Services Co. Ltd., "Within this strategy we have in place local marketing teams in each international market who work with direct mail agencies in their markets to create packs, in local languages, which are totally relevant and applicable to that marketplace."[11]

What are the primary applications of direct marketing in the United Kingdom? As in the United States, financial services, insurance, computer products, mail order companies, book clubs, charities, and some retailers use this technique. More offers go to business customers than to consumers.

A survey done by the D.M. Group (UK) Ltd. found that U.K. direct marketers increased their activities in 1990 and expected direct market-

11. Marilyn Much, "American Express Set to Conquer New Europe" *DM News* (September 24, 1990), pp. 31, 34, 36.

ing to be even more important in 1991. A damper might be the economy. From those that responded to the study, 96 percent used direct mail. Both newspapers and inserts were utilized by 70 percent of respondents. Telemarketing was used by 48 percent, followed by television and household delivery, at 26 percent each. Radio received 17 percent utilization.[12] More than 700 million items are mailed each year. Fifty percent of this business is handled by 100 list brokers. Approximately 4,000 lists are available.[13] This suggests that direct marketing is at a mature stage in the United Kingdom.

Newspapers and inserts are very popular direct marketing tools in England as well as in Europe as a whole. The average person in the United Kingdom reads two or three newspapers a day. Unfortunately, however, very few readers own credit cards.

Government and postal regulations in Western Europe are much more stringent than in the United States. For example, sweepstakes entry in the United Kingdom has to be free, and no proof of purchase can be required. Yet the post office is very helpful to direct marketers. It provides quick delivery, discounts, and a new presort rebate system. Lists cannot be exchanged freely, nor can the data in them be given out. The British passed their own Data Protection Act in 1984. However, it is not as stringent as those in other European countries or the one expected to be passed by the European Council. For example, Germany requires that consumers give approval before their names can be traded to third parties.

## Germany

Direct marketing has been very beneficial to Germany. As Table 17-3 shows, international mail orders came to approximately $13.512 billion in 1989, and that was without East Germany. Otto Versand and Quelle were first and second in the ranking of the 10 leading mail order companies worldwide. Both sell general merchandise. Another German company, Bertelsmann, was listed eighth.

Quelle, the German catalog house, is trying to increase its German-speaking customer base in the United States by 20 percent per year. Most of these customers tend to have an "affinity" for German products. Many of these buyers were obtained through newspaper ads for the catalog.[14] Similarly, American firms are seeking out English-speaking customers in Germany, France, and Spain.

---

12. Ray Schultz, "British DMers Predict a Busy 1991, Rate Vendors in D.M. Group Survey" *DM News* (October 22, 1990), p. 6.
13. Frank MacGinty, "When the Walls Come Down," *Direct Marketing* (February 1990), pp. 22, 24.
14. Ray Schultz, "Quelle Is Seeking Ways to Increase German Speaking U.S. Audience" *DM News* (October 15, 1990), p. 2.

Germany has over 100 direct marketing agencies and a comparable number of mailing houses. Yet it only has six to eight list brokers selling very defined lists. In Germany, a database owner must notify every new potential entry when he or she is to be added to a list. The subject may delete any information on file. Further, a list owner must get permission from each person before selling any information to a third party. The data protection laws of Germany are among the strictest in the world. Most countries' data protection laws are much tighter than those in the United States, which imposes very few legal restrictions on list owners.

The post office in Germany is very cooperative to direct marketers. It gives rebates of up to 30 percent depending on the type of mail order used and whether or not presorting is done.[15] In doing business overseas, firms must be aware of the postal and legal regulations. For example, the words *free* and *gift* in Germany cannot be connected to the sale of a product. Items of a negligible value (3 percent of the product price) are permitted if they are used with the product. Despite these regulations, companies such as American Express, Reader's Digest, Franklin Mint, and National Pen Corp. have been successful in Germany.

## France, The Netherlands, Norway, Spain, and Italy

Significant growth has occurred in database management and electronic media in European direct marketing. Yet the countries in Europe are far behind the United States in exploiting the opportunities in this field. This is due to the fact that the Europeans started much later in the use of direct marketing. They have benefited by installing the latest technology in telemarketing, computers, and printing. List availability is limited in these countries due to their data protection laws.

Since 1985 France's national videotex network can be accessed around the clock from anywhere in France and from abroad via a simple telephone call using common Minitel terminals. The used car business was put on-line in late July and responded to 5,000 inquiries the first month. The system is supported by advertising fees. There is no fee for accessing the used car database except for the cost of a local phone call (7 cents).[16]

Fragrances from Hermes, a Parisian company, has been marketing to U.S. customers since 1986. Customers can simply dial a 1-800 telephone number to purchase clothes or perfumes and can choose their purchases from an elegant, annually designed magalog produced in

15. Frank MacGinty, "If the Walls Come Down," *Direct Marketing* (December 1989), pp. 53–55.
16. Kevin Hanley, "Nouveau Way to Sell Used Cars," *Zip Target Marketing* (November 1985), p. 64.

France. In 1987 the firm mailed 155,000 copies of the magalog to U.S. customers.[17] Galleries Lafayette, "the Bloomingdale's of Paris," tested the U.S. market by advertising an international 800 number to sell its "faux furs."[18] Manufacturers from the Netherlands, Norway, and Spain have sold their crystal and glassware through catalogs for at least 20 years.

The postal services in these countries are excellent, except for Italy. Here the service is unreliable, inefficient, and often hampered by strikes. This is one of the major reasons why direct marketing has not been successful in Italy. In France, the Netherlands, Norway, and Spain bulk mailers receive discounts from the post office. Figure 17-3 shows a Norwegian direct mail promotion for film development. Note the similarity to promotions found in America.

Coupons are a popular form of advertising in France. The majority of newspapers in France contain color supplements. This is done to compete with the glossy advertising in news magazines. In Spain there is a lack of magazines. As a result, Sunday newspapers are filled with supplements.

## Japan

The Japanese market offers direct marketers some major opportunities and one of the most difficult challenges. Japan's population stood at 123.6 million in 1990. It has a large, affluent middle class that wants American goods. Table 17-3 indicates that the Japanese international mail order business came to $11.443 billion in 1989. Mail order has been growing at an average rate of 16 percent per year since 1980, according to the Japan Direct Marketing Association. There were 25 large, established direct marketing companies in Japan in 1990.[19]

Japan's channels of distribution present a formidable barrier. Other obstacles include cultural differences, a different language and currency, no rate reductions for bulk mailings, and the difficulty of securing a reliable list. The lack of an accurate and up-to-date list squanders all of the money invested in a direct mail campaign.

One way firms have handled the channel dilemma is through joint ventures or by using licensees or distributorships. The Sharper Image has had licensees in Germany, Switzerland, and Japan since 1986.[20]

---

17. Michele Whitney, "Direct Marketing Becomes Essential in U.S. for Hermes, Paris Retailer," *DM News* (April 1, 1988), p. 27.
18. Lou Grabowsky, "Globalization: Reshaping the Retail Marketplace," Arthur Anderson & Co. *Retailing Issues Letter* (November 1989), p. 2.
19. Stanley J. Fenvessy, "Fulfillment Lessons From Japan" *DM News* (December 3, 1990), pp. 14–22.
20. Bass, *op.cit.*

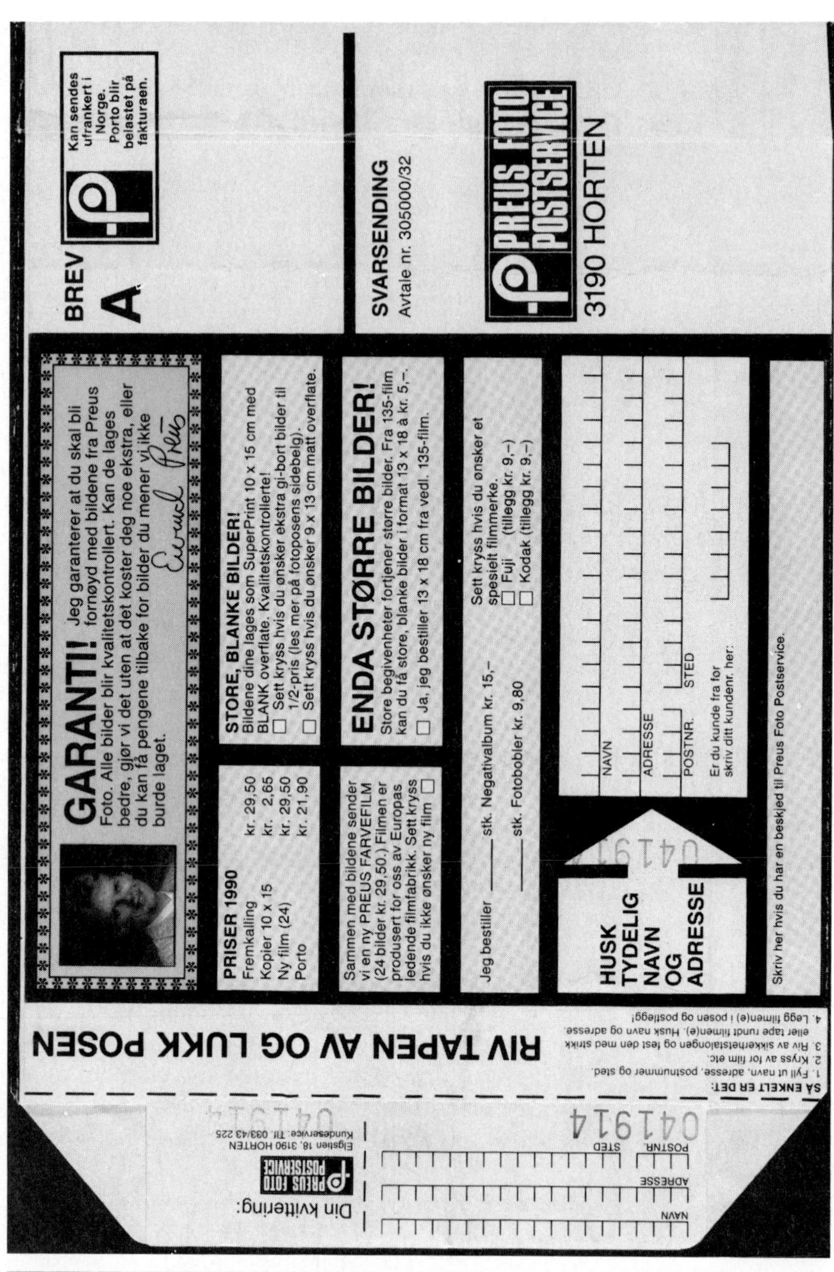


**FIGURE 17-3 Norwegian Film Development Firm Promotes by Mail**
*Source*: Reprinted with permission of Preus Foto.

**FIGURE 17-3 (Continued)**

Other firms that have a licensee agreement in Japan include the Austad Co., Eddie Bauer, and Day-Timers. One of the cultural differences is that the Japanese favor face-to-face marketing. A way of getting around this problem as well as that of not having a reliable list is to place inserts in Japanese newspapers. The advertisement should be in Japanese, and the payment should be in Japanese currency. Further, the compelling benefits of buying the advertised product should be stressed. The Japanese will buy the product if it is to their advantage, and the purchases will produce a mailing list. Direct response advertising in newspapers through inserts is currently the most popular form of direct marketing in Japan, according to Michael Golding of Sedona International.[21] Excellent sources of Asian lists are Amercian business publications such as *Business Week, Fortune,* and the *Asian Wall Street Journal.*

Other sources are national trade publications. Black Box Corp. uses a Japanese mailing team to build up its list.[22]

Catalogs for apparel and kitchenware did well during the 1980s in Japan. To overcome the high postal rates, direct marketers such as The Sharper Image have come out with a magalog to qualify for magazine rates. This requires at least a 50 percent editorial content. Some catalogers are currently experimenting with videotex catalogs.

# Summary

International direct marketing provides significant opportunities for corporations. U.S. mail order sales were estimated to be $183.30 billion in 1989. Companies that provide financial services, information, education, and collectibles operate overseas.

The corporation derives many benefits from globalization and standardization. These include growth, survival, diversification, improved technology, and economies of scale in production and marketing.

Firms that decide to do international direct marketing have to select an entry strategy. A firm can use one of six foreign-market entry strategies or any combination thereof. These include exporting, licensing, joint venture, contract manufacturing, direct investment, and management contracting. Only in exporting can a company sell its products from its home country without sending any of its people overseas.

Regulations concerning business mailing lists vary significantly from country to country. For example, the United States has no data protec-

21. "Marketer Discusses Rules for Success in Japan" *DMA'S Direct Line,* vol. 6, no. 1. (January 1989), p. 2.
22. Miller, *op. cit.*

tion laws, whereas the majority of the European countries have stringent regulations.

The United States has the highest mail order penetration in the world. Second in international mail order sales as of 1989 was Germany, recording $13.512 billion. Japan was third at $11.443 billion, followed by Canada with $6.6 billion. The United Kingdom was fifth with $6.36 billion. Significant growth in international direct marketing has occurred in the aforementioned countries over the last 10 years. Other countries are starting to derive the benefits of direct marketing.

## REVIEW QUESTIONS

1. Discuss the following statement by Naisbitt and Aburdene: "We are in an unprecedented period of accelerated change."
2. What are the direct marketing products and services that the United States sells abroad and that non-U.S. firms sell in America? Explain.
3. **a.** List the benefits of international business.
   **b.** Discuss three benefits in detail. Provide examples for each one other than those listed in this textbook.
4. Explain how exporting goods and services is different from the other foreign-market strategies. Provide three new examples.
5. Discuss the strategies of licensing, joint venture, contract manufacturing, and direct investment. Include new examples for each one.
6. Why should firms interested in selling abroad first try Canada? Explain.
7. What are the benefits to a direct marketer of selling in the United Kingdom? Explain.
8. Discuss the differences in the regulations concerning business mailing lists between the United States and Germany.
9. Discuss the differences in the post office services provided to direct marketers in Germany, Italy, and France.
10. Why is it difficult for direct marketers to enter the Japanese market? What are some solutions to the problem?

# APPENDIX F

# Legal Aspects of International Direct Marketing

John S. Manna, J.D.

## INTRODUCTION

This appendix will familiarize you with the special types of legal issues facing companies involved in international direct marketing. Awareness of these issues and the methods of recognizing and handling them will help international direct marketers avoid unnecessary business disruption, financial loss, and legal penalties.

Laws relating to international direct marketing vary (and often conflict) in purpose, emphasis, and scope from nation to nation. The large number of existing nations makes these laws a maze in which direct marketers can become lost and confused. Various international treaties and conventions add to the large volume of regulations affecting international direct marketers. The rapid pace at which these laws are created and changed further increases the difficulties for direct marketers.

In such an unstable and expanding environment, it would be of little value simply to describe the current laws that affect international direct marketers in each nation. The list would be outdated by the time of publication, and such a description would be too extensive to be of practical use. This is generally true of any area of international business law, and

---

The author is an assistant professor of law at the Colleges of Business Administration of St. John's University. He also is a partner in the law firm of Wander & Manna and specializes in international business law. The author gratefully acknowledges the extensive research assistance given by Janet S. Poriadjian and Sylvia Cuevas.

it should alert you to the need to constantly update your knowledge of the current law in your own country and in foreign countries by retaining attorneys who specialize in these matters.

Rather, this appendix will familiarize you with the general categories of legal issues facing international direct marketers with specific nations used only as examples. This approach will sensitize your ability to recognize legal problems at an early stage, and it will provide suggestions for minimizing the negative effects of legal issues. You will gain a practical and conceptual understanding of the various aspects of these legal issues that will be adaptable to future experience in different nations and with changing laws.

---

## PRIVACY OF INFORMATION

U.S. notions about privacy, as in many other areas of law, must be discarded for the marketer to comprehend the extremely different approaches that foreign nations take to privacy issues. Today, the United States has no broad national privacy protection law. U.S. protections are limited to piecemeal state and federal legislation in some legal areas, a loose patchwork of regulatory privacy protections, and an embryonic theory of a Constitutional right to privacy that is being developed by case law. The lack of broad privacy regulation in the United States is also partially due to the distaste Americans generally have for government involvement in business affairs. The U.S. approach is more favorable to self-regulation by business industries and associations.

The European approach to privacy issues is far different from that of the United States. Broad protection of personal privacy is extremely important to many Europeans. European nations have passed strict privacy laws that place great financial and bureaucratic hardships on businesses and individuals alike. Despite these hardships, strict and broad privacy laws are popular throughout most of Europe, especially in the north.

Member nations of the Council of Europe are required to pass national laws that meet the minimum requirements of the 1981 Convention for the Protection of Individuals with Regard to Automatic Processing of Personal Data. The convention requires that individuals have the ability to access and correct any information about themselves, and that personal information cannot be used without the subject's permission. As of 1990, 7 of the 12 member nations of the European Community had passed national data protections laws broadly protecting the privacy of individuals and some businesses.

GREAT BRITAIN. Great Britain's 1984 Data Protection Act is a relatively mild European privacy law, although it exceeds the requirements of the convention. It does not require a business to notify consumers when their names will be used for the purposes of the business. However, it does require a business to notify consumers that their names may be transferred to other parties at the time a sale is made. This gives individuals the right to decide whether they want such information released. If a business does not give the required notice to a consumer, it must solicit and obtain the consumer's express consent (e.g., by checking a "yes" box on a printed form) before releasing to third parties any information about the consumer. Such consent is called a *positive option* and is very difficult to obtain since direct mail response to such solicitations usually is below 10 percent.

A *negative option* is required when data are collected involuntarily, such as pursuant to law. Negative options require the recipient to send a "no" response in order to keep his or her name and information from being released. Direct marketers prefer negative options because the negative response rate usually is less than 25 percent.

GERMANY. Germans are far more serious about privacy protection than the British. Germany's federal constitution specifically guarantees individual privacy. Germany has adopted a very strict federal privacy law that allows Germans to limit the use of their personal information even by state agencies, except for criminal and national matters. It requires that individuals be notified when an entity holds information about them. Germans also have the right to access and correct this information.

German states are free to pass privacy laws that are stricter than the federal law. Many states have done so, and some require the restrictive positive option–style consent in many situations.

OTHER NATIONS. Broad national privacy laws have been adopted by many nations, including Denmark and Australia. French law limits the exchange of information about noncustomers of a business. Businesses may compile and use information about their own customers and may exchange basic information such as names, addresses, and phone numbers. However, other types of information needed to create useful character profiles may not be exchanged.

Austria has one of the toughest national privacy laws. It requires the restrictive positive option–style consent in nearly all situations where information about individuals is used.

Nations in Asia, Latin America, and Africa generally have not shown much eagerness to pass privacy laws.

THE EUROPEAN COMMUNITY PROPOSAL. December 31, 1992, is the target date for the centralization of many of the European Community's regulatory and financial matters. Many new laws will apply throughout all European Community member nations. A draft proposal has been made to adopt an EC privacy law, and its chances of passage, with some modifications, are high.

The law would establish a code of conduct applicable to all direct marketers located in any EC nation. The law would give individuals strict privacy rights. Individuals would have the right to be informed of details regarding the purpose and use of information compiled about them, and individual preferences would have to be noted and followed. Some believe that this law could require a business to inform subject individuals each time a mailing is made to them. Certainly, a business would have to obtain the subject's consent to its use of sensitive personal information at one time or another.

The accuracy and currency of information would be the responsibility of direct marketers. It is possible that the use of merge-purge and profile technology would be prohibited entirely.

This draft privacy law most reflects the current, strict German law. It poses tremendous problems for U.S. companies who want to create or continue a business presence in the EC and who are not accustomed to dealing with these limitations. They must either adopt the foolish alternative of not doing business in the EC or become familiar with the law and adjust their practices to suit the EC's requirements. However, additional problems face U.S. and other non-EC businesses who want to mail to individuals in the EC. The law would not allow information about individuals to be released outside the EC unless the country to which the data will flow provides adequate protection of such information.

The combined effect of these provisions could stymie the U.S. company's EC marketing efforts. It might not receive important credit and other demographic information crucial to its marketing and other business decisions. Lists and references might be denied to it. Even the authorization of credit card payment from EC sources could be prevented.

U.S. companies may need to set up a European presence with sufficient capability to handle the entire informational side of a transaction to avoid these problems.

---

## RESTRICTION ON TELEMARKETING

Telemarketing in the United States has been subject to few legal restrictions, largely because a strong Constitutional right of free speech is well entrenched. Also, there is little hesitation here to give such a fundamental Constitutional right to business because the United States is a relatively pure capitalist nation that closely associates the rights of businesses with the rights of their individual owners. The combination of the free speech doctrine and capitalism in the United States imposes a philosophical and cultural impediment to laws that would severely restrict the right of telemarketers to call subjects.

Countries that are not democracies do not place much significance on the right of free speech. Even other democracies generally do not place nearly as great an emphasis on the right of free speech as the United States does, regardless of whether the issue is individual or business free speech.

Many nations limit telemarketers' free speech through the measures restricting telemarketers' compilation and use of subject lists. A small number of nations impose direct limits on telemarketers' free speech by restricting or prohibiting the making of phone calls even when list information is available. Some nations' legal restrictions, such as prohibitions on late-night or harassing phone calls, would be viewed as reasonable limits on free speech in any nation. Other nations have imposed very severe restrictions on telemarketers' free speech.

Germany prohibits telemarketers from making outbound "cold" calls to consumers. Outbound calls to businesses are allowed if the telemarketer is making an offer directed to the business, or if the business called is not disturbed by the call. Therefore, business calls can be made to the customers of a business and to noncustomers who have asked to be called, and in order to make business customer contacts. This still allows a telemarketer some freedom to update its list information, to do market research, to determine customer preferences, and to sell items to current customers and businesses. Also, inbound telemarketing generated by activities other than phone calls is allowed.

Germany's limitations on telemarketers are among the most severe in the world. Germany currently is considering additional restrictive rules governing phone use for customer service and soliciting subscriptions. Many telemarketers effectively avoid Germany's harsh rules by calling subjects from Holland. However, this will no longer work if the German rules are adopted as law by the European Community.

## POSTAL AND SHIPPING REGULATIONS AND LEGAL ISSUES

International direct mail efforts must deal with a myriad of postal regulations since each nation has its own mailing laws and rate schedules. The differences in rate schedules are compounded further by continual currency fluctuations, which rapidly change mailing costs and introduce unpredictability to mailing budgets of U.S. firms mailing overseas. It is wise to consider managing the financial risks of expensive mailing plans by purchasing foreign currency contracts in the target nations' currency.

In some nations, the central government has maintained a monopoly over express and other package delivery services. This can artificially drive up costs to direct marketers and can drastically diminish the level of service provided. The European Community has addressed these problems by passing standards requiring Spain to allow private express companies to compete with the Spanish postal service for international deliveries. The European Community is also reviewing a similar situation in Denmark and may impose a Spanish style solution on the Danes.

Shipping terms are the contractual conditions under which a shipment will be forwarded to its destination. They include determining who will pay for certain costs and expenses (shipping, insurance, etc.), who will incur the risk of loss, who is responsible for shipment, and the terms under which title to the shipment will pass to another. The parties to a shipping contract can expressly determine the shipping terms. If they fail to do so, applicable law will determine the terms.

The Convention on Contracts for the International Sale of Goods (CISG), discussed later in this appendix, contains rules providing shipping terms for international shipping contracts that are missing some or all of the terms. The Uniform Commercial Code and the local law of other nations will apply to international shipping contracts where the CISG does not.

Over the next decade, falling trade barriers may result in a marked decrease in the complexity of documentation required to ship goods internationally. The European Community may implement one system of documentation for all shipments to the 12 EC member nations. A presence in one EC nation will ensure simplified mailings to all EC nations. The Canadian and Mexican free trade agreements with the United States may accomplish the same thing in these three nations. If these agreements treat such shipments the same as shipments to other parts of the U.S., as is intended, United States direct marketers will use a uniform and reduced set of documents for shipments to points in all three nations. If this trend is expanded by these groups, or if other regional groups such as the Association of South East Asian Nations or the Asean Common Market adopt similar measures, shipping legalities can become further simplified.

Legal requirements pertaining to labeling should largely reflect the unification trends occurring with respect to shipping documents. Yet the details of labeling requirements will remain with us, however they may be simplified. Therefore, the contents of packages should be identifiable so that customs and postal inspectors can readily know what is inside. The country of origin, the country of destination, and the number of items in the package should be clearly shown. All required documentation should be securely attached to the package, and special warnings or instructions required by law should be clearly visible.

Many international carriers have no legal responsibility for shipments lost at sea or by plane. Insurance should be purchased to cover the value of a shipment whenever its loss would be significant to the shipper.

## TAXES RELATED TO THE SALE OF GOODS BY DIRECT MARKETERS

In the United States, nearly all states impose taxes on the sale of goods. Under such laws, a local tax must be collected by the seller at the time of sale or, if the purchaser is from another state, a use tax must be paid by the purchaser when the goods are brought into the purchaser's state.

A purchaser from a state different from the seller's state can avoid paying a sales or use tax by bringing goods across state borders. If, as is usual, the seller is not required to collect the other state's use tax, the purchaser can avoid taxation by not voluntarily paying the use tax to his state. Most purchasers do not even know that a use tax exists.

Outside the United States, most nations impose a *value-added tax* (VAT). In simple terms, this is a tax on the value added to the goods from the time the seller obtained the goods or their derivative components until the time the goods are sold.

All of these taxes pose a severe collection problem for marketers who have a presence in one or more foreign nations or who are otherwise compelled to collect and pay such taxes to the nation(s). How can direct marketers efficiently monitor and comply with sales tax, use tax, and VAT laws when these differ in every jurisdiction in which a direct marketer makes sales? The direct marketer must know and document on a current basis: whether the tax imposed on each sale is a sales, use, or value-added tax; the particular percentage of the tax that the jurisdiction has chosen to apply to the price of the goods; and the usually long and varying list of goods that the particular jurisdiction has chosen to tax.

Consider that Ireland imposes a VAT of 25 percent, Italy 17 percent, and Great Britain 15 percent—and these nations are part of the same European Community trade union designed to unify all trade conditions among its members! The problem increases for each nation in which the direct marketer does business and each time a tax law is changed. Add to this the problems of paying each nation in its own currency and the risk of currency fluctuation inherent in this. The software, processing, and logistical problems, and the cost of current compliance with these laws are tremendous.

Even the proposed EC VAT rules for the 1992 merger give direct marketers little short-term hope in the EC since they are required to collect VAT in all EC countries if they have a presence directly or through an agent in any one of them. Also, the VAT percentage and lists of goods taxes will continue to differ in each EC nation. What is worse is that the method of collection will reverse itself in a few years. From 1993 until

1996 direct marketers must collect local VAT imposed by the destination country. Effective 1996 they must collect the VAT of the country from which the goods were sold.

The penalties and repercussions of failing to collect sales, use, and value-added taxes usually are great. Direct marketers must invest the time, technology, and money to ensure proper compliance.

## TRADEMARK PROTECTION

A direct marketer doing international business must know how to protect its trademarks and the trademarks of its suppliers and clients. The business of a direct marketer would be hurt seriously if it spends the time and money to create goodwill and demand for the products it sells to foreign customers, when another company can illegally create the same or similar goods and sell them to the direct marketer's foreign customers using trademarks that usurp the direct marketers' goodwill. This problem can be minimized by proper trademark filings.

The International Convention for the Protection of Industrial Property of 1883, generally called the Paris Convention, is an agreement among its member nations to adopt uniform trademark laws. The United States was a latecomer to the Paris Convention's rules. On November 16, 1989 modifications of U.S. law designed to meet the Paris Convention's rules became effective.

The Paris Convention allows U.S. companies to register a trademark even before it is used. Firms can now conduct product and market testing before spending a great deal of money putting a product into use. In the past, a company could spend a great deal of money putting a product in use and then discover that another company had registered the trademark before it. The new "intent to use" provision diminishes the frequency and financial risk of such situations for U.S. companies. The Paris Convention has additional disincentives for those businesses that hoard trademarks but do not use them.

A major benefit of the Paris Convention is that if a U.S. direct marketer owns a trademark registered in the United States, it can register the mark in any other Convention member nation and receive the same protection under the laws of other member nations that it would receive in the United States. This makes it very wise to register a trademark early in all member nations in which it is used or expected to be used. Better still, the convention also protects well-known trade names which are not registered, even if such trade names are not part of a trademark.

Other trademark treaties exist, most notably the Madrid arrangement. The Madrid arrangement provides that if a trademark is registered in a member country, it can be filed in all other member countries through the International Bureau in Switzerland. After a one-year review period, the trademark would, if there are no similar trademarks already registered, be considered registered in all nations that are parties to the arrangement. Member nations are mostly European and include Algeria, Austria, Belgium, the Netherlands, Luxembourg, Czechoslovakia, Egypt, France, Germany, Hungary, Italy, Liechtenstein, Monaco, Morocco, Portugal, Vietnam, Rumania, San Marino, the USSR, Spain, Switzerland, Tunisia, and Yugoslavia.

Although the United States is not a member of the Madrid arrangement, there is a way that a U.S. direct marketer can take advantage of its simultaneous filing arrangements. The U.S. company can make a simultaneous filing in all Madrid Arrangement nations if it has an affiliate in any member nation and any affiliate files the trademark in that nation. Once this is done, the affiliate may file with the International Bureau in Switzerland.

## GIFTS, TIPS, AND BRIBERY

U.S. culture tends to view bribery of public officials very negatively despite the influence of capitalism. Capitalist influences should tend to make the U.S. government indifferent to bribery as a business practice designed to enhance or accomplish business results. However, the traditional U.S. distaste for bribery was carried over by the first English settlers and is part of American philosophy and jurisprudence. Morally, this is proper. Politically, antibribery laws allow Americans to have greater assuredness that their government is acting fairly and providing justice.

Bribery is illegal throughout the United States at both federal and state levels. Even gifts and tips given to public officials are becoming increasingly illegal in this country because of the subconscious or tacit influence they can have on government officials. Some companies, such as IBM, apply this policy to their employees and prohibit them from receiving any gifts except those of nominal value. Certainly, IBM stockholders can feel assured that bribery has little influence on the company's business decisions.

U.S. antibribery laws extend to the activities of a U.S. company doing business overseas. The relevant U.S. law is the Foreign Corrupt Practices Act (FCPA), which makes the bribery of foreign officials, whether directly or knowingly through a third party, a crime in the United States. Punishment includes monetary fines for individuals and corporations, and jail time for individuals. The offense is considered a felony.

Direct marketers who deal directly or through agents with foreign officials must be cautious to avoid violating this act. The FCPA bribery prohibition extends only to government officials, those who have the authority to use discretion to make decisions. It includes not only the payment of money but the giving of anything of value, including illegal items and services.

The FCPA does not consider expediting or grease payments to be illegal bribery. Expediting payments include payments to minor ministerial employees of foreign governments to get them to do their jobs (e.g., payments to postal employees who will not process or deliver your properly mailed items unless a payment is made). Expediting payments also include payments to a more senior government official to ensure that the official will perform in a timely manner a routine government action that the official should perform anyway (e.g., the granting of a license to do business in the nation where all requirements have been met by your company).

The FCPA puts U.S. companies at a competitive disadvantage with businesses from other nations. The FCPA makes the United States the only nation with a law that expressly prohibits bribes to foreign officials, places such severe penalties on those who violate the law, and imposes tax disincentives and detailed record-keeping requirements on such transactions.

Other nations generally prohibit bribery of their own government officials but do not prohibit bribery of officials of other nations. Although this may appear to even the playing field, it should be noted that an extremely large number of nations, primarily in Latin American and Asia, do not enforce seriously their antibribery laws.

LATIN AMERICA. Bribery is rampant throughout Latin America. Businesses pay bribes of hundreds to thousands of dollars to Colombian officials to allow non-Colombian employees to do business in Colombia in violation of its labor laws. Relatively small bribes of hundreds of dollars are paid in Mexico to have the government do almost anything. This is so common that Mexicans refer to it as the official's *mordida* (bite).

The fact that higher officials do not receive bribes directly should not be viewed as an indication that they are avoiding the temptation of taking bribes. The bribes that businesses pay are often shared among all levels of management of the government. Depending on the size and type of bribe, the lowly official shares the money with his supervisor, who shares it with his manager, who shares it with the department head. The higher officials avoid more direct involvement in bribery usually to maintain their sense of dignity. They do not want to show others that they need or want such payments. However, many low officials who collect small bribes for minor routine functions and do not share the bribes due to their small size, still obtain and keep their jobs by the regular payment of bribes to higher officials.

USSR AND EASTERN EUROPE. The USSR and Eastern Europe is another hotbed of bribery. Import licenses, border crossing, customs approvals, visas, and other ordinary activities are subject to bribery payments. However, bribes to employees of one agency may not protect a business from having to pay another bribe to another agency for the same transaction. There is a great deal of autonomy and competition among such agencies. A scorecard of these agencies would be helpful. It might even help your business to distinguish the many "importers" who claim to be government officials or who invent legal requirements to create the need for a bribe. The democratization of these nations is having little if any effect on their bribery practices, with the exception of the former East Germany, which had fewer problems with bribery than other Eastern European nations and is being assimilated (slowly) into West Germany's political culture.

WESTERN EUROPE. Western Europe is a mix of different attitudes toward bribery. Some nations, like Great Britain, have a distaste for bribery that approaches the U.S. view. Others, especially those in the southern portion of Western Europe, view bribery in the same manner as Latin America. Spain and Portugal are rife with government officials who must receive bribes to do their jobs. Italians have institutionalized the practice of bribery for licenses and other "privileges" dispensed by the government. Payment is made by placing cash in a small envelope called a *bustarella*, and it is received with the same enthusiasm and expectation as the *busta* envelope traditionally given to the bride at an Italian wedding.

French officials do not engage in bribery on the level of those in other southern European nations. The French have strong laws imposing severe penalties on officials who accept bribes, and these laws are enforced. French officials content themselves with Christmas gifts, entertainment, or personal favors rather than blatant bribes. However, French businesses regularly give bribes to foreign officials where this will help business.

Germany typifies most Northern European nations. Bribery of German officials is not tolerated, but bribes to foreign officials are acceptable. German tax law allows a tax deduction for bribes to foreign officials if the person who received the bribe provides a receipt. Otherwise, the German company is penalized only to the extent that the bribe cannot be deducted for tax purposes.

MIDDLE EAST. In the more Westernized Middle Eastern nations such as Kuwait officials often accept bribes. The more fundamentalist nations such as Iran view bribery of officials harshly.

ASIA. Generally, officials in Asian nations view bribery in the same manner as Latin Americans, except that the infrastructure for bribery has been in place for a longer time—thousands of years in the case of China. In Japan, bribery of officials is pervasive, but Japanese middlemen are required because of the sensitivity of the recipients to appearances and the cultural importance of achieving a greater effect by having one Japanese deal with another.

In sum, when dealing with payments to foreign officials, you must know the law of the nation you are dealing with. If expediting payments are acceptable, you must determine whether the person you are dealing with can accomplish what he says, or whether he is an imposter or simply ineffective. You also must know whether an agent or middleman is necessary or more appropriate to make the payment. Sometimes middlemen are sophisticated enough about U.S. law that they make true FCPA bribes without even telling the U.S. company to avoid criminal exposure to it.

Finally, remember that the U.S. view of bribery is in the great minority. Most of the world views giving expediting payments and influential gifts as morally acceptable. Many view these payments and gifts as the proper thing to do when an official has done a favor. Such payments and gifts are viewed in the same way that *tips* originated—*to insure proper service.* Failure to make a payment or gift would be viewed as rude.

## EMPLOYMENT LAW

In many situations, U.S. direct marketers find it beneficial or are required to have a business presence in the target nation. Local employees often are needed by such businesses. Direct marketers who hire employees in other nations usually must drastically adjust their way of thinking about employment issues. Like the case of bribery, the U.S. view of employment issues is extreme compared to most of the world.

In general, the United States legally views employment as an "at will" relationship unless a labor or other collective bargaining agreement exists. Lacking such an agreement, the employer can terminate the employee at any time. The employer is required only to pay severance payments that are provided in the employment contract, if any exists, or that are implicitly promised to employees through company policies. Recently, some exceptions have been made to these principles on the state and federal levels, but such changes do not appear to be part of a substantial trend.

Various nations in Europe and Latin America require large payments to be made to terminated employees. The longer an employee has worked for the employer, the larger the severance payment. It is not unusual for employers to be required to pay an amount equal to one month's salary for each year the employee has worked for the employer.

European labor law generally requires that contracts be written for a specific period of time. Unlike U.S. employment, such contracts cannot be terminated during the stated period. The contracts are renewable automatically, for increasing duration with each renewal.

In some nations, employee representatives must be appointed to the board of directors of many companies. Such employee representatives are granted up to 50 percent of the voting rights with respect to all significant non–day-to-day strategic decisions of the company, which in the United States usually are exclusively reserved to shareholders. This severely diminishes the influence of shareholders, corporate or otherwise.

U.S. or other expatriate employees are not a viable long-term alternative for avoiding these problems. Such employees are very expensive to train and maintain in foreign nations. A direct marketer who needs a foreign presence should become very familiar with the labor law of the target nation and should retain a practical legal expert to advise the business as to its best course of action.

## SALES TRANSACTIONS WITH FOREIGN COMPANIES

A direct marketer who begins to do business in another country may expect to confront strange foreign laws that can sharply increase the marketer's legal exposure. However, it has been the case that a New York direct marketer could expect only familiar local law to apply when it met in New York with a foreign manufacturer and ordered inventory or supplies to be delivered in New York pursuant to a contract providing that the law of New York State applies. This is no longer true.

On January 1, 1988, the Convention on Contracts for the International Sale of Goods (CISG) became effective in the United States. The CISG is a treaty among various nations, including Argentina, Australia, Austria, China, Egypt, Finland, France, Germany, Hungary, Italy, Lesotho, Mexico, Norway, Sweden, Syria, the United States, Yugoslavia, and Zambia. It continues to receive a slow but steady stream of ratification by nations and will eventually apply as pervasively to international sales of goods as the Uniform Commercial Code does to sales of goods within the United States.

For U.S.-based companies, the CISG potentially applies to all international sales of goods between merchants, but not to consumer sales. For the CISG to apply, each merchant must conduct the sale from a relevant place of business in a CISG member nation, and more than one member nation must be involved. The place of business that has the closest relationship to the contract and its performance is the relevant place of business for CISG applicability purposes. The nationality of a merchant is irrelevant. For example, a Bulgarian company doing business from France would be subject to the CISG because of its French presence, as would a Polish company doing business from the United States because of its U.S. presence.

The parties to a contract involving the international sale of goods can avoid CISG regulations by expressly stating that the CISG does not apply. A provision stating that the law of New York State applies may not be enough because the U.S. adoption of the treaty makes the CISG part of the law that each state must apply. If the CISG does not apply to a contract made by a company located in the United States, the pertinent law will be the Uniform Commercial Code (UCC), the law of the other party's nation, or the law of another nation if such a choice is allowed.

Since direct marketers are heavily involved in business-to-business transactions, whether with suppliers or customers, dealing with CISG issues can be a daily occurrence. Unfortunately, due to the dearth of knowledge about the CISG, many U.S. and foreign parties to CISG contracts do not know when the CISG applies. In fact, many U.S. businesses, lawyers, and judges are not even aware that the CISG exists, and international contract cases are routinely resolved without anyone raising CISG issues.

It is crucial for a businessperson to be aware of the circumstances that cause the CISG to apply. A business also must establish procedures to best protect the rights of the business under the law. Where the CISG does apply, specialized legal counsel should be retained to resolve dangerous issues. Also, a prudent businessperson should become aware of the more important provisions of the CISG in order to handle issues as they arise and deal intelligently with legal advisors. Following are some important provisions of the CISG.

When the CISG is applicable to a contract, it governs the requirements for forming the contract and the performance rights and obligations of the parties to the contract. The validity of the contract, the rights of third parties, and title issues are governed by local law.

The CISG does not define "goods." It specifically excludes stocks, shares, investment securities, negotiable instruments, money, ships, vessels, hovercraft, and aircraft, but the status of other items, such as growing crops and railroad rolling stock, is unresolved.

Unlike the UCC, the CISG does not require the parties to act in good faith with respect to the contract. The CISG also does not have a statute of frauds, which means that an unwritten contract is enforceable regardless of the amount of money involved.

Unlike U.S. contract law, the CISG does not require consideration as one of the essential elements of a contract. A CISG contract is formed simply when the acceptance of an offer becomes effective. The goods, their quantity, and their price must be defined sufficiently for a contract to exist. This appears to cover most flexible price contracts, but some difficulty could arise if price is not stated at all. Under the UCC, price is not necessary to form a valid contract. Open-quantity contracts are valid under both laws.

The CISG parallels the UCC concept in that offers are revocable unless a "firm offer" is made. However, the UCC requirement that firm offers be in writing is discarded by the CISG, which allows offers to become irrevocable through oral statements by the offeror or reasonable reliance by the offeree. If a fixed time period is not stated, it is unclear how to determine the length of the irrevocability.

Under the CISG, the offeree's acceptance of an offer is not effective until it reaches the offeror, but the offeror cannot terminate the offer once it is sent by the offeree. Since the offeree is not bound by the acceptance until the offeror receives it, an offeree can mail an acceptance or a rejection and then reverse the decision sending an effective contradictory message by a method ensuring that it will reach the offeror before the mailed response (e.g., by hand delivery or a fax).

Ambiguous statements in a CISG contract can be resolved by reference to known customs of international trade. However, one or both parties just beginning to deal in international trade probably are unfamiliar with most trade customs and must resort to other provisions of the CISG to resolve the ambiguity. The first CISG method used to resolve novices' ambiguities is a party's subjective intent where the other party knew or should have known the intent. If this does not apply, the CISG will use the understanding that a reasonable party of the same kind as the party who made the statement would have under the circumstances.

This reliance on subjective intent creates a limitless field of potential problems. For example, assume that your company sues a foreign manufacturer who did not perform its contract with your company, and that neither party has reason to know the other's intent. The foreign manufacturer can startle you with the defense that, in its nation, written contracts are just formalities and are not meant to be enforced to the letter. In such a case, the foreign manufacturer can claim that he never meant to be bound by what was written, and that any reasonable party from his nation would not have considered the contract to be a binding agreement. It is possible that the court will find that no contract exists.

In addition to the existence of unusual CISG provisions, you should be aware that the same CISG does not apply to all member nations. A member nation can, when signing the CISG, declare that certain portions of the CISG will not apply to contracts that relate to it. This has been done by various nations, including the United States.

The CISG creates various problems and confusions for international direct marketers. It behooves you to become familiar with its provisions and nuances, and to consult frequently with an attorney familiar with its provisions.

The Soviet Union and most Eastern European nations have not been receptive to the flexibility of the CISG. Their laws tend to be detailed, perhaps even ponderous, reflecting their preference for certainty and predictability. Their laws generally require specific references to price (as opposed to open or flexible pricing contracts) and written contracts. These nations do not even rely on trade practices, customs, and usages to supply terms missing from a contract.

# CASE STUDIES

# CASE 1

# Arts & Entertainment Network: A Case Study in Market Strategy (July 1, 1991) Part A: Choices for Developing A&E

**INTRODUCTION** The Arts & Entertainment Network (A&E) is one of the premiere cable television networks in North America. A&E is dedicated to bringing exclusive, high-quality programming to its subscribers. Its viewer offerings fall into four primary genres: comedy, drama, documentary, and performing arts.

Jointly owned by two broadcast networks and a major publisher, A&E continues to be one of the faster-growing cable networks. By the year-end 1990, A&E had over 48 million subscribers, and ranked 12th among the 100 cable TV networks in terms of total annual revenue. Highly profitable, it has been a major success for its joint venture investor/parents.

While A&E attributes its success in part to the general environment of growth which affected all parts of the cable business through the 1980s, in a major way credit must go to all of the A&E people who contributed to making the company successful, and to the strategies

 Information in this case has been prepared with the cooperation of Arts & Entertainment Network. All financial and industry information has been obtained from public sources and does not necessarily reflect actual operating data proprietary to Arts & Entertainment Network.

they employed in developing the business. Many in the industry were skeptical about A&E's potential when it started in 1984. Its future was far from certain.

## BACKGROUND

In the late 1970s, cable television began a period of robust growth. Deregulation in the early 1980s helped to accelerate the process. Households wired for cable increased significantly each year as cable system operators responded to viewer demand for cable TV.

New programming services and networks emerged to pursue the growing subscriber market opportunities. Some of these new services focused on a "narrowcasting" approach to programming, targeting niches which appeared to be of interest to specific viewing audiences, and which differentiated the new offerings from other targeted networks, and from those offering a mix of services.

"Cultural" programming was perceived as one of the potential target niches for narrowcasting. Building on the precedent created by public broadcasting, and with a vision of addressing the "wasteland" of broadcast TV, several organizations undertook business development with the objective of establishing successful cultural programming networks. The concept developed considerable trade, public, critical, and viewer appeal. Perhaps surprisingly, despite this strong interest, none of the ventures was able to achieve sustained commercial success.

Kirsten Beck, in *Cultivating the Wasteland*, noted "In April, 1981, there were three satellite-delivered program services devoted entirely to culture, two actually in operation, and one close to launch. There were also three general audience channels featuring some cultural programming.

"Two years later, only two of the cultural services remained, and one of those had become 60 percent movies and 40 percent performing arts. Of the general audience channels, only one continued to offer any cultural programming."[1]

Shortly after Beck's writing, another major player had discontinued operations as a cultural programming network. By year-end 1983, there had been these significant casualties:

- Alpha Repertory Television Services (ARTS), a joint venture by ABC, Inc., and the Hearst Corporation, was the first cultural programming network, having been launched in early 1981. Although it offered only a three-hour service, it managed to survive the longest, ending its service in late 1983.

1. Kirsten Beck, *Cultivating the Wasteland* (New York: 1983.), American Council of the Arts, p.39.

- CBS Cable, launched in the fall of 1981, invested millions of dollars in programming, and additional funds in development of the business. Despite the effort, CBS Cable was unable to produce sufficient revenues and was discontinued by its parent, CBS, Inc., in early 1983.
- A comparable venture in Canada, C Channel, was licensed in the spring of 1982. Launched later that year, it fared no better than its U.S. counterparts. C Channel terminated operations in June 1983.
- The Entertainment Channel (TEC), a joint venture of RCA and Rockefeller Center, Inc., was launched in 1982, and lasted only nine months before being terminated.

Despite investment of tens of millions of dollars during a time of rapid industry growth, these networks were unable to find the path to commercial success as for-profit ventures in cultural television.

With several public failures having occurred almost simultaneously, it would have been quite understandable if the various investors had walked away from cultural programming as high-risk opportunity offering little if any potential. But rather than give up, some of the joint-venture partners of ARTS and The Entertainment Channel vowed to try again.

The Arts and Entertainment Network grew out of a merger of ARTS and The Entertainment Channel, and was launched nationwide in February 1984 into homes of an estimated 9 million viewers.

## THE CABLE INDUSTRY

While the full potential for its growth was only beginning to be realized in 1984, the cable industry today has become a major force in television which has taken a significant share from the once-dominant major broadcast networks—ABC, CBS, and NBC—and the independent broadcasters.

Essentially, through the 1980s and into the present, the industry has been made up of these elements:

- *Production companies and program syndicators* who obtain and/or develop original and off-network programming and films which appear on cable TV
- *Cable TV networks,* which acquire and/or produce programming for distribution through cable system operators
- *Advertisers,* who purchase advertising time directly from networks (for "national" advertising) and/or from cable system operators (for "local" advertising)
- *Federal legislators and regulators,* particularly the Federal Communications Commission staff, who establish the guidelines under which the industry operates

- *Local regulatory authorities* (for example, town and regional governments), who award franchises which permit cable operators to establish operations
- *Manufacturers of equipment* (dishes, converters, other cable technology) used to deliver the cable signal from networks to operating companies, and from the individual operating company to its subscribers
- *Cable system operating companies,* who obtain franchises for installing cable systems in communities and who offer cable service to viewers
- *Cable subscribers,* who purchase cable services for consumption by viewers in homes, hotels, motels, food service establishments, and other locations.

## ECONOMICS

Cable networks purchase "programming" (their products) from suppliers, and also produce their own programming. The nature of programming varies among networks. A network like CNN produces virutally all of its programming "live." By contrast, American Movie Classics acquires films produced by others for viewing on its network.

The typical "basic service" cable network obtains revenue from two primary sources.

- It sells advertising time to a broad range of advertisers interested in reaching the viewers who watch cable TV.
- It also obtains subscriptions fees from cable operators for providing the TV service offered by the network.

There are also a number of networks, described as "pay services," which obtain revenue exclusively from viewer fees, and do not carry advertising. Home Box Office (HBO) is a primary example of this category.

There are other more specialized services. For example, pay-per-view cable networks obtain revenues from a fee per viewing, offering programming which can include movies, sports, and other special events.

The cable system operator typically has four primary sources of revenue.

- A major share of revenue is obtained from monthly subscription fees received from individual and institutional subscribers to the cable operator's service.
- A much smaller but growing source of revenue is generated by the sale of local advertising, run in "local avail" time (several minutes per hour allocated to local advertising) provided by basic service cable networks.
- Some local revenues are also derived from pay-per-view services and events.
- Additional revenues may be obtained from income-generating basic services like home shopping networks.

## INDUSTRY COMPETITION

The cable business is highly competitive.

- At the local system operator level, franchises give companies the right to build systems and offer services. However, these franchises are closely watched by local authorities and community interest groups. Operators must go through a rigorous process of review each time franchises come up for renewal. The operators must serve the needs of their local communities and are confronted with the requirement to understand, interpret, and respond to consumer needs and interests, both to keep subscribers enrolled and to preserve their franchises to operate.
- Channel capacity is limited, and cable networks compete vigorously for channel space and channel position. In 1984 there were over 62 national and 25 regional networks, both basic service and pay service. The total grew to more than 110 by 1990.

  By contrast, the average cable viewer had 18 channel choices in 1984: 3 network channels, 1 or 2 independent stations, 1 PBS channel, 1 pay service cable channel, 10 basic service cable channels, and perhaps 2 other services. While there has been growth of capacity since then, many cable systems still have relatively limited capacity (24 to 52 channels available).

  In serving community needs, operators are required to carry certain services; the cable networks contend with each other for other available channels on the basis of fee per subscriber, distinctiveness of offering, service to the operator, local merchandising and marketing to attract viewers, and other comparable factors.
- New networks are constantly in formation, each focusing on a particular theme or viewer interest. From 1984 through 1990, approximately 60 new programming services and networks were proposed or put into development, and some 15 survived to become commercial operations. At the beginning of 1991, it was projected that over one dozen new cable services might move forward to launch.
- The more carefully focused and distinctively different its programming, the more likely that a network might attract a particular viewer segment. In turn, this can make it possible for the network to promote itself for "carriage," or signal transmission to subscribers by operators, through demonstating that it will appeal to viewers in the communities served by the operators.

  Distinctive focus can also make it possible for the network to appeal to advertisers by guaranteeing to deliver viewer "demographics" which the advertiser wishes to target. The cost per thousand households (CPM) available through cable networks is usually lower than broadcast TV. Although audiences are much smaller, the precision with which cable can deliver targeted audiences, combined with the competitive CPMs, makes cable advertising of considerable interest to many TV advertisers.

## EVOLUTION OF DISTRIBUTION

In the early days of development, cable distribution was a local affair. Individuals and groups of investors and businesses worked locally, community by community, to obtain franchises and establish operations. Much of the early development occurred in rural and remote urban areas at the fringes of broadcast TV service.

As more cable networks became available, local system operators grouped broadcast and cable signals together to offer ever-more-attractive viewing packages to subscribers. The number of local systems expanded quickly.

The building of cable systems is a capital-intensive business. It quickly became apparent that major financial support would be a primary requirement for expansion, and that economies of scale would make the business attractive to major institutional investors—banks, insurance companies, pension funds, etc.

Several organizations emerged as multiple system operators (MSOs). The MSOs grew by obtaining and providing investment funds to acquire and expand existing local systems, and to obtain franchises for building new systems.

The growth of MSOs also gave rise to consideration of network ownership. Through partial ownership of cable TV networks, MSOs could obtain greater control over the sourcing of programming offered on their systems, and realize improved financial results through ever-greater economies of scale.

For their part, many newer networks saw in this relationship the opportunity to obtain the significant funding required to build new businesses, and to obtain preferred access to the limited number of channels available on local systems.

From the point of view of cable TV networks, building effective relationships with MSOs and local system operators is of high priority, since it is through these relationships that the cable TV networks obtain subscriber revenues, and access to viewers which provides the basis for advertising revenue.

## DYNAMICS OF THE SYSTEM OPERATOR ENVIRONMENT

In 1984, a number of factors affected the decisions made by "affiliates," as local system operators and MSOs are known, in pursuing their business and financial objectives.

- *Subscriber rates.* Regulation of cable provided little flexibility in pricing of basic. Cable operators implemented price increases primarily by adding extra programming services at extra cost as a means of delivering greater value for the money to subscribers.

- *Growth prospects.* A majority of operators sought to obtain growth primarily through increasing basic subscriber penetration, that is, getting more of the cable homes passed to become subscribers.
- *Customer service.* Anecdotal horror stories about the service provided to subscribing customers illustrated the importance of improved customer service as a means of retaining subscribers. Reduction of subscriber "churn," or customers who subscribed and then discontinued service, provided operators with a more predictable revenue stream, a better return on investment, and reduced subscriber complaints to local regulatory authorities.
- *Community interests.* As locally regulated franchises, system operators were required to stay constantly attuned to the apparent needs of the communities they served. Understanding the conflicting needs of various consumers and providing the programming services of interest to the community as a whole is a never-ending challenge.
- *Technology.* Channel capacity was limited. Rebuilding to expand channel capacity was very costly to the operator. Thus, decisions about placement of programming networks on channels and addition or substitution of new services were very much constrained by the physical limitations of local systems.

Two years later, in 1986, matters changed somewhat with the emergence of deregulation. Cable system operators were somewhat freer to set rates for basic service to customers. Tiering, or the combining of networks into groups of services, was replaced by the bundling of basic and other services under a single, increased price.

After another four years' evolution, consumer complaints about pricing and service opened the threat of reregulation. Tiering has again emerged as a matter of concern to cable networks in their selling efforts to cable system operators, since tiering can eliminate many subscribers to a particular network within a given system, thereby reducing both subscriber count and revenue to that network.

## THE ROLE OF ADVERTISING

The sale of advertising time represents an important business element of every basic cable service. Factors which affect the sale of advertising by cable networks include:

- *The size of audience available as viewers of the network.* The larger the audience, the more value it has to the advertiser, and therefore the higher the rate that the network can charge for advertising. The standard for measuring the viewing audience is set by A.C. Nielsen, whose ratings system is accepted generally within the industry as a reliable third-party means of documenting size of audience.

  Nielsen ratings are measured in points; a rating of 1.0 means that a network is delivering 1 percent of the total available audience. In the case of cable networks, this typically means 1 percent of the universe of subscribers to a given network. Although almost all major networks are now rated, in 1984 a number of cable network services were not rated by Nielsen. The lack of proof was a source of constant challenges from potential advertisers.

- *Overall cost efficiency.* This is a direct measure of the price of a given unit of advertising (typically a 30-second spot commercial) in terms of the number of households delivered. Comparative costs are evaluated in terms of cost per thousand households, or CPM. In 1984, efficiency was primarily a measure of number of cable TV households delivered. Two years later, additional measurement data made it possible for networks to refine this measure with the inclusion of demographic data on viewing audience gender and age.
- *Audience selectivity.* The consideration here for advertisers is how well a given network delivers a particular type of audience. MTV, for example, is able to deliver teenage viewers.
- *Audience value.* Closely related to selectivity, this dimension describes the ability a given network has in enabling advertisers to reach individuals not readily available from other cable environments, for example, adult audiences of higher-than-average education and income.

All of these factors were important in 1984, and continue to be important today, although in somewhat more refined forms.

In 1984, cable competed effectively against broadcast network advertising by offering lower absolute rates and lower CPMs. As cable growth continued, advertisers bought more cable advertising to adjust for network erosion (loss of share of viewers). Surveys indicated, not surprisingly, that cable households tended to watch significantly less broadcast network TV than noncable households; given a range of choices, viewership migrates to sample and use all of the available choices. By buying cable advertising, advertisers could make up for viewers lost in broadcast advertising.

In addition to these fundamental factors, advertisers also consider other issues in deciding to buy cable advertising, including:

- The potential for advertisers to develop more meaningful, closer associations with programming on cable networks and to obtain added-value merchandising support from networks
- The service provided by networks (scheduling ads in accordance with advertiser wishes, assuring that the proper ads appear when scheduled, providing feedback on audiences delivered, billing properly for ads run, etc.)
- The level, quality, and frequency of contact by the network ad sales representatives with ad agency buyers (who actually contract for space under direction of advertisers) and with the advertising and marketing managers within client organizations
- The degree to which agency buyers themselves can identify with the network's overall theme, position, and programming content

## A&E: EARLY STAGES OF DEVELOPMENT

From the outset, A&E was confronted with the challenge of creating its own identity and convincing both cable subscribers and advertisers that it could succeed. It began by searching for the correct programming mix, one which would maintain quality programming and offer broad viewer appeal.

At the same time, A&E also had to resolve how it would deliver its service to cable operators. In 1984, A&E provided 20 hours of programming per day, providing the signal to operators through two leased satellites.

Because of satellite sharing arrangements, the less attractive satellite (from the cable operator's perspective) provided 20 hours of programming, whereas the more attractive satellite provided only 8 hours of programming. In order to deliver a predictable audience to advertisers, A&E had to find a way to convince a great majority of cable operators to take the full 20-hour "feed," or transmission of programming signal, from the less attractive satellite.

A&E inherited the distribution of the 3-hour service offered by ARTS: approximately 9 million subscribers available through some 1,500 local cable operators and MSOs. The merging of the ARTS and TEC services occurred so quickly at the end of 1983 that A&E had little advance opportunity to develop an integrated marketing program for working with cable system operators. It also faced the challenge of convincing many systems to pay a monthly subscriber fee; the ARTS service had been provided to system operators without a fee per subscriber.

A&E also had to contend with advertiser acceptance of the A&E network. A major factor in the failure of CBS Cable had been its inability to produce projected advertising revenues. It had forecast ad revenues of $40 million in its final year of operations, and had actually achieved only $8 million. For complex reasons, it seemed that advertisers in general had not responded to the proposition for reaching the "cultural viewer."

In its early months of operation, A&E had sponsorship arrangements with two major advertisers, but had not had time to sort out a preferred approach toward advertisers. For their part, advertisers apparently were adopting a "wait-and-see" attitude about A&E.

- A&E was at a disadvantage in the sale of advertising in that it was not Nielsen-rated.
- The rapid transition from ARTS/TEC to A&E left advertisers somewhat uncertain about A&E's programming approach, and concerned that programming would be too "highbrow" for advertising purposes.
- Finally, the A&E ad sales organization was small, and therefore did not have the resources available for the longer-term relationship building so important in establishing advertising sales momentum.

## STRATEGY FORMULATION

Over a several-month period in early 1984, the senior management team of Arts & Entertainment Network conducted a series of strategic planning meetings. The meetings were held for the purpose of formulating a business plan for 1985, and a longer-range strategy which would guide the growth of the business into the future.

The chart below identifies the individuals who made up the planning team.

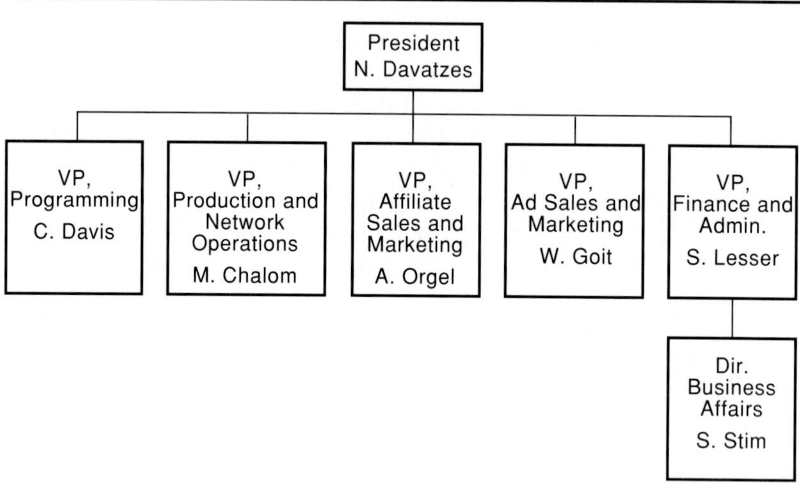


The functions represented by the planning team had these responsibilities within A&E:

- *Programming:* Design of overall programming concept and programming strategy; contacts with suppliers to identify and select programs to be offered to viewers; scheduling of programs for transmission to viewers
- *Production & Network Operations:* Preparation of programs for transmission over the network; development of on-air promotional materials; transmission of the program signal from the operations facility via uplink to the satellite for distribution to cable system operators
- *Affiliate Sales & Marketing:* Marketing and trade show support to the affiliate field sales organization; preparation of advertising, public relations, and collateral material used to promote the network to viewers; sales contact with cable operators at local system and MSO levels
- *Advertising Sales & Marketing:* Market research on viewers; preparation of advertising and collateral material used to promote the network to advertisers; sales contact with advertisers and agencies

- *Finance & Administration:* Human resources; financial and accounting services (billing, collections, etc.); computer and management information services
- *Business Affairs:* Legal and other services required to negotiate contracts for use of programs which were to be transmitted over the network; negotiation of distribution contracts with affilliates

---

## STRATEGIC OPTIONS

From the outset, there was general agreement among the members of the planning team that A&E had to expand its viewership and build distinctive viewership demographics. Accomplishing these objectives would make the network of greater interest to cable operators, thereby increasing the likelihood of obtaining commitments to carriage of A&E. It would also attract the interest of advertisers who wished to reach the viewers available in the A&E audience.

As part of creating a distinctive identity for the network, A&E management realized that it would have to work carefully to position the network effectively to advertisers, affiliates, community leaders, program suppliers, viewers, and to the industry in general.

Deliberations during the planning process resulted in the development of these options for consideration.

PROGRAMMING. Given the programs available from its predecessors (ARTS and The Entertainment Channel), it seemed logical to draw on this inventory. Additionally, A&E had access to a significant quantity of programming from the British Broadcasting Corporation, having taken over the remainder of the 10-year programming contract which had given The Entertainment Channel access to British Broadcasting Corporation programs.

However, A&E thought that it would be important to expand the appeal of the network by reaching beyond the highbrow segment to reach the better-educated viewer through a variety of genres—stage, movies, classical and performing arts, documentaries, comedy, variety. By emphasizing quality and unearthing and offering unique programs, the programming function believed it could obtain critical acclaim for A&E programs and attract additional viewers. Further, by presenting prime-time programming in a series of "theme" nights, A&E would be able to highlight its variety and distinctiveness to advertisers and affiliates, and make it easier for viewers to find programs of preference.

Through extensive search into BBC and other materials in inventory, the programming function felt it would be able to increase its inventory of programming at relatively nominal cost, thus avoiding the significant front-end investment which had placed considerable financial pressure on CBS Cable. Nevertheless, the proposed total funding required to achieve the programming strategy was a good deal more than had been anticipated when the initial financial forecasts had been developed.

PROMOTION. It also appeared to make sense to increase promotion overall, to raise the quantity of on-air promotion, and to improve the overall "look" of the network.

By giving viewers reasons to seek out A&E, and making it easier for viewers to find A&E, it appeared likely that A&E could stimulate increases in viewership. Once the viewer came to A&E, the overall quality of the network's "look" and frequent reminders of programs to come would convert increasing portions of the audience into regular A&E viewers.

It seemed that promotion would increase general awareness and acceptance of A&E. In turn, this would make it possible to present a more convincing case to advertisers and to affiliates. The funding proposed would accomplish the objectives described. However, the proposed budget was considerably greater than had been anticipated.

COMMUNITY DEVELOPMENT. In addition to appealing to and promoting directly to viewers, a strong case was also made for creating interest about A&E among community leaders, community groups, and cable operators. The thinking here was that libraries, educators, cultural organizations, and other comparable groups would find the mix of A&E programming of particular appeal.

By knowing more about A&E, and by being able to take advantage of links between A&E offerings and their efforts, it appeared likely that community leaders and cable operators would be more positively disposed toward A&E.

Genuine "grass roots" appeal of A&E, particularly among the more influential voices in a community, was thought likely to exert strong influence on cable system operators, particularly because of the cable system operators' interests in serving their communities.

It was proposed that A&E's objective for such community development effort be to get community leaders to see that A&E should be an integral part of the basic programming mix available locally—as important to the community as news, weather, sports, children's programming, information, and music, the other comparable categories.

Recommended funding was not out of line with the potential for payoff, but the effort was felt likely to require a greater allocation of staff time than had been planned.

AFFILIATE SALES. At the start of operations in February 1984, A&E had some 9 million subscribers and relationships with some 1,500 affiliate cable system operators and MSOs. The total universe was quite a bit larger. In 1984, there were about 6,100 cable systems overall, and approximately 35 million basic subscribers.

Further penetration of the cable universe would offer A&E the opportunity to increase viewership significantly. Thus, it appeared that A&E would have to give high priority to building relationships with additional affiliates, and to obtain expansion of services with existing affiliates.

The case was therefore advanced to invest significantly in selling to affiliates. By developing high-visibility, high-impact contacts at multiple levels in major systems and MSOs, it appeared likely that A&E could accelerate commitments to carriage by affiliates. To do this, it would be necessary to obtain an in-depth understanding of operator needs and interests, then to build marketing, selling, and support programs which would respond to these needs and interests. Perhaps not surprisingly, the proposed funding required to carry out the effort exceeded the financial guidelines set out at the beginning of the planning process.

ADVERTISING SALES. Initial contacts with prospective advertisers after startup in February 1984 showed that A&E could anticipate positive response to its concept. Potential advertisers could see the probable link between A&E's programming and its ability to deliver an audience with a demographic profile of considerable interest: a balance between male and female viewers, in preferred age ranges, with above-average education and income.

However, at this early stage, advertisers and agencies were not able to obtain A&E ratings data from A. C. Nielsen, on which all advertisers and agencies rely for proof of viewership.

For the time being, A&E thus had to rely on a "concept sell," appealing primarily to those organizations which wanted to emphasize institutional advertising to consumers, or which could justify spot advertising to selected target populations even though they lacked quantitative data on audience delivery.

Nevertheless, the case was advanced strongly that A&E should invest in building its relationships with advertisers and agencies, both to build immediate revenue and to set the foundation for strong future ad revenue growth once quantitative data was available.

Additionally, funding was recommended for research into A&E audiences, so that A&E might provide demographic data for sales support in both advertising and affiliate sales, as well as obtain further insight into viewers to help with programming decisions.

In keeping with the pattern that had become all too familiar to the members of the A&E planning team, the funding initially proposed for the advertising sales efforts exceeded financial guidelines which had been established for the next operating plan.

## STRATEGIC RECOMMENDATIONS

The A&E planning team was confronted with a set of circumstances not at all unusual for a new, growing business: how to reconcile funding requirements considerably in excess of funding resources. The decisions which they had to make were likely to have a considerable impact on the future prospects of the network.

While the actual financial data is proprietary information, the magnitude of the decisions which faced the A&E management team can be inferred from the summary which follows.

| 1985 Budget Category | Planning Guideline: Percent of total | Initial Budget Recommendation Relative to guideline |
|---|---|---|
| Programming | 45 | 1.8x |
| Promotion | 10 | 1.6x |
| Community development | 5 | 1.5x |
| Affiliate sales | 25 | 2.1x |
| Advertising sales | 15 | 1.8x |
| Totals | 100 | 1.8x |

## ASSIGNMENT

1. Assume the role of the A&E planning team, at the time in the fall of 1984 when they had to reach decisions on a strategic approach for A&E, and develop their funding and operational recommendations to the joint-venture partners.
   a. What strategy or strategies would you employ to accomplish the objectives?
   b. What priorities would you place on the possible strategies? For example, would you attempt to apply efforts against all opportunities at a proportionately reduced level of funding? Would some activities be given higher priority, and some lower priority? Would you tackle some opporunities immediately, and postpone action on others until a later time? Would you place emphasis on developing advertisers? Affiliates? Viewers? A combination of these?
   c. How would you adjust your proportionate levels of funding to accommodate the budget requests to the financial guidelines? Would you find a way to stay within the guidelines, or would you attempt to persuade your investors that they should exceed the guidelines in order to achieve the objectives?

Develop a summary presentation which responds to the questions. Be prepared to defend your recommendations.

# CASE 2

# Arts & Entertainment Network: A Case Study in Market Strategy (July 1, 1991) Part B: Implementation of A&E Strategy

## A&E MARKET STRATEGY: 1985 OPERATING PLAN

In the fall of 1984, A&E presented a proposed 1985 operating plan to its investors and received their concurrence on proceeding with implementation. The plan embodied these core elements of strategy. A&E intended to

1. Focus primary attention on developing distribution as a central priority, by building relationships with cable system operators and MSOs, in order to expand the numbers of subscribers to the network.
2. Initiate a program of community development through direct contact with community organizations (libraries, cultural organizations, educational institutions, etc.). All communications and programs would be designed to better acquaint targeted communities with A&E. In taking these steps, A&E intended to assure involvement of the cable operator in the communication and decided to present the cable operator as an important resource to the community organizations.

3. Draw upon existing programming resources to the maximum possible extent, thereby minimizing additional expenditures for programming while at the same time pushing to build greater balance among the various genres. A&E intended to work at shedding the "highbrow" image left over from its ARTS/TEC heritage, feeling that its greatest potential for building viewership among targeted higher-education, higher-income subscribers lay in providing an eclectic programming mix.
4. Invest selectively and carefully in general consumer awareness advertising and promotion, but hold back any major additional investment until potential viewership had been further expanded through building the subscriber base.
5. Focus advertising sales effort primarily on carefully targeted accounts, but hold back any major advertising sales efforts until the network had increased the subscriber base significantly. It was felt that certain advertising prospects would find a natural home with A&E, and these were targeted for pursuit. A&E determined that a more general and aggressive selling approach would have to wait until there were a number of viewers to sell.

---

## 1985 OPERATING PLAN BUDGET

A greater share of the budget was given to affiliate sales and community development. The programming budget was maintained within guidelines. Budgeted funds for advertising sales and promotion were reduced somewhat. Overall, the 1985 operating plan was maintained within budget guidelines.

---

## ACTIONS TO IMPLEMEMT THE 1985 MARKET STRATEGY

The January 21, 1985, edition of *CableVision*, a cable industry trade journal, carried a cover story on A&E.[1] Highlights from the article indicated the industry's perception of the steps A&E was taking to implement its plan.

- *Consumer promotion* was the first topic covered in the *CableVision* article, which noted that A&E had launched a consumer advertising campaign "designed to make the public aware of A&E and dispel what [A&E management termed] an ill-deserved reputation for delivering narrow, high-brow programming of the type associated with A&E's cultural-cable service ancestors, CBS Cable and ARTS." According to the article, A&E's president and CEO, Nickolas Davatzes,

---

1. Cecilia Capuzzi, *Playing A&E in the Key of E: Arts &Entertainment Enters Year 2*, (New York: International Thomson Communications, Inc., 1985), p. 24ff.

saw that making consumers aware of the network and its offerings was the network's biggest challenge.

The ad campaign was to last four months and was targeted at the 12 major markets representing 40 percent of A&E's distribution. It promoted investigation of A&E as a viewing alternative. Consumer research carried out by A&E indicated that overall awareness of A&E was very low, but also showed that those who had watched A&E had found the experience very satisfying.

- *A&E programming* was another topic addressed by *CableVision*. The magazine noted that A&E investors "believed that A&E had a role to play in determining the success of the next level of cable. . . . A&E's mission, simply put, [was] to build the audience for differentiated and distinguished programming."

  The article stated that A&E intended to build the audience in two ways: first, by providing "high quality entertaiment" grouped into "theme nights" and second, by "positioning [the network] as a must in any well-rounded system channel lineup."

  In keeping with its commitment to be responsive to potential customers, A&E engaged in focus group research to determine consumer reactions to A&E programming. Thereafter, the network tested some 20 shows with consumers, to determine which were the most popular. Local promotions featuring these shows were launched in eight markets, and results indicated awareness increases of 30 percent and viewership increases up to 110 percent.

  Andrew Orgel, then-head of A&E's affiliates sales and marketing function, was quoted by *CableVision*. "What we are in fact doing is taking the best of what the arts services were and combining it with the best of the broader-based entertainment." In the opinion of management, A&E's strategy of broadening the scope and the appeal of its programming, as well as aligning itself as the access vehicle to arts programming was "working."
- *Advertising opportunities* were also addressed in the article. *CableVision* observed that A&E had started with one major advertiser, Ford Motor Co., and was to finish the year with 24 sponsors, including BMW, Exxon, IBM, General Motors, and Pfizer. It noted that there was general interest in the advertising community "about how the network [could] be used for corporate clients and high-ticket items."

  According to the article, Whitney Goit, responsible for A&E's advertising sales and marketing function, observed that A&E's format was best suited for corporate sponsors concerned with image maintenance who also had products and services to sell. Goit noted that A&E had developed a small sales staff "to service 'corporate America' as well as agencies with product-oriented clients." He also was quoted as indicating that A&E's biggest problem in attracting more clients was the fact that it was not yet metered by Nielsen.
- *Overall strategy* also received some comment in the article. *CableVision* quoted Mr. Davatzes as saying that A&E had "chosen a 'conservative' business route with a 'reality based' business plan which [would] allow the network to accomplish its 'mission' of making entertaining arts programming a viable viewing alternative and successful

business venture." It also noted that Mr. Davatzes believed that "success . . . [would] be measured in very traditional business terms, by meeting projections and building distribution quickly."

The article also noted that A&E management believed that financial objectives would be met only if the network obtained revenue from multiple revenue streams: subscriber fees, advertising revenue, "ancillary" revenue (for example, revenues received from licensing A&E original productions to other networks), and international business, of which Canada would be first.

*Affiliate sales effort* received only passing mention in *CableVision*. At the time, Mr. Davatzes had made a conscious decision not to reveal this central element of his strategy, feeling that to do so would give A&E's competitors some potential advantage. Although it did not state so publicly, A&E records show that the company mounted a significant effort to sign up affiliates. Additionally, A&E developed a new satellite leasing arrangement to enable it to deliver its full 20-hour service more readily to cable system operators.

## A LATER STAGE IN A&E'S DEVELOPMENT

Another article about A&E appeared in *Wide World Magazine*, an internal publication of Capital Cities/ABC, in April 1986. It documented further evolution and implementation of A&E's market strategy. The article is reproduced below in its entirety.

### Arts & Entertainment Enters Its Third Year

Timing is everything in the television business—even more so in the competitive cable television field, where deregulation is nurturing a "back to basics" movement among many cable system owners.

The Arts & Entertainment Network (A&E)—owned jointly by ABC Video Enterprises, the Hearst Corporation and RCA Cable—has recently entered its third year of operation. At its genesis, A&E's management wisely sought to steer the 20-hour-a-day service away from the front lines of the cable network wars of a few years ago, where the intense competition of the times claimed some bigger and better-heeled rivals. A&E's owners chose instead to hang back, waiting with the quiet determination of the stalwart characters who populate many of A&E's award-winning classic programs.

The patience of the past has paid off. As basic cable's "only premium entertainment service," A&E is currently riding the crest of popularity among cable operators, who are beefing up their stable of basic cable program offerings.

According to A&E President Nickolas Davatzes, "Pay movie services are no longer cable's safe anchor. Today cable operators recognize that subscriber growth is tied to achieving the proper mix of basic and pay services. And experience has demonstrated that subscribers find A&E to be an increasingly valuable part of that mix."

Indeed, A&E is rapidly moving into the black as 2,200 cable systems have affiliated with it over the past two years, paying a monthly per-subscriber fee and propelling the A&E subscriber count to 18 million homes.

A&E is also becoming increasingly visible on Madison Avenue. "Back in 1983, we could count the network's advertisers on one hand," Davatzes recalls. "Today A&E boasts a client roster of nearly 100, including such giants as AT&T, Campbell's, Exxon, Ford Motor Company, General Mills, General Motors, IBM and Sara Lee."

Operators, subscribers *and* advertisers have responded enthusiastically to A&E's diverse and distinctive mix of American and internationally produced programs, which feature comedy and drama, music and dance, movies and specials, and productions from the British Broadcasting Corporation and the Broadway Stage.

With 150 program premieres last year, A&E has been living up to its hard-earned reputation for presenting some of the best and the brightest entertainment on cable television. A&E's critically acclaimed recent program offerings have included award-winning stage presentations as *Mornings at Seven* and Agatha Christie's *Spider's Web*; top movies like John Schlesinger's *An Englishman Abroad* starring Alan Bates and *The Stranger* starring Orson Welles; comedy fare such as *An Evening at the Improv* and Larry Gelbart's series *United States*; and provocative documentaries such as *The Man Who Hid Anne Frank* and *The Architecture of Frank Lloyd Wright.*

Coming up in 1986 are the reprise of *Buffalo Bill* starring Dabney Coleman; *Wynton Marsalis: Catching a Snake* starring the jazz great of the same name; the eight-part series *Africa* and the documentary *The Indomitable Teddy Roosevelt.* Two new A&E/BBC co-productions scheduled for the future are John LeCarre's *A Perfect Spy* and *Silas Marner* starring Academy Award winner Ben Kingsley.

"A&E," says Vice President of Programming Curtis Davis, "has been throwing a very interesting television party with a lot of very interesting guests." Every day, A&E offers entertainers like Eileen Brennan, Dudley Moore, Burgess Meredith, Lee Remick, Billy Crystal, Luciano Pavarotti, Joan Collins and Beau Bridges, along with a roster of hosts that includes Gregory Peck, Burt Lancaster, Edwin Newman, Estelle Parsons and Joan Fontaine.

A&E's daytime programming is organized around educational and family-oriented umbrellas: *The Classics,* featuring dramatization of great literary works; *Family Theater,* offering exciting adventure, dramatic and comedy series; *In Performance* featuring the world's best-loved and most stimulating music and dance; and *Horizons,* focusing on people and their extraordinary achievements.

In addition to its program schedule, another key to A&E's success has been its direct involvement with its viewers and the communities and cable affiliates the network serves. A&E's ongoing community marketing program is designed to help cable operators work with education, arts and civic groups. Through fund-raising projects and tape donations, A&E has assisted in developing healthy resources within the community, including study guides for its family viewing programs and co-sponsorship of the annual "Ruby Slipper Award" with Group W in Los Angeles and the American Center of Films for Children.

In another part of the country, A&E joined Colorado Governor Richard Lamm and the Colorado Council for Arts and Humanities in hosting a reception at the Denver Center for the Performing Arts, to announce the creation of a new video series documenting Colorado folk artists, set to premiere on A&E.

"These projects," says Davatzes, "along with tape donations of A&E programs to institutions like New York's Museum of Broadcasting and successful fund-raisers for libraries such as the Ludington Library in Bala Cynwyd, Pennsylvania, prove that developing community resources is good business."

How will A&E maintain its success story? "With the support and dedication of our employees and our continuing close attention to fiscal management," Davatzes explains. "And of course, we will continue to air the exciting, quality product that makes A&E the cable industry's most unique service."

---

SOURCE: "Wide World of Video Enterprises," *Wide World Magazine,* April 1986.

## SUBSEQUENT GROWTH: SELECTED DATA ABOUT THE CABLE INDUSTRY

The data below, obtained from published sources, illustrate the dimensions of actual and projected cable TV growth from 1986 through 1991, and provide comparable estimated data about A&E for the same period.

**Basic Cable Networks.**

| U.S. Cable Universe | 1986 | 1987 | 1988 | 1989 | 1990 | 1991 |
|---|---|---|---|---|---|---|
| Gross ad billings (millions) | 734 | 869 | 1,125 | 1,420 | 1,780 | 2,062 |
| Subscriber fees (millions) | 257 | 415 | 534 | 723 | 1,021 | 1,179 |
| Net ad revenue (millions) | 624 | 739 | 956 | 1,207 | 1,513 | 1,753 |
| Other revenue (millions) | 12 | 17 | 39 | 22 | 67 | 70 |
| Total net revenue (millions) | 893 | 1,171 | 1,529 | 1,952 | 2,601 | 3,002 |

Estimates of Paul Kagan Associates, Inc., Carmel, CA.

**Summary of Cable Subscriber Data.**

| U.S. Cable Universe | 1986 | 1987 | 1988 | 1989 | 1990 | 1991 |
|---|---|---|---|---|---|---|
| Cable systems (000) | 6.5 | 6.6 | 7.2 | 7.3 | 7.4 | 7.5 |
| TV households (millions) | 85.9 | 87.4 | 88.6 | 90.4 | 92.1 | 93.6 |
| Homes passed (millions) | 68.0 | 71.5 | 74.6 | 80.3 | 83.0 | 85.2 |
| Basic subscribers (millions) | 39.2 | 41.6 | 44.0 | 49.3 | 51.8 | 54.1 |
| Basic penetration of homes passed (%) | 57.6 | 58.2 | 59.0 | 61.4 | 62.4 | 63.5 |

Estimates of Paul Kagan Associates, Inc., Carmel, CA.

**Estimates of Selected A&E Operating Data.**

| A&E | 1986 | 1987 | 1988 | 1989 | 1990 | 1991 |
|---|---|---|---|---|---|---|
| Number of subscribers (millions) | 22.0 | 31.9 | 37.1 | 42.7 | 48.9 | 53.8 |
| Number of affiliates (000) | 1.8 | 2.3 | 2.9 | 4.6 | 6.2 | 6.8 |
| Subscriber revenue (millions) | 15.0 | 22.0 | 30.5 | 36.0 | 45.0 | 50.0 |
| Net ad revenue (millions) | 6.8 | 11.5 | 19.7 | 30.8 | 41.3 | 50.0 |
| Total revenue (millions) | 21.8 | 33.5 | 50.2 | 66.8 | 86.3 | 100.0 |
| Total cash flow (millions) | (4.5) | 2.0 | 4.0 | 10.2 | 14.6 | 18.0 |

Estimates of Paul Kagan Associates, Inc., Carmel, CA.

**ASSIGNMENT**

1. Compare the information about A&E provided in Case 1 with the results obtained by A&E as reported in Case 2.
   a. From your perspective, what factors had the greatest impact on A&E's ability to obtain the estimated operating results, as reported?
   b. Did A&E overlook or miss any significant strategic opportunities? What other steps might A&E have considered in attempting to develop its business?

Develop a presentation which outlines your observations. Prepare to defend your answers.

# CASE 3

## Ford New Holland, Inc: Full-Line Insert

**BACKGROUND** The following information was taken from the Ford New Holland, Inc., brochure.

Your Ford New Holland dealer knows a thing or two about helping you farm better. He knows that selling you quality-built tractors and agricultural implements is only the first step in helping you farm more productively and profitably.

The next steps include comprehensive service and parts support and good advice on everything from equipment financing to crop irrigation.

Your Ford New Holland dealer is one of more than 4,000 respected dealers worldwide entrusted by Ford New Holland to help you farm better.

Your dealer maintains a large parts inventory, which lets him respond to your parts needs quickly and virtually round the clock. If the part you need is not in stock, it can be ordered from the Ford New Holland parts depot for fast shipment.

As for service, our technicians are experts at keeping your equipment operating reliably and efficiently. At the dealership or on your farm, fast dependable service means continuous productivity.

So come into your Ford New Holland dealer today and arrange to take a look at the broad range of Ford tractors and material handling equipment and New Holland harvesting machines he has available. You won't find better equipment or more knowledgeable people to tell you about how it can help you work better.

**OBJECTIVES**

1. Position Ford New Holland as a worldwide leader that offers a complete line of quality and innovative tractors and harvesting equipment.
2. Stimulate prospects with immediate buying intentions to identify themselves.
3. Build a database of Ford and New Holland prospects for future direct response programs.

**ASSIGNMENT**

1. Assume the role of the Ogilvy & Mather Direct account person in developing strategies and promotional literature to accomplish the objectives.
   a. What strategy or strategies would you employ to accomplish each of the given objectives? Explain in outline form.
   b. Develop appropriate promotion pieces to meet the objectives. It is fine to work in black and white. If you prefer, you may do it in color. A paste job is also approved. Neatness and clarity count as part of the grade.

# CASE 4

## Kayeville College Rescinds Its Decision to Admit Men

Kayeville College voted on January 10, 1991, to rescind its decision to admit men to the 125-year-old women's college. Bowing to pressure from striking students and supporting faculty and alumnae, Daniella Pinezic, chairperson of the board, held up a banner that read "Kayeville is for Women."

During an interview, Dr. Barbara Kimmerle, president of Kayeville, told the students that "certain goals had to be met for Kayeville to remain a women's college. Enrollment had to increase from the current 1,200 students to a full-time undergraduate student body of 1,800 by fall of 1994 and 2,500 by the fall of 1996. Financial difficulties had to be resolved by that date." The earlier trustee vote would have admitted men as undergraduates in the fall of 1992. They have been attending as graduate students since the 1960s.

Students opposed co-education, citing studies that showed that women educated in women's colleges achieved higher positions in both the private and public sectors after graduation. They also feared that men would usurp leadership roles on campus and would dominate classroom dynamics. Students conducted a strike and a blockade of the administration offices, barring school officials. Some of the students shaved their heads or taped their mouths closed to imply that the trustees had not heard what they were saying.

---

**QUESTIONS**

1. Formulate the major issue (sometimes called a problem) as a direct question and write it in one sentence.

2. State five facts and explain what they mean in relation to the major issue.
3. Indicate what further information you would want, why it is needed, how it can be obtained, and how it can be used.
4. Formulate various courses of action, considering only direct marketing techniques. State the pros and cons of each alternative.
5. State your decision in one sentence. List the specific steps you would take to resolve the problem. State the results you anticipate from the steps you recommended. Substantiate your recommendations with reasoning based on facts.
6. Create three promotion pieces, at the minimum, for Kayeville College. It is fine to work in black and white. If you prefer, you may do it in color. A paste job is also approved. Neatness and clarity count as part of the grade.

# CASE 5

## Golf View Village

Golf View Village is a real estate development for retirees located just 10 miles away from Los Angeles, California. The average temperature ranges between 75 and 80 degrees year-round. The development overlooks the Pasadena golf course. Luxury townhouses are being offered to upper-income, active adults nearing retirement age.

Promotional advertisements of Golf View Village read as follows:

> Start with a great Pasadena location. Our site is heavily wooded, on level ground, in a private setting, facing the Pasadena golf course. Scheduled bus service is provided to nearby shopping centers. Within the Village you'll find a recreation center with planned activities such as ceramics, painting, lectures, parties, dances as well as various sports activities. Included here are luxurious indoor and outdoor swimming pools, exercise and steam rooms and tennis courts.
>
> Our homes speak for themselves. There are 12 plans to choose from. They feature such standards as eat-in kitchens, formal dining rooms, oversized walk-in closets, and beautiful 1 and 2 bedrooms and oversized garage. All our homes include a fireplace, dual heating and central air conditioning systems, wall to wall carpeting, microwave ovens, washer and dryer. All our homes feature energy efficient construction that insure your comfort while saving you money.
>
> Best of all, while enjoying the benefits of home ownership, you'll have the time to do the things you want to do because all the exterior maintenance is taken care of by a professional staff. Interior services are available.
>
> So drive over this weekend and tour our beautiful models priced from just $399,000.

## QUESTIONS

1. Who would be your target audience? Why?
2. How would you develop a list of potential buyers?
3. What type of marketing strategy would you consider if you are limited to direct marketing? Be creative in your approach.
4. Discuss five alternative direct marketing campaigns including all the pros and cons.
5. State your decision in one sentence. Substantiate your recommendation.
6. Create three promotion pieces, at the minimum, for Golf View Village. It is fine to work in black and white. If you prefer, you may do it in color. A paste job is also approved. Neatness and clarity count as part of the grade.

APPENDIX

# Careers in Direct Marketing

**PROFILE**

**SUSAN SCHROTHER**

**A Success Story.** Susan Schrother is an advertising manager for the Dreyfus Corporation. She earned an M.B.A. in marketing and a B.F.A. in photography from St. John's University.

When Susan began college, she had an affinity for photography; she loved taking pictures as a hobby and thought that she could turn it into a career. While in school, Susan worked as an assistant photographer for various studios in Manhattan, gaining valuable experience and, most of all, establishing a network of contacts. After completing her B.F.A. and working for a few years, Susan began to develop an interest for the business side of art and enrolled in the Graduate School of Business at St. John's.

Majoring in marketing with a concentration in advertising, Susan had the goal of combining art and business in the exciting world of advertising. Getting started wasn't easy. With help from her professors at St. John's, Susan began to pursue a career in direct marketing. Upon graduation, Susan got a job as an assistant account executive at Wunderman Worldwide, the world's largest direct marketing agency at that time. Working on one of the largest accounts, the Columbia House Music Club, she got a firsthand look at how an ad is created from beginnning to end, how it is tracked through sourcing, how the responses are analyzed, and what future strategies should be explored based on the results. Characteristic of agency life, it was very fast-paced and exciting, it involved long working hours, and it was a terrific learning experience.

After establishing a strong network of professional contacts while at Wunderman, Susan was approached by a number of headhunters and was actively recruited by other organizations. Through careful screening, she decided that The Dreyfus Corporation would provide a good career move and the opportunity for Susan to enhance her future marketability by learning the "general" side of direct marketing. ■

Students go to college to broaden their knowledge and horizons, to meet the opposite sex, to please their parents, or to prepare for a particular career path. The search for a career should start well before the senior year. It is not necessary to make a lifetime decision about a first job. College students should be prepared for change. It is important to make sure that options are available and to be prepared to leave a job when necessary.

Now that you have gone through a course in the principles of direct marketing you should have a good idea of the significant opportunities in the field. Several hundred of the authors' former students are working in direct marketing. They find their jobs challenging, interesting, rewarding, and stimulating. These positions have proved to offer excellent opportunities for advancement and for working with other people.

You should let your professor get to know you, if for no other reason than to ask him or her for advice or direction in your job search. If your professor doesn't know you, how can he or she write a recommendation for you?

One of the authors, through his contacts at Wunderman Worldwide, recommended Susan Schrother, a former student, as a possible candidate for a position as assistant account executive. Susan sold herself. She showed the various interviewers at Wunderman her portfolio of photographs and various research projects she had done in direct marketing. She was one up on the other job seekers and was offered the position. True, she did not expect to work the long hours that were required. However, she eventually became acclimated to the business-world hours and received a promotion and raise.

To present themselves in a good light to potential employers, several of this professor's successful job seekers have incorporated their direct marketing projects with other school assignments in their portfolio. This has helped to compensate for their lack of experience in the field in the eyes of the job interviewer. Sixty percent of those successful in finding jobs and being promoted were women. "Ad agency executives and consultants who help companies find agencies say that half or more of agency new-business directors are women. The trend is significant, these people say, because the new position may be a possible path to agency leadership, which until recently was nearly closed to women."[1]

---

1. Randall Rothenberg, "Women Gain Foothold in Drive for Accounts," *New York Times*, July 25, 1989, pp. D1, D23.

# Description of Direct Marketing Positions

The number of career opportunities in direct marketing is gigantic. Students should not be preparing themselves for a job; rather, they should be preparing themselves for a career. This can be achieved by learning a broad range of skills that will permit students to adapt and to take on new positions and careers in this ever-changing society. Various studies point out that about one-third of the Fortune 1,000 CEOs came through the ranks of marketing. Sixteen of the leading direct marketing positions are described next.

*Account executives* are the liaisons between agency and client, receiving all client approvals, requests, and complaints. They muster all the agency's services for the benefit of the client.

*Advertising managers* are responsible for the administration, planning, and budgeting of advertising activities; supervision of outside advertising services; and coordination with other company departments.

*Art directors* are responsible for the visual presentation of the ad.

*Brand managers* of consumer and industrial firms coordinate sales promotion and merchandising of a product or line of products.

*Catalog managers* select merchandise for inclusion in catalogs, work with manafacturers, order catalogs, and monitor order fulfillment.

*Copywriters* create the words and concepts for ads and commercials.

*Database processors* keep up-to-date lists of consumer information, including names, addresses, and telephone numbers; psychographic and demographic data; and figures on recency, frequency, and monetary value of purchases.

*Fulfillment managers* handle the back end of a direct marketing business. These duties include receiving mail and telephone orders, processing orders, checking credit, billing, maintaining inventory, sending goods, and handling complaints.

*List brokers* are middlemen and specialists who make all necessary arrangements for a mailer. They select, evaluate, and recommend lists. They research the size and potential of a market while checking out mechanics and delivery dates.

*Marketing researchers* are individuals who study consumers and businesses through information gathered on identifying and defining marketing opportunities and problems. They also generate, refine, and analyze marketing actions; monitor marketing performance; and improve understanding of marketing as a process.

*Media directors* evaluate media according to efficiency and cost, and then recommend the best medium or media combination to use.

*Media persons* in advertising agencies are concerned with the placement of direct advertising messages and the negotiation for time and space.

*Photographers* produce product photographs and other setup shots required by an agency or in-house advertising department.

*Sales promotion managers* plan and execute sales programs and sales promotion giveaways.

*Telemarketers* sell products and services by using the telephone to contact prospective customers.

*Traffic department personnel* in advertising agencies coordinate all phases of production. They follow the progress of every job, ensuring that everything is completed on time.

## Direct Marketing Salaries in 1991

Crandall Associates, Inc. of New York City publishes an annual direct marketing national salary guide, usually in April. It presents regional variances in salary ranges for all 50 states and major metropolitan direct marketing centers (see Table 1). The salary ranges vary according to experience in the particular job. Also, salaries are typically 10 percent higher than the base level in major cities, including Boston, Chicago, Washington, D.C., Los Angeles, Philadelphia, and San Francisco. New York City employees generally receive salaries that are 15 percent above base.

# Choosing and Getting a Position

One of the most difficult tasks a person must face is finding a job. It does not make much difference whether it is a person's first job or if she or he is a proven executive. Many people do not know how to look for the position that is ideally suited to them. Choosing and finding a job calls for applying some of the skills you learned in your marketing courses. Following are the steps necessary to select, look for, and find the position that will get you started.

## Getting to Know Yourself

It is extremely important that you evaluate yourself. Career success comes from pursuing your innermost feelings and interests. If you want your output to reflect you, and you take pride in your work, firms will appreciate you and pay you what you are worth.

Self-assessment is the first step and one of the most important components of the job search. Let us suppose you do not know what position to look for. You have average reading, writing, and speaking skills; you are able and willing to make decisions; you want to maximize your self-image; you desire a position that utilizes your abilities and interests at the optimum level; and you are a hard worker. The last is the most critical ingredient, since looking for a job is a lot of hard work. It will pay for you to work through the self-assessment worksheet in Figure 1, developed by the St. John's University Placement and Career Development Center, to acquire better insight into yourself.

**TABLE 1. 1991 Salaries for Direct Marketing Positions.**

Crandall Associates, Inc. have determined the salaries by the following process 1) Discussion with employers, from presidents to personnel officers throughout the country, in companies varying in geographic areas, number of employees, and sales volume. 2) Personal interviews and discussions with the professionals in Direct Marketing at all salary levels, working from coast to coast. 3) Search assignments that have been received nationally, enabling Crandall Associates, Inc. to confirm salary levels that prove to be effective in recruiting candidates from each experience range, and serve as a double check on the figures.

| Position Title And Description | Years Exp. | Base Salary Range (excluding benefits) | | Leading Firms |
|---|---|---|---|---|
| ADVERTISING MANAGER: Corporate responsibility for conversion of marketing plan into communication using creative tools and media. | 1–3 | $34,900 | $46,900 | $47,100 |
| | 4–7 | $46,000 | $50,100 | $54,600 |
| | 7 + | $53,600 | $56,800 | $59,900 |
| AGENCY ACCOUNT EXECUTIVE: Liaison with clients, development of marketing, media, copy and art to secure client's goals within budget. | 1–3 | $21,400 | $25,600 | $29,800 |
| | 4–7 | $26,200 | $34,100 | $37,800 |
| | 7 + | $35,300 | $39,400 | $45,000 |
| AGENCY ACCOUNT SUPERVISOR: Manages account executives, develops new business programs and helps guide the agency's course. | 1–3 | $36,500 | $40,800 | $46,200 |
| | 4–7 | $43,600 | $47,500 | $53,900 |
| | 7 + | $52,400 | $57,000 | $59,900 |
| ART DIRECTOR/Catalog: Sets graphic tone, color, format, type, photography, images and paper for maximum sales at minimum cost. | 1–3 | $22,300 | $24,500 | $29,900 |
| | 4–7 | $26,400 | $32,000 | $38,800 |
| | 7 + | $36,600 | $41,700 | $48,300 |
| ART DIRECTOR/Direct Mail, Space: Conceptualize and design graphics for maximum readership to achieve the marketing objectives. | 1–3 | $28,400 | $31,300 | $35,500 |
| | 4–7 | $34,300 | $36,400 | $40,600 |
| | 7 + | $37,800 | $44,900 | $52,700 |
| ART STAFF: Responsible for the creation of comps, type spec'ing, camera-ready mechanicals, under the direction of the art director. | 1–3 | $18,900 | $20,400 | $23,000 |
| | 4–7 | $20,800 | $24,900 | $26,500 |
| | 7 + | $25,900 | $29,000 | $33,400 |
| CIRCULATION DIRECTOR/Consumer: Identifies the target audience, marketing policy and pricing and guides creative efforts and audits. | 1–3 | $48,100 | $52,400 | $57,800 |
| | 4–7 | $55,700 | $61,000 | $64,800 |
| | 7 + | $62,800 | $67,300 | $76,700 |
| CIRCULATION MANAGER/Consumer: Execution of master plan. Responsible for subscriptions, renewals, newsstand and fulfillment. | 1–3 | $31,700 | $36,100 | $38,900 |
| | 4–7 | $37,400 | $45,900 | $51,100 |
| | 7 + | $48,200 | $54,200 | $62,400 |
| CIRCULATION DIRECTOR/Trade: Penetrates defined audience with specific emphasis on positioning, renewals and audit bureau rules. | 1–3 | $23,600 | $34,200 | $39,900 |
| | 4–7 | $36,700 | $41,500 | $49,400 |
| | 7 + | $46,600 | $52,000 | $56,700 |

(continued)

**TABLE 1. (continued)**

| Position Title And Description | Years Exp. | Base Salary Range (excluding benefits) | | Leading Firms |
|---|---|---|---|---|
| CIRCULATION MANAGER/Trade: Helps develop controlled and/or paid subscriptions and renewals; supervises the fulfillment operation. | 1–3 | $22,100 | $25,600 | $29,000 |
| | 4–7 | $28,200 | $31,500 | $36,700 |
| | 7 + | $34,300 | $38,800 | $40,400 |
| COPY CHIEF: Conceptualizes, supervises, inspires and directs copywriters in creation of written promotional materials for all media. | 1–3 | $28,600 | $31,600 | $36,200 |
| | 4–7 | $33,800 | $38,700 | $42,900 |
| | 7 + | $40,600 | $45,300 | $50,900 |
| COPYWRITER/Catalog: Ability to write copy that sparkles and accurately sells products, generally in very limited space on the page. | 1–3 | $16,900 | $19,200 | $23,400 |
| | 4–7 | $21,900 | $25,600 | $28,900 |
| | 7 + | $27,000 | $34,600 | $38,900 |
| COPYWRITER/Direct Mail, Space: With knowledge of the product or service, ability to sell effectively with solo "packages" or space ads. | 1–3 | $20,300 | $26,400 | $29,500 |
| | 4–7 | $27,700 | $33,800 | $39,000 |
| | 7 + | $34,900 | $42,200 | $46,900 |
| CREATIVE DIRECTOR/Agency: With account group, uses talent and experience to develop copy and graphics for the agency's clients. | 1–3 | $41,800 | $45,600 | $53,600 |
| | 4–7 | $52,400 | $57,200 | $62,800 |
| | 7 + | $59,900 | $64,800 | $71,100 |
| CREATIVE DIRECTOR/Corporate: Guides staff in developing art and copy capabilities for creative communications with customers. | 1–3 | $31,600 | $36,200 | $39,400 |
| | 4–7 | $36,700 | $41,600 | $45,900 |
| | 7 + | $42,900 | $51,800 | $56,800 |
| CUSTOMER SERVICE MANAGER: Responsible for diplomatic, effective satisfaction of customer relations within company's guidelines. | 1–3 | $18,200 | $19,400 | $23,600 |
| | 4–7 | $22,400 | $24,800 | $28,900 |
| | 7 + | $26,300 | $32,300 | $34,600 |
| DATA PROCESSING MANAGER: Responsible for the management information services and systems, design, analysis and programming. | 1–3 | $36,400 | $41,600 | $46,200 |
| | 4–7 | $44,200 | $48,900 | $53,400 |
| | 7 + | $50,200 | $55,600 | $60,100 |
| FULFILLMENT MANAGER/Magazine: Responsible for list maintenance, cashiering and order processing, billing and renewal scheduling. | 1–3 | $25,100 | $28,600 | $32,100 |
| | 4–7 | $29,800 | $34,600 | $37,700 |
| | 7 + | $36,100 | $39,700 | $45,300 |
| FULFILLMENT MANAGER/Product: Supervises merchandise order entry and processing, customer service, inventory, and warehousing. | 1–3 | $33,000 | $37,800 | $41,400 |
| | 4–7 | $39,600 | $42,600 | $46,900 |
| | 7 + | $44,800 | $49,500 | $54,300 |
| LIST MANAGER/Corporate: Supervises, maintains, selects, analyzes, promotes and sells house lists and buys/exchanges outside lists. | 1–3 | $27,700 | $30,200 | $33,900 |
| | 4–7 | $31,800 | $37,000 | $40,300 |
| | 7 + | $38,100 | $43,200 | $44,400 |
| MARKETING DIRECTOR/Consumer Catalog: Determines marketing position, guides merchandise direction and carries the P&L duty. | 1–3 | $41,600 | $46,800 | $53,700 |
| | 4–7 | $50,900 | $57,200 | $65,000 |
| | 7 + | $58,800 | $70,900 | $77,900 |
| MARKET RESEARCH MANAGER: Gathers and distills data into intelligent information utilizing the complete gamut of research tools. | 1–3 | $24,900 | $30,200 | $34,900 |
| | 4–7 | $31,900 | $35,200 | $40,800 |
| | 7 + | $37,900 | $39,000 | $44,000 |

(continued)

**TABLE 1. (continued)**

| Position Title And Description | Years Exp. | Base Salary Range (excluding benefits) | | Leading Firms |
|---|---|---|---|---|
| MARKET RESEARCH/Analyst: Generally using computer-generated material, analyzes raw data with sophisticated statistical techniques. | 1–3 | $20,000 | $22,200 | $24,600 |
| | 4–7 | $23,700 | $25,600 | $28,700 |
| | 7 + | $27,600 | $29,900 | $32,000 |
| MEDIA DIRECTOR: Directs staff in all media expenditures to solve marketing problems at the most efficient cost to client or company. | 1–3 | $29,900 | $34,000 | $36,600 |
| | 4–7 | $35,800 | $37,700 | $40,300 |
| | 7 + | $39,000 | $41,300 | $43,900 |
| MEDIA PLANNER/BUYER: Depending on the size of organizations, develops plans and buys print, broadcast and other media efficiently. | 1–3 | $19,500 | $21,600 | $24,500 |
| | 4–7 | $23,300 | $27,000 | $29,000 |
| | 7 + | $27,900 | $30,400 | $31,600 |
| MERCHANDISE MANAGER: Eye for value and uniqueness, identifies, develops, and buys goods of constant quality in sufficient quantities. | 1–3 | $32,000 | $38,600 | $40,400 |
| | 4–7 | $37,200 | $41,000 | $43,900 |
| | 7 + | $42,400 | $52,300 | $59,000 |
| MERCHANDISE BUYER: Develops products, shops, covers markets, meets and negotiates with vendors and keeps tabs on inventory. | 1–3 | $22,300 | $23,500 | $28,600 |
| | 4–7 | $26,400 | $30,100 | $33,300 |
| | 7 + | $31,600 | $35,900 | $38,000 |
| OPERATIONS DIRECTOR: In large organizations responsibilities include manufacturing, production, procedures, budgets, fulfillment. | 1–3 | $40,600 | $46,000 | $51,200 |
| | 4–7 | $49,600 | $54,800 | $61,800 |
| | 7 + | $60,100 | $67,800 | $72,400 |
| PRODUCTION MANAGER: Knows about processes, particularly printing, to buy or produce materials, with emphasis on costs and quality. | 1–3 | $24,000 | $26,500 | $30,100 |
| | 4–7 | $27,600 | $32,700 | $36,400 |
| | 7 + | $34,200 | $42,300 | $46,500 |
| TELEMARKETING DIRECTOR/Outbound: Complete marketing, strategic and operations responsibility for company's telephone sales. | 1–3 | $40,200 | $46,000 | $50,800 |
| | 4–7 | $51,700 | $59,900 | $64,400 |
| | 7 + | $61,500 | $70,300 | $75,000 |
| TELEMARKETING MANAGER/Outbound: Manages department, its programs and personnel, integrating lists, scripts and marketing plans. | 1–3 | $31,300 | $34,900 | $37,000 |
| | 4–7 | $38,000 | $43,100 | $48,400 |
| | 7 + | $45,500 | $54,200 | $56,700 |
| TELEMARKETING MANAGER/Inbound: Complete responsibility for equipment and integration of order taking and/or customer service. | 1–3 | $28,600 | $32,700 | $38,500 |
| | 4–7 | $37,300 | $39,800 | $43,100 |
| | 7 + | $40,400 | $44,000 | $47,200 |
| TELEMARKETING SUPERVISOR/Inbound: Oversees telemarketing sales representatives in order taking and providing customer service. | 1–3 | $20,800 | $21,600 | $22,100 |
| | 4–7 | $21,800 | $23,800 | $26,700 |
| | 7 + | $24,200 | $25,500 | $29,300 |
| TELEMARKETING TRAINER: Interviews, hires and trains telemarketing sales representatives for continual quality control and motivation. | 1–3 | $24,900 | $27,400 | $28,800 |
| | 4–7 | $27,600 | $31,300 | $36,100 |
| | 7 + | $34,300 | $38,500 | $40,500 |

SOURCE: Crandall Associates, Inc.; DMA Statistical Fact Book, 1991.

## SELF-ASSESSMENT WORKSHEET

Self-assessment is the first step in a successful job search. In order to assist you in this process, the following worksheets have been developed.

Initially the questions below may seem difficult and require a considerable amount of thinking, but you will soon discover that responses to these questions provide valuable insight for you. This knowledge will provide building blocks on which to base your resume writing and interview preparation. If you complete this section of the handbook you should be well prepared for the interview, since the most difficult questions seem to deal with who you are and what you want!

### I. ACHIEVEMENTS

What do you want to achieve?

Imagine that you are writing your autobiography 30 years from now and you are reviewing your past achievements. First list five achievements related to work and then five other achievements which might have occurred during your life. For example, professional honors, political leadership, family security and happiness.

#### Achievements Related to Work

1. ____________________
2. ____________________
3. ____________________
4. ____________________
5. ____________________

#### Achievements Related to Other Areas

1. ____________________
2. ____________________
3. ____________________
4. ____________________
5. ____________________

**FIGURE 1 Self-Assessment Worksheet**

## II. VALUES CLARIFICATION

In the above exercise you listed specific achievements. Each achievement indicates something you value. Check those values which your achievement indicate.

| | | | |
|---|---|---|---|
| _____ | honesty | _____ | live in prestigious places |
| _____ | ambition | _____ | nonconformity |
| _____ | prestige | _____ | rule oriented |
| _____ | wealth | _____ | learning |
| _____ | power | _____ | competition |
| _____ | free time | _____ | creativity |
| _____ | hard work | _____ | independence |
| _____ | loyalty | _____ | stand up for your rights |
| _____ | leadership | _____ | persuasiveness |
| _____ | happiness | _____ | goal oriented |
| _____ | security | _____ | your image or social self |
| _____ | respect | _____ | education |
| _____ | making a contribution | _____ | community belonging |
| _____ | tolerance | _____ | urban environment |
| _____ | obedience | _____ | country environment |
| _____ | diversity | _____ | helping others |
| _____ | being needed | _____ | family life |
| _____ | know important people | _____ | small family |
| _____ | travel | _____ | large family |
| _____ | sports | _____ | other |

---

## ACTIVITIES

List five activities you have enjoyed and why you enjoyed them. They can be activities inside or outside college or community life. For example: Travel—meet different types of people, different backgrounds, cultures, etc. Enjoy diversity of people.

| ACTIVITY | ASSETS |
|---|---|
| 1. ______ | 1. ______ |
| 2. ______ | 2. ______ |
| 3. ______ | 3. ______ |
| 4. ______ | 4. ______ |
| 5. ______ | 5. ______ |

## ASSETS

View yourself as a product which you must sell. What factors will be attractive to your customers (the organizations or firms)? Which assets will sell your talents accurately to the particular firm? List five activities in which you have proven or demonstrated your assets. These should present a positive image to others. For example; as a member of The President's Society, I demonstrated the positive attributes of leadership, public relations and communications.

| ACTIVITY | ASSETS |
|---|---|
| 1. ______ | 1. ______ |
| 2. ______ | 2. ______ |
| 3. ______ | 3. ______ |
| 4. ______ | 4. ______ |
| 5. ______ | 5. ______ |

## IDEAL JOB OBJECTIVE TODAY

Indicate the ideal job for you today based on your answers to the previous exercises. If the labor market was open and supply did not exceed demand, what would your present career/job objective be?

______

______

______

______

______

______

## REALISTIC JOB OBJECTIVE TODAY

Indicate your job objective based on your answers to the previous exercises and the tight job market where supply exceeds demand and in some cases specific fields are virtually closed. What would your job strategy be?

## REALISTIC THREE-YEAR JOB OBJECTIVE

SOURCE: St. John's University Placement Guide as laid out with the spacing and bold headings.

TESTS. If you still have some questions about your interests, skills, and values, you might consider taking some standardized aptitude, ability, or personality tests. The Strong-Campbell Interest Inventory matches a number of the test taker's traits with those of people involved in specific professions. For example, if you share personal and professional characteristics with marketing researchers, the test will reveal a "fit" with this field, and you will probably enjoy the work.

The Myers-Briggs Type Indicator attempts to discover your "personality type," such as whether you are intuitive or facts-oriented, emotional or analytic, extroverted or introverted. The test may direct you to become a list broker instead of a computer analyst.

BOOKS. For those that have the drive, stamina, and interest, a trip to the library, placement office, or local bookstore can be very beneficial. There are some excellent books available, many written in a humorous, easy-to-read style. Among the recommended books are the following:

*What Color Is Your Parachute?* by Richard N. Bolles, (Berkeley, CA: Ten Speed Press), 1991.

*Exploring Careers in Advertising* by E. L. Deckinger and Jules B. Singer, (New York, NY: Rosen Publishing Group), 1985.

*Guerilla Tactics in the Job Market* by Tom Jackson, (Bantam Books), 1991.

COMPUTER PROGRAMS. There are some excellent computer programs available to speed your job search. The first one listed will assist you in self-analysis and in designing and organizing your resume. The second one provides information on 500 major companies, with information on addresses, number of employees, and most recent annual revenues. The last one provides an activity journal, a word processor, a guided letter-writing system, and an appointment scheduler.

The Perfect Resume, by Bill Buckingham and Tom Jackson
Permax Systems Inc.
5008 Gordon Avenue
Madison, WI 53716

Jobhunt
Scope International
P.O. Box 598
Alexandria Bay, N.Y. 13607-0598

ResumeMaker
Individual Software Inc.
125 Shoreway Road, Suite 3000
San Carlos, CA 94070

INTERNSHIPS. Significant benefits can be derived from internships while going to college, whether you receive course credit or not, whether you get paid or not. It is a way for students to determine if the line of work or industry is attractive to them. This is a means of getting acclimated to the business world. One can write it up as experience on the resume. An internship is like a honeymoon. Both sides see if they are made for each other. Often it leads to future employment. Here one develops confidence and marketability to others. More colleges are beginning to develop internship programs.

## The Job Search

SETTING PERSONAL GOALS AND OBJECTIVES. The following procedure should help you find the position that is for you. It is assumed that you have done a self-assessment and that you know your strengths and weaknesses.

1. You must decide exactly what you want to do.
2. You must decide exactly where you want to do it, through your own research and personal survey.
3. You must research the organizations that interest you at great length, and then approach the one individual in each organization who has the power to hire you for the job that you have decided you want to do.[2]

---

2. Richard Nelson Bolles, *What Color Is Your Parachute?* (Berkeley, CA: Ten Speed Press).

You can do this on your own. Go after those occupations in which a combination of skills results in synergies and in which you have a differential advantage. You'll be surprised at the many jobs you can handle.

After further analysis of your desires, you must decide whether the position you are seeking is for the purpose of gaining experience, advancement opportunities, monetary, compatible and intelligent associates, security, permanence, or any combination of these or other reasons. For example, Terry Byrne was interested in getting into the direct marketing field. When she heard at a trade show that *Direct Marketing* magazine was looking for a sales trainee, she applied for the position. Here was an applicant with little experience who jumped with joy at the chance to apply. She accepted the offer, which provided this young person with a solid foundation for growth and advancement.

The decision must be made as to where you would be willing to work. In other words, you must decide whether you are willing to relocate. For example, Bill Holden was offered a position as assistant account executive with Ogilvy & Mather in Los Angeles. At the time, he was a St. John's University student working in an internship program in their New York office. After discussing it with his girlfriend, he accepted the job.

It is important to figure out your minimum salary requirements before going for an interview. Develop several budgets, ranging from one of "subsistence" to one of "heaven." To each of the budgets add 20 percent, since people habitually underestimate their needs. The mean of these budgets should aid you in determining to which salary offer you should agree.

## Sources of Information

If you know the companies you want to work for, read their annual reports, brochures, and other materials about them in periodicals in your school library or college placement office. Figure 2 is a listing of all information available at the St. John's University Placement and Career Development Center.

Additional information can be derived at trade shows, career days, and direct marketing conferences and workshops. Other sources are:

Direct Marketing Association
Direct Marketing Educational Foundation, Inc.
6 East 43rd Street
New York, NY 10017
212/689-4977

Direct Marketing Day in New York
Education Committee
1626-1-A Locust Avenue
Bohemia, NY 11716
516/563-3880 (DMD Desk)

## INTRODUCTION

Planning your individual career is an important and detailed process. The Placement and Career Development Center realizes your potential. Our wide array of services, coupled with your fine academic background will give you a competitive edge in the job market.

This brochure outlines the various elements regarding your individual needs that are critical to a professional and successful job search. We want you to become familiar with and take full advantage of all resources available.

The responsibility is yours. We stand ready to assist your every need in a comprehensive and detailed manner. Feel free to contact us at:

**PLACEMENT**
**AND CAREER**
**DEVELOPMENT CENTER**
MARILLAC HALL — SB. 36
(718) 990-6375

## SERVICES

CAREER COUNSELING.

Employment advisement is an integral part of the Placement function. Specially trained counselors can assist you in analyzing your interests, aptitudes, personal needs and goals as well as to review occupational information including "alternate careers."

ON-CAMPUS INTERVIEW PROGRAM.

The On-Campus Interview Program brings to campus a number of representatives from companies within every field of study to interview graduating students for a variety of professional positions.

FULL TIME EMPLOYMENT OPPORTUNITIES.

The Center provides full-time job referrals to all students and alumni that are currently seeking positions. Individuals can repeatedly take advantage of this service whenever the need arises.

PART TIME EMPLOYMENT OPPORTUNITIES.

A composite listing of part time vacancies is available to the entire St. John's community. New openings are posted daily in various fields. Part time employment helps the student meet academic expenses while gaining practical experience in their chosen field.

**FIGURE 2 Professional Services Available at Placement Center**

## CAREER RESOURCE LIBRARY.

A comprehensive collection of career development and placement information is available for students and alumni. This includes employer directories, career literature, annual reports and career information. In addition, trade journals are available regarding up to date information on various career areas.

## SPECIAL CAREER AWARENESS PROGRAMS.

These Programs are to assist you in understanding the realities of the marketplace and help you relate realistically to individual interests and demands of the current labor market. Workshops include self assessment, resume preparation, dressing for success, senior employment advisement, and handling the interview. Information is posted daily in the center regarding upcoming programs and workshops.

## VIDEOTAPE LIBRARY.

The videotape library includes a comprehensive collection of videotape productions which gives the student an opportunity to explore various career fields from successful St. John's alumni. Also available are videos regarding interviewing techniques for different situations. A composite listing is available at the Placement and Career Development Center.

## RESUME WRITING WORKSHOPS.

These workshops are geared toward an in-depth analysis of individual resume preparation. In addition to format structure, further areas of discussion include printing, layout and styles. Consideration is also given to cover letter preparation, successful resume distribution and follow up procedures.

## MOCK INTERVIEW SESSIONS.

Students and alumni are invited to sharpen their individual skills by participating in a taped mock interview. This is then evaluated and suggestions are made on improving effectiveness. Individuals are given the opportunity to repeat the mock interview process to further improve.

## JOB SEARCH MANUAL.

This placement manual is designed to provide practical information in the areas of resume writing and employment interviewing. Several model resumes are included for review. Additionally, the manual contains a list of area directories and specialized resource books.

## EDUCATION CREDENTIAL FOLDERS.

The Center maintains a complete credential service for individuals in Education. Credentials are forwarded to prospective employers upon request by individuals. Once opened, these non-confidential folders may be viewed by the individual during normal business hours.

**FIGURE 2 (continued)**

**TABLE 2. Successful Job Finding Methods for SJU Graduates, 1980-86.**

| | All | | Males | | Females | |
|---|---|---|---|---|---|---|
| Method | Number | Percent | Number | Percent | Number | Percent |
| Own initiative | 158 | 30 | 96 | 30 | 62 | 31 |
| Networking | 115 | 22 | 70 | 22 | 45 | 22 |
| College placement | 76 | 15 | 45 | 14 | 31 | 15 |
| Worked for firm | 59 | 11 | 36 | 11 | 23 | 11 |
| Employment agency | 59 | 11 | 34 | 11 | 25 | 12 |
| Other | 35 | 7 | 26 | 8 | 9 | 4 |
| Classified | 22 | 4 | 14 | 4 | 8 | 4 |
| Total | 524 | | 321 | | 203 | |

Publications:

*Advertising Age*
*Catalog Age*
*Direct Marketing*
*DM News*
*Journal of Direct Marketing*
*Target Marketing*
*Teleprofessional*
*Wall Street Journal*

## Job Finding Methods

What is the best method for finding a position? According to a study done by one of the authors, using one's own initiative was most successful during the years 1980 to 1986 for St. John's University College of Business Administration students (see Table 2).

Networking and college placement were other successful methods. Using newspapers had limited value. Graduates of 1990 and Seniors of 1991 ranked professors' recommendations, internships, and college placement very high in terms of job search success. Many believed that networking was an important factor in their finding a position.

Two other necessary skills are writing a resume and selling yourself in an interview. Once learned, these skills will prove invaluable throughout your climb up the career ladder.

## Writing A Resume

The goal of a resume is to sell yourself. It should gain a positive response from the employer for whom you want to work. Go to your college placement office and study the brochures on resume writing. Read some of the books on the subject. If you are a computer buff, go through some of the excellent programs available on writing a resume.

First, study the layout of a resume. Use bold type to emphasize your name; headings for major sections such as *Education, Honors, and Awards, and Employment*; extracurricular activities; and each employment position by title. Typefaces that are especially effective for resumes include Helvetica, Times Roman and Palatino. Select type sizes between 9 and 12 points.[3] Sections should be separated by double spacing or rules. Important entries can be highlighted by bullets or dashes. There should be adequate margins.

Second, use action words to promote your competence, maturity, positive attitude, and leadership qualities. Use phrases such as the following: "received a cum laude degree"; "worked my way through college"; "hired, supervised, selected five employees"; "introduced, developed three new programs"; "led a team project"; "listed on the dean's list in the senior year".

Third, keep the resume simple—limited to one page, yet interesting. Present only positive items. Use white paper and black ink.

Fourth, cover letters should be addressed to an individual. Here state why you picked this company to write to; your objective, which should be supported by the information in the resume; and, if possible, something unique about yourself that will make you an attractive prospect.

Fifth, follow up the resume with a telephone call. It shows that you are serious about the job. However, don't overdo calling back.

## Interviewing

Company recruiters regard interviews as part of their job of evaluating you face to face, getting further information on you, and, if they like what they see, selling you on working for their company. Recruiters are interested in hiring hardworking, smart, dedicated, and dependable new employees. Before going for an interview, practice with someone who has gone through this process. At St. John's University all students in the College of Business have to practice interviewing by taking a "Marketing Yourself" module as part of the class in principles of marketing. You might help yourself by observing the following recommendations.

### PLANNING PRIOR TO INTERVIEW

1. Do homework on the corporation that will interview you so that your research shows.
2. Do homework on yourself so that you have the ability to sell yourself to the interviewers.

3. Myra Fournier "Looking Good on paper" *College Edition of the National Business Employment Weekly*, (Spring 1990), pp. 34–35.

3. Practice interviewing with a counselor, friend, or parent and ask for an evaluation.
4. Set up a support group in which you discuss and review your interviews. Other classmates seeking employment will go through the same frustrating experiences that you will. The support group is a method of improving your interview skills and letting go of anxieties. Through discussion everyone participating will benefit.
5. Prepare answers for likely questions such as the following.
    a. What qualities do you believe this company should look for in a person for this position?
    b. What has been your greatest success? Disappointment?
    c. What do you consider to be your greatest strengths? Weaknesses?
    d. Would you talk about the best supervisor you ever had? The worst supervisor you ever had?
    e. Why do you want to join our firm?
    f. Would you tell me how you spent your spare time each day last week?
    g. Would you tell me about your health over the last seven years?
6. Prepare at least three questions to ask about the company. Do not ask about the salary for the position at the first interview.
7. Dress conservatively for the interview.
8. Check how you look in front of a mirror before the interview. Check such aspects of your appearance as hair, makeup, nails, suit, shirt and tie, cleanliness, socks, and polished shoes.
9. Review all the points you expect to bring up during the interview.
10. Arrive about 15 minutes before the interview. If the interview is being conducted at the company, reconnoiter the grounds. If the interview is being conducted at school, check the schedule, room number, and name of the interviewer.
11. Be respectful of the secretary if the interview is being conducted at the company. Don't pick your nose or show your nervousness while waiting. At times, secretaries are part of the interviewing team.

## PLAN FOR INTERVIEW

1. Be confident, and show that you are prepared for the interview. Give it all you have; that is all that is expected from you.
2. Give a firm handshake to the interviewer. Say "hello" and state your name.
3. Let the interviewer control the discussion. If she or he is close to your age and proffers a first name, then you may use it. Otherwise leave it on a last name basis. The discussion will probably start with chitchat for the first two minutes. The information exchange will start shortly thereafter.
4. Be yourself with the interviewer, but not chummy.

5. Maintain good posture, eye contact, and clear speech. Do not smoke or play with your hair or clothing. Wear minimal jewelry.
6. Have available extra copies of your resume.
7. Show your portfolio of class projects if this is relevant to the position.
8. Point out your marketable skills such as:
   a. The ability to comprehend written material and to speak and write effectively
   b. The ability to work effectively with others
   c. The ability to gain acceptance of your ideas, motivate others, and work with the public
   d. The ability to work independently and manage your time effectively.[4]
9. Answer the questions in sentences; don't give one-word answers. Explain your responses when appropriate.
10. Ask your prepared questions before the end of the interview.
11. State that you "enjoyed the interview and are very much interested in the job offer" before leaving.
12. Give a firm handshake and say, "Thank you for your time and interview. When will I hear your decision?"

## Plan for After Interview

1. Write down all the important factors. Record the name of everyone that spoke with you and their titles. Will you hear from them, or do you have to follow up by a certain date?
2. Review the interview with your support group. What can you learn from your experience? What did you do right? What did you do wrong and should change in the future?
3. Listen to your classmates and give your advice and support.
4. Remember that it takes time to find the right job for you or anyone else. At times it will be frustrating. However, you have your support group to stand by you.
5. If you have some advice that you would like to share with others, please write to the following address:

   Dr. Herbert Katzenstein
   St. John's University
   Jamaica, New York 11439

4. Lee A. Lewis, "Buy me! Buy me!" *The College Edition of the National Business Employment Weekly*, published by the Wall Street Journal, Fall 1990, pp. 21–22.

# GLOSSARY

**Access Time:** The time it takes a computer to locate a piece of information in memory or storage and to take action (i.e., the "read" time). Also, the time it takes a computer to store a piece of information and to complete action (i.e., the "write" time).

**Account Executive:** The liaison between agency and client, receiving all client approvals, requests, and complaints. The account executive musters all the agency's services for the benefit of the client.

**Action Devices:** Items and techniques used in a mailing to initiate the response desired.

**Active Buyer:** A buyer whose latest purchase was made within the last 12 months. (See *Buyer*.)

**Active Customer:** A term used interchangeably with *active buyer.*

**Active Member:** Any member who is fulfilling the original commitment or who has fulfilled that commitment and has made one or more purchases in the last 12 months.

**Active Subscriber:** One who has committed for regular delivery of magazines, books, or other goods or services for a period of time still in effect.

**Actives:** (1) Customers on a list who have made purchases within a prescribed time period, usually not more than one year. (2) Subscribers whose subscriptions have not expired.

**Additions:** New names, either of individuals or companies, added to a mailing list.

**Add on Service:** A service of the Direct Marketing Association that gives consumers an opportunity to request that their names be added to mailing lists.

**Address Coding Guide (CG):** A listing that contains the actual or potential beginning and ending house numbers, block group and/or enumeration district numbers, ZIP codes, and other geographic codes for all city delivery service streets served by 3,154 post offices located within 6,601 ZIP code regions.

**Address Correction Requested:** An endorsement that, when printed in the upper-left corner of the address portion of the mailing piece (below the return address), authorizes the U.S. Postal Service, for a fee, to provide the known new address of a person no longer at the address on the mailing piece.

**Advertising Managers:** Those responsible for the administration, planning, and budgeting of advertising activities, supervision of outside advertising services, and coordination with other company departments.

**A.I.D.A.:** The most popular formula for the preparation of direct mail copy. The letters stand for *Get Attention. Arouse Interest. Stimulate Desire. Ask for Action.*

**Alphanumeric:** A contraction of *alphabetic* and *numeric,* a term that applies to any coding system that provides for letters, numbers (digits), and special symbols such as punctuation marks. Synonymous with *alphameric.*

**Art Directors:** Those responsible for the visual presentation of the ad.

**Assigned Mailing Dates:** The dates on which the list user has the obligation to mail a specific list. No other date is acceptable without specific approval of the list owner.

**Audience:** The total number of individuals reached by a promotion or advertisement.

**Audit:** A printed report of the counts involved in a particular list or file.

**Back End:** (1) The activities necessary to complete a mail order transaction once an order has been received. (2) The measurement of a buyer's performance after he or she has ordered the first item in a series offering.

**Bangtail:** Promotional envelope with a second flap that is perforated and designed for use as an order blank.

**Batch Processing:** Techniques of executing a set of computer programs/selections in batches as opposed to executing each order/selection as it is received. Batches can be created by computer programing or a manual collection of data into groups.

**Batched Job:** A job that is grouped with other jobs as input to a computing system, as opposed to a transaction job entry where the job is done singly to completion.

**Bill Enclosure:** Any promotional piece or notice enclosed with a bill, an invoice, or a statement not directed toward the collection of all or part of the bill, invoice, or statement.

**Binary:** A selection, choice, or condition involving two possibilities, such as the use of the symbols 0 and 1 in a numbering system.

**Bingo Card:** A reply card inserted in a publication and used by readers to request literature and samples from companies whose products and services are either advertised or mentioned in editorial columns.

**Bit:** A single element in a binary number (digit). The smallest element of binary machine language represented by a magnetized spot on a recording surface or a magnetized element of a storage device.

**Bounce-Back:** An offer enclosed with mailings sent to a customer in fulfillment of an order.

**BPI (Bytes per Inch):** The number of characters, represented by bytes, per inch.

**Brand Managers:** Managers of consumer and industrial firms who coordinate sales promotion and merchandising of a product or line of products.

**Broadcast Medium:** A direct response source, such as radio, television, and cable TV.

**Broadside:** A single sheet of paper, printed on one or both sides, folded for mailing or direct distribution and opening into a single, large advertisement.

**Brochure:** Strictly, a high quality pamphlet with especially planned layout, typography, and illustrations. The term is also used loosely for any promotional pamphlet or booklet.

**Bucktag:** A separate slip attached to a printed piece containing instructions to route the material to specific individuals.

**Bulk Mail:** A category of third-class mail involving a large quantity of identical pieces addressed to different names that are specially processed for mailing before delivery to the post office.

**Burst:** To separate continuous-form paper into discrete sheets.

**Business List:** Any compilation or list of individuals or companies based on a business-associated interest, inquiry, membership, subscription, or purchase.

**Buyer:** One who orders merchandise, books, records, information, or services. Unless a qualifying word is used, it is assumed that a buyer has paid for all merchandise to date.

**Byte:** A sequence of adjacent binary digits operated on as a unit and usually shorter than a computer word. A character is usually considered a byte. (A single byte can contain either two numeric characters or one alphabetic or special character.)

**C/A:** Change of address.

**Cash Buyer:** A buyer who encloses payment with the order.

**Cash Rider:** Also called *cash up* or *cash option* a situation where an order form offers installment terms. But a postscript offers the option of sending full cash payment with the order, usually at some saving over the credit price as an incentive.

**Catalog:** A book or booklet showing merchandise, with descriptive details and prices.

**Catalog Buyer:** A person who has bought products or services from a catalog.

**Catalog Managers:** Those who select merchandise for inclusion in catalogs, work with manufacturers, order catalogs, and monitor order fulfillment.

**Catalog Request:** (Paid or unpaid) One who sends for a catalog (prospective buyer). The catalog may be free, there may be a nominal charge for postage and handling, or there may be a more substantial charge that is often refunded or credited on the first order.

**Census Tract:** A small geographic area established by local committees and approved by the Census Bureau, containing a population segment with relatively uniform economic and social characteristics with clearly identifiable boundaries, averaging approximately 1,200 households.

**Cheshire Label:** Specially prepared paper (rolls, fanfold, or accordion fold) used to reproduce names and addresses to be mechanically affixed, one at a time, to a mailing piece.

**Circulars:** General term for printed advertising in any form, including printed matter sent out by direct mail.

**Cleaning:** The process of correcting or removing a name and address from a mailing list because it is no longer correct or because the listing is to be shifted from one category to another.

**Cluster Selection:** A selection routine based on taking a group of names in series, skipping a group, taking another group, and so on. For example, a cluster selection on an nth-name basis might be the first 10 out of every 100 or the first 125 out of every 175. A cluster selection using limited ZIP codes might be the first 200 names in each of the specified ZIP codes.

**Coding:** (1) Devices used with replies to identify the mailing list or other source from which the address was obtained. (2) A structure of letters and numbers used to classify characteristics of an address on a list.

**Collate:** (1) To assemble individual elements of a mailing in sequence for inserting into a mailing envelope. (2) A program that combines two or more ordered files to produce a single ordered file. Also, the act of combining such files. Synonymous with *merge* in *merge purge*.

**Commission:** A percentage of a sale, by prior agreement, paid to the list broker, list manager, or other service arm for their part in the list usage.

**Compile:** The process by which a computer translates a series of instructions written in a programing language into actual machine language.

**Compiled List:** Names and addresses derived from directories, newspapers, public records, retail sales slips, trade show registrations, and other sources to identify groups of people with something in common.

**Compiler:** An organization that develops lists of names and addresses from directories, newspapers, public records, registrations, and other sources, identifying groups of people, companies, or institutions with something in common.

**Completed Cancel:** One who has completed a specific commitment to buy products or services before canceling.

**Comprehensive:** Complete and detailed layout for a printed piece.

**Computer:** A data processor that can perform substantial computation, without intervention by a human.

**Computer Compatibility:** The ability to interchange the data or programs of one computer system with one or more other computers.

**Computer Letter:** Computer-printed message providing personalized, fill-in information from a source file in predesignated positions. May also be a fully printed letter with personalized insertions.

**Computer Personalization:** The printing of letters or other promotional pieces by a computer using names, addresses, special phrases, and other information based on data appearing in one or more computer records. The objective is to use the information in the computer records to tailor the promotional message to a specific individual.

**Computer Program:** A series of instructions or statements prepared to achieve a certain result.

**Computer Record:** All of the information about an individual, company, or transaction stored on a specific magnetic tape or disk.

**Computer Service Bureau:** An internal or external facility providing general or specific data processing services.

**Consumer List:** A list of names (usually at home address) compiled or resulting from a common inquiry or buying activity indicating a general or specific buying interest.

**Continuity Program:** Products or services bought as a series of small purchases rather than all at one time. Generally based on a common theme and shipped at regular or specific time intervals.

**Continuous Form:** Paper forms designed for computer printing that are folded, and sometimes perforated, at predetermined vertical measurements. These may be letters, vouchers, invoices, cards, or other forms.

**Contributor List:** Names and addresses of persons who have given to a specific fundraising effort. (See *Donor List.*)

**Controlled Circulation:** Distribution at no charge of a publication to individuals or companies on the basis of titles or occupations. Typically, recipients are asked from time to time to verify the information that qualifies them to receive the publication.

**Controlled Duplication:** A method by which names and addresses from two or more lists are matched (usually by computer) in order to eliminate or limit extra mailings to the same name and address.

**Conversion:** (1) The process of changing from one method of data processing to another, or from one data processing system to another. Synonymous with *reformatting.* (2) To secure specific action such as a purchase or contribution from a name on a mailing list or as a result of an inquiry.

**Co-op Mailing:** A mailing of two or more offers included in the same envelope or other carrier, with each participating mailer sharing mailing costs according to some predetermined formula.

**Copywriters:** Those who create the words and concepts for ads and commercials.

**Coupon:** Part of an advertising promotion piece intended to be filled in by the inquirer or customer and returned to the advertiser.

**Coupon Clipper:** One who has given evidence of responding to free or nominal cost offers out of curiosity, with little or no serious interest or buying intent.

**C.P.I. (Cost per Inquiry):** A simple arithmetical formula derived by dividing the total cost of a mailing or an advertisement by the number of inquiries received.

**C.P.M. (Cost per Thousand):** Refers to the total cost per thousand pieces of direct mail "in the mail."

**C.P.O. (Cost per Order):** Similar to *cost per inquiry* but based on actual orders rather than inquiries.

**C.T.O.:** Contribution to overhead (profit).

**Database Processors:** Those whose duties include keeping up-to-date lists of consumer information, including names, addresses, and telephone numbers; psychographic and demographic data; and data on recency, frequency, and monetary value of purchases.

**Deadbeat:** One who has ordered a product or service and, without just cause, hasn't paid for it.

**Decoy:** A unique name specially inserted in a mailing list for verifying list usage.

**Delinquent:** One who has fallen behind or has stopped scheduled payment for a product or service.

**Delivery Date:** The date a list user or a designated representative of the list user receives a specific list order from the list owner.

**Demographics:** Socioeconomic characteristics pertaining to a geographic unit (county, city, sectional center, ZIP code, group of households, education, ethnicity, income level, etc.).

**Direct Mail:** A promotional medium whereby postal services provide the means of communicating with would-be buyers.

**Direct-Mail Advertising:** Any promotional effort using the U.S. Postal Service or other direct delivery service for distribution of the advertising message.

**Direct Marketing:** Paid-for communication in media expressly eliciting a direct, measurable response, such as an order, an inquiry, or a visit to a store or showroom.

**Direct Response Advertising:** Sending out sales messages by any medium.

**Donor List:** A list of persons who have given money to one or more charitable organizations. (See *Contributor List.*)

**Doubling Day:** A point in time established by previous experience when 50 percent of all returns to a mailing will normally be received.

**Dummy:** (1) A mock-up giving a preview of a printed piece, showing the placement and nature of the material to be printed. (2) A fictitious name with a mailable address inserted into a mailing list to check on usage of that list.

**Dupe (Duplication):** Appearance of identical or nearly identical entities more than once.

**Duplication Elimination:** A specific kind of controlled duplication providing that no matter how many times a name and address is on a list, and how many lists contain that name and address, it will be accepted for mailing only once by that mailer. Also referred to as *dupe elimination.*

**Editing Rules:** Specific rules used in preparing name and address records that treat all elements the same way at all times. Also, the rules for rearranging, deleting, selecting, or inserting any needed data, symbols, or characters.

**Envelope Stuffer:** Any advertising or promotional material enclosed in an envelope with business letters, statements, or invoices.

**Exchange:** An arrangement whereby two mailers exchange equal quantities of mailing list names.

**Expiration:** A subscription that is not renewed.

**Expiration Date:** The date when a subscription expires.

**Expire:** A former customer who is no longer an active buyer.

**Field:** (1) A reserved area in a computer that services a similar function in all records of the file. (2) A location on a magnetic tape or disk drive that has definable limitations and meaning (e.g., Position 1-30 is the name field).

**File Maintenance:** The activity of keeping a file up to date by adding, changing, or deleting data (all or part). Synonymous with *list Maintenance.* (See *Update.*)

**Fill-in:** A name, address, or other words added to a preprinted letter.

**First-Time Buyer:** One who buys a product or service from a specific company for the first time.

**Fixed Field:** A way of laying out or formatting list information in a computer file that puts every piece of data in a specific position relative to every other piece of data, and limits the amount of space assigned to that data. If a piece of data is missing from an individual record, or if its assigned space is not completely used, that space is not filled (every record has the same space and the same length). Any data exceeding its assigned space limitation must be abbreviated or contracted.

**Former Buyer:** One who has bought one or more times from a company but has made no purchase in the last 12 months.

**Freestanding Insert:** A promotional piece loosely inserted or nested in a newspaper or magazine.

**Frequency:** The number of times an individual has ordered within a specific period of time. (See *Monetary Value* and *Recency.*)

**Friend of a Friend:** The result of one party sending in the name of someone considered to be interested in a specific advertiser's product or service; a third-party inquiry. Also called *friend recommendation.*

**Front End:** Necessary activities leading to an order or a contribution.

**Fulfillment:** Activity covering everything that happens from the receipt of an order to the shipment of the product to the customer or subscriber.

**Fulfillment Managers:** Personnel who handle the back-end operations of direct marketing business. These include receiving mail and telephone orders, processing orders, checking credit, billing, maintaining inventory, sending goods, and handling complaints.

**Fund-Raising List:** Any compilation or list or individuals or companies based on a known contribution to one or more fund-raising appeals.

**Geographics:** Any method of subdividing a list, based on geographic or political subdivisions (ZIP codes, sectional centers, cities, counties, states, regions).

**Gift Buyer:** One who buys a product or service for another.

**Gimmick:** Attention-getting device, usually dimensional, attached to a direct mail printed piece.

**Guarantee:** A pledge of satisfaction made by the seller to the buyer and specifying the terms by which the seller will make good this pledge.

**Hotline List:** The most recent names available on a specific list, but no older than three months. In any event, use of the term *hotline* should be qualified by *weekly, monthly,* or other specified period.

**House List:** Any list of names owned by a company as a result of compilation, that is used to promote that company's products or services.

**House List Duplicate:** Duplication of name and address records between the user's own lists and any list being mailed by the user on a one-time-use arrangement.

**Inquiry:** One who has asked for literature or other information about a product or service. Unless otherwise stated, it is assumed that no payment has been made for the literature or other information. (*Note:* A catalog request is generally considered a specific type of inquiry.)

**Installment Buyer:** One who orders goods or services and pays for them in two or more periodic payments after delivery.

**Interlist Duplicate:** Duplication of name and address records between two or more lists, other than house lists, being mailed by a list user.

**Intralist Duplication:** Duplication of name and address records within a given list.

**K:** Used in reference to computer storage capacity, generally accepted as 1,000. Analogous to *M* in the direct marketing industry.

**KBN (Kill Bad Names):** Action taken with undeliverable addresses (i.e., *nixies*). You KBN a nixie.

**Key:** One or more characters within a data group that can be used to identify it or control its use. Synonymous with *key code* in mailing business.

**Key Code:** A group of letters and/or numbers, colors, or other markings used to measure the effectiveness of media, lists, advertisements, offers, and so forth, or any parts thereof.

**Keyline:** Any one of many partial or complete descriptions of past buying history coded to include name and address information and current status.

**Label:** A piece of paper containing the name and address of the recipient, applied to a mailing for address purposes.

**Layout:** (1) Artist's sketch showing relative positioning of illustrations, headlines, and copy. (2) Positioning subject matter on a press sheet for most effective production.

**Letter Shop:** A business organization that handles the mechanical details of mailings, such as addressing, imprinting, and collating. Most letter shops offer some printing facilities, and many offer some degree of creative direct mail services.

**Letterhead:** The printing on a letter that identifies the sender.

**List:** Also called *mailing list*, names and addresses of individuals and/or companies having in common a specific characteristic or activity of interest.

**List Brokers:** Middlemen and specialists who make all necessary arrangements for a mailer. They select, evaluate, and recommend lists. They research the size and potential of a market and check out mechanics and delivery dates.

**List Buyer:** Technically, one who actually buys mailing lists. In practice, however, also one who orders mailing lists for one-time use.

**List Cleaning:** The process of correcting or removing a name and/or address from a mailing list. Also used in the identification and elimination of house list duplication.

**List Compiler:** One who develops lists of names and addresses from directories, newspapers, public records, sales slips, trade show registrations, and other sources, for identifying groups of people or companies with something in common.

**List Exchange:** A barter arrangement between two companies for the use of a mailing list. May be list for list, list for space, or list for comparable value—other than money.

**List Maintenance:** Any manual, mechanical, or electronic system for keeping name and address records (with or without other data) up to date.

**List Manager:** One who, as an employee of a list owner or as an outside agent, is responsible for the use by others of a specific mailing list. The list manager generally serves the list owner in several or all of the following capacities: list maintenance (or advice thereon), list promotion and marketing, list clearance and record keeping, collecting for use of the list by others.

**List Owner:** One who, by promotional activity or compilation, has developed a list of names having something in common; or one who has purchased (as opposed to rented, reproduced, or used on a one time basis) such a list from the developer.

**List Rental:** An arrangement whereby a list owner furnishes names to a mailer, together with the privilege of using the list on a one-time basis only (unless otherwise specified in advance). For this privilege, the list owner is paid a royalty by the mailer. (*list rental* is the term most often used; however, *list reproduction* and *list usage* more accurately describe the transaction, since *rental* is not used in its ordinary sense of leasing property.)

**List Royalty:** Payment to list owners for the privilege of using their names on a one time basis.

**List Sample:** A group of names selected from a list in order to evaluate the responsiveness of that list.

**List Segmentation:** See *List Selection*.

**List Selection:** Characteristics used to define smaller groups within a list (essentially, lists within a list). Although very small, select groups may be very desirable and may substantially improve response, increased costs often render them impractical.

**List Sequence:** The order in which names and addresses appear in a list. Most lists today are in ZIP code sequence, and some are alphabetical by name within the ZIP code; others are in carrier sequence (postal delivery), and still others may use some other order within the ZIP code. Some lists are still arranged alphabetically by name, chronologically, or by some other variation or combination.

**List Sort:** The process of putting a list in a specific sequence from another sequence or from no sequence.

**List Test:** Part of a list selected in order to determine the effectiveness of the entire list. (See *List Sample*.)

**List User:** One who uses names and addresses on someone else's list as prospects for the user's product or service; similar to *mailer.*

**Load Up:** The process of offering a buyer the opportunity of buying an entire series at one time after the customer has purchased the first item in that series.

**Magnetic Tape:** A storage device for electronically recording and reproducing, by use of a computer, defined bits of data.

**Mail Date:** The date at which a list user, by prior agreement with the list owner, is obligated to mail a specific list. No other date is acceptable without specific approval of the list owner.

**Mail Order:** A device that advertises goods and services through any medium—television, magazines, newspapers, and others.

**Mail Order Action Line (MOAL):** A service of Direct Marketing Association that assists consumers in resolving problems with mail order purchases.

**Mail Order Buyer:** One who offers, and pays for, a product or service through the mail. (Generally, an order telephoned in response to a direct response advertisement is considered a direct substitute for an order sent through postal channels.)

**Mail Preference Service (MPS):** A service of Direct Marketing Association wherein consumers can request to have their names removed from or added to mailing lists. These names are made available to both members and nonmembers of the association.

**Mailer:** (1) A direct mail advertiser who promotes a product or service using lists of others, house lists, or both. (2) A printed direct mail advertising piece. (3) A folding carton wrapper or tube used to protect materials in the mails.

**Mailgram:** A combination telegram-letter, with the telegram transmitted to a postal facility close to the address and then delivered as first-class mail.

**Mailing Machine:** A machine that attaches labels to mailing pieces and otherwise prepares such pieces for deposit in the postal system.

**Marketing Research:** The function that links consumer, customer, and public to the marketer through information used to identify marketing opportunities and problems; to generate, refine, and evaluate marketing actions; to monitor marketing performance; and to improve understanding of marketing as a process.

**Master File:** A file that is of a permanent nature or regarded in a particular job as authoritative, or one that contains all subfiles.

**Match:** A direct mail term referring to the typing of addresses, salutations, or inserts onto letters with other copy imprinted by a printing process.

**Match Code:** A code determined by either the creator or the user of a file for matching records contained in another file.

**Media Directors:** Individuals who evaluate media according to efficiency and cost and then recommend the best medium or medium combination to use.

**Media Persons:** In advertising agencies, those concerned with the placement of direct advertising messages and the negotiation for time and space.

**MOAL:** Acronym for *Mail Order Action Line*.

**Monetary Value:** Total expenditures by a customer during a specific period of time, generally 12 months.

**MPS:** Acronym for *Mail Preference Service.*

**Multiple Buyer:** One who has bought two or more times (not one who has bought two or more items, one time only). Also called a *multibuyer* or *repeat buyer.*

**Multiple Regression:** A statistical technique used to measure the relationship between responses to a mailing with census demographics and list characteristics of one or more selected mailing lists. Used to determine the best types of people/areas to mail. This technique can also be used to analyze customers, subscribers or other groups.

**Name:** A single entry on a mail list.

**Name Acquisition:** Soliciting a response to obtain names and addresses for a mailing list.

**Name Removal Service:** A portion of the Mail Preference Service offered by Direct Marketing Association, wherein a consumer is sent a form that, when filled in and returned, constitutes a request to have the individual's name removed from all mailing lists used by participating members of the association and other direct mail users.

**Negative Option:** A buying plan in which a customer or club member agrees to accept and pay for products or services announced in advance at regular intervals unless the individual notifies the company, within a reasonable time after announcement, not to ship the merchandise.

**Nesting:** Placing one enclosure within another and inserting both into a mailing envelope.

**Net Name Arrangement:** An agreement, at the time of ordering or before, whereby the list owner agrees to accept adjusted payment for use of fewer than the total number of names shipped to the list user. Such arrangements can be for a percentage of names shipped or a percentage of names actually mailed (whichever is greater), or for only those names actually mailed (without a percentage limitation). They may or may not provide for a running charge.

**Nixie:** A mailing piece returned to a mailer (under proper authorization) by the postal service because of an incorrect or undeliverable name and address.

**No-Pay:** One who has not paid (wholly or in part) for goods or services ordered. *Uncollectible, deadbeat,* and *delinquent* are also often used to describe such a person.

**North/South Labels:** Mailing labels that read from top to bottom and can be affixed with Cheshire equipment.

**Novelty Format:** An attention-getting direct mail format.

***N*th-Name Selection:** A fractional unit that is repeated in sampling a mailing list. For example, in an "every tenth" sample, you would select records 1, 11, 21, 31, and so forth; or records 2, 12, 22, 32, and so forth.

**OCR(Optical Character Recognition):** Machine identification of printed characters through the use of light sensitive devices.

**Offer:** The terms promoting a specific product or service.

**One-Time Buyer:** A buyer who has not ordered a second time from a given company.

**One-Time Use of a List:** An intrinsic part of normal list usage, list reproduction, or list exchange agreement, where it is understood that the mailer will not use the names on the list more than one time without specific prior approval of the list owner.

**Open Account:** A customer record that, at a specific time, reflects an unpaid balance for goods and services ordered, without delinquency.

**Optical Scanner:** An input device that optically reads a line of printed characters and converts each character into its electronic equivalent for processing.

**Order Blank Envelopes:** An order form printed on one side of a sheet with a mailing address on the reverse. The recipient simply fills in the order, and folds and seals it like an envelope.

**Order Card:** A reply card used to initiate an order by mail.

**Order Form:** A printed form, designed to be mailed in an envelope, on which a customer can provide information to initiate an order by mail.

**Package:** A term used to describe all of the assembled enclosures (parts or elements) of a mailing effort.

**Package Insert:** Any promotional piece included in a product shipment. It may be for different products (or refills and replacements) from the same company or for products and services of other companies.

**Package Test:** A test of some or all of the elements of one mailing piece against another.

**Paid Cancel:** One who completes a basic buying commitment, or more, before canceling the commitment (See *Completed Cancel*.)

**Paid Circulation:** Distribution of a publication to individuals or organizations that have paid for a subscription.

**Paid During Service:** A term used to describe a method of paying for magazine subscriptions in installments, usually weekly or monthly, and usually collected in person by the original salesperson or a representative of the company.

**Peel-off Label:** A self-adhesive label attached to a backing sheet that is attached to a mailing piece. The label is intended to be removed from the mailing piece and attached to an order blank or card.

**Penetration:** Relationship of the number of individuals or families on a particular list (by state, ZIP code, SIC, etc.) compared to the total number possible.

**Personalizing:** Individualizing direct mail pieces by adding the name or other personal information about the recipient.

**Phone List:** A mailing list compiled from names listed in telephone directories.

**Photographer:** One who photographs products and other setup shots required by an agency or in-house advertising department.

**Piggy-Back:** An offer that hitches a free ride with another offer.

**Poly Bag:** A transparent polyethylene bag used in place of envelopes for mailing.

**Pop-up:** A printed piece containing a paper construction pasted inside a fold that, when the fold is opened,"pops up" to form a three dimensional illustration.

**Positive Option:** A method of distributing products and services incorporating the same advance-notice technique as the negative option but requiring a specific order each time from the member or subscriber. Generally, it is more costly and less predictable than the negative option.

**Post Card:** Single-sheet self-mailer on card stock.

**Post Card Mailers:** Booklet containing business reply cards that are individually perforated for selective return, for ordering products or obtaining information.

**Postal Service Prohibitory Order:** A communication from the postal service to a company indicating that a specific person and/or family considers the company's advertising mail to be pandering. The Order requires the company to remove from its own mailing list and from any other lists used to promote that company's products or services all names listed on the order. Violation of the order is subject to fine and imprisonment. Names listed on the order are to be distinguished from those names removed voluntarily by the list owner at an individual's request.

**Premium:** An item offered to a buyer, usually free or at a nominal price, as an inducement to purchase or obtain for trial a product or service offered via mail order.

**Premium Buyer:** One who buys a product or service to get another product or service (usually free or at a special price), or who responds to an offer of a special product (premium) on the package or label (or sometimes in the advertising) of another product.

**Preprint:** An advertising insert printed in advance and supplied to a newspaper or magazine for insertion.

**Private Mail:** Mail handled by special arrangement outside the Postal Service.

**Program:** A sequence of steps to be executed by the computer to solve a given problem or achieve a certain result.

**Programming:** The design, writing, and testing of a program.

**Prospect:** A name on a mailing list considered to be a potential buyer for a given product or service, but who has not previously made such a purchase.

**Prospecting:** Mailing to get leads for further sales contact rather than to make direct sales.

**Protection:** The amount of time, before and after the assigned mailing date, in which a list owner will not allow the same names to be mailed by anyone other than the mailer cleared for that specific date.

**Psychographics:** Any characteristics or qualities used to denote the lifestyle(s) or attitudes(s) of customers and prospective customers.

**Publisher's Letter:** A second letter enclosed in a mailing package to stress a specific selling point.

**Purge:** The process of eliminating duplicates or unwanted names and addresses from one or more lists.

**Pyramiding:** A method of testing mailing lists in which one starts with a small quantity and, based on positive indications, follows with increasingly larger quantities of the list balance until the entire list is mailed.

**Questionnaire:** A printed form to a specified audience to solicit answers to specific questions.

**Random Access:** An access mode in which records are obtained from or placed into a mass storage file in a nonsequential manner so that any record can be rapidly accessed. Synonymous with *direct access*.

**Recency:** The latest purchase or other activity recorded for an individual or company on a specific customer list. (See *Frequency* and *Monetary Value*.)

**Reformatting:** Changing a magnetic tape format from one arrangement to another, more usable format. Synonymous with *conversion* (list or tape).

**Renewal:** A subscription that has been renewed prior to or at expiration time or within six months thereafter.

**Rental:** (See *List Rental*.)

**Repeat Buyer:** (See *Multiple Buyer*.)

**Reply Card:** A sender-addressed card included in a mailing on which the recipient may indicate his or her response to the offer.

**Reply-o-Letter:** One of a number of patented direct mail formats for facilitating replies from prospects. It features a die cut opening on the face of the letter and a pocket on the reverse. An addressed reply card is inserted in the pocket and the name and address thereon shows through the die-cut opening.

**Reproduction Right:** Authorization by a list owner for a specific mailer to use that list on a one-time basis.

**Response Rate:** Percent of returns from a mailing.

**Return Envelopes:** Addressed reply envelopes, either stamped or unstamped (as distinguished from business reply envelopes that carry a postage payment guarantee) included with a mailing.

**Return Postage Guaranteed:** A legend imprinted on the address face of envelopes or other mailing pieces when the mailer wishes the postal service to return undeliverable third-class bulk mail. A charge equivalent to the single-piece, third-class rate will be made for each piece returned. (See *List Cleaning*.)

**Return Requested:** An indication that a mailer will compensate the postal service for return of an undeliverable mailing piece.

**Returns:** Responses to a direct mail program.

**RFMR:** Acronym for *Recency–Frequency–Monetary Value Ratio*, a formula used to evaluate the sales potential of names of a mailing list.

**Rollout:** To mail the remaining portion of a mailing list after successfully testing a portion of that list.

**R.O.P. (Run of Paper or Run of Press):** Usually refers to color printing that can be placed on any page of a newspaper or magazine.

**Rough:** Dummy or layout in sketchy form with a minimum of detail.

**Royalties:** Sum paid per unit mailed or sold for the use of a list, imprimatur, patent, or other right.

**Run of Paper:** (1) A term applied to color printing on regular paper and presses, as distinct from separately printed sections made on special color presses. (2) Sometimes used to describe an advertisement positioned by publisher's choice—as opposed to a preferred position—for which a special charge is made.

**Running Charge:** The price a list owner charges for names run or passed but not used by a specific mailer. When such a charge is made, it is usually to cover extra processing costs. However, some list owners set the price without regard to actual cost.

**Sales Promotion Manager:** The person who plans and executes sales programs and sales promotion giveaways.

**Salting:** Deliberate placing of decoy or dummy names in a list to trace list usage and delivery. (See *Decoy* and *Dummy*.)

**Sample Buyer:** One who sends for a sample product, usually at a special price or for a small handling charge, but sometimes free.

**Small Package (Mailing Piece):** An example of the package to be mailed by the list user to a particular list. Such a mailing piece is submitted to the list owner for approval prior to commitment for one-time use of that list. A sample package may, due to time pressure, differ slightly from the actual package used. The list user agreement usually requires the user to reveal any material differences when submitting the sample package.

**Scented Inks:** Printing inks to which a fragrance has been added.

**Sectional Center:** A postal service distribution unit comprising different post offices whose ZIP codes start with the same first three digits.

**Selection Criteria:** Definition of characteristics that identify segments or subgroups within a list.

**Self-Cover:** A cover made of the same paper as the inside text pages.

**Self-Mailer:** A direct mail piece mailed without an envelope.

**Sequence:** An arrangement of items according to a specified set of rules or instructions. Refers generally to ZIP codes or customer numbers.

**SIC (Standard Industrial Classification):** Classification of businesses as defined by the U.S. Department of Commerce.

**Software:** A set of programs, procedures, and associated documentation concerned with operation of a data processing system.

**Solo Mailing:** A mailing promoting a single product or a limited group of related products, usually consisting of a letter, brochure, and reply device enclosed in an envelope.

**Source Code:** Unique alphabetical and/or numeric identification for distinguishing one list or media source from another. (See *Key Code*.)

**Source Count:** The number of names and addresses, in any given list, for the media (or list sources) from which the names and addresses were derived.

**Split Test:** Two or more samples from the same list, each considered to be representative of the entire list, used for package tests or to test the homogeneity of the list.

**State Count:** The number of names and addresses in a given list for each state.

**Statement Stuffer:** A small, printed piece designed to be inserted in an envelope carrying a customer's statement of account.

**Step Up:** The use of special premiums to get a mail order buyer to increase his or her unit of purchase.

**Stock Art:** Art sold for use by a number of advertisers.

**Stock Cut:** Printing engravings kept in stock by the printer or publisher for occasional use.

**Stock Formats:** Direct mail formats with preprinted illustrations and/or headings to which an advertiser adds custom copy.

**Stopper:** Advertising slang for a striking headline or illustration intended to attract immediate attention.

**Stuffer:** Advertising enclosure placed in another medium, such as newspapers, merchandise packages, or mailings for other products.

**Subscriber:** An individual who has paid to receive a periodical.

**Swatching:** Attaching samples of material to a printed piece.

**Syndicated Mailing:** Mailing prepared for distribution by firms other than the manufacturer or syndicator.

**Syndicator:** One who makes available prepared direct mail promotions for specific products or services to a list owner for mailing to his own list. Most syndicators also offer product fulfillment services.

**Tabloid:** A preprinted advertising insert of four or more pages, usually about half the size of a regular newspaper page, designed for inserting into a newspaper.

**Tape Density:** The number of characters (bytes) that can be included in a specific magnetic tape (e.g., 556 BPI, 800 BPI, 1600 BPI,).

**Tape Dump:** A printout of data on a magnetic tape to be edited and checked for correctness, readability, consistency, and other qualities.

**Tape Layout:** A simple "map" of the data included in each record and its relative or specific location.

**Tape Record:** All the information about an individual or company contained on a specific magnetic tape.

**Teaser:** An advertisement or promotion planned to excite curiosity about a later advertisement or promotion.

**Telecommunications:** Data transmission between a computer system and remotely located devices via a unit that performs the necessary format conversion and controls the rate of transmission over telephone lines, microwaves, or other medium. Synonymous with *transceiver.*

**Telemarketer:** A party who sells products and services by using the telephone to contact prospective customers.

**Terminal:** Any mechanism that can transmit and/or receive data through a system or communications network.

**Test Panel:** A term used to identify each of the parts or samples in a split test.

**Test Tape:** A selection of representative records within a mailing list that enables a list user or service bureau to prepare for reformatting or converting the list to a form more efficient for the user.

**Throwaway:** An advertisement or promotional piece intended for widespread free distribution. Generally printed on inexpensive paper stock, it is most often distributed by hand to passersby or from house to house.

**Tie-In:** Cooperative mailing effort involving two or more advertisers.

**Til Forbid:** An order for service that is to continue until specifically canceled by the buyer. (Also *T.F.*)

**Time Sharing:** Multiple utilization of available computer time, often via terminals, usually by different organizations.

**Tip-on:** An item glued to a printed piece.

**Title:** A designation before (prefix) or after (suffix) a name to more accurately: identify an individual. (Prefixes: Mr., Mrs., Dr., Sister, etc. Suffixes: M.D., Jr., President, Sales Manager, etc.)

**Token:** An involvement device, often consisting of a perforated portion of an order card designed to be removed from its original position and placed in another designated area on the order card, to signify a desire to purchase the product or service offered.

**Town Marker:** A symbol used to identify the end of a mailing list's geographical unit. (Originated for towns but now used for ZIP codes, sectional centers, etc.)

**Traffic Builder:** A direct mail piece intended primarily to attract recipients to the mailer's place of business.

**Traffic Department Personnel:** In advertising agencies, they coordinate all phases of production, following the progress of every job to ensure that everything is completed on time.

**Trial Buyer:** One who buys a short-term supply of a product or buys the product with the understanding that it may be examined, used, or tested for a specified time before he or she decides whether to pay for it or to return it.

**Trial Subscriber:** A person ordering a publication or service on a conditional basis. The condition may relate to delaying payment, the right to cancel, a shorter-than-normal term, and/or a special introductory price.

**Uncollectible:** One who hasn't paid for goods and services at the end of a normal series of collection efforts.

**Universe:** The total number of individuals that might be included on a mailing list; all of those fitting a single set of specifications.

**Update:** Recent transactions and current information added to the master (main) list to reflect the current status of each record on the list.

**Up Front:** Payment secured for a product offered by mail order before the product is sent.

**UPS:** Acronym for United Parcel Service.

**Variable Field:** A way of laying out for formatting list information that assigns a specific sequence to the data but doesn't assign them specific positions. This method conserves space on magnetic tape, but it is generally more difficult to work with.

**Verification:** The process of determining the validity of an order by sending a questionnaire to the customer.

**WATS (Wide Area Telephone Service):** A service that provides a special line allowing calls within a certain zone, on a direct-dialing basis, for a flat monthly charge.

**White Envelope:** Envelope with a die-cut portion on the front that permits viewing the address printed on an enclosure. The die-cut window may or may not be covered with a transparent material.

**White Mail:** Incoming mail that is not on a form sent out by the advertiser. All mail other than orders and payments.

**Wing Mailer:** Label-affixing device that uses strips of paper on which addresses have been printed.

**ZIP Code:** A group of five to nine digits used by the U.S. Postal Service to designate specific post offices, stations, branches, buildings, or large companies.

**ZIP Code Count:** The number of names and addresses in a list, within each ZIP code.

**ZIP Code Sequence:** Arranging names and addresses in a list according to the numeric progression of the ZIP code in each record. This form of list formatting is mandatory for mailing at bulk third-class mail rates, based on the sorting requirements of postal service regulations.

# INDEX